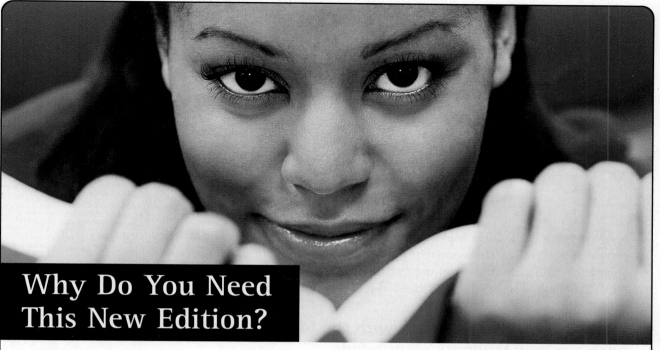

Why Do You Need This New Edition?

If you're wondering why you should buy this new edition of *Writing for Life: Paragraphs and Essays*, here are 10 good reasons!

1. There is an emphasis on the Connection between Reading and Writing: Chapter 1, "Preparing to Learn about Writing," presents the reading process and reading strategies to strengthen your writing. Not only will you learn about the similarities between the reading and writing processes but also you will explore your own reading and writing processes.

2. A new feature, Learning Outcomes, tells you what you will know or be able to do as a result of a learning activity. Outcomes are stated as knowledge, skills, or attitudes. Chapter 1 introduces a chart that describes the five basic outcomes: (1) Structure (of a paragraph and an essay), (2) Writing Process, (3) Connect Reading and Writing, (4) Self-Evaluation, and (5) Use of Sources/Documentation. Icons for each of these learning outcomes appear throughout the text to keep your focus on your learning.

3. Updated, high-interest exercises throughout the text reflect current events and popular interests to engage your interest.

4. Updated graphic organizers, pictures, and student writing samples help you use patterns of organization to develop your paragraphs. In Part 2, the following chapters have fresh material relevant to your life: Narrative (Ch. 5), Example (Ch. 7), Classification (Ch. 8), Comparison and Contrast (Ch. 9), Definition (Ch. 10), and Persuasive Paragraphs (Ch. 12).

5. The Writer's Journal for Making a Point: One Student Writer's Response has been highlighted in Chapters 4–12. These interactive activities give you the skills you need to be an effective peer editor.

6. A new feature, the Writer's Journal, not only helps you review what you are reading and learning but also helps you give and receive peer feedback.

7. There is improved and streamlined instruction on essay writing, with less bulk and the same great instruction. In Chapter 13, you will learn essay writing skills as a natural progression based on the key concepts of paragraph development. A new flow chart illustrates the parts and levels of information in an essay.

8. There are 8 new engaging reading selections written by people who shape our culture, such as President Barack Obama, Amy Tan, Oprah Winfrey, Deborah Tannen, and Dr. Martin Luther King, Jr. You will see examples of effective writing while you read about topics such as Twitter, the surprisingly negative view of youth about the effects of technology, a key difference between men and women, or the visions of Dr. King and President Obama.

9. A new Portfolio Appendix, found in the Instructor's Manual and online at the *Writing for Life: Paragraphs and Essays* 2/e MyWritingLab site, supplies you with rubrics, reflection forms, and self-evaluation forms of the reading and writing process flow charts. The Portfolio Appendix is a companion to the instruction in Chapter 1 about creating your portfolio.

10. The MyWritingLab (www.mywritinglab.com) prompts have been moved to the end-of-chapter "Writing Assignments" in order to fully integrate Pearson's dynamic learning system for additional online instruction and practice.

D1122758

PEARSON

If practice makes perfect, imagine what *better* practice can do . . .

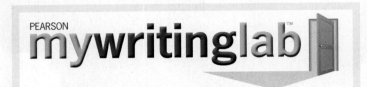

PEARSON
mywritinglab™

MyWritingLab is an online learning system that provides better writing practice through progressive exercises. These exercises move students from literal comprehension to critical application to demonstration of their ability to write properly. With this better practice model, students develop the skills needed to become better writers!

When asked if they agreed with the following statements, here are how students responded:

97%
The MyWritingLab Student-user Satisfaction Level

"MyWritingLab helped me to improve my writing." **89%**

"MyWritingLab was fairly easy to use." **90%**

"MyWritingLab helped make me feel more confident about my writing ability." **83%**

"MyWritingLab helped me to better prepare for my next writing course." **86%**

"MyWritingLab helped me get a better grade." **82%**

"I wish I had a program like MyWritingLab in some of my other courses." **78%**

"I would recommend my instructor continue using MyWritingLab." **85%**

Student Success Story

"The first few weeks of my English class, my grades were at approximately 78%. Then I was introduced to MyWritingLab. I couldn't believe the increase in my test scores. My test scores had jumped from that low score of 78 all the way up to 100% (and every now and then a 99)."

—Exetta Windfield, *College of the Sequoias* (MyWritingLab student user)

TO PURCHASE AN ACCESS CODE, GO TO
WWW.MYWRITINGLAB.COM

SECOND EDITION

Writing *for* Life

Paragraphs and Essays

D. J. Henry

Daytona State College

Longman
Boston   Columbus   Indianapolis   New York   San Francisco   Upper Saddle River
Amsterdam   Cape Town   Dubai   London   Madrid   Milan   Munich   Paris   Montreal   Toronto
Delhi   Mexico City   São Paulo   Sydney   Hong Kong   Seoul   Singapore   Taipei   Tokyo

Dedication

To my foremost teacher, my mom, Mary Maxine Powell

PEARSON

Acquisitions Editor: Matthew Wright
Editorial Assistant: Haley Pero
Senior Development Editor: Katharine Glynn
Senior Supplements Editor: Donna Campion
Marketing Manager: Tom DeMarco
Production Manager: Ellen MacElree
Project Coordination: Nesbitt Graphics, Inc.
Cover Designer/Manager: Wendy Ann Fredericks
Cover Photos: *Digital camera*: dem10/istockphoto;
 Sunflower: maodesign/istockphoto
Photo Researcher: Rona Tuccillo
Senior Manufacturing Buyer: Roy L. Pickering, Jr.
Printer and Binder: Courier/Kendallville
Cover Printer: Coral Graphic Services, Inc.

Managing Art Editor:
 Richard Czapnik
Designers: Anthony Limerick
 and Ian Midson
Design Director: Stuart Jackman
Publisher: Sophie Mitchell

For permission to use copyrighted material, grateful acknowledgment is made to the copyright holders on pp. 684–686, which are hereby made part of this copyright page.

Library of Congress Cataloging-in-Publication Data
Henry, D. J. (Dorothy Jean)
 Writing for life : paragraphs and essays / D.J. Henry.—2nd ed.
  p. cm.
 Includes bibliographical references and index.
 ISBN 978-0-205-66871-7
 1. English language—Composition and exercises—Study and teaching
(Higher) 2. Rhetoric—Study and teaching (Higher) 3. Creative writing
(Higher education) I. Title.
 PE1404.H3975 2010
 808'.042076—dc22

                                           2009049836

ISBN-13: 978-0-205-66871-7 (student ed.)
ISBN-10:   0-205-66871-2 (student ed.)

ISBN-13: 978-0-205-66872-4 (instructor's ed.)
ISBN-10:   0-205-66872-0 (instructor's ed.)

 3 4 5 6 7 8 9—CRK—13 12 11 10

Longman
is an imprint of

Detailed Contents

PART 1 Getting Ready to Write

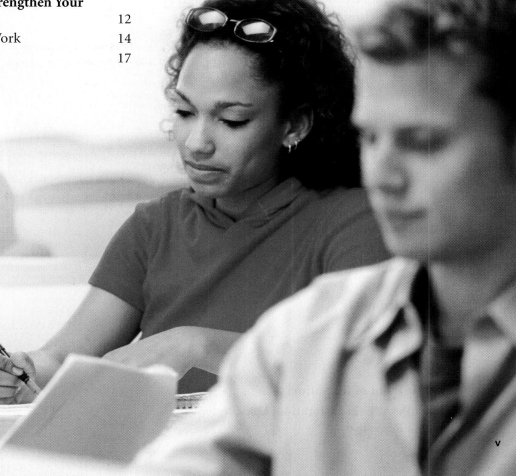

v

PART 3
How to Write an Essay

PART 6 Recognizing and Avoiding Errors

PART 8
Reading Selections

Preface to the Student

Writing requires confidence and courage. Every word that flows from mind to paper reveals something about who we are in that moment—our depth of thought, our mastery of language, our ability to connect to others. But you already know this to be true. As a student writer, you have a gut-level understanding of the risks posed by writing, particularly in the writing classroom. Too often, assignments can seem artificial, and grades, editing marks, and high-stakes exit exams often make writing a nerve-wracking experience. In a few short weeks, you need to master text structure, improve vocabulary, comprehend writing situations, develop a writing process, grasp grammar rules, change life-long habits, and find your voice.

To reach your goals, think of your teacher as a mentor and guide. And think of this textbook as a system of learning. *Writing for Life* aims to engage you with high-interest activities that promote success and foster deep growth as quickly as possible. *Writing for Life* offers a consistent approach that addresses your specific needs as a writer. *Writing for Life* emphasizes the power and importance of writing in everyday, college, and work situations. *Writing for Life* guides you step by step through writing instruction while showing you how to take responsibility for your learning.

On a final and most important note, if I could speak directly to each one of you who holds this book, I would offer the following encouragement. Writing well is a learned behavior, and you can learn most anything you put your mind to. Always remember, every minute you spend learning to write is an investment in yourself and your future. You're worth the effort. A great writer named Emerson once said, "Look to yourself and do good because you are good." Emerson expresses great faith in and respect for our individual abilities. I share his faith and have great confidence in *your ability* to master writing for life. You *can* do it—you can *write for life!*

Sincere wishes for your success,
D. J. Henry

Letter to Instructors

Dear Colleagues:

Allow me to extend my gratitude and respect for the work you do on behalf of your students. Your work is of the utmost value—beyond what you may ever witness in your daily interactions with your students. Like so many of today's students, I began my educational journey as a developmental student whose lack in the ability to write was only exceeded by my lack of faith in my ability to overcome all the barriers I faced. In truth, a few caring, dedicated teachers saved me, pushed me, believed in me, and taught me more than just how to write—they taught me how to learn. This textbook is the fruit of their belief in me and stands as much a tribute to their diligence and faith as to my own effort. It is an honor to partner with you as you seek to impact the lives of your students.

As I composed *Writing for Life,* I always kept before me the hard truth of all that must be accomplished in one semester. In a few short weeks, your students seek to master text structure, improve vocabulary, comprehend writing situations, develop a writing process, grasp grammar rules, change lifelong habits, and find a voice. To foster achievement of these goals, *Writing for Life* embodies best practices based on academic research and nearly 30 years of classroom experience. *Writing for Life* taps into brain-based learning, fosters metacognition, places instruction and activities in meaningful contexts, and engages students with high-interest content and visual presentation.

The art of teaching is an act of great faith. My teachers' hope for me has been realized—far beyond all that I had dared to imagine for myself. I wish this same success for all our students. My hope is that *Writing for Life* complements your aspirations as a teacher and inspires your students to realize their potential.

Thank you!
D. J. Henry

Introducing the *Writing for Life* Series

Writing for Life answers the question "What's the point (of this course material)?" by providing students with specific learning objectives, real-world contemporary examples, and ultra-engaging visuals.

Writing for Life, a two-book series consisting of both a sentences and paragraphs book and a paragraphs and essays book, answers the question students often ask about why they should learn to write well—"What's the point?" *Writing for Life* does more than motivate students, however; it teaches them to take charge of their own learning and helps them transfer the strategies they currently apply to reading visuals over to the tasks of reading and writing text.

Words of praise for *Writing for Life*

"In the inspiring preface, I met an author clearly in love with writing, thoroughly aware of students' and instructors' challenges; [and] sincerely devoted to empowering students through writing. What's the Point? is absolutely one of my favorite features in the textbook!" —Sharon Davidson, *Baton Rouge Community College*

"Writing for Life is an excellent text that addresses all of the major topics, concepts and skills that are important for an introductory college writing class. It is superior to other works of its kind due to its commitment to addressing the absolutely crucial need for students to connect to a topic before becoming engaged in it." —Erin T. Martz, *Northern Virginia Community College*

"I really like the design of the text. I am finding that the majority of students in any of my classes are visual [learners], and they respond well to color coding. One of the features that most impressed me when I first leafed through the book is the highlighting of words and punctuation in the grammar chapters. This feature is very helpful for students. It makes the explanation of a particular point crystal clear." —Justina M. Sapna, *Delaware Technical & Community College*

"The photographic organizers are a great feature. Many of my students are stronger visually than verbally, so this is a most helpful resource." —Julia I. Hoesel, *Iowa Central Community College*

"Writing for Life provides clear, simply stated principles of almost all aspects of basic writing in a format that allows students to take a more active role in their own improvement." —Tina L. Bennett, *Wichita State University*

Writing for Life highlights and promotes...

- Motivation and Preparation
- Illustration and Visuals
- Purpose and Core Learning Objectives (Outcomes)
- Application, Grammar Instruction, and Connecting with Today's Student

- **Motivation and Preparation:** Would you like a book that systematically motivates your students to become better and more productive learners? What do you do to show them the relevance of this course? Do students need to be motivated to see the importance of writing skills in their lives?

  Writing for Life places students within "real world" situations and proves to them that sharpening their writing/reading skills will enable them to succeed in college, work, and everyday life situations while emphasizing the importance of their audience and purpose. *Writing for Life* is a highly motivational book geared to actively engage students and inspire confidence in their own success.

- **Illustration and Visuals:** How many of your students would you describe as visual learners? How do you meet the needs of today's visual learners in and out of class?

  Designed in partnership with Dorling Kindersley, *Writing for Life* employs a dynamic visual design specifically created for today's visual learner. Stimulating images, engaging visual pedagogy, and multi-colored highlighting in the annotated examples make mastering writing skills more attainable and appealing than ever before. Today's developmental writing student needs to be engaged and presented material in a completely new way. Photographic organizers and color-coded annotations of essay, paragraph, and grammatical concepts activate and develop the psychomotor domain. *Writing for Life* will change the way teachers teach and the way learners learn. It will increase class retention rates and boost success rates. *Writing for Life* (along with MyWritingLab) will revolutionize your classroom!

- **Purpose and Core Learning Objectives (Outcomes):** Do you (or your department) have course learning objectives that you want your students to master by the end of the course? Do you want a textbook that provides core purpose and drives success?

  Many people think of a goal as an "outcome." For example, for each goal, people ask "What is the outcome of this goal? What should I know or be able to do once I reach this goal?" In a writing class, a learning

LO-S: Learning Outcomes—Structure

- **Identify/Apply the *Structure* of a paragraph and an essay**
  - Introduction
  - Main Idea
  - Body: Major, Minor Supporting Details
  - Conclusion

LO-WP: Learning Outcomes—Writing Process

- **Identify/Apply the phases of the *Writing Process***
  - **Prewrite**
    - Analyze the three aspects of the **writing situation**
      - Topic
      - Purpose
      - Audience
    - Brainstorm, Map, Outline
  - **Draft** paragraphs and essays
    - Compose **a main idea**: topic sentence, thesis sentence
    - Generate **adequate and relevant details**
    - Use **logical order** of ideas
  - **Revise** drafts for **effective expression**
    - Control sentence structure
    - Use words appropriately
  - **Proofread** drafts for **effective expression**
    - Identify and **correct errors** in grammar

LO-RW: Learning Outcomes—Connect Reading and Writing

- **Read to Write; Think Critically**
  - Analyze a piece of writing
  - Write a summary
  - Provide constructive criticism to others

LO-SE: Learning Outcome—Self-Evaluation

- **Self-evaluate; Think Critically**
  - Reflect on writing **progress**
  - Reflect on writing **process**

LO-DOC: Use of Sources

- **Document sources according to the MLA format**
  - Find relevant outside sources
  - Evaluate outside sources
  - Format sources in text and in Works Cited

outcome states what a student writer should know or be able to do as the result of a lesson or a course of study. The chart above outlines five major learning outcomes (goals) for student writers in the *Paragraphs and Essays* book. Each major learning outcome is built upon its listed set of skills and concepts.

To help them make the most of their studies, the icons for the learning outcomes appear in the margins throughout the book.

- **Application, Grammar Instruction, and Connecting with Today's Student:** Does your current textbook reflect who your students are? Does it supply them with application exercises needed to master writing skills effectively?

  Writing for Life draws students into the writing process by tapping into topics that are of high interest to the contemporary learner. Instructional examples, writing models, practice exercises, workshops, student essays, reading selections, and writing situations/assignments reflect the wide range of topics relevant to today's student, such as fashion, music, health, technology, relationships, green living, natural disasters, reality television, celebrities, and role models. *Writing for Life* reflects the cultural issues of contemporary society that are most interesting to students, but it also addresses each student's individual academic needs in real time as a developing writer. First, *Writing for Life* enables the student to identify and reflect upon his or her strengths and needs as a writer. Then, *Writing for Life* guides the student through a step-by-step process of taking responsibility for his or her own learning. *Writing for Life* shows students how to adopt and adapt instruction into their own writing process. The strategies in *Writing for Life* move students from just learning about writing to using writing as a powerful means of expression in their everyday, college, and working lives.

Features of *Writing for Life*

How Does *Writing for Life* Effectively Motivate and Prepare Students for Success?

The focus of *Writing for Life* is apparent in the comprehensive and systematic approach to learning it provides by motivating and preparing students; engaging students with high-interest and meaningful illustrations and visuals; establishing purpose and clear statements of core learning objectives; offering relevant applications; and meeting today's students where they are.

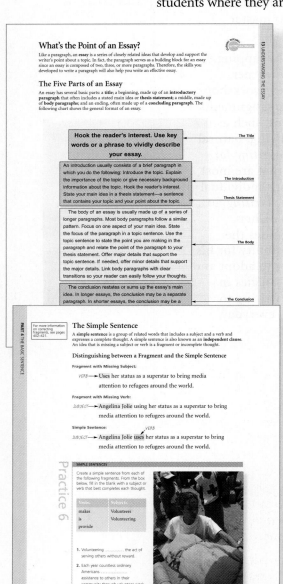

▲ Highlighted examples and grammar sentences

WHAT'S THE POINT? is a motivational teaching strategy that addresses the basic question on most students' minds: *Why do I need to know this?* The question and the instructional answer establish the student writer's purpose for studying the chapter.

OVERALL INSTRUCTIONAL VOICE establishes a clear, direct, respectful tone that honors adult learners.

EMPHASIS ON ACTIVE LEARNING *Writing for Life* motivates students to become active learners who assume responsibility for their individual learning, who reflect upon their progress, and who can and will improve their writing skills. In Part 1, students discover the writing process and assess their own use of the writing process.

WRITING ASSIGNMENTS are presented in fully developed prompts that create realistic writing situations where students can practice proofreading and editing. The writing prompts direct students to consider audience and purpose as they employ the full writing process. Additional assignments provide topics and situations relevant to "Everyday Life," "College Life," and "Working Life."

How Does *Writing for Life* Engage Students with Illustrations and Visuals?

HIGH-INTEREST VISUALS include four-color annotations, graphic organizers, concept maps, outlines, checklists, and photographs to stimulate interest, clarify concepts, and facilitate student responses.

GRAMMATICAL CONCEPTS are comprehensively covered in an approach that combines an illustrated handbook with intensive practice. Examples are clearly annotated visuals with color-coded highlights that make key concepts jump off the page.

PHOTOGRAPHIC ORGANIZERS activate the thinking process, introduce and illustrate a pattern of organization, and stimulate prewriting activities. A set of photographs is arranged in a concept map that illustrates the structure of a particular pattern of organization.

VISUAL LEARNING ACTIVITIES such as photographic organizers introduce and facilitate writing assignments; concept maps, charts, graphs, and annotated examples enable students to "see" the concept clearly.

VISUAL INSTRUCTION offers annotated visuals with color-coded highlights that make key concepts jump off the page. Concepts and rules are further defined, explained, and illustrated with charts and graphs.

THE WRITING PROCESS lays the foundation of ongoing instruction; the writing process is introduced and illustrated in Chapter 2 with a two-page spread of a four-color graphic with explanations of the entire writing process: Prewriting, Drafting, Revising, and Editing. Appropriate writing process icons appear throughout the textbook as signals to guide students through the writing process of particular assignments.

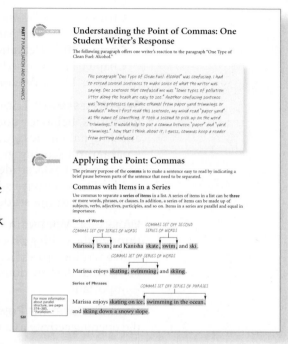

▲ Visual Instruction and "Applying the Point" feature

How Does *Writing for Life* Provide Students with Purpose and Core Learning Objectives (Outcomes)?

LEARNING OUTCOMES Learning Outcomes are statements that specify what learners will know or be able to do as a result of a learning activity. Outcomes are usually expressed as knowledge, skills, or attitudes. Chapter 1, "Preparing to Learn about Writing," introduces a chart of five core outcomes: (1) Structure (of a paragraph and an essay); (2) Writing Process; (3) Connect Reading and Writing; (4) Self-Evaluation; and (5) Use of Sources. Each of these five outcomes represents a domain of knowledge, skills, and attitudes necessary to write effectively. Research based, these outcomes state the learning outcomes expressed by classroom teachers across the country as well as the Writing Program Administrators (WPA). To encourage students to self-assess and track their own progress as writers, icons for each learning outcome appear next to key instruction in every chapter, In fact, every learning outcome is addressed in every chapter. Thus, every assignment in *Writing for Life* is an opportunity to prove mastery of one or more of these learning outcomes.

PREPARING YOURSELF TO LEARN ABOUT WRITING in Chapter 1 teaches students to evaluate their attitudes, identify learning outcomes, generate a study plan, and create a portfolio that helps them "to track growth … organize work … and think about" their learning and their writing. Simple and easy-to-follow advice guides students to use checklists, reflective questions, and journal entries as they think about their writing and what they are learning.

MY FIRST THOUGHTS sustains student engagement in the writing process by prompting a brainstorming session in response to the photographic organizer.

GRAMMAR IN ACTION directly addresses some of the most commonly occurring errors in student writing. A specific common error is discussed in the context of a particular pattern of organization. In the last phase of the step-by-step instruction of the Workshop, students study a grammatical concept and then proofread and edit a sample piece of writing to ensure correct application of the concept. The correlation among chapters and grammar concepts are as follows:

Chapter 4	Descriptive	Dangling and Misplaced Modifiers
Chapter 5	Narrative	Unnecessary Shifts in Verb Tense
Chapter 6	Process	Eliminating Fused Sentences
Chapter 7	Example	Using Commas in a Series
Chapter 8	Classification	Eliminating Comma Splices
Chapter 9	Comparison/Contrast	Commas after Introductory Elements
Chapter 10	Definition	Commas with Nonessential Information
Chapter 11	Cause/Effect	Commonly Confused Words
Chapter 12	Persuasion	Consistent Use of Point of View

SELF-ASSESSMENT TOOLS AND GUIDES include learning outcomes, reflective questions, behavior and attitude surveys, guidelines, checklists, scoring rubrics, and journal entries, complete with examples and explanations. For example, a paragraph scoring guide is introduced and explained and followed by a practice that asks students to score a set of paragraphs using the scoring guide. These activities transfer the responsibility of learning and assessment of learning to the student.

WORKSHOP: WRITING A PARAGRAPH STEP BY STEP guides students one step at a time through the writing process from prewriting to editing, and each phase is highlighted with a writing process icon (based on the graphic introduced in Chapter 2), so students know what they are doing at each point in the process, how they are to do it, and why it is important.

UNDERSTANDING THE POINT reinforces the need to know by offering a student response to the opening activity as a think-aloud that models critical thinking. These activities model effective learning practices.

ACADEMIC LEARNING LOG is an end-of-chapter activity that tests students' comprehension of the chapter's instruction.

EMPHASIS ON THE PROCESS is also embedded in instruction throughout the textbook. Many of the activities that emphasize active learning also emphasize the writing process. Directed thinking activities encourage students to actively self-assess how well they handle the writing process as they prewrite, draft, revise, and proofread their work. Students are also guided to think about how to apply what they are learning to improve their writing. For example, "A Writer's Journal" records a student's thinking about his or her writing process during a particular assignment.

TEXT STRUCTURE is covered extensively at every level, including word, sentence, paragraph, and essay levels. Lessons systematically guide students to consider the types and structures of words, phrases, and sentences; patterns of organization; levels of ideas; traits and function of a main idea; major supporting details; minor supporting details; parts of the paragraph; and parts of the essay. Writing prompts encourage students to adapt text structure to realistic writing situations.

▲ Student self-assessment feature

How does *Writing for Life* drive grammar instruction and key applications to connect with today's student?

GRAMMATICAL INSTRUCTION Student motivation, always vital, seems to be even more crucial when it comes to mastering grammatical concepts. Unfortunately, too many times, grammar instruction is met with apathy and dread. Grammar has purpose. It's worth the effort to learn it. The purpose of instruction is to foster confidence and mastery. The core features of this text—designed to inspire and motivate—have been adapted to match the nature of instruction for grammatical concepts.

THE WRITING SITUATION is explained and illustrated in Chapter 2 in discussions and engaging activities about how the relationships among topic, audience, and purpose impact the creation of a piece of writing. Writing prompts are realistic writing situations based on everyday life, college life, and working life. These writing prompts stimulate role playing and critical thinking skills and illustrate the importance of *writing for life*.

HIGH-INTEREST TOPICS such as tattoos, stress, obesity, eating disorders, pop culture icons, fashion, movies, music, relationships, natural disasters, heroes, and current events engage student interest and foster self-expression.

DIRECT INSTRUCTION follows a logical order to best ensure comprehension and foster student ownership of the material. Each lesson moves systematically through three distinct phases: before learning activities, during learning activities, and after learning activities. Before, during, and after learning activities make excellent portfolio entries that foster student self-assessment.

BEFORE LEARNING ACTIVITIES that prepare students to learn include "What's the Point?," "My First Thoughts," "One Student Writer's Response," and "A Writer's Journal." These activities set the purpose of the lesson, activate critical thinking, and engage the student.

DURING LEARNING ACTIVITIES emphasize understanding concepts and developing skills. Labeled "Understanding the Point," "Developing Your Point," or "Applying the Point," this phase of the lesson offers direct instruction, examples, explanations, checklists, charts, graphics, practices, and workshops.

AFTER LEARNING ACTIVITIES test students' abilities to recall and apply what they have learned. After learning activities include chapter reviews, writing assignments, and reflective-critical thinking activities.

MAKING A POINT: One Student Writer's Response is a twofold model of writing and thinking about writing that illustrates and encourages critical thinking. This section first offers a model

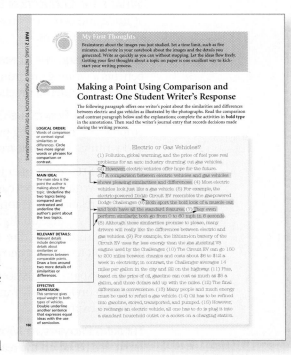

▲ Student Model

writing sample based on the photographic organizer. Students immediately see the relationship between a particular writing prompt and a piece of writing. Each writer's response is annotated with direct instruction about the main idea, supporting details, logical order, and effective expression. The annotations also include directed thinking activities that actively engage students to provide additional (personal) annotations.

APPLYING THE POINT offers direct instruction that includes definitions, explanations, annotated examples, and ample practice to foster mastery of the grammatical concept.

THE WRITER'S JOURNAL is a "think-aloud" that models reflective thinking about a piece of writing; this journal entry functions as the second part of "Making a Point." The Writer's Journal captures the thinking of the writer of the paragraph featured in "One Student Writer's Response." These writing journals teach students to "think aloud" about their writing. The journals record the barriers, the decisions, and the improvements made by writers as they moved through the writing process. The Writer's Journal serves as a model of student engagement—showing students how to create "think-alouds" about their own writings throughout the semester.

DEVELOPING YOUR POINT offers direct instruction, including explanations, annotated examples, student writing samples, and practice to enhance student understanding about how to develop an idea using a particular pattern of organization. Instruction focuses on four core areas: Main Idea, Logical Order, Relevant Details, and Effective Expression. Direct instruction includes a practice that illustrates the use of the pattern of organization in an academic course.

REVIEW OF THE WRITING PROCESS offers a fill-in form that students can tear out and use to reflect about their writing process after they respond to a writing assignment. By asking students to reflect upon and record the choices they made about the main idea, logical order, relevant details, and effective expression, the form helps students generate a journal entry about their writing experience. The activity also serves as a chapter review.

Reading Selections

We know that reading enhances our ability to write well. Therefore, the major emphasis within the in-book reader is the connection between reading and writing.

WHAT'S THE CONNECTION BETWEEN READING AND WRITING? This opening activity offers an attitude and behavior survey that asks students to reflect about their individual reading and writing experiences.

UNDERSTANDING THE CONNECTION BETWEEN READING AND WRITING This section explains the benefits a writer gains from reading, illustrates in a chart the similarities between reading and writing, and offers a practice that models the connection between reading and writing skills.

APPLYING THE POINT: THE CONNECTION BETWEEN READING AND WRITING This section emphasizes the thinking processes students can use to make the connection between reading and writing. Students learn how to annotate a text, summarize a text, and read like a writer.

READING SELECTIONS offer high-interest essays, both contemporary and classical, as models of effective writing. Topics cover a wide range of subjects including poverty, culture, careers, and race relations. The tone and purpose of these essays vary and include distinctive voices such as Maya Angelou, Rachel Carson, Amy Tan, Stephen King, and President Barack Obama. Students are directed to annotate the text and maintain a vocabulary journal of new or difficult terms they encounter.

AFTER READING DISCUSSION QUESTIONS: MEANING, STRUCTURE, AND EXPRESSION focus student attention on four basic traits of an essay: Main Idea, Relevant Details, Logical Order, and Effective Expression.

THINKING PROMPTS TO MOVE FROM READING TO WRITING offer two fully developed writing situations based on the reading. These prompts ask students to consider audience and purpose as they form a response to what they have read.

Developmental Writing Resources

Book-Specific Ancillary Material

Instructor's Manual and Test Bank for *Writing for Life: Paragraphs and Essays* (0-205-66873-9) is a practical supplement useful in any classroom setting. The Instructor's Manual includes a summary of each chapter as well as sample syllabi to assist with designing a course around *Writing for Life: Paragraphs and Essays*. There is also a complete discussion of how to use each chapter in the classroom, including supplementary assignments and class discussions. The Test Bank consists of multiple-choice and true/false questions designed to test each student's comprehension of every chapter. The Writer's Portfolio appendix is also included in this instructor supplement. This combined supplement has something to offer all instructors.

Additional Instructor Resources

The Pearson Developmental Writing Package
Pearson is pleased to offer a variety of support materials to help make teaching developmental English easier on teachers and to help students excel in their coursework. Many of our student supplements are available free or at a greatly reduced price when packaged with *Writing for Life: Paragraphs and Essays*. Contact your local Pearson sales representative for more information on pricing and how to create a package.

Media Resources

MyWritingLab: Where better practice makes better writers! (www.mywritinglab.com)
MyWritingLab, a complete online learning program, provides better practice exercises to developing writers. What makes the practice in MyWritingLab better?

- **Diagnostic Testing:** MyWritingLab's diagnostic test comprehensively assesses student skills in grammar. Students are given an individualized learning path based on the diagnostic's results, identifying the modules in areas where they most need help.

- **Progressive Learning:** The heart of MyWritingLab is the progressive learning that takes place as students complete the Recall, Apply, and Write exercises within each module. Students move from literal comprehension (Recall) to critical comprehension (Apply) to demonstrating concepts to their own writing (Write). This progression of critical thinking, not available in any other online resource, enables students to truly master the skills and concepts they need to become successful writers.

- **Online Gradebook:** All student work in MyWritingLab is captured in the Online Gradebook. Students can monitor their own progress through reports detailing scores on all of the exercises in the course. It also shows which topics students have mastered. Instructors have detailed reports, such as class summaries that track the progress of their entire class and show individual student detail, as well as topical views and alerts.

Acknowledgments

The publication of a text like this requires the effort and sacrifice of many people. I would like to begin with a heartfelt expression of appreciation for the Pearson Longman English team. *Writing for Life* has afforded me the opportunity to work with and learn from a talented group of people. I thank the editorial team for giving me the opportunity to partner with Dorling Kindersley (DK), whose design so beautifully appeals to visual and verbal learners. I would like to specifically thank Richard Czapnik, Anthony Limerick, and Ian Midson from DK for their hard work on this project. Matt Wright, Acquisitions Editor, is a wonderful partner to whom I am indebted and grateful for his enthusiastic support and active involvement throughout this process. I have been fortunate to work with a talented, insightful, and gracious developmental editor, Katharine Glynn. I also extend my heartfelt gratitude to Heather Brady, whose work as my assistant is of immeasurable value.

I would like to acknowledge the production team for *Writing for Life* beginning with Kathy Smith from Nesbitt Graphics, Inc., who served as copy-editor and project coordinator, and Genevieve Coyne, proofreader. I am also grateful to Ellen MacElree, Production Manager. And I would like to acknowledge Dustin Weeks, Senior Professor of Library Sciences, Daytona State College, for his contributions of writing samples for student activities, and Steve Yarborough, Bellevue Community College, for composing the Instructor's Manual.

Finally, I would like to gratefully recognize the invaluable insights provided by the following colleagues and reviewers. I deeply appreciate their investment of time, energy, and wisdom.

Nina Bannett, *New York City College of Technology CUNY;* **Liz Barnes,** *Daytona State College—Main;* **Carolyn Barr,** *Broward College;* **Craig Bartholomaus,** *MCCKC—Penn Valley;* **Elisabeth Bass,** *Camden County College;* **Kathleen Beauchene,** *Community College of Rhode Island;* **Nicholas Bekas,** *Valencia Community College;* **Tina L. Bennett,** *Wichita State University;* **James Bernarducci,** *Middlesex Community College;* **Linda Black,** *St. John's River Community College—Orange Park;* **Kay Blue,** *Owens Community College;* **Randy Boone,** *Northampton Community College;* **Brad Bostian,** *Central Piedmont Community College;* **Patricia Bostian,** *Central Piedmont Community College;* **Aaron Bradford,** *American River College;* **Kathy Britton,** *Florence Darlington Technical College;* **Tracy Brunner,** *Broward Community College;* **Jeff Burdick,** *Willow International College Center;* **Cheryl Cardoza,** *Truckee Meadows Community College;* **Jessica Carroll,** *Miami Dade College—Wolfson;* **Cynthia Cash,** *Southwest Tennessee Community College;* **Gail Harrison Charrier,** *Delaware Technical and Community College;* **Karen Chow,** *DeAnza College;* **Terry Clark,** *Kennedy-King College;* **Jennifer M. Condon,** *Iowa Central Community College;* **Kennette Crockett,** *Malcolm X College;* **Susan Cunningham,** *Ohlone College;* **Kathy Daily,** *Tulsa Community College;* **Sharon Davidson,** *Baton Rouge Community College;* **Nancy Davies,** *Miami Dade College—Homestead;* **Brenda K. DelMaramo,** *Thiel College;* **Marjorie Dernaika,** *Southwest Tennessee Community College;* **Marianna Duncan,** *Angelina College;* **Cynthia M. Dunham-Gonzalez,** *Seminole Community College;* **Marie G. Eckstrom,** *Rio Hondo College;* **Margot A. Edlin;** *Queensborough Community College, CUNY;* **Cheryl Elsmore,** *Antelope Valley College;* **Gwyn Enright,** *San Diego City College;* **Laurie Esler,** *Southern Wesleyan University;* **Cathy Fagan,** *Nassau Community College;* **Karen Feldman,**

Seminole Community College; **Robert Ficociello,** *SUNY Albany and Middlesex Community College;* **Catherine Fraga,** *Sacramento State University;* **Deborah Fuller,** *Bunker Hill Community College;* **Paul T. Gallagher,** *Red Rocks Community College;* **Maria Garcia-Landry,** *Palm Beach Community College—North;* **Lois Garrison,** *Tacoma Community College;* **Tom Ghering,** *Ivy Tech Community College of Indiana;* **Wendy Goodwin,** *Miami Dade College—Homestead;* **James Gray,** *St. Petersburg College;* **Jeremy L. Griggs,** *Lewis & Clark Community College;* **Judy Haisten,** *Central Florida Community College;* **Denise Haley,** *Bunker Hill Community College;* **Cynthia Halstead,** *Broward Community College;* **Beth Hammett,** *College of the Mainland;* **Greg Hammond,** *New Mexico Junior College;* **Anna Harrington,** *Jackson State Community College;* **Julia I. Hoesel,** *Iowa Central Community College;* **Ken Holliday,** *Southern State Community College;* **Tai L. Houser,** *Broward College—North;* **Kalpana M. Iyengar,** *St. Mary's University;* **Richard Johnson,** *Kirkwood Community College;* **Peter Kearly,** *Henry Ford Community College;* **Christine Kling,** *Broward College—South;* **Helene Kozma,** *Housatonic Community College;* **Catherine Lally,** *Brevard Community College—Cocoa;* **Valerie Lazzara,** *Palm Beach Community College—Lake Worth;* **Angela Leeds,** *Brevard Community College;* **Reginald Lockett,** *San Jose City College;* **Erin Lofthouse,** *City College of San Francisco;* **Dana Thiry Dildine Lopez,** *Eastern New Mexico University-Ruidoso;* **John Luukkonen,** *TCI College of Technology;* **Joseph Marshall,** *Villa Julie College;* **Erin T. Martz,** *Northern Virginia Community College;* **Carl Mason,** *UMass Lowell;* **Dr. James S. May,** *Valencia Community College—East;* **Charlene McDaniel,** *Cincinnati State Technical and Community College;* **Diane McDonald,** *Montgomery County Community College;* **Judy McKenzie,** *Lane Community College;* **David Merves,** *Miami Dade College, North Campus;* **John Miller,** *Normandale Community College;* **Rosemary Mink,** *Mohawk Valley Community College;* **Kelley Montford,** *Colorado Technical University;* **Dave Moutray,** *Kankakee Community College;* **Andrea Neptune,** *Sierra College;* **Julie Nichols,** *Okaloosa–Walton College;* **Sandra Offiah,** *Daytona State College—Main;* **Kelly Ormsby,** *Cleveland State Community College;* **Elizabeth Patterson,** *Melton–Delta State University;* **Jay Peterson,** *Atlantic Cape Community College;* **Dawn Pickett,** *Blinn College;* **Diane L. Polcha,** *Tulsa Community College, Southeast Campus;* **Jesus Quintero,** *DeAnza College;* **Jennifer Ratcliff,** *North Central Texas College;* **Brian L. Reeves,** *Tomball College;* **Dana Resente,** *Montgomery County College;* **Charlotte Teresa Reynolds,** *Indiana State University Southwest;* **Leigh Ann Rhea,** *Calhoun Community College;* **Doug Rigby,** *Lehigh Carbon Community College;* **Elizabeth Robbins,** *University of Alaska Southeast;* **Tina Royer,** *Folsom Lake College;* **Sara Safdie,** *University of California, San Diego;* **Rebecca Samberg,** *Housatonic Community College;* **Justina M. Sapna,** *Delaware Technical and Community College–Owens;* **Lisa Sapra,** *Folsom Lake College;* **Tracy Schneider,** *Solano Community College;* **Albert C. Sears,** *Silver Lake College;* **Cherise Shane,** *Community College of Philadelphia;* **Sharon Shapiro,** *Naugatuck Valley Community College;* **Deneen Shepherd,** *St. Louis Community College, Forest Park;* **Rachel Shreve,** *Palm Beach Community College—North;* **Carmen Simpson,** *St. Petersburg College—Clearwater;* **Jac-Lyn Stark,** *Bunker Hill Community College;* **James Suderman,** *Okaloosa-Walton College;* **Holly J. Susi,** *Community College of Rhode Island;* **Nanette Tamer,** *Villa Julie College;* **Etheline Thomas,** *Delaware Technical & Community College—Wilmington;* **Joseph W. Thweatt,** *Southwest Tennessee Community College;* **Tara Timberman,** *Rowan University;* **Trisha Travers,** *Penn State University—Abington;* **Thomas Treffinger,** *Greenville Technical College;* **Sharisse Turner,** *Tallahassee Community College;* **Christopher Z. Twiggs,** *Florida Community College at Jacksonville,* **Cynthia M. VanSickle;** *McHenry Community College,* **Linda VanVickle,** *St. Louis Community College–Meramec;* **Maria Villar-Smith,** *Miami Dade College—Wolfson;* **Kymberli G. Ward,** *Southwestern Oklahoma State University;* **Michael T. Warren,** *Maple Woods Community College;* **Jeff Westfall,** *Skyline College;* **Kathleen G. White,** *Bellevue Community College;* **Margie Wilkoff,** *St. Petersburg College;* **Rachael Williams,** *West Georgia Technical College;* **Jilani Worsi,** *Queensborough Community College;* **Elizabeth Zarubin,** *City College of San Francisco*

1

LEARNING OUTCOMES

● What's the Point of Preparing to Learn about Writing?

● Making a Point about Preparing to Learn about Writing: One Student Writer's Response

● Preparing Yourself to Learn about Writing

Preparing to Learn about Writing

In countless situations in life, preparation is essential to success. Even a trip to the grocery store requires some planning in order to get all the items needed to feed a family and run a household in the most economical way. A careful shopper may create a menu, check the pantry and make a list of what is needed, read the ads for sale items, or clip coupons. In short, an effective shopper thinks about the outcome or goal of each shopping trip before going shopping.

Just as a wise shopper prepares to shop, a wise student writer prepares to learn about writing. Writing is an essential life skill, and learning to write well allows you to express yourself, influence others, succeed in college, and compete in the job market. By starting your academic career with this writing course, you are preparing for success. You are laying a sturdy foundation for writing for life. If you are like many others, you may have a few qualms about writing, but take heart! With the right attitude, a clear set of learning outcomes, and a study plan, you *can* learn to write well. Get ready to learn about writing!

What's the Point of Preparing to Learn about Writing?

Like any other worthwhile endeavor, learning requires preparation. Preparation usually involves setting a goal, adopting an attitude for success, setting aside time to accomplish the task, gathering tools or supplies, and planning a course of action.

PHOTOGRAPHIC ORGANIZER: PREPARING TO LEARN

The following pictures represent one student's effort to prepare to learn about writing. Write a caption for each photograph that identifies her efforts to prepare to learn.

LEARNING OUTCOMES
READING AND WRITING

Practice 1

WRITING FROM LIFE

What is this?

What is this?

What is this?

What is this?

What's the point?

Making a Point about Preparing to Learn about Writing: One Student Writer's Response

The following paragraph records one student's efforts to prepare to learn about writing. As you read the paragraph, underline specific steps he took that you might use as well.

Prepared to Learn

(1) I began preparing to learn about writing on the first day of class. (2) First, I read the course syllabus, which listed the books and materials I needed; later that day, I bought everything listed, and I brought everything I needed with me to every class. (3) I found three people who wanted to learn as much as I did so we formed a study group. (4) We helped each other a lot throughout the whole semester. (5) If one of us was sick, we made sure he or she got the notes and assignment for that day, and we read each other's papers to make sure they made sense and didn't have any careless errors. (6) I also used a daily planner to record assignments and set aside time to study and write. (7) I arrived a few minutes early when possible, so that when class began, I was prepared to get to work. (8) I have to admit I had to work on my attitude. (9) I was so shy and afraid of sounding silly that asking questions in class was really hard, so for a while, I stayed after class to ask my questions, but eventually, I gained enough confidence to ask them during class. (10) I also had to learn how to deal with feedback on my papers. (11) I worked so hard on each essay, yet for a long time, my papers came back to me with grades and edits that showed I still needed to improve. (12) It took a while for my hard work to pay off, but I was determined to succeed. (13) I am proud to say, all my preparation and hard work paid off. (14) Not only did I earn an "A," but I also improved my ability to write.

Preparing Yourself to Learn about Writing

As you prepare to learn about writing, take some time to evaluate yourself as a student writer. Think about your attitude, ways you can become an active learner, your relationship with your teacher, your study plan, and how you will track your growing writing abilities. The more you reflect and the more you prepare, the more likely you are to learn about writing and to become an effective writer.

The Attitude of Learning

Use Positive Self-Talk

Many people have negative thoughts going through their minds that constantly repeat "I can't" phrases: "I can't write… I can't spell." Often these negative attitudes are the result of a prior negative event. A basic step to success is changing that script in your head. Replace "I can't" thoughts with "I can." Then, take steps to prove that you can. For example, instead of believing "I just can't spell," think, "I can use a spell checker," or "I can make a list of words I often misspell and memorize their correct spellings." Success begins in your mind!

Be an Active Learner

Come to class. Be on time. Sit where you can see—and be seen. Take notes. Ask questions. Do your work—on time! Make connections between assignments and learning outcomes. Apply what you learn. Seek help. Find a study partner. Take responsibility for your own learning. The more you do, the more you learn!

Trust Your Teacher

One of the toughest tasks in a writing class is getting and accepting feedback on your writing. Many of us take the teacher's feedback as a personal rejection. Some of us become defensive. Think of feedback as a form of coaching from a personal trainer. A personal trainer assesses your strengths and needs, creates an exercise program, and corrects your form to ensure that you make progress. Likewise, your teacher is your writing coach who offers expert advice. So accept feedback as helpful advice. Take note of those errors, study the rules, and revise your work. Turn feedback into an opportunity to learn!

Practice 2

Read the following reflection written by a student that records how she feels about writing and why. On a separate sheet of paper, write a letter to her, giving her advice to help her overcome her anxiety.

To this day, the very thought of writing an essay and turning it in for a grade makes my hands sweat and my stomach churn. I have pretty painful memories of writing classes. For example, in one class, I always sat at the back of the class. One day the teacher gave my paper back by handing it to the person in the front of the row to pass back. Every one in my row got to see the large red "D" at the top of my paper and all the red marks pointing out each one of my errors. I always thought that teacher had it in for me! I never could bring myself to read the comments, and I was too embarrassed to ask questions. It didn't seem to matter, anyway because I just can't write. Besides, I never really had time to write.

Create a Study Plan

A vital part of preparing to learn about writing is creating a study plan.

Gather Your Tools

Foster success by preparing a study place that is equipped with all the tools you will need: reference materials such as your textbook, a dictionary, a thesaurus, magazines, newspapers, and other reading materials of interest to you; pens (blue or black ink), pencils, and paper; a stapler and 3-hole punch. Optional items include a computer and a printer. In addition, you will need a 3-ring binder to hold the teacher's syllabus, handouts, assignments, class notes, textbook notes, and lab work. Be sure that you bring your textbook, binder, pens, and pencils to class every day.

Set Goals

Students who set goals reduce stress, improve concentration, and increase self-confidence. Use the following guidelines to set effective goals. *Aim high:* Demand your best effort. *Write goals down:* Recording goals makes them clear and important. *Be specific:* Instead of writing "Stop procrastinating," write "Study English on Monday, Tuesday, and Wednesday evenings between 7 and 9 o'clock." *Be positive:* Instead of writing "Don't make stupid errors," write "Use commas properly." *Set priorities:* Rank goals based on need so you can pace your work. *Set daily goals based on larger goals:* Break a larger goal such as "Understand how to use semicolons" into a series of steps such as "Study the rule, take notes, and do the exercises; then proofread my paper for proper use of semicolons."

Take Action

Turn your goals into action steps by setting up a time schedule for your study. The following study plan is easy to use, flexible, and will help you set long-term, intermediate, and short-term goals.

SAMPLE STUDY PLAN	
Long-Term Schedule:	Record ongoing weekly commitments such as job hours, class meetings, church, and so on, for the entire semester.
Intermediate Schedule:	Make a short list of the events taking place and the tasks to be completed in your class (or classes) this week. Make a fresh list each week, as these activities will change from week to week: Writing assignment Tuesday; Math quiz Tuesday; Chapter 3 in English by Wednesday.
Short-Term Schedule:	On an index card every morning (or the night before), list your daily schedule. Be specific! Then, carry this card with you and cross off each goal as you accomplish it. Monday: 9:00–9:30 Revise writing assignment; 12:00–12:30 Review math for quiz; 3:30 Return books to library; 7:00–9:00 Read first 30 pages of Chapter 3 for English.

Practice 3

CREATE A STUDY PLAN

Complete the following chart to create your own study plan. Discuss your plan with your class or in a small group. How will your plan change throughout the semester?

MY STUDY PLAN	
Long-Term Schedule:	
Intermediate Schedule:	
Short-Term Schedule:	

Practice 4

ATTITUDE AND BEHAVIORS OF LEARNING

Complete the survey. Then on your own paper, answer the following question: "What can you do to improve your writing attitude or behaviors?"

Writing Attitude and Behavior Survey	Strongly Agree	Agree	Disagree	Strongly Disagree
1. I enjoy writing.				
2. I respond to teacher feedback.				
3. I enjoy sharing what I write with peers.				
4. I appreciate the chance to revise.				
5. I want to improve my writing.				
6. I have a quiet, well-equipped study place.				
7. I always come to class prepared.				
8. I complete assignments on time.				
9. I read and study to improve my writing.				
10. I manage my time wisely.				

Learning Outcomes for Student Writers

Now that you understand some of the basic guidelines for setting goals and the importance of your attitudes and behaviors, you are ready to think about your specific goals as a student writer. Many people think of a goal as an "outcome." For example, for each goal, ask "What is the outcome of this goal? What should I know or be able to do once I reach this goal?" In a writing class, a **learning outcome** states what a student writer should know or be able to do as the result of a lesson or a course of study.

The following chart outlines five major learning outcomes (goals) for student writers. Each major learning outcome is built upon its listed set of skills and concepts. Notice that the learning outcomes are stated as actions. Every assignment is an opportunity to prove mastery of one or more of these learning outcomes.

LO-S: Learning Outcomes—Structure

- **Identify/Apply the *Structure* of a paragraph and an essay**
  - Introduction
  - Main Idea
  - Body: Major, Minor Supporting Details
  - Conclusion

LO-WP: Learning Outcomes—Writing Process

- **Identify/Apply the phases of the *Writing Process***
  - **Prewrite**
    - Analyze the three aspects of the **writing situation**
      - Topic
      - Purpose
      - Audience
    - Brainstorm, Map, Outline
  - **Draft** paragraphs and essays
    - Compose **a main idea**: topic sentence, thesis sentence
    - Generate **adequate and relevant details**
    - Use **logical order** of ideas
  - **Revise** drafts for **effective expression**
    - Control sentence structure
    - Use words appropriately
  - **Proofread** drafts for **effective expression**
    - Identify and **correct errors** in grammar

LO-RW: Learning Outcomes—Connect Reading and Writing

- **Read to Write; Think Critically**
  - Analyze a piece of writing
  - Write a summary
  - Provide constructive criticism to others

LO-SE: Learning Outcome—Self-Evaluation

- **Self-evaluate; Think Critically**
  - Reflect on writing **progress**
  - Reflect on writing **process**

LO-DOC: Use of Sources

- **Document sources according to the MLA format**
  - Find relevant outside sources
  - Evaluate outside sources
  - Format sources in text and in Works Cited

You will achieve these outcomes as you study *Writing for Life*. To help you make the most of your studies, the icons for these learning outcomes appear in the margins throughout this textbook. Use the icons to connect a lesson to its learning outcome.

Practice 5

CONSIDER YOUR LEARNING OUTCOMES

To begin your learning process about writing, identify what you already know about writing and what you need to learn. Answer the following questions.

1. Which three learning outcomes pose the greatest challenge? Why?

....

....

2. Which three learning outcomes have you already mastered? How could you prove mastery?

....

....

Make the Connection between Writing and Reading

Writing and reading are closely related thinking processes. Writing is the process of expressing meaning with written symbols. Reading is the process of getting meaning from written symbols. A writer sends a message, and a reader receives a message. An effective writer thinks about the reader (audience). An effective reader thinks about the writer (author). Thus, writing and reading rely on and strengthen each other.

Reading benefits a writer in many ways. For example, by reading, a writer gains the following:

- New vocabulary
- Different opinions on a topic
- Additional facts about a topic
- Details that support an opinion

- Varying ways to apply writing techniques
  - Ways to use punctuation
  - Ways to use fresh or creative expressions
  - Ways to write sentences
  - Ways to organize ideas
  - Ways to open and close an essay

The more you read, the more you know and the more you have to write about.

A major similarity between reading and writing is that each is a thinking process best accomplished in specific stages. Careful thought before, during, and after reading a selection or writing a piece improves your ability to do both. The following chart correlates the stages of the reading and the writing processes.

The Thinking Process Connects Writing and Reading		
Thinking	**Writing**	**Reading**
Before	**Pre-write:** Ask questions and skim details to discover your audience, purpose, and point for writing; read for information to use in your writing.	**Pre-read:** Ask questions and skim the text; note headings, words in bold or italics, or graphics; predict the author's audience, purpose, and point.
During	**Draft:** Express your purpose and point through the use of key words, main ideas, and supporting details. **Revise:** Rephrase or reorganize ideas to clearly support your point; help readers to see your purpose and point; use details to create a mental picture for your reader.	**Read:** Comprehend the writer's purpose and point with the use of key words, main ideas, and supporting details. **Apply fix-up strategies:** Use context clues to understand new words; reread a few sentences or a paragraph; make a mental picture of the point.
After	**Edit and Publish:** Create an error-free draft that expresses your new insights and skills as a writer.	**Reflect and Record:** Adjust your views based on new information gained through reading; write in response to what you have read; restate the writer's main points; agree or disagree with what you have read.

CONNECT WRITING TO READING

In your notebook, describe the process you use to write. Then describe the process you use to read. Discuss the following questions with a peer or in a small group:

1. How are your thinking processes similar to or different from the ones described in the chart?

2. How can each of you use the connection between reading and writing to improve as a writer?

Practice 6

Use the Reading Process to Strengthen Your Writing

Reading is a thinking process made up of a series of phases. The process is recursive; the reader may loop or combine any of the stages at any point during the process. The following graphic illustrates the highly recommended **SQ3R** reading process.

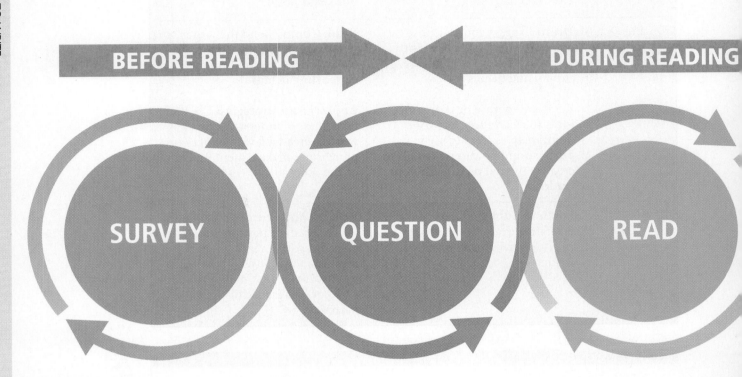

BEFORE READING

DURING READING

SURVEY

QUESTION

READ

Skim the selection to note the following: titles, subheadings, key terms in bold or italic type, graphics, pictures.

Ask the following: What is the topic? What do I already know? What is the author's purpose? How are the ideas organized? What is my purpose for reading?

Read to answer questions; adjust pace based on difficulty; reread to understand.

AFTER READING

RECITE

REVIEW

Annotate the text; underline main ideas; circle key terms; record questions and short summaries in margins; restate ideas out loud.

Review questions based on headings; review new words; connect new ideas to prior knowledge; write a response.

CONNECT WRITING TO READING

Working with a peer or small group of classmates, answer the following questions:

1. How is each chapter in *Writing for Life* (such as Chapters 6 and 16) based on SQ3R?

2. How will the use of SQ3R to study this textbook help you improve as a writer?

3. Besides this textbook, what else can you, as a writer, read?

4. As a writer, how would you use SQ3R to get information from a magazine or newspaper?

5. How could you use SQ3R to edit a peer's paper?

Practice 7

Create a Portfolio of Your Work

To ensure that you learn about writing and to develop writing skills, you need to track your strengths, your needs, and your growth. A portfolio enables you to organize your work and think about what you are learning.

What Is a Portfolio?

A portfolio is a collection of **all** the work you do as a writer organized in a notebook or electronic folder. Your portfolio shows your hard work and your growth because its contents document how much time and effort you put into your writing. A portfolio allows you to assess your own strengths, needs, and goals.

What Should I Include in My Portfolio?

Your portfolio may include class notes and activities, textbook notes and exercises, grammar tests, lab activities, reflective journal entries, and drafts of your writing. By collecting and organizing your work, you are better able to reflect upon your strengths and needs. As a result, you are able to achieve specific learning outcomes as a writer. For example, to prove mastery of the learning outcome "identify and apply the phases of the writing process," you should file in your portfolio all the prewrites, drafts, and final copies of your writings. In addition, the lessons, practices, workshops, and learning logs in this textbook are tied to one or more learning outcomes. An icon appears next to an activity to identify its learning outcome. The learning activities in *Writing for Life* are excellent entries for your portfolio. You can tear out the pages of this textbook and organize them in your portfolio to prove your progress toward specific learning outcomes.

What Is a Reflective Journal Entry?

Reflective journal entries are tied to the learning outcome "Self-Evaluation." In this type of journal entry, you reflect upon your "writing process" and your "writing progress." (See page 88.) A reflective journal entry is an informal piece of writing in which you analyze some aspect of your work as a student writer. In each of the chapters about writing paragraphs, you will read a writer's journal that records this kind of thinking. By writing your own reflective journal entries, you can track and overcome your writing barriers.

Reflective Journals: Self-Assessment

Critical Thinking Questions

To deepen your critical thinking about the feedback you have received, your reflective journal entry also should answer the following questions:

- [ ] What steps did I take to write this piece? Did I prewrite, write, revise, and proofread? Do I need to spend more time on any one step?

- [ ] Which of my errors are proofreading errors? What steps will I take to catch these proofreading errors on my next piece of writing?

- [ ] Which of these errors results from the need to study a certain rule? Where in my textbook is this rule found? How much time do I need to learn this rule? How will I study this rule (take notes, complete exercises)?

What Is the Best Way to Set Up My Portfolio?

Many students purchase a 3-ring binder and tabbed dividers to section off different types of study and writing tasks. Be sure to date and label all work.

All work that is turned in for feedback should include the following information: At the top of the first page and flush with the left margin, place your name, your professor's name, the course name or number (include the section number if the course has multiple sections), and the date you're turning in the paper, each on a separate line with double-spacing throughout.

> Iama Writer
>
> Dr. Richards
>
> ENC 001: Section 32
>
> September 24, 2010

All independent work that is created for your notebook or portfolio should be labeled with the date and by the type of work or learning outcome.

> Oct. 9, 2010   Outcome: Self-Evaluation
> Reflective Journal Entry for Narrative Paragraph

> Oct. 10, 2010   Outcome: Structure, Reading-Writing
> Comma Splices, Chapter 21, pp. 422–437

> Oct. 12, 2010   Outcome: Structure, Reading-Writing
> The Process Paragraph, Class notes

The point of labeling is to help you see and discuss your strengths, needs, and growth as they occur in real time.

Practice 8

To get the best use of this textbook, learn more about the connection between the learning outcomes on page 9 and the lessons in *Writing for Life*. Answer the following questions.

1. Go to page 53 in Chapter 3 "Understanding the Paragraph." List the headings in bold, and list the learning outcome for this section.

_____

2. Go to page 68 in Chapter 3. List the headings in bold print, and list the learning outcome for this section.

_____

_____

3. Go to page 73 in Chapter 4 "The Descriptive Paragraph." List the learning outcome(s) for the Photographic Organizer.

_____

4. Go to page 105 in Chapter 5. List the learning outcome for the Writing Assignments.

_____

5. Go to page 357, Chapter 18 "Sentence Variety." List the learning outcome for the Writing Assignments.

_____

6. Go to page 537, Chapter 29 "Commas." List the learning outcome for the Academic Learning Log.

_____

Practice 9

THE PORTFOLIO

Write an e-mail to a classmate who was absent. Explain the portfolio process. Explain how portfolio assessment will improve your writing skills.

_____

_____

_____

_____

QUESTIONS FOR PREPARING TO LEARN ABOUT WRITING

Academic Learning Log

To test and track your understanding of what you have studied, answer the following questions.

1. What are some of the materials and supplies needed by a writing student?

----

2. What are the three attitudes of learning discussed in this chapter?

----

3. What three general steps can you take to create a study plan?

----

4. What is a learning outcome?

----

5. What are the four major learning outcomes?

----

6. What is a portfolio?

----

7. What is included in a portfolio?

----

8. What is a reflective journal entry?

----

mywritinglab
WANT A BETTER GRADE?
For more practice with preparing to learn about writing, go to **www.mywritinglab.com**
> Getting Ready to Write
> Prepare to Learn about Writing.

2

Thinking Through the Writing Process

The writing process has four stages: prewriting, drafting, revising, and proofreading.

Writing develops, records, and communicates your thoughts to other people. Careful writers rely on the writing process to discover, organize, and record information in response to a specific writing situation.

What's the Point of the Writing Process?

The following photographs document some of the situations in which we use writing in our everyday, college, and working lives. Write a caption for each picture that includes a reason for writing well in that situation. Then, state the point of writing well.

Practice 1

PHOTOGRAPHIC ORGANIZER: REASONS TO WRITE

WRITING FROM LIFE

What's the point of writing well?

My First Thoughts: A Prewriting Activity

Set a time limit, such as five minutes, and jot down in your notebook your thoughts about the importance of writing. Do not let your pen or pencil stop, even if you must repeat ideas. Keep writing until the time limit is up.

PREWRITING

LEARNING OUTCOMES
SELF-EVALUATION

Making a Point about the Writing Process: One Student Writer's Response

The following paragraph is one writer's response to the question "What's the point of writing?"

> Writing can increase our academic, personal, and economic power. Of course, writing is necessary to succeed in college, yet writing is also important outside the classroom. For example, if I have strong writing skills, I am much more likely to get a job, promotions, and higher pay. In addition, writing allows me to express myself in everyday life. For example, I am really worried about forest fires started by careless campers. A well-written letter to the editor might make just one person think about campfire safety. And a thank you note allows me to express my appreciation for someone who has supported me; it's a way of giving back. Really, writing is thinking on paper. Writing allows me to think, remember, organize, record, learn, and share ideas.

LEARNING OUTCOMES
READING AND WRITING

Understanding the Point: Assessing the Writing Situation

When you write, you develop a point about a topic to fulfill a purpose for a specific audience. To develop your point, you need to think about two aspects of writing: the writing situation and the writing process.

A piece of writing develops in response to a specific **writing situation** that is composed of the **topic** (your subject), the **purpose** for writing (your goal), and the **audience** (your reader).

TOPIC
What you write

AUDIENCE
Who reads your writing

PURPOSE
Why you write

The Topic: What You Write

When writing about situations in our personal lives, we may choose to compose a letter of complaint to a business or an e-mail to a friend. Often in these circumstances, the topic of our writing naturally emerges from our need to communicate. However, when writing for college, many of us face writer's block in our search for a topic. You can break through writer's block by building a topic bank for college writing.

The following thinking guide can help you generate a bank of topics.

The Writing Situation Step by Step:

Topic

Build a bank of topics by listing ideas in a special section in your notebook. Use the following prompts to create several lists:

- ☐ Write down the major topics of importance in a specific course (such as biology, psychology, history).
- ☐ Find interesting or important current events.
  - ☐ Topics most often covered in magazines and newspapers
  - ☐ Controversial topics from television (such as news and talk shows)
  - ☐ Topics about which you want to learn more
  - ☐ Topics about which you feel deeply
  - ☐ Hobbies and personal interests
- ☐ Share your lists with your classmates; use class discussion to generate more ideas.
- ☐ Review and expand your list on a regular basis.

As you continue to build your bank of general topics, read, read, and read some more. Read newspapers, magazines, and textbooks for additional topics. Many textbooks provide writing topics at the end of sections or chapters; in addition, headings and subheadings of chapters or sections are excellent sources of topics for your writing.

TOPICS

Skim a newspaper, a magazine, and a textbook and write a list of five topics from each one. Then, share your list with your class or in a small group.

TOPICS FROM A NEWSPAPER: ....

....

TOPICS FROM A MAGAZINE: ....

....

TOPICS FROM A TEXTBOOK: ....

....

Practice 2

The Purpose: Why You Write

Good writing focuses on a goal or purpose. Your writing will flow much more easily when you write with purpose. The following chart presents four basic purposes for writing.

Informative

When writing informatively, your purpose is to share, explain, or demonstrate information.

EXAMPLE:
An **informative essay** that explains the steps of photosynthesis to your reader; a paragraph that answers an exam question about the major causes of stress.

Persuasive

When writing persuasively, your purpose is to change your reader's opinion or call your reader to take action.

EXAMPLE:
An **argumentative essay** that convinces your reader to begin a physical fitness program; a letter to the editor that argues in favor of a law that requires the use of seatbelts.

Expressive

When writing expressively, your purpose is to share with the reader your personal opinions, feelings, or reactions to a topic.

EXAMPLE:
An **expressive piece**—a poem, short story, or personal essay, for example— that expresses your view about a social problem such as poverty or drug abuse.

Reflective

When writing reflectively, your purpose is to record your understanding about what you have experienced or learned.

EXAMPLE:
An **informal essay** that explores what you think is significant about a current event; a journal entry that discusses the strengths of a paper written by you or a peer.

The following thinking guide can help you identify your purpose in writing.

The Writing Situation Step by Step:

Purpose

- ☐ Annotate the lists of topics in your topic bank to indicate possible purposes for each topic: Beside each topic write **I** for informative, **P** for persuasive, **E** for expressive, or **R** for reflective.

- ☐ Generate four sets of topics based on different purposes for writing, using "The Writing Situation Step by Step: Topic" box on page 21 to guide your thinking.

- ☐ Select one topic for each of the four purposes and complete the following statements:

  - ☐ This topic will inform the reader about...

  - ☐ This topic will persuade the reader to...

  - ☐ This topic will express...

  - ☐ This topic will reflect upon...

PURPOSE

State the purpose of each of the following topic sentences. Discuss with your class or in a small group how a writer's purposes may be combined in certain situations.

1. My experience and education make me an excellent candidate for this job.

- -

2. Adult stem cell research should be funded by the government.

- -

3. The gentle breeze, the lapping water, and the dappled shade soothe the human soul.

- -

4. Eating disorders fall into several categories based on their symptoms.

- -

5. Based on my unit exam, I need to review the following topics.

- -

Practice 3

The Audience: Who Reads Your Writing

When we take part in a conversation, we know exactly to whom we are speaking, and we adjust our tone, word choice, and examples to match the situation. For example, contrast how you talk with a friend with the way you talk to the dean of your college. Audience has the same impact in the writing situation.

Assume that you have chosen to write about the topic of marijuana. What main points do you want each of the following audiences to consider about this drug? Use the blanks below each picture to record your ideas.

The following thinking guide can help you identify your audience.

The Writing Situation Step by Step:

Audience

☐ Choose a specific topic and purpose for writing.

☐ List the traits of your audience that are relevant to your topic and purpose:

    ☐ Age

    ☐ Gender

    ☐ Education level

☐ If you are writing for a general audience of mixed traits, identify the main traits most relevant to your topic and purpose.

☐ Identify three or four points about the topic of most interest to a specific audience.

☐ Choose several key words to describe your topic and hook the interest of a specific audience. Use a thesaurus to find the words best suited for your audience.

AUDIENCE

Based on your first thoughts about the audiences represented by the four pictures on page 24, write a brief response to the following questions. Then, discuss your answers with your class or in a small group.

- What are the most important traits of each audience represented by the pictures?

- Did your main points differ based on the audience? Why or why not?

- Will your word choice or examples differ based on the audience? Why or why not?

Practice 4

Practice 5

AUDIENCE

Each of the following four pieces of writing appeals to one of the audiences depicted by the photos on page 24. Write the letter of the piece of writing in the picture that shows its audience.

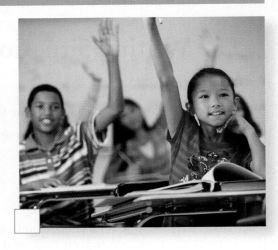

A. Scientists funded by the National Institute on Drug Abuse (NIDA), a federal government agency, have found that the damage to the brain's thinking abilities that results from smoking marijuana can last up to 28 days after an individual last smoked the drug.

B. Marijuana use today starts at a younger age—and more potent forms of the drug are available to you. Marijuana use is a serious threat—do not use it!

C. Under the influence of marijuana, you can forget your best friend's phone number, watch your grade point average drop like a stone, or get into a car accident.

D. Welcome to the Mothers Against Drugs speaker series. During today's speaker panel, we'll investigate the fascinating facts about marijuana. You may have heard it called pot, weed, grass, ganja, or skunk, but marijuana by any other name is still a drug that affects the brain.

When student writers are asked "Who is your audience?" most reply, "The teacher." Of course, the teacher is your immediate audience, and you must carefully consider his or her expectations. However, many teachers understand the value of writing to a real-life audience. College is preparing you for success in life. You are learning to write for life.

TOPIC AND AUDIENCE

The following writing prompts apply an academic topic to a real audience.

Write the name of the college course(s) for each prompt and describe the traits of each audience. Discuss your answers with your class or in a small group. Talk about how each audience affects the writer's choice of words and details.

1. Write a letter to the editor of a newspaper that compares the war in Iraq to the Vietnam War.

COURSE(S): ....

AUDIENCE: ....

....

....

2. Write a report for the school board that explains the benefits of smaller class sizes.

COURSE(S): ....

AUDIENCE: ....

....

....

3. Write an e-mail to a classmate explaining the five steps for problem solving.

COURSE(S): ....

AUDIENCE: ....

....

....

4. Write a memo to a new, young employee at a fast food restaurant that explains how the cost of his insurance is based on his age.

COURSE(S): ....

AUDIENCE: ....

....

....

Understanding the Point: Using the Writing Process

Writing is a process that comprises a series of phases or steps. The process approach focuses on the writer, the way writing is produced, and how the writer can improve his or her personal writing process. The process approach is recursive; the writer may loop or combine any of the stages at any point during the writing process. The key outcome at the end of the process is a published piece of writing. Throughout each stage, think about the relationships among your topic, purpose, and audience.

PREWRITING

Planning or rehearsing

DRAFTING

Getting ideas down in a preliminary form

PREWRITING

During the prewriting stage, you create a plan for your piece of writing.

This phase of writing is made up of the following steps:

- Decide on a topic.
- Determine your purpose for writing.
- Gather information.
- Generate details by using clusters, lists, and freewrites.
- Organize the details into an outline.

The rest of this chapter covers specific prewriting techniques.

DRAFTING

During the drafting stage, you create a draft of your writing.

This phase may include the following steps:

- Decide on an audience.
- Choose a format (such as an essay or a letter).
- Create an introduction, body, and conclusion for longer pieces.

Chapters 3–12 guide you through the entire writing process as you learn how to write paragraphs.

REVISING

PUBLISHING

Taking another look at
one's work

Preparing the piece for
publication

PROOFREADING

REVISING

During the revision phase, you fine tune the ideas in your essay. After you have written a draft, allow some time to pass so that you can examine your writing with fresh eyes.

This phase includes the following steps:
- Delete details that are not relevant.
- Add details to ideas that need more support.
- Reorder ideas for clarity.
- Insert transitions between details for a smooth flow of ideas.
- Replace vague or weak words with vivid, strong words.
- Write a new draft if necessary.

Part 5 covers specific skills to consider while revising.

PROOFREADING

During the editing phase of the writing process, you polish your draft so your reader will not be distracted or confused by careless errors.

This phase includes correcting errors such as:

- fragments
- fused sentences
- shift in tenses
- spelling
- punctuation

Part 6 covers the skills to consider during editing.

Prewriting

Have you ever stared at a blank piece of paper with a blank mind, unable to think of how to start a writing task? Or, have you ever had so many ideas that they jumble up in chaos so that you can't even begin to write? Finding those first few words to put on paper can grind a writer's thinking process to a complete halt and cause writer's anxiety.

▲ Students writing an exam

Some level of anxiety about writing is often a sign that you care about doing well. However, in excess, writer's anxiety can become a barrier. The first step to overcoming writer's anxiety is to understand why you feel anxious and how your anxiety affects your writing. Identifying the causes and effects of your writer's anxiety makes it easier to overcome.

SELF-EVALUATION OF WRITER'S ANXIETY

Complete the following survey to identify the causes and effects of your writer's anxiety. Then in your writer's journal, discuss the following: your level of writer's anxiety; the main causes of your anxiety; the main effects of your anxiety on your writing.

Causes of Writer's Anxiety	High/Often			Low/Never		
I worry about my grade.	6	5	4	3	2	1
Deadlines make me nervous.	6	5	4	3	2	1
I feel pressure to excel.	6	5	4	3	2	1
I fear failure.	6	5	4	3	2	1
I am competitive by nature.	6	5	4	3	2	1
I am distracted by my personal life or social issues.	6	5	4	3	2	1
My professor seems intimidating.	6	5	4	3	2	1
The writing assignment seems irrelevant or boring.	6	5	4	3	2	1
In the past, I have received harsh criticism on my writing.	6	5	4	3	2	1
Effects of Writer's Anxiety						
I put off writing assignments until the last minute.	6	5	4	3	2	1
I get writer's block and cannot think of ideas.	6	5	4	3	2	1
I am unable to understand the writing assignment.	6	5	4	3	2	1
I think about my anxiety more than I do the assignment.	6	5	4	3	2	1
I turn in assignments late or not at all.	6	5	4	3	2	1

Even the best writers experience writer's anxiety now and then. Although no cure-all for writer's anxiety exists, prewriting fuels thinking, triggers the writing process, and fires past the block. Experienced writers have learned to spend time thinking about what they are going to write before they begin drafting.

In general, writing occurs long before you pick up your pen or your fingers touch the keyboard. **Prewriting** includes reading, listening, discussing, and thinking about your topic before you write a rough draft, capturing your prewriting thinking on paper. It allows you to explore ideas and plan your strategies without worrying about polishing them.

> **Prewriting** is the act of generating, exploring, developing, and roughly organizing ideas. Prewriting can help you choose a topic, narrow a topic, and put details related to a topic in logical order.

The rest of this section guides you through six prewriting techniques:
- Asking Questions:
    The Reporter's Questions
    Reflective Questions

- Freewriting
- Keeping a Journal
- Listing
- Concept Mapping
- Outlining

As you write for life, try out each one. Combine a few to stretch your thinking. Experiment with all of them. Discover which one(s) best suit you as a writer or in a particular writing situation.

Asking Questions

Asking questions helps you identify a topic and develop details about it based on thoughtful insights. Asking and answering questions helps you discover both what you already know and what you need to learn about the topic. Your goal as a writer is to share a point or main idea about a topic. Usually, a main idea or point is made up of the topic and the writer's opinion about the topic. Two types of questions enable you to explore topics and your opinions about those topics: the reporter's questions and reflective questions.

THE REPORTER'S QUESTIONS

To describe a newsworthy event, effective reporters gather the facts by asking six basic questions:

- Who?
- What?
- When?
- Where?
- Why?
- How?

At first, the answers to these questions may help you identify and narrow a topic that grabs your interest; once you have narrowed your topic, these questions also yield many details of support for your topic.

REFLECTIVE QUESTIONS

Reflective questions also help you discover your purpose for writing by revealing your attitude toward a topic. By using these questions to reflect, identify, and add your opinion about a topic to your writing, you can also narrow a writing topic that is too general.

Although reflective questions will vary based on the writing topic, the following three questions are good examples of some reflective questions that you can use to explore your views about most topics.

- What is the significance of this topic?
- Who should be interested in this topic?
- How can I best express my point to those who do not agree with me?

Asking and answering questions before writing will also guide you to make logical decisions about which details to select and highlight when you do begin to write.

Practice 8

TOPIC AND AUDIENCE

Assume you are writing a report on the power of propaganda for a history class. Discuss the use of the following poster by Norman Rockwell to raise support for World War II. Use the reporter's questions and reflective questions to brainstorm your first thoughts.

Reporter's Questions:

Who is the intended audience of the poster?

What is the relationship between this image and war?

Reflective Questions:

What do I know or need to know about World War II and Norman Rockwell?

In what ways could this poster relate to current events?

Should propaganda be used to support a war? Why or why not?

OURS...to fight for

FREEDOM FROM WANT

When you are ready to explore ideas about a topic on paper, the following thinking guide can help you use questions as a prewriting technique.

The Writing Process Step by Step:

Prewriting by Asking Questions

Use the reporter's questions to identify a topic, purpose, and audience.

- ☐ What?
- ☐ Why?
- ☐ Who?

Use the reporter's questions to generate details about the topic.

- ☐ When?
- ☐ Where?
- ☐ How?

Use reflective questions to identify attitudes and generate additional details about the topic.

- ☐ What are my attitudes or feelings about this topic?
- ☐ What are my audience's attitudes or feelings about this topic?
- ☐ Why is this topic important?
- ☐ How will my audience respond to my point?
- ☐ How can I make this topic interesting and relevant to my audience?

QUESTIONING

Assume you are reporting on the 9/11 attack on the World Trade Center. Using the box "The Writing Process Step by Step: Prewriting by Asking Questions," write a list of questions to identify your point and generate details. Share your ideas with the class or in a small group.

QUESTIONING

Ask questions to brainstorm your first thoughts about one of the following topics:

- Road Rage
- Graffiti
- Drug Abuse
- Positive Thinking
- Workplace Stress

Practice 9   Practice 10

Freewriting

During **freewriting**, you record your thoughts as they stream through your head. The key to this brainstorming strategy, like all prewriting activities, is to turn off the critic inside your head. At this point, no thought is wrong, off base, or silly. The idea is to warm up your thinking muscles, flex your creativity, and set your ideas free. The following thinking guide can help you use freewriting as a prewriting technique.

The Writing Process Step by Step:

Prewriting by Freewriting

☐ Set a time limit, such as ten minutes, and write whatever comes to mind as fast as you can, without stopping at all.

☐ If you get stuck, write the same word or phrase until a new idea comes along. Do not stop writing. Do not worry about wording, organization, or grammar. Later in the writing process, you will organize and polish your ideas—tell that critic inside your head to pipe down for now.

☐ When the time limit is up, read what you wrote and underline interesting ideas.

☐ Use one of the ideas you underlined as a starting point for a focused freewrite. A **focused freewrite** occurs when you freewrite about a specific topic you have chosen or been assigned.

FREEWRITING

Read the following two freewrites. Discuss with your class or in a small group how ideas develop using freewriting and focused freewriting. What are the advantages of freewriting? What are the disadvantages?

Well it is time for another writing assignment, and the teacher said we could choose our own topic, but I don't know what to write I always have a hard time coming up with topics writing is so hard I know I am a terrible at this but I need to find a topic not write about not finding a topic let's see what can I write about? It is so cold in here I can't think think think think think think well wats going on in the news oh, what about all the missing and abused children and the how child molesters are everywhere. Things seem to be getting worse all the time. Pretty depressing. I think things ar worse now than when I was growing up. My hometown was so safe no one locked their doors they didn't have too. We spent hours roaming the neighborhood on our bicycles, swimming in Lake Martha, enjoying being a kid. Now small towns seem as dangerous as crime ridden big cities.

Focused Freewrite

We spent hours roaming the neighborhood on our bicycles, swimming in Lake Martha, enjoying being a kid. There were about 20 of us kids pretty close in age who lived in my neighborhood, so we always had someone to play with or fight with, and we did both passionately. Our neighborhood was surrounded by orange groves, so we all learned at a pretty young age how to throw and dodge rotten oranges in our on-going orange wars. My brother earned the reputation of the best warrior. He could throw an orange further and straighter than any one any time. The best wars ended with a bike race to Lake Martha to rinse off the sticky juices and dirt that clung to us. I can still hear the ice cream truck's merry music and feel the hot sand beneath my feet as we dashed from the waters edge to catch the ice cream man as he rounded the corner during his afternoon route. Life seemed so simple, so safe, so fun.

FOCUSED FREEWRITING

Step 1: Choose one of the following topics and freewrite for five minutes. Ask and answer the reporter's and reflective questions before you begin freewriting.

- Popular Music

- Useful Technology

- A Favorite Place

- An Influential Person

Step 2: Read your freewrite and highlight ideas. Write a focused freewrite for an additional five minutes using the idea(s) you highlighted.

Keeping a Journal

Many people keep a **journal** to record how they feel about the events of their daily lives, current events, or life in general. A journal allows the writer to explore experiences in a personal way and store them in a private place. Some writers use a spiral notebook; others use a diary or a pre-made journal. The point is to create a specific place where you can record and review your private thoughts and personal experiences. Journal entries are often freewrites with your main purpose being to get ideas on paper, but they may take on different creative forms, such as a letter or a poem. Many writers use journals as a place to practice their writing and experiment with language. The key to keeping a journal is to write on a regular basis. Writing and reflecting on what you have written on a consistent basis leads to a deeper understanding of yourself and your world—and improves your writing!

The following thinking guide can help you use journaling as a prewriting technique.

The Writing Process Step by Step:

Prewriting by Journaling

☐ Create a section in your notebook for journal entries or buy a spiral notebook, diary, or pre-made journal that you will use only for journal writing.

☐ Commit to writing in your journal on a regular basis for the next two weeks. Select a time of day that you can write in your journal, such as during your lunch break or at the end of the day. Set a time limit, such as fifteen minutes, for each journal entry.

☐ Ask and answer the reporter's questions and reflective questions to stimulate your thinking.

Use the following topics to get started:

☐ Record events, images, or scenes of interest to you; write as many details as you can.

☐ Record a favorite memory; explore why that memory is so important.

☐ Write a brief autobiography.

☐ Recount a news event and your reactions to it.

☐ Write a letter to yourself or to someone else, giving advice about a particular matter.

☐ Vent about something that really bothers you.

☐ Reread a previously written journal entry and develop an idea in greater detail.

JOURNALING

Read the following journal entry. Identify the academic courses that are relevant to the personal experiences recorded in the journal. Discuss with your class or in a small group the ways in which the ideas in the journal entry might be developed into an essay in each course.

> April 20: 8:00 p.m.: Well, here I am again, eating once more out of stress. Today was incredibly stressful. For some reason I have a hard time communicating with my boss, so once again she scheduled me to work when I needed to be off for a doctor's appointment. I have been gaining weight like crazy, but I absolutely crave carbohydrates. And on days like this, a warm bowl of macaroni and cheese soothes my soul. My mom thinks I might have a thyroid problem which is making me gain weight, but I think it's just from eating too much, and too much stress. I wish I had more time. I would love to go to the beach tonight and observe the turtle nests. I wonder why they always come to this beach to nest. The county has made all the businesses along the beach dim their lights so the turtles won't be disturbed. I wonder why the light is such a problem.

Academic topics related to journal entry:

_____

Now that you have analyzed a journal entry, write your own journal entry in your notebook. Choose a topic from the journal entry you just read in this practice, and write an entry dated with today's date. Write about your chosen topic without stopping for at least three to five minutes. After writing, reread your journal entry and underline ideas that you could use for a future writing assignment.

Listing

A common way to brainstorm ideas is to **create a list.** If you have a free choice of topics, then create a topic bank: List ideas about which you want to learn more or topics about which you already know something and that you enjoy discussing. To create a list of topics for an academic course, look at the table of contents, the index, and the glossary of your textbook. Use these resources to create a list of topics based on what you will be studying throughout the semester. If you already have a topic, then create a list of everything that comes to mind as you think about your topic. Write your list as quickly as you can. Just as in freewriting, quiet your inner critic. Once you make a thorough list, then you can organize your ideas.

The following thinking guide can help you use listing as a prewriting technique.

The Writing Process Step by Step:

Prewriting by Listing

- [ ] Write a topic at the top of your page.
- [ ] List ideas as quickly as possible in the order that they occur to you.
- [ ] Use words or short phrases.
- [ ] List all ideas that occur to you; reject nothing.
- [ ] If you run out of ideas, choose one idea you have already recorded and begin a new list about that idea.
- [ ] Review your list and group ideas into logical relationships.
- [ ] Label each group of ideas as possible points of development for a piece of writing.

Practice 14

LISTING

Prewriting for an academic course: The following lists are based on the table of contents of two textbooks. Identify the academic courses to which each list is related. Then, brainstorm a list of additional writing topics based on an idea from each list.

COURSES: _____   COURSES: _____

_____   _____

List 1
Mass Media and Politics
The Power of the Media
Sources of the Media
Bias in the Media
Freedom versus Fairness

New Lists of Additional Ideas

_____

_____

_____

List 2
Coping with Stress
Eating Smart
Maintaining Proper Weight
Keeping Fit
Controllable Health Risks

New Lists of Additional Ideas

_____

_____

_____

Prewriting for Business Writing: Assume you have just been given two weeks' notice because your company is downsizing and eliminating your job. To locate job opportunities, take the following steps:

Step 1: Go to the classified section of your local newspaper and make a list of available jobs in your area.

Step 2: Choose one of the advertised positions and list the skills needed to compete for the job.

Step 3: List the skills you already possess that qualify you for the job.

Step 4: On your own paper, repeat steps 2 and 3 for each of the jobs you listed in Step 1.

Practice 14

Concept Mapping

Concept mapping, also known as **clustering** or **webbing**, creates a visual picture of the relationships among the ideas you generate. Think of what you already know about a map. Someone can tell you how to get somewhere, but it is much easier to understand the directions when you can study a map and see how each road connects to other roads. Likewise, a concept map shows how a topic connects to supporting details—how each idea connects to another idea and how the main idea connects to supporting details. Sometimes, as you use a concept map, the idea that first occurred to you might be a great example for a supporting detail. Rarely do ideas occur to us in a logical order. Concept mapping helps a writer figure out the logical order of ideas. Chapters 4 through 12 will show you how to adapt concept maps to specific writing situations and thought patterns.

The following thinking guide can help you use concept mapping as a prewriting technique.

The Writing Process Step by Step:

Prewriting by Concept Mapping

- [ ] Draw a circle in the middle of your page and write your topic in the circle.
- [ ] Write a word that relates to the topic, circle the word, and connect it to the topic circle with a line.
- [ ] Repeat this process so that a set of major supports radiates out from the topic circle.
- [ ] Write a word that relates to one of the major supports, circle it, and connect it to that major support circle.
- [ ] Repeat this process for each of the major supports to create clusters of minor supports.

MAPPING

The writer of the following paragraph used a concept map to brainstorm ideas. Read the paragraph. Then, recreate her concept map by filling in the appropriate blanks with ideas from her paragraph. Discuss how the concept map differs from her final draft.

According to *Merriam-Webster's Collegiate Dictionary*, a role model is "a person whose behavior in a particular role is imitated by others." In other words, a role model is anyone who has influence over us. A role model can be anyone including celebrities, such as actors, athletes, or politicians or plain folks, such as teachers, parents, and friends. Role models can be positive or negative. For example, a positive role model possesses several traits. A positive role model reflects an ideal, such as courage or honesty, has an upstanding reputation, and uses his or her influence for the greater good. In contrast, a negative role model negates an ideal by being cowardly or dishonest, has a damaged reputation, and uses his or her influence for selfish gain. Still, ideals such as courage, cowardice, honesty, and dishonesty are often a matter of opinion. For example, many thought Tom Cruise acted as a strong role model when he spoke out against the psychiatric profession. He claimed that vitamins and exercise, not therapy and drugs, are the best treatments for postpartum depression. He even condemned Brooke Shields as a role model for relying on drug therapy for her postpartum depression. However, many others saw his criticism as an unfair attack that damaged his reputation in their eyes. In the end, a role model actually reflects our own values.

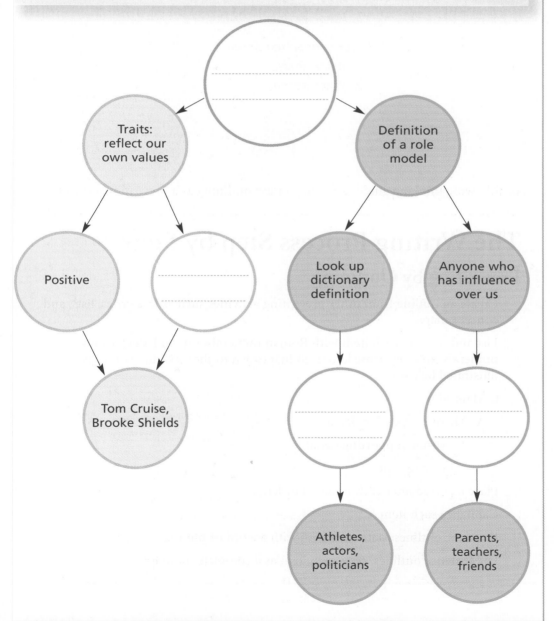

Practice 15

Outlining: A Writing Plan

In addition to brainstorming first thoughts, a prewrite also organizes ideas into a writing plan. A concept map is one way to create a writing plan because it shows the flow of ideas among the topic, major details, and minor details. An outline is another way to create a writing plan. An **outline** lists ideas in blocks of thought, as shown in the following outline for a paragraph.

Main Idea Statement: Topic Sentence

    A. *Major supporting detail*
        1. *Minor detail*
        2. *Minor detail*

    B. *Major supporting detail*
        1. *Minor detail*
        2. *Minor detail*

    C. *Major supporting detail*
        1. *Minor detail*
        2. *Minor detail*

The following thinking guide can help you use outlining as a prewriting technique.

The Writing Process Step by Step:

Prewriting by Outlining

☐ Create an outline from other prewriting activities such as freewrites, lists, and concept maps.

☐ List and identify each item with Roman numerals, capital letters, Arabic numerals, and lowercase letters, in that order, to show the flow of ideas, as illustrated below:

I. Main Idea

    A. Major supporting detail

        1. Minor supporting detail

           a. subpoint

☐ Place a period after each numeral or letter.

☐ Capitalize each item.

☐ For topic outlines, state each item with a word or phrase.

☐ For sentence outlines, state each item as a complete thought.

OUTLINING

The following reflection and concept map was created by a student during the prewriting phase of an assignment. Complete the outline with ideas from the concept map.

Laura's First Thoughts:

I am going to write about the topic "My Ideal Mate," and my classmates are my audience. I am going to focus my topic by discussing three traits of an ideal mate and how my boyfriend is a perfect example of an ideal mate. My purpose is to let the reader know what a great boyfriend I have.

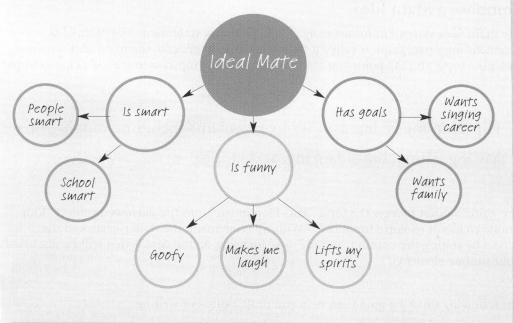

Main idea statement: My boyfriend Kelly is my ideal mate.

A. ....

   1. He excelled in high school and college.

   2. ....

B. Kelly is funny.

   1. ....

   2. He keeps me laughing.

   3. ....

C. ....

   1. He is working toward a singing career.

   2. ....

Drafting

The **drafting** stage of the writing process may include several tasks, depending on the writing situation. An essay or letter may require the drafting of an introduction, a main idea, supporting details, and conclusion. A stand-alone paragraph may require only a main idea and supporting details.

> **Drafting** is putting your ideas into sentences and paragraphs.

Compose a Main Idea

The **main idea statement** for an essay is called a **thesis statement**. The main idea statement for a paragraph is called a **topic sentence**. In general, the main idea sentence presents a topic and the point you are making about the topic, as in the following example:

TOPIC

Hip-Hop music has four unique elements including rapping or MCing, DJing, breakdancing, and graffiti. ← *WRITER'S POINT*

The writer's point focuses the topic "Hip-Hop music" into the narrowed subject "four unique elements of Hip-Hop music." With this statement, the writer narrowed the subject by stating the opinion "unique" and focusing on the details that will be discussed: "four unique elements."

The following thinking guide can help you draft a piece of writing.

The Writing Process Step by Step:

Drafting

- [ ] Write your main idea in a complete sentence.
- [ ] As you write a thesis statement or topic sentence, assert an idea instead of announcing your topic. Avoid the following announcements:
  - "I am going to write about…"
  - "My paragraph (or essay) is about…"
  - "My topic is…."
- [ ] As you write your first draft, do not worry about issues such as spelling and grammar.
- [ ] Generate major and minor details to support your main idea.
- [ ] As you write, include new ideas as they occur to you without self-criticism or editing before you have a complete draft; this first draft does not need to be perfect. You will use the revision process to evaluate details for logic and relevance once your draft is complete.
- [ ] Use the first draft to discover how your ideas flow and fit together.
- [ ] Resolve to write multiple drafts to produce your best work.

STATING THE MAIN IDEA

Revise the following main idea statements so they are more effectively expressed. Identify the hint you used to revise each one. Discuss your work with your class or in a small group.

1. I am going to write about how the automobile costs too much, pollutes the environment, and traps us in isolation.

....

Hint: ....

2. The annoying and rude manners of people while talking on cell phones in public places.

....

....

Hint: ....

3. Minimum wage is a controversial issue.

....

Hint: ....

Write a Draft of Your Paragraph

A draft of a paragraph or essay is the result of careful thought based on prewriting activities. Creating a first or rough draft allows you to get a working copy of your ideas that can be improved upon during the revision process.

COMPOSE A TOPIC SENTENCE AND A DRAFT

Step 1. Choose a topic from a previous practice exercise and compose a main idea statement. (Remember that your **main idea statement** is also called a **topic sentence** if you are writing a paragraph. If you are writing an essay, your main idea statement is also called a **thesis statement**.)

Step 2. Write a draft using your own paper.

AUDIENCE AND PURPOSE: ....

TOPIC: ....

WRITER'S POINT: ....

MAIN IDEA STATEMENT (topic sentence or thesis statement): ....

....

Revising

Now that you have gotten your ideas on paper, you can review your work to make sure your paragraph offers a focused, unified, well-supported, and coherent chunk of information. As you revise your draft, review and apply what you have learned.

> **Revising** is re-seeing your work through the eyes of your reader. Revising is reworking your draft for clarity, logic, interest, and credibility.

The following thinking guide can help you revise a piece of writing.

The Writing Process Step by Step:

Revising

- ☐ Read your draft out loud (either on your own or to a peer). This is an easy way to identify parts of your draft that may be unclear or awkward.
- ☐ Make sure your main idea is stated clearly in a topic sentence or thesis statement.
- ☐ Make sure that the details in the body of your paragraph or essay fully support your topic sentence or thesis statement.
- ☐ Make sure every sentence in a paragraph relates to your main idea so that a reader can easily follow the logic of your ideas.
- ☐ Move information as needed into the most logical order.
- ☐ Add transitions as needed to clarify the relationship between ideas.
- ☐ Add details and examples as needed to strengthen or clarify the main idea and supporting points.
- ☐ Replace vague words and details with vivid and precise expressions.
- ☐ Delete irrelevant details.
- ☐ If your paragraph or essay draft seems to end abruptly, add a concluding sentence (or paragraph, if you are writing an essay), restating and summing up your main points.

REVISING

Read Laura's first draft of her paragraph "My Ideal Mate." Then, complete the activity that follows. Share your work and thoughts with a small group of your peers.

My Ideal Mate

(1) My ideal mate is a man who is intelligent, funny, and goal oriented. (2) Kelly, my current boyfriend, has all of these wonderful traits. (3) Kelly has to be one of the smartest people I know. (4) He excelled academically in high school and college. (5) He is not only book smart but is people smart also. (6) He knows exactly how to keep the people he loves protected and safe from this cruel world. (7) Kelly has to be the funniest person I know. (8) If we didn't have fun and goof around, our relationship would be boring. (9) He can be serious when necessary, and like everyone, has his dark days. (10) Whenever I am down about something, he is the one to make me overcome the sadness and laugh. (11) The most important trait of all though is that Kelly is goal oriented; he knows what he wants out of life. (12) He has a plan to succeed. (13) Not too many guys know what they want. (14) Kelly wants to become a professional musician, have a family, and earn enough money to support his family. (15) All of these traits make Kelly my ideal mate.

–Laura Bender, English Student

1. Locate the topic sentence by underlining the topic once and the writer's point about that topic twice.
2. Cross out any details that are not related to the topic sentence.
3. Circle any ideas that need more examples to fully support the main idea.
4. Choose three words to revise; cross out the words you chose, and above them, write stronger, more vivid words. Use a thesaurus.
5. Insert the following transitions where they best show the logical flow of ideas: First, In addition, Finally.

REVISING

Review a draft you have written. Annotate or mark your paragraph with the changes you need to make, and write a journal entry about your revision. Do you need to brainstorm more details for certain ideas? Identify those ideas and describe or explain the kinds of details you need. Do you need to use a thesaurus to improve word choice? List and discuss the words that need to be replaced. Based on your review, revise to create a new draft of your work.

Proofreading

Once you have revised your paragraph, take time to carefully proofread your work. Publishing a clean, error-free draft proves you are committed to excellence and that you take pride in your work. Many student writers struggle with common errors, and every writer has her or his own pattern or habit of careless errors. To create a polished draft, a writer masters the rules of writing and edits to eliminate careless errors.

> **Proofreading** is preparing your work for publication.
> Proofreading is correcting errors in punctuation, capitalization, mechanics, grammar, and spelling.

The following thinking guide can help you proofread a piece of writing.

The Writing Process Step by Step:
Proofreading

- ☐ Allow some time to pass between revising and proofreading.
- ☐ Read your work one sentence at a time from the *end* to the *beginning*. Reading your work from the end to the beginning allows you to focus on each sentence.
- ☐ Read again from the beginning with a cover that you slide down the page as you read so that you focus on one sentence at a time.
- ☐ Use a highlighter to mark mistakes.
- ☐ Proofread more than once; focus on one type of error at a time.
- ☐ Proofread for the types of errors you commonly make.
- ☐ Use word processing spell checkers carefully (they don't know the difference between words such as *there, their,* or *there*).
- ☐ Use a dictionary to double check your spelling.
- ☐ Have someone else read over your work.

PROOFREADING

The following draft by a student writer reveals her struggle with two common errors: pronoun agreement and subject-verb agreement. The box on the next page sums up the rules for pronoun agreement and subject-verb agreement and includes correct sentence examples. Read the rules and examples in the box, and then use them as a guide to correct the same kind of errors in pronoun agreement and subject-verb agreement in the student's draft.

Student draft

The Bride to Be

(1) In a traditional wedding, the center of attention revolves around the bride. (2) Although brides vary in temperament and style, most often they fall into three common types: bridezilla, coldarella, and bellaella brides.

(3) First, the bridezilla is the typically testy, irritated and acerbic bride. (4) The best known trait of a bridezilla is the tendency to have high voltage temper tantrums. (5) For example, they cannot settle a single, simple issue without blowing off the handle and making something out of nothing. (6) The second type of bride, coldarella, is also known as a runaway bride. (7) Though she may come across as calm and understanding, deep down they are repressing all their bottled tension. (8) A runaway bride often smiles until the day she skips town and leaves the man of her dreams waiting at the altar. (9) The third and best bride is the bellaella bride, the beautiful bride. (10) Her inner beauty makes them the most delightful ones to be around. (11) She loves the intrinsic details and although she wants everything to be perfect, they don't fuss if it is not. (12) This bride is gentle, easy going, and understanding. (13) She doesn't fret over unexpected circumstances. (14) This bride is the bride to be and the bride to marry!

Pronoun Agreement

If a noun is singular (*I, you, he, she,* or *it*), then the pronoun that refers to the noun must be singular. If a noun is plural *(we, you, they),* then the pronoun that refers to the noun must be plural.

Subject-Verb Agreement

If a subject of a sentence is singular, then the verb and object of the verb must be singular. If the subject of a sentence is plural, then the verb and object of the verb must be plural.

Practice 21

Academic Learning Log

PORTFOLIO

To test and track your understanding of what you have studied, answer the following questions.

1. A piece of writing develops in response to a specific situation that is composed of the

   _____, the _____ for writing, and the _____.

2. The four basic purposes for writing are _____,

   _____, _____, and _____.

3. The four phases of the writing process are _____,

   _____, _____, and _____.

4. The writing process is _____: Any step can be repeated as necessary.

5. Several prewriting techniques are _____, _____,

   _____, _____, and _____.

6. Drafting is putting your ideas into _____ and _____.

7. Revising is _____ your work through the eyes of your reader.

8. Revising is reworking your draft for _____, _____,

   _____, and _____.

9. Proofreading is preparing your work for _____.

10. Proofreading is correcting errors in _____, _____,

    _____, _____, and _____.

11. What did I learn about the writing process?

_____

_____

_____

_____

_____

_____

_____

12. What about the writing process do I need to continue studying or working on?

_____

_____

_____

_____

_____

_____

_____

_____

PORTFOLIO

Academic Learning Log

mywritinglab

WANT A BETTER GRADE?
For more practice with thinking through the writing process, go to **www.mywritinglab.com** > **Getting Ready to Write** > **Thinking Through the Writing Process.**

3

CHAPTER PREVIEW

LEARNING OUTCOMES

● What's the Point of a Paragraph?

● Three Parts of a Paragraph

● Developing Your Point Using a Paragraph

● Workshop: Analyzing the Effectiveness of a Paragraph

Understanding the Paragraph

A paragraph is a well-planned sequence of sentences coupled together to convey a main point.

A paragraph allows a writer to express clearly and powerfully one main idea about a narrowed subject. A well-written paragraph can express a valid consumer complaint, a compelling reason to be hired, a sincere apology to a loved one, or a concept tested by a written exam in a college course.

What's the Point of a Paragraph?

A paragraph is a well-thought-out chunk of information. A writer narrows a topic into a focused main idea, selects enough relevant details to support the main idea, and organizes these supporting details in a logical flow of information.

Three Levels of Information in a Paragraph

The following flow chart shows the three levels of information within a paragraph.

Subject
- A narrowed topic

1 Main idea
- Is often stated as a topic sentence
- Explains the author's one main point about the subject
- Is a more general statement than any of the supporting details

2 Major detail
- Explains the main idea
- Provides primary support to the main idea
- Is more general than a minor detail

3 Minor detail
- Explains a major detail
- Provides secondary support to the main idea
- Is the most specific idea in the passage

Practice 1

WRITING FROM LIFE

PHOTOGRAPHIC ORGANIZER: LEVELS OF INFORMATION

Study the following outline based on an article about types of tattoos that was published in the journal *Dermatology Nursing*. In the blanks, identify each piece of information as the narrowed topic, main idea, major supporting detail, or minor supporting detail.

Four Types of Tattoos ....

There are four major types of tattoos: traumatic, amateur, professional, and cosmetic. ....

A. Traumatic ....

   1. Cause: accidental embedding of colored material, which leaves pigment after healing

   ....

   2. Examples: motorcycle rash, "graphite tattoo" from a puncture injury with a pencil

   ....

B. Amateur ....

   1. Cause: placed by the person being tattooed or by a friend with little experience

   ....

   2. Examples: boyfriend's name; gang tattoo

   ....

C. Professional ....

   1. Cultural ....

      a. Cause: placed by time-honored method by members of certain cultural groups

      ....

      b. Example: Samoan tattoos

      ....

   2. Modern ....

      a. Cause: placed by "tattoo gun" by experienced, paid artists ....

      b. Example: Tattoo parlors ....

D. Cosmetic ....

   1. Cause: placed by a cosmetic specialist as permanent makeup or camouflage ....

   2. Example: eyeliner ....

▲ **Gang tattoos**

▲ **Cultural**

▲ **Modern**

▲ **Permanent makeup**

Read the paragraph developed from the previous outline. Circle the main idea. Underline the four sentences that state the major supports.

Four Types of Tattoos

(1) There are four major types of tattoos: traumatic, amateur, professional, and cosmetic. (2) The first type, the traumatic tattoo, is caused by the imbedding of dirt or debris beneath the skin, which leaves an area of pigmentation after healing. (3) For example, this commonly occurs in "road rash" after a motorcycle accident or after a puncture injury from a lead pencil, called a "graphite tattoo." (4) The second type, the amateur tattoo, is placed by the person being tattooed or by a friend and often shows little artistry or detail. (5) A boyfriend's or girlfriend's name or a gang symbol is tattooed using a pin and India ink, pen ink, charcoal, or ashes as the pigment. (6) The third type, the professional tattoo, takes two forms: cultural and modern. (7) Cultural tattoos are placed using the time-honored methods of certain cultural ethnicities. (8) For example, the Samoans use tattoos to display the artistry of their particular heritage. (9) Modern tattoos are performed using a "tattoo gun" and are placed by experienced, paid artists. (10) The fourth type, the cosmetic tattoo, is a rapidly growing area of the tattoo industry. (11) Permanent makeup, including eyeliner, lip liner, rouge, and eyebrow pencil, can be placed by a tattoo specialist. (12) Finally, another aspect of cosmetic tattooing is the camouflaging of an undesired tattoo or other physical flaw.

–Adapted from Terrence A. Cronin Jr. *Dermatology Nursing*. Oct 2001 v13 i5 p 380(4).

Practice 3

Read the following paragraph. Then fill in the sentence outline with the main idea and missing supporting details.

Alligators and Rocketships

(1) Sharing a boundary with Merritt Island's National Wildlife Refuge on the east coast of Florida, John F. Kennedy Space Center serves as a refuge for several endangered species. (2) For example, the endangered manatee flourishes in the shadows of launch platforms. (3) Just south of launch pad 39A, more than 300 manatees graze protected in a sanctuary in the northern end of Banana River. (4) Manatees are so abundant at the Center that they make up around 30 percent of Florida's total manatee population. (5) Another endangered species at the center is the beloved sea turtle. (6) Between May and September, thousands of endangered sea turtles come ashore on this barrier island in the dark of night to lay their eggs. (7) With its protected shoreline, Kennedy has one of the most dense turtle populations in the northern hemisphere. (8) Bald eagles also find

▲ **Merritt Island's National Wildlife Refuge**

▲ **Launch platforms**

refuge at the space center. (9) At least five active bald eagle nests exist around the Center. (10) Nests can reach more than six feet in diameter and are usually inhabited from September through May. (11) The eagles usually produce one or two chicks per year. (12) No discussion of wildlife at Kennedy is complete without mentioning alligators! (13) While the interactions between man and alligator are few, the biggest problem is during Shuttle landings. (14) Prior to each Kennedy Shuttle landing, it is the task of a special crew to clear the runway of all debris, including any alligators that might be sunning themselves on the runway surface.

–Adapted from *"Alligators and Rocketships."* NASA.
http://www.nasa.gov/centers/kennedy/shuttleoperations/alligators/kscovrv.html

Main idea (Topic Sentence): ....

....

A. Major support: ....

....

   1. Minor support: Just south of launch pad 39A, more than 300 manatees graze protected in a sanctuary in the northern end of Banana River.

   2. Minor support: Manatees are so abundant at the Center that they make up around 30 percent of Florida's total manatee population.

B. Major support: ....

....

   1. Minor support: Between May and September, thousands of endangered sea turtles come ashore on this barrier island in the dark of night to lay their eggs.

   2. Minor support: ....

....

C. Major support: Bald eagles also find refuge at the space center.

   1. Minor support: ....

   2. Minor support: ....

....

   3. Minor support: The eagles usually produce one or two chicks per year.

D. Major support: ....

....

   1. Minor support: ....

....

   2. Minor support: ....

....

....

Practice 3

LEARNING OUTCOMES
STRUCTURE

Three Parts of a Paragraph

A paragraph is a series of closely related sentences that develop and support the writer's point about a narrowed subject. Often, the paragraph serves as a building block for a longer piece of writing such as an essay, since an essay is composed of two, three, or more paragraphs. In many situations a writer can make a point through one well-developed paragraph. Sometimes, a writer provides a stand-alone paragraph with a title. In addition to a title, a paragraph has three basic parts:

A Beginning:
An introduction of one or more sentences: A topic sentence that states the author's purpose and main point

A Middle:
A body of major and minor details that support the topic sentence

An Ending:
A conclusion of one or more sentences that reinforces the author's purpose and main point

The following graphic describes the function of each part of a paragraph and shows the general format of a paragraph.

Title:
Use Key Words or a Phrase to Vividly Describe the Point of Your Paragraph

Introduction:
An introduction is usually one or more sentences that explain the importance of the topic or give necessary background information about the topic.
<u>Your topic sentence states your narrowed subject and your point about the subject.</u>

Body:
The body of a paragraph is made up of a series of sentences that offer major details in support of your topic sentence. If needed, provide minor details that support the major details. Link sentences within the paragraph with clear transitions so your reader can easily follow your thoughts.

Conclusion:
The conclusion restates or sums up your paragraph's main idea in one or more sentences.

PARTS OF A PARAGRAPH

The following student essay by Adam Stewart illustrates the use of a title and the three parts of a paragraph. Underline the topic sentence. Circle each of the three parts of the paragraph: Introduction, Body, and Conclusion. Provide a title for the paragraph.

▲ **Ambitious worker**

▲ **Mediocre worker**

▲ **Lazy worker**

(1) Although everyone has to work at one point in his or her life and a strong work ethic is looked upon very highly, unfortunately not all workers understand the importance of hard work and a good attitude. (2) Depending upon which category they represent, workers are judged by their coworkers and employers. (3) Three different types of workers make up the workforce, and each type works toward a very different future. (4) First, the ambitious worker comes to work on time, has a good attitude, stays on task, and is always willing to help in any way. (5) Supervisors and coworkers highly value the work ethic of ambitious workers because they always get the job done and do it well beyond expectations. (6) The second type of worker is satisfied with mediocrity. (7) This type of worker comes to work on time, but he or she is not always on the required task. (8) Mediocre workers do what is required and nothing more. (9) Employers and coworkers tolerate mediocre workers because even though they don't always have a good attitude, the job does get done and usually meets expectations. (10) The third type is the lazy worker, also known as the slacker. (11) Everyone hates the slacker. (12) Slackers consistently show up late, rarely accomplish the required task, and continuously try to get the rest of their coworkers off task as well. (13) The slacker, looking for the easy way out, rarely meets expectations. (14) In conclusion, the ambitious workers will be the leaders and high-wage earners; the mediocre workers will likely remain at some dead-end jobs; and the slackers will probably be fired from job after job, never rethinking their work ethic.

Developing Your Point Using a Paragraph

An effective paragraph is *focused*, *logical*, *detailed*, and *well expressed*. A writer (1) narrows a topic into a focused main idea; (2) offers only those details that are relevant to the main idea; (3) provides adequate details to support the main idea; (4) organizes these supporting details in a logical flow of information; and (5) uses effective expression through the purposeful choice of words, sentence structure, and grammar.

The Point: The Main Idea

A focused main idea presents a narrowed subject and the writer's controlling point about the narrowed subject. The controlling point often indicates both the writer's opinion and a pattern of organization. A topic sentence states the focused main idea in a complete sentence.

Narrow the Topic

Use the following suggestions to guide your thinking as you focus a general topic into a narrowed subject or topic.

- Narrow the topic based on your **opinion**. An opinion is expressed by using words such as *amazing, alarming, beautiful, best, likely, should,* or any other word that states personal values, judgments, or interpretations. Use questions, freewriting, mapping, listing, or another brainstorming technique to discover your opinion about a topic.

Example:	General Topic	Narrowed Subject
	Seatbelts	Seatbelts can be dangerous
		Seatbelts save lives

- Narrow the topic based on a **pattern of organization**. A writer may use a pattern of organization to narrow a subject and generate details. Patterns of organization are also used to develop, organize, and express a main idea, major details, and minor details in a logical order. The following list provides a few examples of patterns of organization and signal words for each one.

Pattern of Organization	Signal Words
Space Order	*above, below, next to, underneath, scene*
Time Order	*first, now, then, before, after, process, use*
Example	*for example, exemplify, includes, such as*
Classification	*types, kinds, levels*
Compare/Contrast	*similar, likewise, just as / however, in contrast*
Cause/Effect	*source, origin / results, impact*

Example:	General Topic	Narrowed Subject
	Graffiti	The effects of graffiti
		The types of graffiti

- Combine topic, opinion, and pattern of organization to generate a narrowed subject.

Example:	General Topic	Narrowed Subject
	Seatbelts	Three reasons seatbelts can be dangerous
		Proper use of seatbelts saves lives
	Graffiti	The negative effects of graffiti
		Graffiti: A type of artistic expression

FOCUS A TOPIC INTO A NARROWED SUBJECT

Combine the topic with an opinion and pattern of organization signal words to narrow the topic. In the blank items, practice narrowing topics of your choice.

1. GENERAL TOPIC: *Health Issue: Weightlifting*

   OPINION: *positive*   SIGNAL WORD: *effects*

   NARROWED SUBJECT:

2. GENERAL TOPIC: *A Public Figure: Tyra Banks*

   OPINION: *admirable*   SIGNAL WORD: *traits*

   NARROWED SUBJECT:

3. GENERAL TOPIC: *Historical Place: Gettysburg*

   OPINION: *most decisive battle in history*   SIGNAL WORD: *scene*

   NARROWED SUBJECT:

4. GENERAL TOPIC: *Business: Saving Money*

   OPINION: *smart*   SIGNAL WORD: *steps to*

   NARROWED SUBJECT:

5. GENERAL TOPIC: *Health Issue: Cancer*

   OPINION: SIGNAL WORD:

   NARROWED SUBJECT:

6. GENERAL TOPIC:

   OPINION: SIGNAL WORD:

   NARROWED SUBJECT:

7. GENERAL TOPIC:

   OPINION: SIGNAL WORD:

   NARROWED SUBJECT:

8. GENERAL TOPIC:

   OPINION: SIGNAL WORD:

   NARROWED SUBJECT:

Write the Topic Sentence

Once you have focused a topic into a narrowed subject with your opinion and a pattern of organization, you are ready to write a complete sentence to state the main idea. Each of the following topic sentences offers a subject and a controlling point: a **topic** narrowed by the writer's **opinion** and a suggested **pattern of organization**.

TOPIC   *WRITER'S OPINION*   *PATTERN OF ORGANIZATION*

Seatbelts can be dangerous for three reasons.

WRITER'S OPINION   *TOPIC*   *WRITER'S OPINION*

Proper use of seatbelts saves lives. *TOPIC*

TOPIC   *PATTERN OF ORGANIZATION*   *WRITER'S OPINION*

Graffiti leads to several negative effects.

TOPIC   *PATTERN OF ORGANIZATION*   *WRITER'S OPINION*

Graffiti is a type of artistic expression. *TOPIC*

Practice 6

WRITE A TOPIC SENTENCE

Write topic sentences for each of the following narrowed subjects.

1. Narrowed Subject: Benefits of weightlifting

TOPIC SENTENCE: _____

_____

2. Narrowed Subject: The admirable traits of Tyra Banks

TOPIC SENTENCE: _____

_____

3. Narrowed Subject: Gettysburg: Scene of the Most Decisive Battle in History

TOPIC SENTENCE: _____

_____

4. Narrowed Subject: Smart Steps to Saving Money

TOPIC SENTENCE: _____

_____

Logical Order

Use a writing plan to establish a logical order for details and a clear flow of ideas. A writing plan includes one or more of the following elements.

A Pattern of Organization As discussed on page 60, a writer uses a pattern of organization to arrange major details and minor details in a logical order. The following chart provides a few examples of patterns of organization and signal words for each one (see Chapters 4–12 for in-depth instruction about patterns of organization and signal words).

Patterns of Organization	Signal Words
Description (Space order)	above, below, next to, underneath, scene
Narrative/Process (Time order)	first, now, then, before, after, next, stage
Example	for example, exemplify, includes, such as
Classification	types, kinds, levels
Compare/Contrast	similar, likewise/however, in contrast
Cause/Effect	source, origin/results, impact, reasons
Persuasion	must, should, ought to

Order of Importance Often, a writer decides upon and arranges details according to his or her opinion about the importance of the details, known as **climactic order**. Usually, climactic order moves from the least important point and builds to the paragraph's climax, the most important point.

Order of Topic Sentence Often the controlling point of the topic sentence divides the subject into chunks of information. The order of the ideas in the topic sentence often reflects a pattern of organization or an order of importance for details.

LOGICAL ORDER

Read the following paragraph from a college textbook. Underline the topic sentence. Circle the pattern of organization's signal words. Then, identify the type of logical order used by the author.

> (1) Interpersonal communication is a continuous series of processes that blend into one another. (2) For convenience of discussion we can separate them into five stages. (3) During the first stage, we sense, we pick up some kind of stimulation. (4) Next, we organize the stimuli in some way. (5) Third, we interpret and evaluate what we perceive. (6) Then, we store it in memory, and finally, in stage five, we retrieve it when needed.
>
> –Adapted from DeVito, *The Interpersonal Communication Book*, 10th Ed., p. 91.

Practice 7

Type of Logical Order: ....

Relevant and Adequate Details

Relevant and adequate details support and develop the main idea. As you narrow a topic, usually you generate many ideas before you decide on one main point. You must evaluate each detail based on its relationship to the point you want to make.

Relevant details explain and support only the writer's point. Once you narrow a subject into a focused main idea, you then include only those details that relate to your opinion and pattern of organization.

Check for Relevant Details

Apply the following questions to each detail to see if it is relevant to a main idea. If the answers are "no" to these questions, then the detail is most likely irrelevant and should not be included as a support.

- Does the detail reinforce the writer's opinion?
- Does the detail carry out the pattern of organization?
- Does the detail support the main idea?
- Does the detail support a major detail?

Practice 8

RELEVANT DETAILS

The following prewrite list includes a focused main idea and a set of details. Use the "Check for Relevant Details" questions given above to identify the irrelevant detail, and cross it out.

Main Idea: Aerobic exercise leads to several benefits.

First Benefit	Second Benefit	Third Benefit
stronger bones	stronger muscles	better health
builds bone mass	tones muscles	improved looks
reduces brittleness	increases range of motion	reduces body fat

Adequate details offer in-depth explanations and supports for the writer's opinion and pattern of organization. In-depth support of a main idea often requires both major and minor details. Major details directly support the main idea. Minor details support and explain the major details (review the chart on page 53 of this chapter).

Check for Adequate Details

Apply the following questions to see if you have adequate details to support your main idea. If the answer is "yes" to these questions, then additional details are most likely needed to fully support the main idea.

- Is more information needed to explain the writer's opinion?
- Is more information needed to carry out the pattern of organization?
- Does a major detail need a minor detail of support or explanation?

Read the following rough draft of a paragraph. Cross out the irrelevant detail. Underline the point that needs more information to adequately support the main idea.

A Winter Wonder or Winter Haven Vacation?

(1) Many families take advantage of the winter break in school calendars across the country to enjoy a vacation together. (2) A winter-time vacation actually offers distinct choices in activities, food, and clothing. (3) On the one hand, a family may choose to enjoy the wonder of winter. (4) Fresh snow offers plenty of opportunities for winter sports such as skiing, sledding, snowmobiling, snowboarding, or ice skating. (5) Plus, nothing beats the warmth of a fire and a cup of hot soup after a hard day of play in the cold, fresh air. (6) Of course, the family will need to plan on packing additional special clothing. (7) On the

other hand, a family may prefer to visit a winter haven in a tropical climate. (8) Balmy beaches offer plenty of fun options such as sunbathing, snorkeling, surfing, and swimming. (9) Then, after a day drenched in sun and sand, nothing satisfies more than an air-conditioned restaurant serving fresh fish and cold drinks. (10) And the family can travel light. (11) In the tropics, all they really need are their swimsuits and a few causal clothes such as shorts, t-shirts, and sandals. (12) Of course, many people just stay home.

Effective Expression

Effective expression enhances the writer's purpose through the precise choice and use of words, sentence structure, and grammar.

Word Choice

Precise word choice communicates exact meaning. Writers choose words that effectively communicate tone, purpose, and order. For example, strong transitions and signal words clue the audience into the logical order of the writer's thoughts. Another example of effective expression is the clear and consistent use of pronouns. In addition, words chosen for their emotional or visual impact create strong mental images in the reader's mind and carry out the writer's purpose.

Ineffective Expression

SINGULAR PRONOUN   DISAGREES WITH   PLURAL PRONOUN

Everyone on the soccer team was tired; they were upset about losing.

VAGUE WORDING

Effective Expression

SIGNAL WORD

PRONOUNS AND NOUNS AGREE IN NUMBER

As everyone on the soccer team dragged into the locker room, each player drooped her head in defeat.

WORDS CHOSEN FOR EMOTIONAL IMPACT

Sentence Structure

Four types of sentences serve as the basis for all sentences in the English language: simple sentence, complex sentence, compound sentence, compound-complex sentence. Effective expression uses a variety of sentence types to express ideas in clear and interesting statements. (You will learn more about sentence structure in Chapters 16–17.)

Simple Sentences:

Michaella had been out of school for years. She was insecure about her abilities.

Complex Sentence:

Michaella, who had been out of school for years, didn't want to fail.

Compound Sentence:

She studied for two hours every day; as a result, she earned a 4.0 GPA.

Compound-Complex Sentence:

Michaella studied for two hours every day because she didn't want to fail; as a result, she earned a 4.0 GPA.

Grammar

Grammar is a tool of effective expression. Writers use grammar to clarify and polish ideas. Grammar includes a wide variety of language rules such as the following: tense, agreement, and punctuation. (You will learn more about grammar throughout your studies in this text.) During the revision process, many writers focus on one element of expression at a time.

EFFECTIVE EXPRESSION

Revise the following paragraph for effective expression through word choice. With a small group of your peers, revise the underlined parts of the following paragraph for effective expression. Use the following word(s) in your revision. Discuss how the revision improves the effectiveness of the paragraph.

is

Justine's brand new Maxima

landed

shattered

suddenly swerved into

the car's

wrapped

A Frightful Moment

(1) Justine was driving her friend Jeremy to his house after a concert last Tuesday evening. (2) An oncoming car <u>is in</u> her lane. (3) Justine jerked her steering wheel to avoid a head-on collision. (4) Her car spun 360° and off the road. (5) The car <u>lands</u> in the middle of a stand of trees. (6) Thankfully, Justine and Jeremy walked away without injury; unfortunately, <u>their</u> car was totaled. (7) The windshield <u>is broke</u>. (8) The rear-end of the car <u>wraps</u> around a tree. (9) <u>Its</u> trunk was shoved into the backseat. (10) Because of that frightful moment, Justine <u>was</u> still afraid to drive.

Workshop

Analyzing the Effectiveness of a Paragraph

Many student writers benefit from the study of a scoring guide. A scoring guide identifies and describes levels of writing effectiveness. The following scoring guide describes the traits of an effective paragraph as discussed in this chapter: A score of "5" indicates a highly effective paragraph. In a small group of your peers, discuss the differences between a "5" paragraph and a "3" level paragraph.

Scoring Guide for a Paragraph

5 A focused main idea presents the narrowed subject and the writer's point, and suggests a pattern of organization. Relevant and in-depth details convincingly support and develop the main idea. Strong transitions indicate careful ordering of details based on a logical pattern of organization. Effective expression enhances the writer's purpose through the precise choice and use of words, sentence structure, and grammar.

4 A focused main idea presents the narrowed subject and the writer's opinion, and suggests a pattern of organization. Relevant and adequate details support and develop the main idea. Clear transitions indicate an order of details based on a logical pattern of organization. Effective expression carries out the writer's purpose through the competent use and choice of words, sentence structure, and grammar.

3 A focused main idea presents the narrowed subject and the writer's opinion or a pattern of organization. Relevant details offer enough support to develop the main idea. Occasional transitions indicate the use of a pattern of organization, but details are not always logically ordered. Expression does not interfere with the writer's purpose, even though occasional errors in use and choice of words, sentence structure, and grammar occur.

2 The main idea presents a general subject or a broad opinion. Details are generalized statements or lists that do not offer enough information to support the main idea. Weak or misused transitions and confused order of details indicate little use of a pattern of organization. Weak expression interferes with the writer's purpose through frequent errors in use and choice of words, sentence structure, and grammar.

1 The main idea presents a vague, weakly worded opinion about a general subject. Details are missing, superficial, or rambling. Lack of transitions and illogical order of details indicate no use of a pattern of organization. Confused expression interferes with the writer's purpose through pervasive errors in choice and use of words, sentence structure, and grammar.

EVALUATE THE EFFECTIVENESS OF A PARAGRAPH

Use the scoring guide to assign a score to each of the following paragraphs written by students about the following topic: *An Important Lesson Everyone Should Learn*. Be prepared to discuss your reasons for each score.

.... Life is full of changes and drama. Never know what is going to happened next step. With ups and downs I had learn lot of things. At this point of our life you cannot trust anyone. You learn more about life everyday. Experience make us learn something new and give us a lesson what we should expect next. My life was full of thrill but it's good to have something like that in your life. How life has teach me a good lesson and how you can learn something from my experience. I want to tell others that never give up in your life, never think that life is ending when u loose something out of your life, because it's always a hope that bring your confidence back. Never depend on others not even your close family. Trust yourself and you will make it. Success never comes easy it's always tuff ways to find it. Unless you don't give up life goes on.

.... A friendly attitude can bring us more reward than a frown any day. We all need to learn the importance of a smile. Before I learned this lesson, I didn't know how to react at work to a disgruntled person or a grumpy coworker. In fact, most of the time I would simply call on a supervisor for help. Unfortunately, this move made me seem incapable of handling a problem on my own. Then one day, someone smiled at me for no reason. A friendly face in the crowd made me feel good. If one person with a smile on her face could make me feel lighter, then a smile might be a powerful way to change how other people felt. Over the next few months, I smiled at every person who looked in my direction, even the nastiest of patrons. As a result, most people were friendlier towards me, and I even felt better about myself. I also became easily able to handle those pesky daily problems. I wish more of us could learn that we have the opportunity to change the world within in us and outside of us, when we smile.

.... Everyone should learn an important lesson in life. Some lessons about being honest. Everyone should learn honesty. Parents teach honesty. Don't shoplift. Don't cheat on tests. Don't lie to friends, even white lies. Everyone should learn kindness. Parents and friends teach kindness. Peers are not kind to them. Too many school yard bullies hurt people. If everyone learned important lessons in life, they would be better off.

.... My mom taught how to deal with stress. As a young child, I was diagnosed with attention deficit disorder. This condition makes many every day situations very stressful. So mom taught me three things that have helped me reduce stress. First, she taught me to think ahead. For example every evening, I lay out my clothes for the next day. Planning what I want to wear the night before saves me time and gives me one less thing to worry about in the morning rush to get out the door. Second, she taught me to be organized. Not only do I plan what I am going to wear, but I make a daily list of assignments and appointments so I know exactly what I need to do and where I need to be. I also keep a backpack filled with supplies such as bottled water, healthy snacks, pen, paper, or any other item I might need. Finally, mother taught me to ask questions and take notes. Asking questions and taking notes keep me focused on a task and keeps my mind from wandering in a million different directions. I am grateful that my mom taught me how to reduce stress. I bet everyone would be better off if they could learn what my mom taught me about coping with stress.

.... Steeling is wrong! Unfortunately not everyone knows this. If every one respected others' property as they do there own we would have less chaos. If everyone that was caught steeling had a good beating put on them I am sure they would second guess doing it again, I am not saying that is how this problem should be resolved but I think it would work. Whether you are a child or a full grown adult I believe this concept should be stressed, let alone it is against the law. The world would be a better place if no one stole, and we would all have more respect for each other and there property.

Academic Learning Log

1. The three levels of information in a paragraph are the _____, _____, and _____.

2. The three parts of a paragraph are a _____, a _____, and an _____.

3. The beginning of a paragraph includes a _____, the _____, and the _____.

4. The middle or the _____ of the paragraph offers major and minor details in support of the topic sentence.

5. The ending or conclusion of the paragraph reinforces _____.

6. An effective paragraph is _____, _____, _____, and _____.

7. A topic sentence states the focused main idea in a _____.

8. To establish logical order, a writing plan includes one or more of the following elements: a _____, order of _____, and order of _____.

9. Relevant details explain and support only the writer's point; _____ details offer in-depth explanations and supports for the writer's point.

10. Effective expression enhances the writer's purpose through the precise choice and use of _____, _____, and _____.

11. What did I learn about the paragraph?

_____

_____

_____

_____

_____

_____

_____

_____

12. What about the paragraph do I need to continue studying or working on?

_____

_____

_____

_____

_____

_____

_____

_____

_____

_____

_____

_____

_____

_____

_____

Academic Learning Log

mywritinglab
**WANT A
BETTER GRADE?**
For more practice with
understanding the para-
graph, go to
www.mywritinglab.com
> Writing Paragraphs
**> Understanding the
Paragraph.**

4

The Descriptive Paragraph

A description is an account that creates a vivid mental image.

The ability to describe people, places, or objects accurately is a useful life skill. Whether you are talking with a stylist about the exact hairstyle you want, sharing a funny or startling scene from your day with a friend in an e-mail, or reporting on the structure of a plant cell for a biology class, you will use description to make your point.

> "Snow blows across the highway before me as I walk—little, wavering trails of it swept along like a people dispersed. The snow people—where are they going? Some great danger must pursue them. They hurry and fall, the wind gives them a push, they get up and go on again."
>
> JOHN HAINES, FROM "SNOW"

What's the Point of Description?

In a descriptive paragraph, the writer uses sensory details such as sights, sounds, smells, tastes, feelings, and textures to create vivid images in the reader's mind. An experienced writer relies on sense memories of a specific experience to evoke these details. In addition, the writer often uses spatial order to create a clear visual image of a person, place, object, or scene: the location or arrangement in space from top to bottom, bottom to top, right to left, left to right, near to far, far to near, inside to outside, or outside to inside.

Every day, we experience rich sensory details from television, movies, music DVDs, and daily life. Think of a scene that grabbed your attention recently. What is your main impression of the scene? What are several details that make this impression so vivid or memorable?

Description also may include or suggest time order because a person, place, or object usually appears in a situation, or an incident usually occurs or suggests a scene.

Descriptive transition words signal that the details follow a logical order based on one or more of the following elements:

1. The arrangement in space of a person, place, object, or scene

2. The starting point from which the writer chooses to begin the description

3. The time frame as relevant to the description (see Chapter 5 for information about time order)

Getting a mental picture of the person, place, object, scene, or situation helps a writer discover his or her point about the subject being described. Study the following photograph of a popular destination for travelers: the Riverwalk in San Antonio, Texas. Use your sense memory of this or similar scenes to call up sensory details. Fill in the graphic with captions that capture the particular details of specific locations on the Riverwalk. Then answer the question "What's the point or impression you are trying to make?" with a one-sentence statement of the overall main idea.

PHOTOGRAPHIC ORGANIZER: DESCRIPTION

Practice 1

A Where is this detail in the scene?

....

What are the sensory details?

SIGHT: ....

SOUND: ....

SMELL: ....

TASTE: ....

TOUCH: ....

B Where is this detail in the scene?

....

What are the sensory details?

SIGHT: ....

SOUND: ....

SMELL: ....

TASTE: ....

TOUCH: ....

C Where is this detail in the scene?

....

What are the sensory details?

SIGHT: ....

SOUND: ....

SMELL: ....

TASTE: ....

TOUCH: ....

D Where is this detail in the scene?

....

What are the sensory details?

SIGHT: ....

SOUND: ....

SMELL: ....

TASTE: ....

TOUCH: ....

E Where is this detail in the scene?

....

What are the sensory details?

SIGHT: ....

SOUND: ....

SMELL: ....

TASTE: ....

TOUCH: ....

What's the point?

....

....

....

....

Practice 1

My First Thoughts: A Prewriting Activity

Brainstorm about the images you just studied. Set a time limit, such as five minutes, and write in your notebook about the images you just studied and the details you generated. Write as quickly as you can without stopping. Getting your first thoughts about a topic on paper is an excellent way to overcome writer's block and set your mind to thinking.

PREWRITING

Making a Point Using Description: One Student Writer's Response

The following descriptive paragraph, written as an online review for tourists, offers one writer's point about the Riverwalk in San Antonio. Read this description and the explanations; complete the activities in **bold type** in the annotations. Then read the writer's journal entry about her experience writing the paragraph.

Main Idea:
The main idea is the point the author is making. The topic is "Paseo Del Rio, the San Antonio Riverwalk." **Underline the author's point.**

Spatial Order:
The phrase "left bank" establishes spatial order. **Circle four more words or phrases that indicate spatial order.**

Relevant Details:
Relevant details describe elements of the scene to support the point "shimmers with color and light." **Draw a box around three additional details that support this point.**

Effective Expression:
Sensory details such as "cool, damp evenings," "spicy fajitas," "salty margaritas," "lights" and "sunset glimmer" create a vivid mental picture. **Double underline 3 more sensory details.**

Paseo Del Rio: A Festival of Color and Light

(1) The Texas spirit of fun and hospitality lights up Paseo Del Rio, the San Antonio Riverwalk. (2) This festive and popular travel destination shimmers with color and light. (3) Along the left bank, two lines of brightly colored café umbrellas—tropical red, Cancun blue, emerald green, lemon yellow—shelter outdoor diners and adorn the cobblestone walk. (4) Above the rainbow rows of umbrellas, white lights strung between oak trees along the walking path glimmer softly in the dusk. (5) Miniature white lights rim the eaves and roofs of the buildings behind the diners and illuminate the graceful drape of the oak branches bending over them. (6) Diners can stay warm on cool, damp evenings with spicy fajitas and salty margaritas as they watch the lights of the Riverwalk and the sunset glimmer upon the water. (7) As they watch, a steady flow of purple trimmed boats putter to midstream from under the bridge on the right side of the river. (8) On this side of the river, the rock walls and the footbridge showcase the rough beauty of the area's natural elements and earth tones. (9) Colorful lights trace the arch under the footbridge. (10) Luminaries sit atop both sides of the bridge's stone-grey railings. (11) At the far side of the bridge, more luminaries light the path along the water's edge. (12) People fill the path with laughter and conversation as they stroll beneath trees shimmering with countless tiny lights. (13) All along the river, this canopy of lights buffers the Riverwalk from the buildings rising in the distance. (14) The lights, the good food, the water, the spectacle of color, the festive atmosphere provide a luscious retreat—Texas style!

Writer's Journal

PEER EDITING

The student writer of "Paseo Del Rio: A Festival of Color and Light" completed the following reflection to record her thinking about her use of details. Read her writer's journal that describes a few key choices she made as she wrote. Then, in the given space, answer her questions about her use of details in her paragraph. Work with a peer or a small group of classmates.

RELEVANT DETAILS: *During one revision, I discovered that my sentence about the boats wasn't relevant to my point. I had included the boats because they were in the picture, not because they supported the point I wanted to make. So I revised that sentence to include the color of the boats, which does add to the festive atmosphere of the Riverwalk and directly supports my point.*

RELEVANT DETAILS: Did I use too many details to support my main idea? Should I leave out any details? Which ones and why? Which details are the most effective? Why?

Developing Your Point Using Description

Writers use descriptive paragraphs to make a point through the vivid details they observe and share about a person, place, object, scene, or situation. To make a point by describing details, a writer often relies on spatial order transitions and sensory details. At times, a writer also uses time order to describe an experience.

The Point: The Main Idea

When you write a description, you limit your topic to concrete details based on sight, sound, smell, taste, and touch. Your opinion or attitude about the subject you are describing is your point or main idea. In a description, your main idea may also include logical order signal words; other times, the logical order is implied without including the signal words.

For example, the first of the following two topic sentences includes (1) the topic, (2) the writer's opinion about the topic, and (3) spatial order signal words. The second topic sentence only includes (1) the topic and (2) the writer's attitude about the topic.

PATTERN OF ORGANIZATION:
SPATIAL ORDER   THE TOPIC

From head to toe, Latoya dressed to appear professional and confident.

THE WRITER'S OPINION

Miguel's office reveals his careful attention to organization.

THE TOPIC   THE WRITER'S OPINION

Practice 2

TOPIC SENTENCES

Practice creating topic sentences. The first two items present a topic, an opinion, and logical order signal word(s). Combine the ideas in each group to create a topic sentence for a descriptive paragraph. Then complete the practice by composing your own topic sentences.

1. TOPIC: (a favorite place) *Grandmother's kitchen*

OPINION: *offered a haven of old-fashioned country warmth*

LOGICAL ORDER SIGNAL WORDS: *A small room at the rear of the house*

TOPIC SENTENCE: ....

....

....

2. TOPIC: (a treasured possession) _The handmade well-pump lamp_

OPINION: _is an eye-catching and whimsical family treasure_

LOGICAL ORDER SIGNAL WORDS: _implied: such as in top to bottom_

TOPIC SENTENCE: _____

_____

3. TOPIC: (a useful product) _____

OPINION: _sleek, lightweight, flexible, easy to use_

LOGICAL ORDER SIGNAL WORDS (as needed): _____

_____

TOPIC SENTENCE: _____

_____

4. TOPIC: (a person of character) My mother (or father, brother, sister, friend, etc.)

OPINION: _kindness_

LOGICAL ORDER SIGNAL WORDS (as needed): _____

_____

TOPIC SENTENCE: _____

5. TOPIC: _____

OPINION: _____

LOGICAL ORDER SIGNAL WORDS (as needed): _____

_____

TOPIC SENTENCE: _____

_____

Practice 2

Logical Order

Once you have chosen a topic and focused on a main idea, you are ready to generate and organize details. To organize visual details, spatial order transition words are helpful during the prewriting phase as well as during the drafting part of the writing process. During prewriting, spatial signal words such as *top*, *middle*, or *bottom* can be used as headings to list details. During the drafting stage, explicitly stating spatial transition words creates a picture in your reader's mind of how your subject is arranged in space. Strong transition words establish coherence, a clear and easy-to-follow flow of ideas.

Transition Words Used to Signal Visual Description

above	at the top	beyond	farther	left	right
across	back	by	front	middle	there
adjacent	behind	center	here	nearby	under
around	below	close to	in	next to	underneath
at the bottom	beneath	down	inside	outside	within
at the side	beside	far away			

Practice 3

SPATIAL ORDER DETAILS

Determine the logical order of the following details taken from Maya Angelou's autobiography *I Know Why the Caged Bird Sings. Hint:* Underline the words that signal spatial order. Complete the exercise by answering the question "What's the point?"

_____ And when they put their hands on their hips in a show of jauntiness, the palms slipped the thighs as if the pants were waxed.

_____ When they tried to smile to carry off their tiredness as if it was nothing, the body did nothing to help the mind's attempt at disguise.

_____ In the store the men's faces were the most painful to watch, but I seemed to have no choice.

_____ Their shoulders drooped even as they laughed.

What's the point Maya Angelou makes with her use of spatial details?

_____

Relevant Details

A writer narrows a topic into a focused main idea by generating descriptive details that answer questions such as *who, what,* and *where.* As a writer brainstorms, the thinking process brings to mind many sensory as well as spatial details. A writer evaluates the relevance of each detail and uses only those that illustrate the main idea. Some relevant details describe the appearance of a person, object, place, or scene; other relevant details explain the author's opinion about the topic. Many descriptive details appeal to sight, sound, smell, taste, and touch. A **concept map**, or **graphic organizer**, helps in several ways. First, the graphic can prompt your thinking, memory, and creativity. In addition, the graphic helps to order ideas as they occur to you. A graphic organizer also allows you to visualize the details and determine if you have enough to make your point. Irrelevant details do not explain, support, or illustrate the focused point of the paragraph. In addition to the graphic organizer, writers use the revision process to double check details for relevance and to eliminate irrelevant ones.

During the prewriting phase, a writer naturally generates irrelevant details. In fact, an effective writer evaluates the details and uses only the details that support the main idea. All descriptive details should work together to create a strong, unified impression, a mental image of the author's main point.

Concept Chart: Description					
TOPIC: *Latoya and professional attire for a job interview*					
WHERE	SIGHT	SMELL	SOUND	TASTE	TOUCH
Top: Hair	*hair gathered and smoothed into a neat and stylish twist*				
Face	*light touch of blush and lip gloss; small gold earrings*		*calm, assured tone of voice*		
Middle: Blouse and Jacket	*white dress cotton button-up collared shirt; dark blue jacket with a rich pin stripe*				*firm handshake*
Skirt	*below the knee; dark blue, A-line*				
Bottom: Shoes	*dark blue, polished, low heels, attractive*				

RELEVANT DETAILS

The following paragraph develops the ideas recorded in the graphic organizer about Latoya and her professional attire. Circle the main idea. Underline the spatial signal words and the sensory details. Cross out the two details that are not relevant to the main idea.

Dressed to Impress

(1) Latoya Bond had been job hunting for months; finally, she landed an interview with a company that she was eager to join. (2) Latoya felt confident that she was well qualified for the position. (3) After all, she was one of the three final candidates chosen from over 100 applications, yet she also knew the importance of making a good impression. (4) From head to toe, Latoya dressed to appear professional and confident. (5) Latoya gathered her hard-to-manage curls into a neat and stylish twist. (6) To complement her no-nonsense hairstyle, Latoya used makeup sparingly but effectively. (7) A little black mascara on her lashes, a touch of blush across her cheeks, and bit of tinted lip balm brought attention to her interested eyes and her earnest smile. (8) She would also be sure to speak with a calm and assured voice. (9) The neatly pressed collar of a white cotton shirt contrasted nicely with her tailored blue pinstriped jacket. (10) Her dark blue A-line skirt reached to just below her knees. (11) Latoya finished her outfit with a flattering pair of blue low-heeled pumps that matched her briefcase and purse. (12) She would offer her prospective employer a firm handshake. (13) Latoya looked as professional and confident as she felt.

Effective Expression: Concrete Word Choice

Precise word choice communicates exact meaning. Words chosen for a specific emotional or visual impact create strong images in the reader's mind and carry out the writer's purpose. As you move through the writing process, think about the impact you want to have on your reader. For the greatest impact, choose concrete and precise words and phrases instead of general or vague expressions. Choose words that *show* instead of *tell*. Consider the following examples.

General or vague words that tell:

> This property has curb appeal.

Concrete words that show:

> This beachfront cottage charms potential buyers with its colorful
> garden, wrap-around porch, and ocean view.

Practice 5

CONCRETE WORD CHOICE

Each item below presents a general sentence using vague words. The phrase in parentheses before each sentence— (A customer to a mechanic) in item 1, for example—describes the speaker of the sentence and the person hearing it. Revise each sentence to eliminate vague wording. Consider the point of the writing situation; express ideas with words that have concrete and precise meanings for a specific impact. Discuss your revisions with your class or with a small group of peers.

1. (A customer to a mechanic): My car makes a funny sound sometimes.

----

2. (A student commenting to his or her companion): The restaurant was disappointing.

----

3. (A weather reporter to a commuter): The weather is nice (or horrible).

----

4. (A staff assistant to Technology Support): The printer is broken.

Using Description in Your Academic Courses

Many college courses in subjects such as literature, composition, history, psychology, ecology, and biology use description. As you study these subjects, you will read descriptions of historical places, influential people, natural elements, and scientific experiments. In addition, you will write descriptions to learn or demonstrate what you have learned.

USING DESCRIPTION IN A HISTORY ASSIGNMENT

Student writer Jean Powell composed the following descriptive paragraph of an important historical site for a report in her American History course. Complete the following activities: (1) Insert appropriate transition words in the blanks; (2) underline the words or phrases used to create sensory details; (3) discuss the point of her report with a small group of peers or with your class.

> The Vietnam Memorial is made up of two black granite walls joined in a wide-angled V shape. A study of just one of the walls reveals the significance of the memorial. A polished black granite slab stretches hundreds of feet long. At its highest tip, it stands 10 feet tall and then tapers to a height of 8 inches at its end point. Its low tip points _____ the Lincoln Memorial. _____ its polished face are the carved names of service men and women who gave their lives during the Vietnam War. Starting at the highest point on the first panel, thousands of names are listed in chronological order. The high polish of the black granite reflects the image of the world _____ the wall. The reflection of earth, sky, and visitors are seen along with the inscribed names. On the wall, the present and the past mingle. A path runs _____ the base of the wall so visitors can walk the path to read the names. Many create pencil rubbings or leave tokens such as flowers, flags, and personal notes. To the side of the path, a wide grassy park adds to the sense of serenity. The memorial is a quiet place where one can come to terms with loss and grief. Its tranquility is a fitting memorial to a controversial war that cost so many their lives.

▲ The Vietnam Memorial

Workshop: Writing a Descriptive Paragraph Step by Step

Workshop

PORTFOLIO

Prewrite Your Paragraph

The various activities below will walk you through the steps of the prewriting stage of the writing process: choosing a topic, focusing your point, and generating and organizing relevant details.

Choose Your Topic

The following activities are designed to help you choose a topic.

1. Create a bank of topics. Use the following headings and brainstorm or list as many topics as you possibly can. Don't analyze your thoughts; just jot down topics as quickly as they occur to you. Compare your bank of topics with those of your classmates.

   - The Scene of an Accident
   - A Nature Scene
   - A Pop Icon
   - An Advertisement
   - Emotions (such as fear)

2. Reread the freewrite you composed based on the photograph of the San Antonio Riverwalk. Underline ideas that could be used for a descriptive paragraph. Map out the logical order of details.

3. Select a photograph of a special place. Write captions, brainstorm sensory details, and freewrite about the photograph. Remember to ask "What are the sensory details and how are the details arranged in space?" and "What's the point?" as you generate ideas.

Focus Your Point

Think about a prewrite you have generated for a descriptive topic. Underline or generate words that suggest your values, opinions, or attitudes about what you described. Think about what strikes you as important about your subject. Consider your audience. Who would be interested in this information and why? Choose a purpose. Write a list of adjectives and sensory details that relate the essence of what you are describing. Use a thesaurus and choose several vivid words to express your thoughts. State in one sentence the point of your description.

AUDIENCE: ....

PURPOSE: ....

SENSORY DETAILS: ....

WHAT'S THE POINT? ....

Generate and Organize Relevant Details

Using the ideas you have already recorded and the concept chart for a description, generate and organize sensory and spatial details that support your point. (*Hint*: Fill in the "Where" column with spatial signal words such as *left, right, near, far, above.*)

		Concept Chart: Description			
TOPIC:					
WHAT'S THE POINT?					
WHERE	SIGHT	SMELL	SOUND	TASTE	TOUCH

Write a Draft of Your Paragraph

Using ideas you generated during the prewriting phase, compose a draft of your paragraph. Return to the prewriting process at any time to generate additional details as needed. Use your own paper.

Revise Your Draft

Once you have drafted a description, read the draft and answer the questions in the "Questions for Revising a Descriptive Paragraph" box that follows on the next page. Indicate your answers by annotating your paper. If you answer "yes" to a question, underline, check, or circle examples. If you answer "no" to a question, write needed information in the margins and draw lines to indicate placement of additional details. Revise your paragraph as necessary based on your reflection. (*Hint*: Experienced writers create several drafts as they focus on one or two questions per draft.)

Questions for Revising a Descriptive Paragraph:

☐ Have I stated or implied a focused main idea? Have I created a strong impression? Can I state my point in one sentence?

☐ Is the logical order of the details clear? Have I used strong transitions to indicate spatial order? Time order?

☐ Have I created a vivid mental image through the use of sensory details?

☐ Have I made my point with adequate details?

☐ Do all the details support my point?

☐ Have I chosen concrete words to make my point?

Proofread Your Draft

Once you have made any revisions to your paragraph that may be needed, proofread your paper to eliminate unnecessary errors, such as dangling or misplaced modifiers.

Grammar in Action: Eliminate Dangling or Misplaced Modifiers

Modifiers are words and phrases that describe other words. A **dangling modifier** occurs when a writer uses a modifier without including the word that the modifier describes.

- **Dangling modifier:**
  INCORRECT: Entering the museum of shrunken heads, my stomach lurched with queasiness.

  (The missing word is "I": It was I, not my stomach, that entered the museum.)

- **Revised sentence:**
  CORRECT: As I entered the museum of shrunken heads, my stomach lurched with queasiness.

A **misplaced modifier** occurs when a writer separates the modifier from the word it is describing.

- **Misplaced modifier:**
  INCORRECT: Scattering in a million directions, Tyrone hustled to scoop up the spilled ball bearings.

  (The ball bearings scattered, not Tyrone)

- **Revised sentence:**
  CORRECT: Tyrone hustled to scoop up the spilled ball bearings scattering in a million directions.

Workshop

Edit the following student paragraph to eliminate one dangling modifier and two misplaced modifiers.

The Amazing Ruby Falls

(1) The caves at Ruby Falls are one of the wonders of the world, eerie yet intriguing. (2) Our tour group was a small one of about ten people. (3) We all piled onto an elevator, stuffy from all the bodies and stinking like a dirty sock, to sink 250 feet underground. (4) We exited the elevator, gasping for air because of the lack of oxygen and the dampness of the cave. (5) The cave was dark with barely any light. (6) We wore helmets mounted with lights. (7) I looked like a real spelunker. (8) We saw stalactites hanging from the ceiling and stalagmites growing up from the ground. (9) The columns, drapes, and flow stone were phenomenal. (10) We walked through an onyx jungle flowing with layers of limestone. (11) The massive monuments were smooth and damp. (12) Some were slimy like a snail. (13) Water trickled from the ceiling in my hair and down my face, a kiss from the cave. (14) We squeezed through stone pathways littered with rock shapes resembling everything from bacon, to a dragon foot, to a form that looked like New York City, all natural. (15) We came across a huge formation; that appeared to be lifelike; the ice sickle stalactites looked like they could break free and assault us. (16) A breathtaking formation that appeared to be lifelike. (17) The caves are amazing.

Review

MY WRITER'S JOURNAL

Work with a classmate to give and receive feedback about your descriptive paragraphs. Use the following form to record your thinking about your writing process for your descriptive paragraph. Use the writer's journal on page 77 as a model for your own journal. Discuss the decisions you made as you wrote, and describe what you have learned by writing. Also, ask for advice about how to improve your paragraph.

MAIN IDEA: _____

_____

_____

_____

LOGICAL ORDER: _____

_____

_____

_____

RELEVANT DETAILS: _____

_____

_____

_____

EFFECTIVE EXPRESSION: _____

_____

_____

_____

Writing Assignments

Considering Audience and Purpose

Study the photographs at the beginning of the chapter. Assume you are a member of the Riverwalk business community, and the community leaders have asked you and other interested parties for needed safety improvements along the Riverwalk. Suggest and describe one or more specific safety improvements.

Writing for Everyday Life

Assume you are separated from your family or loved ones during a holiday or a special occasion. Write a letter in which you describe a significant element of the event. For example, describe the decorations of the season or event, a bride's dress, a favorite birthday gift, or the spread of food at a party or dinner. Choose words that reflect one of the following: (1) approval and enjoyment or (2) disapproval and disappointment.

Writing for College Life

Assume you are writing a report in your psychology class about how a person's mood is reflected in the clothes he or she chooses on any given day. Describe an outfit that reflects an individual's mood.

Writing for Working Life

Assume you have invented a product that will make life much easier; also assume that the Small Business Association finances the production and marketing of useful new inventions. Write a paragraph describing your product to submit your idea to the Small Business Association.

mywritinglab

WANT A BETTER GRADE?
For more practice with description, go to
www.mywritinglab.com >
Using Patterns of Organization to Develop Paragraphs > The Descriptive Paragraph.

5

The Narrative Paragraph

CHAPTER PREVIEW

● What's the Point of Narration?

● Making a Point Using Narration: One Student Writer's Response

● Developing Your Point Using Narration

● Using Narration in Your Academic Courses

● Workshop: Writing a Narrative Paragraph Step by Step

● Writing Assignments

Narration is an account of events told in chronological order to make a specific point.

All of us love a good story. Think of a good story that you have heard, read, or watched on TV or in a theater.

A good story is about personalities or characters, whether real or imagined. A good story is full of vivid action and details. A good story makes a point.

A writer uses narration to tell a story to make a specific point. Often we tell stories to warn about dangers, to teach important lessons, to record important historical events, or to amuse and entertain each other. Narration is a chain of events. These events unfold in chronological order—the order in which they occur. Thus, details follow a logical order based on time. The writer presents an event and then shows when and how each of the subsequent events flows from the first event. In addition to relaying an event, a writer also uses vivid actions and details to show the point of the story. Vivid details may include specific sights, sounds, smells, tastes, textures, feelings, and actions.

What's the Point of Narration?

Getting a mental picture of an event helps a writer to discover the point he or she wishes to make. The following sequence of photographs documents a series of events that took place in the life of Jennifer Hudson over the course of several years. Study each photograph in the timeline. Write a caption that states the topic of each picture. Then answer the question "What's the point?" with a one-sentence statement of the overall main idea.

PHOTOGRAPHIC ORGANIZER: NARRATION

FIRST EVENT

▲ *American Idol, 2004*

What happened?

_____

_____

_____

SECOND EVENT

◄ *Oscar ceremony, 2007*

What happened?

_____

_____

_____

THIRD EVENT

◄ October 24, 2008, a memorial for Hudson's mother and brother

What happened?

_____

_____

_____

What's the point?

TOPIC SENTENCE: _____

_____

My First Thoughts: A Prewriting Activity

Set a time limit, such as five minutes, and write in your notebook about the images you just studied. Do not let your pen or pencil stop. Even if you must repeat ideas, keep writing until the time limit is up. Let the ideas flow freely. Getting your first thoughts about a topic on paper is one excellent way to kick-start your writing process.

Making a Point Using Narration: One Student Writer's Response

The following paragraph offers one writer's narrative inspired by photographs of Jennifer Hudson. Read the narrative paragraph and the explanations; complete the activities in **bold type** in the annotations. Then, read the writer's journal that describes a few key choices she made as she wrote.

Chronological Order:
Chronological order is established with the phrase "in the moment." **Circle four more words or phrases that indicate time order.**

Main Idea:
The main idea is the point of the narration. Notice the topic is Jennifer Hudson. **Underline the author's point.**

Vivid Verbs:
Vivid verbs such as "exploded" creates a mental image and emphasizes action. **Double underline three more vivid verbs.**

Relevant Details:
Relevant details describe events to support the point about Hudson's faith and determination.

Jennifer Hudson's Faith and Determination

(1) All of us, at some point in our lives, face great disappointment or loss. (2) Often, in the moment of such challenges, we want to give up or give in to hopelessness. (3) Jennifer Hudson's story shows us how to overcome loss with faith and determination. (4) In 2004, fans booted Hudson off of the third season of *American Idol*. (5) Many critics following the show that season had expected her to win. (6) Suddenly, however, she sank to seventh place and was sent home. (7) For the most part, the general public forgot about her. (8) However, losing did not stop Hudson. (9) She hoped and watched and worked for her next big break. (10) Then in 2006, Hudson exploded back onto the national stage with the release of the smash-hit movie *Dreamgirls*. (11) By 2007, her show-stopping performance as Effie White in *Dreamgirls* had won her an Academy Award, a British Academy of Film and Television Award, a Golden Globe Award, and a Screen Actors Guild Award. (12) In 2008, she snagged a Grammy as Outstanding New Artist; she had achieved her own dreams. (13) At the height of her success, Jennifer Hudson endured a horrible tragedy. (14) On October 24, 2008, Hudson's mother, Darnell Donerson, and her brother Jason Hudson were found shot to death in Donerson's home. (15) Three days later, Hudson's nephew, 7-year-old Julian King, was also found shot and killed in a sport-utility vehicle belonging to Jason Hudson. (16) Even in the middle of her own suffering, Hudson revealed her faith and determination. (17) Immediately, she and her family created *The Hudson-King Foundation for Families of Slain Victims* in honor of her mother, brother, and nephew.

Writer's Journal

PEER EDITING

The student writer of "Jennifer Hudson's Faith and Determination" completed the following reflection to record her thinking through the writing process. Read her writer's journal that describes a few key choices she made as she wrote. Then, in the given space, answer her questions about her use of details in her paragraph. Work with a peer or a small group of classmates.

LOGICAL ORDER: *When I read over my first draft, I noticed that the paragraph didn't really flow smoothly. I had used contrast and addition transition words instead of time order words. So I revised to include chronological transitions because this is a narrative. For example, the signal word "suddenly" replaced the contrast signal word "however," and the signal word "immediately" replaced the addition signal word "and."*

LOGICAL ORDER: Does the paragraph flow smoothly now? Which transitions are most effective? Are more time order transition words needed? Where and why?

Developing Your Point Using Narration

A narrative tells a story. The story illustrates the writer's point or main idea. To make a point by telling a story, a writer relies on the use of time order transitions, relevant sensory details, and vivid word choice.

The Point: The Main Idea

When you choose to write a narrative, you limit your topic to the details of a specific event based on time order. Most likely, you also have an opinion or point of view about the event. Your opinion or attitude about the event is your point or main idea. Many writers of narrative paragraphs create topic sentences to state the points illustrated by the events.

For example, the following topic sentence contains (1) the topic, (2) the writer's opinion about the topic, and (3) the pattern of organization used to organize details.

Aaron Ralston **bravely** survived a **five-day ordeal.**

TOPIC IS AARON RALSTON

WRITER'S OPINION IS STATED WITH THE WORDS "BRAVELY" AND "ORDEAL"

PATTERN OF ORGANIZATION: NARRATION TIME ORDER IS ESTABLISHED WITH THE PHRASE "FIVE-DAY ORDEAL"

This example illustrates the relationships of the topic, the author's opinion, and the pattern of organization in this particular topic sentence. Note that the word "ordeal" suggests both time order and the writer's opinion.

Practice 2

TOPIC SENTENCES

Practice creating topic sentences. The following items present a topic, an opinion, and time order signal word(s). Combine the ideas in each group to create a topic sentence for a narrative.

1. TOPIC: *Jeff Gordon*

OPINION: *squeaked to narrow victory*

TIME ORDER SIGNAL WORDS: *during the last few laps of the Daytona 500*

TOPIC SENTENCE:

2. TOPIC: *honesty*

OPINION: *I learned the value of*

TIME ORDER SIGNAL WORDS: *during my first job interview*

TOPIC SENTENCE:

Logical Order

Once you have selected your topic and focused on a main idea, you are ready to generate additional details and organize your ideas into a logical sequence based on time order. Each event in a narrative is developed by describing the individual actions and details that make up that event. Just as time order words in the topic sentence signal a narrative, time order transition words also show the flow of events as they unfold in the narrative. Strong transitions establish coherence, a clear and understandable flow of ideas.

Transition Words Used to Show Time Order

after	during	later	previously	ultimately
afterward	eventually	meanwhile	second	until
as	finally	next	since	when
before	first	now	soon	while
currently	last	often	then	

TIME ORDER SIGNAL WORDS

The following paragraph was first published by Linda M. Hasselstrom in *High Country News* to explain her choice for self-defense. Fill in the four blanks with appropriate time order signal words based on the logical order of ideas.

A Peaceful Woman Explains
Why She Carries a Gun

(1) As I drove home one night, a car followed me. (2) It passed me on a narrow bridge .... a passenger flashed a blinding spotlight in my face. (3) I braked sharply. (4) The car stopped, angled across the bridge, and four men jumped out. (5) I realized the locked doors were useless if they broke the windows of my pickup. (6) I started forward, hoping to knock their car aside so I could pass. (7) Just .... another car appeared, and the men hastily got back into their car. (8) They continued to follow me, passing and repassing. (9) I dared not go home because no one else was there. (10) I passed no lighted houses. (11) .... they pulled over onto the roadside, and I decided to use their tactic: fear. (12) Speeding, the pickup horn blaring, I swerved as close to them as I could .... I roared past. (13) It worked: they turned off the highway. (14) But I was frightened and angry. (15) Even in my vehicle I was too vulnerable.

Relevant Details

A writer narrows a topic into a focused main idea by generating details that answer questions such as *who, what, when, where, why,* and *how.* A writer evaluates the relevance of each detail and uses only those that illustrate the main idea. Some relevant details show the action of the event; other details explain the author's opinion about the event. Relevant details also often include sensory details, which appeal to sight, sound, smell, taste, and touch. These vivid details work together to create a mental image of the author's main point. During the prewriting phase, a timeline can help a writer organize ideas as they are generated. Study the following concept map that was used to generate details about the topic "Aaron Ralston's Ordeal."

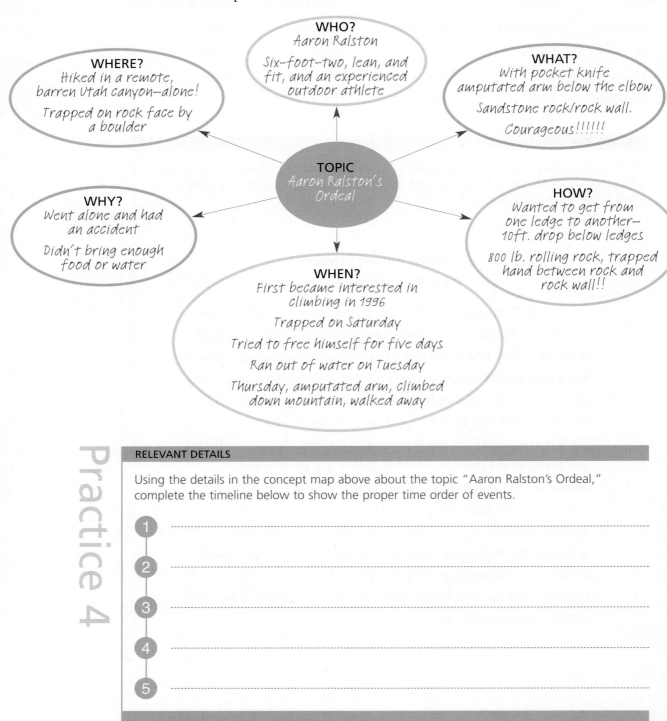

RELEVANT DETAILS

Using the details in the concept map above about the topic "Aaron Ralston's Ordeal," complete the timeline below to show the proper time order of events.

Practice 4

1 ....

2 ....

3 ....

4 ....

5 ....

During the prewriting phase, a writer naturally generates irrelevant details. In fact, an effective writer often produces far more details than can be used to make a specific point. Irrelevant details do not explain, support, or illustrate the focused point of the paragraph. Often, writers use the revision process to double check details for relevance and to eliminate irrelevant details.

RELEVANT DETAILS

The following paragraph develops the ideas recorded in the brainstorming list about Aaron Ralston. Circle the main idea. Underline the relevant sensory details. Cross out the two details that are not relevant to the main idea.

The Courage to Survive

(1) Aaron Ralston courageously survived a five-day ordeal.
(2) Ralston began his ordeal Saturday morning when he made an attempt to climb over a ten-foot drop between two ledges.
(3) Suddenly, an 800-pound rock roared down upon him from above. (4) He quickly scrambled to get out of its path in time.
(5) In the next second, the mammoth stone trapped him on the barren rock face. (6) The boulder had smashed and pinned his right hand between it and a sandstone wall. (7) Six-foot-two, lean, and fit, Ralston is an experienced outdoor athlete. (8) He first became interested in climbing in 1996. (9) For five days, Ralston chipped away at the boulder with a pocket knife.
(10) Finally, on Tuesday, he ran out of his meager ration of food and water. (11) By Thursday rescue seemed unlikely, so Ralston, parched with thirst, made the gutsy decision to amputate his own hand. (12) Knowing his flimsy pocket knife would not cut through bone, he used the force of the rock to snap his bones just below the elbow. (13) Then after applying a tourniquet, Ralston cut through his own muscles, veins, and arteries. (14) Once he completed the hour-long amputation, he rappelled down the mountain. (15) At last, a haggard Ralston hiked out of the canyon.

Effective Expression: Vivid Verbs

Show, don't tell! Some of the verbs most commonly used by student writers belong to the *to be* family of verbs. However, *to be* verbs such as *am, is, are, was,* and *were* are vague and lifeless. They *tell* instead of *show* action, as in the following sentence: *Ivan was angry.* This sentence tells us about Ivan's emotion, but it doesn't show how he acts when he is angry or how his anger fits into the flow of events.

A writer draws a mental picture for the main idea through the use of vivid verbs.

Vivid verbs show the action that is taking place:

Ivan stomped to the trash can and hurled the report into it.

The verbs "stomped" and "hurled" are biased words. Another witness may have chosen objective language to describe Ivan's actions:

Vivid verbs reflect the author's opinion:

Ivan walked to the trash can and tossed the report into it.

Vivid verbs express sensory details:

Ivan snorted with contempt.

Many writers dedicate one full revision to focus on word choices.

Practice 6

VIVID VERBS

Revise each of the following sentences by using vivid verbs to replace *to be* verbs such as *am, is, are, was,* and *were.*

1. The coffee was hot.

----

2. Ryanne was injured during the race.

----

3. Lance Armstrong was the winner of Tour De France six times.

----

4. We were so excited; we were screaming and jumping all around like lunatics.

----

5. I am afraid of my next door neighbor's pit bull.

Using Narration in Your Academic Courses

Many college courses in subjects such as history, psychology, composition, and literature use narration. As you study these subjects, you will read narrations of historical events, case studies, short stories, and novels. In addition, you will write narratives to demonstrate what you have learned. For example, an essay exam may ask you to relate the key events of a major war or the important events in the life of an influential person. Some college writing assignments ask you to draw upon your personal experience and relate it to what you are learning.

USING NARRATION IN AN INTERPERSONAL COMMUNICATION ASSIGNMENT

Read the following information from a college communications textbook. On a separate sheet of paper, write a response to the writing assignment, given in the last sentence of the text.

Ethics in Interpersonal Communication

Because communication has consequences, interpersonal communication involves ethics, a moral aspect of right or wrong. It is believed that there are certain universal ethical principles: you should tell the truth, have respect for another's dignity, and not harm the innocent.

In the U.S. legal system, you have the right to remain silent and to refuse to incriminate yourself. But you don't have the right to refuse to reveal information about the criminal activities of others that you may have witnessed. Psychiatrists and lawyers are often exempt from this general rule. Similarly a wife can't be forced to testify against her husband nor a husband against his wife. In interpersonal situations, however, there aren't any written rules so it's not always clear if or when silence is ethical.

What would you do? While at the supermarket, you witness a mother verbally abusing her three-year-old child. You worry that the mother might psychologically harm the child, and your first impulse is to speak up and tell this woman that verbal abuse can have lasting effects on the child and often leads to physical abuse. At the same time, you don't want to interfere with a mother's right to say what she wants to her child. Nor do you want to aggravate a mother who may later take out her frustration on the child. Write a short narrative that illustrates what you would do in this situation.

Workshop

PORTFOLIO

Workshop: Writing a Narrative Paragraph Step by Step

Prewriting for Your Paragraph

The various activities that follow will walk you through the steps of the prewriting stage of the writing process: choosing a topic, focusing your point, and generating and organizing relevant details.

Choose Your Topic

The following activities are designed to help you choose a topic.

1. Create a bank of topics. Use the following headings and either brainstorm or list as many topics as you possibly can. Don't be critical of what you write; just get as many topics written down as quickly as possible. As you think of new topics, add them to the list. Compare your bank of topics with those of your classmates.

   - Heroes
   - Health
   - Pop Culture
   - Memories

2. Generate ideas with a freewrite. Choose one of the topics from your topic bank and think of an event related to the topic. Write about the event for ten minutes without stopping. Include sensory details: sight, sound, smell, taste, and touch.

3. Select a photograph of a special event. Write a caption, brainstorm topics, and freewrite about the photograph. Remember to ask "What happened?" and "What's the point?" as you generate ideas.

Focus Your Point

Read a freewrite you have generated for a narrative. Underline words that suggest your values, opinions, or attitudes about the event. Think about what interests you about the event. Use a thesaurus and choose several vivid words to express your thoughts. Identify your audience and purpose. Write a list of vivid verbs that show the actions that occur during the event. State in one sentence the point of the story you are going to tell.

AUDIENCE: _____

PURPOSE: _____

VIVID VERBS: _____

WHAT'S THE POINT? _____

Generate and Organize Relevant Details

Using ideas you have recorded so far and the timeline graphic, generate and organize details that support your point.

What's the point?

TOPIC SENTENCE: _____

_____

_____

What happened?

1 _____

2 _____

3 _____

4 _____

5 _____

 # Write a Draft of Your Paragraph

Using the ideas you generated during the prewriting phase, compose a draft of your paragraph. Return to the prewriting process at any time to generate additional details as needed. Use your own paper.

 # Revise Your Draft

Once you have created a draft of a narrative, read the draft and answer the questions in the "Questions for Revising a Narrative Paragraph" box that follows. Indicate your answers by annotating your paper. If you answer "yes" to a question, underline, check, or circle examples. If you answer "no" to a question, write additional details in the margins and draw lines to indicate their placement. Revise your paragraph based on your reflection. (*Hint:* Experienced writers create several drafts as they focus on one or two questions per draft.)

 Portfolio Workshop

Workshop Practice 8

Questions for Revising a Narrative Paragraph:

☐ Have I stated or implied a focused main idea? Have I created a strong impression? Can I state my point in one sentence?

☐ Is the logical order of the events clear? Have I used strong transitions to indicate time? And space?

☐ Have I made my point with adequate details?

☐ Do all the details support my point?

☐ Have I used vivid verbs to keep my readers interested in what I am saying? Have I used sensory details to make my point?

☐ What impact will my paragraph make on my reader?

Proofread Your Draft

Once you have made any revisions to your paragraph that may be needed, proofread your paragraph to eliminate careless errors such as shifts in verb tense.

Grammar in Action: Unnecessary Shifts in Verb Tense

Verb tense tells your reader when an event occurred. "Sandra laughed" is past tense. "Sandra laughs" is present tense. "Sandra will laugh" is future tense. A shift in tense for no logical reason is confusing to the reader.

- **A Shift in Verb Tense:**

  INCORRECT: Monica sighed loudly, rolled her eyes, and stomps off angrily.

- **Consistent Use of Tense:**

  CORRECT: Monica sighs loudly, rolls her eyes, and stomps off angrily.

TENSE SHIFTS

Edit these sentences for unnecessary shifts in tense.

1. Raul works two jobs and attends a community college. He wanted to become a registered nurse and join the Peace Corps.

....

....

....

....

2. Hurricane Ivan destroyed property along the coast in Pensacola, Florida. The hurricane force winds and waves would batter hotels to pieces and rip roofs off restaurants and homes.

----

3. Vitali and Carl had fun at the Daytona 500 race. They always pay to sit in the infield. They will grill hamburgers and hot dogs. As they ate, they watched the cars zoom around them.

----

4. Joe and Jarvonna had a wonderful first date. Joe makes reservations at the Japanese Steak House. After dinner, he surprises her with tickets to watch her favorite team, the Orlando Magic, play the Miami Heat. On the way home, Jarvonna suggested stopping for coffee. Losing track of time, the two talk for hours.

Practice 8

Review

MY WRITER'S JOURNAL

Work with a classmate to give and receive feedback about your narrative paragraphs. Use the following form to record your thinking about your writing process for your narrative paragraph. Use the writer's journal on page 93 as a model for your own journal. Discuss the decisions you made as you wrote, and describe what you have learned by writing. Also, ask for advice about how to improve your paragraph.

MAIN IDEA: ....

....

....

....

LOGICAL ORDER: ....

....

....

....

RELEVANT DETAILS: ....

....

....

....

EFFECTIVE EXPRESSION: ....

....

....

....

Writing Assignments

Considering Audience and Purpose

Study the sequence of photographs of Jennifer Hudson at the beginning of the chapter. Assume the pictures are to be used to document her achievements on a website designed to promote her career. Write a narrative that will be recorded as a voice-over and heard as the pictures flash on the screen.

Writing for Everyday Life

Assume you or someone you know recently took action in an emergency situation. Write a paragraph for a letter to a friend relaying the event as it unfolded. Choose words that reflect one of the following: (1) approval of a courageous act or (2) concern for a foolish act.

Writing for College Life

Assume you have witnessed an important historical event such as the invention of the wheel, the first flight into space, landing on the moon, the last battle fought in the Civil War, or 9/11. Write a paragraph for a local paper documenting the event as it occurred.

Writing for Working Life

Assume you are filing for worker's compensation for an injury that occurred on the job. Write a paragraph for a report to your supervisor in which you record the events as they occurred.

6

CHAPTER PREVIEW

LEARNING OUTCOMES

The Process Paragraph

A process is a series of steps, occurring in chronological order.

Every day we repeat countless processes, from cooking a meal to flossing our teeth. Effective use of processes allows us to perform efficiently in every aspect of our lives. In our personal lives, we follow specific processes to file our taxes or enhance our health. In our professional lives, most of us go through an interview process to secure a job and an evaluation process to get a raise. In our academic lives, we follow set procedures to enroll in classes, learn, and achieve high GPAs.

A process may describe the steps necessary to complete a task such as changing a tire, activating an iPod, or creating a web page. A process may also describe the phases, stages, or cycle of a recurring event such as the phases of the moon, the stages of human development, or the cycle of grief. To write a process paragraph, a writer identifies and explains the logical time order of the individual steps or stages in the task or cycle. An effective process paragraph also relies heavily on concrete descriptive details and vivid images so the reader can mentally see the process as it unfolds.

What's the Point of Process?

Visualizing a process helps a writer discover his or her point about the procedure. The following sequence of photographs documents a series of steps in a set of Pilates exercises called "spine stretch and roll like a ball." Study each photograph in the timeline. Write a caption that briefly describes each picture. Then answer the question "What's the point?" with a one-sentence statement of the overall main idea.

PHOTOGRAPHIC ORGANIZER: PROCESS

STEP ONE

What is happening?

_____

_____

_____

_____

STEP TWO

What is happening?

_____

_____

_____

_____

STEP THREE

What is happening?

_____

_____

_____

_____

STEP FOUR

What is happening?

_____

_____

_____

_____

What's the point?

_____

_____

_____

My First Thoughts: A Prewriting Activity

Set a time limit, such as five minutes, and write in your notebook about the images you just studied. Do not let your pen or pencil stop. Even if you must repeat ideas, keep writing until the time limit is up. Let the ideas flow freely. Getting your first thoughts about a topic on paper is one excellent way to overcome writer's block and set your mind to thinking.

LEARNING OUTCOMES
STRUCTURE

Making a Point Using Process: One Student Writer's Response

The following paragraph offers one writer's point about the set of exercises depicted in the photographs. Read the process and the explanations; complete the activities in **bold type** in the annotations. Then read the writer's journal entry that records decisions made during the writing process.

Main Idea:
The main idea is the point the author is making about the topic. The topic is "an exercise sequence." Underline the author's point about this topic.

Chronological Order:
The transition "First" signals time order. Circle four more time order signal words.

Effective Expression:
Vivid details such as "sitting tall and straight ... as if you were sitting next to a wall" creates a mental picture for the reader. Double underline three more vivid descriptive details.

Relevant Details:
Relevant details explain specific steps that build strength and flexibility. Strength is required to curve the spine and pull in the stomach. Draw a box around a step in the process that builds flexibility.

Spine Stretch and Roll Like a Ball

(1) "Spine stretch and roll like a ball" is an exercise sequence that builds strength and flexibility in the core area of your body supported by the spine. (2) First, assume the proper starting position. (3) Begin by sitting tall and straight on your mat as if you were sitting next to a wall. (4) Open your legs slightly wider than hip-width apart, placing your heels on the outside edges of the mat. (5) Pull your navel up and in. (6) Extend your arms at shoulder height parallel to your legs and flex your feet, pressing through your heels and pointing your toes toward the ceiling. (7) Next, tighten your buttocks and round your torso up and over. (8) Continually press your lower back behind you and scoop in your abdominals. (9) As you deepen the curve of your spine, press your navel further in as if it could kiss your spine. (10) Imagine your body forming a U-shape. (11) Once you are fully extended, hang your head between your shoulders, and hold the stretch. (12) To roll like a ball from this position, bend your knees and draw both ankles toward the core of your body and balance on your sit bones. (13) Grasp an ankle in each hand; pull your feet close to your buttocks, and place your head snugly between your knees. (14) Imagine your body taking the shape of a small, tight C. (15) Then, inhale and roll back. (16) As you roll, keep your feet close to your body and your head tucked between your knees. (17) Roll until you are balanced on your shoulder blades, but do not roll onto your neck. (18) Throughout the roll, maintain your C-shape and keep your navel pressed into your spine. (19) Finally, exhale as you roll back into your starting position.

The Writer's Journal

PEER EDITING

The student writer of "Spine Stretch and Roll Like a Ball" completed the following reflection to record his thinking through the writing process. Read his writer's journal that describes a few key choices he made as he wrote. Then, in the given space, answer his question about the main idea of his paragraph. Work with a peer or a small group of classmates.

MAIN IDEA: *Even though I really like this topic, I know a lot of people just aren't into exercise. As I reread the paragraph, it sounds like I am only talking to people who already care about exercise, but I really want to inspire everyone to exercise. How can I make my topic interesting to people who need to exercise but don't?*

Developing Your Point Using Process

A process shows how to do something or how something works. To describe a process, a writer uses chronological order (also called time order), relevant concrete descriptive details, and vivid images.

The Point: The Main Idea

When you write a process paragraph, you limit your topic to a specific set of details based on time order. Most likely, you also have an opinion or point of view about the process, and this opinion or attitude is your point or main idea. A topic sentence states the point or purpose of the steps, directions, or phases.

For example, the following topic sentence contains (1) the topic, (2) the writer's opinion about the topic, and (3) the pattern of organization used to organize details.

The topic is "grief." The writer's opinion is stated with the phrase "emotional work" and time order is established with the phrases "the six phases" and "in progress."

The six phases | of grief | represent an emotional work | in progress.

PATTERN OF ORGANIZATION: TIME ORDER   TOPIC   AUTHOR'S OPINION   PATTERN OF ORGANIZATION: TIME ORDER

This example illustrates the relationships of the topic, the author's opinion, and the pattern of organization in this particular topic sentence. Note that the phrase "the six phases of grief" combines the topic and the pattern of organization.

Practice 2

TOPIC SENTENCES

Practice creating topic sentences. The following items present a topic, an opinion, and time order signal word(s). Combine the ideas in each group to create a topic sentence for a process.

1. TOPIC: Test-taking anxiety

OPINION: can be overcome

TIME ORDER SIGNAL WORDS: in several steps

TOPIC SENTENCE: ....

2. TOPIC: Checking the oil and changing the oil in a car

OPINION: easy and quick

TIME ORDER SIGNAL WORDS: process

TOPIC SENTENCE: ....

Logical Order

A process describes the individual actions that make up each step or phase within the process. Just as time order words in the topic sentence signal a process, time order transition words show the flow of events as the process unfolds. Strong transitions establish coherence, a clear and understandable flow of ideas.

Transition Words Used to Show Time Order

after	currently	last	now	since	until
afterward	eventually	later	often	soon	when
as	finally	meanwhile	previously	then	while
before	first	next	second	ultimately	

Practice 3

TIME ORDER

The following information appears in the safety publication *How to Survive a Submerging Car* sponsored by the Florida Highway Patrol. Determine the logical order of the sentences. *Hint:* Underline the time order transition words. Then answer the question "What's the point?"

_____ Then, while the car is still floating, **get out**; crawl through the opened window and swim to shore.

_____ The first thing to do in a floating car is to **push** the button to unbuckle your seatbelt.

_____ Next, **open** the window; electric windows should still work while the car is floating.

_____ When a car plunges into a lake or river, it should float for about three minutes, giving you enough time to safely exit the car before it sinks.

_____ P.O.G.O. stands for Push, Open, and Get Out.

_____ Once the car sinks, the P.O.G.O. method still works.

_____ In a submerged car, first **push** the button that releases your seatbelt.

_____ Finally, **get out**; push yourself out of the car and quickly swim to the surface.

_____ Then, **open** your car door.

What's the point?

_____

Relevant Details

As a writer narrows a topic into a focused main idea about a process, the thinking process brings to mind many details of time and space. A writer evaluates the relevance of each detail and uses only those that illustrate the main idea. Some relevant details show the action of the process; other details explain the author's opinion about the process. Relevant details also include vivid descriptive and sensory details. These details work together to create a vivid mental image of the author's main point about the process. During the prewriting phase, a timeline can help a writer organize ideas as they are generated. Study the following timeline that was used to generate details about the phases of grief.

The Six Phases of Grief

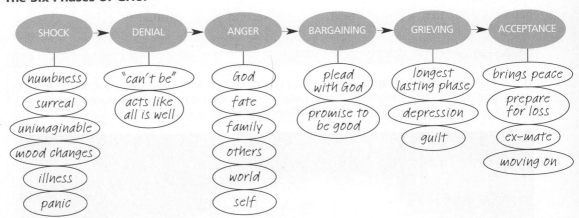

RELEVANT DETAILS

Assume you are going to write about the major stages of the human life cycle for a college psychology course. Create a timeline similar to the one above for the stages of grief. Compare your timeline with that of a peer or a small group of classmates.

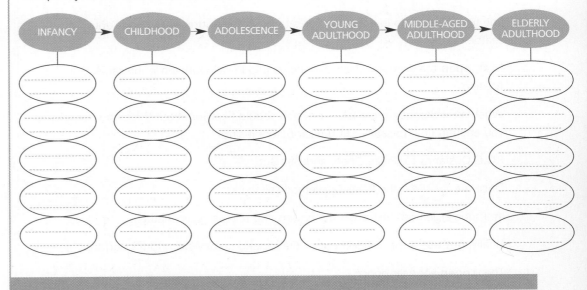

During the prewriting phase, a writer naturally generates irrelevant details. In fact, an effective writer often produces far more details than can be used to make a specific point. Irrelevant details do not explain, support, or illustrate the focused point of the paragraph. A careful writer uses the revision process to double check details for relevance and to eliminate irrelevant details.

RELEVANT DETAILS

The following paragraph develops the ideas recorded in the brainstorming list about the six phases of grief. Circle the main idea. Underline at least three concrete details. Cross out the two details that are not relevant to the main idea.

1. Shock

2. Denial

3. Anger

4. Bargaining

5. Grief

6. Acceptance

The Phases of Grief

(1) In her book, *On Death and Dying*, Dr. Elizabeth Kübler-Ross explains the phases of grief we experience when we learn that a loved one is terminally ill. (2) The six phases of grief represent an emotional work in progress. (3) The first phase is shock. (4) During this initial phase, we experience a fog of numbness; life seems surreal as it crumbles around us, and the chore ahead of us seems unimaginable. (5) Throughout the second phase, denial, we work hard to erect the illusion that recovery is possible or that life is still normal. (6) We simply think, "This can't be happening to me." (7) Once we move past denial, we then grapple with the third phase of grief—anger. (8) We aim our anger at God, fate, doctors, family, the world, or even ourselves. (9) Thoughts such as "If only I had…" or "How can others just go on with their lives?" occupy our minds. (10) During traumas such as divorce, we often become angry with our ex-mate. (11) During the fourth phase, known as bargaining, we negotiate with God to cure the problem in exchange for our good behavior. (12) The fifth phase, usually the longest lasting, is grieving. (13) We often labor in mourning for months or years. (14) Chipping away at depression, guilt, physical illness, loneliness, panic, and abrupt mood changes employs all our energies. (15) The final phase of grief occurs as acceptance. (16) Often, for those of us facing our own death, acceptance brings the wage of peace. (17) As survivors of loss, such as divorce, we usually find ourselves working to re-build our lives and move on.

Effective Expression: Vivid Images

Show, don't tell! Create vivid word pictures that deepen your reader's understanding of your point. Two figures of speech create vivid images: simile and metaphor.

A **simile** is an indirect comparison between two different ideas or things that uses *like, as, as if,* or *as though.*

Example:

As Robin crossed the finish line, his legs pumped like pistons.

A **metaphor** is a direct comparison between two different ideas or things that does *not* use *like, as, as if,* or *as though.* Often a metaphor uses words such as *is, are,* or *were* to make the direct comparison between the two ideas.

Example:

As Robin crossed the finish line, his legs were pumping pistons.

Practice 6

VIVID IMAGES

Revise each of the following sentences to create vivid images by using similes and metaphors suggested by the photos. Discuss your work with your class or in a small group of your peers.

1. To ensure a healthful serving size, limit meat portions to 3 ounces.

2. Adolescence is a stage of human development made up of great change leading to adulthood.

Using Process in Your Academic Courses

Many college courses in subjects such as biology, ecology, history, political science, psychology, and composition use process in their discussions. As you study these subjects, you will learn about processes involving the physical world, mental health, government, and writing. In addition, you will record processes to learn or demonstrate what you have learned. For example, a science lab may require you to conduct an experiment, record the steps you took, and evaluate the process. Some college writing assignments ask you to reflect upon your personal writing process so you can strengthen your writing skills.

USING PROCESS IN A COMPOSITION ASSIGNMENT

During a composition class, a student wrote the following paragraph in her writer's journal to reflect upon the effectiveness of her writing process. Assume you are her peer editor, and, based on what you have learned in this chapter about writing a process paragraph and in Chapter 2, offer her some advice.

Kristen Elizabeth Spengler

Writing 101

September 27, 2010

My Writer's Journal: My Writing Process

(1) I start my writing process by mapping. (2) I make what is like a spider web with one basic idea in the middle of the page and supporting ideas branching off all around it. (3) After brainstorming for a while, I go on the computer and put the ideas I came up with into sentences. (4) Usually, I like to lay it all out on the computer and print it out because it is easier for me to see it while I'm typing my draft. (5) After I type up all the ideas I brainstormed, I print it out and turn it in.

Workshop: Writing a Process Paragraph Step by Step

Prewrite Your Paragraph

The various activities below will walk you through the steps of the prewriting stage of the writing process: choosing a topic, focusing your point, and generating and organizing relevant details.

Choose Your Topic

The following activities are designed to help you choose a topic.

1. Create a bank of topics. Use the following headings and brainstorm or list as many processes about each topic as you possibly can. Don't criticize your thoughts; just get as many relevant processes written down as quickly as possible. Compare your bank of topics with those of your classmates.

   - Recycling Trash
   - Auditioning
   - Studying
   - Training an Animal

2. Generate ideas with a freewrite. Choose one of the topics from your topic bank and think of the steps necessary to complete the process. Write about the process for ten minutes without stopping.

3. Select a photograph or series of photographs that illustrates a process. Write captions; brainstorm steps, directions, or phases; and freewrite about the photograph(s). Remember to ask "What is happening?" and "What's the point?" as you generate ideas.

Focus Your Point

Read a freewrite you have generated for a process. Underline words that suggest your values, opinions, or attitudes about the process. Use a thesaurus and choose several vivid words to express your thoughts. Think about why the steps are important. Identify your audience and purpose. Create a list of concrete details and vivid images that show the actions that occur during the process. State in one sentence the point of the process.

AUDIENCE: ....

PURPOSE: ....

....

LIST OF CONCRETE DETAILS: ....

....

WHAT'S THE POINT? ....

....

Generate and Organize Relevant Details

Using ideas you have recorded so far and the process flowchart, generate and organize details that support your point.

What's the point?

TOPIC SENTENCE: ....

....

....

What is happening?

First Step

↓

Second Step

↓

Third Step

↓

Fourth Step

 ## Write a Draft of Your Paragraph

Using the ideas you generated during the prewriting phase, compose a draft of your process paragraph. Return to the prewriting process at any time to generate additional details as needed. Use your own paper.

 ## Revise Your Draft

Once you have created a draft of a process, read the draft to answer the questions in the "Questions for Revising a Process Paragraph" box that follows. Indicate your answers by annotating your paper. If you answer "yes" to a question, underline, check, or circle examples. If you answer "no" to a question, write needed information in margins and draw lines to indicate placement of additional details. Revise your paragraph based on your reflection. (*Hint:* Experienced writers create several drafts as they focus on one or two questions per draft.)

Portfolio Workshop

Questions for Revising a Process Paragraph:

☐ Have I stated or implied a focused main idea? Have I created a strong impression? Can I state my point in one sentence?

☐ Is the order of the steps, directions, or phases within the process clear? Have I used strong transitions?

☐ Have I made my point with adequate details?

☐ Have I included only the details that are relevant to my topic sentence?

☐ Have I used vivid images to make the process clear to my readers?

☐ Have I used concrete details to make my point?

Proofread Your Draft

Once you have made any revisions to your paragraph that may be needed, proofread your paragraph to eliminate careless errors such as fused sentences.

Grammar in Action: Eliminating Fused Sentences

A **fused sentence** occurs when two or more independent clauses are punctuated as one sentence. Correct a fused sentence by applying any of the following four edits: (1) separate independent clauses with a period and capital letter; (2) insert a coordinating conjunction (*for, and, nor, but, or, yet,* or *so*) and a comma between independent clauses; (3) insert a semicolon between the independent clauses; or (4) insert a semicolon with an appropriate transition between independent clauses.

PORTFOLIO

Workshop

- **A fused sentence:**

  Plants take in water through their roots they take in the gas carbon dioxide through their foliage plants use sunlight to turn water and carbon dioxide into food through the process of photosynthesis.

- **Two ways to correct the above fused sentence:**

  ADDED COMMA AND COORDINATING CONJUNCTION "AND" TO SEPARATE INDEPENDENT CLAUSES

  1. Plants take in water through their roots, and they take in the gas carbon dioxide through their foliage; plants use sunlight to turn water and carbon dioxide into food through the process of photosynthesis.

  ADDED SEMICOLON TO SEPARATE INDEPENDENT CLAUSES

ADDED PERIOD TO SEPARATE INDEPENDENT CLAUSES; THE FIRST LETTER OF THE SECOND INDEPENDENT CLAUSE IS NOW CAPITALIZED

2. Plants take in water through their roots. In addition, they take in the gas carbon dioxide through their foliage; then, plants use sunlight to turn water and carbon dioxide into food through the process of photosynthesis.

ADDED SEMICOLON AND TRANSITION WORD "THEN" TO SEPARATE INDEPENDENT CLAUSES

Workshop Practice 8

ELIMINATING FUSED SENTENCES

Edit to eliminate fused sentences.

1. Using anabolic steroids is a fast way to increase body size some athletes are willing to cheat at a sport they take these steroids to increase body mass beyond what hard work alone could produce.

----

2. Effective questioning occurs in an order that draws out the exact information needed questions should focus on easy-to-answer factual information that puts the person at ease then the interviewer can move to ideas that can't be stated as a fact.

LEARNING OUTCOMES
SELF-EVALUATION

Review

MY WRITER'S JOURNAL

Work with a classmate to give and receive feedback about your process paragraphs. Use the following form to record your thinking about your writing process for your process paragraph. Use the writer's journal on page 109 as a model for your own journal. Discuss the decisions you made as you wrote, and describe what you have learned by writing. Also, ask for advice about how to improve your paragraph.

MAIN IDEA: _____

_____

_____

_____

LOGICAL ORDER: _____

_____

_____

_____

RELEVANT DETAILS: _____

_____

_____

_____

EFFECTIVE EXPRESSION: _____

_____

_____

_____

Writing Assignments

Considering Audience and Purpose

Study the sequence of photographs about the set of Pilates exercises at the beginning of the chapter. Draft a process paragraph based on one of the following two writing situations:

Assume you are keeping a personal exercise journal. Write a paragraph in which you describe the steps in your exercise sequence. Include the challenges you might face in each phase of the process.

Assume you are an instructor of an exercise class for an elderly group. Think about specific movements in each step of the exercise that might have to be adapted due to poor balance or stiffness of joints. Write a paragraph for the Senior Citizens' Health Club Newsletter that describes these adapted exercises.

Writing for Everyday Life

Assume that a friend or family member has asked you for advice about how to open a bank account; write a paragraph that explains how to do so. Be sure to include information about necessary personal identification and available banking services. Choose words that reflect one of the following: (1) endorsement of the banking services or (2) warning against possible problems.

Writing for College Life

Assume you are in a college course called Student Success, and you have been assigned to write a brief oral report about how to study. Write a paragraph that records the text for your speech in which you describe the most effective way to take notes during class.

Writing for Working Life

Assume you are the director of the Human Resources department for a corporation, and you are volunteering your services at a job fair designed to help unemployed citizens secure jobs. You have agreed to teach participants how to handle the interviewing process. Write a paragraph as part of your handout that describes the steps necessary to prepare for an interview.

PEARSON
mywritinglab
WANT A
BETTER GRADE?
For more practice with process, go to
www.mywritinglab.com
> Using Patterns of
Organization to Develop
Paragraphs > The Process
Paragraph.

7

The Example Paragraph

An example, also called an exemplification, is a specific illustration of a more general idea.

When we communicate—with family members, employers, teachers, or friends—we often use examples to clarify a point we want to make. Think of a situation you were in recently where you used examples to make a point. What makes an example effective?

In everyday life, we illustrate our decorating ideas with paint chips and swatches of fabric. In working life, we offer examples of our hard work and successes when we apply for jobs and promotions. In college life, professors and textbook authors use examples to teach concepts in every discipline.

To write an example paragraph, a writer moves from a general idea to specific examples that support and clarify the main point. Sometimes, as in a science lab report, a writer may present the specific examples first and then come to a general conclusion based on the examples. An effective example paragraph also relies heavily on concrete details, the logical order of importance, and, often, parallel expression.

What's the Point of Examples?

Generating and organizing examples help a writer to discover his or her point about a particular topic. The following photographs offer three examples of a thrifty lifestyle. Study each photograph. Write a caption that briefly describes each example of thrifty living. Then, answer the question, "What's the point?" with a one-sentence statement of the overall main idea.

WRITING FROM LIFE

PHOTOGRAPHIC ORGANIZER: EXAMPLES

EXAMPLES OF A THRIFTY LIFESTYLE

Example 1:

What is this?

....

....

Example 2:

What is this?

....

....

Example 3:

What is this?

....

....

What's the point?

....

....

My First Thoughts: A Prewriting Activity

PREWRITING

Set a time limit, perhaps five minutes, and write in your notebook about the images you just studied. Do not let your pen or pencil stop. Even if you must repeat ideas, keep writing until the time limit is up. Let ideas flow freely. Getting your first thoughts about a topic on paper is one excellent way to kick start your writing process.

Making a Point Using Examples: One Student Writer's Response

The following paragraph offers one writer's point about what the people in the photographs exemplify on the previous page. Read the exemplification and the explanations; complete the activities in **bold type** in the annotations. Then read the writer's journal entry that records decisions made during the writing process.

Main Idea:
The main idea is the point the author is making about the topic. The topic is "A thrifty lifestyle." **Underline the author's point about this topic.**

Listing Order:
The transitional phrase "for example" signals that the paragraph is developed by examples. **Circle two more transitional phrases that indicate a list of examples.**

Effective Expression:
Parallelism refers to the way ideas of equal importance are worded. To achieve parallelism, a writer uses the same form of wording for a set, series, or list of ideas or details. Repeating a form of wording or type of phrase makes your ideas easier to follow. **Double underline two more ideas with –ing phrasing.**

Relevant Details:
Concrete details list specific minor details for each major example of "a thrifty lifestyle." **Draw boxes around two more concrete minor details that support a major example.**

Be Thrifty: Save Money

(1) When hard times hit the economy, most of us get back to the basics. (2) That old saying "a penny saved is a penny earned" states some good basic advice. (3) A thrifty lifestyle saves money. (4) For example, adjusting our thermostats can lower our energy bill up to 10% a month. (5) In the winter, we should set the thermostat to 68°F while we're awake and even lower while we're asleep or away from home. (6) In the summer, we should set the thermostat to 78°F. (7) If we usually pay $300.00 a month for energy, we could save $30.00 a month. (8) A second example of thrifty living is saving loose change. (9) Most of us have tons of change in our wallets, at the bottom of our purses and backpacks, in our cars, and even in our sofas and chairs. (10) We can put that money to good use by rolling loose change and depositing the rolls into a savings account. (11) Saving 50 cents a day in loose change adds up to $15 a month. (12) Another example of thriftiness is packing a lunch. (13) Typically, each of us spends $6 to $12 every time we eat out during a work or school day. (14) If one person packed a lunch every day, he or she would save $60 to $120 a week! (15) That means we could save as much as $480 a month, and that's just for one person. (16) Think of what a family could save by packing lunches. (17) As these three examples prove, living a thrifty lifestyle can save each of us thousands of dollars in just one year.

The Writer's Journal

PEER EDITING

The student writer of "Be Thrifty: Save Money" completed the following reflection to record some of her thinking about her writing process. Read her writer's journal that describes a few key choices she made as she wrote. Then, in the given space, answer her questions about her use of details in her paragraph. Work with a peer or a small group of classmates.

RELEVANT DETAILS: My first draft was way too long. Once I had a topic, I did a freewrite about it, and within 5 minutes, I had filled two pages with lots of examples for saving money by being thrifty. It was kind of hard to figure out what to cut. For example, I wanted to give some hints about rolling coins (like how often, where to get supplies, etc.) and packing lunches (like nutrition, variety, and weight loss/gain). Do you think I should include some of these details? Why or why not? If so, which details and where?

Developing Your Point Using Examples

An exemplification illustrates a main point with one or more examples. To exemplify a point, a writer lists the examples, often according to the order of importance; explains each example with relevant concrete details; and often uses parallel expression.

The Point: The Main Idea

When you write an exemplification, you limit your topic to a set of specific examples, instances, or cases. Most likely, you also have an opinion or point of view about the examples, and this opinion or attitude is your point or main idea. You may reveal your opinion by listing the examples in a particular order of importance. A topic sentence states the point or purpose of the examples.

For example, the following topic sentence contains (1) the topic; (2) the writer's opinion about the topic; and (3) the pattern of organization used to organize details.

The topic is "body art." The pattern of organization is established with the phrase "such as tattooing and piercing" and the verb "exemplifies." The writer's opinion is stated with the phrase "self-expression."

Sometimes in an example paragraph, a topic sentence only implies the pattern of organization as in the following version.

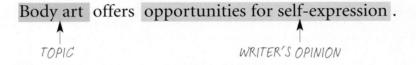

When the example pattern of organization is only implied by the topic sentence, then transitions that signal and list examples establish the pattern of organization within the body of the paragraph. Notice in the following example that the two major detail sentences state the topic, pattern of organization, and writer's opinion.

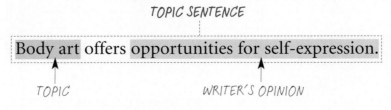

MAJOR DETAIL SENTENCE #1

Tattooing is one example of body art as self-expression.

PATTERN OF ORGANIZATION: TOPIC   WRITER'S OPINION
EXEMPLIFICATION

MAJOR DETAIL SENTENCE #2

Piercing is another example of artistic self-expression.

PATTERN OF ORGANIZATION: TOPIC   WRITER'S OPINION
EXEMPLIFICATION

Practice 2

TOPIC SENTENCES

The items below present a topic, an opinion, and example signal word(s). Combine the ideas in each group to create a topic sentence for an example paragraph.

1. TOPIC: *Foods* .... OPINION: *inflame the condition diverticulitis*

EXAMPLE (OR LISTING) SIGNAL WORDS: *Certain* ....

TOPIC SENTENCE: ....

....

2. TOPIC: *A good friend* .... OPINION: *compassion and honesty*

EXAMPLE (OR LISTING) SIGNAL WORDS: *illustrates* ....

TOPIC SENTENCE: ....

....

3. TOPIC: *Solar energy* .... OPINION: *is versatile and cheap*

EXAMPLE (OR LISTING) SIGNAL WORDS: *not included; only implied* ....

TOPIC SENTENCE: ....

....

4. TOPIC: *SUV drivers* .... OPINION: *rugged, aggressive*

EXAMPLE (OR LISTING) SIGNAL WORDS: ....

TOPIC SENTENCE: ....

....

Logical Order

Once you have selected your topic and focused on a main idea, you are ready to generate additional details and list your ideas based on their order of importance. To use examples to illustrate a main point, a writer moves from a general idea to a major support to a minor support. To signal the movement between these levels of ideas, a writer uses transitions to signal or list examples. Strong transitions establish coherence, a clear and understandable flow of ideas.

Transitions Used to Signal Examples

an illustration	for instance	once	to illustrate
for example	including	such as	typically

Transitions Used to List Examples

also	final	for one thing	last of all	second
and	finally	furthermore	moreover	third
another	first	in addition	next	
besides	first of all	last	one	

Practice 3

LOGICAL ORDER

▲ Injury from overuse

Fill in the blank with appropriate transitions to signal or list examples.

In the drive to become physically fit, many risk injury by overtraining. Overuse injuries develop through the daily stresses placed on various parts of the body (1) .... tendons, muscles, (2) .... joints. Plantar Fasciitis is (3) .... of an overuse injury from walking, jogging, (4) .... running. This injury is an inflammation of the band of tissue that stretches across the sole of the foot. (5) ...., the foot is tender from the ball to the heel, making it painful to walk.

Practice 4

The following information was published on a government website for consumer protection. Determine the logical order of the sentences. Complete the exercise by answering the question "What's the point?" Discuss your answers with your class or with a small group of peers.

Consumer Beware!

.... The third and most common example of fraud is phishing.

.... Phishing is an email message that lures a consumer to a phony website.

.... The email sender pretends to be from a legitimate government organization, bank, or retailer.

.... The phishy email stated, "We recently reviewed your account, and we need more information to help us provide you with secure service."

.... The message also directed the receiver "to visit the Resolution Center and complete the 'Steps to Remove Limitations.'"

.... A recent instance of phishing came from a phony PayPal site.

.... A second example of fraud is the phone scam; a caller pretends to represent a trusted organization or company.

.... In one instance, a caller claims to work for the court and says the listener has been called for jury duty.

.... The caller then demands personal information such as a social security number, birth date, and credit card numbers.

.... The first and least common example of fraud is the handyman sting.

.... The handyman offers to fix the problem, such as replacing a roof or removing a fallen tree, for a cash fee lower than any reputable company could offer.

.... The handyman shows up on the doorstep of a home in obvious need of repair, usually after severe weather such as a tornado or hurricane.

.... Most often, the money is paid upfront, and the work is never completed.

What's the point?

....

....

....

Relevant Details

As a writer narrows a topic into a focused main idea, the thinking process brings to mind many details that answer the questions *who, what, when, where, why,* and *how.* A writer evaluates the relevance of each detail and uses only those that exemplify the main idea. Some relevant details express major examples of the main point; minor details may further illustrate major examples. Some major and minor details may explain the author's opinion about the examples. During the prewriting phase, a list can help a writer organize ideas as they are generated. Study the following list generated about the topic "Examples of State Gun Laws."

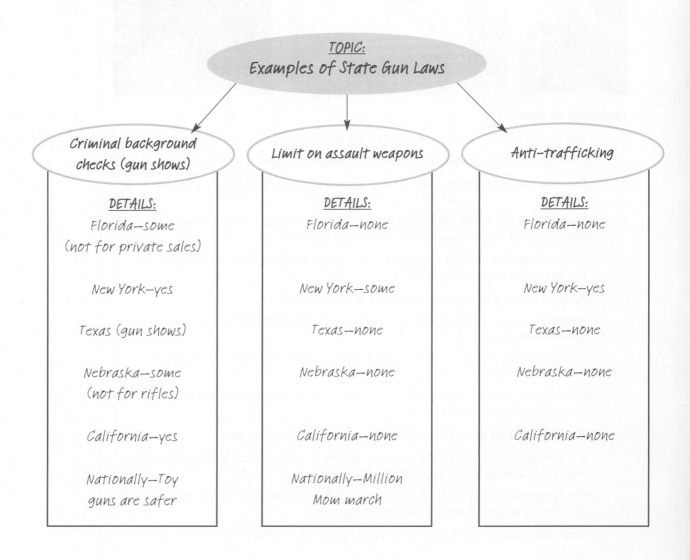

During the prewriting phase, a writer naturally generates irrelevant details. In fact, an effective writer often produces far more details than can be used to make a specific point. Irrelevant details do not exemplify, explain, or support the focused point of the paragraph. A careful writer uses the revision process to double check details for relevance and to eliminate irrelevant ones.

The following paragraph, adapted from the *stategunlaws.org* website, develops the ideas recorded in the brainstorming list about state gun laws. Circle the main idea. Underline three concrete major examples. Cross out the two details that are not relevant to the main point.

State Gun Laws

(1) New York, Florida, Texas, Nebraska, and California gun control laws vary greatly from state to state. (2) For example, of the five states—New York, Florida, Texas, Nebraska, and California—only New York has an anti-trafficking law that places a one-handgun-per-month limit on gun sales. (3) In the other four states, anyone can easily traffic guns to criminals by buying as many handguns as they want from gun stores and turning them over for profit on the streets. (4) Unbelievably, toy guns face stricter safety regulations than do real guns. (5) In addition, only two states, California and New York, require criminal background checks at gun shows. (6) Florida and Nebraska require partial background checks; for example, Florida requires a criminal background check for handguns, but no background check is necessary to purchase an assault rifle such as AK47. (7) Alarmingly, Texas does not require background checks at gun shows. (8) Perhaps the most alarming example of our uneven approach to gun control is the overall lack of limits on assault weapons. (9) Of the five states, only California bans the sale of semiautomatic assault weapons such as the Uzi. (10) New York has a partial limit on such sales; for example, the state does not ban the sale of "rapid fire ammunition magazines that hold up to 100 rounds." (11) Texas, Nebraska, and Florida have no limits on assault weapons and magazines. (12) A national network of volunteers known as the Million Mom March works to strengthen and unify gun laws.

Effective Expression: Parallel Language

Parallel language is the use of similar and balanced expressions in a pair or series of words, phrases, or clauses. Parallelism makes a piece of writing more enjoyable, more powerful, and more readable. Study the following examples from a student's first thoughts about the seasons of the year.

Non-Parallel Words:

Summer time is ideal for swimming, boating, and a picnic.

Revised Words for Parallelism:

Summer time is ideal for swimming, boating, and picnicking.

THIS SERIES OF WORDS (NOUNS) ALL END IN –ING.

Non-Parallel Phrases:

The seasons can go from the fire of summer to the freezing winter.

Revised Phrases for Parallelism:

The seasons can go from the fire of summer, to the chill of fall, to the freeze of winter, to the breeze of spring.

THIS SET OF IDEAS REPEATS A PATTERN OF PREPOSITIONAL PHRASES.

Non-Parallel Clauses:

I love the fall because the leaves turn colors, and it's football season.

Revised Clauses for Parallelism:

I love the fall because the leaves turn colors, and television programming turns to football.

THESE CLAUSES ARE NOW BOTH DEPENDENT CLAUSES THAT BEGIN WITH THE SAME SUBORDINATING CONJUNCTION ("BECAUSE") AND USE THE SAME VERB ("TO TURN").

Practice 6

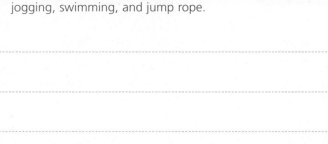

PARALLEL EXPRESSION

Revise the following sentences so ideas are expressed in parallel language. Discuss your work with your class or with a small group of your peers.

1. Examples of activities that strengthen the heart include jogging, swimming, and jump rope.

2. A healthy heart lifestyle includes the following: getting plenty of sleep, eating a balanced diet, and regular exercise.

....

....

....

Using Examples in Your Academic Courses

Every college course uses examples to clarify ideas. As you study these subjects, you will learn about examples of governments, important historical figures, psychological concepts, scientific principles, effective speeches, and so on. In addition, you will prove what you have learned by providing examples of the concepts and skills you have studied.

Practice 7

USING EXAMPLES IN A SHORT-ANSWER COMMUNICATION ESSAY EXAM

Assume you are taking a college class in communication. Your professor has given your class a set of study questions to help you prepare for an upcoming exam. A peer in your study group started the following prewrite to one of the study questions. Study her notes; then fill in the blank with a one-sentence answer to the study question. Finally, on your own paper, write a draft of a paragraph. Include appropriate example transition words. Work with a peer or in a small group.

Study Question: What is the purpose of listening?

Answer to Study Question *Listening serves several purposes.* ....

....

....

....

....

Example	**Example**	**Example**
We learn from others.	We relate to others.	We influence others.
We learn from parents, teachers, and others.	We develop long-lasting relationships.	We respect others.
We learn about others, the world, and ourselves.	We increase understanding.	We earn the respect and trust of others.
	We avoid conflict.	

Workshop: Writing an Example Paragraph Step by Step

Prewrite Your Paragraph

The various activities that follow will walk you through the steps of the prewriting stage of the writing process: choosing a topic, focusing your point, and generating and organizing relevant details.

Choose Your Topic

The following activities are designed to help you choose a topic.

1. Create a bank of topics. Use the following headings to brainstorm or list as many examples about each topic as you possibly can. Don't criticize your thoughts; just get as many relevant examples written down as quickly as possible. Add more topics and examples as they occur to you. Compare your bank of topics with those of your classmates.

   - Pollution
   - Job Skills
   - Effective Teachers
   - Alternative Energy Supplies

2. Generate ideas with a freewrite. Choose one of the topics from your topic bank and think of examples that illustrate the topic. Write about the topic and examples for ten minutes without stopping.

3. Select a photograph or series of photographs that illustrates a topic. Write captions, brainstorm examples, and freewrite about the photograph(s). Remember to ask "What do(es) the picture(s) illustrate?" and "What's the point?"

Focus Your Point

Read a prewrite you have generated for an exemplification. Underline words that suggest your values, opinions, or attitudes about the topic and the examples. Think about why the details are important. Identify your audience and purpose. Write a list of additional concrete examples that illustrate your point. State in one sentence the point of the examples.

AUDIENCE: ....

PURPOSE: ....

LIST OF CONCRETE DETAILS: ....

....

WHAT'S THE POINT? ....

....

Generate and Organize Relevant Details

Using ideas you have recorded so far and the following idea map, generate and organize details that support your point.

Example: Illustrations of an Idea

What's the point?

Topic:

| Major Detail: Example 1 | Major Detail: Example 2 | Major Detail: Example 3 |

Minor Details

Minor Details

Minor Details

 DRAFTING
Write a Draft of Your Paragraph

Using the ideas you generated during the prewriting phase, compose a draft of your example paragraph. Return to the prewriting process at any time to generate additional details as needed. Use your own paper.

 REVISING
Revise Your Draft

Once you have created a draft of an example paragraph, read the draft and answer the questions in the "Questions for Revising an Example Paragraph" box that follows. Indicate your answers by annotating your paper. If you answer "yes" to a question, underline, check, or circle examples. If you answer "no" to a question, write the additional details in the margin and draw lines to indicate their placement. Revise your paragraph based on your reflection. (*Hint:* Experienced writers create several drafts as they focus on one or two questions per draft.)

 PORTFOLIO

Workshop

Questions for Revising an Example Paragraph:

- ☐ Have I stated or implied a main idea? Have I made my point? Can I state my point in one sentence?
- ☐ Have I used concrete details to make my point?
- ☐ Have I included only the details that are relevant to my point?
- ☐ Have I used order of importance effectively? Have I used strong transitions?
- ☐ Have I used parallel language to make my ideas clear to my readers?

Proofread Your Draft

Once you have made any revisions to your paragraph that may be needed, proofread your paragraph for proper usage and punctuation, such as using commas in a series.

Grammar in Action: Using Commas in a Series

Use commas to separate three or more words, phrases, or clauses in a series. One of the following conjunctions is used between the last two items of a series: *for, and, nor, but, or, yet,* or *so*; for example, sending, receiving, *and* forwarding emails. Some experts state that the comma before the conjunction is optional. However, leaving the last comma of the series out may cause confusion, so many experts advise including it. In writing for college, we suggest you include it. Study the following examples:

- **Using Commas to Separate Three or More Words:**

    Dave Chappelle is candid, creative, and comical.

    Coordinating conjunction

- **Using Commas to Separate Three or More Phrases:**

    Texas offers vacation experiences that are enjoyable and educational: exploring Big Ben National Park, visiting The Alamo, and touring the NASA Space Center.

    Coordinating conjunction

- **Using Commas to Separate Three or More Clauses:**

    Our company is looking for employees who can find solutions, who can work as a team, and who can excel in their roles.

    Coordinating conjunction

PORTFOLIO

Workshop

USING COMMAS IN A SERIES

Edit these sentences for proper use of commas in a series. Rewrite them on the lines below.

1. I only need three pairs of shoes—running shoes low-heeled pumps and reef sandals.

----

2. The study of psychology includes units such as the biology of the brain the development of the mind and the social behaviors of a human being.

----

3. Those who snore are those who are more likely to have heart attacks who are more likely to be in an automobile accident and who are more likely to suffer from daytime fatigue.

----

4. Heart disease is linked to diet exercise and genetics.

----

5. You need better fitting shoes if you have to dig the corner of your toenail from under your skin if you have a build-up of dead skin such as corns or calluses or if you have tired aching feet at the end of a long hard day.

----

6. Snoring can be caused by a variety of factors such as alcohol consumption nasal problems sleep apnea and the structure of your mouth.

LEARNING OUTCOMES
SELF-EVALUATION

Review

Work with a classmate to give and receive feedback about your example paragraphs. Use the following form to record your thinking about your writing process for your example paragraph. Use the writer's journal on page 125 as a model for your own journal. Discuss the decisions you made as you wrote, and describe what you have learned by writing. Also, ask for advice about how to improve your paragraph.

MAIN IDEA: ....

....

....

....

LOGICAL ORDER: ....

....

....

....

RELEVANT DETAILS: ....

....

....

....

EFFECTIVE EXPRESSION: ....

....

....

....

....

Writing Assignments

Considering Audience and Purpose

Study the set of photographs of examples of thrifty living at the beginning of the chapter. Assume you are a volunteer working with HOPE, a nonprofit group that assists families. Your task this month is to write a column for the group's newsletter. Write a paragraph that identifies and explains additional examples of money-saving ideas for family life.

Writing for Everyday Life

Assume that you are keeping a personal journal and you want to capture the essence of your daily life so your children and grandchildren will know about the customs, fashions, or nature of this time in your life and our society. Use examples to make your point. Choose words that reflect one of the following attitudes: (1) realistic, (2) idealistic.

Writing for College Life

Assume you are a member of the Student Government Association, and you are helping with freshman orientation. Identify two or three aspects of college life about which new students should be aware. Use examples to make your point.

Writing for Working Life

Assume a peer is applying for a job as a supervisor of a sales team at Best Buy or Radio Shack (or some other job that requires leadership and commitment) and has asked you for a recommendation. Interview the peer; then write a one-paragraph recommendation in which you use examples to support your recommendation.

mywritinglab

WANT A BETTER GRADE?
For more practice with exemplification, go to **www.mywritinglab.com** > Using Patterns of Organization to Develop Paragraphs > The Example Paragraph.

8

The Classification Paragraph

A classification is a division of a topic into one or more subgroups.

CHAPTER PREVIEW

LEARNING OUTCOMES

- What's the Point of Classification?

- Making a Point Using Classification: One Student Writer's Response

- Developing Your Point Using Classification

- Using Classification in Your Academic Courses

- Workshop: Writing a Classification Paragraph Step by Step

- Writing Assignments

Whether we are grocery shopping, studying, job hunting, or searching for that special someone, we often gather and group information based on types. For example, most of us have experienced or observed the social cliques that form in high schools, neighborhoods, and on the job.

A writer uses classification to sort, group, and label items and ideas based on shared traits or types. In everyday life, we fulfill various social roles such as life-partner, parent, sibling, friend, employee, or student. In working life, we promote people to higher levels of responsibility and pay based on particular types of skills and attitudes. In college life, each of us probably prefers certain kinds of courses, likes certain types of teachers, and does better on certain types of tests.

To write a classification paragraph, a writer divides a topic into subgroups based on shared traits or qualities. The writer lists and often labels each subgroup, describes its traits, and offers examples that best represent the group. Because groups and subgroups are listed, transitions are often used to signal logical order and ensure coherence. An effective classification paragraph uses details of description and examples, logical order, and (as in any effective paragraph) sentence variety.

What's the Point of Classification?

Identifying and labeling groups or types helps a writer to discover his or her point about a particular topic. Study the following set of photographs. In the space provided, (1) identify the types of music represented by the three photographs; (2) list the traits of each subgroup; (3) describe specific examples based on the photographs; and (4) answer the question "What's the point?" with a one-sentence statement of the overall main idea.

PHOTOGRAPHIC ORGANIZER: CLASSIFICATION

TOPIC: TYPES OF MUSIC

1ST TYPE	2ND TYPE	3RD TYPE

▲ Garth Brooks   ▲ Ludacris and Queen Latifah   ▲ Marc Anthony

WRITING FROM LIFE

1. What type of music does each artist in the photographs represent?

_____

2. Traits: Traits: Traits:

3. Examples: Examples: Examples:

What's the point?

_____

My First Thoughts: A Prewriting Activity

Brainstorm about the images you just studied. Set a time limit, such as five minutes, and write in your notebook about the images and the details you generated. Write as quickly as you can without stopping. Let the ideas flow freely. Getting your first thoughts about a topic on paper is one excellent way to overcome writer's block and set your mind to thinking.

LEARNING OUTCOMES
STRUCTURE

Making a Point Using Classification: One Student Writer's Response

The following paragraph offers one writer's point about the types of music illustrated by the photographs. Read the classification paragraph below and the explanations; complete the activities in **bold type** given in the annotations. Then read the writer's journal that records decisions made during the writing process.

Effective Expression:
Parallelism refers to the similarity in the way ideas are worded. To achieve parallelism in this sentence, the writer repeats the subject "music" and uses the same form to express each verb. **Double underline three other expressions that repeat a pattern of wording.**

Main Idea:
The main idea is the point the author is making about the topic. The topic is "popular music." **Underline the author's point about this topic.**

Listing Order:
The transitional phrase "first major type" signals that the paragraph is developed based on classification. **Circle two more phrases that signal a list of types.**

Relevant Details:
Relevant details use descriptive details of traits and examples. Descriptive details include sensory details such as "fast, energetic tempo stirs the urge to dance." **Draw a box around two more details that appeal to the senses.**

Music's Variety Is Music's Power

(1) Music expresses our individuality; music connects us to one another; music carries our culture. (2) The power of music comes from the variety of the lives it expresses. (3) Three major types of popular music illustrate the powerful variety of music. (4) The first major type of music is country music. (5) Country music is based on the traditional folk music of the rural South and the cowboy music of the West. (6) Country songs express strong personal emotions about topics such as mother, home, love, hard work, prison, the rambling man, and religion. (7) Country musicians like Garth Brooks typically play such instruments as the guitar and fiddle. (8) The second major type of music that reveals the diversity of music is Hip Hop or rap music. (9) Rap music is a form of music that came about in African American urban communities. (10) Rap is characterized by beat-driven rhymes spoken over instruments or mixed recordings. (11) Rappers like Queen Latifah and Ludacris often express strong political and social views. (12) A third major type that illustrates the powerful variety in music is Salsa music. (13) Salsa, with its origin in Cuba, is a popular form of Latin-American dance music. (14) Salsa is characterized by Afro-Caribbean rhythms; its fast, energetic tempo stirs the urge to dance. (15) Performers like Marc Anthony use percussion instruments such as claves, congas, and cowbells.

The Writer's Journal

PEER EDITING

The student writer of "Music's Variety Is Music's Power" completed the following reflection to record her thinking through the writing process. Read her writer's journal that describes a few key choices she made as she wrote. Then, in the given space, answer her questions about the main idea for her paragraph. Work with a peer or a small group of classmates.

MAIN IDEA: Getting started was really hard for me. I spent a lot of time staring at a blank page, unable to come up with a way to get started. I knew what to say about each type of music, I just couldn't figure out how to word the beginning. Finally, I gave up and just started writing the body of the paragraph, so I think the title and introduction are weak, and there isn't a conclusion. Could you suggest a better title? What would you do to make the opening more interesting? And is the conclusion okay as it is? Or do I need to add something? If so, what?

Developing Your Point Using Classification

A classification makes a main point by grouping or sorting ideas. To support a point through classification, a writer divides a topic into subgroups based on common traits or principles. Writers offer relevant concrete details of descriptions and examples, and (as in every piece of writing) control sentence structure.

The Point: The Main Idea

When you write a classification, you limit your topic to a set of ideas or groups based on types, shared traits, and common principles. Most likely, you also have an opinion or point of view about the groups, traits, or common principles. This opinion or attitude is your point or main idea. You also reveal your opinion by discussing the groups or traits in a particular order of importance. A topic sentence states the point or purpose of the groups, types, or traits.

For example, the following topic sentence contains (1) the topic; (2) the writer's opinion about the topic; and (3) the pattern of organization used to organize details.

The topic is "friendship." The pattern of organization is established with the phrase "three types of." The writer's opinion is stated with the phrase "equally important interpersonal relationships."

TOPIC   PATTERN OF ORGANIZATION: CLASSIFICATION SIGNAL WORDS

Friendships offer three types of equally ◄—
important interpersonal relationships. ◄— ——WRITER'S OPINION

The example above illustrates the relationship of the topic, the writer's opinion, and the pattern of organization in this particular topic sentence.

Practice 2

TOPIC SENTENCES

Practice creating topic sentences. You are given a topic, an opinion, and classification signal word(s). Combine the ideas in each group to create a topic sentence for a classification.

1. TOPIC: *leisure activities*   OPINION: *relaxing and inexpensive, strengthen family ties*

CLASSIFICATION SIGNAL WORDS: *two types of*

TOPIC SENTENCE: ....

2. TOPIC: *diet*   OPINION: *healthful*

CLASSIFICATION SIGNAL WORDS: *several traits*

TOPIC SENTENCE: ....

Logical Order

Once you have divided a topic into groups, types, or traits and focused on a main idea, you are ready to generate additional details and list your ideas in their order of importance. To make a point using classification, a writer moves from a general idea (the group) to a major support (a particular trait of the group) to a minor support (an example of the trait). To signal the movement between these levels of ideas, a writer uses transitions to signal or list groups, types, or traits. Strong transitions establish coherence, a clear and understandable flow of ideas.

Words That Are Used to Signal Groups, Types, or Traits

aspect	classify	group	quality	style
attribute	classification	ideal	rank	trait
branch	collection	kind	section	type
brand	division	level	set	typical
categories	element	order	sort	variety
characteristic	feature	part	status	
class	form	principle	stratum	

Transitions That Combine with Signal Words to List Groups, Types, or Traits

also	final	for one thing	last of all	second
and	finally	furthermore	moreover	third
another	first	in addition	next	
besides	first of all	last	one	

LOGICAL ORDER

Based on the logical order of ideas, fill in the blanks with the appropriate classification signal words. Compare and discuss your answers with a peer or in a small group of your classmates.

I write in support of Henry William's promotion in _____ and pay. Mr. William has several _____ that will make him an effective manager. _____ of these _____ are his communication _____ and his _____ of commitment. He is the _____ who listens and learns. He is the _____ who works for the success of his whole _____.

Relevant Details

As a writer narrows a topic into a focused main idea, the thinking process brings to mind many details that answer the questions such as *who*, *what*, *when*, *where*, *why*, and *how*. A writer evaluates the relevance of each detail and uses only those that clarify or support the main idea based on classification. Some relevant details identify subgroups, types, or traits of the main point. Minor details may offer examples of subgroups, types, or traits. Some major and minor details may explain the writer's opinion about the topic and how it is being classified. During the prewriting phase, a list can help a writer organize ideas as they are generated. Study the following concept map that was used to generate ideas about the topic "Two types of comedy that dominate television."

Concept Map

Topic: *Two types of comedy that dominate television*		
Traits	Type 1: *Sketch comedy*	Type 2: *Situation comedy*
Length:	*Short scenes or sketches (1–10 mins.)*	*30 min. story line*
Material:	*Actors improvise/write scripts Avoids violence, uses bad language*	*Writers create scripts Avoids violence and bad language*
Focus:	*Politics, current events, issues, ensemble acting*	*Social relationships at home and work, ensemble acting*
Examples:	*Colgate Comedy Hour, Monty Python's Flying Circus, SNL, Mad TV, Chappelle's Show, Ed Sullivan (best show of all)*	*I Love Lucy, Friends, Seinfeld, Everybody Hates Chris*

During the prewriting phase, a writer naturally generates irrelevant details. In fact, an effective writer often produces far more details than can be used to make a specific point. Irrelevant details do not explain or support the focused point of the paragraph. A careful writer uses the revision process to double check details for relevance and to eliminate irrelevant ones.

Practice 4

The following paragraph develops the ideas recorded in the brainstorming list about comedy. Circle the main idea. Underline a trait for each group. Cross out the two details that are not relevant to the main point.

Television Comedy: Sketches and Sitcoms

(1) Two types of comedy have long dominated television. (2) One type is sketch comedy. (3) Sketch comedy is a series of short comedy scenes that typically range from one to ten minutes. (4) Often the actors improvise the sketch, making it up as they go; then they write the script based on their improvisation. (5) This kind of humor avoids violence, often uses offensive language, and focuses on politics, issues, and current events. (6) Well-known examples of sketch comedy include *Monty Python's Flying Circus, Saturday Night Live, Mad TV,* and *Chappelle's Show.* (7) However, *The Ed Sullivan Show* remains the all time best variety show to have appeared on television. (8) A second type of comedy dominating television is the sitcom or situation comedy, also an ensemble routine. (9) Sitcoms are usually set in a specific location such as a home or office, and they present amusing story lines about a group of characters such as a family, friends, or co-workers in an office. (10) Often episodes are self-contained stories that are resolved in less than 30 minutes; some sitcoms do use ongoing story lines based on developing relationships between characters. (11) This type of humor avoids violence, rarely uses offensive language, and focuses on social relationships. (12) Well-known examples of situation comedy include *I Love Lucy, Friends, Seinfeld,* and *Everybody Hates Chris.* (13) Overall, sitcoms are more appropriate for family viewing than sketch comedy.

Effective Expression: Controlled Sentence Structure

Control of sentence structure enhances effective expression. You can express ideas through the use of four sentence types: simple, compound, complex, and compound-complex. Study the following definitions and examples of these four types of sentences.

1. A **simple sentence** contains one independent clause.

INDEPENDENT CLAUSE

The food pyramid classifies food into six groups.

2. A **compound sentence** contains two or more independent clauses. These clauses can be joined with:

    a. A comma and a coordinating conjunction (*for, and, nor, but, or, yet, so*: FANBOYS),

INDEPENDENT CLAUSES

We must eat healthfully, and we must exercise regularly.

    b. A semicolon,

INDEPENDENT CLAUSES

The food pyramid has two roles; it classifies food and features physical activity.

OR

    c. A semicolon with a conjunctive adverb.

INDEPENDENT CLAUSES

MyPyramid.gov is helpful; for example, experts explain calorie values.

3. A **complex sentence** contains one independent clause and one or more dependent clauses. A dependent clause begins with a subordinating conjunction (such as *although, because, when, who, which,* and *that*) placed immediately before a subject and verb. Sometimes, the subordinating conjunction also serves as the subject of the verb in the dependent clause.

INDEPENDENT CLAUSE   DEPENDENT CLAUSE

Physical activity means movement of the body that uses energy.

4. A **compound-complex** sentence contains two or more independent clauses and one or more dependent clauses. This sentence type combines the traits of the compound and complex sentences.

DEPENDENT CLAUSE   INDEPENDENT CLAUSES

When we eat well and move often, we feel better, and we do more.

▲ Food Pyramid poster to promote healthy eating

Label each of the following sentences as a simple, compound, complex, or compound-complex sentence. Revise each sentence into the new type of sentence indicated. Discuss your work with your class or with a small group of your peers.

----------------------- **1.** Foods from wheat, rice, oats, cornmeal, barley, or another cereal grain are grain products. Bread, pasta, oatmeal, breakfast cereals, tortillas, and grits are examples of grain products.

REVISE INTO A COMPOUND SENTENCE: --

----------------------- **2.** Oils are fats that are liquid at room temperature, like canola, olive, and other vegetable oils used in cooking.

REVISE INTO A COMPOUND-COMPLEX SENTENCE: --

Using Classification in Your Academic Courses

Classification plays two roles in most academic courses: (1) to narrow a topic and (2) to research a topic. First, any academic topic can be narrowed by breaking a larger topic into subgroups. For example, the following concept map was created for a paper about leadership in a sociology class.

General Topic:	LEADERSHIP	
Subgroups: Authoritarian leader	**Subgroups:** Democratic leader	**Subgroups:** Liberal leader
Traits: Gives orders	**Traits:** Builds agreement	**Traits:** Gives freedom

Practice 6

USING CLASSIFICATION TO NARROW AN ACADEMIC TOPIC

Use the following classification concept map to narrow a topic for a history class. Work with a peer or small group of classmates.

General Topic:	TYPES OF GOVERNMENT	
Subgroups:	**Subgroups:** Democracy	**Subgroups:**
Traits:	**Traits:**	**Traits:** Power is seized by an individual or group.

Second, classification plays a key role in research because information is organized based on types. Two well-known methods of classifying information are the Dewey Decimal System and the Library of Congress System. Your college library uses one of these two types to arrange books on the shelves by labeling them with a system of letters and numbers. When you are assigned a research topic, you will use classification to find the information you need.

Listed below are the letters and titles of the main classes and one subgroup of the Library of Congress Classification. Study the list and answer the questions.

A – GENERAL WORKS
B – PHILOSOPHY. PSYCHOLOGY. RELIGION
C – AUXILIARY SCIENCES OF HISTORY
D – WORLD HISTORY AND HISTORY OF EUROPE, ASIA, AFRICA, AUSTRALIA, NEW ZEALAND, ETC.
E – HISTORY OF THE AMERICAS
F – HISTORY OF THE AMERICAS
G – GEOGRAPHY. ANTHROPOLOGY. RECREATION
H – SOCIAL SCIENCES
   H – Social Sciences (General)
   HA – Statistics
   HB – Economic theory. Demography
   HC – Economic history and conditions
   HD – Industries. Land use. Labor
   HE – Transportation and communications
   HF – Commerce
   HG – Finance
   HJ – Public finance
   HM – Sociology (General)
   HN – Social history and conditions. Social problems. Social reform

HQ – The family. Marriage. Women
HS – Societies: secret, benevolent, etc.
HT – Communities. Classes. Races
HV – Social pathology. Social and public welfare. Criminology
HX – Socialism. Communism Anarchism
J – POLITICAL SCIENCE
K – LAW
L – EDUCATION
M – MUSIC AND BOOKS ON MUSIC
N – FINE ARTS
P – LANGUAGE AND LITERATURE
Q – SCIENCE
R – MEDICINE
S – AGRICULTURE
T – TECHNOLOGY
U – MILITARY SCIENCE
V – NAVAL SCIENCE
Z – BIBLIOGRAPHY. LIBRARY SCIENCE. INFORMATION RESOURCES (GENERAL)

—"Library of Congress Classification Outline."
Library of Congress 5 July 2005. 14 August 2009
http://www.loc.gov/catdir/cpso/lcco/lcco.html

1. Write the letter of the group that would contain the following book titles:

.... *Dealing with Relatives (—even if you can't stand them): Bringing Out the Best in Families at Their Worst* by Rick Brinkman and Rick Kirschner

.... *Encyclopedia of Family Health*

2. Write the letter of the group that you would search for the following information:

.... The principles of Islam

.... The author Toni Morrison, winner of the Nobel Prize for Literature

Workshop: Writing a Classification Paragraph Step by Step

Prewrite Your Paragraph

The various activities below will walk you through the steps of the prewriting stage of the writing process: choosing a topic, focusing your point, and generating and organizing relevant details.

Choose Your Topic

The following activities are designed to help you choose a topic.

1. Create a bank of topics. Use the following headings to brainstorm or list as many categories and subgroups about each topic as you possibly can.
   Don't analyze your thoughts; just get as many relevant categories written down as quickly as possible. Add more topics and categories as they occur to you. Compare your bank of topics with those of your classmates.

   - Birth Order (traits of oldest, middle, youngest, only child)
   - Music
   - Technology
   - Vehicles
   - Life Roles

2. Generate ideas with a freewrite. Choose one of the topics from your topic bank and think of the traits that set a group or subgroup apart. Write about the traits of the group and subgroups for ten minutes without stopping.

   OR

   Select a photograph or series of photographs that illustrates a group or subgroup. Write captions, brainstorm traits, and freewrite about the photograph(s). Remember to ask "What is the group or subgroup represented by this picture(s)?" and "What's the point?"

Focus Your Point

Read a freewrite you have generated for a classification. Underline words that suggest your values, opinions, or attitudes about the topic and its subgroups or categories. Think about why the traits are important. Think about what examples best represent the group, categories, or subgroups. Identify your audience and purpose. Write a list of additional concrete traits and examples that explain your point. State in one sentence the point of the groups, traits, and examples.

AUDIENCE: ....

PURPOSE: ....

LIST OF TRAITS: ....

WHAT'S THE POINT? ....

Generate and Organize Relevant Details

Use the graphic organizer below to either organize the ideas you have already created or to generate details to support your point.

Types (groups) of		

1st Type/group	2nd Type/group	3rd Type/group

Traits:	Traits:	Traits:

Examples:	Examples:	Examples:

What's the point?

_____

_____

Workshop

PORTFOLIO

Write a Draft of Your Paragraph

DRAFTING

Using the ideas you generated during the prewriting phase, compose a draft of your classification paragraph. Return to the prewriting process at any time to generate additional details as needed. Use your own paper.

Revise Your Draft

Once you have created a draft of a classification paragraph, read the draft and answer the questions in the "Questions for Revising a Classification Paragraph" box. Indicate your answers by annotating your paper. If you answer "yes" to a question, underline, check, or circle examples. If you answer "no" to a question, write the additional details in the margin and draw lines to indicate their placement. Revise your paragraph based on your reflection. (*Hint:* Experienced writers create several drafts as they focus on one or two questions per draft.)

Questions for Revising a Classification Paragraph:

☐ Have I made my point? Can I state my point in one sentence?

☐ Have I divided my topic into types, groups, or categories? Have I clearly labeled each group? Have I discussed the common traits and examples of each group?

☐ Have I used strong transitions of classification?

☐ Have I used concrete details to make my point?

☐ Have I included only the details that are relevant to my topic sentence?

☐ Have I used the following to make my ideas clear to my readers: vivid verbs and images, parallel language, controlled sentence structure?

Proofread Your Draft

Once you have made any revisions to your paragraph that may be needed, proofread your paper to eliminate distracting errors such as comma splices.

For more information on eliminating comma splices, see pages 386–401.

Grammar in Action: Eliminating Comma Splices

Comma splices and fused sentences have been categorized as two of the most common errors in student writing. Both the comma splice and the fused sentence occur when writers join ideas without the proper punctuation.

A **comma splice** occurs when a writer uses *only a comma* to join two or more independent clauses.

COMMA SPLICE

Americans enjoy many vacation options, some choose family bonding activities such as trips to family reunions or theme

COMMA SPLICE

parks, others choose special-interest activities such as Bike Week in Daytona Beach or spring break in Cancun.

A **comma splice** can be corrected in three different ways.

Three Rules for Properly Joining Two or More Independent Clauses

A writer can properly join two or more independent clauses in several ways:
1. Use a comma AND a coordinating conjunction (*for, and, nor, but, or, yet, so*: FANBOYS).
2. Use a semicolon.
3. Use a semicolon with a transition (*for example, in addition, however, therefore, thus,* etc.).

Study the following examples:

1. Americans enjoy many vacation options; some choose family bonding activities such as trips to family reunions or theme parks, but others choose special-interest activities such as Bike Week in Daytona Beach or spring break in Cancun.

2. Some choose family bonding activities such as trips to family reunions or theme parks; others choose special-interest activities such as Bike Week in Daytona Beach or spring break in Cancun.

3. Americans enjoy many vacation options; for example, some choose family bonding activities such as trips to family reunions or theme parks.

ELIMINATING COMMA SPLICES

Edit these sentences to eliminate comma splices. *Hint:* Underline subjects once and verbs twice to identify independent clauses.

1. My car matches my personality, we are both dependable and conservative.

-----

2. Both of us are dependable, for example, I have perfect attendance, put in long hours, and meet my goals.

-----

3. I have perfect attendance, put in long study hours, and maintain a high GPA, my Toyota Camry has a perfect maintenance record, gets great gas mileage, and lives up to its reputation.

PORTFOLIO

Workshop Practice 8

Review

MY WRITER'S JOURNAL

Work with a classmate to give and receive feedback about your classification paragraphs. Use the following form to record your thinking about your writing process for your classification paragraph. Use the writer's journal on page 143 as a model for your own journal. Discuss the decisions you made as you wrote, and describe what you have learned by writing. Also, ask for advice about how to improve your paragraph.

MAIN IDEA: ....

....

....

....

LOGICAL ORDER: ....

....

....

....

RELEVANT DETAILS: ....

....

....

....

EFFECTIVE EXPRESSION: ....

....

....

....

Writing Assignments

Considering Audience and Purpose

Study the set of photographs about the types of music at the beginning of the chapter. Assume you are a mentor to a young person who is just becoming interested in music. You have decided to start a collection of music for him or her. First, identify the type(s) of music you want to include in this gift collection. Create a list of specific artists and songs for the type or types of music you have chosen. Then, write a note to go with the gift; write a paragraph that explains the type(s) of music in the collection.

Writing for Everyday Life

Assume you have just experienced an event as an invited guest, and you would like to follow up with a written thank you note. Write a one-paragraph thank you note in which you include the following information: the type of event, the quality of your experience, the most vivid aspects of the event, and the traits of your host that you appreciate. Choose words that reflect one of the following: (1) polite and reserved or (2) warm and enthusiastic.

Writing for College Life

Assume you are in a college psychology class. Your teacher has assigned a chapter on "The Six Basic Emotions and Their Combinations" as the basis of discussion for your next class meeting. The teacher also requires you to keep a learning log. You have decided to record in your learning log what you currently know about these ideas before you begin your reading assignment. Write one paragraph in which you identify, describe, and classify six basic types of emotions you have observed or experienced.

Writing for Working Life

Assume you are compiling information for a résumé for a position as manager trainee at a business such as Target, Best Buy, or Olive Garden. Use the following categories to create your résumé.

Personal Information: Name, address, phone number, and e-mail address

Objective: Manager Trainee position with <u>name of business</u>

Education:

Work Experience:

Activities:

mywritinglab

**WANT A
BETTER GRADE?**
For more practice with classification, go to **www.mywritinglab.com > Using Patterns of Organization to Develop Paragraphs > The Classification Paragraph.**

9

The Comparison and Contrast Paragraph

A comparison examines how two or more things are similar. A contrast looks at how two or more things are different.

Comparing and contrasting ideas is an essential part of critical thinking. When we choose between Subway and McDonald's or Apple and Dell computers, we are weighing the similarities or differences of products and services and making a choice by comparison shopping. What are some basic comparable points for any consumer to consider when shopping? What are some other situations in which we use comparable points as the basis of our thinking or actions?

In everyday life, we compare or contrast the neighborhoods we want to live in and the prices of homes we want to buy, or the honesty and policies of political candidates as we decide for whom we will vote. In working life, we compare or contrast the salaries, benefits, and working conditions among several career opportunities. In college life, we compare and contrast leaders, governments, cultures, literature, technology, writers, or philosophies in a wide range of courses.

To write a comparison or a contrast paragraph, identify the comparable points between two (or more) topics. Once you identify the points of comparison, brainstorm a list of similarities and differences for each one. Then, list and explain examples of each similarity or difference.

158

What's the Point of Comparison and Contrast?

LEARNING OUTCOMES
READING AND WRITING

Often ideas become clearer when they are analyzed based on how they relate to one another. The comparison and contrast patterns of organization allow a writer to explore the ways in which ideas are related. The following set of photographs document some similarities and differences between electric and gas vehicles. Study the sets of images. Answer the following questions about each comparable point. Then answer the question "What's the point?" with a one-sentence statement of the overall main idea.

Practice 1

WRITING FROM LIFE

PHOTOGRAPHIC ORGANIZER: COMPARE AND CONTRAST

SIMILAR TO OR DIFFERENT FROM

GAS VEHICLES
(DODGE CHALLENGER)

ELECTRIC VEHICLES
(DODGE CIRCUIT EV)

What is the **1st** comparable point?

SIMILAR TO OR DIFFERENT FROM

What is the **2nd** comparable point?

SIMILAR TO OR DIFFERENT FROM

What is the **3rd** comparable point?

ELECTRIC VEHICLE CHARGING STATION

What's the point?

My First Thoughts

Brainstorm about the images you just studied. Set a time limit, such as five minutes, and write in your notebook about the images and the details you generated. Write as quickly as you can without stopping. Let the ideas flow freely. Getting your first thoughts about a topic on paper is one excellent way to kick-start your writing process.

Making a Point Using Comparison and Contrast: One Student Writer's Response

The following paragraph offers one writer's point about the similarities and differences between electric and gas vehicles as illustrated by the photographs. Read the comparison and contrast paragraph below and the explanations; complete the activities in **bold type** in the annotations. Then read the writer's journal entry that records decisions made during the writing process.

LOGICAL ORDER: Words of comparison or contrast signal similarities or differences. **Circle two more signal words or phrases for comparison or contrast.**

MAIN IDEA: The main idea is the point the author is making about the topic. **Underline the two topics being compared and contrasted and underline the author's point about the two topics.**

RELEVANT DETAILS: Relevant details include descriptive details about similarities or differences between comparable points. **Draw a box around two more details of similarities or differences.**

EFFECTIVE EXPRESSION: This sentence gives equal weight to both types of vehicles. **Double underline another sentence that expresses equal ideas with the use of semicolon.**

Electric or Gas Vehicles?

(1) Pollution, global warming, and the price of fuel pose real problems for an auto industry churning out gas vehicles. (2) However, electric vehicles offer hope for the future. (3) A comparison between electric vehicles and gas vehicles shows pleasing similarities and differences. (4) Most electric vehicles look just like a gas vehicle. (5) For example, the electric-powered Dodge Circuit EV resembles the gas-powered Dodge Challenger. (6) Both sport the bold look of a muscle car, and both have all the standard features. (7) They even perform similarly; both go from 0 to 60 mph in 6 seconds. (8) Although these similarities promise to please, many drivers will really like the differences between electric and gas vehicles. (9) For example, the lithium-ion battery of the Circuit EV uses far less energy than the gas guzzling V8 engine used by the Challenger. (10) The Circuit EV can go 150 to 200 miles between charges and costs about $6 to $12 a week in electricity; in contrast, the Challenger averages 14 miles per gallon in the city and 22 on the highway. (11) Plus, based on the price of oil, gasoline can cost as much as $5 a gallon, and those dollars add up with the miles. (12) The final difference is convenience. (13) Many people and much energy must be used to refuel a gas vehicle. (14) Oil has to be refined into gasoline, stored, transported, and pumped. (15) However, to recharge an electric vehicle, all one has to do is plug it into a standard household outlet or a socket on a charging station.

The Writer's Journal

LEARNING OUTCOMES
READING AND WRITING

PEER EDITING

The student writer of "Electric or Gas Vehicles?" completed the following reflection to record his thinking through the writing process. Read his writer's journal that describes a few key choices he made as he wrote. Then, in the given space, answer his questions about his use of effective expression in his paragraph. Work with a peer or a small group of classmates.

ELECTRIC VEHICLE
CHARGING STATION

EFFECTIVE EXPRESSION: I used coordination to state most of my ideas because I wanted to be sure to cover each point equally, like in sentences 6, 7, and 10. Does the repeated use of signal words for comparison and contrast make my paragraph boring or interesting? Why? I also had trouble with some of my word choices. I really support electric vehicles, but I couldn't find the right words to get my support across. For example, I am not really satisfied with the word "pleasing" in sentence 3. Should I leave it out, or could you suggest another word? Is it important to give my opinion, or should I stick with just the facts?

Developing Your Point Using Comparison and Contrast

A **comparison** makes a point by discussing the *similarities* between two or more topics. A **contrast** makes a point by discussing the *differences* between two or more topics. To support a point through comparison or contrast, a writer identifies the comparable points of the topic, offers relevant and concrete descriptions and examples for each comparable point, and effectively uses coordination and subordination of ideas.

The Point: The Main Idea

When you write a comparison or a contrast piece, you limit your thoughts to a set of topics based on their relationship to each other. Most likely you have an opinion or belief about the two topics and their comparable points. Your opinion is your point or main idea. In a comparison or contrast paragraph, you also reveal your opinion by discussing the topics and their points of similarities or differences in the order of your own choosing. A topic sentence states the overall point of the comparison or the contrast between the two topics.

For example, the following topic sentence contains (1) the comparable topics, (2) the writer's opinion about the topic, and (3) the pattern of organization used to organize details.

The comparable topics are "Giada De Laurentiis" and "Rachael Ray, celebrity chefs." The pattern of organization is established with words "even though" and "differ." The writer's opinion is stated with the clause "styles differ greatly."

PATTERN OF ORGANIZATION: TRANSITION
WORDS THAT SIGNAL CONTRAST

TOPIC

Even though Giada De Laurentiis and Rachael Ray are both

celebrity chefs, their styles differ greatly. ← WRITER'S OPINION

Practice 2

TOPIC SENTENCES

Practice creating topic sentences. The first two items present a topic, an opinion, and comparison and contrast signal word(s). Combine the ideas to create a topic sentence for a comparison or a contrast. Then, complete the practice by making your own topic sentences.

1. TOPIC: *the communication styles of men and women*

OPINION: *significant*

COMPARISON OR CONTRAST SIGNAL WORDS: *differ three ways*

TOPIC SENTENCE:

Logical Order

Once you have identified the comparable points between your topics and have focused on a main idea, you are ready to generate and organize additional details. To make a point using comparison or contrast, a writer moves from a general idea (the comparison or contrast of two or more topics) to a major support (a comparable point about the topics) to minor supports (details or examples of the comparable point about the topics). To signal the movement among these levels of ideas, a writer uses transitions to signal similarities or differences and examples. Strong transitions establish coherence, a clear and understandable flow of ideas.

Words That Signal Comparison

alike	equally	in the same way	likewise	similarity
as	in a similar fashion	just as	resemble	similarly
as well as	in a similar way	just like	same	
equal	in like manner	like	similar	

Words That Signal Contrast

although	conversely	differently	more	on the other hand
as opposed to	despite	even though	most	still
at the same time	difference	in contrast	nevertheless	to the contrary
but	different	in spite of	on the contrary	unlike
by contrast	different from	instead	on the one hand	yet

LOGICAL ORDER

Based on the logical order of ideas, fill in the blanks with the appropriate comparison or contrast signal words. Compare and discuss your answers with a peer or in a small group of your classmates.

Practice 3

If you could build your ideal mate, he or she would probably look, act, and think very much _____ you. By being attracted to people _____ yourself, you validate yourself. You tell yourself that you're worthy of being liked. _____ there are exceptions, the _____ factor probably means that you will be attracted to your own mirror image. You will be attracted to people who are _____ to you in nationality, race, ability, physical traits, intelligence, attitudes, and so on. If you were to ask a group of friends, "To whom are you _____ attracted?" they would probably name the _____ attractive people they know. _____ if you were to watch these friends, you would find that they have relationships with people who are about _____ in attractiveness.

--adapted from DeVito, Joseph A. *The Interpersonal Communication Book*, 11th ed., 2007. p. 236.

Relevant Details

As a writer narrows a topic into a focused main idea, the thinking process brings to mind many details that answer the questions *who, what, when, where, why,* and *how.* A writer evaluates the relevance of each detail and uses only those that clarify or support the main idea. In a comparison or contrast paragraph, some relevant major details include those that identify comparable topics or points. Relevant minor details offer examples and explanations of the similarities or differences between comparable points. Relevant details include descriptions, explanations, and examples of similarities or differences between two or more topics. Details are logically ordered to best support the point.

Comparable Topics in a Venn Diagram

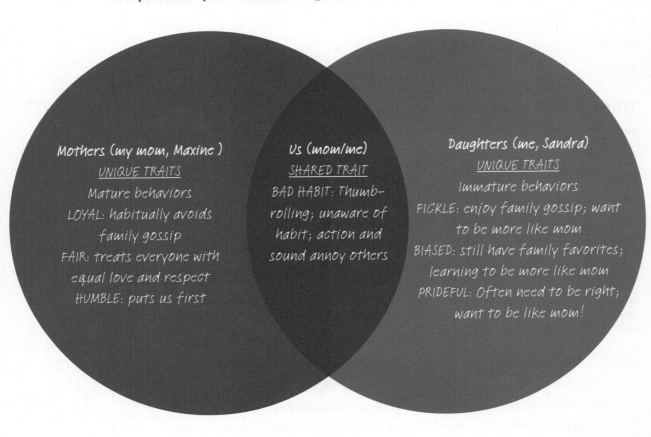

Mothers (my mom, Maxine)
UNIQUE TRAITS
Mature behaviors
LOYAL: habitually avoids family gossip
FAIR: treats everyone with equal love and respect
HUMBLE: puts us first

Us (mom/me)
SHARED TRAIT
BAD HABIT: Thumb-rolling; unaware of habit; action and sound annoy others

Daughters (me, Sandra)
UNIQUE TRAITS
Immature behaviors
FICKLE: enjoy family gossip; want to be more like mom
BIASED: still have family favorites; learning to be more like mom
PRIDEFUL: Often need to be right; want to be like mom!

During the prewriting phase, a writer naturally generates irrelevant details. In fact, an effective writer often produces far more details than can be used to make a specific point. Irrelevant details do not explain or support the focused point of the paragraph. A careful writer uses the revision process to double check details for relevance and to eliminate irrelevant ones.

The following paragraph explains and illustrates the ideas generated using the Venn diagram. Circle the main idea. Underline the words that signal similarities or differences and double underline three supporting points of similarities discussed in the paragraph. Cross out two details that are not relevant to the main point.

Bonds of Habits Tie Us Together

(1) I never realized how similar parents and their children can be. (2) My mother, Maxine, has a habit of rolling her thumbs. (3) She sits with her hands clasped, fingers laced, and thumbs rolling. (4) The action creates a soft rhythmic swish as the pad of one thumb brushes the top of her other thumb. (5) I don't know why, but the sight and sound of mother's thumb-rolling drives me to distraction. (6) Sometimes, I can hardly concentrate on my thoughts. (7) She remains completely unaware of the habit or how much it bothers me. (8) The one time I mentioned the behavior, she was embarrassed, and she tried for a while to break herself of the habit. (9) Although I vowed never to develop any such quirk, I recently caught myself in the middle of my own mother-like thumb roll. (10) As my husband described his golf swing, his eyes kept darting to my hands in the same way my own eyes react to Mom's thumb roll. (11) Suddenly he fell silent mid-sentence. (12) We heard a sound just like the one made by mother's thumb roll. (13) Just like my mother, I sat with my hands clasped, fingers laced, and thumbs rolling. (14) My husband asked, "Maxine," (he called me by mother's name instead of my name!) "Maxine, are you aware that you are a thumb-roller? (15) And that, for some reason, it gets on my nerves?" (16) My habit of leaving lids loose on containers also drives my husband nuts. (17) Now I know just how maddeningly similar parents and their children can be.

Effective Expression: Use of Coordination and Subordination

Effective expression reflects a writer's thoughtful match of ideas to words and structure. Two types of sentence structures enable effective expression of comparison or contrast: coordination and subordination.

Coordination expresses an **equal** relationship between **similarities** with words such as: *and, likewise, similarly, also.* Coordination expresses an **equal** relationship between **differences** with words such as *but, yet, or, however, in contrast.*

A **compound sentence** is an example of **coordination.**

Example

An athlete trains the body for competitions; *likewise,* a student trains the mind for final exams.

Subordination expresses an **unequal** relationship between **similarities** with words such as: *as, just as, just like, like.* **Subordination** expresses an **unequal** relationship between **differences** with words such as *although, even though, while.*

A **complex sentence** is an example of **subordination**.

Example

Just as an athlete trains the body for competitions, a student trains the mind for final exams.

For more information on coordination and subordination, see pages 343–344.

Practice 5

USING COORDINATION AND SUBORDINATION

Label each of the following sentences as a compound or a complex sentence. Identify the pattern of organization expressed by each sentence as comparison, contrast, or both.

1. Although the pessimist and the optimist face many of the same challenges in life, they differ greatly in their actions, words, and thoughts.

SENTENCE TYPE: ....

PATTERN OF ORGANIZATION: ....

2. Just as the pessimist faces rejection and disappointments, the optimist endures those same hardships common to all humans.

SENTENCE TYPE: ....

PATTERN OF ORGANIZATION: ....

3. The pessimist focuses on problems and remains passive; in contrast, the optimist focuses on solutions and takes action.

SENTENCE TYPE: ....

PATTERN OF ORGANIZATION: ....

Using Comparison and Contrast in Your Academic Courses

College writing assignments are often based on information gathered through class lectures, textbook reading assignments, and research. For example, essay exams often test students on material given in class or assigned in readings. Note-taking is an excellent pretest and prewriting activity. When you take or revise notes, set up a graphic organizer into which you can plug information from your class notes or reading assignments. A popular note-taking graphic divides an 11-inch by 8.5-inch page into three sections: a 8-inch by 3-inch left margin for key terms; a 8-inch by 5-inch right margin for notes; and a 3-inch by 8.5-inch wide bottom margin for a summary. This format allows you to write, reflect, and write for understanding as you study.

Key Terms	Notes
Summary	

USING COMPARISON AND CONTRAST IN AN ART APPRECIATION COURSE: TAKING NOTES

Study the following set of notes taken during a lecture in a college art appreciation class. In the bottom margin, write a short paragraph that states and supports the main idea of the notes.

Tragic hero	Virtuous, admirable, rich, powerful, and male, but flawed; inner conflict and guilt; accepts responsibility for suffering; loses all.
Example	5th Century BCE: In Oedipus the King, Oedipus loses power, wealth, family, and independence due to his limited wisdom and great pride.
Melodramatic hero	A symbol of good, male or female, a stereotype of courage and honesty, etc. No flaws; no inner conflict or guilt; fights against and defeats evil; all ends well.
Example	Pauline, the heroine of Perils of Pauline, is a "damsel in distress" who escapes many life-threatening, thrilling perils (dangers) due to her courage and ingenuity.

Summary: What are the differences between a tragic hero and a melodramatic hero?

_____

_____

_____

_____

_____

Practice 6

Workshop: Writing a Comparison and Contrast Paragraph Step by Step

Choose Your Topic

The following activities are designed to help you choose a topic.

1. Create a bank of topics. Use the headings given below to brainstorm, or list as many similarities or differences about sets of topics as you possibly can. Don't criticize your thoughts. Add more topics, similarities, or differences as they occur to you. Revisit topic banks created during your study of previous chapters and identify comparable topics. Compare your bank of topics with those of your classmates.

   - Family Members
   - Natural Disasters
   - Neighborhoods
   - Movies

2. Generate ideas with a freewrite. Choose one of the topics from your topic bank and think about the points of similarities or differences. Write about the similarities or differences for ten minutes without stopping.

   OR

   Select a set of photographs that illustrates the similarities or differences between two topics. Write a caption, brainstorm comparable points, and freewrite about the photograph(s). Remember to ask, "What are the similarities or differences represented by these images?" and "What's the point?"

Focus Your Point

Read a prewrite you have generated for a comparison or contrast paragraph. Identify your audience and purpose. Annotate the text: Underline or insert words that suggest your values, opinions, or attitudes about the topics and their points of similarity or difference. State in a sentence or two the importance of each similarity or difference between the comparable topics. Generate one or more concrete examples for each comparable point. Finally, state the point of the comparison or contrast paragraph in one sentence.

AUDIENCE: ....

PURPOSE: ....

LIST OF CONCRETE EXAMPLES: ....

....

WHAT'S THE POINT? ....

....

Generate and Organize Relevant Details

Using ideas you have recorded so far and the concept chart below, generate and organize details that support your point.

Concept Chart: Comparison/Contrast			
COMPARABLE TOPICS:	TOPIC A	LIKE OR UNLIKE	TOPIC B
1st attribute, point, basis of comparison		Like or unlike	
2nd attribute, point, basis of comparison		Like or unlike	
3rd attribute, point, basis of comparison		Like or unlike	

What's the point?

....

....

....

....

PORTFOLIO

Workshop

Write a Draft of Your Paragraph

Using the ideas you generated during the prewriting phase, compose a draft of your comparison or contrast paragraph. Return to the prewriting process at any time to generate additional details as needed. Use your own paper.

Revise Your Draft

Once you have created a draft of your comparison or contrast paragraph, read the draft and answer the questions in the "Questions for Revising a Comparison and Contrast" box that follows. Indicate your answers by annotating your paper. If you answer "yes" to a question, underline, check, or circle examples. If you answer "no" to a question, write the additional details in the margins and draw lines to indicate their placement. Revise your paragraph based on your reflection.

Questions for Revising a Comparison and Contrast Paragraph:

- ☐ Have I chosen appropriately comparable topics? Have I clearly labeled each comparable point as a similarity or a difference?

- ☐ Have I made my point? Can I state my point in one sentence?

- ☐ Are my ideas logically and clearly ordered? Have I used strong transitions of comparison or contrast?

- ☐ Have I used concrete details to make my point?

- ☐ Have I included only the details that are relevant to my topic sentence?

- ☐ Have I used the following to make my ideas clear and interesting to my readers: vivid verbs and images, parallel language, controlled sentence structure, coordination, or subordination?

Proofread Your Draft

Once you have revised your paragraph, proofread to ensure precise usage and grammar, such as editing for proper use of a comma after introductory elements.

Grammar in Action: Commas after Introductory Elements

Commas are used after introductory elements: a word, phrase, or dependent clause that comes before an independent clause.

A dependent clause—an incomplete thought containing a subject and a verb—is signaled by a subordinating conjunction *(although, because, while…)* or a relative pronoun *(who, which, that…)*.

An independent clause is a complete thought containing a subject and a verb.

- **Introductory word used with independent clause**

  Similarly, Sandra twiddles her thumbs.

- **Introductory phrase used with independent clause**

  In contrast, comedy's main purpose is to entertain.

- **Introductory dependent clause used with independent clause**

  Although Bob and Tom are both baby boomers, they differ greatly in values and lifestyles.

PORTFOLIO

Workshop

Practice 7

COMMAS AND INTRODUCTORY ELEMENTS

Edit the following sentences for proper use of a comma after an introductory element. Identify the type of introductory element used in each sentence.

Hint: To identify a dependent clause, look for subordinating conjunctions and relative pronouns immediately in front of a subject and verb. To identify an independent clause, underline subjects once and verbs twice; then check to be sure a subordinating conjunction or relative pronoun does not come first.

.... 1. Unlike those who are habitually late Consuelo has received three merit raises for prompt, efficient work.

.... 2. Like a fire hydrant opened full force Deborah poured out her grief.

.... 3. However the traveling nurse program offers better pay and greater mobility.

.... 4. The oldest child enjoyed the full attention of her parents; in contrast the youngest child always had to share her parents' attention with her siblings.

Review

MY WRITER'S JOURNAL

Work with a classmate to give and receive feedback about your comparison and contrast paragraphs. Use the following form to record your thinking about your writing process for your comparison and contrast paragraph. Use the writer's journal on page 161 as a model for your own journal. Discuss the decisions you made as you wrote, and describe what you have learned by writing. Also, ask for advice about how to improve your paragraph.

MAIN IDEA: ....

....

....

LOGICAL ORDER: ....

....

....

....

RELEVANT DETAILS: ....

....

....

....

EFFECTIVE EXPRESSION: ....

....

....

....

Writing Assignments

Considering Audience and Purpose

Study the set of photographs that show the similarities and differences between electric and gas vehicles. Write a letter to your United States Senator or to the editor of your local newspaper. In your letter call for support for either the electric or the gas vehicle. Explain the points of comparison that prove one better than the other.

Writing for Everyday Life

Assume that you have just experienced a life-altering event, such as a near-death experience, a graduation, a marriage, the birth of a child, a severe loss, or the breaking of a bad habit. You have been asked to talk about "Change" to a specific audience such as the Rotary Club, a civic group. Identify your audience and write a short speech in which you discuss three before-and-after comparable points. Allow your tone through word choice to reflect either sadness and regret or pride and encouragement.

Writing for College Life

Assume you are in a biology class and you read the following textbook question on the study guide for the final exam: "In what ways did the human skeleton change as upright posture and bipedalism evolved? Describe the changes by comparing the human skeleton and the skeleton of a quadruped such as a baboon." – Campbell, Mitchell, and Reece. *Biology: Concepts and Connections*, 5th ed. 2005 Longman. p. 620.

Test what you already know about the subject by writing a paragraph. Identify the comparable points of similarities and/or differences between the two topics. Look up words in your dictionary as needed.

Writing for Working Life

Assume that you are applying for a management position at a local business or mid-sized company. You had the following positions and experiences, which are listed on your résumé: Treasurer, Student Government Association; Certified in various computer programs and software; Member of Toastmasters, a public-speaking organization. Write a paragraph in which you compare the skills you've developed with the skills needed at the job for which you are applying.

mywritinglab

WANT A BETTER GRADE? For more practice with comparison and contrast, go to **www.mywritinglab.com > Using Patterns of Organization to Develop Paragraphs > The Comparison and Contrast Paragraph.**

10 The Definition Paragraph

A definition explains what a word or concept means.

We are all familiar with the word *definition*. In fact, we apply or create definitions in every aspect of life. Call to mind what you already know about a definition. Answer the following questions: How would you define "a good life"? What are the traits and examples of "a good life"? What information should be included in a definition?

The definition pattern of organization is helpful in all areas of life. In personal life, you rely upon a doctor's definition of your symptoms when you seek medical treatment. In working life, you define your job duties to ensure your best performance. In college life, you will define the specialized meanings and examples of words in each content area.

To write a definition paragraph, the writer names a concept, explains its traits, describes the concept using similar terms, and offers examples of the concept. Often a contrast clarifies meaning; thus, a writer may also include an example and explanation of what the term or concept is *not*.

What's the Point of a Definition?

The following definition-concept chart shows three visual examples of a concept and one visual example of what the concept is not. Study the chart and the visual examples. Then, write answers to the questions asked in the chart. Consider these questions as you write your answers: What is the concept being defined? What are some examples? What traits does each example represent? Then, answer the question "What's the point?" with a one-sentence statement of the overall main idea.

Practice 1

PHOTOGRAPHIC ORGANIZER: DEFINITION

Definition Concept Chart

What are the traits or characteristics of the concept?

What are some examples?

WRITING FROM LIFE

What is it NOT?

Concept?

What is the concept similar to?

What's the point?

Concept map adapted from following sources:

Frayer, D., Frederick, W. C., and Klausmeier, H. J. (1969). *A Schema for Testing the Level of Cognitive Mastery*. Madison, WI: Wisconsin Center for Education Research.

Schwartz, R., & Raphael, T. (1985). "Concept of definition: A Key to Improving Student's Vocabulary." *The Reading Teacher*, 39, 198-205.

My First Thoughts: A Prewriting Activity

Brainstorm about the images you just studied. Set a time limit, such as five minutes, and write in your notebook about the images and the details you generated. Write as quickly as you can without stopping. Let the ideas flow freely. Getting your first thoughts about a topic on paper is one excellent way to overcome writer's block and set your mind to thinking.

LEARNING OUTCOMES
STRUCTURE

Making a Point Using Definition: One Student Writer's Response

The following paragraph offers one writer's point about the concept depicted in the photographs. Read the definition and the explanations; complete the activities in **bold type** in the annotations. Then read the writer's journal entry that records decisions made during the writing process.

An Everyday Hero

(1) Every evening, the news reminds us that times are difficult and our needs are great. (2) Even in this nation, one of the wealthiest in history, we see too many who are hungry or homeless. (3) We see too many suffering with diseases such as AIDS and cancer. (4) We see too many who don't have the literacy skills needed to get and hold a job. (5) It would be great if life were like the movies, and a superhero could swoop into our world and defeat hunger, disease, and illiteracy. (6) Unfortunately, in the real world, we can't find solutions as fast as a speeding bullet. (7) In the real world, we need real-life everyday heroes. (8) First, we need compassionate people who care about others as much as they care about themselves. (9) Second, we need humble people who want to serve others without looking for a reward. (10) Third, we need dedicated people who won't quit no matter what. (11) A real hero is an ordinary person who makes a significant difference in the lives of others. (12) A real hero seeks out the hungry and homeless to serve them hot meals and give them safe, warm beds. (13) A real hero hands out water at a charity walk to defeat disease. (14) A real hero volunteers to read to a child. (15) A real hero doesn't have x-ray eyesight, superhuman strength, or supersonic speed. (16) A real hero has better gifts--a vision of hope, the strength of faith, and the speed of good-will.

EFFECTIVE EXPRESSION:
Vivid images make your point interesting and memorable. This phrase paints a vivid picture in the reader's mind. **Double underline three more vivid images.**

RELEVANT DETAILS:
Relevant details include descriptive details about traits and examples. **Draw boxes around two additional traits of a hero.**

LISTING ORDER:
The transition "third" indicates that a list of at least three traits are listed. **Circle two other transitions that introduce supporting details.**

MAIN IDEA:
The main idea states the author's point about a concept. The concept being defined is "hero." **Underline the writer's point about the concept.**

The Writer's Journal

PEER EDITING

The student writer of "An Everyday Hero" completed the following reflection to record her thinking through the writing process. Read her writer's journal that describes a few key choices she made as she wrote. Then, in the given space, answer her questions about her use of main idea, relevant details, and effective expression in her paragraph. Work with a peer or a small group of classmates.

MAIN IDEA: *I didn't state my main idea until sentence 11. Should I have stated it earlier in the paragraph? Why or why not?*

RELEVANT DETAILS: *Sentences 8–10 give examples of a real hero. Are these examples specific enough? Or should I have named names and told little stories about each example?*

EFFECTIVE EXPRESSION: *I tried to use vivid images to make my paragraph interesting. For example, I used words like "swoop" and "defeat" and "as fast as a speeding bullet." And I rewrote the last two sentences a lot just for vivid images; I want to show the difference between a make-believe hero and a real hero. Do these vivid images help make my point? Why or why not? Do you have any suggestions to improve my wording? Also does my paragraph sound choppy? If so, where?*

Developing Your Point Using Definition

A definition clarifies the meaning of a concept. A definition makes a point by classifying a concept, describing its traits, describing what it is *like*, describing what it is *not like*, and illustrating it with examples. To support a point by definition, a writer may also use figurative language.

The Point: The Main Idea

When you write a definition paragraph, most likely, you have an opinion or belief about the concept, characteristics, or examples. Your opinion is your point or main idea. A topic sentence states the overall point of the definition. Often a definition topic sentence emphasizes one aspect of the definition: its class, its traits, what it is like, or what it is not like.

For example, each of the following two topic sentences contains (1) a concept, (2) the writer's attitude about the concept, and (3) the pattern of organization used to organize details.

Definition by Classification: Group or Traits

TOPIC   PATTERN OF ORGANIZATION: WRITER'S OPINION
          DEFINITION SIGNAL WORDS

A classical hero is a male character who suffers due to his pride.

Definition by Comparison: Synonyms or Analogies

TOPIC   PATTERN OF ORGANIZATION:
          DEFINITION SIGNAL WORDS

Faith is like a tree. ← WRITER'S OPINION

Practice 2

TOPIC SENTENCES

The items present a topic, an opinion, and definition signal words. Combine the ideas in each group to create a topic sentence for a definition.

1. TOPIC: *depression*

OPINION: *treatable illness that affects the body and mind*

DEFINITION SIGNAL WORDS: *is a*

TOPIC SENTENCE:

2. TOPIC: *a hypocrite*

OPINION: *a spy or traitor*

DEFINITION SIGNAL WORDS: *is*

TOPIC SENTENCE:

Logical Order

Once you have narrowed your topic into a focused subject, you are ready to generate and organize additional details. To make a point using definition, a writer moves from a general idea (the concept to be defined) to major and minor supporting details. These include traits and examples of *what it is, what it is like,* or *what it is not like.* To signal the relationship between these levels of ideas, a writer often uses the following pattern of wording: "A concept is…"; "A term means…"; "for example."   Strong signal words establish coherence, a clear and understandable flow of ideas.

Key Words and Transition Words That Signal Definition

also	constitutes	in particular	means
another trait	defined as	indicates	one trait
are	denotes	is	specifically
connotes	for example	is not	such as
consists of	in addition	like	suggests

RELATIONSHIP OF DETAILS

Fill in the blanks with the appropriate transition or signal words for definition. Work with a peer or in a small group of your classmates.

Sexual Harassment

Sexual harassment .... a form of sex discrimination. ------------------------------, unwelcome sexual advances, requests for sexual favors, and other verbal or physical conduct of a sexual nature is sexual harassment when submission to or rejection of this conduct affects an individual's employment, interferes with an individual's work performance, or creates a hostile or offensive work environment. Sexual harassment can occur in a variety of situations, ----------------------- the following. ------------------------------, the victim as well as the harasser may be a woman or a man. The victim does not have to be of the opposite sex. Second, the harasser can be the victim's supervisor, an agent of the employer, a supervisor in another area, a co-worker, or a non-employee. -----------------------, the victim does not have to be the person harassed but could be anyone affected by the offensive conduct. -----------------------, unlawful sexual harassment may occur without economic injury to or discharge of the victim. -----------------------, the harasser's conduct must be unwelcome. An example is a co-worker who regularly tells sexually explicit jokes and makes demeaning comments about male coworkers and clients.

—Adapted from United States Equal Employment Opportunity Commission.
"Facts about Sexual Harassment." 15 April 2009

Relevant Details

As a writer narrows a topic into a focused main idea, the thinking process brings to mind many details that answer questions such as *who, what, when, where, why,* and *how.* A writer evaluates the relevance of each detail and uses only those that clarify or support the main idea. In a definition paragraph, some relevant major details include those that classify and describe the traits of a term or concept. Relevant minor details offer examples and illustrations of the term or concept as defined. Some major and minor details may explain the writer's opinion about the concept. Relevant details include types, traits, descriptions, and examples of the concept being defined.

During the prewriting phase, a concept chart can help a writer organize ideas. Study the following Definition Concept Chart about the topic "graffiti."

Definition Concept Chart

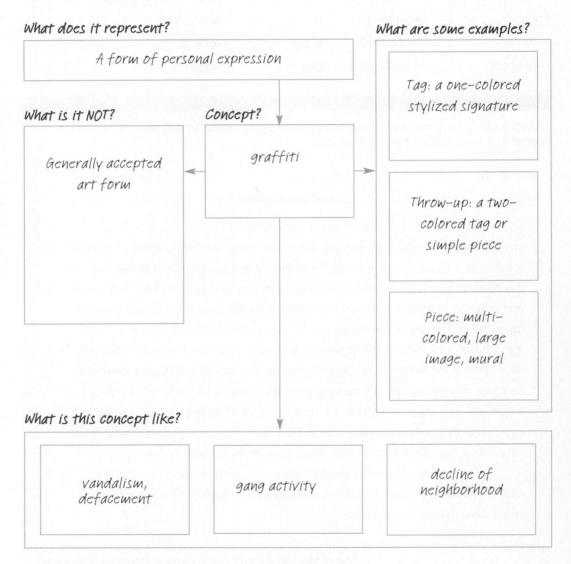

What does it represent?

A form of personal expression

What are some examples?

Tag: a one-colored stylized signature

Throw-up: a two-colored tag or simple piece

Piece: multi-colored, large image, mural

What is it NOT?

Generally accepted art form

Concept?

graffiti

What is this concept like?

vandalism, defacement

gang activity

decline of neighborhood

During the prewriting phase, a writer naturally generates irrelevant details. In fact, an effective writer often produces far more details than can be used to make a specific point. Irrelevant details do not explain or support the focused point of the paragraph. A careful writer uses the revision process to double check details for relevance and to eliminate irrelevant ones.

RELEVANT DETAILS

The following paragraph develops the ideas generated about graffiti during the brainstorming and prewriting phases. Circle the main idea. Underline the three major details. Cross out two details that are not relevant to the main point.

Graffiti

(1) Although graffiti is a common sight, many do not understand its true nature: vandalism. (2) Graffiti, a form of personal expression, is the unlawful markings of an individual or group on private and public surfaces. (3) One type of graffiti is known as a tag, a stylized signature of a tagger or writer. (4) A tag is quickly created with one color that starkly contrasts with the background upon which it is written. (5) Tags can be written with spray paint, fat-tipped markers, etching tools, or pre-tagged stickers. (6) Another kind of graffiti is the throw-up, a two-dimensional image made with large bubble letters that are outlined in black or white and filled in with another color. (7) A writer often uses throw-ups to bomb an area in a short amount of time. (8) A third type of graffiti, similar to a mural, is the piece, short for masterpiece. (9) Time-consuming to create, a piece is a large, colorful, and complex image that usually reflects a political or social issue. (10) Piecing demonstrates a high level of aerosol paint control. (11) Unlike more widely accepted forms of art, graffiti is not generally regarded as aesthetically pleasing, nor is it thought of as a means to explore or enhance the appreciation of beauty. (12) Graffiti is much more likely to be labeled as vandalism and defacement, and seen as evidence of a gang or a neighborhood in decline. (13) Instances of graffiti are evident in both urban and suburban public areas such as parks, restrooms, buildings, and trains. (14) Graffiti can be removed by scraping, power washing, chemically treating, or painting the affected surface. (15) Many communities fight graffiti by offering legal walls as concrete canvases for graffiti writers.

▲ An example of "throw-up" graffiti

▲ Mural-style graffiti

▲ An example of tagging

Effective Expression: Sound Structure and Vivid Images

Effective expression reflects a writer's thoughtful match of ideas to words and structure. Writers rely heavily on the various forms of the *to be* verb (such as *is*) to write a definition. Often the use of *is* leads to nonstandard phrasing or bland expressions. To add interest and maintain clarity, consider the following hints.

Hint 1: Avoid *is when* and *is where* to construct your definition. One way to eliminate *is when* and *is where* is to follow the verb with a synonym that renames the subject of the sentence.

Nonstandard

Addiction is when a person has a compulsive need for a habit-forming substance such as alcohol.

Revised

Addiction is a compulsive need for a habit-forming substance such as alcohol.

Hint 2: Use *is* to create a vivid image. A vivid image often allows the writer to express a point about the concept being defined.

Addiction is a self-made prison of compulsive need.

Hint 3: Replace *is* with an action verb. An action verb often allows the writer to express a point about the concept being defined.

Addiction imprisons a person in the compulsive need for habit-forming substances such as alcohol.

Practice 5

SOUND STRUCTURE AND VIVID IMAGES

Revise the following sentences to avoid nonstandard phrasing or bland expressions. Discuss your work with your class or with a small group of your peers.

1. An input device is where a machine feeds data into a computer, such as a keyboard.

REVISED: ....

....

2. A character is when any symbol requires a byte of memory or storage in computer software.

REVISED: ....

....

▲ Input device

Using Definition in Your Academic Courses

The definition paragraph serves as an excellent way to write for understanding. By defining key concepts and specialized vocabulary in your content courses, you will deepen your learning.

USING DEFINITION IN A COMMUNICATIONS ASSIGNMENT: DEFINING SPECIALIZED VOCABULARY

The following definition concept chart is based on information taken from a college communications textbook. Demonstrate your understanding of the concept and the relationship among the details in the definition. Using your own words, write a definition of the concept in the space below.

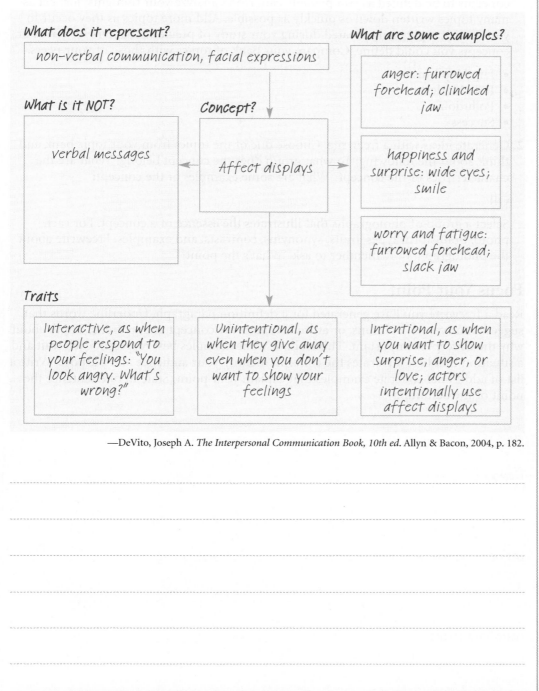

What does it represent?

non-verbal communication, facial expressions

What is it NOT?

verbal messages

Concept?

Affect displays

What are some examples?

anger: furrowed forehead; clinched jaw

happiness and surprise: wide eyes; smile

worry and fatigue: furrowed forehead; slack jaw

Traits

Interactive, as when people respond to your feelings: "You look angry. What's wrong?"

Unintentional, as when they give away even when you don't want to show your feelings

Intentional, as when you want to show surprise, anger, or love; actors intentionally use affect displays

—DeVito, Joseph A. *The Interpersonal Communication Book, 10th ed.* Allyn & Bacon, 2004, p. 182.

Workshop: Writing a Definition Paragraph Step by Step

Choose Your Topic

The following activities are designed to help you choose a topic.

1. Create a bank of topics. Use the headings below to brainstorm or list as many concepts to be defined as you possibly can. Don't analyze your thoughts; just get as many topics written down as quickly as possible. Add more topics as they occur to you. Revisit topic banks created during your study of previous chapters for terms or concepts you could define. Compare your bank of topics with those of your peers.

   - Hip Hop Music
   - Role Models
   - Pollution
   - Success

2. Generate ideas with a freewrite. Choose one of the topics from your topic bank and think about the following: To what group does the concept belong? What are the characteristics of the concept? What are some examples of the concept?

   OR

   Select a group of photographs that illustrates the essence of a concept. For each photo: brainstorm types, traits, synonyms, contrasts, and examples. Freewrite about the photograph(s). Remember to ask "What's the point?"

Focus Your Point

Read a freewrite you have generated for a definition paragraph. Underline words that suggest your values, opinions, or attitudes about the concept and its traits. Think about why the concept is important. Think about what examples best represent each trait and a situation that best illustrates the concept. Identify your audience and purpose. Write a list of additional concrete examples that explain your point. State in one sentence the point of the definition.

AUDIENCE: ....

PURPOSE: ....

....

LIST OF DETAILS AND EXAMPLES: ....

....

WHAT'S THE POINT? ....

....

Generate and Organize Relevant Details

Using ideas you have recorded so far and the following definition concept chart, generate and organize details that support your point.

Definition Concept Chart

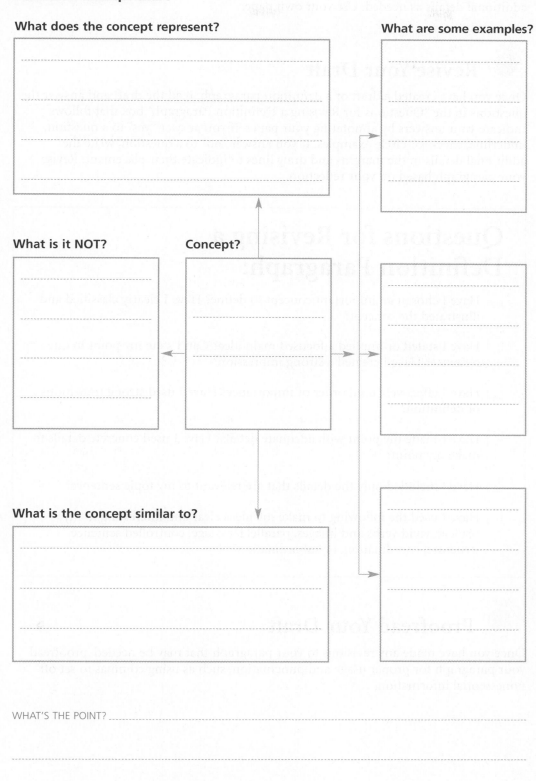

What does the concept represent?

What are some examples?

What is it NOT?

Concept?

What is the concept similar to?

WHAT'S THE POINT?

PORTFOLIO

Workshop

Write a Draft of Your Paragraph

Using the ideas you generated during the prewriting phase, compose a draft of your definition paragraph. Return to the prewriting process at any time to generate additional details as needed. Use your own paper.

Revise Your Draft

Once you have created a draft of a definition paragraph, read the draft and answer the questions in the "Questions for Revising a Definition Paragraph" box that follows. Indicate your answers by annotating your paper. If you answer "yes" to a question, underline, check, or circle examples. If you answer "no" to a question, write the additional details in the margins and draw lines to indicate their placement. Revise your paragraph based on your reflection.

Questions for Revising a Definition Paragraph:

☐ Have I chosen an important concept to define? Have I clearly classified and illustrated the concept?

☐ Have I stated or implied a focused main idea? Can I state my point in one sentence? Have I created a strong impression?

☐ Have I effectively used order of importance? Have I used strong transitions of definition?

☐ Have I made my point with adequate details? Have I used concrete details to make my point?

☐ Have I included only the details that are relevant to my topic sentence?

☐ Have I used the following to make my ideas clear and interesting to my readers: vivid verbs and images, parallel language, controlled sentence structure, coordination, or subordination?

Proofread Your Draft

Once you have made any revisions to your paragraph that may be needed, proofread your paragraph for proper usage and punctuation, such as using commas to set off nonessential information.

PORTFOLIO

Workshop

Grammar in Action: Proper Use of Commas with Nonessential Information

For more information on using commas with nonessential information, see pages 527–529.

In a sentence, some information that describes or modifies a word is nonessential. Nonessential information doesn't restrict the meaning of the word being described or modified. Nonessential information can be words, phrases, or clauses. If you can leave the information out of the sentence without changing the meaning of the sentence, then the information is nonessential. Use **commas before** and **after** nonessential words, phrases, and clauses. Use commas after nonessential words, phrases, and clauses that introduce a sentence.

- **Nonessential Word:**

Regular physical activity, moreover, promotes health, psychological well-being, and a healthy body weight.

My husband, Bob, runs six miles every other day.

- **Nonessential Phrase:**

A healthful diet, for example, includes a variety of fruits and vegetables each day.

Janine, eating a healthful diet and exercising, has lost 25 pounds.

- **Nonessential Clause:**

My great-grandmother, who is nearly 90 years old, goes bowling every week.

Sandra's diet, which is laden with high-fat, high-calorie foods, must change to ensure her good health.

Workshop Practice 7

PROPER COMMA USE WITH NONESSENTIAL INFORMATION

Edit these sentences for proper use of commas before and after nonessential words, phrases, or clauses. Underline the nonessential information and insert the commas as needed.

1. Patience however is not tolerance of harmful wrongdoing.

2. Jerome who has been my friend since childhood does not tolerate gossip.

3. Jerome wanting to stand on his principles broke up with a girl who was a gossip.

4. Patience is on the other hand acceptance based on forgiveness.

5. Once Iva who was a gossip until Jerome broke up with her changed her ways, Jerome asked her out again.

LEARNING OUTCOMES
SELF-EVALUATION

Review

MY WRITER'S JOURNAL

Work with a classmate to give and receive feedback about your definition paragraphs. Use the following form to record your thinking about your writing process for your definition paragraph. Use the writer's journal on page 177 as a model for your own journal. Discuss the decisions you made as you wrote, and describe what you have learned by writing. Also, ask for advice about how to improve your paragraph.

MAIN IDEA: ....

....

....

....

LOGICAL ORDER: ....

....

....

....

RELEVANT DETAILS: ....

....

....

....

....

EFFECTIVE EXPRESSION: ....

....

....

....

....

....

Writing Assignments

Considering Audience and Purpose

Study the set of photographs about the people and situations at the beginning of the chapter. Assume you have benefited personally from the efforts of one of the people depicted in the images. Brainstorm a list of attributes of this person. Write a one-paragraph thank you letter to this person in which you define what he or she means to you.

Writing for Everyday Life

Assume that you have agreed to seek counseling to improve a relationship with a family member or coworker. The counselor has asked you to define your role in the relationship. Identify the type of relationship you have with your family member or coworker, the major traits of the relationship, and examples or incidents that illustrate the nature of your relationship. Allow your tone—through your word choice—to reflect one of the following: (1) concern or (2) resentment.

Writing for College Life

Assume you are a first-semester college student who is enrolled in a study skills class, and you have been assigned to write a paragraph that defines student success. Based on your experience and observations, write a definition of student success that addresses attitudes, behaviors, and skills.

Writing for Working Life

Assume that you work in a retail store that sells clothes, electronics, or some other specialized merchandise. Also assume that sales and morale are down. Write a one-paragraph memo to your supervisor in which you define the morale problem.

11

The Cause and Effect Paragraph

A cause is the reason an event took place. An effect is the result of an event. Cause leads to effect.

Understanding the relationship between cause and effect is a vital critical thinking skill used in all aspects of life. For example, when an illness strikes us, our physician must correctly identify the cause of our symptoms in order to treat us. In addition, the side effects of any medication to treat the illness must be taken into account. What are some other instances in which we consider causes and effects?

Thinking about cause and effect points out the relationship between events based on reasons and results. For example, in your personal life, you may have identified that stress causes you to eat for comfort. In working life, you may have identified the need to master certain software programs to be competitive in the job market. In college life, you may have identified how logical causes and effects play a role in the study of history, science, or economics. To write a cause and effect paragraph, identify a set of related events, objects, or factors. Then, label each event, object, or factor within the group as either a cause or an effect. Be sure to test each event as a true cause. Events that occur at or near the same time may be coincidental and unrelated. Then, present your details in a logical order that explains why each cause leads to a specific effect.

What's the Point of Cause and Effect?

Often ideas become clearer when they are analyzed based on how they relate to one another. The cause and effect pattern of organization allows a writer to explore the ways in which ideas are related based on reasons and results. The following set of photographs documents a set of causes and effects. Study the images and write captions that identify the appropriate causes and effects illustrated. Answer the following questions: What is this? Why did it happen? What is this further effect? Answer the question "What's the point?" with a one-sentence statement of the overall main idea.

WRITING FROM LIFE

PHOTOGRAPHIC ORGANIZER: CAUSE AND EFFECT

What is this?

Why did it happen?

What is this further effect?

Why did it happen?

▲ A volunteer organization

▲ Volunteers building homes

What is this?

Why did it happen?

What is this?

Why did it happen?

What's the point?

My First Thoughts: A Prewriting Activity

Brainstorm about the images you just studied. Set a time limit, such as five minutes, and write in your notebook about the images and the details you generated. Write as quickly as you can without stopping. Let the ideas flow freely. Getting your first thoughts about a topic on paper is one excellent way to kick-start your writing process.

Making a Point Using Cause and Effect: One Student Writer's Response

The following paragraph offers one writer's point about the causes and effects illustrated by the photographs. Read the cause and effect paragraph and the explanations; complete the activities in **bold type** in the annotations. Then read the writer's journal entry that records decisions made during the writing process.

EFFECTIVE EXPRESSION:
Precise word choice makes your point credible. Writers often confuse the word "affect," a verb that means to influence with "effect," a noun which means result. **Double underline a verb that can be replaced with "affects." Double underline two nouns that can be replaced with "effect."**

STRONG TRANSITIONS:
The transitional word "because" signals that "natural disasters and poverty" occur as causes before "Habitat for Humanity calls for volunteers." **Circle two more transitional words or phrases that signal cause or effect.**

RELEVANT DETAILS:
Relevant details include descriptive details that describe the qualities of a cause or effect. "Quality and affordable" are important traits of the homes built by Habitat for Humanity. These traits become the effect or goals. **Draw boxes around three more relevant details that describe a cause or effect.**

MAIN IDEA:
The main idea is the point the author is making about the topic. The topic is Habitat for Humanity. **Underline the author's point about this topic.**

A Noble Response: A Joyous Result

(1) Volunteer work is a noble response to human need, and one basic human need is safe and comfortable shelter. (2) Habitat for Humanity affects this basic need. (3) Because of the impact of natural disasters and poverty on housing, Habitat for Humanity calls for volunteers to build quality and affordable houses that results in home ownership for those in need. (4) In recent years, natural disasters such as earthquakes, mudslides, hurricanes, and tsunamis have caused countless homes to be reduced to rubble or obliterated. (5) As a result, hundreds of thousands of people are left homeless and without resources to rebuild. (6) Currently, poverty influences many around the world by causing families to live in shoddy structures with little hope of improving their living conditions. (7) Habitat for Humanity was established to meet these very needs. (8) Consequently, strangers voluntarily come together to accomplish one goal: to build a house for a family. (9) The end results are obvious. (10) First, the family, who also helped build their home, owns their home. (11) In addition, and just as importantly, along with home ownership comes the joy and pride of an improved quality of life. (12) Habitat for Humanity is a noble response to human need with joyous results.

The Writer's Journal

PEER EDITING

The student writer of "A Noble Response: A Joyous Result" completed the following reflection to record his thinking through the writing process. Read his writer's journal that describes a few key choices he made as he wrote. Then, in the given space, answer his questions about his use of relevant details and effective expression in his paragraph. Work with a peer or a small group of classmates.

RELEVANT DETAILS: Once I decided on my topic, the graphic organizer really helped me think of details. I divided my details into two groups. I gave two reasons Habitat for Humanity was created, and I gave a few of the effects HH has had on people. Do you think I gave enough details? Should I have mentioned specific disasters like Hurricane Katrina? Why or why not?

EFFECTIVE EXPRESSION: I proofread several times to make sure I used "effect" and "affect" correctly. Could you proofread it one more time? Did I use these words correctly? Should I have used these two words more often, since this is a cause and effect paragraph? For example in sentence 8, I used the word "goal." Should I have used "effect" or "affect" here? Or is "goal" more effective? Why? Do you see other words that should be replaced to make my point?

© Pearson Education, Inc.

11 THE CAUSE AND EFFECT PARAGRAPH

193

Developing Your Point Using Cause and Effect

A cause and effect paragraph makes a point by discussing the reasons and results among a set of events, objects, or factors. To support a point through cause and effect, a writer identifies a set of events, objects, or factors. A writer then identifies the specific details of cause and effect between each of the events, objects, or factors. The writer tests each reason and result to weed out true causes and effects from coincidence. The writer discusses the specific details in the order that reflects the logical relationship among causes and effects. In addition, the writer uses precise word choice for effective expression.

The Point: The Main Idea

When you write a cause and effect paragraph, you limit your thoughts to a set of topics based on their relationship to each other. Most likely you have an opinion or belief about the topics and their causes and effects; your opinion is your point or main idea. A topic sentence states the overall point of the causes and effects.

For example, the following topic sentence contains (1) the topic, (2) the writer's opinion about the topic, and (3) the pattern of organization used to organize details.

TOPIC   WRITER'S OPINION

Addiction to television has led to several negative effects on

American students.   PATTERN OF ORGANIZATION: CAUSE AND EFFECT SIGNAL WORDS

The topic is the "addiction to television [of] American students." The pattern of organization is established with the signal words "led to several effects." The writer's opinion is stated with the modifier "negative."

Practice 2

TOPIC SENTENCES

The items present a topic, an opinion, and cause or effect signal word(s). Combine the ideas in each group to create a topic sentence for a cause and effect.

1. TOPIC: _smoking cigarettes_   OPINION: _adverse_

CAUSE OR EFFECT SIGNAL WORDS: _leads to physical effects_

TOPIC SENTENCE: _____

2. TOPIC: _bullying_   OPINION: _low self-esteem and anger_

CAUSE OR EFFECT SIGNAL WORDS: _stems from_

TOPIC SENTENCE: _____

_____

Logical Order

Once you have identified a topic, a set of factors, their relationships based on cause and effect, and have focused on a main idea, you are ready to generate and organize additional details. To make a point using cause or effect, a writer moves from a general idea (the overall causal relationship) to a major support (a specific cause or effect of the topic) to minor supports (details or examples of a specific cause or effect). To signal the movement among these levels of ideas, a writer uses transitions to signal causes, effects, and examples. Strong transitions establish coherence, a clear and understandable flow of ideas.

Transitions That Signal Cause and Effect

accordingly	consequently	hence	on account of	so
as a result	due to	if…then	results in	therefore
because of	for that reason	leads to	since	thus

Verbs That Signal Cause and Effect (sample list)

affect	constitute	create	force	institute	restrain
cause	construct	determine	induce	preclude	stop
compose	contribute	facilitate	initiate	prevent	

Nouns That Signal Cause and Effect (sample list)

actor	consequence	end	influence	product
agent	creation	event	issue	result
author	creator	grounds	outcome	source
condition	effect	impact	outgrowth	

CAUSE AND EFFECT

Fill in the blanks with the appropriate transition or signal words for cause and effect. Work with a peer or in a small group of your classmates.

How Is Stroke Prevented?

A stroke is the _____ of a disease of the blood vessels in the brain, and underlying health conditions can _____ a stroke. For example, heart disease, high blood pressure, high cholesterol, and diabetes can _____ to a stroke. _____ you have any of these conditions, _____ take your medication as prescribed by your health care provider. Second, a healthful diet lowers your risk for a stroke. _____, eat a diet low in saturated fat and rich in fruits, vegetables, and whole grains. For example, eating too much meat and whole milk dairy products can _____ in high cholesterol, which raises your risk for a stroke.

Practice 3

Relevant Details

As a writer narrows a topic into a focused main idea, the thinking process brings to mind many details that answer questions such as *who*, *what*, *when*, *where*, *why*, and *how*. A writer evaluates the relevance of each detail and uses only those that clarify or support the main idea. In a cause and effect paragraph, some relevant major details include those that identify a specific cause or effect. Relevant minor details offer examples and explanations of the cause or effect. Relevant details include descriptions, examples, and explanations of the causal relationship between a set of events, situations, objects, or factors.

One writer generated these ideas while brainstorming using a fishbone cause and effect concept map.

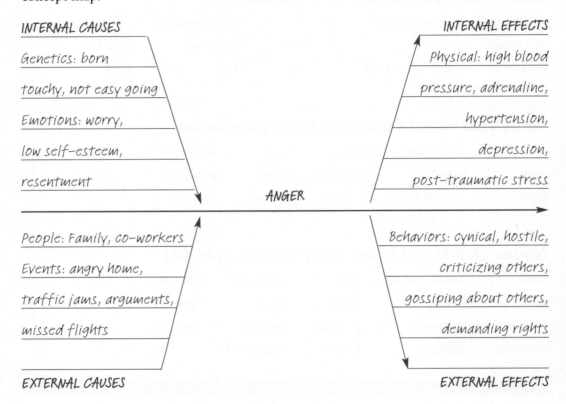

INTERNAL CAUSES

Genetics: born

touchy, not easy going

Emotions: worry,

low self-esteem,

resentment

ANGER

INTERNAL EFFECTS

Physical: high blood

pressure, adrenaline,

hypertension,

depression,

post-traumatic stress

People: Family, co-workers

Events: angry home,

traffic jams, arguments,

missed flights

EXTERNAL CAUSES

Behaviors: cynical, hostile,

criticizing others,

gossiping about others,

demanding rights

EXTERNAL EFFECTS

During the prewriting phase, a writer naturally generates irrelevant details. In fact, an effective writer often produces far more details than can be used to make a specific point. Irrelevant details do not explain or support the focused point of the paragraph. A careful writer uses the revision process to double check details for relevance and to eliminate irrelevant ones.

Baseball manager argues with home plate umpire ▶

RELEVANT DETAILS

The following paragraph develops the ideas generated about anger during the brainstorming phase using the fishbone cause and effect concept map shown on page 201. Circle the main idea. Underline two causes and two effects. Cross out two details that are not relevant to the main point.

Anger Inside and Out

(1) Anger can be a normal, healthy emotion, yet anger can also spiral out of our control and lead to problems that affect our work, our families, and our lives. (2) To control anger, we need to understand its causes and effects. (3) Basically, anger is the result of both internal and external forces. (4) Genetics and emotions are two internal forces that give rise to anger. (5) According to experts, some people are born innately touchy and easily angered. (6) Others of us are born with mild, easy-going tendencies. (7) Another internal force is the complex mixture of our emotions. (8) Worry, low self-esteem, anxiety, or resentment can cause anger to flare. (9) In addition, external forces such as people and events can trigger anger. (10) For example, if we have been raised in an environment of anger without learning how to cope with negative feelings, we are much more likely to be easily angered. (11) As a result, a disagreement with a family member or coworker, a traffic jam, or a cancelled airline flight ignites angry feelings. (12) Not only does our anger arise from internal and external forces, but also our anger has internal and external effects. (13) Anger has immediate physical effects: it causes our heart rate, blood pressure, and adrenaline to rise. (14) Ultimately, chronic anger can lead to hypertension or depression. (15) Post-traumatic stress syndrome also leads to depression. (16) Chronic anger also may result in cynical and hostile behavior towards others. (17) When we feel angry, we may act out our hostility by criticizing others, gossiping about them, or rudely demanding our rights. (18) Ultimately, uncontrolled anger damages our relationships with others and diminishes our quality of life. (19) We need to understand the reasons and results of our anger before we can hope to control this volatile emotion.

Effective Expression: Correct Use of Words

Effective expression reflects a writer's thoughtful choice of words for impact on the reader. Some words, such as *affect* and *effect*, seem closely related because they are similar in their sounds and spellings. These similarities often cause confusion and lead to the misuse of the words. However, their meanings are clearly distinct, so thoughtful writers use the correct word for effective expression.

Affect is a verb that means **to influence.**

Example

Video games **affect** learning by improving concentration and visual skills.

Effect is a noun that means **result.**

Example

Video games have a positive **effect** on learning by improving concentration and visual skills.

Effect is a verb that means **to bring about.**

Example

The new law will **effect** a change in the sentencing of sex offenders.

Practice 5

CORRECT USE OF AFFECT AND EFFECT

Complete the following sentences with the correct use of the words *affect* and *effect*. (*Hint:* Substitute the words *influence* or *result* as a test for exact meaning in the context of the sentence.)

1. The lack of bright light during winter months produces an .... known as Seasonal Affective Disorder (SAD), a form of depression.

2. The long, dark hours of winter .... as much as 6 percent of the population.

3. The .... of SAD include loss of energy, social withdrawal, overeating, weight gain, and difficulty concentrating.

4. Researchers believe that reduced sunlight .... the biological rhythms that control the body's internal clock.

5. Researchers also believe that heredity, age, and the body's chemical balance .... the onset of SAD.

6. Exposure to sun and sun lamps for one to three hours a day .... a positive change in the mood of one who suffers from SAD.

Using Cause and Effect in Your Academic Courses

Often college writing assignments require that you combine information you learn from your textbooks with your observations about how that information applies to real-world situations. Textbooks may provide graphic organizers to emphasize key concepts and make them easy to understand. Use these graphic organizers to learn and apply the concept. A good way to review your textbook notes is to add examples you have observed in life to the concept you are studying.

Practice 6

USING CAUSE AND EFFECT IN A SOCIOLOGY ASSIGNMENT

Study the following graphic taken from a college sociology textbook. In a small group or with a classmate, add examples of each concept that you and your classmate(s) have observed. Then, write a paragraph in answer to the question at the end of the practice. Use a dictionary as necessary.

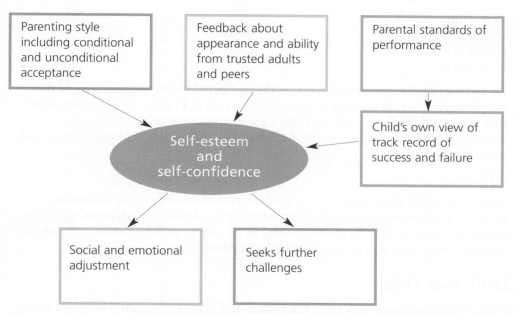

—Jaffe, Michael L. *Understanding Parenting, 2nd Ed*. Allyn & Bacon. 1997 p. 241.

EXAMPLE OF PARENTAL STANDARD: ....

EXAMPLE OF CHILD'S VIEW OF SUCCESS AND FAILURE: ....

EXAMPLE OF FEEDBACK: ....

EXAMPLE OF PARENTING STYLE: ....

EXAMPLE OF FURTHER CHALLENGE: ....

EXAMPLE OF ADJUSTMENT: ....

On a separate sheet of paper, answer the following question:
What factors influence children's self-esteem and self-confidence?

Workshop

PORTFOLIO

Workshop: Writing a Cause and Effect Paragraph Step by Step

Choose Your Topic

The following activities are designed to help you choose a topic.

1. Create a bank of topics: Use the following headings to brainstorm or list as many causes and effects as you possibly can. Don't criticize your thoughts; just get as many relevant causes and effects written down as quickly as possible. Add more topics, causes, or effects as they occur to you. Revisit topic banks created during your study of previous chapters; identify causes and effects. Compare your bank of topics with those of your peers.

   - YouTube
   - Friendship
   - Fuel-efficient Cars
   - Romance

2. Reread a freewrite you created (such as the one based on the photographs of the people in the chapter opening or the one generated in Practice 4). Underline ideas that you could use for a cause and effect paragraph. Number the points you recorded to indicate a logical order. Add major or minor details of explanation and examples as needed.

   OR

   Select a group of photographs that illustrate a set of related events, situations, objects, or factors. Generate a list that identifies the details of each event, situation, object, or factor as either a cause (reason) or an effect (result). Freewrite about the photograph(s). Remember to ask "What's the point?"

Clarify Your Point

Read a prewrite you have generated for a cause and effect paragraph. Underline words that suggest your values, opinions, or attitudes about the events. Think about why the information is important. Think about what examples best represent each cause or effect. Think about a situation that best illustrates the concept. Identify your audience and purpose. Write a list of additional concrete examples that explain your point. In one sentence, state the point of the cause and effect paragraph.

AUDIENCE: ....

PURPOSE: ....

LIST OF CONCRETE DETAILS: ....

WHAT'S THE POINT? ....

....

Generate and Organize Relevant Details

Use the graphic organizer below to either organize the ideas you have already created or to generate details to support your point.

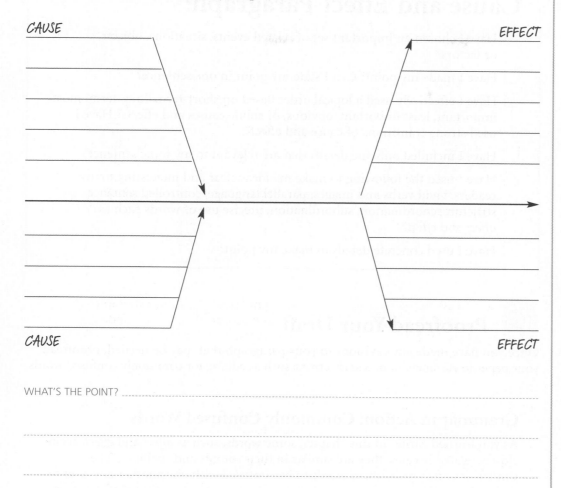

CAUSE

EFFECT

CAUSE

EFFECT

WHAT'S THE POINT? _____

_____

_____

Write a Draft of Your Paragraph

Using the ideas you generated during the prewriting phase, compose a draft of your cause and effect paragraph. Return to the prewriting process at any time to generate additional details as needed. Use your own paper.

Revise Your Draft

Once you have created a draft of your cause and effect paragraph, read the draft and answer the questions in the "Questions for Revising a Cause and Effect Paragraph" box that follows. Indicate your answers by annotating your paper. If you answer "yes" to a question, underline, check, or circle examples. If you answer "no" to a question, write the additional details in the margins and draw lines to indicate their placement. Revise your paragraph based on your reflection.

Workshop

PORTFOLIO

Questions for Revising a Cause and Effect Paragraph:

- [ ] Have I chosen an important set of related events, situations, objects, or factors?

- [ ] Have I made my point? Can I state my point in one sentence?

- [ ] Have I effectively used a logical order based on short-term, long-term, most important, least important, obvious, or subtle causes and effects? Have I used strong transitions of cause and effect?

- [ ] Have I included only the details that are relevant to my topic sentence?

- [ ] Have I used the following to make my ideas clear and interesting to my readers: vivid verbs and images, parallel language, controlled sentence structure, coordination, subordination, precise use of words such as *affect* and *effect*?

- [ ] Have I used concrete details to make my point?

Proofread Your Draft

Once you have made any revisions to your paragraph that may be needed, proofread your paper to eliminate unnecessary errors, such as editing for commonly confused words.

Grammar in Action: Commonly Confused Words

As you learned earlier in this chapter, some words, such as *affect* and *effect,* seem closely related because they are similar in their sounds and spellings. The similarities often cause these words to be confused with one another and lead to their misuse. However, their meanings are clearly distinct, so thoughtful writers choose the precise word for effective expression. The following list presents a group of words that are commonly confused. Memorize this list of words and their meanings so you can use each one precisely in your writing.

its, it's	**its** (possessive form of it); **it's** (contraction of *it is* or *it has*)
their, they're, there	**their** (possessive of they); **they're** (contraction of *they are*); **there** (points to a place)
to, two, too	**to** (suggests movement or direction); **two** (a number); **too** (also)
whose, who's	**whose** (possessive form of *who*); **who's** (contraction of *who is* or *who has*)
your, you're	**your** (possessive form of *you*); **you're** (contraction of *you are*)

PORTFOLIO

Workshop

Edit the following rough draft of a paragraph written by student Seiko Kaneyama about the effects of stress due to a language barrier. Cross out the words used incorrectly and insert the correct word.

The Main Cause of My Stress: The Language Barrier

(1) For me, the language barrier is the biggest source of stress. (2) Four years ago, I lost my husband to heart failure. (3) He passed away in the hospital. (4) Because I could not express myself in English, no matter how I tried, no one could understand me or what I wanted. (5) The stress reached too the point that I was shaking and collapsed in tears. (6) Its still one of the most difficult and frustrating memories of my life. (7) Today, my stress is from language problems at work with some co-workers. (8) For example, when a mistake is made, someone always blames me. (9) They say, "Your two hard too understand." (10) Or they say that I do not understand what there saying. (11) As a result, I have to do my job better than anyone else. (12) Some people try to take advantage of me because there sure that I would not complain because of my imperfect English.(13) Its very difficult their. (14) School causes me stress, to. (15) I speak and write Chinese, Japanese, and Korean. English is very difficult; its a very frustrating language. (16) One of the most stressful moments is when I ask questions at school. (17) Most professors interrupt me before I can fully express myself; I feel miserable, and it keeps me from asking questions at school. (18) This language problem at work, at school, and in everyday life causes me great stress. (19) In the past, I have had headaches, and I have become irritable. (20) However, I feel that I have become a person whose able to handle these stressful situations better, and as my language skills improve, I feel more confident and less and less stressful.

LEARNING OUTCOMES
SELF-EVALUATION

Review

Work with a classmate to give and receive feedback about your cause and effect paragraphs. Use the following form to record your thinking about your writing process for your cause and effect paragraph. Use the writer's journal on page 193 as a model for your own journal. Discuss the decisions you made as you wrote, and describe what you have learned by writing. Also, ask for advice about how to improve your paragraph.

MAIN IDEA: _____

_____

_____

_____

LOGICAL ORDER: _____

_____

_____

_____

_____

RELEVANT DETAILS: _____

_____

_____

_____

_____

EFFECTIVE EXPRESSION: _____

_____

_____

_____

_____

_____

Writing Assignments

Considering Audience and Purpose

Study the set of photographs at the beginning of the chapter. Assume you are the one who now owns the home built by Habitat for Humanity. Assume that as you worked beside the volunteers to build your home, you became friendly with the project director, Wilma Weindmyer. Write a one-paragraph thank you letter to Ms. Weindmyer that explains the impact of building and owning your own home.

Writing for Everyday Life

Assume that you are the mentor of a young person who is a member of your family or community. Assume the young person is making some choices that can have lasting negative consequences. Perhaps the youth is hanging out with the wrong crowd, or skipping school, or experimenting with drugs. Write a one-paragraph letter that explains the dangers of the wrong choices or the benefits of mature choices. Choose your words to reflect one of the following: (1) stern warning or (2) warm encouragement.

Writing for College Life

Assume you are applying for a scholarship set up to aid a person currently enrolled as a full-time college student with at least a 3.0 GPA. Assume you must compete with other students to win the scholarship by writing a one-paragraph essay on the topic "Education Matters." Write a paragraph that explains one or both of the following: (1) the impact the education has had and will have on you or (2) the impact you hope to have as an educated member of society.

Writing for Working Life

Assume that you are applying for a job with a company or organization. Perhaps you are applying for a job as a health care provider, teacher, office manager, or computer programmer. Write a one-paragraph cover letter that explains the impact you can have on the job due to your skills, work ethic, and character.

mywritinglab

WANT A BETTER GRADE?
For more practice with cause and effect, go to **www.mywritinglab.com** > **Using Patterns of Organization to Develop Paragraphs > The Cause and Effect Paragraph.**

12

The Persuasive Paragraph

A persuasive claim is a strong stand on a debatable topic supported by facts, examples, and opinions.

In almost every area of our lives, we engage in some form of persuasion. Whether convincing a friend to see a particular movie or proving we are the right candidate for a particular job, we use reasons, logic, and emotion to get others to agree with our views. What are some other situations that use persuasion to influence our beliefs and behaviors? Why are certain arguments or points of view so persuasive?

To be persuasive, a writer asserts a strong stand on one side of a debatable issue. Then the writer supports that stand by offering convincing evidence such as reasons, facts, examples, and expert opinions. In everyday life, our court system is based on proving claims of guilt or innocence. In working life, we use reasons to resolve workplace disputes. In college life, we encounter debatable claims in every discipline. In addition to asserting a claim and supporting it with evidence, a persuasive writer acknowledges and rebuts (disproves, challenges) the opposition.

What's the Point of Persuasion?

The purpose of persuasion is to convince the reader to agree with a particular claim about a debatable topic. Persuasion is a call to action or a call to a change of mind. The following photos represent several reasons against building a Target store in the location of a popular neighborhood park. Study the photographs. In the space provided, identify the claim, reasons, and an opposing point of view about removing the park to build a Target store. Answer the question "What's the point?" with a one-sentence statement of the overall main idea.

PHOTOGRAPHIC ORGANIZER: PERSUASION

What is the issue?

_____

_____

Practice 1

WRITING FROM LIFE

SUPPORTING POINTS

What is this reason?

OPPOSING POINT

What is this point?

_____

_____

What is this reason?

_____

_____

SUPPORT THAT REFUTES OPPOSING POINT

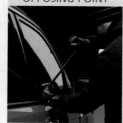

What is this reason?

_____

_____

What is this reason?

_____

_____

What's the point?

_____

_____

_____

My First Thoughts: A Prewriting Activity

Brainstorm about the images you just studied. Set a time limit, such as five minutes, and write in your notebook about the images and the details you generated. Write as quickly as you can without stopping. Let the ideas flow freely. Getting your first thoughts about a topic on paper is one excellent way to overcome writer's block and set your mind to thinking.

LEARNING OUTCOMES
STRUCTURE

Making a Point Using Persuasion: One Student Writer's Response

The following paragraph offers one writer's point that argues against building a new Target store in her neighborhood, as illustrated by the photographs. Read the persuasive paragraph and the explanations; complete the activities in **bold type** in the annotations. Then read the writer's journal entry that records decisions made during the writing process.

MAIN IDEA:
The main idea is the point the author is claiming about the topic. **Underline the topic and circle the writer's claim about this topic.**

EFFECTIVE EXPRESSION:
To persuade a reader, an author uses subjective words that express opinions, attitudes, and values. **Double underline at least three more subjective words or phrases.**

STRONG TRANSITION:
The transition phrase "First of all" signals that the author is offering a reason in support of her claim. **Circle three more transitional words or phrases that signal a reason of support.**

RELEVANT DETAILS:
In persuasion, relevant details not only include facts and consequences, but also refute opposing points. Here, the writer offers another location better suited to a retail store. **Draw a box around one other opposing point and the writer's counter point.**

Let the Children Play: No Target

Dear Mayor and Commissioners:

(1) I strongly oppose relocating our community's invaluable recreational center at the corner of Nova Road and Main Trail to make space for a Target store. (2) I am outraged and shocked that you even think moving our playground so it sits on top of a land field behind a new Target is an option. (3) Most likely, you think a Target will stimulate the economy, but a Target in this location is not worth the money it would generate. (4) First of all, the intersection will not be able to sustain the kind of traffic that a Target will draw. (5) This type of traffic will create added dangers for the children commuting to their "relocated" park. (6) Secondly, the development will destroy one of the few remaining ecological parks; Nova Park is not only a natural habitat, but also a shady oasis for the many families that live nearby. (7) Why pave over this natural refuge when there is so much bare land out Williamson and US 1? (8) Those roads can better bear the added traffic. (9) Thirdly, a park at the edge of the neighborhood adds more value to the neighborhood than a Target. (10) I am an expectant mother and have planned on walking my child to this park just as my parents did with me. (11) I grew up playing on those monkey bars and swinging under the beautiful canopy of oaks that you now threaten to destroy with a lame, hot parking lot and an unattractive, square building. (12) I do not wish to take my child to the back of a Target store to play. (13) Finally, this type of mega-retail store often increases crime in the surrounding area. (14) This nearsightedness is not the kind of leadership I will vote for. Respectfully, A Concerned Citizen

The Writer's Journal

PEER EDITING

The student writer of "Let the Children Play: No Target" completed the following reflection to record her thinking through the writing process. Read her writer's journal that describes a few key choices she made as she wrote. Then, in the given space, answer her questions about her use of logical order and effective expression in her paragraph. Work with a peer or a small group of classmates.

LOGICAL ORDER: I wanted to use an order that would make my argument sound strong and smart. So rather than just telling them I was angry about the issue, I also included three examples of why their consideration of this development made me upset. Once I had recorded my three major ideas that began with "First of all, Secondly, and Thirdly" I saw that each of those ideas needed support to be more effective. So I added an additional sentence after each major idea to help explain how I felt. Do you agree with the order of my ideas? Why or why not? How could I improve on the order of my ideas?

EFFECTIVE EXPRESSION: When I first sat down to write my city officials about why a Target store should not relocate my neighborhood park, I was angry. I just wanted them to know I was disappointed with them. But as I wrote, I became anxious. The longer I thought about the issue, more and more points against the development flooded my mind. I wanted to address them all without sounding boring. Is my tone okay? Do I come across too strong? How could I improve my tone?

Developing Your Point Using Persuasion

A persuasive paragraph makes a point by supporting one side of a debatable topic and refuting the opposing side. The details that support and refute the point include reasons based on facts, examples, effects, and expert opinions on the topic. In addition, a writer uses effective expression to qualify ideas and control the point of view.

The Point: The Main Idea

A persuasive paragraph gives your opinion or stand on an issue. A topic sentence states the debatable topic, the writer's persuasive opinion, and, possibly, a pattern of organization. Because persuasion is a purpose, the writer may choose any particular pattern of organization to support a claim. In addition, the writer's persuasive opinion is often signaled by the following types of subjective words or phrases: *all, always, only, must, must not, should, should not,* or *too.*

For example, the following topic sentence contains (1) the debatable topic, (2) the writer's persuasive opinion, and (3) a pattern of organization used to organize details.

DEBATABLE TOPIC   WRITER'S OPINION   DEBATABLE TOPIC

Colleges and universities should provide substance free housing for students for several reasons.

PATTERN OF ORGANIZATION: PERSUASION SIGNAL WORDS

Practice 2

TOPIC SENTENCES

The items present a debatable topic, the writer's opinion, and a pattern of organization. Combine the ideas in each group to create a topic sentence for a persuasive paragraph.

1. TOPIC: *education about crystal meth*

OPINION: *horrific, is our best hope to end this plague*

PATTERN OF ORGANIZATION: *the consequences of*

TOPIC SENTENCE: ....

....

2. TOPIC: *procrastination by students, academic*

OPINION: *is the leading, failure*

PATTERN OF ORGANIZATION: *cause of*

TOPIC SENTENCE: ....

....

Logical Order

Once you have identified a debatable topic, you are ready to generate and organize the details. To make a persuasive point, a writer moves from a general idea (the claim) to a major support (a reason, fact, example, expert opinion, or reason against the opposing view) to a minor support (also a reason, fact, example, expert opinion, or argument against the opposing view). Transitions and signal words indicate the importance and movement among details. Strong transitions and signal words establish coherence, a clear and understandable flow of ideas.

Transitions That Signal Persuasion

accordingly	even so	however	nonetheless	therefore
admittedly	finally	in conclusion	obviously	thus
although	first (second,	indeed	of course	to be sure
because	third, etc.)	in fact, in truth	on the one hand	truly
but	for	in summary	on the other hand	undoubtedly
certainly	furthermore	last	since	
consequently	granted	meanwhile	some believe	
despite	hence	nevertheless	some may say	

Signal Words That Qualify an Idea as Persuasive (sample list)

all	every	may	often	probably, probable	think
always	has/have to	might	only	seem	too
believe	it is believed	must	ought to	should	usually
could	likely	never	possibly, possible	sometimes	

LOGICAL ORDER

Fill in the blanks with the appropriate transition or signal words for persuasion. Work with a peer or in a small group of your classmates.

Practice 3

For the Sake of the Children

For their safety and well-being, children .... be removed from homes that house meth labs. According to John W. Gillis, the director of the Office for Victims of Crime, "children who live at or visit home-based meth labs face acute health and safety risks." A few of these risks include fire hazards, chemical explosions, physical and sexual abuse, and medical neglect. In addition, because of the hand to mouth behavior of young children, they are .... to ingest toxic chemicals used to make the drug. ...., removal of a child from his or her home is a traumatic experience. However, the dangers posed by the "meth" lifestyle .... outweigh the risks posed by removing the child from these chaotic homes.

—Swetlow, Karen. *"Children at Clandestine Methamphetamine Labs: Helping Meth's Youngest Victims."* OVC Bulletin. Office for Victims of Crime. U.S. Department of Justice. June 2003. 3 April 2006. <http://www.ojp.usdoj.gov/ovc/publications/bulletins/children/197590.pdf>.

Relevant Details

As a writer narrows a topic into a focused main idea, he or she generates supporting details that answer the questions such as *who*, *what*, *when*, *where*, *why*, and *how*. A writer evaluates the relevance of each detail and uses only those that clarify or support the main idea. The supports of a persuasive claim are reasons, facts, examples, effects, expert opinions, and details that refute the opposing view.

Compare the following chart of Persuasive Supporting Details with the ideas in the Persuasive Thinking Map about metal detectors in public schools.

Persuasive Supporting Details	
REASON	A cause of an event or action. An explanation. A basis or foundation of an idea.
FACT	A specific detail that is true based on objective proof. Objective proof can be physical evidence, an eyewitness account, or the result of accepted scientific investigation.
EXAMPLE	An illustration or instance of a general idea.
EFFECT	A result or consequence of an event or action. Consider positive effects of claim and negative effects of opposing views.
EXPERT OPINION	A view based on much training and extensive knowledge in a given field. Be sure to stay with opinions of experts in the field of the topic that is being debated. For example, a physician, an expert in medicine, is not an expert in criminal justice.
SUPPORTS THAT REFUTE	To refute is to disprove or counter an opposing point; supports include reasons, facts, effects, examples, and expert opinions.

Persuasive Thinking Map

Supporting Points

Effects:
• Prevent loss of life and injury
• Provide safe schools

Facts:
• From 1992–1999, 56% of homicides and suicides at school used firearms.
• Thousands of students carry guns.

Expert Opinion:
• National Education Association
• Centers for Disease Control and Prevention

Debatable Topic

Must have metal detectors in public schools

Opposing Points

Metal detectors foster jail house atmosphere and condemn students without cause.

Costs too much money.

Supports that Refute Opposing Point

Examples:
• Columbine High School, Colorado
• Red Lake High School, Minnesota

During the prewriting phase, a writer naturally generates irrelevant details. In fact, an effective writer often produces far more details than can be used to make a specific point. Irrelevant details do not explain or support the focused point of the paragraph. A careful writer uses the revision process to double check details for relevance and to eliminate irrelevant ones.

RELEVANT DETAILS

The following paragraph develops the ideas about metal detectors in public schools generated using the persuasive thinking map. Circle the main idea. Underline one example of each of the following: fact, example, effect, and a support that refutes the opposing view. Cross out the detail that is not relevant to the main point.

Pay the Price: Stop the Shootings

(1) Public school officials should use metal detectors to screen students for possession of firearms in order to reduce the numbers of injuries and deaths. (2) The use of metal detectors signals students that safety measures are in place and that violence will not be tolerated. (3) Some oppose the use of metal detectors as a step that fosters a jail house atmosphere and condemns students as guilty without cause. (4) These opponents to metal detectors also decry the economic cost of screening students for possession of firearms. (5) Unfortunately, evidence indicates that the need to provide a safe school and the right to a safe school far outweigh these concerns. (6) According to the Centers for Disease Control and Prevention, from 1992 to 1999, 56% of homicides and suicides occurring at school involved firearms. (7) In addition, the National Education Association estimates that "on a daily basis, 100,000 students carry guns to school, 160,000 miss classes due to fear of physical harm, and 40 are injured or killed by firearms." (8) Tragic school shootings have already occurred and signal that the danger is clear and present. (9) For example, in 1999 at Columbine High School, in Colorado, two students massacred 12 fellow students and a teacher, injured 24 other people, and then committed suicide. (10) As recently as 2005, at Red Lake High School in Minnesota, a student killed five students and injured seven others after he had killed his grandfather and his grandfather's girlfriend at home. (11) He also shot himself. (12) All of these shooters obviously suffered mental health problems. (13) Though these incidents are extreme, they are not isolated. (14) These incidents show that public schools must screen students for weapons. (15) The cost of not doing so is too high!

Works Cited

Centers for Disease Control and Prevention. "Source of Firearms Used by Students in School-Associated Violent Deaths—United States, 1992–1999." *Morbidity and Mortality Weekly Report* 52(09): 169-72. 7 March 2003. Web. 14 Aug. 2009.

"School Violence." National Education Association. Washington, D.C.: 1993.

Effective Expression: Use of Subjective Words to Persuade

Effective expression is the result of a writer's thoughtful choice of words for impact on the reader. Subjective words reflect a strong stand because they express opinions, emotions, value judgments, and interpretations. Because subjective words express personal opinions, they can bring meanings and stir reactions in the reader not intended by the writer. Therefore, a thoughtful writer carefully chooses subjective words for effective expression. Note the differences between the neutral words and the subjective words in the following list:

Neutral Words	Subjective Words
injury	wound, gash
perpetrator	criminal, delinquent, achiever
shelter	haven, hut

Practice 5

EFFECTIVE EXPRESSION: USE OF SUBJECTIVE WORDS TO PERSUADE

Use your dictionary and thesaurus to find an effective biased word to fill in the blank in each sentence. In the spaces after each sentence, describe the impact you intend to have on your reader through your choice of words. Discuss your work with your class or small group.

1. Spanking is a ....

....

2. Laws that require cyclists to wear helmets are ....

....

3. Completion of a college education requires ....

....

4. Burning the United States flag is an act of ....

....

5. President Barack Obama is ....

....

Using Persuasion in Your Academic Courses

Often college textbooks present situations to help you think critically and come to your own conclusions about a debatable topic. An excellent study technique is to write a paragraph in response to the information and questions. Many professors of these courses will also ask you to write an essay in which you explain your understanding of a controversial issue. You may find that you can use the information from the textbook as a resource for your writing assignment.

USING PERSUASION IN A COLLEGE BUSINESS ASSIGNMENT: RESPONDING TO A CONTROVERSIAL ISSUE

Read the following study prompt about an ethical issue based on a college business textbook lesson. Then follow the directions given in the section "The Dilemma."

Taking a Stance: Ethics in Business

The Situation

An on-going debate revolves around the roles and activities of business owners in contributing to the greater social good. Promoting a proactive stance, some people argue that business should be socially responsible. In a proactive stance, businesses should seek opportunities to benefit the community in which they do business. Others say that businesses exist to make profits for owners, so they have no further obligation to society than that (the defensive stance). The defensive stance gives credit to businesses because they create jobs and pay taxes.

The Dilemma

Pair up with a classmate. Choose one side of this debate. On your own sheet of paper, create a persuasive thinking map to support the side you have chosen. Then, take the opposite side of the debate and create a persuasive thinking map to support that side of the issue. Use the persuasive thinking map on page 212 as a model.

--Adapted from Griffin and Ebert. *Business.* Prentice Hall 2006, p. 86.

Workshop

PORTFOLIO

Workshop: Writing a Persuasive Paragraph Step by Step

Choose Your Topic

The following activities are designed to help you choose a topic.

1. Create a bank of topics: Use the following debatable topics to brainstorm or list as many facts, effects, and examples as you possibly can. Don't analyze your thoughts; just get as many ideas written down as quickly as possible. Add more debatable topics and examples as they occur to you. Revisit topic banks created during your study of previous chapters. Compare your bank of topics with those of your peers.

   - Violence in Cartoons
   - Sex Education
   - Teenage Drivers
   - Conserving Energy

2. Choose a list of topics from Activity 1. Brainstorm possible points the opposition could use to challenge your ideas. Identify relevant expert opinions you will need to include. Determine where you could locate those opinions. For example, can you interview an expert? Locate an expert opinion on the Internet? Read a newspaper or magazine article?

   OR

   Select a group of photographs that illustrate a debatable topic. Generate a list that includes facts, effects, examples, and opposing points. Search for expert opinions to include. Freewrite about the photograph(s). Remember to ask "What's the point?"

Focus Your Point

Read a prewrite you have generated for a persuasive paragraph. Underline words that suggest your values, opinions, or attitudes about the events, situations, objects, or factors. Why is the subject important? Think about the reasons, facts, effects, and examples that best represent your claim. Identify your audience. Think about what specific reaction you want from your audience. Do you want to change your audience's mind about an issue, raise your audience's awareness about an issue, or call your audience to take a specific action? In one sentence, state the claim of your persuasion.

AUDIENCE: ....

PURPOSE—AUDIENCE REACTION: ....

....

CONCRETE EXAMPLES: ....

....

WHAT'S THE POINT? STATE YOUR CLAIM: ....

....

Generate and Organize Relevant Details

Use the persuasive thinking map below to either organize the ideas you have already created or to generate details that support your point.

Persuasive Thinking Map

The Debatable Topic: What is the issue? ....

....

Supporting Points

Reason 1: ....

....

Reason 2: ....

....

Reason 3: ....

....

Opposing Point

....

....

Support that Refutes Opposing Point

....

....

What's the point?

....

....

Write a Draft of Your Paragraph

Using the ideas you generated during the prewriting phase, compose a draft of your persuasive paragraph. Return to the prewriting process at any time to generate additional details as needed. Use your own paper.

Revise Your Draft

Once you have created a draft of a persuasive paragraph, read the draft and answer the questions in the "Questions for Revising a Persuasive Paragraph" box that follows. Indicate your answers by annotating your paper. If you answer "yes" to a question, underline, check, or circle examples. If you answer "no" to a question, write the additional details in the margins and draw lines to indicate their placement. Revise your paragraph based on your reflection.

Workshop

Questions for Revising a Persuasive Paragraph:

- ☐ Have I chosen an important debatable topic?

- ☐ Have I made my point? Can I state my point in one sentence?

- ☐ Have I effectively used reasons, facts, effects, examples? Have I used strong signal words of persuasion?

- ☐ Have I used concrete details to make my point?

- ☐ Have I included only the details that are relevant to my topic sentence? Have I used effective and relevant expert opinions? Have I addressed important opposing points effectively? Have I documented my sources properly?

- ☐ Have I used the following to make my ideas clear and interesting to my readers: vivid verbs and images, parallel language, controlled sentence structure, coordination, subordination, precise use of words such as *affect* and *effect*, and thoughtful use of biased words?

- ☐ Have I used subjective words to persuade my reader?

Proofread Your Draft

Once you have made any revisions to your paragraph that may be needed, proofread you paper to ensure appropriate usage and grammar, such as the consistent use of point of view.

Grammar in Action: Consistent Use of Point of View

Point of view is established with the use of personal pronouns. Personal pronouns identify three points of view: first person, second person, and third person.

Personal Pronouns and Points of View

- **First Person** (informal tone)
  I, me, mine, myself, my
  we, us, ours, our, ourselves

- **Second Person** (informal tone)
  you, your, yours, yourselves

- **Third Person** (formal tone)
  he, him, his, himself
  she, her, hers, herself
  it, its, itself
  they, them, their, theirs, themselves

Common sense tells us that we cannot shift between several individuals' points of view. However, often, we shift point of view carelessly, as in the following sentence.

> Television addiction contributes to our obesity. When you choose to sit in front of a television from the minute you get home until you go to bed, you leave no time for exercise.

Consistent use of point of view strengthens coherence or the clear flow of ideas. Therefore, carefully edit your writing to ensure consistent use of point of view, as in the following edited version of the sentence above.

> Television addiction contributes to our obesity. When we choose to sit in front of a television from the minute we get home until we go to bed, we leave no time for exercise.

CONSISTENT USE OF POINT OF VIEW

Edit these sentences for consistent use of point of view. Cross out the pronoun that causes a shift in point of view and insert a noun or pronoun that establishes consistent use of point of view. Discuss your answers with a small group of peers or with your class.

1. A parent must monitor children's access to the Internet because you are vulnerable to predators in chat rooms and virtual communities like MySpace.com.

2. Some people believe that abstinence is the only way you can prevent unwanted pregnancies and the spread of sexually transmitted diseases.

3. People should not talk on the cell phone and drive at the same time. I was run off the road by a man who was obviously having an intense cell phone conversation while he was driving.

4. Getting enough sleep is crucial to a person's long-term health. When you deprive yourself of sleep, you deprive the body of its ability to repair itself through rest.

5. Women should limit their intake of alcohol to one serving of red wine per day; keep in mind that one serving is five ounces.

Review

MY WRITER'S JOURNAL

Work with a classmate to give and receive feedback about your persuasive paragraphs. Use the following form to record your thinking about your writing process for your persuasive paragraph. Use the writer's journal on page 209 as a model for your own journal. Discuss the decisions you made as you wrote, and describe what you have learned by writing. Also, ask for advice about how to improve your paragraph.

MAIN IDEA: ....

....

....

LOGICAL ORDER: ....

....

....

....

RELEVANT DETAILS: ....

....

....

....

EFFECTIVE EXPRESSION: ....

....

....

....

Writing Assignments

Considering Audience and Purpose

Study the set of photographs at the beginning of the chapter. Assume you are the mayor or a commissioner who has received this letter from "A Concerned Citizen." Write a one-paragraph response that states your official stand on the issue. Or assume you are a representative for Target. Write a one-paragraph response to support the building of a Target at the Nova Park location.

Writing for Everyday Life

Assume that you and your family, or you and a group of your friends, have decided to take a vacation together. Each of you has a different destination and activity in mind. Write a one-paragraph e-mail to your family or group of friends in which you convince them to travel to your choice of destinations. Be sure to include facts, effects, examples, expert opinions, and reasons that counter any opposition to your choice. Allow your word choice and tone to reflect your enthusiasm.

Writing for College Life

Assume that you disagree with a grade you have received for a course or an assignment. Write a one-paragraph letter to your professor in which you argue for the grade you believe you have earned. Be sure to include facts that prove what you have learned, examples of what you have learned, and explanations of the benefits of what you have learned. As part of your proof, include ideas and concepts you have learned from your professor (as an expert in the field). Allow your word choice and tone to reflect both respect for the professor and self-confidence in your abilities.

Writing for Working Life

Assume that you are a supervisor of a shift of workers at a fast food restaurant or department store. Assume that you are short of staff, and the busy season is approaching: You need more workers. Write a one-paragraph memo to your district manager, Derwood Kuntz, persuading him to authorize you to hire three additional workers. Be sure to include reasons, facts, examples, effects, and points that will counter any opposition he may pose.

mywritinglab
WANT A BETTER GRADE? For more practice with persuasion, go to **www.mywritinglab.com** > Using Patterns of Organization to Develop Paragraphs > The Persuasive Paragraph.

13

Understanding the Essay

An essay is a series of closely related ideas.

All of us of have had some experience studying, writing, or reading essays. What do you already know about essays? Where have you seen essays? What are the traits of an essay?

Perhaps the most common and flexible form of writing, an essay allows powerful personal expression. The essay is used for academic papers, business reports, business letters, newspaper and magazine articles, Web articles, and personal letters, as well as letters to the editor of a newspaper or journal. By mastering the task of writing an essay, you empower your ability to think, to reason, and to communicate.

What's the Point of an Essay?

Like a paragraph, an **essay** is a series of closely related ideas that develop and support the writer's point about a topic. In fact, the paragraph serves as a building block for an essay since an essay is composed of two, three, or more paragraphs. Therefore, the skills you developed to write a paragraph will also help you write an effective essay.

The Five Parts of an Essay

An essay has several basic parts: a **title**; a beginning, made up of an **introductory paragraph** that often includes a stated main idea or **thesis statement**; a middle, made up of **body paragraphs**; and an ending, often made up of a **concluding paragraph**. The following chart shows the general format of an essay.

> **Hook the reader's interest. Use key words or a phrase to vividly describe your essay.**

The Title

> An introduction usually consists of a brief paragraph in which you do the following: Introduce the topic. Explain the importance of the topic or give necessary background information about the topic. Hook the reader's interest. State your main idea in a thesis statement—a sentence that contains your topic and your point about the topic.

The Introduction

Thesis Statement

> The body of an essay is usually made up of a series of longer paragraphs. Most body paragraphs follow a similar pattern. Focus on one aspect of your main idea. State the focus of the paragraph in a topic sentence. Use the topic sentence to state the point you are making in the paragraph and relate the point of the paragraph to your thesis statement. Offer major details that support the topic sentence. If needed, offer minor details that support the major details. Link body paragraphs with clear transitions so your reader can easily follow your thoughts.

The Body

> The conclusion restates or sums up the essay's main idea. In longer essays, the conclusion may be a separate paragraph. In shorter essays, the conclusion may be a powerful sentence or two at the end of the last body paragraph.

The Conclusion

For more on creating effective titles, introductions, and conclusions, see pages 251–256.

Making a Point Using an Essay: One Student Writer's Response

Read the following essay from the U.S. Bureau of Labor Statistics' Web site. Study the annotations and complete the activities suggested in the annotations.

The Introduction:
The writer begins with a bold statement designed to hook the reader's interest. The next several sentences offer important background information about an associate degree. The introduction ends with the thesis statement. Notice that the thesis statement states the topic, "associate degree," and the writer's focus, "many advantages" and "many resources."

The Title:
The writer used a phrase to appeal to the reader's desire to get a "jump start" on the future. The title introduces the topic "Associate Degree" and sums up the point of her essay in just a few words.

The Body:
The body of this essay is made up of several paragraphs. This topic sentence states a primary support for the thesis—one advantage of an associate degree: "increased earning power." By repeating the key term "advantage," the writer ties this body paragraph to the thesis statement.

This detail supports the topic sentence and is introduced with the transition "First."

This sentence is a **minor detail** that supports a major detail. **Underline the phrase that introduces this detail.**

Second major detail that supports the topic sentence. Note the transition word "also."

Third major detail that supports the topic sentence is introduced with the transition "However."

Associate Degree: Two Years to a Career or a Jump Start to a Bachelor's Degree

by Olivia Crosby

(1) In two years, you can increase your earnings, train for some of the fastest growing jobs in the economy, and pave the way for further education. (2) How? (3) Earn an associate degree. (4) An associate degree is a college degree awarded after the completion of about 20 classes. (5) It either prepares students for a career after graduation, or it allows them to transfer into a bachelor's degree program. (6) An associate degree offers many advantages, and many resources exist to help you decide upon a specific degree and college.

(7) One advantage of an associate degree is increased earning power. (8) First, people with associate degrees earn more money. (9) For example, compared with workers whose highest held degree was a high school diploma, workers with an associate degree averaged an extra $128 a week in 2001, according to the Bureau of Labor Statistics (BLS). (10) People with associate degrees are also more likely to find jobs. (11) The unemployment rate in 2001 was more than 30 percent lower for people with associate degrees compared with high school graduates. (12) And, according to several studies, advantages in the job market might be even greater for those just starting their careers. (13) However, for most people, the best part about earning an associate degree is the opportunity to enter interesting professions. (14) Training is available for those with nearly any interest, from technical fields like electronics and health care to liberal arts areas, such as design and social work. (15) And according to the BLS, careers in which workers often are required to have an associate degree are growing faster than careers that require other types of training.

(16) Another advantage of an associate degree is that it is widely ◄ available, offering a variety of experiences. (17) Degrees are available from public community colleges, private two-year colleges, for-profit technical institutes, and many four-year colleges and universities. (18) Taking classes from home is more common in associate degree programs than in any other type of educational program. (19) More than 9 percent of associate degree students used distance learning in 1998, according to the U.S. Department of Education. (20) Other students have a more traditional college experience. (21) These students choose schools that offer on-campus housing and meals. (22) And nearly all schools offer extracurricular activities—as well as academics.

This topic sentence states another primary support for the thesis—"another advantage" of an associate degree. This phrase links this paragraph to the previous paragraph with the transition "another," and the word "advantage" ties this body paragraph to the thesis statement. Underline the words in the topic sentence that state the author's point in this paragraph.

(23) In addition to the many advantages of an associate degree, many ◄ resources exist to help you make the best decisions about your career. (24) First, most libraries and career centers have the Encyclopedia of Associations and the *Occupational Outlook Handbook.* (25) These books offer information about work-related associations. (26) The *Handbook* also describes hundreds of careers and how to train for them. (27) Second, counselors at colleges and career centers have information about local associate degree programs, labor markets, and financial aid. (28) Third, the easiest way to learn about specific degree programs is to request information from the schools that offer them. (29) Nearly every school provides free publications and has Web sites that describe programs and facilities. (30) For more details, consider calling, writing, or visiting prospective teachers. (31) Faculty and counselors are usually happy to speak with would-be students about courses and careers.

This topic sentence offers another primary support for the thesis. The sentence begins with a transitional phrase "In addition to the many advantages of an associate degree." This phrase links this paragraph to the previous paragraphs and the thesis statement. Circle the words that state the author's focus in this paragraph. Underline the three major supporting details in this paragraph. Remember to look for transition words.

(32) An associate degree increases your chance for financial power ◄ and personal fulfillment—in just two years. (33) And with the many resources to help you decide on a degree and school along with the flexible paths to access, a bright future awaits you. (34) So don't delay; begin today!

The Conclusion: This essay ends by restating the writer's main idea and calling the reader to action. Underline the words that restate the essay's main point.

—Adapted from Olivia Crosby, "Associate Degree: Two Years to a Career or a Jump Start to a Bachelor's Degree," US Department of Labor.

Practice 1

WRITING FROM LIFE

Test your understanding of the essay's structure. Read the student essay below straight through once. Complete the activities on the next page as you read the essay a second time. After reading, complete the outline with information from the essay.

Lacey Durrance
Professor Ragan
ENC 1101: Section 47
October 10, 2009

Traits of a Successful College Student

(1) First-time college students don't realize the reality shock they will receive when they get to college. (2) High school and college atmospheres are extremely different in many ways. (3) College campuses and classes are often larger, college teachers have different expectations, and college students face many new challenges. (4) To get through college successfully, all first-time college students must be dedicated, responsible, and independent. (5) Many won't realize this until it is too late.

(6) Dedication is a primary part of being successful in college. (7) Students must work hard and take action to learn at a college level. (8) Assignments can't be left until the last minute like they might have been in high school. (9) College students must be willing to speak up in class and ask questions when they don't understand. (10) Dedication means setting priorities for success; dedication means putting off going out with friends and caring about producing the best work possible. (11) Dedicated students will do their work and do it well, spending hours reading textbooks, reviewing notes, and revising essays.

(12) For many, being responsible during high school wasn't really necessary. (13) Students might forget to do their homework and the teacher most likely would extend the deadline. (14) In contrast, college students must be responsible for their actions and accept the consequences. (15) Paying attention to what's due and when assignments should be turned in is a prime example. (16) Most college teachers stick to their deadlines and expect students to do so also. (17) Being on time to class is another example of being responsible. (18) Responsibility plays a key role in a successful college career.

(19) However, having dedication and being responsible aren't the only traits college students need to survive. (20) College students must also be independent. (21) Teachers expect students to take notes without assigning them to do so. (22) In high school, teachers often gave out notes to study from or told students where and when to take them. (23) College students must do their work without being reminded everyday. (24) However, teachers are there to help their students understand the class material. (25) They will guide their students yet not help complete their work. (26) Being independent is a skill to acquire for college success, as well as life-long success.

(27) College is hard work, and students must have these traits to be successful. (28) Most first-time college students will struggle with the new experience, yet by being dedicated, responsible, and independent, they will thrive in the college world.

1. Based on the title of the essay, what is the writer's topic and main point?

---

2. In the introduction, how does the writer "hook" the reader's interest?

---

3. Underline the thesis statement. Rewrite the thesis statement using your own words here.

---

4. What ideas did the writer restate in her conclusion?

---

5. The writer used a brief outline to plan and organize her ideas before she wrote her essay. Recreate her plan by completing the following outline. Fill in the blanks with her thesis statement and topic sentences.

I. INTRODUCTION

THESIS STATEMENT: _____

II. FIRST BODY PARAGRAPH TOPIC SENTENCE: _____

III. SECOND BODY PARAGRAPH TOPIC SENTENCE: _____

IV. THIRD BODY PARAGRAPH TOPIC SENTENCE: _____

V. CONCLUSION TOPIC SENTENCE: _____

Practice 1

Developing Your Point: Writing an Essay

The Four Levels of Information in an Essay

In addition to being made up of several parts, an essay offers several levels of information that range from general to specific. Understanding these levels of information helps a writer create and organize ideas throughout the writing process.

▲ Ladders to different levels

Titles, Introductions, and Conclusions Express General Ideas

Titles, introductions, and conclusions introduce and summarize ideas. Chapter 14 offers helpful hints about how to effectively use titles, introductions, and conclusions.

Thesis Statement

The thesis statement is a one-sentence summary of the main idea of the essay. All the details in the body paragraphs support the thesis statement.

Types of Supporting Details

Two types of details are often needed to thoroughly explain a main idea: primary and secondary details. **Primary details** directly explain or support the thesis statement. **Secondary details** indirectly support the thesis statement. In an essay, topic sentences of the body paragraphs are the primary supports for the thesis statement. The examples, reasons, and facts within the body of a paragraph support the topic sentence. They serve as secondary details that support the thesis statement.

Levels of Supporting Details

Secondary supports can also be divided into two levels: major details and minor details. A **major detail** supports a topic sentence. A **minor detail** supports a major detail. Thus, a topic sentence supports the thesis statement, and secondary supports explain a topic sentence. The following flow chart illustrates these levels of information in an essay. This chart represents a basic three-paragraph essay. This format is often expanded to include two or more body paragraphs.

THE LEVELS OF INFORMATION IN AN ESSAY

Compare this chart to the chart about levels of information in a paragraph on page 53.

Introduction
Explains importance of topic and writer's point.

Offers background information about the topic.

Hooks reader's interest.

Thesis Statement
States the main idea in a complete sentence.

Uses specific, effective wording.

Relates to all the details in the essay.

Topic Sentence
States the main idea of the paragraph.

Offers one primary support for the thesis statement.

Relates to all the details in the paragraph.

Major Detail
Supports the topic sentence.

Is a secondary support for the thesis statement.

Is more general than a minor detail.

Minor Detail
Supports a major detail.

Is a secondary support for the thesis statement.

Offers the most specific details in the essay.

The Body

Conclusion
Reinforces the importance of the writer's overall point.

Practice 2

Read the following three-paragraph essay. Underline the thesis statement. Next, underline the three major details in the body paragraph.

Street Luging for the Extreme Thrill

(1) Extreme sports take athletic competition to new levels of danger and excitement. (2) They often offer a combination of speed, height, danger, and mind-blowing stunts. (3) Street luging illustrates the allure of extreme sports.

(4) Street luging, like many extreme sports, involves high levels of speed, danger, and adrenaline. (5) First, street luging is all about speed. (6) A pilot lies on his or her back on a luge (a type of skateboard, eight and a half feet long) and flies through a street course at speeds of around 70 miles per hour. (7) As a result, the urethane wheels of the luge may actually flame fire and melt during a run due to the high speeds. (8) Second, street luging courses are known for their rough, hazardous road surfaces and obstacles. (9) For example, very dangerous courses are known as *bacon* while less dangerous ones are labeled *scrambled eggs*. (10) And frequently, luges snag or hook together, wobble, wipe out, or slam into barriers that mark the course. (11) Finally, the dangers of street luging are related to another important attraction of extreme sports—the thrilling rush of an adrenaline high. (12) The adrenaline rush is due to high levels of dopamine, endorphins, and serotonin produced by the body in response to the danger. (13) Adrenaline floods the body with additional surges of energy, power, and well-being so that a person can either fight or flee the danger. (14) Many extreme sports participants are called adrenaline junkies. (15) Luge pilots refer to this feeling as being "amped."

(16) Extreme sports include a wide variety of thrill-seeking sports such as wave surfing, wind surfing, BASE jumping (jumping from buildings, antennas or towers, spans or bridges, or cliffs), parachuting, and drag racing. (17) Overall, street luging offers athletes all the dangers and thrills that all extreme sports enthusiasts find so attractive.

The Traits of an Effective Essay

The word *essay* means attempt, to make an effort to accomplish an end. An essay is a writer's attempt to share his or her unique and specific point about a specific subject to a specific audience for a specific purpose. An effective essay supports a **main idea** or **thesis statement** with **relevant details** in **logical order,** using **effective expression.**

The Point: Main Idea or Thesis Statement

What's the point of a focused main idea? To make a clear and powerful point to your reader! An effective essay makes a clear point by focusing a main idea. A focused main idea is the result of several thinking steps: selecting and narrowing a topic and drafting a **thesis statement.**

For more on using prewriting techniques and selecting a topic, see pages 20–21.

Select and Narrow a Topic

Many writers break this step into two parts. First, a writer often generates a list of topics. This list serves as a bank of ideas that can be applied to a wide variety of writing situations. Second, a writer considers the writing situation.

Understanding the writing situation helps the writer narrow the topic. For example, the length of an essay often depends on your audience and purpose. A paper for an academic audience such as a history professor may have a required length of 1,000 words. In contrast, a local newspaper may limit the length of letters to the editor to 500 words. The scope of the topic needs to match the required length. For example, the 500-word letter to the editor cannot cover all the reasons one should volunteer at the local soup kitchen for the poor. Instead, you would need to narrow the topic to just two or three reasons. And you would choose only those details that are of interest to your specific audience.

For more on the writing situation, and topic, purpose, and audience, see pages 22–27.

THE WRITING SITUATION

The following pictures present specific writing situations. Each picture represents an audience, and each caption states the purpose for writing to that audience. First, match the audience and purpose to its appropriate topic. Then, write the letter of the topic in the appropriate space. Finally, discuss your answers with your class or in a small group.

Topics: a. The importance of a specific lesson

b. Wisdom gained from an education

c. The proper way to discipline a child

d. Why voting is important

Practice 3

.... Writing Situation 1: To Inform — to share, explain or demonstrate information

.... Writing Situation 2: To Persuade — to change this audience's opinion or call them to action

.... Writing Situation 3: To Express — to share personal opinions, feelings, or reactions

.... Writing Situation 4: To Reflect — to record your understandings about what you have experienced or learned

Draft a Thesis Statement

After choosing and narrowing a topic, a writer composes a working draft of the thesis statement. A **thesis statement** shares the same traits of a topic sentence for a paragraph. Just as the topic sentence states the main idea of a paragraph, the thesis sentence states the main idea of the essay. Both statements answer the question "What's the point?" This point is the opinion about the topic that you are explaining and supporting in the essay. In fact, your point further narrows your topic. The writer's point or opinion is often referred to as the controlling idea.

The controlling idea often includes a pattern of organization as well as the writer's opinion. You learned about patterns of organization as you studied how to develop paragraphs in Chapters 3 to 12. The following graphic illustrates an effective thesis statement.

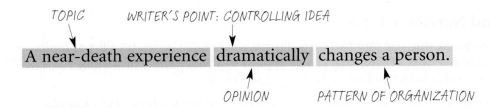

The word "dramatically" is an opinion that must be explained or supported. In addition, the word "changes" suggests a pattern of organization. This word indicates that the writer is going to compare what the person was like before the near-death experience to what the person is like after the near-death experience. The controlling idea answers the question "What's the point?" of the essay.

Hints for Drafting a Thesis Statement
Use specific statements. Replace vague, general words with vivid, exact words. "Football is a dumb game" is too vague and general. "Football glorifies violence" is specific and vivid.
Always state your thesis statement as a complete sentence.
Avoid announcing your topic. Never say, "I am going to write about football and violence," or "My essay is about football and violence," or "My topic is football violence."
Review and, if necessary, revise your thesis statement after you have written a rough draft. As you think about a topic, the point you want to make often becomes clearer.

Practice 4

CREATING AND REVISING THESIS STATEMENTS

These items present a topic and a writer's point about the topic. Combine the ideas in each group to create a thesis statement. Discuss your ideas with your class or in a small group.

1. TOPIC: *workplace aggression*

WRITER'S POINT: *is on the rise and takes on several forms of behavior*

THESIS STATEMENT: ....

....

2. TOPIC: *cardiovascular disease*

WRITER'S POINT: *although certain factors are unavoidable, other factors*

we can influence

THESIS STATEMENT: ....

....

....

3. TOPIC: *major depressive disorder*

WRITER'S POINT: *a common type of mood disorder with several long-term effects*

THESIS STATEMENT: ....

....

4. TOPIC: *use of chat rooms and online discussion boards*

WRITER'S POINT: *five tips for effectiveness*

THESIS STATEMENT: ....

....

5. TOPIC: *weight training machines and free weights*

WRITER'S POINT: *similarities and differences*

THESIS STATEMENT: ....

....

Logical Order

In an effective essay, body paragraphs are arranged in a clear, logical order for a coherent flow of ideas. Likewise, effective writers link each paragraph to the next so that readers can follow their chain of thought.

You can achieve a coherent flow of ideas in several logical ways.

1. *Follow the order of ideas as presented in the thesis statement.* Often the controlling idea of the thesis statement divides the topic into chunks of information.

2. *Follow space order.* At times, a writer describes how something is arranged in space to develop a main idea. Description moves from top to bottom, side to side, front to back, or the reverse of these.

3. *Follow time order.* A writer may record an event or a process as it unfolds in time.

4. *Present ideas in order of importance.* Often, a writer decides upon and arranges details according to his or her opinion about the importance of the details, known as **climactic order**. Usually, climactic order moves from the least important point in the first body paragraph and builds to the essay's climax, the most important point in the final body paragraph.

Practice 5

COHERENCE TECHNIQUES: THESIS STATEMENT, SPACE, TIME, AND CLIMACTIC ORDER

Complete the exercises, and share your responses with your class or in a small group.

1. **Follow space order**. Write and arrange in space order three topic sentences (primary supports) suggested by the following thesis statement. Use the photograph to generate your primary supports.

   I.   Introduction

   THESIS STATEMENT: *Although Goth fashion varies widely, the*

   look makes a bold, nontraditional fashion statement.

   II. ....

   III. ....

   IV. ....

   V.   Conclusion

◄ Goth fashion

2. **Follow time order.** Write and arrange in time order three topic sentences (primary supports) suggested by the following thesis statement. Use the photographs to generate your primary supports.

I.   Introduction

THESIS STATEMENT: *Technology plays a key role in the restoration of Sand Key Beach, Florida.*

II. _____

III. _____

IV. _____

V. _____

VI.   Conclusion

▲ Before restoration

▲ During restoration

▲ After restoration

3. **Present ideas in order of importance.** Write and arrange in climactic order three topic sentences (primary supports) suggested by the following thesis statement.

I.   Introduction

THESIS STATEMENT: *Stress challenges us in almost every aspect of our lives.*

II. _____

III. _____

IV. _____

V.   Conclusion

Practice 5

Connecting Paragraphs

In addition to ordering paragraphs coherently, writers clearly connect each paragraph to the next so that readers can follow their chain of thought. The following chart lists and illustrates several options to connect paragraphs to each other.

Connecting Paragraphs
Echo or repeat important words or phrases from the thesis statement in body paragraphs.
I. Thesis statement: We can *ease* the *pain* that occurs from illness or injury in several different ways.
II. Topic sentence: *Pain* can be *eased* by deep breathing.
III. Topic sentence: Visualization and imagery *ease pain*.
Refer to the main idea of the previous paragraph in the topic sentence of the present paragraph.
I. Thesis statement: Applying the principles of computer ergonomics reduces the chances of injury and fatigue.
II. Topic sentence: The *computer screen* should be *placed properly* to avoid painful injuries to the neck.
III. Topic sentence: *Proper placement* of the *monitor* not only *reduces* the possibility of *neck injury* but also eases eye fatigue.
Use transitional words, phrases, or sentences.
I. Thesis statement: Sleep disorders can deprive sufferers of much needed rest and complicate their lives.
II. Topic sentence: *One type* of sleep disorder is known as night terrors.
III. Topic sentence: *Another type* of sleep disorder, nightmares, torments many people.
IV. Transition sentence and topic sentence: *At least the previous two disorders occur in the privacy of one's home.* Narcolepsy, a *third kind* of sleep disorder, can occur suddenly anywhere, and at any time without warning.
Tie the last idea in one paragraph to the opening of the next paragraph.
I. Thesis statement: Hurricane activity is on the rise, is likely to increase, and calls for new methods of preparation.
II. Topic sentence and ending idea of paragraph: Hurricane activity is on the rise because of higher ocean temperatures and lower vertical wind shear. Therefore, these *climate changes* are likely to continue for as many as 10 to 40 years.
III. Topic sentence: *These shifts in climate* call for new methods of hurricane preparation.

Practice 6

CONNECTING PARAGRAPHS

Read the following essay. Underline the connections between paragraphs. Circle the key ideas that are repeated throughout the essay. Discuss with your class or in a small group the different types of connections the writer used and evaluate their effectiveness.

A Song of Humility

(1) The neighborhood of my youth hummed with the songs of our carefree play. (2) The beat of hammers building forts and the zings of the over-ripe ammunition of our orange wars in Winter Haven, Florida, blended beautifully with the music of the times. (3) The Beatles, and all the other really far-out groups, deafened us to any world but our very own. (4) No one was more deaf than I.

(5) At that time, I was particularly deaf to the family that lived two streets over and halfway down a dusty clay side road. (6) This out of sync family lived poorer than we did. (7) They grew their own food, raised chickens, and loved loud country music. (8) Every time I passed their house, I felt sorry for them, in a smug sort of way. (9) One afternoon the mama of that family labored up the hill to our house. (10) Her son had cut a record, and she "would be obliged if we was to listen to it" and tell her what we thought. (11) I was too busy marveling at her stained clothes and dusty feet to hear how respectfully my mother responded.

(12) Mother treated everyone with respect and tried to teach her children to do so as well. (13) She insisted that the whole family listen to the twangy tune about love and shirttails, but only I took great joy in mocking it. (14) Mother told me to return the record and say she thought it "a fine tune." (15) When I objected, she said, "Consider this an avoidable duty!" (16) I stood a long time studying the rusty door of that family's dust-covered house, wondering why I hadn't the courage to do my duty.

(17) Finally, my good friend Florence appeared at the end of the alley. (18) "Florence," I cried in great relief, "come here quick." (19) I ran to meet her, and we stood a few feet away with our backs turned from the door I so dreaded. (20) In the loud, exuberant tones of an inconsiderate child, I belted out the details of my dilemma. (21) "You ought to hear this … stupid … only hicks … and I have to … Hey, wait for me," I said to her retreating back. (22) I had hoped to push my obligation into her hands. (23) "Naw," she said without looking back, "I'm already late."

(24) So, I turned to do my hated duty. (25) Then I saw the son, the singer, dart from the door into the shadows of the house. (26) I wheeled about and cried, "Florence, come back." (27) I ran to her, begging, "He heard me. (28) What should I do? (29) He heard everything I said." (30) Florence shrugged and turned away. (31) I pivoted and marched to the steps. (32) The son stepped out to meet me. (33) My words resonated in the silence that loomed between us, and I cursed the supper time desertion of the dusky streets. (34) "Young lady," he said gently. (35) I looked at him. (36) "Thank ya for bringing back my demo."

(37) To this day, the timbre of his voice shames me. (38) I had mocked him, yet he sought to soothe my soul. (39) And, now, when I feel the deafness of prejudice threaten me, I remember the song of humility I learned that day from a fine young singer.

Practice 6

For concept maps of specific patterns of organization, such as narration, classification, and definition, see pages 96, 146, and 180.

Relevant Details

In an effective essay, the writer provides enough relevant details to adequately or thoroughly support the essay's main idea.

Generate Details with a Writing Plan

Most writers generate details during the prewriting stage by listing or freewriting. Once you have generated an adequate amount of details, you need to organize them into a writing plan. Many writers use clustering or outlining to help them create a plan for the essay. Clustering and outlining are excellent ways to see if you have enough details to support the point of your essay.

Some writers begin the writing process by generating details, then drafting a thesis statement, while other writers draft a working thesis statement first and then generate details. The following two practice exercises offer you an opportunity to work with both approaches. In your own writing, you should experiment to see which approach works best for you.

Often, a writer uses a prewriting technique, such as a concept map, to generate primary and secondary details. Then, the writer drafts a working thesis statement to summarize the point of the details generated with the concept map.

Practice 7

GENERATE DETAILS, DRAFT A THESIS, CREATE A WRITING PLAN

Study the following list of details. Create a writing plan by filling in the concept map with groups of details from the list. Then, write a one-sentence summary (a thesis statement) of the main point that they support.

respects others

functions of effective communication on the job

builds consensus

fosters team work

diffuses confrontations

states clear expectations

seeks solutions

remains professional

encourages input from others

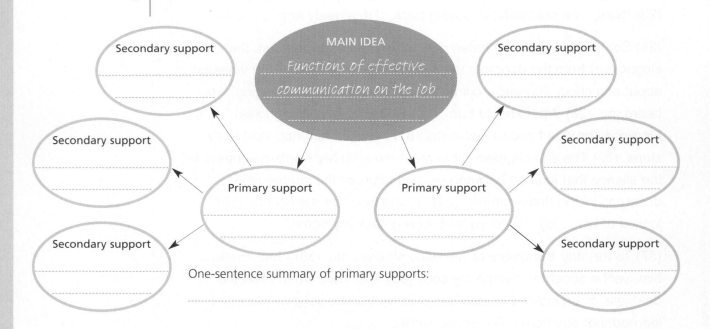

Evaluate Details

In an effective essay, every detail supports the thesis statement. *All* the details work together as a unit to explain and support the writer's point. During the prewriting process, a writer brainstorms many details, some of which may not be related to the focus of the main idea. Therefore, as you create your writing plan, you should test the details to be sure that each one is relevant to the thesis statement. Drop those details that do not support either the thesis statement or the thesis statement's primary supports. You also may want to check details for relevance once more during the revision stage of the writing process.

TESTING DETAILS FOR RELEVANCE

Study the following writing plan. Cross out details that are not relevant to the thesis statement. The following questions will help you test details for unity. Share your work with your class or in a small group of peers.

- What is the topic and controlling idea of the thesis statement? Circle the topic. Underline the controlling idea.

- Which details are the primary supporting details (the ones that will be used as topic sentences for body paragraphs)? Number the three primary supports A, B, and C.

- What are the secondary details? Number each secondary detail to correspond to a primary point: A1, A2, and so on; B1, B2, and so on; and C1, C2, and so on.

THESIS STATEMENT: *Due to the nature of lightning, you must follow lightning safety guidelines to reduce risk of injury or death.*

_____ Lightning is a complex event.

_____ Lightning is described as having two components: leaders and strokes.

_____ The leader is the probing feeler sent from the cloud.

_____ The return streaks of light are a series of strokes that produce the actual lightning bolt or flash that we see.

_____ Lightning is also common, unpredictable, and dangerous.

_____ At any given moment, there are 1,800 thunderstorms in progress somewhere on the earth. This amounts to 16 million storms each year.

_____ Lightning has been seen in volcanic eruptions, extremely intense forest fires, surface nuclear detonations, heavy snowstorms, and in large hurricanes.

_____ No one can predict the location or time of the next stroke of lightning.

_____ Lightning has been the second largest storm killer in the U.S. for the last 40 years, exceeded only by floods.

_____ Following proven lightning safety guidelines can reduce your risk of injury or death.

_____ Count the seconds between the time you see lightning and the time you hear the thunder.

_____ You should already be in a safe location if that time is less than 30 seconds.

_____ The safest location during lightning activity is an enclosed building.

_____ Stay inside until 30 minutes after you last hear thunder.

Effective Expression: Using a Thesaurus

One aspect of effective expression is choosing the precise word to convey your point with power and clarity. Effective writers often refer to a thesaurus to avoid repetition and to find the exact words needed to make their point. A thesaurus is a collection of words, their synonyms (words of similar meaning), and their antonyms (words of opposite meaning). Some thesauruses list words alphabetically: A–Z. Other thesauruses list words by types or groups of related words. You can find both kinds on the Internet. For example, *Roget's II: The New Thesaurus* 3rd ed. online at Bartleby.com offers both versions. You can find words by looking at the headwords as in the following two illustrations:

Alphabetical Index:			**Categorical Index:**
A-1	to	all right	like, dislike
all-round	to	atrocity	restraint, unrestraint
atrophy	to	big	explosion, collapse

Features vary from thesaurus to thesaurus, so be sure to read the instructions on how to use a specific one. Some features include a main entry, parts of speech, a definition, a list of synonyms, a list of antonyms, field or usage labels (such as Law or slang), and a *see also* cross reference.

Practice 9

EFFECTIVE EXPRESSION: USING A THESAURUS

Study the two entries from *Roget's II: The New Thesaurus* 3rd ed.* Then, answer the questions.

spew

VERB: To send forth (confined matter) violently: belch, disgorge, eject, eruct, erupt, expel. Geology : extravasate. See EXPLOSION.

extravasate

VERB: Geology. To send forth (confined matter) violently: belch, disgorge, eject, eruct, erupt, expel, spew. See EXPLOSION.

1. What part of speech are these two words? ....

2. Is the word "Geology" a synonym, an antonym, or a field label? ....

3. Is the word "Explosion" in both entries a field label, a cross reference,

   or a synonym? ....

4. Insert a word from the entries that best completes the point of the following statement:
   Jeremiah's parents .... their breath in relief as he safely completes
   his parachute jump.

*All examples from *Roget's II: The New Thesaurus* 3rd ed. Boston: Houghton Mifflin, 1995.

Workshop: Writing an Essay Step by Step

To create an effective essay, use the complete writing process. Begin by prewriting; then, move on to drafting, revising, and editing. Writing rarely develops in a neat and orderly process. Some writers need to generate details before they can compose a working thesis statement. Others have to know exactly what their main point is before they can generate details. The following series of workshops encourages you to follow the prewriting steps in a certain order. Feel free to move between steps or to return to any step in the process as needed.

 Prewriting

During the prewriting stage, you figure out what you want to say, why you want to say it, and to whom you want to say it.

Select and Narrow Your Topic

Select a topic on your own, pick a topic from a previous practice or workshop, or choose one of the following topics. Identify your audience and purpose.

- Movie heroes (or villains)
- Violence in sports
- Technology everyone should own
- A great achievement
- A fun activity
- Common fears

TOPIC
What you write

AUDIENCE
Who reads your writing

PURPOSE
Why you write

For an overview of the writing process, see pages 28–29.

For more on the prewriting stage of the writing process, see pages 30–42.

Create a Tentative Thesis

Then, draft a tentative thesis statement.

TOPIC: ....

AUDIENCE: ....

PURPOSE: ....

....

THESIS STATEMENT: ....

....

....

Generate Supporting Details with a Writing Plan

Generate primary and secondary supporting details by listing a writing plan or use the concept map to create a writing plan. Use the reporter's questions *who? what? when? where? why?* and *how?* to produce details.

PORTFOLIO

Workshop

Now that you have generated some details to support your tentative thesis, you probably have a clearer sense of your controlling idea. The following thesis statement has been revised to focus the topic by including the writer's opinion and a pattern of organization.

TOPIC   WRITER'S POINT: CONTROLLING IDEA

Voter turnout remains dismal for several reasons.

OPINION   PATTERN OF ORGANIZATION
               (CAUSE AND EFFECT)

Revise Your Thesis Statement

Revise your thesis so that it includes the topic, your point about the topic, and, if appropriate, a pattern of organization.

REVISED THESIS STATEMENT:

_____

_____

Evaluate Your Details

Use a writing plan to test your details. Complete the following outline with your revised thesis statement and details from your list or concept map. Make sure you have an adequate amount of details to convince your reader of your point. If you do not have the necessary major and minor details to support each topic sentence, brainstorm additional details. Delete details that are not related to your thesis statement or to the topic sentences (the primary supports for your thesis statement).

I. INTRODUCTION

REVISED THESIS STATEMENT: _____

_____

_____

II. _____

_____

   A. _____

   B. _____

III. _____

_____

   A. _____

   B. _____

IV. CONCLUSION: _____

_____

Workshop

For more on the drafting stage of the writing process, see page 44.

Write a Draft of Your Essay

Often, a writer pauses during the drafting stage of the writing process to scan what has been written so far, particularly when using a computer to write. Sometimes, while scanning, a writer may begin to make small revisions. Scanning may help a writer stay focused and can help with expression. However, you should resist the urge to spend very much time revising at this point. Your main purpose is to get a rough draft written. You can make effective revisions once you have a working draft.

Using your writing plan, write a rough draft of the body of your essay. Don't worry about the introduction and conclusion for now. Have a dictionary and thesaurus nearby just in case you get stuck trying to think of a word.

Revise Your Essay Draft

For more on the revising stage of the writing process, see page 46.

Revision is much more than simply recopying the essay so that it is neater. A good revision requires time. So, put your essay aside for an hour or two, or even better, a day or two. You want to look at your essay with fresh eyes. Then, set aside enough time to revise your essay more than once—that way, you do not have to think of everything in one sitting. During the revising stage of your writing, think about your essay on two different levels: logic and style. The following chart offers you some helpful questions to guide you through your revision.

For more information about sentence variety, see pages 340–359.

Questions for Revising an Essay:

☐ Does the essay have a clearly stated thesis statement?

☐ Are my topic sentences clearly stated?

☐ Have I provided relevant support?

☐ Is each body paragraph fully developed with major and minor details as needed?

☐ Which ideas need more support?

☐ Is each topic sentence directly related to my thesis statement?

☐ Is each detail in each body paragraph related to its topic sentence?

☐ Have I used logical order?

☐ Have I provided clear connections between paragraphs?

☐ Have I provided clear connections between sentences within paragraphs?

☐ Have I used effective expression?

☐ Do my sentences vary in type and length?

Reread your essay, and as you revise, mark up your rough draft with the changes you intend to make: (1) cross out irrelevant details and vague, weak, or trite expressions, and write stronger words directly above or near them; (2) draw arrows to show where you want to move information; (3) add more details in the margin and draw a line to indicate where you will put them.

One Student Writer's Revision Process

At the beginning of this chapter, you read the essay Lacey Durrance composed for her English class. Take a moment to reread her final draft on pages 226–227. Then, study her revisions of one draft of the essay's first two paragraphs. How does this draft differ from her final draft?

Traits of a Successful College Student

(1) First-time college students don't realize the reality shock they will receive when they get to college. (2) High school and college atmospheres are extremely different in many ways. (3) Schools are larger; there are different teachers with different expectations, and different experiences. (4) College is a big part of growing up, and with growing up comes certain traits that you need to have to make it in college. (5) All first-time college students must have dedication, be responsible, and be independent, to get through college successfully. (6) Many won't realize this until it is too late and without these traits, they won't succeed.

(7) Dedication is the biggest part of being successful in college. (8) Students must want a good grade, and know what they need to do to achieve it. (9) Among my own personal experiences of being a first time college student, dedication has played a major part of being successful. (10) I had to change my learning process to adapt to college and so have former students. (11) Students must be hard working and take action to learn at a college level. (12) Things can't be left until the last minute like they might have been in high school. (13) College students can't only want a good grade, but must do the work to get that grade. (14) Dedication will get their work done and do it well. (15) College is very different in the sense that a lot is expected from students, and they won't be walked through anything.

PORTFOLIO

Workshop

Workshop Review

PORTFOLIO

Proofreading Your Essay

Once you have revised your essay to your satisfaction, take time to carefully proofread your work. Check for the mistakes that you commonly make such as spelling errors, misplaced or missing commas, shifts in verb tense, or shifts in point of view. Publishing a clean, error-free draft proves you are committed to excellence and that you take pride in your work.

Proofread to correct spelling and grammar errors. Mark the corrections you need to make directly on the most recent draft of your essay. Create a neat, error-free draft of your essay.

For more on the proofreading stage of the writing process, see pages 48–49

REVIEW: UNDERSTANDING THE ESSAY

1. What are the four parts of an essay?

a. ....

b. ....

c. ....

d. ....

2. What are the four levels of information in an essay?

a. ....

b. ....

c. ....

d. ....

3. What are two types of details in an essay?

a. ....

b. ....

4. What are the two levels of secondary supports?

a. ....

b. ....

5. An effective essay supports a .... idea with .... details in .... order and .... expression.

6. What are the four phases of the writing process for composing an essay?

a. ....

b. ....

c. ....

d. ....

7. How will I use what I have learned about writing an essay? Discuss how you will apply to your own writing what you have learned about writing an essay.

_____

_____

_____

_____

_____

_____

_____

8. What do I still need to study about writing an essay? Discuss your ongoing study needs by describing what, when, and how you will continue studying about how to write an essay.

_____

_____

_____

_____

_____

_____

_____

PORTFOLIO

Review

14

Effective Titles, Introductions, and Conclusions

Titles, introductions, and conclusions work together to emphasize the writer's point.

The importance of effective titles, introductions, and conclusions is obvious in the composition of a movie. Think of a good movie you have seen lately. How did its title hook your interest? How did the title relate to the point of the movie? How effective was the opening of the film? How was the conclusion of the movie related to its beginning?

Just as in a successfully constructed movie, an essay with an effective title, introduction, and conclusion is more likely to have a strong impact on your audience.

What's the Point of Effective Titles, Introductions, and Conclusions?

Effective titles, introductions, and conclusions work together to emphasize the writer's point in an essay.

PHOTOGRAPHIC ORGANIZER: TITLES, INTRODUCTIONS, AND CONCLUSIONS

Study the following series of pictures of Mount St. Helens before, during, and after an eruption. First, answer the questions below for each of the photographs to identify the major details that could be used in an essay about the event. Then, write captions that provide a title, an introduction, and a conclusion for the point made by the images.

Title: ....

Introduction: ....

....

FIRST EVENT   SECOND EVENT   THIRD EVENT

What is this?

....

....

What is this?

....

....

What is this?

....

....

What the point?

....

....

Conclusion:

....

....

My First Thought Box: A Prewriting Activity

Set a time limit, such as five minutes, and write in your notebook about the images you just studied. Do not let your pen or pencil stop. Even if you must repeat ideas, keep writing until the time limit is up. Let the ideas flow freely. Getting your first thoughts about a topic on paper is a great way to start the writing process.

Title:
An effective title can be a word or phrase that helps the reader understand the writer's point by stating the topic and suggesting the writer's opinion about the topic.
Underline the topic and circle the writer's opinion.

Introduction:
An effective introduction stirs the reader's interest, establishes the relevance of the topic, and often suggests or states the main idea.
Underline the sentence that states the main idea.

Conclusion:
An effective conclusion restates the main idea to reinforce the writer's point in the reader's memory.
Underline the words that restate the topic and the writer's opinion.

Making a Point Using Effective Titles, Introductions, and Conclusions: One Student Writer's Response

The following paragraph offers one writer's response to the call to write a title, introduction, and conclusion based on the images of Mount St. Helens'. Read the text below and the annotations. Complete the activities in bold type given in the annotations. Then, read the writer's journal that records decisions she made during the writing process.

> Nature's Fierce Power Humbles Humanity
>
> An ancient Chinese proverb states, "Human will can conquer nature." However, the 1980 eruption of Mount St. Helens in Washington makes a mockery of such a thought. The 1980 eruption of Mount St. Helens demonstrates the devastating power of nature and the powerlessness of humanity.
>
> As Maya Angelou stated, "Nature has no mercy at all."

THE WRITER'S JOURNAL

The student who wrote "Nature's Fierce Power Humbles Humanity" wrote the following journal entry to record her thoughts about using a title, introduction, and conclusion. Read her writer's journal that describes a few key choices she made as she wrote. Underline any strategies that you might be able to use in your own writing.

> When I first saw the images of the 1980 eruption of Mount St. Helens, I was blown away by the devastating power of nature. I guess being so coddled by technology, I never really thought about how little control we have over nature. Of course, since then, Hurricane Katrina has made it quite clear to me just how vulnerable we are. Yet, just as we did before Katrina struck, many have forgotten this terrible truth. I had an idea about the point I

wanted to make, but I waited until after I composed the body of my essay before I worked on my title, introduction, and conclusion,. It's really hard for me to introduce a point until I know exactly what that point is, and I like to tie my conclusion to my introduction so that my essay creates an unbroken circle of thought. Hey, I just noticed that my title, introduction, thesis statement, and conclusion create a summary of my essay. I am going to use this strategy when I read information for my academic courses. What a great way to take notes!

Developing Your Point Using Effective Titles, Introductions, and Conclusions

Thoughtful titles, introductions, and conclusions enhance the effectiveness of an essay. Often these three aspects of the essay are written after the thesis statement and body paragraphs have been drafted. Although titles are the first part of the essay that catches the reader's attention, many writers create them after the introduction and conclusion.

Effective Titles

An **effective title** fulfills the following purposes:

- It hooks the reader's interest.
- It vividly describes the topic of your essay.

You should write your essay, reread your essay for its overall impact, and then create your title. Your title should be brief, and you should not use italics, quotations, or underlining for emphasis. Instead, center the title on the page about an inch above the introductory paragraph. Capitalize the first word and other key words of the title, except for prepositions such as *in, on, for, at* and articles such as *a, an,* and *the.* The following chart describes and illustrates several types of effective titles.

Types of Titles		
The question title: States the main point as a question.	**EXAMPLES:**	Is Cloning Moral? Why Clone?
The descriptive title: Uses key words to form the thesis statement.	**EXAMPLES:**	The Arrogance of Cloning Cloning Offers Hope
The recommendation title: Calls for action.	**EXAMPLES:**	Cloning Must Be Banned Clone On!

The general-specific title: States the general topic, followed by a controlling point.	EXAMPLES:	Cloning: An Unethical Procedure Cloning: The Scientific Method Working for Progress
The pattern(s) of organization title: Uses the words that establish the essay's central pattern(s) of organization.	DESCRIPTION EXAMPLES:	The Town of My Birth The Beauty of the Beach
	NARRATION EXAMPLES:	Sojourner Truth's Journey An Unforgettable Memory
	PROCESS EXAMPLES:	How to Deal with Cranky Customers Starting Your Own Business
	EXAMPLE/ILLUSTRATION EXAMPLES:	Winning Isn't Easy Pets Are People Too
	CLASSIFICATION EXAMPLES:	Types of Sexual Harassment Kinds of Camps for Kids
	COMPARISON/CONTRAST EXAMPLES:	The Differences between Male Talk and Female Talk
	DEFINITION EXAMPLES:	The Forgiving Heart The Meaning of Bravery What It Means to Be Compulsive
	CAUSE/EFFECT EXAMPLES:	Why Parents Send Their Kids to Camp The Reasons Students Cheat The Effects of Hurricane Katrina
	PERSUASION EXAMPLES:	The Need for Smaller Classes in Public Schools We All Have the Right to Die Commit to Life to the Very End

Practice 2

TITLES

Read the following three-paragraph business memo and supply a title in the blank labeled RE (for the topic of the memo).

Memo

To: Sales Associates

From: Shanika Thomas, Store Manager

Date: 3 November 2009

RE: ....

Do you want to win the $200 bonus promised to each employee of the store which best represents our company's ideals: professional, friendly, fast service? Corporate representatives will be popping in unannounced sometime over the next few weeks to rate us as individuals and as a team.

To ensure our win, keep the following tips in mind. Reflect professionalism in your personal attire, the store's appearance (keep shelves stocked and orderly), and in your work ethic. Reflect friendliness in your attitudes to supervisors, coworkers, and, most importantly, to our customers. Finally, be quick to help each other and the customer. Greet the customer promptly and politely. The moment a customer walks in through our door, make that person feel as if he or she is the most important person on earth.

If each and every one of you continues to do the fine job that has put our store in the finals of this competition, we will all be winners!

Effective Introductions

An effective introduction serves the following purposes:

- It introduces the essay topic.
- It explains the importance of the essay topic and/or gives necessary background information about the topic.
- It hooks the reader's interest.
- It presents the essay's main idea in a thesis statement.

Many writers choose to end the introductory paragraph with the thesis statement.

The following chart describes and illustrates several types of introductions you can use to effectively begin your essay. The thesis statement in each introduction is underlined.

Types of Introductions	
An interesting illustration or anecdote	**EXAMPLE:** The Wooten family makes a point of sharing the evening meal as special family time. Every evening, just as the family begins to dine and enjoy each other's company, the phone begins its non-stop ringing with unwanted harassment from telemarketers. Thankfully, the family can now put a stop to the harassment. <u>The National Do Not Call Registry is open for business, putting consumers in charge of the telemarketing calls they get at home.</u>
A surprising fact or statement	**EXAMPLE:** Nearly one in seven Americans has key clinical data missing from their medical files, according to a report in *The Journal of the American Medical Association* (JAMA). And in 44 percent of cases the absent information would have impacted a doctor's diagnosis, potentially putting patients' health at risk. <u>You can take a few simple steps to maintain accurate and accessible personal-health records and safeguard your well-being.</u> – Adapted from "Read This Before Your Next Doctor's Appointment," First Magazine

Types of Introduction	*(continued)*
A direct quotation	**EXAMPLE:** In 1961 a copy writer named Shirley Polykoff was working for the Foote, Cone & Belding advertising agency on the Clairol hair-dye account when she came up with the line: "If I've only one life to live, let me live it as a blond!" <u>In a single slogan she had summed up what might be described as the secular side of the Me Decade.</u> "If I've only one life to live, let me live it as _____!" (You have only to fill in the blank.) – Tom Wolfe, *"The Me Decade and the Third Great Awakening"*
A definition	**EXAMPLE:** Hope is belief that the impossible is possible. Hope is the future counted in the present. Hope is a light, a map, and a compass. <u>Hope gave me the will to fight and survive cancer.</u>
A contradiction or opposing view	**EXAMPLE:** Many wanna-be runners don't even try because they believe they don't have the right physique. Their legs are too short. Their stomach is too big. Their shoulders are too broad. Their body weight is too much. These people are wrong. The body is unimportant. The mind is everything. Running is not a physical sport. <u>It's mental.</u> – *"Mind Over Body,"* Running Fit Prevention Guide
A vivid description	**EXAMPLE:** Two gas stations. A car repair shop barely visible through the rusty open hoods of dismantled race cars. A man clad in overalls selling roasted peanuts from the back of his truck. These are a few sights at the unpretentious intersection that is the small town of Barberville in Northwest Volusia. <u>To some, the settlement along the corner of U.S. 17 and State Road 40 represents one of the area's last strongholds of unspoiled country life.</u> – Maria Herrera, *"Rural Residents Wary of Road Project"*
A general or historical background	**EXAMPLE:** In 1831, when Darwin was 22 years old, he secured a position as "gentleman companion" to Captain Robert Fitzroy of the HMS *Beagle*. The *Beagle* soon embarked on a 5-year surveying expedition along the coastline of South America and then around the world. <u>Darwin's voyage on the *Beagle* sowed the seeds for his theory of evolution.</u> In addition to his duties as companion to the captain, Darwin served as the expedition's official naturalist, whose task was to observe and collect geological and biological specimens. The *Beagle* sailed to South America and made many stops along its coast. There Darwin observed the plants and animals of the Tropics and was stunned by the greater diversity of species compared with that of Europe. Although he had boarded the *Beagle* convinced of the permanence of species, Darwin's experiences soon led him to doubt it. – Audesirk, Audesirk, and Byers. *Biology: Life on Earth*, 8th ed. p. 282

INTRODUCTIONS

Read the following four introductory paragraphs. Underline the thesis statement and identify the type of introduction used in each one. Discuss your answers with your class or in a small group of peers.

a. An interesting illustration or anecdote
b. A surprising statement or fact
c. A direct quotation
d. A definition

e. A contradiction or opposing view
f. A vivid description
g. General or historical background

.... **1.** Heat kills! In fact, excessive heat is the number one weather-related killer, causing more fatalities per year than floods, lightning, tornadoes, hurricanes, winter storms, and extreme cold, according to the National Weather Service's storm data from 1994 to 2003. Therefore, when you exercise in warm, humid temperatures, protect yourself by taking a few sensible safety measures.

.... **2.** To Frederick Douglass is credited the plea that, "the Negro be not judged by the heights to which he has risen, but by the depths from which he has climbed." Judged on that basis, the Negro woman embodies one of the modern miracles of the modern World.
– Mary McLeod Bethune, "A Century of Progress of Negro Women"

.... **3.** The roll of honor read at the 9/11 ceremonies was a tapestry of America, of native-born Americans of all ethnic origins and more recent immigrants. Of course, we know too well that some of the assassins and others plotting against America were immigrants who betrayed our ideas, so it is natural that many people feel we should now close the door altogether, beginning with immigrants from Muslim countries. Natural, and wrong. What is long overdue, however, is a sustained national dialogue on immigration.
– Mortimer B. Zuckerman, "Our Rainbow Underclass"

.... **4.** When we first saw Henry, we knew he had to be ours. He had only been recently rescued from a cruel breeder who supplied greyhounds to local race tracks. We were told that the breeder caged Henry in a metal crate with shredded newspaper for bedding for 18-22 hours each day. He fed Henry cheap 4-D meat for Greyhounds. The 'D' stands for dying, diseased, disabled and dead livestock. Henry had barely survived the E. coli poisoning from this feed. At one time, almost every detail of Henry's skeleton could be seen beneath his thin skin. The fact is that these kinds of abuses are more common than not. Greyhound racing should be outlawed.

Effective Conclusions

An **effective conclusion** fulfills the following purposes:

- It brings the essay to an end.
- It restates the essay's main idea and sums up the major points in the essay.

In longer essays, the conclusion may be a separate paragraph. In shorter essays, the conclusion may be a powerful sentence or two at the end of the last body paragraph. Just remember that a conclusion must stay on point, so don't introduce new information.

The following chart describes and illustrates several types of conclusions you can use to effectively and powerfully end your essay.

Types of Conclusions	
A question	**EXAMPLE:** Don't you want to experience the well-being that results from a healthful diet and regular exercise?
A quotation	**EXAMPLE:** Just as renowned coach of the Green Bay Packers Vince Lombardi said, "The difference between a successful person and others is not a lack of strength, not a lack of knowledge, but rather in a lack of will."
A call to action	**EXAMPLE:** This is not a time for indecision or hesitation. This is a time for commitment and action. Tell your federal, state, and local governments that you demand a coordinated response plan for natural disasters.
A suggestion	**EXAMPLE:** Your best friend is the one who will tell you a hard truth for your own good.
A warning about consequences	**EXAMPLE:** If instruments used for ear and body piercing are not properly cleaned and sterilized between clients, then you could contract HIV, hepatitis B, or hepatitis C.
A vivid image	**EXAMPLE:** And when this happens, when we allow freedom to ring, when we let it ring, when we let it ring from every village and every hamlet, from every state and every city, we will be able to speed up that day when all God's children, black men and white men, Jews and Gentiles, Protestants and Catholics, will be able to join hands and sing in the word of the Old Negro Spiritual – Free at last! Free at last! Thank God Almighty, we are free at last! –Martin Luther King, "I Have a Dream"
A summary	**EXAMPLE:** Therefore, it is especially important to wash your hands before, during, and after you prepare food, before you eat, after you use the bathroom, after handling animals or animal waste, when your hands are dirty, and more frequently when someone in your home is sick. –National Center for Infectious Diseases, "Wash Your Hands Often"

Practice 4

CONCLUSIONS

Read the following four conclusions. Identify the type of conclusion for each selection. Discuss your answers with your class or in a small group of peers.

a. A question **d.** A suggestion **f.** A vivid image
b. A quotation **e.** A warning about consequences **g.** A summary
c. A call to action

_____ **1.** Fellow citizens, we will meet violence with patient justice—assured of the rightness of our cause and confident of the victories to come.
 –President George W. Bush, "Address to a Joint Session of Congress and the American People, 2001."

...... **2.** The crew of the space shuttle Challenger honored us by the manner in which they lived their lives. We will never forget them, nor the last time we saw them, this morning, as they prepared for their journey and waved goodbye and "slipped the surly bonds of earth" to "touch the face of God."
—*President Ronald Reagan, Eulogy for the Challenger Astronauts, 1986.*

...... **3.** The measure of a student's achievement is not in the grade from a teacher, too often these days a symbol of high inflation and low value, but in the wisdom gained from learning. Daniel Pederson stated it best in *Newsweek*, March 3, 1997: "When *A* stands for average, do grades mean anything at all?"

...... **4.** Our life on earth has already reaped many benefits from past and current space exploration. The establishment of a human colony on the moon would further enhance the quality of life on this planet. Products designed for independent life on the moon will someday become part of everyday life on Earth, advancing research in robotics, communications, medicine, computer technologies, food and nutrition, clothing, environmental and architectural design, rocketry, fuel and energy, building materials, and agriculture. We should shoot for the moon!

REVIEW: EFFECTIVE TITLES, INTRODUCTIONS, AND CONCLUSIONS

Complete the chart by filling in the blanks with information from the chapter:

Types of Titles

- The Question Title
- The Descriptive Title
- ....
- The General-Specific Title

The Patterns of Organization Title:

....

- Description
- Narration
- Process
- Example/Illustration
- Classification
- Comparison/Contrast
- Definition
- Cause/Effect
- Persuasion

Types of Introductions

- An interesting illustration or anecdote
- A surprising fact or statement
- A direct quotation
- A definition
- A contradiction or opposing view
- ....
- ....

Types of Conclusions

- A question
- ....
- ....
- A suggestion
- A warning about consequences
- A vivid image
- A summary

mywritinglab
WANT A BETTER GRADE? For more practice with effective introductions, conclusions, and titles, go to **www.mywritinglab.com** > Writing an Essay > **Effective Titles, Introductions, and Conclusions.**

15

Using Patterns of Organization to Develop Essays

Patterns of organization help arrange, present, and develop ideas into an essay.

We use patterns of organization to clearly arrange and present thoughts and ideas as we engage in academic, business, and everyday life. Students who go to RateMyProfessor.com are looking for certain traits in and ratings about a teacher and may compare these qualities with those of another teacher. Factory owners must think about the effects of commonly used chemicals in the manufacturing process and train their employees on safety procedures. To make a particular dish or dessert, cooks must closely follow a recipe's steps and instructions and do those steps in order. Similarly, many writers use patterns of organization to develop their ideas into an essay.

What's the Point of Using Patterns of Organization to Develop Essays?

PHOTOGRAPHIC ORGANIZER: USING PATTERNS OF ORGANIZATION IN ESSAYS

Study the following series of pictures. First, answer the questions below each of the photographs to identify the major details that could be used in an essay about the event.

NARRATION: _A Chain of Events_   TOPIC: _My New York Experience_

| FIRST EVENT | SECOND EVENT | THIRD EVENT |

WRITING FROM LIFE

What happened?

What happened?

What happened?

What's the point of the narration?

Now that you have used a pattern of organization to brainstorm about a topic, think about how patterns of organization can help you write an essay. Answer the question:

What's the point of learning about using patterns of organization to write an essay?

My First Thoughts: A Prewriting Activity

PREWRITING

Set a time limit, such as five minutes, and jot down in your notebook your thoughts about using patterns of organization. In addition to the examples mentioned above, what are some other situations that require thinking about time sequences, comparisons, contrasts, definitions, or persuasive ideas?

Making a Point Using Patterns of Organization: One Student Writer's Response

THE WRITER'S JOURNAL

Read the following student journal entry that records the writer's thoughts about using patterns of organization to develop an essay.

Earlier in the semester, I learned about using patterns of organization to develop paragraphs, so I see how useful they will be during the writing of essays. Based on the timeline for "My New York Experience," I can see that an essay uses several paragraphs to discuss a topic. The graphic also shows that each paragraph discusses just one part of the topic. It also occurred to me that the topic is "New York" and the pattern of organization is time order (based on "experience"). So all the details in the essay have to be details of time, but I also think some description is also going to be needed. Patterns of organization can help me limit a topic and think up details of support. Patterns of organization can help me keep on topic and put my ideas in the order that makes the most sense.

Developing Your Point in a Descriptive Essay

The ability to describe people, places, or things accurately is a useful life skill.

For information on writing a descriptive paragraph, see pages 72–89.

In your personal life, you may need to file a police report or insurance claim about the damage, loss, or theft of your property. You must be able to describe the damaged, lost, or stolen goods.

In your college life, you will rely upon description in many content courses. For example, you may need to describe a natural environment for a science class or a piece of artwork for a humanities class.

In your working life, you may need to describe the physical specifications of office equipment.

To write a **descriptive essay**, a writer describes a person, place, or object based on its location or the way it is arranged in space. Spatial order describes an arrangement of details from top to bottom, from bottom to top, from right to left, from left to right, from near to far, from far to near, from inside out, or outside to inside. The writer also relies upon sensory details such as sight, sound, smell, taste, and touch to create vivid mental images so that the reader can see what is being described. Descriptive transition words signal that the details follow a logical order based on two elements:

1. How the person, place, or object is arranged in space.

2. The starting point from which the writer chooses to begin the description.

Transition Words Used to Signal Description

above	at the side	beneath	close to	here	nearby	there
across	at the top	beside	down	in	next to	under
adjacent	back	beyond	far away	inside	outside	underneath
around	behind	by	farther	left	right	within
at the bottom	below	center	front	middle		

A Descriptive Essay: One Student Writer's Response

Read the following descriptive essay written by student Allyson Melton for an English class. Read the essay a second time. Then complete the activities and answer the questions that follow.

The Brilliance of Nature

1   (1) Too often, the brilliance of nature goes unnoticed. (2) This became very apparent to me, early one morning, on my way to work. (3) As I merged with the flock of procrastinating people, late as usual, I sped along, aware of the neon yellow dashes on the road flashing by as I sped along. (4) The flock of us grudgingly slowed to a stop as we approached a red light. (5) While waiting impatiently for the signal to go green, I diverted my eyes from the glare of the traffic light. (6) The sights and sounds around me revealed a vision of color and movement.

2   (7) The view to my left filled my vision with color and movement. (8) The road was lined with trees, each one proudly standing tall. (9) Dressed in their brightly colored costumes of jade, olive, emerald, and lime, they stood against the heavens as a magnificent tribute to the earth. (10) Their brown trunks, solid and strong-willed, stood unwaveringly in the face of time. (11) A skirt of green grass encircled the weathered tree roots. (12) To my right, a gleaming shopping center towered above the people who milled around its base. (13) Shoppers constantly lined in and out of the mall doors; they reminded me of ants carrying grains of sand or tiny crumbs to and from their anthill. (14) The light gray sidewalk provided a path mostly for bicyclists, spinning their wheels in an effort to gain ground, and joggers, bobbing along with the iPod ear buds plugged in like drooping antennae.

3   (15) The view ahead wavered in a vapor of exhaust fumes and noise. (16) The road, packed with cars of all colors and shapes, stretched before me. (17) Everything from the small, bright red sports car to the gigantic, black Hummer had come to a stop on this stretch of asphalt. (18) I rolled my window down to feel the cool morning air only to be

greeted by honking horns and obnoxious music from nearby cars. (19) The bass from the music of the car beside me was so loud I could feel the boom, boom, boom move through my frame and land at the top of my head with an extra "boom" for emphasis. (20) Before quickly rolling my window up again, I caught a whiff of the sharp smell of exhaust fumes.

4   (21) The red light still burned brightly, so I ventured a quick look up at the sky and couldn't look away. (22) It contained every hue imaginable, moving from pink to purple, blue to gray, and orange to yellow. (23) The newly risen sun, so yellow it was nearly white, shimmered in the mist of the new day. (24) Golden sun rays sprayed a flock of birds with a splendid display of light and shadow. (25) Their wings had hypnotic powers in their rhythmic beatings. (26) Hundreds, even thousands formed a fluid ribbon of birds, winding through the topaz sky in a graceful stream, never fraying from its curve. (27) Though I couldn't see even one bird up close, I could imagine their feathers blowing in the cool morning air as they swept through the sky. (28) As I watched, the stream continued to speed across the sky without hesitation, as if they all knew exactly where they were going. (29) When I finally broke my gaze, I looked around again.

5   (30) The people in their cars around me were still staring fixatedly forward at that commanding red light while the glory of nature flew over their heads. (31) As the birds continued to flow across the heavens, the light switched to green. (32) As much as I wanted to linger and watch them, I had to move forward again.

READING AND EVALUATING THE ESSAY

Complete the activities below after you have read the essay a second time.

1. What kind of title does the writer use? ....

2. What type of introduction does the writer use? ....

....

3. Underline the thesis statement.

4. For each of the body paragraphs, underline the topic sentence. Circle the descriptive transition words. List two major details for each paragraph below.

Major Details (Paragraph 2): ....

....

Major Details (Paragraph 3): ....

....

Major Details (Paragraph 4): ....

....

5. What type of conclusion does the writer use? ....

6. What is the purpose of the essay? Explain your answer. ....

....

7. Who is the audience for the essay? Explain your answer. ....

....

8. What did you like best about the essay? Why? ....

....

....

9. What about the essay could be improved? ....

....

Writing Assignments for a Descriptive Essay

Plan and illustrate your essay with one or more photographs of your own choosing. Write caption(s) for the photograph(s) that reflect your point(s).

Considering Audience and Purpose

Assume you are a witness or victim of an ATM robbery, and authorities have asked you to write a description of the two thieves and the getaway car. Your description will be included in the official police report, will be used by a sketch artist to create a picture of the thieves and their car, and may be distributed to the media to alert the public.

Writing for Everyday Life

Most of us have a favorite spot or place to which we return or that we reminisce about with fondness. Describe your favorite place or the favorite spot of someone you know. Write an essay that describes the site's special qualities for the regional newspaper of this favorite location.

Writing for College Life

Assume you are writing an essay about popular culture for a sociology class. Describe a person or object that represents an aspect of pop culture: a film actor; the costume or instrument of a singing artist; a cartoon character.

Writing for Working Life

Assume you work for a travel agency, and your clients—parents with three children ranging in ages from 3 to 15—ask you for advice about where to go for a one-week vacation. The family has expressed an interest in going someplace that offers natural beauty and outdoor activities. Write a letter to the parents describing the destination you recommend for their vacation.

Additional Descriptive Topics

A scene that provokes strong emotions	A person of interest
A vandalized or dilapidated neighborhood	An exotic animal and its habitat
Ideal gifts for a loved one	The scene after violent weather

Developing Your Point in a Narrative Essay

Narration is a fundamental part of everyday life.

- In your personal life, you may wish to share an important moment or event you experienced with a friend or family member in a letter or e-mail.

- In your college life, you will study biographies and write essays about important figures in subjects such as history, science, and the arts. You will also study and narrate significant events that have occurred in various fields of study, such as wars in history or case studies in psychology.

- In your working life, you may need to narrate an individual or departmental accomplishment in a report, memo, or letter.

> For information on writing a narrative paragraph, see pages 90–105.

In a **narrative essay,** a writer recounts a series of events or actions that occurred during a specific period of time. The writer presents an event and then shows when each of the additional events occurred in relation to it. Thus, narrative details follow a logical order based on time or chronological order. The following transition words establish the flow of ideas or coherence of a narration essay by signaling when actions or events occurred and in what order.

Transition Words Used to Signal Narration

after	currently	first	next	second	ultimately
afterward	during	last	now	since	until
as	eventually	later	often	soon	when
before	finally	meanwhile	previously	then	while

A Narrative Essay: One Writer's Response

Read the following narrative essay. Read the essay a second time. Then complete the activities and answer the questions that follow.

The Meanest Fish

1   (1) The Gar is the ugliest of any fresh water fish—olive brown with black spots and a yellow-white belly. (2) These fish have a long crooked snout filled with very sharp teeth. (3) They also are the meanest of all fish, a fact which I discovered three days after my eleventh birthday during a fishing trip on the Tomoka River in East Central Florida.

2   (4) Like many rivers in Florida, the Tomoka is a narrow, sluggish, tea colored river that snakes its way through dense hammocks of palms, live oak, and palmettos. (5) Canoes are about the only mode of transportation that can make it through some of the long, almost impenetrable stretches of the river. (6) On weekends, we would launch from the dock at Sanchez Park and often paddle for hours, dropping a fishing line every now and then, and most of the time losing our bait to the catfish living along the banks. (7) This particular trip was a special

one. (8) I had just received a new fishing pole and was anxious to try it out. (9) My paddling was enthusiastic, but not very efficient because, whenever possible, I would pull my paddle out of the water to knock down the banana spider webs strung between the low branches of the overhanging trees. (10) I would tell my brother that the spider was going to fall on his head. (11) He would yell and start jumping around, and then Dad would yell at him to sit still and me to stop teasing him. (12) It was all great fun!

3   (13) Eventually, we pulled around a bend in the river to a favorite fishing hole, known to be home to some extra large catfish. (14) We decided to eat our baloney sandwiches and drink our root beer before it got too hot. (15) Of course, eager to try out my new fishing gear, I was soon threading a hunk of my baloney onto my hook. (16) Catfish will bite at just about anything, but baloney seems to be one of their favorite snacks.

4   (17) I dropped my hook in the water and was just getting ready to settle down when something hit the bait hard. (18) Suddenly, my pole was bent almost double. (19) Since we were in such shallow water, I only had about six feet of line out, and when I yanked back in surprise, a huge Gar fish popped out of the water, and into my brother's lap! (20) He started screaming at the large slimy fish, and his sandwich and root beer went sailing over his head and right into Dad's lap.

5   (21) My brother and I had sort of leapt in opposite directions so for a frozen moment the canoe was counterbalanced, but then, inevitably, time resumed, and the canoe tipped over. (22) Fortunately, the river was so shallow that our feet hit the mushy bottom, and before we knew what was happening, my Dad's strong hands dug us both up onto the bank. (23) As we spat out the water and baloney and caught our breath, Dad retrieved the canoe, and we managed to paddle back to the dock. (24) Soaked, covered in mud, and empty handed, we presented quite a sight for Mother when we finally showed up in the kitchen.

6   (25) It was a long while before I went fishing again. (26) My new pole had followed the Gar into some far corner of the river, and I had no desire to meet up again with the meanest of all fish.

Practice 3

READING AND EVALUATING THE ESSAY

Complete the activities below after you have read the essay a second time.

1. What kind of title does the writer use? _____

2. What type of introduction does the writer use? _____

_____

3. Underline the thesis statement.

4. For each of the body paragraphs, underline the topic sentence. Circle the narrative transition words. List two major details for each paragraph below.

Major Details (Paragraph 2): _____

_____

Major Details (Paragraph 3): _____

_____

Major Details (Paragraph 4): _____

_____

5. What type of conclusion does the writer use? _____

6. What is the purpose of the essay? Explain your answer. _____

_____

7. Who is the audience for the essay? Explain your answer. _____

_____

8. What did you like best about the essay? Why? _____

_____

_____

9. What about the essay could be improved? _____

_____

Writing Assignments for a Narrative Essay

Plan and illustrate your essay with one or more photographs of your own choosing. Write caption(s) for the photograph(s) that reflect your point(s).

Considering Audience and Purpose

Assume you have been asked to speak to a group of teenagers about peer influences on their development. You have decided to use a personal childhood experience to develop your ideas. Your purpose is to explain how one childhood experience with a peer influenced you.

Writing for Everyday Life

Most of us, like the writer of "The Meanest Fish," have a vivid memory from childhood that shows the strength of our family, the joy of being young and carefree, or a challenge we have overcome. What does a vivid memory from childhood reveal about you, your family, or someone you know? Recount a vivid memory in an essay that will be published in a newsletter for family members and friends who live far away.

Writing for College Life

Narrate an important event such as the terrorist attack on 9/11, the swearing in of the President of the United States, the launching of a space shuttle, the civil rights march on Washington and Dr. Martin Luther King, Jr.'s "I Have a Dream Speech," as though you had witnessed it. Write a report for your college history class about the event as you saw it unfold.

Writing for Working Life

Assume you are applying for a management job with a retail store such as Wal-Mart, Target, or J.C.Penney. What life and work experiences can you relate that show your ability to listen, solve problems, manage merchandise, and motivate others? Write an essay sharing an incident or series of events that show you are the best candidate for the job.

Additional Narrative Topics

A clash with authority	An ideal day or a horrible day
An important lesson learned	The story behind a celebrity's rise to fame
A life-changing experience	The time you met someone important to you

Developing Your Point in a Process Essay

The ability to clearly communicate the steps in a process is a basic skill for success in all areas of life.

- In your personal life, you may want to share advice with a friend or relative about how to reduce stress or how to handle a job interview.

- In your college life, many academic disciplines, such as biology, sociology, and psychology, rely on process. For example, you may be required to record the process you used in a science lab activity, or you may choose to write a research paper on the stages of grief for a psychology class.

- In your working life, you may need to write a marketing plan, an action plan, or a company procedure.

A **process essay** shows actions that can be repeated at any time, with similar results. Like narration, a process essay is organized by time order (also called chronological order). A writer uses the process pattern of organization for three reasons:

1. To give steps, directions, or procedures for completing a task.

2. To analyze or study the steps, cycles, or phases of a process.

3. To explain how to complete a task and to analyze the process.

The following transition words establish the flow of ideas or coherence of a process essay.

> For information on writing a process paragraph, see pages 106–121.

Transition Words Used to Signal a Process

after	during	later	previously	ultimately
afterward	eventually	meanwhile	second	until
as	finally	next	since	when
before	first	now	soon	while
currently	last	often	then	

A Process Essay: One Writer's Response

Read the following process essay. Read the essay a second time. Then complete the activities and answer the questions that follow.

How to Find Your Keys

1   (1) In order to find your keys, you must first understand the important role keys play in your life. (2) Fortunately, this important role becomes abundantly clear when you are standing in the hallway ready to dash out the door for work or school and you realize your keys are missing. (3) You cannot lock your door. (4) You cannot start your car. (5) You have nothing to jangle impatiently while waiting in line at Dunkin Donuts for coffee. (6) You are going to be late. (7) Keys are indeed important. (8) However, there is no need to panic, even though you may lose your job if you are late one more time or fail the midterm or not have time to stop at Dunkin Donuts.

(9) OK, perhaps a little panic is warranted. (10) The important thing to remember is that if you approach the search for your keys calmly and logically, none of these catastrophes need occur.

2   (11) The first step is to check your person. (12) Start with your hands. (13) You would not be the first person to scour the house or apartment for something you are already holding. (14) This is very similar to the "glasses perched on top of head" phenomenon. (15) Check your pockets. (16) Better yet, empty your pockets so you don't have to guess what all that stuff in your pockets actually is just by touch. (17) Check your coat pockets. (18) Now check your other coat's pockets even though they couldn't possibly be there because you hate that coat and you never wear it. (19) If you have a purse, see appendix A, "Major Excavations." (20) These procedures will establish that you are not, in fact, in physical contact with your keys.

3   (21) Next you will undertake the process of "retracing your steps" which is essentially a form of backward time travel. (22) You may have to travel back several hours so you must be patient. (23) Sometimes it helps if you actually walk backwards, undress, climb back into bed, etc. (24) But be careful! (25) All this backward motion requires a degree of physical coordination and you haven't had your coffee yet. (26) At some point, you will probably have to venture into the dirty clothes hamper. (27) No one said finding lost keys did not require courage and fortitude. (28) If you travel all the way back to the moment when you walked in the door the previous evening and have still not located your keys, you may have to adopt a more creative strategy. (29) But first you will have to travel forward in time to get back to the present. (30) I will wait.

4   (31) As a last resort, think creatively. (32) If you have pets, remember that they always know more than they let on and should always be suspected. (33) Carefully inspect pet bedding, food bowls, and under the sofa. (34) Even if you have caged birds or fish, check the seed cup and the little castle that bubbles in the aquarium. (35) You never know. (36) If all else fails, you can resort to the SDSM or Slow Desperate Spin Maneuver. (37) This is where you stand in the middle of your apartment and slowly spin around, trying to look on every surface simultaneously, hoping for a glimpse of your keys, sparkling like a gold nugget at the bottom of a mountain stream. (38) This of course never works, but sometimes the dizziness created by this move will jog your memory and you will remember you left your keys on the kitchen counter next to the empty peanut butter jar.

5   (39) As you can see, by following this careful and thoughtful process, you will never again be separated from your keys for very long. (40) And keys in hand, you will stride purposefully into a bright and meaningful future or at least until you get to the donut shop.

READING AND EVALUATING THE ESSAY

Complete the activities below after you have read the essay a second time.

1. What kind of title does the writer use? ....

2. What type of introduction does the writer use? ....

3. Underline the thesis statement.

4. For each of the body paragraphs, underline the topic sentence. Circle the process transition words. List two major details for each paragraph below.

Major Details (Paragraph 2): ....

Major Details (Paragraph 3): ....

Major Details (Paragraph 4): ....

5. What type of conclusion does the writer use? ....

6. What is the purpose of the essay? Explain your answer. ....

....

7. Who is the audience for the essay? Explain your answer. ....

....

8. What did you like best about the essay? Why? ....

....

9. What about the essay could be improved? ....

....

Writing Assignments for a Process Essay

Plan and illustrate your essay with one or more photographs of your own choosing. Write caption(s) for the photograph(s) that reflect your point(s).

Considering Audience and Purpose

Assume you are a student-worker in the admissions and registration office at your college. You have been asked to create a brochure for students that illustrates and explains the registration process from a student's point of view. Write several paragraphs that take students through the registration process. Consider creating a brochure based on what you write.

Writing for Everyday Life

At some point in our lives, all of us suffer the loss of a loved one or a valued object. Tell how you or someone you know coped with such a loss. Write a letter to a friend in which you share the steps you or someone you know took to overcome the grief of loss.

Writing for College Life

Assume you are enrolled in the college class Introduction to Psychology, and your professor has assigned a chapter about stress. Your professor wants to know what you already know about stress before you read the chapter. Write an essay that explains several steps one can take to reduce stress.

Writing for Working Life

Assume that you are on a committee at work that is looking into ways in which employees can better manage their time and increase productivity. What recommendations would you make for employees whose tasks include phone calling, e-mailing, writing reports, filing paperwork, and attending meetings? Interview a staff assistant (such as in the English, science, or some other department at your college) for timesaving tips on the job. Write a report in which you outline several timesaving steps. Insert the appropriate information into the following MLA citation format to document your source:

```
Last Name of Person Interviewed, First Name of Person Interviewed.
    Personal Interview. Day Month Year.
```

Additional Process Topics

How to win an argument

How to get a promotion or recommendation

How to develop a friendship

How to save money or shop smart

How to make a piece of art, such as a print, woodcut, or an etching

How to set up a program or piece of technology (such as a cell phone, e-mail, Web site, or blog)

Developing Your Point in an Illustration Essay

Illustration may be the pattern of organization that you will use most often.

- In your personal life, think about how you often rely on examples and illustrations to make your point, such as when you recommend a restaurant or movie to a friend.

- In your college life, illustrations and examples effectively clarify a main point in all areas of study. For example, for a history class, you may choose to explain the contributions Frederick Douglass made to the civil rights of African Americans by offering several examples or illustrations.

- In your working life, examples and illustrations help you prove that you or an employee under your supervision deserve a raise.

> For information on writing an example paragraph, see pages 122–139.

In the illustration essay, a writer offers a focused main idea about a particular topic and then presents a series of examples or illustrations to clarify or support the main idea. Example words signal that a writer is giving an instance of a general idea.

Transition Words Used to Signal Examples and Illustration

an illustration	for instance	once	to illustrate
for example	including	such as	typically

An Illustration Essay: One Student Writer's Response

Read the following example and illustration essay written by student Beth Zivistski for an English class. Read the essay a second time. Then complete the activities and answer the questions that follow.

Fads: POG-Mania

1   (1) In all areas of life, our society is constantly swept up in the latest craze, and with the rise of every new fad comes the depressing downfall of the former fad. (2) Fads make their way into the world as fast as they are shut out. (3) A fad arises out of a particular culture, becomes intensely popular for a brief time, and then loses popularity suddenly and dramatically. (4) Ironically, fad-mania blindly leads to the retirement of great ideas, such as the fabulous milk cap game now known as POGs.

2   (5) Milk cap games were an excellent example of a fad that arose out of a particular culture. (6) Milk cap games originated when milk and juice were sold in glass bottles rather than the current disposable containers. (7) This fad-game first got its name from a brand of a tropical fruit drink made up of passion fruit, orange, and guava juice called POG. (8) Kids collected the round wax coated cardboard disks that sealed the bottles and invented simple games that everyone

could play. (9) Nearly every household, rich or poor, had access to milk caps, which made the game very inclusive. (10) Children enjoyed this popular form of entertainment until the establishment of screw-on lids and disposable containers virtually put an end to milk caps and these engaging games.

3   (11) Most fads, such as milk games, began as a simple, fun idea. (12) For example, the standard rules for POG playing were simple. (13) Two or more players placed an equal number of POGs into a common stack. (14) The milk caps would be piled artwork side up on a level surface. (15) To determine who would go first, players flipped a POG or played Ro-Sham-Bo (Paper, Scissors, Rock). (16) The first player threw his or her "kini" or slammer, an object used to hit the stack of POGs. (17) Usually a slammer was bigger, thicker, and heavier than a POG, often made of plastic or different types of metal. (18) All of the milk caps that landed face down went to that player. (19) The milk caps left over were restacked for the next player's turn. (20) The players exchanged turns until every milk cap had been won, and the player with the most milk caps was the winner. (21) Like all fads, the POG craze started simply, in this instance, with children using the milk caps for inexpensive fun.

4   (22) POGs were also an illustration of the intense popularity to which a fad could rise. (23) As the fad grew in popularity, companies flooded the market with POG products. (24) In the early 1990s, a number of companies started their own series of game pieces to compete in the new craze. (25) For example, the company Tilt, Poison, and Kapz offered POGs decorated with skulls, crossbones, and eight balls. (26) Even fast food restaurants illustrated POG mania as they latched onto the new fad and included POGs in their kid's meals. (27) POGs were not just a source of entertainment through game play. (28) They became available in sets of original artwork, sports and team logos, or even pictures of the latest Saturday morning cartoons. (29) Purchasing POGs became an obsession. (30) For example, people began collecting POGs, and some felt the need to own every single POG in a series. (31) These factors made POGs collectable as well as tradable. (32) The popularity of POGs was also evident in its international following, as illustrated by the World Pog Federation (WPF), created by players who loved POGs so much that they wanted an official body to direct the craze. (33) The WPF created its own official brand that was printed with the POG logo on the back. (34) The front artwork carried a variety of designs including cartoons, POG history, and POG incentives.

5   (35) POGs also illustrated the criticism and blame most fads face for fostering undesirable consequences and behaviors. (36) For example, many criticized POGs for fostering overspending. (37) When so many companies offered such a wide range of POG series available for purchase, expenses for a POG devotee quickly mounted up. (38) Children used their allowances to buy POGs; adults spent exorbitant amounts of money ensuring they had complete sets of brand name POGs for sports teams, athletes, or other popular cultural icons. (39) Another example of the criticism against POGs was the belief that the game was a form of gambling. (40) People would play for keeps in the hopes of enlarging their POG holdings. (41) Oftentimes, players would lose their own POGs in the process; then they would have to purchase more. (42) Many critics opposed POGs as an illustration of the antisocial behaviors that a fad can generate. (43) For example, fights sometimes broke out over POGs. (44) This game, for some children, was much more than entertainment; therefore, if these children lost a certain favored POG, they would react as children often do with tears, insults or even fists. (45) POGs, and especially slammers, were often stolen. (46) In addition, many educators complained that POG playing served as a distraction to school work. (47) Eventually, these negative aspects led to the banning of POGs by many public schools in North America.

6   (48) Like all fads, POGs decreased suddenly and dramatically in popularity. (49) Today, instead of lining the shelves in major retail markets, POGs may possibly be found on eBay or in specialty game and card shops. (50) Like fads, POG playing rose out of its culture, began as a way to have fun, reached intense heights of popularity, garnered criticism, and then faded away as just another one of those crazy trends that swept across the nation and over international borders. (51) Even so, POG playing is still fondly remembered by those who still love them to this day. (52) POGs illustrate the irony of fad-mania: the short-lived devotion to a really good idea.

Practice 5

Complete the activities below after you have read the essay a second time.

1. What kind of title does the writer use? ....

2. What type of introduction does the writer use? ....

3. Underline the thesis statement.

4. For each of the body paragraphs, underline the topic sentence. Circle the example or illustration transition words. List two major details for each paragraph below.

Major Details (Paragraph 2): ....

....

Major Details (Paragraph 3): ....

....

Major Details (Paragraph 4): ....

Major Details (Paragraph 5): ....

....

5. What type of conclusion does the writer use? ....

6. What is the purpose of the essay? Explain your answer. ....

....

7. Who is the audience for the essay? Explain your answer. ....

....

8. What did you like best about the essay? Why? ....

....

....

....

9. What about the essay could be improved? ....

....

Writing Assignments for an Illustration Essay

Plan and illustrate your essay with one or more photographs of your own choosing. Write caption(s) for the photograph(s) that reflect your point(s).

Considering Audience and Purpose

Assume you serve as a member of the Parent-Student-Teacher Association (PSTA), and you have been asked to write a report to be submitted to the principal. The purpose of the report is to explain the improvements your group wants to be funded. Identify and illustrate the need for three improvements at the school.

Writing for Everyday Life

Think about the creativity and cleverness of the human mind as seen through various inventions. Which invention best represents human achievement in our generation? Write an essay for your local newspaper that illustrates the most helpful invention of our time.

Writing for College Life

Think about the importance of integrity, reliability, or candor in our culture. What three people in the news illustrate these concepts? Write an essay for a college course in ethics that gives three illustrations of people who epitomize integrity, reliability, or candor.

Writing for Working Life

Assume that you are a local businessperson and you have been asked to share with a youth group your thoughts on the value of an education. What examples or illustrations would you choose to convince students to make education a top priority? What knowledge or skills did you gain through your education that helped you succeed in your business? Write a speech to be given to the youth and their parents in which you illustrate the importance of an education.

Additional Illustration Topics

Lack of morality on television

The best or worst commercials

Annoying or dangerous driving behaviors

A healthful diet or an outlandish diet

Good gifts that don't cost much money

Acts of kindness

mywritinglab

WANT A BETTER GRADE?
For more practice using patterns of organization to develop essays, go to **www.mywritinglab.com** > Writing an Essay > **Using Patterns of Organization to Develop Essays.**

Developing Your Point in a Classification Essay

Classification allows you to order or group your thoughts based on traits of a category.

- In your personal life, you may want to warn a young person in your family or social group about types of peer pressure or dangerous behaviors to avoid.

- In your college life, you will use classification in the sciences to write about classes of species or habitats; in the humanities, to write about styles of artists, artistic movements, modes of architecture, literature, and branches of philosophies; in business and history classes, to write about different kinds of economic systems and governments.

- In your working life, you may need to write reports that identify types of markets for your products, job descriptions based on the nature of the position you need to fill, or a cover letter that describes the set of skills you bring to the workplace.

For information on writing a classification paragraph, see pages 140–157.

Writers use the **classification essay** to sort or divide ideas into smaller groups and then describe the common traits of each subgroup. The writer lists each subgroup, describes its characteristics, and offers examples that represent the group. Because groups and subgroups are listed, transitions that suggest additional categories are often used to ensure coherence.

Transitions Used to Signal Classification

another (group, kind, type)	first (group, categories, kind, type, order)
characteristics	second (group, class, kind, type, traits)

A Classification Essay: One Student Writer's Response

Read the following classification essay written by Josiah Cobb for a music appreciation class. Read the essay a second time. Then complete the activities and answer the questions that follow.

Types of Guitars

1   (1) When people think of guitars, they most likely think of an oldies band such as the Beatles and their guitars, or an iconic performer like B.B. King and his guitar "Lucille" or, more currently, Mark Tremonti and his signature Paul Reed Smith guitar. (2) However, most people are unaware of the differences among guitars. (3) Not all guitars are alike. (4) True, guitars share fundamental traits: they are stringed instruments with a neck, a flat back, incurving sides, and a flat peg disc with rear tuning pegs. (5) However, apart from these shared traits, a range of guitars from acoustic to electric have evolved that enable musicians to create an array of distinct sounds.

(6) Currently, four types of guitars allow musicians to produce a variety of sounds in today's music.

2   (7) The acoustic guitar is a favored instrument used in most types of current music. (8) Bands today rely on the bright sound of the acoustic guitar to fill in the gaps with the guitar's unique, deep, full sound. (9) The acoustic guitar is simply a hollow body that has a neck and a set of thick bronze strings which together produce a bigger sound than the other types of guitars. (10) Because most acoustic guitars are not amplified by an external device, their sound is not loud and often cannot compete with other instruments in a band or orchestra. (11) However, one of the secrets to a good sounding acoustic guitar is the pick-up, which detects the mechanical reverberations of the strings and acts as a microphone. (12) A pick-up is mounted on the body of the guitar close to the strings. (13) The Simon & Garfunkel folk song "Fifty-Ninth Street Bridge" offers an excellent example of the rhythmic, strumming sound created with the acoustic guitar.

3   (14) The classical or nylon guitar is a kind of acoustic guitar designed especially for finger picking, which is the art of plucking the string with the fingers instead of using a pick to strum over the strings. (15) The classical guitar has nylon strings instead of bronze strings, and the body of the classical guitar is larger than the other types of guitars. (16) This design produces a reverberation as if it were in a large room. (17) In addition, the neck of the guitar is broader than the ones on steel string guitars, allowing for more complex finger work. (18) Classical guitars do have acoustic pick-ups in them most of the time. (19) One of the most popular examples of the classical guitar's crisp, nimble tones can be heard in "Classical Gas" by Mason Williams.

4   (20) A third kind of guitar is the electric guitar. (21) The unique design of the electric guitar makes it a versatile instrument. (22) The body of the electric guitar is solid, small, and can be any shape. (23) Most electric guitars today have two pick-ups. (24) The modern day pick-ups are usually small rectangular pieces of plastic with six small magnets. (25) These pick-ups use the magnets to feel the vibrating string and then transfer the sound through an amplifier so the player can hear the pitch of the strings. (26) Many guitarists love the electric guitar because they can get any sound out of it they want. (27) For instance, by using the neck pick-up, the guitarist can get the really low end sound of a hardcore band, or by using the bridge pick-up, he or she can get the bright high end sound of ska music. (28) The electric guitar also lets the musician mimic the sounds of other types of guitars such as the acoustic, Dobro, or the classical. (29) One illustration of a well-known song performed on the electric guitar is U2's blazing, bone-rattling song "Vertigo."

▲ Acoustic guitar

▲ Electric guitar

▲ Dobro guitar

5 (30) A fourth type of guitar is the Dobro. (31) Though not many people know about the Dobro or think of it as a guitar, it is one of the hardest forms of guitar to learn. (32) The Dobro is an instrument that is very small and is placed on a table so the strings are parallel to the ground. (33) The player then takes a guitar pick and plucks the strings as if finger picking but with a pick. (34) In addition, instead of using fingers to produce certain pitches from the guitar, the player uses a slide. (35) A slide is usually either a small piece of wood with metal, or a glass tube into which a finger is inserted. (36) The Dobro uses an electric guitar pick-up, which gives it a country guitar sound. (37) A prime example of the Dobro twang can be heard in the classic country song "An Old Cowboy's Dream" by Don Edwards.

6 (38) Although guitars come in various shapes and styles and produce a wide range of sounds, each one has the same basic idea: a set of strings pulled to a certain tension to combine different pitches and create something that everyone enjoys—music.

Practice 6

READING AND EVALUATING THE ESSAY

Complete the activities below after you have read the essay a second time.

1. What kind of title does the writer use? ....

2. What type of introduction does the writer use? ....

3. Underline the thesis statement.

4. For each of the body paragraphs, underline the topic sentence. Circle the classification transition words. List two major details for each paragraph below.

Major Details (Paragraph 2): ....

....

....

....

Major Details (Paragraph 3): ....

....

....

....

Major Details (Paragraph 4): _____

_____

_____

Major Details (Paragraph 5): _____

_____

_____

_____

5. What type of conclusion does the writer use? _____

6. What is the purpose of the essay? Explain your answer. _____

_____

_____

7. Who is the audience for the essay? Explain your answer. _____

_____

_____

8. What did you like best about the essay? Why? _____

_____

_____

_____

9. What about the essay could be improved? _____

_____

_____

_____

Practice 6

Writing Assignments for a Classification Essay

Plan and illustrate your essay with one or more photographs of your own choosing. Write caption(s) for the photograph(s) that reflect your point(s).

Considering Audience and Purpose

Assume you are a member of Students Against Destructive Decisions (SADD). The original mission of this group focused on preventing drunk driving. However, SADD has expanded its role to include several types of destructive decisions such as underage drinking, other drug use, violence, depression, and suicide. Many people do not know about this expanded focus. To get the word out about SADD, your local chairperson has asked you to write an essay to accompany short video clips (acted out by other local members) that will be posted on YouTube.com. Your purpose is to describe the different types of destructive decisions for which SADD offers help.

Writing for Everyday Life

Many of us have an ideal in mind when we think about a person who fulfills a particular role in our lives: a mate, a boss, a teacher, a friend, and so on. What are the traits of any one of these ideals? Write a tribute to a boss, company, friend, teacher, or family member in which you describe the ideal traits of a boss, job, friend, mate, or child.

Writing for College Life

Assume that you are a student in a college music appreciation course, and your class is discussing how types of music reveal cultural values. What types of music best reflect American culture? Write an essay that identifies three or four types of American music. (Feel free to change the term "American" to reflect any culture of your choice.)

Writing for Working Life

Assume you are an employee at a grocery store that has been receiving a record number of complaints such as the following examples: empty shelves, rude or slow cashiers, sticky floors, no one to answer questions, and so on. Write a letter for the employee suggestion box in which you classify typical customer complaints and discuss types of employee attitudes that could reduce complaints.

Additional Classification Topics

Kinds of vacations people take

Types of technology that record or play music

The basic food groups in a balanced diet

The market for a particular product, celebrity, or experience: *Harry Potter* novels, Halle Berry, or white water rafting

Styles of personal expression: fashion, hobby, or interior design

Categories of movies, television shows, or books

Developing Your Point in a Comparison and Contrast Essay

Many ideas become clearer when you evaluate them in relation to one another.

- In your personal life, comparing and contrasting products before a purchase makes you a wise shopper.

- In your college life, you will be asked to compare and contrast leaders, governments, cultures, literature, writers, and philosophies in a wide range of courses such as history, humanities, English, science, and economics classes.

- In your working life, you may compare and contrast bids on a job, phone or Internet services for your office, or prospective employees during an interview process.

> For information on writing a comparison and contrast paragraph, see pages 158–173.

The **comparison and contrast essay** shows the similarities and differences between or among topics based on comparable points. The following transition words signal comparison and contrast.

Transition Words That Signal Comparison

alike	in a similar fashion	just as	resemble	similarly
as	in a similar way	just like	same	
as well as	in like manner	like	similar	
equally	in the same way	likewise	similarity	

Transition Words That Signal Contrast

although	conversely	differently	nevertheless
as opposed to	despite	even though	on the contrary
at the same time	difference	in contrast	on the one hand
but	different	in spite of	on the other hand
by contrast	different from	instead	still

A Comparison and Contrast Essay: One Student Writer's Response

Read the following student comparison and contrast essay written by student J. R. Hill for an English class. Read the essay a second time. Then complete the activities and answer the questions that follow.

Reading the Waves

1   (1) Along the edges of Florida's East coast lie miles and miles of inviting blue-green ocean water and alluring sun-bleached beaches to which thousands of bronzed surfers flock on any given day. (2) Each of these beaches varies in its sand composition, reef formations, and surfing conditions. (3) Although the East coast of Florida is made mainly of soft, sandy beaches and a hard ocean bottom, no beach along the Atlantic coast remains the same as the specific conditions change that cause

waves to form and break. (4) Two main surf spots, the Ponce Inlet Jetty and the Sun Glow Pier, only a few miles apart, represent the distinctly different surfing experiences available on Florida's East coast.

2   (5) The first difference between the Ponce Inlet Jetty and the Sun Glow Pier is the shape of the beaches. (6) Many expert surfers looking for a challenge choose the Ponce Inlet Jetty because of its rocky beach formation off which waves form. (7) The Inlet has a long stretch of rocks jutting up from the beach and reaching hundreds of feet out into the ocean, creating a cove. (8) In contrast, the Sun Glow Pier does not have an inlet off which waves can form. (9) Instead this coast stretches out as an unbroken, barrier-free contour of beach, ideal for beginner surfers.

3   (10) The floor of the ocean and thus the depth of the water just off the coast of the Ponce Inlet Jetty and the Sun Glow Pier also differ significantly. (11) On the one hand, because of the protective jetty at Ponce Inlet, the sand on the ocean floor there does not dramatically shift so the depth of the ocean floor near the jetty remains fairly consistent and uniform. (12) On the other hand, since Sun Glow Pier does not have a rock jetty, the sand there constantly shifts and redistributes the depth of the ocean floor near the coast. (13) The few Pier pilings add to the unevenness of the water's depth. (14) Sand gathers around the pilings and leaves holes where sand is swept away between pilings.

4   (15) Not only do the beaches, ocean floor, and water depth differ, but also the formation of waves at the two locations varies greatly. (16) At the Ponce Inlet Jetty, the waves form off the rock jetty and shape into a solid, organized wave. (17) When a wave comes to shore, the jetty pushes it into an A shape, also called an A-frame wave or peak. (18) The A-frame gains size in a matter of seconds to form a clean, structured, and powerful wave. (19) The wave then breaks on the fairly flat or uniform ocean bottom on top of two or three feet of water. (20) Unlike the well-formed, powerful waves of Ponce Inlet, the waves at Sun Glow have no

▼ *Sun Glow Pier* beach

solid objects (such as the rock jetty and the even ocean floor) off which to push. (21) Without solid objects and consistent water depth to help form it, the wave remains in its natural form. (22) In its natural form, the wave breaks in unorganized sections because the uneven depth of the ocean floor does not push the wave to break evenly. (23) The wave may look as if it is crumbling from the top to the bottom.

5   (24) The variations in the waves at these two beaches offer two very different surfing experiences. (25) The duration and flexibility of the surfer's ride differ at each location. (26) The consistent depth of water at the Ponce Inlet Jetty makes the wave break harder and faster, which enables the surfer to gain fast speeds. (27) At these fast speeds, the surfer is able to execute a great number of technical maneuvers. (28) After completing one maneuver, the surfer still has enough wave power to push through into the next maneuver. (29) Many surfers enjoy this long ride with clean conditions, making the Ponce Inlet Jetty a popular surf spot for expert surfers, as well as those who are learning to master more intricate moves. (30) In contrast, due to the uneven bottom and the unorganized, quickly crumbling waves, the waves at the Sun Glow Pier lose a great amount of power. (31) Unlike the longer ride at the Ponce Inlet Jetty, this weaker wave at the Sun Glow Pier leaves the surfer a short amount of time to complete maneuvers. (32) Generally, a surfer can only complete one or two maneuvers, and once a maneuver is completed, the surfer is left to fight for speed to continue on the wave to shore. (33) The wave at the Sun Glow Pier is great for the beginner surfer who needs to learn the basics and understand waves.

6   (34) The Ponce Inlet Jetty and the Sun Glow Pier, though only a few short miles apart, are two entirely different beaches. (35) These two spots are prime examples of the different surfing experiences available to surfers along Florida's East coast. (36) So before surfers grab their boards, they should carefully read their wave!

▼ *Ponce Inlet Jetty*

Practice 7

Complete the activities below after you have read the essay a second time.

1. What kind of title does the writer use? ....

2. What type of introduction does the writer use? ....

3. Underline the thesis statement.

4. For each of the body paragraphs, underline the topic sentence. Circle the comparison and contrast transition words. List two major details for each paragraph below.

Major Details (Paragraph 2): ....

....

....

Major Details (Paragraph 3): ....

....

....

Major Details (Paragraph 4): ....

....

....

Major Details (Paragraph 5): ....

....

....

5. What type of conclusion does the writer use? ....

....

6. What is the purpose of the essay? Explain your answer. ....

....

....

7. Who is the audience for the essay? Explain your answer. ....

....

....

8. What did you like best about the essay? Why? ....

....

....

9. What about the essay could be improved? ....

....

....

Writing Assignments for a Comparison and Contrast Essay

Plan and illustrate your essay with one or more photographs of your own choosing. Write caption(s) for the photograph(s) that reflect your point(s).

Considering Audience and Purpose

Assume you have just moved from a large city to a small town, and other members of your family or friends are considering making the same move. Write a letter that discusses the differences (or similarities) between living in a particular large city (such as Chicago, New York, or Atlanta) and living in a small town of your choice.

Writing for Everyday Life

Assume you have an account on a social networking Web site, such as Facebook or MySpace, and you compose and post your thoughts on a regular basis. Recently, you have noticed that many of us see a tremendous change in our circumstances, attitudes, or beliefs. This week you are writing about the specific ways that you or someone you know has changed over time or due to a specific event. Contrast what someone you know or you were like earlier in life to what that person or you are like currently.

Writing for College Life

Assume you have been working with two of your peers on a required group project and the two students differed greatly in their performance. What were the differences in their attitudes, work habits, and products? Use the goals stated on a course syllabus as the context your evaluation of their performances. Write the required report to your teacher in which you contrast your peers' performance.

Writing for Working Life

Assume you are a realtor, and a client of yours is moving into the area from across the country. Your client has asked you to identify a couple of homes in a specific price range. You have found two homes in which your client may be interested. How do the two homes compare in terms of location, price, square footage, and special features? Write a letter to your client that compares and contrasts the two homes.

Additional Comparison and Contrast Topics

Two pieces of music, art, or books

A scene before and after a terrible storm

Comparable products: Palm Pilots and other personal digital assistants

Communication habits of men and women

Dating customs of different cultures or generations

Disciplining children as opposed to punishing them

An original and a remade movie, or a book and a movie based on it

WANT A BETTER GRADE?
For more practice using patterns of organization to develop essays, go to **www.mywritinglab.com** > Writing an Essay > **Using Patterns of Organization to Develop Essays.**

Developing Your Point in a Definition Essay

You may encounter definitions most often in academic settings. However, the definition pattern of organization is helpful in all areas of life.

For information on writing a definition paragraph, see pages 174–189.

- In your personal life, knowing the definition of "whole grains" and being able to identify examples that fit the definition will protect you against false advertising and enable you to make healthful choices.

- In your college life, you will be expected to know the specialized meanings and examples of many terms in each content area.

- In your working life, you need to understand the terms of your company's insurance policy and examples of what is covered so you can make a claim when needed or offer reasonable coverage to your employees.

In the **definition essay,** the writer explains the meaning of a new, difficult, or special term or concept. A definition may include traits, comparisons, causes, or effects. In addition, a writer may include an explanation of what the term or concept is *not.* Examples are used to illustrate the various components or elements of the term being defined. The following key words and transition words signal the definition pattern of organization.

Key Words and Transition Words That Signal Definition

Key Words:	are	denotes	is	means
	connotes	indicates	is not	suggests
Transition Words:	also	in addition	one trait	
	another trait	in particular	specifically	
	for example	like	such as	

A Definition Essay: One Writer's Response

Read the following definition essay. Read the essay a second time. Then complete the activities and answer the questions that follow.

Just What Is a Blog?

1   (1) What exactly is a blog? (2) Is it a movie creature from outer space that eats clueless teenagers? (3) Is it a Scandinavian Desert? (4) Is it some special type of lumber? (5) Actually, the term blog is a shortening of the phrase "web log." (6) It is essentially an online journal, diary, or collection of articles, which is arranged in reverse chronological order, with the latest articles or "postings" appearing first. (7) "Bloggers" are those individuals or groups who create blogs, and the blogs they write cover a wide range of topics, including personal observations, politics, hobbies, and even official corporate news. (8) In the past few years, the "blogosphere," as the blog community is sometimes known, has exploded in popularity.

(9) A form of online communication, a blog serves as an important alternative source for news, opinion, and information outside the mainstream media.

2   (10) It is important to note that a blog is not a forum of hard news full of carefully verified facts. (11) Thus, a blog is not necessarily a reliable source of information, and any information gained from a blog should be checked against a known to be reliable source. (12) A blog is not private; information posted on a blog is communicated to the World Wide Web. (13) Nor does a blog necessarily offer a true portrait of a blogger. (14) Information on a blog could be erroneous, or even fictitious. (15) Understanding what a blog is not enables full and safe enjoyment of what a blog offers.

3   (16) Blogs appeal to people because of their spontaneity, informality, and passion; they reflect the fact that most of us gather and absorb information in an unstructured way. (17) First, blogs resemble informal conversations with friends, as opposed to the sanitized and filtered content of most types of media. (18) Most blogs are personal, as the following blog excerpt demonstrates: "It's funny how nothing changes between friends. (19) When Matt and Anson arrived, it was as if we had never missed a day. (20) Things just fell into place." (21) Second, blog postings are often spontaneous expressions, like views shared around the water coolers at work; some bloggers have even been fired for their off-the-cuff postings. (22) For example, Amy Nora Burch was fired for posting unflattering comments about her job at Harvard University in 2004. (23) "Most of it is total heat of the moment stuff," Burch said, according to an article published in The Harvard Crimson. (24) Of course not all spontaneous postings lead to such serious outcomes. (25) Third, blog postings are often fueled by controversies. (26) As blogs have grown in popularity and influence, political consultants, news services, and corporations have begun using them as tools to communicate and in some instances, manipulate. (27) When a controversial issue hits the blogs, it sometimes causes what is called a "blogstorm" or "blog swarm." (28) Such a blogstorm occurred the moment CBS national news anchor Dan Rather claimed proof that President George W. Bush received preferential treatment during his National Guard duty.

4   (29) Blogs are easy to set up and offer a rich array of options. (30) Many easy to use software packages, such as Moveable Type and Blogjet, are available for creating blogs, and the many hosting sites available for blogs such as Blogger and LiveJournal are also simple to use and free. (31) For example, the instructions to set up a blog at Blogger (www.blogger.com), read "Create a blog in three easy steps: create an account; name your blog; choose a template." (32) In addition to being easy to set up, blogs offer a rich communication environment. (33) Because blogs are web-based, many of them take advantage of the power of hyperlinking, which allows them to link their content to other sites or other blogs dealing with similar themes or more in-depth information. (34) "Blogrolls" are lists of other blogs linked to a particular article. (35) Feedback comment systems allow blog readers to respond to postings in a blog and create a discussion thread similar to those found on online discussion boards. (36) Some blogs also incorporate audio and video content into their postings. (37) Automation tools have even been developed that allow blogs to talk to each other and keep their content updated!

5   (38) Blogs are a good example of the unexpected effects of new technologies. (39) Because of blogs, friends and family members can enjoy instant and ongoing communication. (40) Pictures of a new baby can be instantly and simultaneously shared with family members who live in various parts of the country or world. (41) Because of blogs, people who would never meet in person are able to connect online. (42) Star Wars junkies, skateboarders, vegans, dog lovers—anyone with any special interest can develop a blog and instantly connect with others who share their passion. (43) Because of blogs, information is easier to access. (44) For example, blogs provided evacuees from hurricane Katrina with coveted information about the neighborhoods and homes they had to leave behind and to which they longed to return. (45) One such blogger, Brian Oberkirch (http://slidell. weblogswork.com), offered information about and photographs of Slidell, Louisiana. (46) Blogs like this one respond to the need of the moment and offer a surprising depth of vital information, as in this case, to homeowners, employers, and employees so they could make reasonable, informed decisions about their futures.

6   (47) If you've never seen a blog before, a good place to start is Google's Blog Search. (48) There you can search blogs by keywords such as "pets" or "movies." (49) And if you have some thoughts you would like to share with the world, you might want to give blogging a try!

Practice 8

READING AND EVALUATING THE ESSAY

Complete the activities below after you have read the essay a second time.

1. What kind of title does the writer use? ....

2. What type of introduction does the writer use? ....

3. Underline the thesis statement.

4. For each of the body paragraphs, underline the topic sentence. Circle the definition signal words. List two major details for each paragraph below.

Major Details (Paragraph 2): ....

....

Major Details (Paragraph 3): ....

....

Major Details (Paragraph 4): ....

....

Major Details (Paragraph 5): ....

....

5. What type of conclusion does the writer use? ....

6. What is the purpose of the essay? Explain your answer. ....

....

7. Who is the audience for the essay? Explain your answer. ....

....

8. What did you like best about the essay? Why? ....

....

9. What about the essay could be improved? ....

....

Writing Assignments for a Definition Essay

Plan and illustrate your essay with one or more photographs of your own choosing. Write caption(s) for the photograph(s) that reflect your point(s).

Considering Audience and Purpose

Assume you are in need of financial aid to continue your education, and you have found several available scholarships from a particular organization such as the following: The Hispanic Scholarship Fund, The United Negro Scholarship Fund, The Organization of Chinese Americans, or the Truman Scholarship. All of these scholarships require essays. Most of these essays ask candidates to define some aspect of themselves. Adapt one of the following topics to the organization of your choice, and write an essay to compete for a scholarship:

1. Define your heritage based on its significance.

2. Define yourself as a leader.

3. Define the kind of contribution you hope to make.

Writing for Everyday Life

Assume a couple in your family or the family of someone you know is going to celebrate their 50th anniversary and their union has served as a model of a strong and loving relationship. What would you say has made their partnership so successful? Write the text for a speech you will deliver at their anniversary celebration in which you define *partnership* and honor their life together.

Writing for College Life

Assume that in a college health class you have been studying about the connection between the mind and body and how important self-understanding is to a healthful lifestyle. How well do you know yourself? What brings you joy? What is your idea of a fulfilling, purposeful life? What is your mission? How do you want to be remembered? Write an essay that expresses a mission statement for your life in which you define your ideals and goals.

Writing for Working Life

Assume you are starting a small business, such as a restaurant, a fitness club, a toy store, or some kind of specialty shop. To receive financial backing from investors, you have been asked to write a mission statement for your business. Write an essay that defines your small business. What service or commodity are you selling? Who are your potential customers? Why is this service or commodity needed? Where is the best location for your business? How will your product or service be superior to other similar products or services?

Additional Definition Topics

A computer term such as a computer virus, spam, or search engine

A disorder such as insomnia, anorexia, Type 2 Diabetes, or Seasonal Affective Disorder

A natural phenomenon such as a sinkhole, tropical depression, fault line, or coral reef

Developing Your Point in a Cause and Effect Essay

Understanding the relationship between cause and effect is a vital critical thinking skill that enhances all areas of life.

- In your personal life, understanding the cause of a misunderstanding, or recognizing the effect of an over-the-counter or prescription drug can protect your relationships and your health.

- In your college life, you will be asked to analyze the causes and effects of wars, inventions, discoveries, natural disasters, economic recessions, or mental and physical diseases. An analysis of causes and effects deepens your understanding of information in every content area.

- In your working life, to ensure success you need to understand why a product sells, reasons for poor performance, or the effects of decisions on employee morale or the company's budget.

> For information on writing a cause and effect paragraph, see pages 190–205.

A writer uses the **cause and effect essay** to explore why something happened or what results came from an event. A cause explores the reason something happens, and an effect examines the result or outcome. The following transition words signal cause and effect.

Transitions That Signal Cause and Effect

accordingly	because of	due to	leads to	since	therefore
as a result	consequently	if…then	results in	so	thus

A Cause and Effect Essay: One Writer's Response

Read the following cause and effect essay from the National Institute on Alcohol Abuse and Alcoholism. Read the essay a second time. Then complete the activities and answer the questions that follow.

Alcoholism: Getting the Facts

1   (1) For most people who drink, alcohol is a pleasant accompaniment to social activities. (2) Moderate alcohol use—up to two drinks per day for men and one drink per day for women and older people—is not harmful for most adults. (3) (A standard drink is one 12-ounce bottle or can of either beer or wine cooler, one 5-ounce glass of wine, or 1.5 ounces of 80-proof distilled spirits.) (4) Nonetheless, a large number of people get into serious trouble because of their drinking. (5) Currently, nearly 17.6 million adult Americans abuse alcohol or are alcoholic. (6) Several million more adults engage in risky drinking that could lead to alcohol problems. (7) These patterns include binge drinking and heavy drinking on a regular basis. (8) In addition, 53 percent of men and women in the United States report that one or more of their close relatives has a drinking problem. (9) Due to the scope of this problem, it is important to understand the effects of alcoholism and alcohol abuse, as well as identify their causes.

2   (10) Alcoholism, also known as "alcohol dependence," is a disease with at least four recognizable effects or symptoms. (11) One impact of alcoholic dependence is a strong craving for alcohol. (12) An alcoholic feels a strong need, or compulsion, to drink. (13) Another impact is a loss of control: alcoholics cannot limit their drinking on any given occasion. (14) People who are not alcoholic sometimes do not understand why an alcoholic can't just "use a little willpower" to stop drinking. (15) However, alcoholism has little to do with willpower. (16) Alcoholics are in the grip of a powerful craving that can be as strong as the need for food or water. (17) Third, alcohol dependence eventually results in physical dependence: withdrawal symptoms, such as nausea, sweating, shakiness, and anxiety, occur when an alcoholic stops drinking. (18) Finally, a tolerance for alcohol develops. (19) Thus the need to drink greater amounts of alcohol in order to "get high" occurs.

3   (20) Alcohol abuse differs from alcoholism in that it does not result in an extremely strong craving for alcohol, loss of control over drinking, or physical dependence. (21) Alcohol abuse, a pattern of drinking, leads to one or more of the following four situations within a 12-month period. (22) Alcohol abuse often leads to failure to fulfill major work, school, or home responsibilities. (23) Drinking occurs in situations that are physically dangerous, such as while driving a car or operating machinery. (24) Alcohol-related legal problems are recurring, such as being arrested for driving under the influence of alcohol or for physically hurting someone while drunk. (25) Finally, drinking continues despite ongoing relationship problems that are caused or worsened by the drinking. (26) Although alcohol abuse is basically different from alcoholism, many effects of alcohol abuse are also experienced by alcoholics.

4   (27) The long-term consequences of alcohol misuse are serious —in many cases, life threatening. (28) Heavy drinking can increase the risk for certain cancers, especially those of the liver, esophagus, throat, and larynx (voice box). (29) Heavy drinking can also cause liver cirrhosis, immune system problems, brain damage, and harm to the fetus during pregnancy. (30) In addition, drinking increases the risk of death from automobile crashes as well as recreational and on-the-job injuries. (31) Furthermore, both homicides and suicides are more likely to be committed by persons who have been drinking. (32) In purely economic terms, alcohol-related problems cost society approximately $185 billion per year. (33) In human terms, the costs cannot be calculated.

5   (34) Many people wonder why some individuals can use alcohol without problems but others cannot. (35) Alcohol misuse occurs for several reasons. (36) One important reason has to do with genetics. (37) Scientists have found that having an alcoholic family member makes it more likely that if a person chooses to drink he or she too may develop alcoholism. (38) Genes, however, are not the whole story. (39) In fact, scientists now believe that certain factors in a person's environment influence whether a person with a genetic risk for alcoholism ever develops the disease. (40) A person's risk for developing alcoholism can increase based on the person's environment, including where and how he or she lives; family, friends, and culture; peer pressure; and even how easy it is to get alcohol.

6   (41) Those who choose to ignore these facts about alcoholism and alcohol abuse may be the very ones who will suffer the devastating effects associated with drinking-related problems.

—Adapted from "Getting the Facts," National Institute on Alcohol Abuse and Alcoholism (2001)

READING AND EVALUATING THE ESSAY

Complete the activities below after you have read the essay a second time.

1. What kind of title does the writer use? ....

2. What type of introduction does the writer use? ....

....

....

3. Underline the thesis statement.

4. For each of the body paragraphs, underline the topic sentence. Circle the cause and effect transition words. List two major details for each paragraph below.

Major Details (Paragraph 2): ....

....

Major Details (Paragraph 3): ....

....

Major Details (Paragraph 4): ....

....

Major Details (Paragraph 5): ....

5. What type of conclusion does the writer use? ....

6. What is the purpose of the essay? Explain your answer. ....

....

....

7. Who is the audience for the essay? Explain your answer. ....

....

....

8. What did you like best about the essay? Why? ....

....

....

9. What about the essay could be improved? ....

....

Writing Assignments for a Cause and Effect Essay

Plan and illustrate your essay with one or more photographs of your own choosing. Write caption(s) for the photograph(s) that reflect your point(s).

Considering Audience and Purpose

Assume you are a volunteer with an organization such as Meals on Wheels, Habitat for Humanity, or Scouts, or that you volunteer at a particular place such as a school, hospital, or animal shelter. You have been asked to give a speech to an audience of college students to raise awareness about volunteering. Write a speech that discusses the need for and benefits of volunteering.

Writing for Everyday Life

Many of us have rebelled against our parents (or another authority figure) or know someone who has. What are some of the things against which youth rebel? Why? Is most youthful rebellion harmless or are serious long-term effects more likely? Why? Write an encouraging letter to a young person who is in conflict with authority that explains some of the causes and possible effects of youthful rebellion.

Writing for College Life

Assume you are enrolled in a sociology class, discussing the ways in which technology has changed society during your lifetime or over the lifetime of your grandparents. What are some of the intended benefits or unexpected outcomes of having televisions, automobiles, dishwashers, digital recorders, cell phones, iPods, or other pieces of technology? Write an essay for this class explaining the effects of a specific piece of technology on modern culture.

Writing for Working Life

Assume your company has asked you to speak about the "elements of success" during an employee training day. Think of highly successful people such as Oprah Winfrey, Bill Gates, Rita Rossi Colwell, Michael Jordan, Hillary Rodham Clinton, Reverend Billy Graham, or Soraya. What motivates or drives people to such high levels of success? Write a speech to motivate a group of work colleagues by explaining the reasons for success.

Additional Cause and Effect Topics

Excessive mood swings or compulsive behavior

Low or high self-esteem

Benefits of a particular exercise: walking, jogging, so on

Benefits of humor

A natural disaster such as a hurricane, tornado, or tsunami

Benefits of team sports

Addiction to or withdrawal from a drug such as nicotine or caffeine

PEARSON
mywritinglab

WANT A BETTER GRADE?
For more practice using patterns of organization to develop essays, go to www.mywritinglab.com > Writing an Essay > Using Patterns of Organization to Develop Essays.

Developing Your Point in a Persuasive Essay

Persuasion is used in every aspect of life.

- In your personal life, you come across attempts to persuade you in magazine, radio, and television advertisements. As a parent, you may persuade your children to eat healthful foods and get lots of exercise. Or you may persuade your partner to go on a much needed vacation.

- In your college life, you will be asked to take stands on issues in all the areas you study. For example, in a social science class, you may want to argue for or against gun control or in a science class, you may take a stand for or against cloning.

- In your working life, you use persuasion when you try to convince a prospective employer that you are the best candidate for the job. Or you may need to write your own advertisement to get people to come to your store or restaurant.

For information on writing a persuasive paragraph, see pages 206–221.

In a **persuasive essay,** a writer takes a strong stand on a debatable issue and offers thoughtful, convincing reasons in its support. To create a credible argument, a writer uses facts and examples, offers expert and informed opinions, considers consequences, and answers the opposition. The following transitions signal persuasion.

Transition Words Used to Signal Persuasion

accordingly	even so	in conclusion	nonetheless	therefore
admittedly	finally	indeed	obviously	thus
although	first (second, third, etc.)	of course		to be sure
because	for	in fact	on the one hand	truly
but	furthermore	in summary	on the other hand	undoubtedly
certainly	granted	last	since	
consequently	hence	meanwhile	some believe	
despite	however	nevertheless	some may say	

A Persuasive Essay: One Writer's Response

Read the following persuasive essay. Read the essay a second time. Then complete the activities and answer the questions that follow.

Ban Cell Phones: Save Lives

1   (1) No one understands the dangers of using a cell phone while driving better than Rob and Patti Pena. (2) On November 3, 1999, their 2-year-old daughter Morgan Lee died as a result of injuries sustained in a car crash the previous day. (3) As she sat securely strapped into her car seat in the back seat of her mother's car, a driver who ran a stop sign while using his cellular phone broadsided their car. (4) The only legal penalty the driver faced was a $50 fine and two traffic tickets.

(5) Regrettably, the tragic loss of Morgan Lee is not an isolated case. (6) According to a study by the Harvard Center for Risk Analysis, researchers estimated that the use of cell phones by drivers caused approximately 2,600 deaths. (7) Cell phone use while driving should be banned.

2   (8) Of course, not everyone agrees that talking on a cell phone while driving should be outlawed. (9) In fact, many believe that this behavior is no more dangerous than the many other tasks drivers perform while driving. (10) Obviously, drivers constantly multitask as they eat, fiddle with the radio or air conditioner, light a cigarette, apply makeup, read a map, and converse with their passengers. (11) Obviously, common sense dictates that these tasks should be kept to a minimum. (12) Certainly, any activity that absorbs a driver's attention has the potential to adversely affect the driver's control of the vehicle and reaction to hazards and traffic signals. (13) However, to suggest that one set of careless behaviors excuses another reckless behavior defies common sense. (14) Common sense also suggests that the dangers posed by these distractions do not compare to the dangers posed by using a cell phone while driving.

3   (15) Human Factors experts study the relationship between human limitations and the design of technology. (16) These experts note that drivers face visual, auditory, mechanical, and cognitive distractions. (17) Using a cell phone while driving incorporates every one of these distractions. (18) Darla Burton offers an excellent example of how using a cell phone while driving combines all four.

4   (19) The cell phone in Darla's purse rings as she speeds down the Interstate. (20) Immediately, she becomes visually distracted as she takes her eyes off the road and leans across the front seat to grab her purse. (21) The insistent ringing serves as an auditory alarm that urges her to hurry her movements. (22) As she rummages for the phone in her purse and fumbles with the mechanics of opening and answering the flip phone, she swerves out of her lane. (23) A passing motorist blares his car's horn in warning; Darla jerks her car back into her own lane. (24) The caller is her boyfriend, and with an angry voice, he continues an argument that began days ago. (25) Darla, distracted cognitively as she argues with her boyfriend, becomes lost in the conversation and unaware of her bearings. (26) Suddenly, she notices that her exit is looming quickly. (27) Without thinking or looking in her rear view and side mirrors, she veers across three lanes to make the exit. (28) Luckily, she narrowly avoids sideswiping another vehicle.

(29) Darla's behavior is typical of many people who use a cell phone while driving.

5   (30) Those who oppose banning cell phone use while driving argue that hands-free cell phones reduce these risks, and they do, but not enough. (31) Hands-free cell phones may limit visual and mechanical distractions, but auditory and cognitive distractions are still issues of concern. (32) Some believe that these distractions are no different than the distraction of talking with a passenger in the car. (33) However, talking on a cell phone is significantly different than talking with a passenger in a car. (34) First, a passenger in a vehicle often contributes to the safety of the driving situation by providing an additional set of eyes and ears to warn against road hazards. (35) When a driving situation demands the focused attention of the driver, a passenger in the car helps control the flow of conversation so that the driver can safely attend to the task of driving. (36) In addition, most people are conditioned to immediately respond to a ringing phone. (37) This need to answer often overrides convenience or safety issues and drags attention away from the challenges of the road.

6   (38) The sheer number of cell phone users also adds to the seriousness of the problem. (39) There are currently 190 million cell phone users in this country alone. (40) A record 24 million new cell phone subscribers signed up between June 2004 and June 2005. (41) According to a 1995 *Prevention Magazine* survey, 85% of cell phone owners drive while using their cell phones. (42) If that trend has continued, then about 162 million drivers currently talk on their phones while driving, at least some of the time. (43) In addition, current in-car communication services allow users to check e-mail and calendars, surf the web, and even send faxes while driving. (44) The wireless industry plans to offer an even wider range of mobile options such as digital streaming, which have the potential to further distract drivers.

7   (45) Remember Morgan Lee Pena and the thousands of other possible victims of someone's need to stay plugged in. (46) Join the fight to ban cell phone use while driving. (47) Write to your politicians, and tell them to support cellular phone legislation. (48) Urge them to ban cell phone use while driving and to enact strong penalties against violators. (49) Write to your cellular provider and ask the company to support laws that restrict cellular phone use while driving. (50) Finally, if you take a cell phone with you in your car, set a good example; pull over and stop before you make or take a call. (51) Tell your friends and family to do the same for their safety and the safety of others. (52) Stay safe! (53) Save lives! (54) Don't talk; just drive!

Practice 10

READING AND EVALUATING THE ESSAY

Complete the activities below after you have read the essay a second time.

1. What kind of title does the writer use? _____

2. What type of introduction does the writer use? _____

3. Underline the thesis statement.

4. For each of the body paragraphs, underline the topic sentence. Circle the persuasion signal words. List two major details for each paragraph below.

Major Details (Paragraph 2): _____

_____

Major Details (Paragraph 3): _____

Major Details (Paragraph 4): _____

Major Details (Paragraph 5): _____

_____

Major Details (Paragraph 6): _____

_____

_____

5. What type of conclusion does the writer use? _____

6. What is the purpose of the essay? Explain your answer. _____

_____

_____

7. Who is the audience for the essay? Explain your answer. _____

_____

8. What did you like best about the essay? Why? _____

9. What about the essay could be improved? _____

Writing Assignments for a Persuasive Essay

Plan and illustrate your essay with one or more photographs of your own choosing. Write caption(s) for the photograph(s) that reflect your point(s).

Considering Audience and Purpose

Assume you are a reporter for your college's newspaper. Identify a problem that affects many people on your campus, such as poor lighting in the parking lot, inadequate parking, or poor food service. Write a column calling for administrative action to correct the problem. Your purpose is to offer compelling evidence that action must be taken.

Writing for Everyday Life

Think about the amount of graphic violence and sexual content on television shows and the numbers of hours people spend watching these images. Should sponsors such as Kellogg, Nike, McDonald's, and Wal-Mart support shows that contain graphic violent and sexual content? Write a letter to a company that sponsors a particularly graphic television show to persuade the company to withdraw its sponsorship.

Writing for College Life

Assume you are taking a sociology course, and you have been studying about the impact of clothes (or fashion) on human behavior. Your professor directs your attention to Northwest High School, where school uniforms will soon be required. What are some of the reasons administrators and parents might have for supporting school uniforms, and what are some of the reasons students may oppose them? Write a letter to the principal of the school taking a strong stand for or against school uniforms for students attending Northwest High School.

Writing for Working Life

Assume you are the manager of a retail store in a local mall, and one of your employees has consistently performed at a high level. Write a letter to your supervisor in which you recommend a promotion and raise for your employee.

Additional Persuasive Topics

Animal testing for cosmetic or medical research

Manned space flights

Abstinence-only sex education courses

Stricter gun laws

Surveillance cameras installed in all public places

Decriminalization of marijuana

Developing Your Point in a Layered-Plan Essay

Often, writers find that the most effective way to express their view about a particular topic is to layer several patterns of organization into one essay.

- In your personal life, you may find it necessary to write an apology for a misunderstanding with a family member or friend. In your letter, you may find it helpful to discuss the *types* of stresses you have been facing, the *effects* such stresses have had upon you, and the *reasons* you value your friend or family member.

- In your college life, you will combine patterns of organization as you study topics in greater depth. For example, in humanities you may choose to write about the *origin*, *types*, and *impact* of art or artifacts produced by a particular culture.

- In your working life, you may need to write a report that *defines* a problem, *compares* several solutions, and *recommends* a course of action.

In an **essay that layers patterns of organization**, a writer divides the topic into subsections based on a series of patterns of organization best suited for each paragraph that develops the main point. For example, "alcoholism," discussed in an earlier essay by using causes and effects, could also be discussed by layering several patterns of organization. As a disease, alcoholism has recognizable stages or cycles that could be discussed using process. In addition, several types of treatment are available and could be discussed using classification. Or perhaps sharing personal testimonies or case histories of recovering alcoholics in the form of narratives could convince someone to seek help. Many other topics also can be developed in greater depth by layering plans.

Transition words used within each paragraph signal the type of pattern of organization used to develop that particular paragraph. Therefore, draw from the lists of transitions given throughout this chapter for each of the specific patterns of organization as needed.

A Layered-Plan Essay: One Student Writer's Response

Study the following layered-plan essay written by student Doug Frazier. Read the essay a second time. Then complete the activities and answer the questions that follow.

The Games People Play

1   (1) Games have always been a part of human culture. (2) Archeologists have uncovered the use of board games as far back as 4000 B.C. in ancient Babylonia. (3) While board games apparently appeared as the first type of game, other forms such as card games and tiled games evolved as people began to understand, enjoy, and develop the concept of games. (4) The variety and enjoyment of games expanded as technology advanced through the millennia. (5) Most recently, over the past 30 years, the newest and perhaps most radical change to games has occurred with the invention of the computer video game. (6) The advent of computer video games enabled a significant jump in gaming evolution. (7) While video games share many of the same traits as traditional games, the distinct qualities of computer games intensify both the dangers and the pleasures of gaming.

2   (8) To appreciate the impact of video games on the gaming experience, a general understanding of a few types and features of traditional games is necessary. (9) Overall, traditional games often reflect three types of intense, real-life experiences: physical combat or skill, intellectual strategy, and chance. (10) The group of games based on physical skills is made up of a wide range of activities such as races, archery, and darts; the outcome of these games relies upon the physical abilities of the players. (11) Another group of games are based on strategy, such as chess, and rely upon the player's ability to make rational decisions. (12) Many games combine the first two types of games so that players need both physical skill and strategy to win such as in organized sports like soccer, baseball, and football. (13) The third type of game utilizes chance and often uses dice or some kind of random number selection that dictates the outcome; examples of these games include bingo and lotteries. (14) Often games of chance also combine with strategy, so that knowledge or skill helps determine the outcome. (15) For example, through a series of plays, Monopoly and poker combine chance and strategy to determine a winner.

3   (16) All of these traditional games share a few basic traits. (17) First, games usually offer an avatar or icon that represents the player; in Monopoly the original avatars were metal tokens based on objects found in households across America (the flat iron, purse, lantern, car, thimble, shoe, top hat, and the rocking horse); in sports the avatars are the team's name and mascot like the Eagle for the Philadelphia Eagles in the National Football League. (18) Traditional games, also, present an environment that challenges the players or allows the players to challenge each other, and traditional games keep track of the player's success or scores. (19) In addition, traditional games foster social interaction; part of the fun of playing is experiencing the game with someone else.

4   (20) A comparison of traditional games to video games finds many similarities. (21) Just like traditional games, video games offer avatars. (22) For example, in the video game King Kong based on director Peter Jackson's version of the classic story, players can choose the adventurer Jack Driscoll as the avatar, or choose Kong, thus playing the game through the eyes of the ape. (23) Both traditional and video games present environments in which challenges are posed by the game player and opponent; in addition, both traditional and video games keep track of a player's success or score and reward the players when they overcome challenges or challengers. (24) Moreover, video games actually combine physical skill, strategy, and chance. (25) Physical skill is needed to rapidly figure out and adapt to the immense amount of visual information provided on the video screen. (26) In addition, the player must make rational decisions based on this information and make moves in a logical sequence. (27) Thus video games, like many traditional games, require strategy. (28) Finally, many video games are programmed to allow apparently random events to occur, so they are similar to games of chance as well.

5 (29) Although traditional and video games are similar, they do indeed differ in drastic ways. (30) Traditional games are much more unpredictable than video games. (31) Traditional board and card games require other players to enrich the environment and to create the uncertainty which generates the fun. (32) Video games, on the other hand, are a form of artificial intelligence (A.I.) programmed into the computer. (33) While A.I. is impressive, it is ultimately limited and lacks the unpredictable flexibility of human thought; therefore, the outcomes of the challenges are ultimately much more predictable. (34) Traditional games and video games differ in the social experiences they offer. (35) A.I. fosters an antisocial experience. (36) Often, video players do not need other players. (37) Traditionally, games have been seen as such an enjoyable activity partly because of the time spent making and enjoying friends. (38) During this time, players learn how to win and lose with dignity and to respect the integrity of others. (39) In contrast, many video games absorb individual players in countless hours of isolated play. (40) The great majority of these games also demand that players engage in simulated antisocial acts of murder and mayhem. (41) For example, "Carmageddon" is described on the package as "The racing game for the chemically imbalanced." (42) The goal of this gory video game is to "waste contestants, pedestrians, and farmyard animals for points and credit." (43) Some critics of video games consider these differences from traditional games alarming and dangerous.

6 (44) Experts warn that violent video games can have a negative impact. (45) These types of video games may increase aggressive thoughts, feelings, and behaviors; arouse hostility; and decrease helping behaviors. (46) Because video game players must make active decisions to choose violent strategies to win, players may learn that violence is fun and rewarding. (47) Another negative effect may be that players become numbed or blunted emotionally to violence and come to accept violence as a normal part of life. (48) Because players view violence as inevitable, they may not develop the skills needed to make nonviolent choices when they are faced with real life challenges.

7   (49) The ways in which video games differ from traditional games may present some reasons for caution; still the distinctive nature of video games offers some positive pleasures. (50) A video game player often learns how to play the game through trial and error by playing. (51) So video games are fun to explore. (52) As the player explores the world of the video game, he or she must rethink choices and come up with strategies based on new information. (53) In addition, to achieve ultimate victory, a player must think about the short-term and long-term effects of each decision or move in the game. (54) Finally, many players enjoy figuring out the limits of the game. (55) The fun lies in figuring how the game's program works and if there are any flaws in the program. (56) Thus, video games make critical thinking enjoyable.

8   (57) Traditional and computer games share many traits. (58) Both require physical skill, chance, and strategy to win. (59) However, video games offer a different kind of gaming experience. (60) Video games are often violent and antisocial by nature, yet they make problem solving a fun activity. (61) Some critics consider video games far more dangerous than traditional games.

Practice 11

READING AND EVALUATING THE ESSAY

Complete the activities below after you have read the essay a second time.

1. What kind of title does the writer use? _____

2. What type of introduction does the writer use? _____

3. Underline the thesis statement.

4. For each of the body paragraphs, underline the topic sentence. Circle the layered-plan signal words. List two major details for each paragraph below.

Major Details (Paragraph 2): _____

_____

Major Details (Paragraph 3): _____

_____

Major Details (Paragraph 4): _____

_____

Major Details (Paragraph 5): _____

_____

Major Details (Paragraph 6): _____

Major Details (Paragraph 7): _____

_____

5. What type of conclusion does the writer use? _____

6. What is the purpose of the essay? Explain your answer._____

_____

7. Who is the audience for the essay? Explain your answer._____

_____

8. What did you like best about the essay? Why? _____

9. What about the essay could be improved? _____

Writing Assignments for a Layered-Plan Essay

Plan and illustrate your essay with one or more photographs of your own choosing. Write caption(s) for the photograph(s) that reflect your point(s).

Considering Audience and Purpose

Assume you are a dissatisfied customer with several complaint issues, and you are writing a formal complaint to the manager. Identify the types of complaints you have; discuss the causes of your dissatisfaction, and list the steps you expect the manager to take to rectify the situation.

Writing for Everyday Life

Technological advances are rapidly accelerating. How important is it to stay abreast of the new technologies? Why? What are the types of new technologies, such as podcasting or multimedia cell phones? Which ones are most accessible, easy to use, affordable, or important? Why? Write a consumer report for an online posting in which you analyze the importance of keeping up with technology.

Writing for College Life

Assume you are taking a college humanities course, and you have been studying the concept of cultural traditions. Many of us have favorite traditions or rituals that have been handed down to us by our families or cultures. How does a tradition or ritual reflect a particular family, culture, heritage, or value? Write an essay in which you analyze the significance of a particular ritual or tradition.

Writing for Working Life

Assume you work in an environment full of conflict, and you have learned effective conflict resolution skills. Identify some typical conflicts that occur on a particular job: Between a team supervisor and a team member at a car dealership? Between a waiter and a diner? Between colleagues at a walk-in health clinic? What causes these conflicts? What are the steps to effective conflict resolution? Write a report for a supervisor that documents a conflict, evaluates the causes of the conflict, and recommends steps to resolve the conflict.

Additional Layered-Plan Topics

Minimum wage	Inspiring or effective teachers
National identity cards	A popular public figure
A living will	Internet fraud

Review

Complete the chart by filling in the blanks with information from the chapter:

A descriptive essay describes a person, place, or object based on its location or the way it is arranged in .... ; relies upon .... details such as sight, sound, smell, taste, and touch to create vivid mental images so that the reader can see what is being described.

A narrative essay recounts a series of .... or actions that occur during a specific period of ....

A process essay shows actions in time order (also called chronological order) that can be repeated at any time, with similar results for three reasons:

1. To give steps, ..., or procedures for completing a task.

2. To analyze or study the steps, ..., or phases of a process.

3. To explain how to complete a task and to analyze the process.

An illustration essay offers a focused main idea about a particular topic and then presents a series of .... or .... to clarify or support the main idea.

A classification essay sorts or divides ideas into smaller groups and then describes the common .... of each subgroup. The writer lists each ...., describes its characteristics, and offers examples that represent the group. Because groups and subgroups are listed, transitions that suggest additional categories are often used to ensure coherence.

A comparison and contrast essay shows the .... and .... between or among two topics based on comparable points.

A definition essay explains the meaning of a new, difficult, or special .... or concept. A definition may include traits, comparisons, causes, or effects. In addition, a writer may include an explanation of what the term or concept is .... Examples are used to illustrate the various components or elements of the term being defined.

A cause and effect essay discusses why something happened or what results came from an event. A cause explores the .... something happens, and an effect examines the .... or outcome.

A persuasive essay takes a strong stand on a debatable issue and offers thoughtful, convincing reasons in its support. To create a credible argument, a writer uses .... and ...., offers expert and informed ...., considers consequences, and answers the ....

A layered-plan essay divides the topic into subsections based on a .... of .... of organization best suited for each paragraph that develops the main point.

16

Subjects, Verbs, and Simple Sentences

A simple sentence, also called an *independent clause*, includes a subject and a verb and expresses a complete thought.

Communicating about a real-life situation helps us to understand the purpose of subjects, verbs, and simple sentences. The photograph on the facing page illustrates one immediate effect of strenuous exercise. Read the statements given in Practice 1 about Venus Williams, and answer the question "What's the point of subjects, verbs, and simple sentences?"

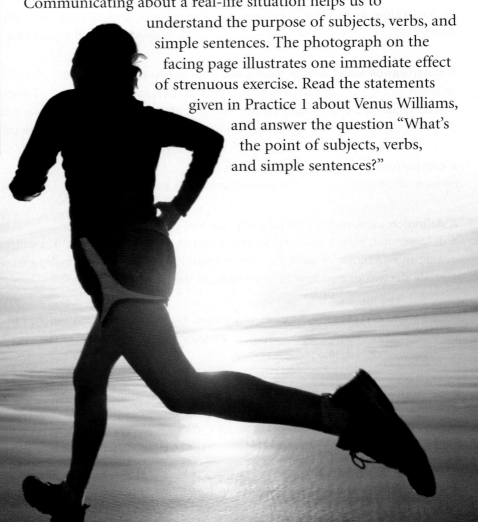

What's the Point of Subjects, Verbs, and Simple Sentences?

PHOTOGRAPHIC ORGANIZER: SUBJECTS, VERBS, AND SIMPLE SENTENCES

Read the following set of statements. Circle the one that makes the most sense. Discuss why the statement you chose makes sense and why the other two do not.

Swigs a bottle of water in one long gulp.

Venus Williams, preparing for the French Open.

Venus Williams, preparing for the French Open, swigs a bottle of water in one long gulp.

What's the point of subjects, verbs, and simple sentences?

Understanding the Point of Subjects, Verbs, and Simple Sentences: One Student Writer's Response

The following paragraph offers one writer's reaction to the statements about Danielle and the importance of subjects, verbs, and simple sentences.

> The first statement "swigs a bottle of water in one long gulp" doesn't make any sense by itself. Who's doing this? "Venus Williams, preparing for the French Open" doesn't make any sense by itself either. I need more information! The ideas do make sense when they are put together. Venus Williams takes a drink because she is preparing for the French Open. It's hard to figure out what someone is saying when a subject or a verb is missing. I think both must be needed to say something.

Applying the Point: Subjects, Verbs, and Simple Sentences

A subject and a verb unite to state a focused and complete thought in a sentence. You already have a great deal of experience using subjects, verbs, and simple sentences. As we think silently, we use subjects and verbs to frame most of our thoughts. Most often, we converse with each other by using subjects and verbs, and much of what we read in newspapers, magazines, and books and on the Internet is expressed by using subjects and verbs.

Subjects

A **subject** is the person, place, object, or topic about which a writer expresses a focused thought or makes an assertion. To identify a subject, ask: Who or what did this? Alternatively, ask: Who or what is this?

Types of Subjects

A subject is expressed in a variety of ways based on the focus of the writer's thought or point. Three common types of subjects include the **simple subject**, the **action/being subject**, and the **compound subject**.

Simple Subjects: Three Types

- **Simple Subject, Type 1:** A single person, place, or topic is the focus of thought.

SUBJECT
↓

Wilma Mankiller served as the first female chief of

the Cherokee Nation from 1985 to 1995.

- **Simple Subject, Type 2:** A group of words expresses the focus of thought.

SUBJECT

What the government knows about the assassination of President Kennedy is still a matter of debate.

- **Simple Subject, Type 3:** A suggestion, command, or order is the focus of thought.

Make a difference by voting.

"YOU" IS UNDERSTOOD, BUT NOT STATED, AS THE SUBJECT OF THE SENTENCE, WHICH IS A COMMAND.

Action/Being Subject: Two Types

- **Action/Being Subject, Type 1:** An action word ending with *-ing* is the point of a focused thought.

Laughing reduces stress.

ACTION SUBJECT

- **Action/Being Subject, Type 2:** A state of being word ending with *-ing* is the point of a focused thought.

BEING SUBJECT

For many Mexican immigrants, **living** in the United States during the 21st century increases economic opportunities.

Compound Subject

- **Compound Subject:** Two or more people, places, objects, or topics are the subjects of a focused thought.

COMPOUND SUBJECTS

Florida, **Texas**, **and California** lead the national growth of online banking.

COMPOUND SUBJECTS ARE OFTEN JOINED BY THE COORDINATING CONJUNCTION "AND."

Practice 2

SUBJECTS

Underline the <u>subject</u> once in each of the following sentences. Then, identify each subject by its type, writing *simple, compound,* or *action/being* in the blanks. (*Hint:* Compound subjects can combine action/being subjects.) Share and discuss your responses in a small group or with your class.

.... **1.** Nurses use their training to perform five basic tasks.

.... **2.** Assessing the patient and aiding in the diagnosis of the illness are two tasks of nurses.

.... **3.** The remaining three tasks include participating in the planning of a patient's care, carrying out the plan, and evaluating the effectiveness of the treatment.

.... **4.** What nurses observe in the daily care of their patients affects the treatment plan and the effectiveness of the treatment.

.... **5.** Nursing offers flexible work schedules in 4, 8, 10, or 12 hour shifts.

.... **6.** Home care, private practice, hospitals, clinics, and hospices are just a few areas of practice for nurses.

.... **7.** Consider entering the rewarding profession of nursing.

....

8. Write a sentence using a simple subject. Suggested topic: An ideal job.

....

Verbs

A **verb** makes an assertion about a subject. A verb states an occurrence (*occur, happen*), a state of being (*is, seems*), or an action (*run, talk*) of the subject. Various verb forms express different kinds of information about the subject of a sentence. Three basic types of verbs include **linking verbs, action verbs,** and **helping verbs.**

Linking Verbs

A **linking verb** connects the subject to a word that renames, describes, or defines the subject. Linking verbs often describe a state of being. The following chart lists common linking verbs and a few examples of their uses in sentences.

Commonly Used Linking Verbs

- *am, is, are, was, were, being, been...*

SUBJECT   LINKING VERB

The ice cream is cold and sweet.

- *appear, become, look, seem, turn*

SUBJECT   LINKING VERB

The cheese turned moldy.

- *feel, smell, sound, taste*

SUBJECT   LINKING VERB

The burrito tasted spicy.

Practice 3

LINKING VERBS

Fill in each blank with a linking verb that best completes the meaning of the sentence. Discuss your responses in a small group or with your class.

1. With an excess of water or mud on normally dry land, a flood _____ a serious danger.

2. Flash floods _____ the result of large volumes of rainfall within a short time.

3. Flooding _____ the most common of all natural disasters.

4. A tsunami flood _____ like a dangerous, sky-high wall of water carrying rocks, mud, and other debris.

5. Write a sentence using a linking verb. Suggested topic: Flood damage to a home.

_____

_____

_____

_____

Action Verbs

An **action verb** shows the behavior of the subject.

SUBJECT   ACTION VERB

Justin and Mia prepared their house for the

upcoming storm.

SUBJECT   ACTION VERB

Before the flood, Justin and Mia raised the furnace,
water heater, washer, dryer, and furniture off the
floors in their home.

Practice 4

ACTION VERBS

Underline the action verb twice in each of the following sentences.

1. Justin installed check valves in sewer traps to prevent floodwater from backing up into the drains of their home.

2. To stop floodwater from entering their home, Justin and Mia constructed barriers of sandbags around all of their doors.

3. They also sealed the walls in their basement with a waterproofing compound to avoid seepage.

4. Just as importantly, Justin and Mia bought flood insurance.

5. Write a sentence using an action verb. Suggested topic: A severe storm.

Helping Verbs

A **helping verb** is used with a main verb to create a verb phrase. Helping verbs are also used to form questions. The verbs *be, do,* and *have* can be used alone or as helping verbs.

VERB PHRASE

Jermaine has prepared a supply kit in case of an emergency.

HELPING VERB   MAIN VERB

VERB PHRASE

Has Jermaine prepared a supply kit?

HELPING VERB   MAIN VERB

VERB PHRASE

Jermaine has not bought all the supplies.

HELPING VERB   MAIN VERB

THE WORD "NOT" IS AN ADVERB THAT NEGATES THE VERB, SO "NOT" IS NEVER PART OF THE VERB PHRASE.

Common Helping Verbs						
be being been am are is was were	do does did	have had has	may might must	should could would	can will shall	have to have got to ought to supposed to used to

HELPING VERBS

Underline the <u>verb phrase</u> twice in each of the following sentences.

1. Most Americans have not prepared for natural disasters.

2. We must increase people's awareness of the possibility of disasters and the need for preparation.

3. Can we increase parents' disaster awareness by teaching their children about disasters?

4. In Japan, children are learning about the dangers of earthquakes, volcanoes, and hurricanes as part of the school curriculum.

5. Write a sentence using a helping verb. Suggested topic: An idea for increasing disaster awareness.

_____

_____

_____

_____

Practice 5

For more information on correcting fragments, see pages 402–421.

The Simple Sentence

A **simple sentence** is a group of related words that includes a subject and a verb and expresses a complete thought. A simple sentence is also known as an **independent clause**. An idea that is missing a subject or verb is a fragment or incomplete thought.

Distinguishing between a Fragment and the Simple Sentence

Fragment with Missing Subject:

VERB ⟶ **Uses** her status as a superstar to bring media attention to refugees around the world.

Fragment with Missing Verb:

SUBJECT ⟶ **Angelina Jolie** using her status as a superstar to bring media attention to refugees around the world.

Simple Sentence:

VERB

SUBJECT ⟶ **Angelina Jolie** **uses** her status as a superstar to bring media attention to refugees around the world.

Practice 6

SIMPLE SENTENCES

Create a simple sentence from each of the following fragments. From the box below, fill in the blank with a subject or verb that best completes each thought.

Verbs	Subjects
makes	Volunteers
is	Volunteering
provide	

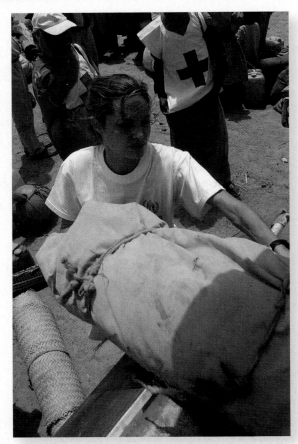

▲ UNHCR Goodwill Ambassador Angelina Jolie

1. Volunteering .... the act of serving others without reward.

2. Each year countless ordinary Americans .... assistance to others in their community through volunteer work.

3. .... improve their job skills, build their resumes, and enhance their experience through their efforts.

4. The Internet _____ matching volunteers with appropriate organizations a simple matter.

5. In short, _____ results in benefits for both volunteers and organizations, as well as the individuals who are helped.

Adapted from "Calculating the Economic Impact of Volunteers," Points of Light Foundation & Volunteer Center National Network

Locating Subjects and Verbs to Identify Complete Thoughts

To avoid fragments and to state ideas as complete thoughts, proofread to identify the subjects and verbs of each sentence. Identifying prepositional phrases as you proofread will help you locate the subject of the sentence.

Understand the Prepositional Phrase

A **preposition** is a word that has a noun or pronoun as its object and states a relationship between its object and another word. A prepositional phrase begins with a preposition and ends with the object of the preposition.

PREPOSITIONAL PHRASE

PREPOSITION ──▶ as the first female chief ◀── OBJECT OF THE PREPOSITION

The following chart lists a few common prepositions and examples of their objects.

Common Prepositions with Possible Objects			
Preposition	**Object**	**Preposition**	**Object**
about	the house	for	Texas
along	the street	from	the past
after	the movie	in	my wallet
as	the parent	of	the boys
below	the surface	on	the chair
by	evening	to	the college
during	the storm	with	patience

Find the Prepositional Phrases

The object of the preposition can never be the subject or the verb of a sentence. Since subjects and verbs are often surrounded by prepositional phrases, you need to identify these phrases. Identifying prepositional phrases keeps you from confusing them with the subject of the sentence. And often, once these phrases are identified, the subject and the verb—or lack of either—becomes easier to recognize.

IDENTIFYING PREPOSITIONAL PHRASES

Place parentheses around all (prepositional phrases) in the following simple sentences.

1. Wilma Pearl Mankiller served from 1985 through 1995 as the first female Chief of the Cherokee Nation.

2. Former Chief Mankiller lives in Oklahoma on the land allotted to her paternal grandfather, John Mankiller, in 1907.

3. Her family name "Mankiller" appears to be an old military title for the person in charge of protecting the village.

4. As Principal Chief of the Cherokee people, she represented the second largest tribe in the United States.

5. As part of the government's Indian relocation policy, Mankiller, along with her family, was forcibly removed from her father's land in Oklahoma to California during her early childhood.

The FIL Process

To identify subjects and verbs, follow these three simple steps:

1. **F**ind Prepositional Phrases: Place parentheses around (prepositional phrases).

2. **I**dentify the Verb: Underline the <u>verb</u> (action or linking) twice.

3. **L**ocate the Subject: Ask: Who or what did this or who or what is this? The answer is the subject. Underline the <u>subject</u> once.

SUBJECT   PREPOSITIONAL PHRASE   VERB

Applicants (for firefighting jobs) generally must pass a written exam (along with tests) (of strength, physical stamina, coordination, and agility).

PREPOSITIONAL PHRASES

IDENTIFYING SUBJECTS AND VERBS

Identify the subjects and verbs in the following simple sentences. Annotate each sentence: Place parentheses around (prepositional phrases), underline the <u>verb</u> twice, and underline the <u>subject</u> once.

1. Firefighters work in dangerous conditions and for long, irregular hours.

2. They often are on duty for 24 hours and work overtime.

3. Even so, competition is keen for firefighting jobs.

4. During duty hours, a firefighting crew goes to fires or other emergencies and provides victims with medical attention.

5. Not surprisingly, after being hired, all firefighters receive considerable training.

Adapted from U.S. Department of Labor, Bureau of Labor Statistics, *Occupational Outlook Handbook, 2008–09 Edition,* "Fire Fighting Occupations."

SUBJECTS, VERBS, AND SIMPLE SENTENCES REVIEW

Read the following paragraph written by a student. Annotate each sentence by underlining <u>subjects</u> once, underlining <u>verbs</u> twice, and placing parentheses around (prepositional phrases). *Hint*: Some sentences use the understood subject *you*. Then write three simple sentences of your own.

(1) Can you improve your job prospects for the future? (2) Sure, you can! (3) Volunteer work is one good way of getting useful experience. (4) Your college may offer advice through its career services. (5) In every job, you can impress your supervisor by your hard work and can gain glowing references for future jobs. (6) Bosses, teachers, and counselors all could be sources of references in the future. (7) Working hard at your job will help you with your job skills. (8) Research your interests through books, on the Internet, and by talking to people. (9) At all times, keep yourself open to different possibilities. (10) It is not always easy! (11) So avoiding discouragement and staying positive are both important! (12) We do not know now about our future. (13) The job of your dreams, with some effort on your part, will become clear to you.

Write three simple sentences. Suggested topic: The ideal job.

1. ....

....

2. ....

....

3. ....

Writing Assignments

Writing for Everyday Life

Read the following thank you note for a surprise birthday party. In each sentence, underline the <u>subject</u> once, underline the <u>verb</u> twice, and place parentheses around the (prepositional phrase). Use your own paper.

Dear Dave and Jennifer:

Please accept my thanks for such a wonderful surprise birthday party. I really was surprised. I was able to visit with so many people. I haven't seen most of them in a long time! Everyone loved the spicy food and cold drinks. The theme of "Mexican Nights" was perfect. Thanks, too, for the great gifts. Bob, along with the children, also sends you a big thank you. We owe you one!

Thanks, again,

Beverly

Writing for College Life

Read the following paragraph written for a psychology class. In each sentence, underline the <u>subject</u> once, underline the <u>verb</u> twice, and place parentheses around the (prepositional phrase). Use your own paper.

Natural disasters, such as tsunamis and hurricanes, are stressors. These stressors can affect the mental well-being of victims. Survivors of a disaster often deal with shock, fear, grief, anger, resentment, guilt, shame, helplessness, and hopelessness. They may feel emotionally numb, lose interest in daily activities, have trouble concentrating, and experience memory loss. In addition, physical symptoms such as tension, fatigue, sleeplessness, and bodily aches or pain are common. Victims may also suffer with nightmares or images from the disaster. These reactions are normal and expected.

Writing for Working Life

Read the following email exchanged between professionals at a bank. Identify subjects, verbs, and prepositional phrases. Insert missing subjects or verbs as needed. *Hint:* Some sentences use the understood subject *you.* Use your own paper.

> TO: Dwayne <Dwayne@ITsolutions.com>
> FROM: Kendis Moore Kendis@ITsolutions.com
> SUBJECT: Promotion
>
> Dear Dwayne,
> Please accept my congratulations for your promotion to Manager of Information Systems. You and your team will handle activities like installation and upgrading of hardware and software. In addition, you will manage programming and systems design, development of computer networks, and implementation of Internet and intranet sites. By the end of the month, please analyze the computer needs of the organization. Once again, congratulations, and feel free to call on me for assistance.
>
> Best regards,
>
> Kendis Moore
>
> Supervisor of Technology

mywritinglab

WANT A BETTER GRADE?
WANT A BETTER GRADE? For more practice with subjects, verbs, and simple sentences, go to **www.mywritinglab.com > The Basic Sentence > Subjects, Verbs, and Simple Sentences.**

WHAT HAVE I LEARNED?

To test and track your understanding, complete the following sentences. Use several sentences as needed for each response.

1. A subject is

2. The three types of subjects are

3. A verb

The three basic types of verbs are

4. A simple sentence is

5. How will I use what I have learned?
In your notebook, discuss how you will apply to your own writing what you have learned about subjects and verbs.

6. What do I still need to study about subjects and verbs?
In your notebook, discuss your ongoing study needs by describing what, when, and how you will continue studying subjects and verbs.

Academic Learning Log

LEARNING OUTCOMES
SELF-EVALUATION

PORTFOLIO

17

Compound and Complex Sentences

CHAPTER PREVIEW

LEARNING OUTCOMES

● What's the Point of Compound and Complex Sentences?

● Understanding the Point of Compound and Complex Sentences: One Student Writer's Response

● Applying the Point: Compound and Complex Sentences

● Writing Assignments

A compound sentence joins together two or more independent clauses. A complex sentence combines one independent or main clause and one or more dependent clauses.

Communicating about a real-life situation helps us to understand the purpose of compound and complex sentences. The photograph on the facing page illustrates some of the benefits of computer games. Read the statements given in Practice 1, complete the activities, and answer the question "What's the point of compound and complex sentences?"

What's the Point of Compound and Complex Sentences?

PHOTOGRAPHIC ORGANIZER: COMPOUND AND COMPLEX SENTENCES

▲ **School children using educational software**

The following ideas are stated using four types of sentences: (1) simple; (2) compound; (3) complex; and (4) compound-complex. Discuss with a small group of peers in what ways these sentences differ from each other.

1. Children can benefit from computer games.

2. Computer games are a lot of fun, and they can promote skill development.

3. Some innovative after-school programs, which have grown in recent decades, use computer games in just this way.

4. Fun games are motivating, and motivation leads to better learning; therefore, after-school programs that use computer games have had success.

What's the point of compound and complex sentences?

Understanding the Point of Compound and Complex Sentences: One Student Writer's Response

The following paragraph offers one writer's thoughts about the differences among sentence types.

> To study the list of sentences, I underlined the subjects and verbs in each one. As I did, I noticed that the first sentence was the only one that focused on one topic. It had only one subject and verb. The rest of the sentences had two or more ideas. I also noticed that some sentences joined ideas with words like "and," "which," and "therefore." Another way the sentences differed was the use of punctuation. Some used commas, and one used a semicolon. I always struggle with commas and semicolons. I need to learn how to use them. Overall, I would say using different types of sentences will give me more ways to say what I want to say.

Applying the Point: Compound and Complex Sentences

A **clause** is a group of related words that includes a subject and a verb. Two types of clauses provide the basis of all sentences: (1) the **independent clause** and (2) the **dependent clause**.

1. The Independent Clause

For more on simple sentences, see pages 310–323.

A focused and complete thought expressed with a subject and a verb; also known as a *main clause* or **simple sentence**.

INDEPENDENT CLAUSE
(COMPLETE THOUGHT)

Severe dehydration may result in shock and death.

SUBJECT   VERB

2. The Dependent Clause

(1) An incomplete thought expressed with a subject and a verb marked by a subordinating conjunction such as *after*, *before*, or *when*.

(2) An incomplete thought marked by a relative pronoun, such as *who* or *which*, acting as the subject of the verb.

TYPES OF CLAUSES

Identify each of the following clauses as **I** for independent or **D** for dependent. *Hint:* Circle subordinating conjunctions and relative pronouns.

.... **1.** Dehydration can occur from extreme exertion such as participating in a triathlon.

.... **2.** Because people sweat a lot when exerting themselves.

.... **3.** Paying attention to signs of dehydration is important.

.... **4.** Which may include dizziness and dry mouth.

.... **5.** Although dehydration can occur even without great exertion, especially in the summertime.

A Compound Sentence

A compound sentence is made up of two or more independent clauses. A **compound sentence** links independent clauses together as **equally important** ideas through one of three methods.

Three Ways to Combine Independent Clauses into a Compound Sentence

1. **A comma and a coordinating conjunction**: The coordinating conjunction serves as a transition that shows the equal relationship of ideas within the sentence. Use the acronym FANBOYS to help you remember the seven coordinating conjunctions—*for, and, nor, but, or, yet,* or *so.*

   [Independent clause,] coordinating conjunction [independent clause.]

Coordinating Conjunctions (FANBOYS) and Meanings							
Coordinating Conjunction	For	And	Nor	But	Or	Yet	So
Meaning	Result	Addition	Negation	Contrast	Choice	Contrast	Result

Many customers pay for their gas at the pump, so fewer customers go into the gas station's store.

SUBJECT   VERB   INDEPENDENT CLAUSE   COMMA ENDS FIRST CLAUSE

SUBJECT   VERB   INDEPENDENT CLAUSE

COORDINATING CONJUNCTION COMBINES INDEPENDENT CLAUSES

2. **A semicolon, conjunctive adverb, and a comma**: The conjunction shows the relationship of ideas within the sentence. In addition, the conjunctive adverb introduces the next clause. A comma follows the conjunctive adverb since it is an introductory element of the next clause.

   [Independent clause;] conjunctive adverb, [independent clause.]

Common Conjunctive Adverbs and the Relationships They Express					
Addition	**Cause or Effect**	**Comparison or Contrast**	**Example**	**Emphasis**	**Time**
also	accordingly	however	for example	certainly	finally
besides	as a result	in comparison	for instance	indeed	meanwhile
further	consequently	in contrast		in fact	next
furthermore	hence	instead		still	then
in addition	therefore	likewise		undoubtedly	thereafter
incidentally	thus	nevertheless			
moreover		nonetheless			
		otherwise			
		similarly			

SUBJECT   VERB   INDEPENDENT CLAUSE   SEMICOLON ENDS FIRST CLAUSE

Gas Station TV embeds 20-inch HD monitors in the gas pump ;

therefore , customers see news and advertisements at the gas pump.

CONJUNCTIVE ADVERB   SUBJECT   VERB   INDEPENDENT CLAUSE

COMMA SIGNALS INTRODUCTORY ELEMENT FOR NEXT CLAUSE

3. A semicolon: A semicolon joins two closely related independent clauses.

[Independent clause;] [independent clause.]

SUBJECT   INDEPENDENT CLAUSE   VERB   SEMICOLON ENDS FIRST CLAUSE

The consumer at the pump is a captive audience ;

Gas Station TV shows ads of products for sale

inside the gas station's convenience store.

SUBJECT   VERB   INDEPENDENT CLAUSE

COMPOUND SENTENCES

Insert the proper punctuation in each of the following compound sentences. *Hint:* Identify the subjects and verbs. Place parentheses around (prepositional phrases); underline the <u>subject</u> once; underline the <u>verb</u> twice.

1. We need to conserve energy hence we should improve our gas mileage.

2. An idling car gets zero miles per gallon and an idling car (with a large engine) wastes a lot of gas.

3. Driving (at a constant speed) improves gas mileage therefore using cruise control saves gas.

4. (In an overdrive gear), the speed (of the car's engine) slows down the use (of the overdrive gears) saves gas and reduces engine wear.

5. Write a compound sentence. Suggested topic: Ways to conserve energy.

Practice 3

For more information on how to identify subjects, verbs, and prepositional phrases, see page 320.

Practice 4

COMPOUND SENTENCES

Create compound sentences by combining the following sets of simple sentences. Vary the ways in which you join ideas. Use appropriate conjunctions and punctuation to show the relationship between the ideas within each new sentence.

1. Both men and women value the handiness of the Internet. They use the Internet for different purposes.

_____

_____

2. Women are more likely to go online for information about personal issues. They get maps, use e-mail, and access information about health and religion.

_____

_____

3. Men are more likely to go online to listen to music, take a class, and use a Webcam. They check the weather and get information about news, sports, politics, jobs, and finances.

_____

_____

4. Men and women equally use the Internet for online banking and shopping. Men are more likely to pay bills, trade stocks, and bid in auctions.

_____

_____

_____

5. Write a compound sentence. Suggested topic: Advantages of the Internet.

_____

_____

Adapted from Jennifer LeClaire, "Study: Men and Women Use Internet Differently." TechNewsWorld. Dec. 29, 2005.

A Complex Sentence

A **complex sentence** contains one independent or main clause and one or more dependent clauses. A **dependent clause** expresses a **subordinate** or minor detail about the idea in the independent clause. A complex sentence joins independent and dependent clauses by placing a subordinating conjunction at the beginning of the dependent clause. **Subordinating conjunctions** state the unequal relationship between the main clause and the subordinate clause.

Subordinating Conjunctions and the Relationships They Express				
Cause	**Contrast**	**Time**	**Place**	**Condition**
as	although	after	where	even if
because	as if	as	wherever	if
in order that	even though	as long as		only if
now that	though	before		unless
since	whereas	once		when
so	while	since		whether or not
		until		
		when		
		whenever		
		while		

A subordinating conjunction always signals the beginning of a dependent clause. However, many subordinating conjunctions can also be other parts of speech.

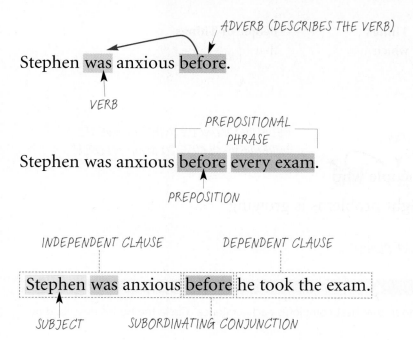

ADVERB (DESCRIBES THE VERB)

Stephen was anxious before.

VERB

PREPOSITIONAL PHRASE

Stephen was anxious before every exam.

PREPOSITION

INDEPENDENT CLAUSE   DEPENDENT CLAUSE

Stephen was anxious before he took the exam.

SUBJECT   SUBORDINATING CONJUNCTION

COMPLEX SENTENCES

Underline the dependent clauses in each sentence. In the blank after each sentence, state the relationship between the dependent clause and the main clause.

1. Since he was an elementary school student years ago, Stephen has always struggled with

test anxiety. _____

2. He feels anxious even if he memorizes all the material. _____

3. Stephen found a tutoring center where students can get tips about dealing with

test anxiety. _____

Practice 5

4. Because he learned tips to use during a test, he now approaches tests with a calm attitude. ....

5. Write a complex sentence using a subordinating conjunction. State the relationship between your dependent and main clauses. Suggested topic: How to deal with anxiety.

....

....

A special kind of subordinating conjunction is the relative pronoun. A **relative pronoun** connects the dependent clause to a noun in the main clause. The choice of a relative pronoun indicates whether the dependent clause is describing a person or a thing.

Relative Pronouns and What They Indicate		
People	**Things**	**People or Things**
who	which	that
whom		
whose		

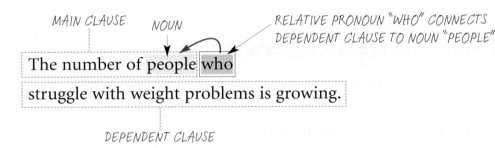

MAIN CLAUSE   NOUN   RELATIVE PRONOUN "WHO" CONNECTS DEPENDENT CLAUSE TO NOUN "PEOPLE"

The number of people who struggle with weight problems is growing.

DEPENDENT CLAUSE

COMPLEX SENTENCES

Insert the relative pronoun that best completes each sentence. Circle the nouns described by the relative pronoun.

1. Mindfulness refers to an attitude .... blends thought and action.

2. Connor, ... lost 40 pounds, wanted to change bad habits.

3. Therefore, he gave up eating hamburgers, French fries, and Coca-Cola, ... were his favorite foods.

4. Instead, he ate a wide variety of foods .... were high in vitamins and low in calories.

5. Write a complex sentence using a relative pronoun. Suggested topic: An important decision.

....

....

Placement and Punctuation of a Dependent Clause within a Complex Sentence

1. Before the main clause: A dependent clause at the beginning of a sentence acts as an introductory element and must be set off with a comma.

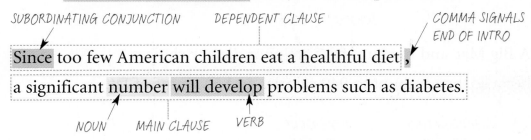

2. In the middle of the main clause: The context of the clause controls the use of commas. Many dependent clauses in the middle of a sentence are **relative clauses.** Relative clauses are either essential or nonessential.

(a) If the dependent clause adds information **essential** to the meaning of sentence, no commas are needed. Most often essential information limits or restricts the meaning of a common noun such as *man* or *woman*.

(b) If the dependent clause adds information that is **nonessential** to the meaning of the main clause, insert commas before and after the dependent clause. Usually a nonessential clause describes a proper noun.

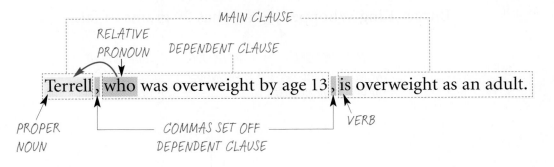

3. After the main clause: The context of the clause controls the use of commas in these instances:

   (a) If the dependent clause begins with a **subordinating conjunction,** no comma is needed.

Main clause *subordinating conjunction* *dependent clause.*

   (b) If the dependent clause begins with a relative pronoun, determine if the information is essential or nonessential. An **essential** dependent clause does not need a comma.

Main clause *dependent clause.*

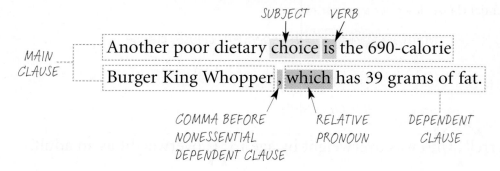

   (c) Insert a comma before a dependent clause that is **nonessential**.

Main clause, *relative pronoun* *dependent clause.*

COMPLEX SENTENCES

Edit each of the following complex sentences for proper punctuation. *Hint:* One sentence is already correctly punctuated.

1. Organic meat, poultry, eggs, and dairy products come from animals that are given no antibiotics or growth hormones.

2. Organic food differs from other foods, because it is produced without pesticides, sewage sludge, or radiation.

3. Organic food is produced by farmers, who work to enhance environmental quality for future generations.

4. Before a product can be labeled organic the farmer must meet USDA organic standards.

5. Write a complex sentence. Suggested topic: A reason to eat organic food.

Adapted from U.S. Department of Agriculture. "Organic Food Standards and Labels: The Facts." April 2002.

COMPLEX SENTENCES

Create five complex sentences by combining the following sets of simple sentences. Use appropriate subordinating conjunctions, relative pronouns, and punctuation to show the relationship between ideas within each new sentence.

1. Organic food has long been available for people. In recent years it has been available for pets.

2. People want their pets to be healthy and happy. They buy their pets organic food.

3. It's not clear that organic food is better for pets. There hasn't been much research on this yet.

4. One reason many people don't buy organic food for their pets is the price. The price is often higher than the price of other pet food.

5. My cat tried a pricey new organic cat food. She would no longer eat anything else.

For more on coordinate and subordinate ideas, see pages 343–344.

A Compound-Complex Sentence

A **compound-complex sentence** contains two or more independent clauses and one or more dependent clauses. A compound-complex sentence joins coordinate and subordinate ideas into a single sentence. All the punctuation rules for both compound and complex sentences apply to the compound-complex sentence.

SUBORDINATING CONJUNCTION   DEPENDENT CLAUSE   COMMA INTRODUCES INDEPENDENT CLAUSES

VERB

INDEPENDENT CLAUSE

Before she took the test for her driver's license ,
Helen studied the rule book , ← COMMA ENDS FIRST CLAUSE
and she practiced driving around town.

NOUN

COORDINATING CONJUNCTION "AND" COMBINES INDEPENDENT CLAUSES

NOUN   VERB

INDEPENDENT CLAUSE

Practice 9

COMPOUND-COMPLEX SENTENCES

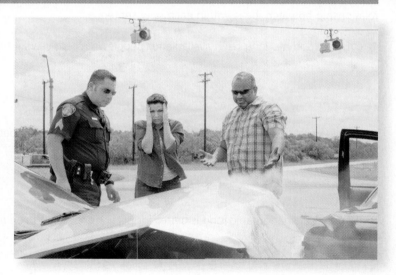

Create and properly punctuate four compound-complex sentences by combining the following simple sentences. Discuss your work with a classmate or a small group of peers.

1. Shelly is a defensive driver. She keeps her eyes moving. She avoids a fixed stare.

----

2. Shelly was first learning to drive. Another driver ran a stop sign. Shelly's car was wrecked beyond repair.

----

3. Shelly didn't cause the accident. The accident left her with three broken ribs. She might have been able to avoid the collision.

_____

_____

4. Shelly wasn't watching the road. She was thinking about her upcoming graduation. She never saw the other car coming.

_____

_____

5. Write a compound-complex sentence. Suggested topic: Dangerous driving habits.

_____

_____

FOUR SENTENCE TYPES REVIEW

Write and properly punctuate four different types of sentences. Suggested topic: A favorite holiday.

1. Simple _____

_____

2. Compound _____

_____

3. Complex _____

_____

4. Compound-Complex _____

_____

_____

Writing Assignments

Writing for Everyday Life

The following journal entry is from the personal diary of a person who wants to lose weight and get healthy. Edit the paragraph for correct punctuation of sentence types. Use your own paper.

> Dear Diary:
>
> Today, I am starting a new lifestyle that will include a healthful diet and regular exercise so I need to identify my current exercising and eating habits. The first is easy because I don't exercise. I will drive around a parking lot for 30 minutes looking for a close parking space and I spend way too much time in front of the television. I watch TV every night from 4:00 p.m. until bedtime which is usually 11:00 p.m. My diet consists mostly of diet sodas and fast food! I sure do have my work cut out for me.

Writing for College Life

Read the following paragraph, written for a humanities course, about the impact of art on the viewer. The assignment asked students to react to a piece of art of their own choosing, such as a sculpture, photograph, or painting. Edit the paragraph for correct punctuation of sentence types. Use your own paper.

> The powerful impact of art on a person is evident in my own response to Michelangelo's statue of David. Although I have seen only photographs of this remarkable sculpture, its beauty and balance are striking. Michelangelo who is perhaps the most gifted artists of all times captured the physical strength and grace of this Jewish hero from the Old Testament. Muscles of perfect proportion reveal David's strength a stance of action reveals his agility and a steady gaze reveals his confidence. Michelangelo's David looks like the hero who could kill a lion with his bare hands, fell a giant with one well placed stone from his sling, and establish a kingdom. I appreciate this piece of art because it captures the essence of the beauty of humanity; David seems strong yet gentle.

Writing for Working Life

Read the following memo written from an employee to a supervisor. Edit the paragraph for correct punctuation of sentence types. Use your own paper.

To: April Gulleme, Manager
From: Ricardo Menendez
RE: Customer Complaints

As you requested, I am submitting a report that includes customer complaints and recommendations gathered from the suggestion box. Some customers complained about slow service in contrast others complained about being interrupted too often by servers while a few servers received rave reviews. Some customers complained during the week about the noisy atmosphere yet others complimented the lively entertainment on the weekends.

I recommend two actions. First, the servers who are efficient and appreciated by customers can mentor the other servers these server-trainers will be paid for their efforts. Second, we can offer and advertise different types of entertainment on different days of the week; for example, on weekends we can offer lively entertainment; on weeknights we can offer toned-down, easy-listening music.

LEARNING OUTCOMES
SELF-EVALUATION

WHAT HAVE I LEARNED?

To test and track your understanding, answer the following questions.

1. What is a clause, and what are the two types of clauses? ....

....

....

2. What is a simple sentence? ....

3. What is a compound sentence? ....

4. What is a complex sentence? ....

....

5. What is a complex-compound sentence? ....

....

6. How will I use what I have learned?
   In your notebook, discuss how you will apply to your own writing what you have learned about sentence types. When will you apply this knowledge during the writing process?

7. What do I still need to study about sentence types?
   In your notebook, discuss your ongoing study needs by describing what, when, and how you will continue studying sentence types.

Academic Learning Log

PORTFOLIO

18

Sentence Variety

Sentence variety is the use of sentences of different lengths, types, and purposes.

Communicating about a real-life situation helps us to understand the purpose of sentence variety. The photograph on the facing page illustrates a woman who deals with stress on a daily basis. Read the accompanying short paragraph about the woman in Practice 1, complete the activities, and answer the question "What's the point of sentence variety?"

LEARNING OUTCOMES

- What's the Point of Sentence Variety?

- Understanding the Point of Sentence Variety: One Student Writer's Response

- Applying the Point: Sentence Variety

- Writing Assignments

What's the Point of Sentence Variety?

PHOTOGRAPHIC ORGANIZER: SENTENCE VARIETY

Read the following short paragraph. What do all the sentences have in common? Describe the overall effect of the paragraph.

Marla has a high-stress lifestyle. She is a single mother of a preschool child. She works as a receptionist for a dentist's office. She is going to school full time. She is training to be a dental hygienist. She is always on the go. She is learning to cope with stress.

What is the point of sentence variety?

Understanding the Point of Sentence Variety: One Student Writer's Response

The following paragraph records one writer's thoughts about the point of sentence variety in the paragraph about Marla in Practice 1.

> In the paragraph about Marla and her stress, every sentence begins the same way, with her name or the pronoun "she," and five of the seven sentences use the verb "is." In addition, the sentences are all about the same length, using six to nine words, and they are all simple sentences. The paragraph seems boring and bland.

Applying the Point: Sentence Variety

Sentence variety adds interest and power to your writing. You can achieve sentence variety by varying the purposes, types, openings, and length of your sentences.

Vary Sentence Purpose

Every sentence expresses a purpose.

Four Purposes for Sentences

1. Declarative sentences make a statement to share information and are punctuated with a period. Declarative sentences are often used to state a main idea and supporting details.

> Half of college undergraduates have four or more credit cards.

2. Interrogative sentences ask a question and are punctuated with a question mark. Usually, the writer also provides an answer to the question. An interrogative sentence may be used to introduce a topic and lead into a topic sentence.

> How can you protect yourself from credit card debt?

3. Imperative sentences give a command that demands an action and are punctuated with a period. Imperative sentences are often used to give directions to complete a process or to persuade a reader to take action.

> Avoid reckless spending. Follow these steps.

4. Exclamatory sentences express a strong emotion and are punctuated with an exclamation point. Exclamatory sentences emphasize a significant point.

> Credit cards will never make you rich!

Most often, you will rely upon the declarative sentence to share information with your reader. However, thoughtful use of a question, command, or exclamation gives your writing variety and adds interest to your ideas.

VARY SENTENCE PURPOSE

Read the following paragraph, adapted from "Choosing a Credit Card: The Deal is in the Disclosures," a June 2008 article on the U.S. Federal Trade Commission website. Identify the purpose of each sentence.

Credit Card Tips

(1) Did you know some credit card plans let the issuer change the APR? (2) This rate change can raise or lower the finance charge on your account. (3) The issuer must tell you that the rate may change and how the rate is determined. (4) In addition, many credit cards charge membership fees. (5) Issuers have a variety of names for these fees, including "annual," "activation," and "monthly maintenance" fees. (6) These fees may appear monthly, periodically, or as one-time charges. (7) When you are choosing a credit card, there are many features to consider. (8) Don't commit to a credit card until you understand how you will be billed. (9) To avoid reckless spending, think about how you plan to use your credit. (10) Using a credit card is a form of borrowing: you have to pay the money back!

Sentence 1. _____   Sentence 6. _____

Sentence 2. _____   Sentence 7. _____

Sentence 3. _____   Sentence 8. _____

Sentence 4. _____   Sentence 9. _____

Sentence 5. _____   Sentence 10. _____

Vary Sentence Types

You learned in Chapters 16 and 17 about the four types of sentences: simple, compound, complex, and compound-complex. When writers rely on one type of sentence more than the others, their work becomes dull and flat, like a speaker delivering a speech in a monotone. As writers combine sentences, they must decide if the combined ideas are equal in importance, or if one idea is more important than another.

Coordinating ideas makes each idea equal in importance. To combine coordinate ideas, use a comma and a coordinating conjunction (FANBOYS: *for, and, nor, but, or, yet,* or *so*).

Subordinating ideas makes one idea dependent on (and less important than) another idea. To make an idea subordinate, use a subordinating conjunction (*after, although, as, because, before, since, unless,* etc.). If the new subordinate clause begins the sentence as an introductory element, include a comma at the end of that clause to set it off from the main independent clause.

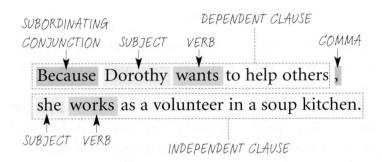

As you study methods of combining sentences, you will learn how to coordinate or subordinate ideas. To add interest and emphasis to your writing, vary the type of your sentences. Many writers use the revision process to combine sentences to achieve variety and interest.

Combine Two or More Simple Sentences into One Simple Sentence

A series of short simple sentences often creates a choppy flow of ideas. Combining closely related short simple sentences into one simple sentence creates a smooth flow of ideas. Short simple sentences can be combined in several ways.

COMBINE SENTENCES WITH A COMPOUND SUBJECT

When two separate simple sentences possess the same verb, they can become one sentence with a compound subject; a **compound subject** is two or more nouns or pronouns joined by the coordinating conjunction **and.** Note that the verb form of a compound subject must be plural. This method of coordinating ideas places equal emphasis on each subject.

> For more about subject-verb agreement, see pages 432–451.

Original Sentences:

Sentences Combined with a Compound Subject:

344

VARY SENTENCE TYPES

Combine the following simple sentences into a new simple sentence using compound subjects. *Hint*: Delete words or reword ideas as needed to create a smooth flow of ideas.

1. Aerobic activities are important for your health. Muscle strengthening activities are also important for your health.

----

2. The heart and the lungs are strengthened by aerobic activities. These activities also make blood vessels stronger.

----

3. Increasing your strength is a benefit of undertaking a physical activity program. Improving your health is another benefit of a physical activity program. Last but not least, spending fun time with family and friends is a benefit of such a program.

----

4. Aerobic activities can be done at a moderate level or a vigorous level. Either level is also possible for muscle strengthening activities.

----

5. Write a simple sentence with a compound subject. Suggested topic: Fun forms of exercise.

COMBINE SENTENCES WITH A COMPOUND VERB

When two separate simple sentences possess the same subject, they can become one sentence with a **compound verb**, two or more verbs joined by a coordinating conjunction of addition or contrast; *and*, *or*, *but*, or *yet*. When only two verbs are joined, no comma is needed before the conjunction. This method of coordinating ideas places equal emphasis on each verb.

Original Sentences:

SUBJECT   VERB

Face-recognition software programs take images of human faces.

The programs analyze the facial images to identify them.

REPEATED SUBJECT   VERB

Sentences Combined with a Compound Verb:

SUBJECT   COMPOUND VERB

Face-recognition software programs take and analyze

images of human faces to identify them.

COORDINATING CONJUNCTION

VARY SENTENCE TYPES

Combine the following simple sentences into a new simple sentence using compound verbs.

1. Face-blindness can be an inherited disorder. Alternatively, it may occur as the result of a head injury.

....

....

2. A person with face-blindness can recognize the faces of family members and other very familiar people. However, he or she is unable to recognize the faces of other people.

....

....

3. Face-blind people have difficulties in social situations. But they can use strategies to minimize these difficulties.

....

....

4. To identify another person, face-blind people can look at visual characteristics such as hair. They can listen for voice cues. They also can pay close attention to other people's reactions and responses.

_____

_____

_____

5. Write a simple sentence with a compound verb. Suggested topic: Overcoming a difficulty.

_____

_____

COMBINE SENTENCES WITH A PARTICIPLE PHRASE

Participle phrases are used as adjectives to describe a noun or a pronoun. A participle phrase is placed directly in front of the noun or pronoun it describes and is set off with a comma. This sentence combination subordinates an idea; it places less emphasis on the idea in the participle phrase.

The **present participle** is the *-ing* form of a verb, such as *causing* or *biting*. A **present participle phrase** begins with a present participle; ends with an object, a noun, or a pronoun; and indicates two actions occurring at the same time.

> For more about participles, see pages 464–479, 506.

Original Sentences:

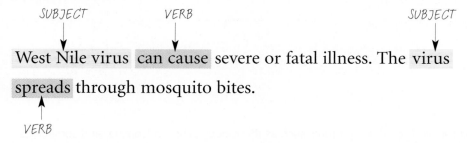

Sentences Combined with a Present Participle Phrase:

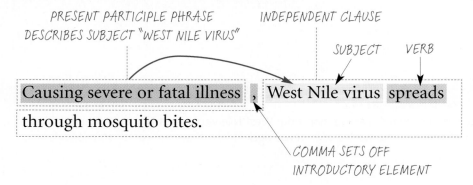

A **past participle** is the *-ed* or *-en* form of a verb, such as *talked* or *bitten*. A **past participle phrase** begins with a past participle; ends with an object, a noun, or a pronoun; and is often created by revising a sentence with a *to be* verb and a past participle into a past participle phrase.

Original Sentences:

SUBJECT   VERB   SUBJECT   VERB

Carlota was bitten by mosquitoes. She feared contracting the West Nile virus.

Sentences Combined with a Past Participle Phrase:

PAST PARTICIPLE PHRASE
DESCRIBES SUBJECT "CARLOTA"   INDEPENDENT CLAUSE

                                    SUBJECT   VERB

Bitten by mosquitoes , Carlota feared contracting the West Nile virus.

COMMA SETS OFF
INTRODUCTORY ELEMENT

Practice 5

VARY SENTENCE TYPES

In each of the items below, combine the two given sentences into one new sentence using a present participle phrase as an introductory element. Use appropriate punctuation.

1. The West Nile virus is a seasonal epidemic in North America. It flares up in the summer and continues into the fall.

----

2. West Nile virus causes symptoms such as fever, body aches, headache, and sometimes swollen lymph glands and rash. West Nile virus lasts only a few days in most cases.

----

3. West Nile encephalitis can develop from West Nile virus. West Nile encephalitis includes symptoms such as headache, high fever, neck stiffness, stupor, coma, and convulsions.

----

4. Kadeem wore long sleeves, long pants, and socks when outdoors. Kadeem attempted to reduce the risk of contracting West Nile virus.

----

5. Write a sentence using the present participle phrase as an introductory element. Suggested topic: Flu medicines.

VARY SENTENCE TYPES

In each of the items below, combine the two given sentences into one new sentence using a past participle phrase as an introductory element. Use appropriate punctuation.

1. DEET is intended to be applied to the skin or to clothing. It primarily protects against insect bites.

----

2. DEET was developed by the United States Army in response to the Army's experience of jungle warfare during World War II. DEET protects against tick and mosquito bites.

----

3. Laboratory rats were exposed to frequent and long-term use of DEET. The rats experienced serious brain cell death and behavior changes.

Practice 6

4. DEET has not proven to be of significant harm to human health. DEET is the most common active ingredient in insect repellents.

....

....

5. Write a sentence using a past participle phrase. Suggested topic: Annoying or dangerous insects.

....

....

COMBINE SENTENCES WITH AN APPOSITIVE

An **appositive phrase** renames or restates a noun or pronoun. This sentence combination subordinates an idea: it places less emphasis on the idea expressed by an appositive. An appositive can appear at the beginning, middle, or end of a sentence since it appears next to the noun or pronoun it renames. The use of commas depends upon where the appositive appears.

Placement of Appositives and Commas

Beginning of sentence: An appositive at the beginning of a sentence is an introductory element. Use a comma to set off an appositive at the beginning of the sentence.

Original Sentences:

Sentences Combined with an Appositive:

Middle of sentence: Use a pair of commas to set off an appositive phrase that interrupts an independent clause.

Original Sentences:

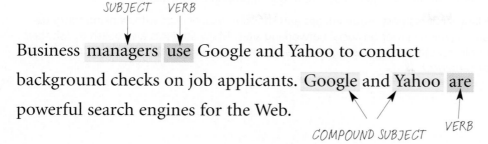

Business managers use Google and Yahoo to conduct background checks on job applicants. Google and Yahoo are powerful search engines for the Web.

SUBJECT VERB

COMPOUND SUBJECT VERB

Sentences Combined with an Appositive:

SUBJECT VERB OBJECT (COMPOUND NOUNS) COMMAS SET OFF APPOSITIVE PHRASE

INDEPENDENT CLAUSE (INTERRUPTED BY APPOSITIVE PHRASE)

Business managers use Google and Yahoo, powerful search engines for the Web, to conduct background checks on job applicants.

APPOSITIVE PHRASE DESCRIBES OBJECT "GOOGLE AND YAHOO"

End of sentence: Use a comma to set off an appositive phrase at the end of a sentence.

Original Sentences:

SUBJECT VERB

Students should be wary of posting personal information on Facebook. Facebook is a popular social networking site.

SUBJECT VERB

Sentences Combined with an Appositive:

SUBJECT VERB INDEPENDENT CLAUSE

Students should be wary of posting personal information on Facebook, a popular social networking site.

OBJECT (NOUN) COMMA SETS OFF APPOSITIVE PHRASE APPOSITIVE PHRASE DESCRIBES OBJECT "FACEBOOK"

Practice 7

VARY SIMPLE SENTENCES

In each of the items below, combine the given simple sentences into one new sentence using an appositive phrase. In your answers, follow the appositive placement suggested in parentheses at the end of each item. Use appropriate punctuation.

1. Many students post risqué images and shocking experiences with drinking, drug use, and sexual behavior on social networking sites. Many students are foolish to risk their public reputations by posting risqué and shocking images and statements. *(beginning of sentence)*

....

....

....

2. Some students experiment with a wide range of personal behaviors. They are eager to explore their new freedom away from home. *(beginning of sentence)*

....

....

....

3. Personal behavior is a reflection of a person's judgment. The personal behavior of an employee may concern an employer. *(middle of sentence)*

....

....

....

4. An employer should not have the legal right to consider personal behavior. Personal behavior is a matter covered by the right to privacy. *(end of sentence)*

....

....

....

5. Write a sentence with an appositive phrase. Suggested topic: A social networking site such as MySpace or Facebook.

....

....

....

For information on how to create compound and complex sentences, see pages 324–339.

Combine Ideas Using Compound and Complex Sentence Types

Combine ideas of equal importance using **coordination**, joining independent clauses into a **compound sentence**. Combine ideas of unequal importance—a main idea and a subordinate, or minor, idea—using **subordination**, joining an independent clause with a dependent clause into a **complex sentence.**

Practice 8

Use subordination and coordination to logically combine the ideas in the ten sentences below into five sentences. Punctuate properly. (*Note:* For more help on how to create compound and complex sentences and punctuate them correctly, see Chapter 17.)

(1) As a departing employee, keep in mind you may want to return to the organization. (2) You should strive to be remembered as professional. (3) To leave a good impression, emphasize the positive experiences. (4) Don't criticize colleagues or supervisors. (5) Leaving a poor impression can lead to a poor recommendation and a series of shut doors. (6) Leaving a positive impression can result in an excellent recommendation and open options for the future. (7) Resist the urge to leave a nasty note to a boss or coworker. (8) Act as professionally on the last day as on the first. (9) For example, Randall left the firm with an excellent last impression. (10) His boss and coworkers have agreed to act as references for future jobs.

Vary Sentence Openings

Most often, we begin our sentences with the subject followed by the verb. To add interest and to shift the emphasis of an idea, you can vary the ways in which you begin a sentence. You have already worked with several types of sentence openings: participle phrases, appositives, and dependent clauses. Two additional ways to begin a sentence include using adverbs and prepositional phrases. As introductory elements in a sentence, both an adverb and a prepositional phrase are set off with a comma.

ADVERB

- Describes or modifies another adverb, a verb, or an adjective.

- Answers the questions: *How? How often? How much? When? Where? and Why?*

- Usually ends in *-ly: angrily, beautifully, frequently.*

ADVERB   COMMA SETS OFF INTRODUCTORY ELEMENT

Eagerly , Emilo shops for an engagement ring.

PREPOSITIONAL PHRASE

- Begins with a preposition and ends with a noun or pronoun, the object of the preposition.

- Object of the preposition describes or modifies another word in the sentence.

- Common prepositions and objects: *about the yard, at the store, by the door, in the house, on the way, to the corner, with you.*

PREPOSITIONAL PHRASE   COMMA SETS OFF INTRODUCTORY ELEMENT

At the store , Emilo finds the perfect diamond ring.

Practice 9

VARY SENTENCE OPENINGS

Revise the openings of the sentences to vary emphasis and expression. Move the adverb or prepositional phrase to the beginning of the sentence as appropriate.

1. Advertisers try to get us to buy products through various appeals.

....

....

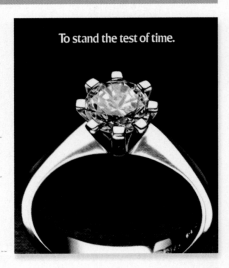

To stand the test of time.

2. They cleverly appeal to emotions such as envy and the desire to be respected and liked.

....

....

3. Your feelings of desire and status are being aroused in jewelry ads.

....

....

4. Advertising appeals to our emotions are undeniably effective.

....

....

5. Write a sentence that begins with an adverb or a prepositional phrase. Suggested topic: An ad I find effective.

Vary Sentence Length

To add interest to your writing, vary the length of your sentences. When a writer relies too heavily on one sentence length, the work will be dull, flat, or uninteresting. Too many long sentences make a piece boring or confusing. Too many short sentences can seem choppy and immature. The sentence-combining techniques you have learned throughout this chapter will also help you create sentences of varying lengths.

VARY SENTENCE LENGTH

Revise the following paragraph written for a college humanities course. Vary the length of the sentences by combining the thirteen sentences into six new sentences.

(1) Conversation is a five-step process. (2) The first step is the greeting. (3) The greeting can be either verbal or nonverbal. (4) The second step is feedforward. (5) Feedforward gives the other person a general idea about the topic of conversation. (6) The third step is business. (7) Business is the conversation's focus and details. (8) The fourth step is feedback. (9) Feedback is verbal and nonverbal responses from the other person. (10) Step five is the closing. (11) The closing is the goodbye. (12) The closing ends the conversation. (13) The closing can be verbal and nonverbal signals.

Adapted from Joseph A. DeVito, *Messages: Building Interpersonal Communication Skills*, 4th Ed.

SENTENCE VARIETY REVIEW

Assume you are acting as a peer editor for a classmate who wrote the following paragraph in response to a question on an exam study guide. Revise the paragraph for sentence variety by varying sentence purposes, types, openings, and lengths.

(1) There are different kinds of dietary fat. (2) Saturated fats are found in animal products such as meat, eggs, milk, and dairy products, and palm oil and coconut oil are saturated fats from plants. (3) Polyunsaturated fats are corn oil, soybean oil, and cottonseed oil, and some fish are sources of polyunsaturated fats. (4) Monounsaturated fats are found in peanut oil, olive oil, and canola oil. (5) Cholesterol is a fat-like substance. (6) The liver manufactures cholesterol, and cholesterol circulates in the bloodstream. (7) Saturated fats raise cholesterol levels, but polyunsaturated fats lower cholesterol. (8) Saturated fats are the most dangerous of the three.

Adapted from B. E. Pruitt and Jan J. Stein, *HealthStyles*, 2nd Ed.

Writing Assignments

Writing for Everyday Life

The following letter to the editor of a local newspaper was written to protest a city's decision to install video cameras and a face-recognition program to reduce crime. Revise the letter to create a variety of purposes, types, patterns, openings, and length of sentences. Use your own paper.

Dear Editor:

A serious violation of our rights has come to my attention. Our city has installed a face-recognition program. They say the program is to reduce crime. The cameras are an invasion of our privacy. These cameras are installed at every major intersection. The government has no right to do this. This will record our actions without our knowledge or consent. I wonder how many rights we will lose in the fight against crime and terror. City and county commissioners voted for this program. We must vote them out of office.

–Julie Q. Public

Writing for College Life

Assume your humanities teacher has assigned a short response paper about the significance of landmarks such as the Golden Gate Bridge. Assume you have composed the following piece of writing. Revise the draft to create a variety of purposes, types, patterns, openings, and length of sentences. Use your own paper.

The Golden Gate Bridge stands as a symbol of human ingenuity. It was completed in 1937. It cost $35 million. The bridge spans the The Golden Gate. The Golden Gate is the strait connecting the San Francisco Bay to the Pacific Ocean. The bridge was once the longest suspension bridge in the world. It is now the second longest one. The bridge is 1.7 miles long. It is 90 feet wide. It has six lanes. The bridge is known for its beauty. Its color is an orange vermilion called International orange. The color was chosen for two reasons. It blends well with the natural environment. It is visible in fog. Lighting outlines the bridge's cables and towers. The lighting enhances the beauty of the bridge. The lights attract many visitors. This bridge is a remarkable engineering feat.

Writing Assignments CONTINUED

Writing for Working Life

Jerome Offiah, a recent graduate looking for employment, knows that many employers surf the Web for information about potential employees. Jerome Offiah maintains a blog on a social networking service such as MySpace and has drafted the following posting to make a positive impression on potential employers. Revise his draft to create a variety of purposes, types, patterns, openings, and length of sentences. Use your own paper.

> I wonder if you are looking for a solid, reliable employee. I am your man. I am a recent college graduate. I majored in business and graduated with a 3.5 GPA. I can identify problems and research solutions. I collaborate with others. I bring these abilities to the workforce. I value hard work. I value being on time. I appreciate constructive criticism. I have several goals. I want to work with a large corporation. I hope to advance into management. I look forward to the opportunity to travel. I am a hard worker and a quick learner. You can count on me.

mywritinglab

WANT A BETTER GRADE?
For more practice with sentence variety, go to **www.mywritinglab.com > Writing Clear Sentences > Sentence Variety.**

LEARNING OUTCOMES
SELF-EVALUATION

Academic Learning Log

WHAT HAVE I LEARNED ABOUT USING SENTENCE VARIETY?

To test and track your understanding of sentence variety, answer the following questions.

1. What are the four purposes for sentences?

(a) ....

(b) ....

(c) ....

(d) ....

2. What are the six ways to combine simple sentences?

(a) ....

(b) ....

(c) ....

(d) ....

(e) ....

PORTFOLIO

Academic Learning Log

(f) _____

3. What are five ways to vary sentence openings?

(a) _____

(b) _____

(c) _____

(d) _____

(e) _____

4. Why is it important to vary sentence length?

_____

5. How will I use what I have learned?
In your notebook, discuss how you will apply to your own writing what you have learned about sentence variety. When will you apply this knowledge during the writing process?

6. What do I still need to study about sentence types?
In your notebook, discuss your ongoing study needs by describing what, when, and how you will continue studying and using sentence variety.

19

Sentence Clarity: Person, Point of View, Number, and Tense

Sentence clarity creates a logical flow of ideas through consistency in person, point of view, number, and tense.

Communicating about a real-life situation helps us to understand the purpose of sentence clarity. The photograph on the facing page illustrates a particular situation. Read the accompanying original and revised sentences about the situation in Practice 1, complete the activities, and answer the question "What's the point of sentence clarity?"

What's the Point of Sentence Clarity?

Practice 1

PHOTOGRAPHIC ORGANIZER: SENTENCE CLARITY

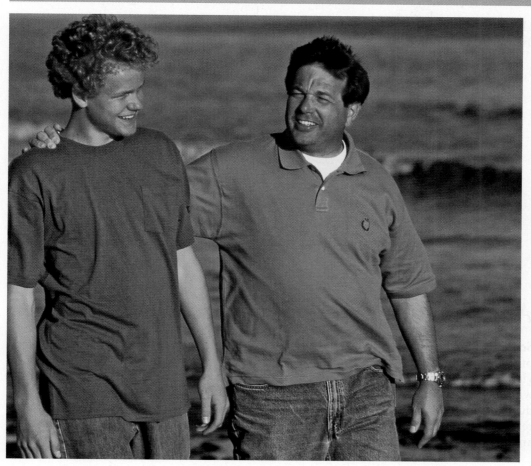

What do you think the following sentence means? How could the sentence seem confusing to some readers?

Original Sentence: Jonathan and his son often walked on the beach and talk about his ups and downs in everyday life.

Is the above sentence describing current or past events? Whose everyday life is being discussed—Jonathan's or his son's, or do they share about both their lives?

Read the revised sentence below for clarity. How is the revised sentence different from the original? Which revised words clarify the meaning of the sentence?

Revised Sentence: Jonathan and his son often walk on the beach and talk about the ups and downs of their everyday lives.

What is the point of sentence clarity?

Understanding the Point of Sentence Clarity: One Student Writer's Response

The following paragraph offers one writer's reaction to the clarity of the sentence about the walk on the beach.

> The first sentence doesn't make much sense because of the way the verbs and pronouns are used. The verb "talk" is in the present tense, yet the verb "walked" is in the past tense. An event can't take place in the present and past at the same time. Also, the use of the pronoun "his" is very confusing. Do they only talk about one person? Then which one? In the revised sentence, the verbs match in time, and the pronoun "their" refers to both people. The revised sentence also changed "life" to "lives" to match "their."

Applying the Point: Sentence Clarity

Sentence clarity is the precise choice of the form and arrangement of words and groups of words within a sentence. A clearly stated sentence is consistent in person, point of view, number, and tense. As a result, sentence clarity helps create a coherent flow of ideas within and among sentences. Often, writers work on sentence and paragraph clarity during the revision process. As you study the sentence clarity techniques in this chapter, revise pieces of your own writing and peer edit for a classmate. Apply and track what you are learning as you go.

Use Consistent Person and Point of View

The term **person** refers to the use of pronouns to identify the difference between the writer or speaker, the one being written or spoken to, and the one being written about or spoken of. **Point of view** is the position from which something is considered, evaluated, or discussed; point of view is identified as first person, second person, or third person. Person and point of view also communicate tone.

Three Points of View

Person	Traits	Pronouns
First Person	The writer or speaker; informal, conversational tone	singular: *I, me* plural: *we, our*
Second Person	The one being written or spoken to; can remain unstated; informal, conversational tone	singular: *you* plural: *you*
Third Person	The one being written about or spoken of; formal, academic tone	singular: *he, she, it, one* plural: *they*

Illogical Shift in Person

An abrupt or **unnecessary shift in person or point of view** causes a break in the logical flow of ideas. The key is to use the same phrasing throughout a paragraph. When you revise for consistency, remember that the number of the verb may need to change as well. (More information on correcting illogical shifts in number appears on page 365 in this chapter.)

> For more information about subject-verb agreement, see pages 432–451.

Illogical Shift in Person:

THIRD PERSON — Everyone wants to improve gas mileage no matter what type of vehicle you drive.
— SECOND PERSON

Revisions:

THIRD PERSON — Everyone wants to improve gas mileage no matter what type of vehicle he or she drives.
PRONOUN AND VERB AGREE IN NUMBER

PRONOUN AND VERB AGREE IN NUMBER

SECOND PERSON — You want to improve gas mileage no matter what type of vehicle you drive. — "–S" IN VERB DELETED

CONSISTENT PERSON AND POINT OF VIEW

Edit the following statements to ensure consistent use of person in each sentence. Change verbs as necessary to agree with their subjects.

More people are choosing hybrid cars to reduce your gas expenses.

If a person is concerned about the environment, you may drive a hybrid car.

When you drive a hybrid, one produces less harmful emissions.

We all will benefit from breathing less air pollution in their daily commute.

When you buy a hybrid vehicle, one is making a responsible decision.

Practice 3

Edit the following paragraph to ensure consistent use of person and point of view.

Proper Storage for Food Safety

(1) Proper food handling and storage protects a person's health; therefore, a cook must wisely defrost, store, and dispose of food. (2) First, we must properly defrost frozen foods. (3) You should never defrost foods at room temperature, which can allow bacteria a better chance to grow. (4) Instead, thaw foods in the refrigerator, microwave, or bowl of cold water that is changed every 30 minutes. (5) In addition, set your refrigerator below 40°F. (6) A wise cook doesn't 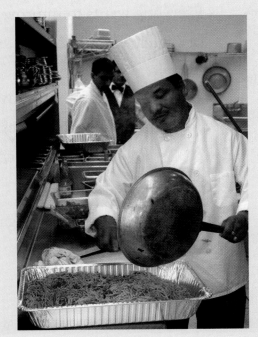 rely on the refrigerator's built-in dial but rather uses a separate thermometer to judge the temperature, as advised by the U.S. Department of Agriculture. (7) Finally, I put cooked food in the refrigerator or freezer within 2 hours of purchase or preparation. (8) Since harmful bacteria and microorganisms grow between 40°F and 140°F, leaving your food at room temperature for long can increase your chance of contracting a food-borne illness. (9) Keep refrigerated leftovers for only four days; then throws them away. (10) A wise cook protects the health of those you serves.

For more information on point of view, see the "Grammar in Action" section in pages 218–219.

Use Consistent Number

The term *number* refers to the difference between a singular noun or pronoun and plural nouns and pronouns. Once you choose a point of view, carefully edit your writing to ensure **consistent use of number**: singular pronouns refer to singular nouns, and plural pronouns refer to plural nouns.

	Singular	Plural
First Person	*I, me, my, mine* *myself*	*we, our, ours* *ourselves*
Second Person	*you, yours, yourself*	*you, yours, yourselves*
Third Person	*he, she, it* *him, her, hers,* *himself, herself, itself* *one, everyone, none*	*they, them,* *theirs,* *themselves*

Illogical Shift in Number

When pronouns act as the subject of a verb, they, too, must agree in number. An abrupt or **unnecessary shift in number** causes a break in the logical flow of ideas.

Illogical Shift In Person:

PLURAL NOUN

Children use many electronic gadgets, yet it is sometimes
hazardous to health.

SINGULAR VERB

SINGULAR, THIRD-PERSON PRONOUN

Revision:

PLURAL NOUN

Children use many electronic gadgets, yet they are sometimes
hazardous to health.

PLURAL VERB

PLURAL, THIRD-PERSON PRONOUN

CONSISTENT NUMBER

Edit the following statements to ensure consistency in number within each sentence.

1. The typical American child spends 900 hours per year studying and learning in their school and over 1,000 hours per year parked in front of their televisions.

2. Children begin using personal computers, video games, CD and DVD players, and cell phones by age seven to nine; they almost seem addicted to it.

3. Experts report that children as young as 8 years old suffer from repetitive strain injury from sending so many text messages on his or her cell phone.

4. A teen can damage their hearing by using an iPod; they, along with other media players, can blast music at more than 115 decibels, a noise level equal to a chain saw.

5. A parent cannot take their children's health for granted.

Practice 4

Practice 5

Revise the following paragraph for consistency of number as well as of person and point of view within and across sentences. Change nouns, pronouns, and verbs as needed. Different changes are possible.

Recycling for the Greater Good

(1) Consumers can recycle much of what they get. (2) One just needs to take several simple steps. (3) A product usually comes in several sizes. (4) Their economy size is not only cheapest but also reduces the amount of packaging to be disposed of. (5) You will often be able to reuse a container, rather than throwing them away. (6) For example, if it is cleaned, jam jars can be used as a juice glass. (7) Old clothes in good shape should be given to people who can use it. (8) Electronic equipment can also be donated, and many communities have centers for donating them. (9) Children should be encouraged to help recycle, as habits one acquires in their early life will stay with them in one's later life. (10) Every day, consumers who recycle make a difference to his or her environment.

Use Consistent Tense

Consistent tense expresses the logical sequence of events or existence. Verb *tense* expresses the time or duration of an action or state of being. Primary tenses include three timeframes: The **past** *was*; the **present** *is*; the **future** *will be*. The following chart outlines several hints to achieve sentence clarity through consistent tense.

<table>
<tr><td colspan="2" align="center">For Consistent Tense</td></tr>
</table>

1. Use the same verb tense for each action or state occurring within the same timeframe.	
Past Tense:	Monica graduated from college and began searching for a job.
Present Tense:	Monica graduates from college and begins searching for a job.
Future Tense:	Monica will graduate from college and begin searching for a job.

2. Change tense to indicate a logical movement in timeframe from one action or state to another.

Past to Present Tense:	Stephen, who changed careers, currently works as an insurance adjuster for Allstate.
Present to Future Tense:	Although Stephen currently holds an entry level position, he will advance into a management position.

3. Choose and remain in one primary tense to express your points.

Past tense expresses completed action:
Monica sat attentively, made direct eye contact, and spoke with confidence. She understood the importance of making a good first impression, so she listened carefully to each question and offered thoughtful responses.

Present tense expresses the immediacy of a current event:
Monica sits attentively, makes direct eye contact, and speaks with confidence. She understands the importance of making a good first impression. So she listens carefully to each question and offers thoughtful responses.

Illogical Shift in Tense

An abrupt change from one verb tense to another without a logical reason, also called an **illogical shift in tense,** breaks the logical flow of ideas and causes confusion.

Illogical Shift In Tense:

PRESENT TENSE

Monica does not rely solely on the classifieds to find a job; she followed other leads.

PAST TENSE

Revisions:

PRESENT TENSE

Monica does not rely solely on the classifieds to find a job; she follows other leads.

PRESENT TENSE

PAST TENSE

Monica did not rely solely on the classifieds to find a job; she followed other leads.

PAST TENSE

Practice 6

Edit the following essay to ensure consistency in tense.

The Winning Interview

(1) The best jobs often go to the candidates with the best interviewing skills. (2) Preparing for a job interview is essential to a successful interview. (3) If you were facing a job interview, consider the following tips. (4) Before the interview, study yourself and the job. (5) First, study your own strengths and weaknesses; be prepared to address both. (6) Second, study the job description and list five reasons you were best qualified for the job. (7) Third, study the company, its products, and its services. (8) During the interview, look and act like you were interested. (9) First, dress professionally. (10) Second, be positive so you showed enthusiasm for the job. (11) Finally, at the end of the interview, ask questions focused on the job and its responsibilities.

Practice 7

To give this paragraph more immediacy, revise the following paragraph making all past tense verbs present tense verbs.

Lakers versus Rockets

(1) Going into the game, the playoff series between the Lakers and Rockets was tied. (2) The Houston crowd jeered Lakers star Kobe Bryant. (3) But the jeers didn't bother Bryant. (4) He drilled shot after shot. (5) He kept frustrating the Rockets with his tough drives to the basket and difficult jumpers. (6) The Rockets were doing everything in their power against Bryant, but they weren't containing him. (7) The Rockets rallied behind Yao Ming, but the Lakers didn't relinquish the

lead. (8) The Rockets' woes grew when Ron Artest was called for a flagrant foul and ejected from the game. (9) When the game ended, the Lakers won by a score of 108 to 94. (10) They now held a two to one lead in this best of seven series.

Adapted from NY Times, 5/9/09, Howard Beck, "Lakers Keep Poise as Artest Loses His."

CONSISTENT TENSE

Many pieces of writing move logically and effectively from past to present tense. Edit the following essay to ensure consistency in tense based on the logical movement of time.

One Successful Man!

(1) Bill Gates was considered by many to be one of the most successful and generous businessmen alive. (2) Husband of Melinda Gates, father to three children, and co-founder of Microsoft, this billionaire sees the widening gap between the rich and the poor as a moral challenge, so he and his wife were dedicating their lives and fortune to helping others. (3) Currently, Microsoft employs over 60,000 workers in 102 countries and regions around the world.

Practice 8 Practice 9

(4) Bill Gates' generosity equaled his business success. (5) In 2000, Gates and his wife Melinda establishes the Bill & Melinda Gates Foundation. (6) Their foundation has the purpose of "reducing poverty inequities in the United States and around the world," according to the foundation's website. (7) Thus, the foundation's $30.6 billion assets were used to improve the quality of technology, education, and health across the globe. (8) Their generosity found a kindred spirit in billionaire investor Warren Buffett. (9) In 2006, Buffett donated an additional $31 billion to the Gates Foundation. (10) In that same year, Gates announces his decision to resign from Microsoft and work full time with the foundation. (11) Bill Gates was indeed a most successful and generous man.

SENTENCE CLARITY REVIEW

Revise the following student paragraph for consistent use of point of view, number, and tense.

(1) It is 5:00 p.m. on a Friday, and the commuters in town are in his car driving home from work. (2) As always, someone is driving carelessly, and they is likely endangering other drivers. (3) Careless drivers rarely think about why he or she drives so recklessly. (4) One major cause of careless driving is the driver's emotions. (5) Any kind of emotion can take your mind off the road. (6) For example, last Saturday, a teenage boy was so excited and happy about winning a football game that he races home at high speeds, nearly sideswiping another car on the way. (7) Another emotion that causes careless driving is anger. (8) When people have heated arguments while driving, for example, sometimes you release the adrenaline running through your body by driving aggressively. (9) You rode the bumpers of other cars and swerved in and out of lanes to pass slower drivers. (10) Emotion, whether positive or negative, is a major cause of careless driving.

Writing Assignments

Writing for Everyday Life

Revise the following short article, written for a neighborhood newsletter, for sentence clarity. Use your own paper.

Attention All Residents: We are going green!

As a community, we have taken several steps to help the environment. First, last week, the neighborhood begins a recycling program. Everyone receives three blue plastic storage bins for their plastic, aluminum, and glass garbage. On Tuesday of each week, put your recycling bins at their curbs for the 9:00 a.m. pick up. Second, watering restrictions will begin next week. Residents can water your yards or wash their cars only on Tuesday, Thursday, and Sunday after 5:00 p.m. or before 8:00 a.m. Finally, to save gas, car pooling for around town errands are available every morning between 9:00 a.m. and noon. Everyone can make a difference! Go green!

Writing for College Life

Edit the following paragraphs, written in response to a short essay question on a history exam, for sentence clarity. Use your own paper.

Test Question: What were the differences between Native American and European combat styles?

Student Answer: Indians conducted warfare very differently from Europeans. Your weapons included bows and arrows, knives, tomahawks, spears, and clubs. War parties do not attack in battle formations but use the forest as their cover and ambushed enemies in guerrilla-like raids. Thus, you did not stand and fight in a "civilized" fashion. Rather, "they were always running and traversing from one place to another," complained de Soto. The tactic made it impossible to shoot you. In addition, a skilled Indian archer easily fires off "three or four arrows" with great accuracy by the time musketeers prepared his awkward weapon for firing. The bowmanship of the Native Americans made combat with him very dangerous because, as de Soto stated, an Indian bowman "seldom misses what he shoots at."

In contrast, Europeans were trained to fight on open fields, during fair weather, and in the daylight hours. Strictly disciplined, European soldiers marched in step and fight in formation. Officers march at the head of the column. At first they used matchlock muskets, which proved to be awkward, inaccurate, and unreliable. So Europeans resorted to "total war." For example in one battle, you encircled the village, set fire to the wigwams, and shoot all escaping Indians. Eventually, the lighter and more accurate flintlock rifle replaced your muskets, yet the total war tactic continued.

Writing Assignments CONTINUED

Writing for Working Life

Edit the following cover letter for a job to ensure sentence clarity.
Use your own paper.

Pete Kramer
200 North Gravel Lane
Murphyville, Georgia 32345
204-573-2345
pkramer@aol.com

March 30, 2009

Ms. Sara Livermore
Director of Human Resources
Livermore Construction
43231 Hightower Road, Suite 300
Jacksonville, Florida 54323

Dear Ms. Livermore:

My teacher, Mr. Connors, told me that you were looking for an electrician's apprentice at your firm, Livermore Construction. I have just finished an intensive 16-week training program. I learn all the parts of the electrician's trade and also pass the test for the Electrical Workers Union Apprentice Certificate. I'm very interested in working for an innovative company that support young people by partnering with the Smokey Mountain Job Corps Center.

I noticed in your advertisements that you includes CAT 5 wiring in all the houses you builds. During the last five weeks of my training, I help install CAT 5 wiring in a local school. My teachers say that I learn new techniques quickly and that I am very responsible and reliable. Once you begin working, you should keep up with training, so once I begin working, I plan on continuing my education at the Jacksonville Community College. I know you are looking for employees who learn quickly, work independently, and constantly improve their skills.

I will be attending a vocational competition in Jacksonville with my teacher Mr. Connors from April 15 to April 19. If it was convenient I would like to visit Livermore Construction and talks with you about the possibility of employment. I will call you next week to schedule a time. My resume is enclosed. If you have any questions regarding my qualifications or my schedule, please call me.

With confidence,
Pete Kramer
enc.

—Adapted from the Job Corps
Wheel of Career Opportunity
Website at <JCStudent.org>,
U.S. Department of Labor

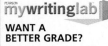
372

WHAT HAVE I LEARNED ABOUT SENTENCE CLARITY?

Academic Learning Log

To test and track your understanding of sentence clarity, answer the following questions. Use several sentences as needed for each response.

1. What is sentence clarity? ....

....

2. What are three techniques used to achieve sentence clarity?

(a) .... ,

(b) .... , and

(c) ....

3. How will I use what I have learned? In your notebook, discuss how you will apply to your own writing what you have learned about sentence clarity. When will you apply this knowledge during the writing process?

4. What do I still need to study about sentence types? In your notebook, discuss your ongoing study needs by describing what, when, and how you will continue studying and using sentence clarity.

PORTFOLIO

20

Parallelism

Parallelism is the expression of equal ideas using similar words, phrases, or clauses in matching grammatical form.

Memorable quotations can help us to understand the purpose of parallelism. The photographs on the next page represent well-known public figures who made powerful statements. Read the quotations, complete the activities, and answer the question "What's the point of parallelism?"

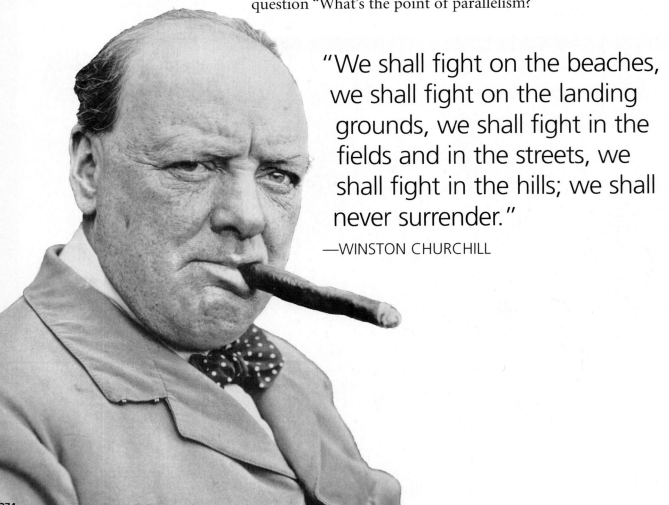

"We shall fight on the beaches, we shall fight on the landing grounds, we shall fight in the fields and in the streets, we shall fight in the hills; we shall never surrender."

—WINSTON CHURCHILL

What's the Point of Parallelism?

PHOTOGRAPHIC ORGANIZER: PARALLELISM

Each of the following well-known quotations uses parallelism to make an idea memorable and powerful. What do these statements have in common?

"I came; I saw; I conquered."

–JULIUS CAESAR

"We have nothing to fear but fear itself."

—FRANKLIN D. ROOSEVELT

"Scratch a lover; find a foe."

—DOROTHY PARKER

What is the point of parallelism?

_____

_____

_____

_____

Understanding the Point of Parallelism: One Student Writer's Response

The following paragraph records one writer's definition of parallelism based on the traits of the example quotations.

The sentences have a few things in common. Each one repeats words or similar types of words. For example, the quote "I came; I saw; I conquered" uses three short simple sentences; they repeat the subject "I" and use the same kind of verb. This quote shows a chain of actions. "Scratch a lover; find a foe" has two short sentences, and both begin with a verb. "Nothing to fear but fear" repeats a word. So I think parallelism repeats the same kind of words, phrases, and sentences. Parallelism is kind of musical. It's got rhythm.

Applying the Point: Parallelism

Parallelism refers to the balance of equal ideas expressed in the same grammatical form. Parallel expressions bring clarity, interest, and power to a piece of writing. You can achieve parallelism by emphasizing equal ideas using similar structures and patterns of words, phrases, or clauses. You can also use certain types of conjunctions and punctuation to signal parallel structures.

Parallel Words

Parallel structure uses a pair or series of closely related compound words to emphasize a point. Parallel words often, but not always, use similar **suffixes** (word endings).

- **Parallel Words**

Nonparallel:

ADJECTIVE OR VERB   *NOUN*

Prehistoric Paleo-Indians were wandering and hunters.

Revised for Parallelism:

PARALLEL NOUNS

Prehistoric Paleo-Indians were wanderers and hunters.

Nonparallel:

ADVERB   *PREPOSITIONAL PHRASE*

Paleo-Indians skillfully hunted game and with diligence gathered berries.

Revised for Parallelism:

PARALLEL ADVERBS

Paleo-Indians skillfully hunted game and diligently gathered berries.

Nonparallel:

NONPARALLEL VERBS

They flaked and crafting flint into spears.

Revised for Parallelism:

PARALLEL VERBS

They flaked and crafted flint into spears.

Practice 2

PARALLEL WORDS

Rewrite the following sentences to achieve parallelism with parallel words.

1. Ancestors of today's Pueblo Indians, the Anasazi were farming and craftsmen.

_____

_____

_____

_____

2. The Anasazi men wove baskets, and the Anasazi women were making pottery.

_____

_____

3. Cleverly and in a gradual way, the Anasazi developed an irrigation system to survive in an arid environment.

_____

_____

4. Write a sentence that uses parallel words. Suggested topic: A good way to make something.

_____

_____

Parallel Phrases

Parallel structure uses a pair or series of closely related compound phrases to emphasize a point. Parallel phrases repeat similar word patterns or groups.

• **Parallel Phrases**

Nonparallel:

INFINITIVE PHRASE

Around A.D. 300, the Mayas learned to build cities, jewelry crafting, and to develop trade.

NOUN PHRASE   *INFINITIVE PHRASE*

Revised for Parallelism:

Around A.D. 300, the Mayas learned to build cities, to craft jewelry, and to develop trade.

PARALLEL INFINITIVE PHRASES

Nonparallel:

PRESENT PARTICIPLE PHRASE

Maya women worked hard, planting the seeds, weeded the crops, and reaped the harvest.

PAST PARTICIPLE PHRASES

Revised for Parallelism:

Maya women worked hard, planting the seeds, weeding the crops, and reaping the harvest.

PARALLEL PRESENT PARTICIPLE PHRASES

Nonparallel:

WORD (NOUN)   *PHRASE (NOUN)*

Architecture and building a system of roads were two major accomplishments of the Incas.

Revised for Parallelism:

PARALLEL NOUN PHRASES

Developing a style of architecture and building a system of roads were two major accomplishments of the Incas.

Practice 3

PARALLEL PHRASES

Revise the following sentences to achieve emphasis through parallel phrases.

1. The Inca empire began in 1200 with the conquest of the Moche culture in Peru and its ending in 1535 with the conquest of the Inca by the Spanish.

----

2. To see their enemies and in self defense, they built enormous fortresses on top of steep mountains, such as the famous Sacasahuman, located in Cuzco, the Inca Empire capital.

----

3. By developing an irrigation system and they used llamas for meat and transportation, the Inca were able to provide ample resources for their population.

----

4. Write a sentence that uses parallel phrases. Suggested topic: An amazing achievement.

Adapted from "Inca," EMuseum@Minnesota State University, Mankato, 2003

Parallel Clauses

Parallel structure uses a set of closely related clauses to emphasize a point. Parallel structure begins with a clause and continues with clauses to create a balanced, logical statement. Parallel structure establishes a pattern of similarly structured clauses to express closely related ideas. Use parallel words and phrases within clauses.

> For more information on sentence types and sentence elements, see pages 310–323, "Subjects, Verbs, and Simple Sentences," and pages 324–339, "Compound and Complex Sentences."

- **Parallel Clauses**

    Nonparallel:

    INDEPENDENT CLAUSE

    Only a few million people inhabited the Americas by 1490,

    yet roughly 75 million people who were living in Europe.

    DEPENDENT CLAUSE
    (ILLOGICAL MIXED STRUCTURE)

    Revised for Parallelism:

    PARALLEL INDEPENDENT CLAUSES

    Only a few million people inhabited the Americas by 1490, yet roughly 75 million people inhabited Europe.

Nonparallel:

DEPENDENT CLAUSE

Myth teaches that Europeans discovered an uninhabited America; in history, Native peoples inhabited a cultivated, civilized America.

INDEPENDENT CLAUSE

Revised for Parallelism:

PARALLEL INDEPENDENT CLAUSES

Myth teaches that Europeans discovered an uninhabited America; history teaches that Native peoples inhabited a cultivated, civilized America.

PARALLEL DEPENDENT CLAUSES

Practice 4

PARALLEL CLAUSES

Revise the following sentences to achieve emphasis through parallel clauses.

1. Native Americans believed that humans were merely a part of the natural world and in the need for humans to revere nature.

----

2. Europeans saw the land as something to own and control, in contrast with Native Americans seeing the land as something to have a place in and sustain.

----

3. Before a hunt Native Americans prepared themselves spiritually, and during a hunt showing great humility.

----

4. Write a sentence that uses parallel clauses. Suggested topic: My beliefs about the environment.

Punctuation for Parallelism

The comma (sometimes along with coordinating conjunctions) and the semicolon signal equal ideas. In addition, numbered, lettered, or bulleted items in a list signal ideas of equal importance. Ideas marked by these pieces of punctuation are best expressed with parallelism.

Coordinating conjunctions always signal an equal relationship among words, phrases, and clauses. Use **commas** between parallel items in a series. Use a comma with a coordinating conjunction to join independent clauses.

Examples

To build a relationship, do not criticize, condemn, or complain.

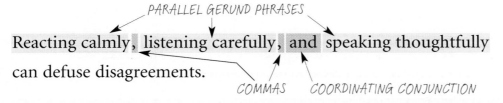

Reacting calmly, listening carefully, and speaking thoughtfully can defuse disagreements.

Criticism makes others resentful, yet praise makes others joyful.

Semicolons signal two or more closely related independent clauses.

Immediacy is the union between people; it is the creation of oneness; it is the communication of interest.

Numbers, letters, or bullets signal items in a list. Lists are often used in résumés, business letters, and presentations. Note that colons can introduce a list, and semicolons can separate items.

Training session suggestions include the following: (1) expressing interest in the customers; (2) using the names of customers; and (3) meeting the needs of customers.

PARALLELISM

Edit the following sentences for proper use of punctuation for parallel expression.

1. Space is an important factor in communication; for example three types of distances are personal social and public distances.

2. Personal distance ranges from 18 inches to about 4 feet social distance ranges from 4 to 12 feet public distance ranges from 12 to more than 25 feet.

3. People interact in three types of territories: (1) primary territories like a bedroom or office; secondary territories like the cafeteria or a classroom seat (3) public territories like a restaurant or shopping mall.

4. Write a sentence using parallelism. Suggested topic: The media and personal space.

Adapted from Joseph A. DeVito, *Messages: Building Interpersonal Communication Skills*, 4th Ed.

PARALLELISM REVIEW

Edit and revise the following paragraph for parallel expression and proper punctuation of parallel expressions.

Interpersonal Silence

(1) In the U.S. legal system, you have the right to remain silent and refusing to incriminate yourself. (2) But you don't have the right to refuse to reveal information about the criminal activities of others, you must reveal details of a crime you wrongly have witnessed. (3) Rightly or wrong, psychiatrists and lawyers are often exempt from this general rule. (4) A wife can refuse to testify against her husband a husband can refuse to testify against his wife. (5) In interpersonal situations, however, there aren't any written rules; therefore, it's not always clear whether silence is ethical or being unethical. (6) For example, most people would agree that you have the right to withhold information that has no bearing on the matter at hand. (7) Private information irrelevant to the workplace includes the following: personal relationships sexual orientation or religion.

Writing Assignments

Writing for Everyday Life

Assume you are putting together a cookbook of your grandmother's favorite recipes to reproduce and give as gifts to family members. Edit the following recipe for parallel expression. Use your own paper.

Chocolate Fudge Square Cake

Cake Batter for Cake:
1 stick of margarine
2 Tbsp. of cocoa
3/4 cup of flour
1 cup of chopped nuts
Mini marshmallows
2 eggs

Cake Icing:
2 Tbsp. of cocoa
2 Tbsp. of melted margarine
2 cups of confectioner sugar
mixed with 2 Tbsp. or more milk

Beat margarine and cocoa. Adding unbeaten eggs one at a time. Add sugar, flour, and salt. Stir in nuts. Poured into greased 7 x 11 inch pan. Bake at 350° for 25 to 30 minutes. Removing from oven. Cover with scant layer of marshmallows and returning to oven until marshmallows are puffy and soft. Remove from oven. Poured and spread icing over marshmallows for marbled effect.

Writing for College Life

Assume you are giving a PowerPoint presentation in your Communication class. Edit the following outline of your PowerPoint slides so that each element is parallel. Use your own paper.

Title Slide:

The Self in Interpersonal
Communication

Slide One:

Dimensions of the Self
Self-Concept
Being Aware of Self
Self-Esteem

Slide Two:

Self-Disclosure
Influences on Self-Disclosure
Rewarding Self-Disclosure
Dangers of Self-Disclosure

Slide Three:

Communication Apprehension
The Nature of Communication
Apprehension
Theories of Communication
Apprehension Management

—From Joseph A. DeVito, *The Interpersonal Communication Book,* 10th ed., Longman 2004, p. viii.

Writing Assignments CONTINUED

Writing for Working Life

Edit the following portion of a résumé to ensure parallel expression.

CAREER OBJECTIVE
- To secure a Management position
- I want to contribute to the success of the organization.

SUMMARY OF QUALIFICATIONS
- Experienced in retail management.
- I am skilled in the following areas: analytical thinking, client orientation, creative thinking, decision-making, problem solving, time management, leading others, interpersonal skills, oral communication, written communication, and computer skills.

WORK EXPERIENCE
- Target, sales associate
  From: 11/6/98 – 6/23/01
- State Farm Insurance, worked as secretary to Team Supervisor of Claims Unit
  From: 7/1/01 – To: Present

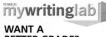
WANT A BETTER GRADE?
For more practice with parallelism, go to **www.mywritinglab.com > Writing Clear Sentences > Parallelism.**

Academic Learning Log

WHAT HAVE I LEARNED ABOUT PARALLELISM?

To test and track your understanding, answer the following questions. Use several sentences as needed for each response.

1. What is parallelism? ....

....

2. Parallel .... often, but not always, use similar suffixes (word endings).

3. Parallel phrases repeat similar ....

4. Repeat parallel patterns of .... to pace ideas through the thoughtful arrangement and sequence of sentence types.

5. What types of punctuation signal parallelism? (a) ....; (b) ....;

and (c) ....

6. Commas are used with .... to join independent clauses.

7. Semicolons signal two or more closely related ....

8. **How will I use what I have learned?** Discuss how you will apply to your own writing what you have learned about parallelism. When will you apply this knowledge during the writing process?

---

9. **What do I still need to study about sentence types?** Discuss your ongoing study needs by describing what, when, and how you will continue studying and using parallelism.

Academic Learning Log

21

Run-ons: Comma Splices and Fused Sentences

A comma splice is an error that occurs when a comma is used by itself to join two sentences. A fused sentence is an error that occurs when two sentences are joined without any punctuation.

According to research, comma splices and fused sentences are two of the most common errors made by student writers. The photograph on these pages shows a natural phenomenon that stirs human emotions and imagination. Read about this special place and then answer the question "What's the point of learning about correcting comma splices and fused sentences?"

What's the Point of Correcting Comma Splices and Fused Sentences?

PHOTOGRAPHIC ORGANIZER: COMMA SPLICES AND FUSED SENTENCES

Read the following short description of Niagara Falls, adapted from a 1913 essay written by Rupert Brooke for the *Westminster Gazette*. This version contains one comma splice and three fused sentences. How do these errors affect the reading of the passage?

Niagara Falls

Half a mile or so above the Falls, on either side, the water of the great stream begins to run more swiftly in confusion it descends with ever-growing speed it begins chattering and leaping, breaking into a thousand ripples, throwing up joyful fingers of spray, sometimes it is divided by islands and rocks sometimes the eye can see nothing but a waste of laughing, springing, foamy waves.

Adapted from "Niagara Falls," Rupert Brooke

What's the point of learning about correcting comma splices and fused sentences?

_____

_____

_____

_____

Understanding the Point of Correcting Comma Splices and Fused Sentences: One Student Writer's Response

The following paragraph offers one writer's response to the opening paragraph about Niagara Falls.

> I had to read the paragraph several times to figure out what the author was saying. I couldn't tell when one sentence ended and another one started. I guess a comma splice or fused sentence occurs because a writer joins sentences without the proper punctuation. Without proper punctuation that signals the end of one thought and the beginning of another, ideas become confusing as they run on. Proper punctuation signals the beginning or end of each sentence. Proper punctuation makes ideas clear and easy to follow.

Applying the Point: Correcting Comma Splices and Fused Sentences

Comma splices and fused sentences are punctuation errors that occur where independent clauses are improperly joined to form a compound sentence. To properly combine clauses into a compound sentence, the end of each independent clause must be signaled by appropriate punctuation, such as a semicolon, a comma followed by a coordinating conjunction, or a period at the end of the sentence.

Comma Splice

A **comma splice** occurs when a comma is used by itself (without a coordinating conjunction) to join two independent clauses.

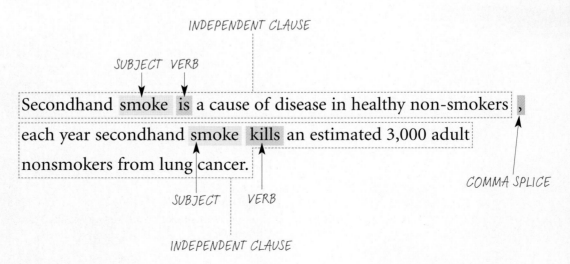

Fused Sentence

A **fused sentence** occurs when two independent clauses are joined without any punctuation.

INDEPENDENT CLAUSE

SUBJECT VERB

FUSED SENTENCES (MISSING PUNCTUATION)

SUBJECT

Secondhand smoke causes respiratory problems it also causes reddening, itching, and watering of the eyes.

VERB

INDEPENDENT CLAUSE

IDENTIFYING COMMA SPLICES AND FUSED SENTENCES

Practice 2

Test your ability to identify comma splices, fused sentences, and properly combined clauses. Write **CS** for comma splice, **FS** for fused sentence, or **C** for correctly punctuated.

.... **1.** More than 126 million nonsmoking Americans are exposed to secondhand smoke in homes, vehicles, workplaces, and public places, almost 60 percent of U.S. children between the ages of 3 and 11—or almost 22 million children—are exposed to secondhand smoke.

.... **2.** There is no risk-free level of secondhand smoke exposure even brief exposure can be dangerous.

.... **3.** Secondhand smoke, also known as environmental tobacco smoke, is a complex mixture of gases and particles including smoke from the burning cigarette, cigar, or pipe tip and exhaled smoke.

.... **4.** Two types of secondhand smoke exist, sidestream smoke is the smoke released from the burning end of a cigarette, exhaled mainstream smoke is the smoke exhaled by the smoker.

.... **5.** Secondhand smoke is a known human carcinogen (cancer-causing agent) more than 50 compounds in secondhand smoke have been identified as known or reasonably anticipated human carcinogens secondhand smoke contains at least 250 chemicals that are known to be toxic or carcinogenic.

Five Ways to Correct Comma Splices and Fused Sentences

As a writer, you have the choice of several ways to correct or avoid comma splices and fused sentences. Each method creates a specific effect. Most experts recommend using a variety of these methods, rather than always relying on the same one.

1. Separate sentences using a period and capital letter

Punctuating the independent clauses as separate sentences is a method often used to correct comma splices and fused sentences.

Incorrect:

Incorrect:

Revised (Correct):

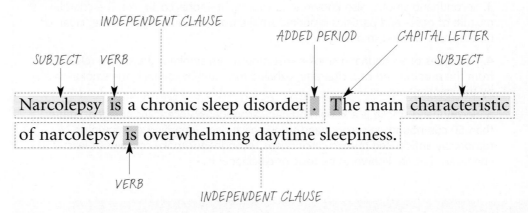

Practice 3

COMMA SPLICES AND FUSED SENTENCES

Edit the following sentences to eliminate comma splices and fused sentences. Separate clauses by inserting a period and capital letter as needed.

1. A person with narcolepsy is likely to become drowsy or to fall asleep, often at inappropriate times and places, daytime sleep may occur with or without warning and may be irresistible.

2. Drowsiness may persist for prolonged periods of time nighttime sleep may be fragmented with frequent awakenings.

3. There is strong evidence that narcolepsy may run in families, eight to twelve percent of people with narcolepsy have a close relative with the disease.

4. Narcolepsy can occur in both men and women at any age, its symptoms are usually first noticed in teenagers or young adults.

5. Write a compound sentence. Suggested topic: Sleep problems.

2. Join sentences with a comma followed by a coordinating conjunction

Sentences can be properly joined by inserting a comma followed by a coordinating conjunction between the independent clauses. The acronym FANBOYS stands for each of the coordinating conjunctions: *for, and, nor, but, or, yet, so.* This method of combining sentences states the relationship between ideas of equal importance.

Incorrect:

SUBJECT *VERB* *INDEPENDENT CLAUSE*

Chief Red Cloud led a successful war against the U.S. government,

he stands as a legendary Lakota leader.

SUBJECT VERB *INDEPENDENT CLAUSE* *COMMA SPLICE*

Incorrect:

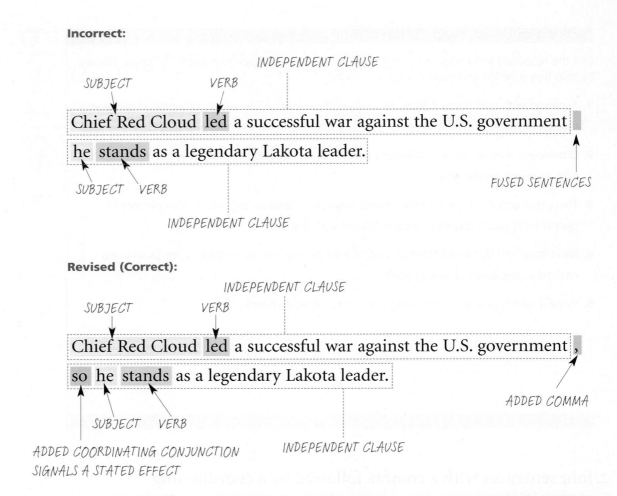

INDEPENDENT CLAUSE

SUBJECT   VERB

Chief Red Cloud led a successful war against the U.S. government

he stands as a legendary Lakota leader.

SUBJECT   VERB

INDEPENDENT CLAUSE

FUSED SENTENCES

Revised (Correct):

INDEPENDENT CLAUSE

SUBJECT   VERB

Chief Red Cloud led a successful war against the U.S. government,

so he stands as a legendary Lakota leader.

SUBJECT   VERB

ADDED COMMA

ADDED COORDINATING CONJUNCTION
SIGNALS A STATED EFFECT

INDEPENDENT CLAUSE

Practice 4

COMMA SPLICES AND FUSED SENTENCES

Edit the following sentences to eliminate comma splices and fused sentences. Join independent clauses with a comma and a coordinating conjunction.

1. Chief Red Cloud waged war against the United States the army had constructed forts along the Bozeman Trail.

2. The Bozeman Trail served as a route to the Montana gold fields for miners and settlers, the trail cut through the heart of Indian Territory.

3. Red Cloud remembered the removal of the Eastern Lakota from Minnesota in 1862 and 1863, he launched a series of assaults on the forts.

4. Chief Red Cloud's successful strategies forced the United States to close the Bozeman Trail he negotiated a treaty resulting in the United States abandoning its forts along the trail.

5. Write a compound sentence using a comma and a coordinating conjunction. Suggested topic: A heroic action.

3. Join sentences with a semicolon

Use a semicolon to join independent clauses when no conjunction is present. A semicolon indicates that the two sentences of equal importance are so closely related that they can be stated as one sentence; however, a semicolon alone does not state the relationship between the two clauses. The relationship between clauses may be one of the following: *time, space, order of importance, general to specific, addition, cause, effect, comparison,* or *contrast.*

Incorrect:

Incorrect:

Revised (Correct):

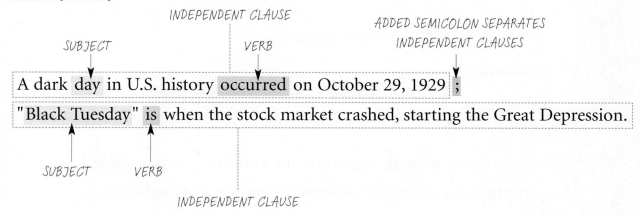

Practice 5

COMMA SPLICES AND FUSED SENTENCES

Edit the following sentences by inserting semicolons as needed to correct comma splices and fused sentences.

1. Unemployment skyrocketed a quarter of the workforce was without jobs by 1933, and many people became homeless.

2. President Herbert Hoover attempted to handle the crisis, he was unable to improve the situation.

3. In 1932, President Franklin Delano Roosevelt promised a "New Deal" for the American people Congress created the Works Progress Administration (WPA), which offered work relief for thousands of people.

4. In 1941, America entered into World War II, the Great Depression ended.

5. Write a compound sentence using a semicolon. Suggested topic: The homeless.

4. Join sentences with a semicolon followed by a conjunctive adverb

For more information about joining ideas of equal importance, see pages 324–329, "Compound and Complex Sentences."

Use a semicolon with a conjunctive adverb to join independent clauses. Conjunctive adverbs are transition words that state the relationships between ideas of equal importance. A few common examples include *also, for example, however, then, therefore,* and *thus.*

Incorrect:

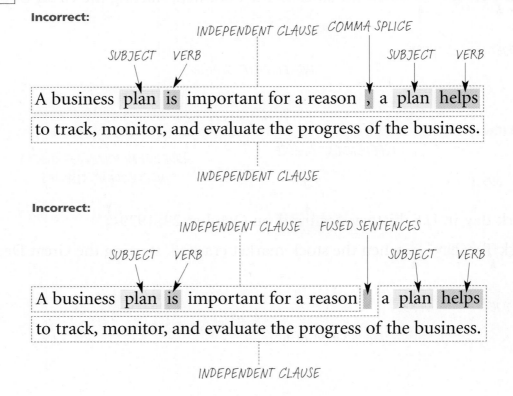

Revised (Correct):

INDEPENDENT CLAUSE

SUBJECT VERB

ADDED SEMICOLON SEPARATES INDEPENDENT CLAUSES

ADDED CONJUNCTIVE ADVERB

A business plan is important for various reasons ; for example ,
a plan helps to track, monitor, and evaluate the progress of the business.

SUBJECT VERB

INDEPENDENT CLAUSE

ADDED COMMA WITH
INTRODUCTORY ELEMENT

Not only do these transitions state the relationship between ideas, but they also introduce
an independent clause and must be set off with a comma.

COMMA SPLICES AND FUSED SENTENCES

Edit the following sentences to correct comma splices and fused sentences. Join independent
clauses with a semicolon and one of the following transitions: *also, for example, however,
therefore*. Use each transition once.

Practice 6

1. You can start a new business of your own, many people would rather buy an existing
   business or a franchise.

2. A business plan will help you to get organized it's almost impossible to get financing for
   your business unless you have a plan.

3. Business plans actually consist of various different plans the marketing plan lays out the
   strategies that help you bring your products or services to the attention of prospective
   customers.

4. Friends, family, and other individuals who could lend you money for your business are likely
   not to have as much money as you need, you will probably decide to apply for a bank
   loan.

5. Write a compound sentence using a semicolon and a conjunctive adverb. Suggested topic:
   Why I would (wouldn't) want to start my own business.

5. Join sentences using a subordinating conjunction

Not all ideas are of equal importance. Frequently, writers choose to join ideas in a complex sentence made up of an independent clause and one or more dependent clauses. A subordinating conjunction signals the beginning of a dependent clause and states its subordinate relationship to the independent clause. Some examples of subordinating conjunctions include *although*, *as*, *because*, *if*, and *when*. Relative pronouns also connect a dependent clause to an independent clause. Examples of relative pronouns include *that*, *which*, and *who*.

> For more information on complex sentences, see pages 330–335, "Compound and Complex Sentences."

Incorrect:

SUBJECT   VERB
INDEPENDENT CLAUSE

I am grateful for the opportunity to work for Southeast Dental Clinic ,
it rewards the excellence and hard work of its staff.

SUBJECT   VERB
INDEPENDENT CLAUSE
COMMA SPLICE

Incorrect:

SUBJECT   VERB
INDEPENDENT CLAUSE

I am grateful for the opportunity to work for Southeast Dental Clinic
it rewards the excellence and hard work of its staff.

SUBJECT   VERB
INDEPENDENT CLAUSE
FUSED SENTENCES

Revised #1 (Correct):

SUBJECT   VERB
INDEPENDENT CLAUSE
COMMA

I am grateful for the opportunity to work for Southeast Dental Clinic ,
which rewards the excellence and hard work of its staff.

VERB
ADDED RELATIVE PRONOUN
(SUBJECT)
DEPENDENT CLAUSE

Revised #2 (Correct):

ADDED SUBORDINATING CONJUNCTION

SUBJECT   DEPENDENT CLAUSE

VERB

Because Southeast Dental Clinic rewards the excellence and hard work of its staff , I am grateful for the opportunity to work for the clinc.

COMMA SETS OFF
INTRODUCTORY ELEMENT   SUBJECT   VERB   INDEPENDENT CLAUSE

COMMA SPLICES AND FUSED SENTENCES

Revise the following sentences into complex sentences to correct comma splices and fused sentences. Use the following subordinating conjunctions: *after*, *as*, *even though*, *which*.

1. You might want to consider careers in dentistry, they include dentist, dental hygienist, and dental assistant.

----

2. The preparation to be a dentist is time consuming, dental school takes four years and is followed by an exam for a state license to practice dentistry.

----

3. To be a dental hygienist, you will also need to take an exam for a license, you won't have to go through dental school.

----

4. You complete the required training then you'll be able to find a rewarding career in the field of dentistry.

----

5. Write a complex sentence using any subordinator. Suggested topic: Dentistry.

Practice 8

Revise the following sentences to correct fused sentences and comma splices.

1. Sleepwalking is a disorder characterized by walking or other activity while seemingly asleep, Lady Macbeth, in Shakespeare's play, is perhaps the most famous sleepwalker.

2. Sleepwalking is associated with deep sleep, sometimes it occurs during lighter sleep.

3. A sleepwalker may just sit up and seem awake, he may walk around, he may perform complicated activities such as moving furniture and even driving a car.

4. A common misconception is that sleepwalkers should not be awakened, experts say that there's no harm in awakening a sleepwalker.

5. Sleepwalking usually doesn't require consultation and treatment by a physician a visit to a physician is appropriate if sleepwalking occurs frequently or in combination with other symptoms.

Adapted from http://www.medicinenet.com/script/main/art.asp?articlekey=39396&pf=3&page=1]

Practice 9

FUSED SENTENCES AND COMMA SPLICES REVIEW

Edit and revise the paragraph below, adapted from the article "Why Sleep Is Important," from the National Institute of Health website, to correct fused sentences and comma splices. Use your own paper.

Sleep Is a Basic Human Need

Sleep is a natural part of everybody's life but many people know very little about how important it is, and some even try to get by with little sleep. Sleep is something our bodies need to do it is not optional. Even though the exact reasons for sleep remain a mystery, we do know that during sleep many of the body's major organ and regulatory systems continue to work actively. Some parts of the brain actually increase their activity dramatically, the body produces more of certain hormones. Sleep, like diet and exercise, is important for our minds and bodies to function normally in fact, sleep appears to be required for survival. Rats deprived of sleep die within two to three weeks, a time frame similar to death due to starvation. An internal biological clock regulates the timing for sleep it programs each person to feel sleepy during the nighttime hours and to be active during the daylight hours. Light is the cue that synchronizes the biological clock to the 24-hour cycle of day and night. Sleepiness due to chronic lack of adequate sleep is a big problem in the United States it affects many children as well as adults. Children and even adolescents need at least 9 hours of sleep each night to do their best most adults need approximately 8 hours of sleep each night.

Writing Assignments

Writing for Everyday Life

Read the following letter of protest written to a county council. Edit to correct comma splices and fused sentences. Use your own paper.

Dear Roberta Clancy, Chairperson of the County Council:

Recent news articles published the council's intention to allow WC Homes, Inc. to cut down a pair of century-old oak trees on the Marsh Loop these trees evidently stand in the way of progress. WC Homes, Inc. plans to develop a neighborhood of 1,000 single homes, the trees will block access to the entrance of the neighborhood. Marsh Loop has long been known for its unique beauty and importance as a wildlife refuge. Developers are rapidly changing this rare and important natural environment into an over-built urban area. Many voters agree with me you cut down these trees you will be out of office.

Sincerely,

Jane Watts

Writing Assignments CONTINUED

Writing for College Life

The following paragraph was written during an essay exam for a health class. The exam question asked the student to explain the need for proper technique in weight training. Edit to correct comma splices and fused sentences. Use your own paper.

Weight training is an excellent exercise you can improve your strength, increase muscle tone, lose fat, gain muscle mass, and improve bone density. You use a sloppy technique, you stand a good chance of doing more harm than good. Common injuries can occur during weight training these include sprains, strains, tendonitis, fractures, and dislocations. The Mayo Clinic offers several suggestions on proper technique. First, remember to breathe holding your breath during weightlifting can increase your blood pressure to dangerous levels. Second, don't overdo it. The amount of weight you lift should make your muscles feel tired after 10 to 15 repetitions. A weight that causes fatigue at 12 repetitions creates muscle strength and toning. Finally, don't rush. And don't jerk the weights up, lift and lower the weights in a slow, fluid movement.

Writing for Working Life

Read the following letter written as a follow-up to a job interview. Edit to correct comma splices and fused sentences. Use your own paper.

Dear Ms. Tucker:

Thank you very much for taking time to talk with me about the position of department manager. I enjoyed meeting you and the members of the department, I am excited about the chance to work with such a dynamic team. I, too, am a self-starter yet a team player. I like to encourage individuals to take ownership of projects but to still involve team members. Based on our meeting, I believe this is the job for me my qualifications are an excellent fit, particularly my training in technology and communication. The position is exactly what I'm looking for I'm confident that I can be a significant contributor to the success of the graphics department. I sincerely hope you agree. Thank you, again, for giving so much of your time I look forward to hearing from you.

Sincerely,

Justin M. Agler

mywritinglab

WANT A BETTER GRADE?
For more practice with fragments, go to **www.mywritinglab.com > Recognizing and Avoiding Errors > Run-ons: Comma Splices and Fused Sentences.**

WHAT HAVE I LEARNED ABOUT CORRECTING COMMA SPLICES AND FUSED SENTENCES?

To test and track your understanding, complete the following ideas. Use several sentences as needed for each response.

1. A comma splice is

2. A fused sentence is

3. What are the five ways to eliminate comma splices and fused sentences?

4. How will I use what I have learned about correcting comma splices and fused sentences?
In your notebook, discuss how you will apply to your own writing what you have learned about comma splices and fused sentences.

5. What do I still need to study about correcting comma splices and fused sentences?
In your notebook, discuss your ongoing study needs by describing what, when, and how you will continue studying comma splices and fused sentences.

22

Fragments

A fragment is an incomplete thought.

Thinking about a real-life situation helps us to understand the impact of fragments on our ability to communicate. The photo illustrates a couple in search of a place to live. Read about the situation and answer the question "What's the point of learning about fragments?"

What's the Point of Correcting Fragments?

PHOTOGRAPHIC ORGANIZER: FRAGMENTS

▲ Apartment for rent

Suppose you are looking for a new apartment. You ask two landlords the same questions. Below are the two replies.

Landlord A:
"If it's a little messy, well ... sometimes partial refunds ... for damages ... not leaving behind personal belongings..."

Landlord B:
"You will get your security deposit back if you leave the apartment in the same or better condition than it is in right now, if you don't leave any of your belongings behind, and if you pay your last month's rent. We can go around the apartment right now and make a list of the condition of each room so we'll have a reference point when you're ready to move out."

With which landlord will you be able to communicate easily and clearly if you move in?

....

What's the point of learning about fragments?

....

....

....

....

....

Understanding the Point of Correcting Fragments: One Student Writer's Response

The following paragraph offers one writer's reaction to the statements about the security deposit given by the landlords.

Landlord A never finishes a thought, so I have no idea what he means. His answers are vague, and he doesn't seem to care about being understood. Maybe he thinks I should just know what he means. In contrast, Landlord B spoke clearly using complete sentences. I know exactly what is expected.

Landlord B is going to be easier to talk to and understand. The difference between the two responses makes me realize how important it is to use complete sentences if you want to be understood. When others can understand your thoughts, you can connect with them and even change how they think about things or how they act. That's real power.

Applying the Point: Correcting Fragments

The ability to write ideas in complete thoughts, or sentences, is an important tool in building coherent paragraphs and essays. A sentence has two traits.

SENTENCE: Complete Thought-Complete Information

   TRAIT ONE: A sentence states a complete and independent thought.

   TRAIT TWO: A sentence contains a subject and a verb.

A **sentence** contains all the information needed to clearly express a complete thought. In contrast, a fragment can often be recognized by what is missing from the thought. A **fragment** is an incomplete thought.

FRAGMENT: Incomplete Thought-Missing Information

A **fragment** is missing a subject, a verb, or both a subject and a verb.

Missing Subject:	Does not disqualify you from exercising.
Missing Verb:	Edward taking a physical exam.
Missing Subject and Verb:	To safely participate and to reduce risk of injury.

Even when a group of words includes both a subject and a verb, it still can be a fragment. A subordinating conjunction signals a fragment that has both a subject and a verb. These types of fragments are missing an independent clause.

Fragment (Missing an Independent Clause):

To identify a fragment, ask the following questions:

- Does the idea have a verb?
- What is the subject of the verb?
- Does the idea express a complete thought?

IDENTIFYING FRAGMENTS

Identify fragments and sentences. Write **F** for *fragment* next to the incomplete thoughts. Write **S** for *sentence* next to the complete thoughts.

.... **1.** Regular physical activity, fitness, and exercise are critically important.

.... **2.** For the health and well being of people of all ages.

.... **3.** Research has proven that all individuals can benefit from regular physical activity.

.... **4.** Whether they engage in vigorous exercise or some type of moderate physical activity.

.... **5.** Might enjoy exercising on a regular basis.

Practice 2

Types of Fragments

This section discusses seven common types of fragments: (1) prepositional phrase, (2) appositive phrase, (3) infinitive phrase, (4) gerund phrase, (5) participle phrase, (6) dependent clause, and (7) relative clause. This section also discusses techniques you can use to revise these fragments into a sentence. Fragments are either phrases or dependent clauses punctuated as if they are sentences. A writer may use two techniques to revise fragments into sentences.

- Combine existing ideas.
- Add missing ideas.

Phrase Fragments

A **phrase** is a group of words that acts as a single unit. A phrase is a fragment because it does not contain both a subject and a verb. To create a sentence, add information (such as a subject, a verb, or both), or join the phrase to an existing sentence.

1. PREPOSITIONAL PHRASE

A **prepositional phrase** begins with a preposition (such as *at, on, in, to, toward, for, since,* and *of*) and ends with the object of the preposition. A prepositional phrase adds information about direction, manner, space, and time, such as *in the house* or *after the game*.

Revised to Combine Ideas:

Revised to Add Ideas:

Practice 3

Build two new sentences using the prepositional phrase. First, combine the existing sentence with the prepositional phrase to create a new sentence. Then, create another new sentence by adding missing information to the prepositional phrase.

Fast food is too often on the menu.
in many American households

1. COMBINE IDEAS: ....

....

2. ADD IDEAS: ....

....

A typical meal from McDonald's is high in fat and calories.
like a Big Mac, a large order of French fries, and a medium Coke
with a total of 64 grams of fat and 1,260 calories

3. COMBINE IDEAS: ....

....

....

4. ADD IDEAS: ....

....

....

....

2. APPOSITIVE PHRASE

An **appositive phrase** contains a noun that renames or describes another noun in the same sentence. An appositive phrase combines with a complete thought to add detail. Place an appositive phrase next to the noun it renames.

APPOSITIVE PHRASE FRAGMENT	SUBJECT	VERB	COMPLETE THOUGHT
A devoted family man.	Jermaine	protects	his health for the sake of his family.

Revised to Combine Ideas:

A devoted family man , Jermaine protects his health for the sake of his family.

INTRODUCTORY PHRASE
SET OFF WITH COMMA

COMPLETE THOUGHT

Revised to Add Ideas:

ADDED VERB

ADDED SUBJECT

Jermaine is a devoted family man.   He protects his health for the sake of his family.

COMPLETE THOUGHT

COMPLETE THOUGHT

Practice 4

APPOSITIVE PHRASE FRAGMENTS

Build two new sentences using the appositive phrase. First, combine the existing sentence with the appositive phrase to create a new sentence. Then, create another new sentence by adding missing information to the appositive phrase.

the range of motion around a joint

Flexibility can help prevent injuries through all stages of life.

1. COMBINE IDEAS: _____

_____

2. ADD IDEAS: _____

_____

A beneficial exercise. Yoga improves flexibility.

3. COMBINE IDEAS: _____

_____

4. ADD IDEAS: _____

_____

_____

3. INFINITIVE PHRASE

An infinitive is a form of a verb, but it is not a verb. Combining *to* with a verb forms an **infinitive,** as in *to go*, *to talk*, and *to think*. An **infinitive phrase** is made up of an infinitive and the object of the infinitive, such as *to quit smoking* or *to run a mile*. An infinitive phrase can act as a noun, adjective, or adverb.

SUBJECT   VERB   COMPLETE THOUGHT   INFINITIVE PHRASE

Jermaine makes beneficial life style choices. To protect his health.

Revised to Combine Ideas:

COMPLETE THOUGHT

Jermaine makes beneficial life style choices to protect his health.

Revised to Add Ideas:

COMPLETE THOUGHT

COMPLETE THOUGHT   ADDED SUBJECT   ADDED VERB

Jermaine makes beneficial life style choices. His priority is to protect his health.

INFINITIVE PHRASE FRAGMENTS

Build two new sentences using the infinitive phrase. First, combine the existing sentence with the infinitive phrase to create a new sentence. Then, create another new sentence by adding missing information to the infinitive phrase.

You may want to use both dynamic and static types of stretches. to improve your flexibility

1. COMBINE IDEAS: _____

2. ADD IDEAS: _____

Stretch a muscle to its farthest point and then hold the position. to perform a static stretch

3. COMBINE IDEAS: _____

4. ADD IDEAS: _____

Practice 5

-ING PHRASES: GERUNDS AND PARTICIPLES

An *-ing* phrase can function as either a noun or an adjective. An *-ing* phrase used as a noun is called a **gerund**. An *-ing* phrase used as an adjective is called a **participle**.

4. GERUND PHRASE

A **gerund** is a form of a verb, but it is not a verb. A gerund is a noun that ends in *-ing,* such as *going, talking,* and *thinking.* A **gerund phrase** is made up of a gerund and the object of the gerund, such as *quitting smoking* or *running three miles.* A gerund phrase functions as a noun. For example, a gerund phrase can be the subject of a sentence or an object of a verb or preposition.

Revised to Combine Ideas:

Revised to Add Ideas:

-ING FRAGMENTS

Build two new sentences using the gerund phrase. First, combine the existing sentence with the *-ing* phrase to create a new sentence. Then, create another new sentence by adding missing information to the gerund phrase.

Keeping fit through yoga.
Sharika is strong and flexible.

1. COMBINE IDEAS: ....

....

2. ADD IDEAS: ....

Practice 6

Yoga often includes dynamic stretches.
moving the body in a sequence of poses

3. COMBINE IDEAS: ....

....

4. ADD IDEAS: ....

....

Practice 6

5. PARTICIPLE PHRASE

A participle is a form of a verb, but it is not a verb. A **participle** is an adjective that ends in *-ing*, such as *going, talking,* and *thinking.* A **participle phrase** is made up of a participle and the object of the participle such as *quitting smoking* or *running a mile.* A participle phrase functions as an adjective; it describes nouns and other adjectives.

–ING PHRASE FRAGMENT (PARTICIPLE)   COMPLETE THOUGHT

Trying to quit smoking.   Justine struggles with nicotine addiction.

SUBJECT   VERB

Revised to Combine Ideas:

COMPLETE THOUGHT

Trying to quit smoking , Justine struggles with nicotine addiction.

ACTS AS AN ADJECTIVE;   COMMA SETS OFF PHRASE
DESCRIBES THE SUBJECT "JUSTINE"   AS INTRODUCTORY ELEMENT

Revised to Add Ideas:

THE PARTICIPLE "TRYING"
BECOMES PART OF A VERB   OBJECT OF VERB

Justine is trying to quit smoking.

COMPLETE THOUGHT

Practice 7

–ING FRAGMENTS

Build two new sentences using the participle phrase. First, combine the existing sentence with the participle phrase to create a new sentence. Then, create another new sentence by adding missing information to the participle phrase.

Worrying about her son's eating habits
Tisha decided to consult a nutritionist.

1. COMBINE IDEAS: ....

....

2. ADD IDEAS: ....

....

Craving sodas, potato chips, and ice cream
10-year-old Sean is already obese.

3. COMBINE IDEAS: ....

....

4. ADD IDEAS: ....

....

Practice 8

PHRASE FRAGMENTS

Read the following sets of ideas. Identify the type of phrase fragment. Then, revise the ideas to eliminate fragments by combining or adding ideas.

1. Bones play many roles in the body. Providing structure, protecting organs, anchoring muscles, and storing calcium.

TYPE OF FRAGMENT: ....

REVISED SENTENCE: ....

....

2. Adequate calcium consumption and weight-bearing physical activity are necessary. To build strong bones and optimize bone mass.

TYPE OF FRAGMENT: ....

REVISED SENTENCE: _____

_____

3. The body cannot produce calcium. A mineral needed to produce bone.

TYPE OF FRAGMENT: _____

REVISED SENTENCE: _____

_____

4. By the age of 20. The average woman has acquired most of her skeletal mass.

TYPE OF FRAGMENT: _____

REVISED SENTENCE: _____

_____

5. Eating foods and drinking beverages that contain lots of calcium during childhood. Builds strong bones.

TYPE OF FRAGMENT: _____

REVISED SENTENCE: _____

_____

6. Rap star Nelly got milk. To build his bones.

TYPE OF FRAGMENT: _____

REVISED SENTENCE: _____

_____

Practice 8

Clause Fragments

A **clause** is a set of words that contains a subject and a verb. An **independent clause** states a complete thought in a sentence that begins with a capital letter and ends with punctuation such as a period or semicolon. In contrast, a **dependent clause** expresses an incomplete thought or fragment.

For more on dependent and subordinate clauses, see page 327.

6. DEPENDENT CLAUSE

A **dependent clause,** also known as a **subordinate clause,** does not make sense on its own. A dependent clause is formed by placing a subordinating conjunction in front of a subject and a verb.

A **subordinating conjunction** states the relationship between two clauses.

The following chart lists common subordinating conjunctions based on the relationships they express.

Subordinating Conjunctions and the Relationships They Express				
Cause	**Contrast**	**Time**	**Place**	**Condition**
as	although	after	where	even if
because	as if	as	wherever	if
in order that	even though	as long as		only if
now that	though	before		unless
since	whereas	once		when
so	while	since		whether or not
		until		
		when		
		whenever		
		while		

To create a sentence, combine the dependent clause with an independent clause. Or revise the dependent clause into an independent clause by dropping the subordinating conjunction.

Revised to Combine Ideas:

DEPENDENT CLAUSE

COMMA SETS OFF
INTRODUCTORY CLAUSE

Because healthy employees are more productive , some
corporations provide health club benefits for their employees.

COMPLETE THOUGHT

Revised to Add Ideas:

INDEPENDENT CLAUSE FORMED
BY DROPPING "BECAUSE"

SEMICOLON JOINS TWO
INDEPENDENT CLAUSES

Healthy employees are more productive ; therefore, some
corporations provide health club benefits for their employees.

COMPLETE THOUGHT

Practice 9

DEPENDENT CLAUSE FRAGMENTS

Build two sentences using the following sets of ideas. First, combine the existing sentence with the dependent clause to create a new sentence. Then, create another new sentence by revising the dependent clause into an independent clause.

because young children grow rapidly and have increased iron requirements
Young children are at risk of iron deficiency.

1. COMBINE IDEAS: ....

....

2. ADD IDEAS: ....

....

7. RELATIVE CLAUSE

One type of dependent clause is the relative clause, such as *who scored the winning home run.* A **relative clause** describes a noun or pronoun in an independent clause. A **relative pronoun** introduces the relative clause and relates it to the noun or pronoun it describes.

Relative Pronouns				
who	whom	whose	which	that

Join the relative clause to the independent clause that contains the word it describes. Or revise the relative clause into an independent clause by replacing the relative pronoun with a noun.

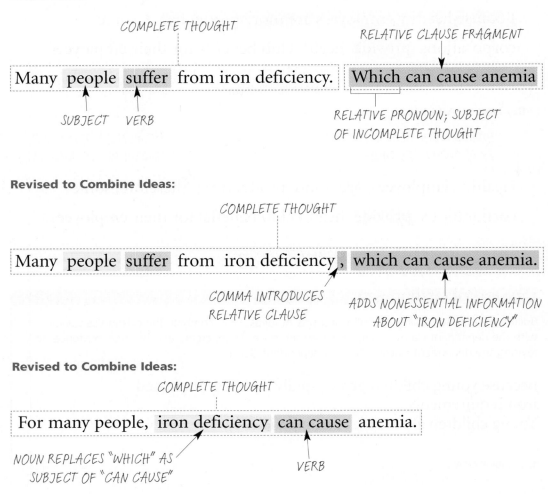

COMPLETE THOUGHT

RELATIVE CLAUSE FRAGMENT

Many people suffer from iron deficiency. Which can cause anemia

SUBJECT   VERB

RELATIVE PRONOUN; SUBJECT OF INCOMPLETE THOUGHT

Revised to Combine Ideas:

COMPLETE THOUGHT

Many people suffer from iron deficiency, which can cause anemia.

COMMA INTRODUCES RELATIVE CLAUSE

ADDS NONESSENTIAL INFORMATION ABOUT "IRON DEFICIENCY"

Revised to Combine Ideas:

COMPLETE THOUGHT

For many people, iron deficiency can cause anemia.

NOUN REPLACES "WHICH" AS SUBJECT OF "CAN CAUSE"

VERB

Practice 10

RELATIVE CLAUSE FRAGMENTS

Build two new sentences using the relative clause. First, combine the existing sentence with the relative clause to create a new sentence. Then, create another new sentence by revising the relative clause into an independent clause.

The most common cause of anemia is iron deficiency.
which impairs mental and physical development in infants and children.

1. COMBINE IDEAS: ....

....

2. ADD IDEAS: ....

....

Practice 11

CLAUSE FRAGMENTS

Revise the ideas to eliminate clause fragments.

1. The heart needs a constant supply of oxygen and nutrients. Which are carried to it by the blood in the coronary arteries.

----

2. When the coronary arteries become narrowed or clogged by cholesterol and fat deposits. They cannot supply enough blood to the heart, and the result is coronary heart disease (CHD).

----

3. Cholesterol is a waxy, fat-like substance. That occurs naturally in all parts of the body. That your body needs to function normally.

----

4. Unlike age, high cholesterol can be controlled. Which is a factor beyond our control.

----

5. You are at higher risk of having coronary heart disease. If you smoke, are overweight, and eat a high-fat diet.

Practice 12

FRAGMENTS

Revise the ideas to eliminate fragments by combining or adding ideas.

1. Sleep apnea is a common disorder. That can be very serious.

----

2. Sleep apnea episodes can occur 20 to 30 times or more an hour. Pauses that typically last 10–20 seconds or more.

----

3. Moving out of deep sleep and into light sleep several times during the night, resulting in poor sleep quality.

----

4. During sleep, enough air cannot flow into your lungs through your mouth and nose even though you try. To grasp a breath.

----

5. Your breathing may become hard and noisy and it may even stop. For short periods of time (apneas).

FRAGMENTS

Proofread the following paragraph for fragments. Revise to eliminate fragments by combining or adding ideas.

How to Maintain Your Weight

(1) In order to stay at the same body weight, people must balance the amount of calories in the foods and drinks they consume. (2) With the amount of calories the body uses. (3) Physical activity is one important way to use food energy. (4) Most Americans spend much of their working day in activities that require little energy. (5) In addition, many Americans of all ages now spend a lot of leisure time each day being inactive. (6) For example, watching television or working at a computer. (7) To burn calories. (8) Devote less time to sedentary activities like sitting. (9) Spend more time in activities like walking to the store or around the block. (10) Use stairs rather than elevators. (11) Less sedentary activity and more vigorous activity may help you reduce body fat and disease risk. (12) Try to do 30 minutes or more of moderate physical activity on most—preferably all—days of the week. (13) The kinds and amounts of foods people eat. (14) Affect their ability to maintain weight. (15) High-fat foods contain more calories per serving than other foods. (16) Which may increase the likelihood of weight gain. (17) However, even when people eat less high-fat food. (18) They still can gain weight from eating too many foods high in starch, sugars, or protein. (19) Eat a variety of foods. (20) Emphasizing pasta, rice, bread, and other whole-grain foods as well as fruits and vegetables. (21) These foods are filling, but lower in calories than foods rich in fats or oils. (22) The pattern of eating may also be important. (23) Snacks provide a large percentage of daily calories for many Americans. (24) Unless nutritious snacks are part of the daily meal plan. (25) Snacking may lead to weight gain. (26) A pattern of frequent binge eating, with or without alternating periods of food restriction, may also contribute to weight problems.

—Adapted from "Balance the Food You Eat With Physical Activity—Maintain or Improve Your Weight." Nutrition and Your Health: Dietary Guidelines for Americans. U. S. Department of Agriculture. Dec. 1995.

Writing Assignments

Writing for Everyday Life

Read the following letter to a doctor requesting information. Edit to eliminate fragments. Use your own paper.

Dear Dr. Alito:

Please send my records to the office of Dr. Alice Godbey. Who is currently treating me for a stress fracture in my right shin. Because your office ordered the x-rays of the injury. You must approve their release. Since you are my primary physician, Dr. Godbey's office will return the x-rays to your office. After my surgery.

Sincerely,

Sandra Acuri

Writing for College Life

Read the following paragraph written for a history class. Edit to eliminate fragments. Use your own paper.

Sojourner Truth who was first known as Isabella Baumfree. Born a slave somewhere around 1797. While in slavery. She had five children with the man she married, Thomas Jeffery Harvey. Fleeing slavery around 1827. She left the country and lived in Canada. Isabella returned to New York. When the state abolished slavery in 1829. She worked with Elijah Pierson preaching on street corners for more than a decade. Later, she became a well-known speaker against slavery and for women's rights. She is still noted today. For her famous speech, "Ain't I a Woman?"

Writing for Working Life

Read the following request for supplies in a department of a retail business. Edit to eliminate fragments. Use your own paper.

To: Office Supply Department
From: Customer Service Department
Re: Order # 3214

According to our records. Our order for three computer desks, three computer chairs, and three filing cabinets was placed three weeks ago. At that time, you assured us that you would deliver this order promptly. Since our need was urgent. To meet the needs of our customers. We have added three new employees. Employees who began reporting to work two weeks ago. If these items are not delivered by the end of the week, I will refer this matter to your supervisor.

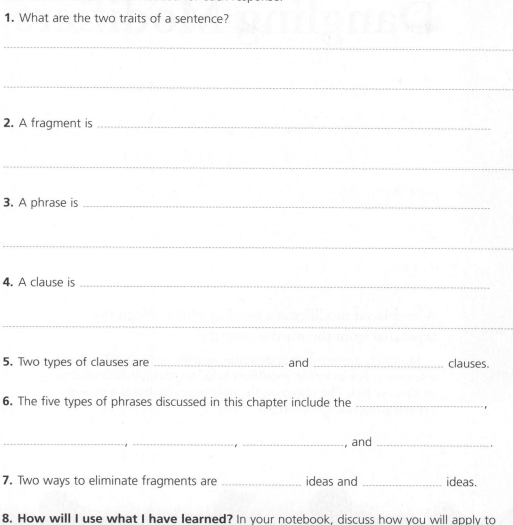

WHAT HAVE I LEARNED ABOUT CORRECTING FRAGMENTS?

To test and track your understanding of correcting fragments, complete the following ideas. Use several sentences as needed for each response.

1. What are the two traits of a sentence?

_____

_____

2. A fragment is _____

_____

3. A phrase is _____

_____

4. A clause is _____

_____

5. Two types of clauses are _____ and _____ clauses.

6. The five types of phrases discussed in this chapter include the _____,

_____, _____, _____, and _____.

7. Two ways to eliminate fragments are _____ ideas and _____ ideas.

8. How will I use what I have learned? In your notebook, discuss how you will apply to your own writing what you have learned about correcting fragments.

9. What do I still need to study about fragments? In your notebook, discuss your ongoing study needs by describing what, when, and how you will continue studying fragments.

Academic Learning Log

LEARNING OUTCOMES
SELF-EVALUATION

PORTFOLIO

23

Misplaced and Dangling Modifiers

A modifier is a word or phrase that describes, clarifies, or gives more information about another word in a sentence.

A misplaced modifier is a word or phrase illogically separated from the word it describes.

Modifiers are words that describe, restrict, or limit other words in a sentence. For example, modifiers help us communicate what we see or how we feel. The photo on the next page illustrates a person experiencing intense feelings.

What's the Point of Correcting Misplaced and Dangling Modifiers?

PHOTOGRAPHIC ORGANIZER: MISPLACED AND DANGLING MODIFIERS

Read the sentence that describes the marathon runner and answer the question.

> Running the marathon,
> her legs cried out in pain.

What is the point of correcting misplaced and dangling modifiers?

....

....

....

....

....

....

Understanding the Point of Correcting Misplaced and Dangling Modifiers: One Student Writer's Response

When I first read the sentence, I kind of laughed because it created such a funny image in my mind of "legs crying." I know the author didn't mean to be funny. But the way the idea is worded takes away from the serious nature of the situation. And as a reader, I don't know who ran the marathon. Information is either jumbled or missing from this sentence. I suggested the following revision: "While running the marathon, Lynda cried out in pain from leg cramps."

LEARNING OUTCOMES
STRUCTURE

Applying the Point: Correcting Misplaced and Dangling Modifiers

Sentence clarity can be achieved through appropriately placed and clearly expressed modifiers. A **modifier** is a word or phrase that describes, clarifies, or gives more information about another word in a sentence. Confusion in meaning occurs when a modifier is misplaced in the sentence or when the word being modified is not stated in the sentence. To avoid confusion, place modifiers next to the word that is being described.

Misplaced Modifiers

A **misplaced modifier** is a word or phrase illogically separated from the word it describes. The result is a lack of clarity. The following chart offers a few examples and revisions of common types of misplaced modifiers.

Misplaced Modifiers

MISPLACED WORD A misplaced word is separated from the word it limits or modifies.

WORD "ONLY" DESCRIBES ?

? ?
Belle Glade, Florida, only has been flooded twice by hurricanes.

Revision #1

WORD "ONLY" DESCRIBES "TWICE"

Belle Glade, Florida, has been flooded only twice by hurricanes.

Revision #2

Only Belle Glade, Florida, has been flooded twice by hurricanes.

WORD "ONLY" DESCRIBES "BELLE GLADE"

MISPLACED PHRASE A phrase that describes a noun is placed next to the wrong noun and separated from the word it modifies.

PHRASE "WITHOUT HER GLASSES" DESCRIBES ?

? ?
She couldn't recognize her mother without her glasses.

Revision

PHRASE "WITHOUT HER GLASSES" DESCRIBES "SHE"

Without her glasses, she couldn't recognize her mother.

ADDED COMMA SETS OFF INTRODUCTORY PHRASE

Example

? ?
Jammed into his backpack, Sean hunted through the papers.

PHRASE "JAMMED INTO HIS BACKPACK" DESCRIBES ?

ADDED COMMA SETS OFF INTRODUCTORY PHRASE

Revision

Sean hunted through the papers jammed into his backpack.

PHRASE "JAMMED INTO HIS BACKPACK" DESCRIBES PAPERS

MISPLACED CLAUSE A dependent clause that describes a particular word is placed next to the wrong word and is separated from the word the clause describes.

Example

CLAUSE "WHO GAVE BIRTH TO TWINS" DESCRIBES ?

The 60-year-old woman was hounded by the reporter who gave birth to twins.

Revision   *CLAUSE "WHO GAVE BIRTH TO TWINS" DESCRIBES "WOMAN"*

The 60-year-old woman who gave birth to twins was hounded by the reporter.

CORRECTING MISPLACED MODIFIERS

Revise the following student sentences to correct misplaced modifiers.

1. The groom dropped the wedding ring, trembling with nervousness. _____

2. Topped with onions and mushrooms, the guests enjoyed filet mignon. _____

3. Only Margarita drinks wine on the weekends. _____

4. Tired and sweaty, the sun beat down on the runners. _____

5. Kirstie Alley had joined Jenny Craig, who claims to have lost 65 pounds. _____

Practice 2

Dangling Modifiers

A **dangling modifier** is a word, phrase, or clause intended to modify a word not stated in the sentence. Therefore, the dangling modifier seems to describe the nearest word, yet it doesn't make sense. To revise dangling modifiers, you may need to add or rephrase ideas.

Dangling Modifiers: Two Revision Tips

A **dangling modifier** is a phrase that describes a word not stated in the sentence.

EXAMPLES What or whom do these phrases describe in each sentence below?

Sentence #1

While cleaning the house, a fifty dollar bill turned up. ?

Sentence #2

Observing the wildlife, the canoe glided through the waters. ?

Sentence #3

Running in second place, the finish line came into view. ?

REVISION TIP #1 Change the dangling modifier into a logical clause with a subject and a verb.

Revised Sentence #1

ADDED SUBJECT AND VERB TO CREATE DEPENDENT CLAUSE

While I was cleaning the house, a fifty dollar bill turned up.

Revised Sentence #2

ADDED SUBORDINATING CONJUNCTION, SUBJECT, AND VERB TO CREATE DEPENDENT CLAUSE

As we were observing the wildlife, the canoe glided through the waters.

Revised Sentence #3

ADDED SUBJECT AND VERB TO CREATE INDEPENDENT CLAUSE

I was running in second place; the finish line came into view.

ADDED SEMICOLON JOINS TWO INDEPENDENT CLAUSES

REVISION TIP #2 Revise the main clause to include the word being modified.

Revised Sentence #1

PHRASE "WHILE CLEANING THE HOUSE" DESCRIBES ADDED SUBJECT

While cleaning the house, I found a fifty dollar bill.

ADDED SUBJECT AND VERB

Revised Sentence #2

PHRASE "OBSERVING THE WILDLIFE" DESCRIBES ADDED SUBJECT

Observing the wildlife, we glided the canoe through the waters.

ADDED SUBJECT

Revised Sentence #3

PHRASE "RUNNING IN SECOND PLACE" DESCRIBES ADDED SUBJECT

Running in second place, I saw the finish line come into view.

ADDED SUBJECT AND VERB

CORRECTING DANGLING MODIFIERS

Revise the following student sentences to eliminate dangling modifiers.

1. Having a job, holidays are really appreciated!

2. Walking down Fifth Avenue, the Empire State Building looked awesome.

3. Voted out of office, their policies were quickly reversed.

4. Thinking about it later, the house seemed too large and expensive.

5. Having scored 19 touchdowns, the game was definitely out of reach.

Practice 3

CORRECTING MISPLACED AND DANGLING MODIFIERS

Revise to correct misplaced and dangling modifiers. Move or add ideas as needed.

1. As a kid, my parents had pretty strict rules. ....

....

2. Marianne Pearl is the widow of Danny Pearl, played by Angelina Jolie in *A Mighty Heart*.

....

3. Joanna gave a dog to her daughter named Spot. ....

....

4. Jamal was referred to a specialist suffering from a rare infection. ....

....

5. After saying good-bye, the train pulled away. ....

....

MISPLACED AND DANGLING MODIFIERS REVIEW

In the space provided on the next page, revise the following paragraph to eliminate misplaced and dangling modifiers.

Who says that the rich only can go on European vacations? You may be an impoverished student, but European travel is well within your reach if you plan carefully. By having some flexibility, plane tickets to Europe can be cheap. For example, prices for tickets in the off-season are far lower than those for tickets during the season. And once you are traveling within Europe, tickets are available from budget carriers like Ryanair that don't cost much money. Traveling by train or bus can also be a low-cost option. Restaurants may be expensive, but grocery stores aren't. Tucked into your picnic basket, you can bring sandwiches, fruit, and delicacies and have a feast on a park bench. And you don't have to stay in hotels. One alternative is hostels, found across Europe. And looking on a website, other possibilities emerge, including people who will take you into their home as a guest.

Practice 5

LEARNING OUTCOMES
WRITING PROCESS

Writing Assignments

Writing for Everyday Life

Edit the following posting for a blog on a social networking site such as MySpace.com. Eliminate misplaced or dangling modifiers. Use your own paper.

Thursday, January 26, 2010

We had the best weekend ever! Only our friends come to visit a couple of times a year. We decided to swim with the dolphins eager to have fun. Surprised by their sleek and smooth skin, our hands gently caressed the dolphins. The dolphins loved swimming with us. They actually made eye contact with us. It was an awesome experience.

Writing Assignments CONTINUED

Writing for College Life

Edit the following part of a report, written for a psychology class. Eliminate misplaced or dangling modifiers. The student was asked to illustrate a personal trait. Use your own paper.

> I go to unfamiliar places by myself. Swimming in shark-infested waters, my parents worry about me. I walk alone through dark areas to get to my car without pepper spray. I make friends with weird people, making poor choices about what is safe and what is threatening. I am too trusting.
>
> As a very young child, my parents had to keep an extra close eye on me. As the story goes, I had a tendency to wander off in search of new companions. At the age of four, my parents, brother, and sister lost track of me on a day trip to Wet N' Wild. Unconcerned, I skipped through the masses, tugging on the shorts of giants, asking "Do you know my Dad? Have you seen my Mom?" Eventually, I spotted a woman who must have been a lifeguard in a red bathing suit. She wasn't, but when I asked her for help to find my family, she obliged, returning me to my panic-stricken mother and father.

Writing for Working Life

Edit the following performance evaluation of an employee. Eliminate misplaced or dangling modifiers. Use your own paper.

To: Human Resources
From: Anna Shrimali, Manager
RE: Evaluation of Joanna Santiago
Joanna Santiago has been employed for three months. As an employee, her work is completed to a level above and beyond expectations. She is well able to deal with any type customer prone to listen carefully and act quickly. In addition, her efforts have saved our diligent company several thousands dollars. Only Ms. Santiago thinks of the good of the team, accepting the hardest assignments without complaint. I fully recommend Ms. Santiago for both a promotion and a raise.

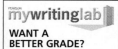

WANT A BETTER GRADE?
For more practice with misplaced and dangling modifiers, go to **www.mywritinglab.com > Recognizing and Avoiding Errors > Misplaced and Dangling Modifiers.**

Academic Learning Log

LEARNING OUTCOMES
SELF-EVALUATION

WHAT HAVE I LEARNED ABOUT MISPLACED AND DANGLING MODIFIERS?

To test and track your understanding, answer the following questions.

1. What is a misplaced modifier?

2. How is a misplaced modifier corrected?

3. What is a dangling modifier?

4. What are two ways to correct a dangling modifier?

5. How will I use what I have learned about misplaced and dangling modifiers?
In your notebook, discuss how you will apply to your own writing what you have learned about misplaced and dangling modifiers. When during the writing process will you apply this knowledge?

6. What do I still need to study about misplaced and dangling modifiers?
In your notebook, discuss your ongoing study needs by describing what, when, and how you will continue to study about misplaced and dangling modifiers.

PORTFOLIO

24

CHAPTER PREVIEW

LEARNING OUTCOMES

- What's the Point of Subject-Verb Agreement?

- Understanding the Point of Subject-Verb Agreement: One Student Writer's Response

- Applying the Point: Subject-Verb Agreement

- Writing Assignments

Subject-Verb Agreement: Present Tense

In the present tense, subjects and verbs must agree in person and number. Singular subjects must take singular verbs; plural subjects must take plural verbs.

Subject-verb agreement in the present tense ranks as one of the most common errors in written and spoken English. Rules for subject-verb agreement in regional dialects may differ from the rules in standard English. It is important to understand the difference between regional speech and standard English and to be able to use the standard English rules. Look at the picture and statements on the following page, and answer the question, "What's the point of correct subject-verb agreement?"

What's the Point of Subject-Verb Agreement?

PHOTOGRAPHIC ORGANIZER: SUBJECT-VERB AGREEMENT

Complete the following activity and answer the question "What's the point of subject-verb agreement?"

Assume you are a manager, and you are interviewing possible candidates for a job opening in your department. Which candidate's response to your question sounds more professional? Why?

Manager's question:
What is a current example of your greatest strength as an employee?

Candidate 1:
My greatest strengths is in listening, following directions, and problem solving. For example, procedures comes to us from the home office, and I listen carefully to understand them. Confusion often happen with deliveries, and I've been working to prevent that.

Candidate 2:
My greatest strengths are in listening, following directions, and problem solving. For example, procedures come to us from the home office, and I listen carefully to understand them. Confusion often happens with deliveries, and I've been working to prevent that.

What's the point of subject-verb agreement?

....

....

....

Understanding the Point of Subject-Verb Agreement: One Student Writer's Response

The following paragraph records one writer's thoughts about the point of subject-verb agreement in the job interview example.

> Candidate 2 sounded more polished and educated. Candidate 1 used a singular subject with a plural verb and plural subjects with singular verbs. In contrast, Candidate 2 always used singular subjects with singular verbs and plural subjects with plural verbs. In our group discussion of the example, we made a chart to show the contrast between the two responses:
>
> Candidate 1:
>
> | Subject | Verb |
> |---|---|
> | strengths | is |
> | procedures | comes |
> | confusion | happen |
>
> Candidate 2:
>
> | Subject | Verb |
> |---|---|
> | strengths | are |
> | procedures | come |
> | confusion | happens |
>
> As our group talked about singular and plural subjects and verbs, I got really confused because of how the letter "s" is used to make a word plural. My group explained to me that "s" is used to make subjects plural, but that "s" is also used to make some verbs singular.

Applying the Point: Subject-Verb Agreement

In the present tense, subjects and verbs must agree in person and in number. So a singular subject must have a singular verb, and a plural subject must have a plural verb. The following chart uses the sample verb "think" to illustrate present tense agreement in number.

	Present Tense Agreement			
	Singular **Subject** and **Verb**		Plural **Subject** and **Verb**	
First Person	I	think	We	think
Second Person	You	think	You	think
Third Person	He She It	thinks	They	think

For standard verbs, only the third-person singular verb is formed by adding -s or -es.

Third-person singular subject	→	present tense verb ends with -s or -es
He	→	apologizes
She	→	accepts
It	→	catches

Practice 2

SUBJECT-VERB AGREEMENT

Fill in the following charts with the correct form of each subject and verb. A few blanks are completed as examples.

1. To Listen	Subject	Verb
First person singular	I	listen
Second person singular/plural		
Third person singular		

2. To Hear	Subject	Verb
First person plural		
Second person singular/plural		
Third person plural	They	hear

3. To Watch	Subject	Verb
First person singular		
Second person singular/plural		
Third person singular		

4. To Hope	Subject	Verb
First person singular		
Second person singular/plural		
Third person singular		

5. To Fax	Subject	Verb
First person plural		
Second person singular/plural		
Third person singular	He	

SUBJECT-VERB AGREEMENT

Circle the verb form that agrees with the subject of each of the following sentences.

1. Drugs (contributes   contribute) to careless driving because a drug (affects   affect) a driver both mentally and physically.

2. For example, Samuel (takes   take) a new headache medicine, and the side effects (includes   include) drowsiness.

3. Then, he (decides   decide) to drive even though he (realizes   realize) he shouldn't because of this new medicine.

4. The medication (makes   make) him drowsy, and it (becomes   become) difficult for him to stay alert.

5. The medication (slows   slow) Samuel's reflexes considerably, so they (causes   cause) a delay in his reactions to driving conditions.

Key Verbs in the Present Tense: *To Have, To Do, To Be*

Three key verbs are used both as main verbs and as helping verbs to express a wide variety of meanings: *to have, to do,* and *to be.* Memorize their present tense singular and plural forms to ensure subject-verb agreement.

To Have: **Present Tense**		
	Singular **Subject** and **Verb**	Plural **Subject** and **Verb**
First Person	I have	We have
Second Person	You have	You have
Third Person	He She — has It	They have

SUBJECT-VERB AGREEMENT: *TO HAVE*

Write the form of the verb *to have* that agrees with the subject in each of the following sentences.

1. My younger brother .... problems with asthma.

2. As a result, he .... to use an inhaler.

3. Researchers .... developed fun inhalers for children.

4. With these inhalers, children .... fewer complaints about taking their medication.

5. Write a sentence using *has* or *have* as a verb. Suggested topic: A useful product.

To Do: Present Tense		
	Singular **Subject** and **Verb**	Plural **Subject** and **Verb**
First Person	I do	We do
Second Person	You do	You do
Third Person	He She does It	They do

SUBJECT-VERB AGREEMENT: *TO DO*

Write the form of the verb *to do* that agrees with the subject in each of the following sentences.

1. A robot currently being developed, Probo .... many things to comfort sick young children in hospitals.

2. Probo's outside feels soft and cuddly; its inside parts .... the hard work of understanding children's emotions and communicating with them.

3. Probo can't give hugs yet, but it .... purr when hugged.

4. The words Probo says aren't words in a real language, but they .... provide comfort because of their warm, sympathetic tone.

5. Write a sentence using *do* or *does* as the verb. Suggested topic: The ideal robot.

The verb **to do** is often used with the adverb *not* to express a negative thought. Frequently this negative is stated in the form of the contractions *doesn't* and *don't*, which combine the verb and adverb into shorter words. The verb part of the contraction must still agree with its subject.

To Do and Not: Contraction Form		
	Singular **Subject** and **Verb**	Plural **Subject** and **Verb**
First Person	I don't agree	We don't agree
Second Person	You don't seem well	You don't seem well
Third Person	He She doesn't care It	They don't care

Practice 6

SUBJECT-VERB AGREEMENT: *TO DO* AND *NOT*

Fill in the blank with the form of the verb *to do* that agrees with the subject of each of the following sentences. Use the contractions *doesn't* and *don't* as needed.

1. He .... have to study to earn high grades, but I have to study for hours.

2. It .... hurt your reputation to admit that you are wrong.

3. Even when we ask politely, they .... turn down the music.

4. You still .... understand why I am so angry.

5. Write a sentence using *do, does, doesn't,* or *don't*. Suggested topic: A helpful piece of advice.

....

....

The ***to be*** verb is unusual because it uses three forms in the present tense: *am, is,* and *are*.

To Be: **Present Tense**				
	Singular **Subject** and **Verb**		Plural **Subject** and **Verb**	
First Person	I	am	We	are
Second Person	You	are	You	are
Third Person	He She It	is	They	are

Practice 7

SUBJECT-VERB AGREEMENT: *TO BE*

Write the form of the verb *to be* that agrees with the subject of each of the following sentences.

1. A cell phone .... a multi-purpose device.

2. Cell phones .... able to take pictures, download music, and access the Internet.

3. We .... delighted with the innovations in cell phones.

4. Made by Digit Wireless, the Fastap keyboard .... a full typewriter keyboard for a cell phone.

5. Write a sentence using a form of the verb *to be*. Suggested topic: A useful tool.

....

....

Subjects Separated from Verbs

The standard order of ideas in a sentence places the subject first, immediately followed by the verb. However, subjects are often separated from their verbs by **prepositional phrases**.

A **preposition** is a word that has a noun or pronoun as its object and states a relationship between its object and another word. A prepositional phrase begins with a preposition and ends with the object of the preposition. The object of the preposition can never be the subject of a sentence. Identifying prepositional phrases keeps you from confusing them with the subject of the sentence. The verb of a sentence agrees with the subject, not the object of the preposition.

Example

The following chart of prepositional phrases lists a few common prepositions and sample objects.

Common Prepositional Phrases			
Preposition	**Object**	**Preposition**	**Object**
at	work	of	concern
from	home	on	the desk
in	the office	with	experience

SUBJECT-VERB AGREEMENT

Choose the verb form that agrees with the subject of each of the following sentences. Cross out prepositional phrases. Underline the subject. Circle the appropriate verb.

1. Counselors at a college career center (assists assist) students and alumni in various ways.

2. A student with a well-crafted resume and good references (has have) an advantage in a tight job market.

3. Many employers in the area (lists list) jobs at the college career center.

4. Students at a large college (benefits benefit) from school-sponsored job fairs with employers from a range of companies.

5. Often, an inventory of interests and strengths (suggests suggest) some possible careers.

Practice 8

Singular or Plural Subjects

To establish subject-verb agreement, first identify a subject as plural or singular. Some subjects may seem singular or plural when actually they are not. The following section identifies and discusses several of these types of subjects and the rules of their agreement with verbs.

Indefinite Pronouns

Indefinite pronouns do not refer to specific nouns. Most indefinite pronouns are singular; a few are plural, and some can be either singular or plural. Consider the context of the indefinite pronoun to achieve subject-verb agreement.

- **Singular indefinite pronouns agree with singular verbs.**

Example

Everyone has a computer.

SINGULAR INDEFINITE PRONOUN

SINGULAR VERB "HAS" AGREES WITH SINGULAR INDEFINITE PRONOUN "EVERYONE"

Singular Indefinite Pronouns					
anybody	each	everyone	neither	no one	somebody
anyone	either	everything	nobody	nothing	someone
anything	everybody	much	none	one	something

- **Plural indefinite pronouns agree with plural verbs.**

Example

Few have a computer.

PLURAL INDEFINITE PRONOUN

PLURAL VERB "HAVE" AGREES WITH PLURAL INDEFINITE PRONOUN "FEW"

Plural Indefinite Pronouns			
both	few	many	several

- **Some indefinite pronouns are singular or plural based on context and meaning. The context determines agreement with singular or plural verbs.**

Example of Indefinite Pronoun That Is Singular Based on Context

All has ended well.

INDEFINITE PRONOUN IS SINGULAR BASED ON CONTEXT

SINGULAR VERB "HAS" AGREES WITH SINGULAR INDEFINITE PRONOUN "ALL"

Example of Indefinite Pronoun That Is Plural Based on Context

All of the students have left.

INDEFINITE PRONOUN IS PLURAL BASED ON CONTEXT

PLURAL VERB "HAVE" AGREES WITH PLURAL INDEFINITE PRONOUN "ALL"

Singular or Plural Indefinite Pronouns Based on Context				
all	any	more	most	some

SUBJECT-VERB AGREEMENT: INDEFINITE PRONOUNS

Choose the verb form that agrees with the subject of each of the following sentences. Underline the subject. Circle the appropriate verb.

1. Everyone (is are) shaped by genes and the environment.

2. Both (plays play) important roles in our development.

3. Few of our characteristics (is are) purely genetic; most (shows show) significant environmental influences.

4. At one time, some experts believed that all (was were) born as blank slates.

5. Write a sentence using an indefinite pronoun. A suggested topic: A common human characteristic

---

Collective Nouns

Collective nouns are singular forms of names of groups. They name a collection of people, animals, or items as a unit. The agreement between a collective noun and a verb depends on the context of the sentence.

- **When a collective noun acts as one unit, a singular verb is needed to achieve agreement.**

Example

The flock of birds is about to take flight.

COLLECTIVE NOUN
"FLOCK" REFERS TO ONE
GROUP (OF BIRDS)

SINGULAR VERB "IS" AGREES WITH
SINGULAR MEANING OF "FLOCK"

- **When a collective noun represents the individuals in a group, a plural verb is needed to achieve agreement.**

Example

PLURAL VERB "ARE" AGREES WITH PLURAL
MEANING OF "FACULTY"

The faculty are disagreeing about the curriculum.

COLLECTIVE NOUN "FACULTY" REFERS
TO THE INDIVIDUALS ON THE FACULTY

Common Collective Nouns				
assembly	class	crowd	gang	staff
audience	clergy	enemy	group	team
band	committee	faculty	herd	tribe
cast	company	family	jury	troop
choir	crew	flock	pride	unit

Practice 10

SUBJECT-VERB AGREEMENT: COLLECTIVE NOUNS

Choose the verb form that agrees with the subject of each of the following sentences. Underline the subject. Circle the appropriate verb.

1. As curtain time approaches, the audience (fills fill) the auditorium and (takes take) their seats.

2. The committee (considers consider) all petitions and in most cases (gives give) its approval.

3. The faculty (has have) many advanced degrees, including some PhDs.

4. The company (manufactures manufacture) a wide range of bolts, screws, nails, and other fasteners, all in its Pittsburgh plant.

5. Write a sentence using a collective noun. Suggested topic: Going to a concert.

_____

_____

Either-Or/Neither-Nor

Either or *neither* often signal a singular subject that requires a singular verb.

- **To ensure subject-verb agreement, identify and cross out prepositional phrases.**

"EITHER" REFERS TO ONE OF "THE MEN" AND THUS IS A SINGULAR SUBJECT

SINGULAR VERB "IS" AGREES WITH SINGULAR SUBJECT "EITHER"

Either ~~of the men~~ is eligible for employment.

PREPOSITIONAL PHRASE

Either-or and *neither-nor* join parts of a subject; the verb agrees with the nearer part of the subject.

- **When all parts of the subject are singular, the verb is singular.**

"EITHER" / "OR" JOINS SINGULAR
SUBJECTS "MIGUEL" AND "TANYA"

SINGULAR VERB "HAS" AGREES
WITH SINGULAR SUBJECTS
"MIGUEL" AND "TANYA"

Either Miguel or Tanya has the key to the house.

SINGULAR SUBJECTS

- **When all parts of the subject are plural, the verb is plural.**

"NEITHER" / "NOR" JOINS PLURAL
SUBJECTS "TREES" AND "BUSHES"

PLURAL VERB "WERE" AGREES
WITH PLURAL SUBJECTS
"TREES" AND "BUSHES"

Neither the trees nor the bushes were damaged
in the storm.

PLURAL SUBJECTS

- **When one part of the subject is singular and the other part is plural, the verb agrees with the nearer part.** For smooth expression, place the plural part of the subject closer to the verb.

"EITHER" / "OR" JOINS SUBJECTS
"TRUCK" AND "CARS"

PLURAL VERB "NEED" AGREES
WITH NEARER (PLURAL)
SUBJECT "CARS"

Either the truck or the cars in the driveway need to
be moved.

SINGULAR SUBJECT   PLURAL SUBJECT

SUBJECT-VERB AGREEMENT: *EITHER-OR/NEITHER-NOR*

Choose the verb form that agrees with the subject of each of the following sentences. Cross out prepositional phrases. Underline the subject. Circle the appropriate verb.

1. Neither of the men (has have) applied for a student loan.

2. For many students, either student loans or scholarships (is are) necessary to pay for higher education.

3. Either the counselors or your faculty advisor (has have) information about financial aid.

4. Neither the President of the Student Government Association nor the campus representatives (does do) the will of the student body.

5. Write a sentence using *either* or *neither*. Suggested topic: Paying for school.

Practice 11

Fractions, Titles, and Words Ending in –s

A **fractional expression** states the quotient or ratio of two real numbers; for example, the fraction ¾ expresses a 3 to 4 ratio, which is also *seventy-five percent* or a *majority*. Fractional expressions can be either singular or plural subjects, depending on the context of the sentence.

Thus, the verbs in fractional expressions match the subjects as singular or plural accordingly. Sums and products of mathematical processes are singular and require singular verbs. To ensure subject-verb agreement, identify and cross out prepositional phrases.

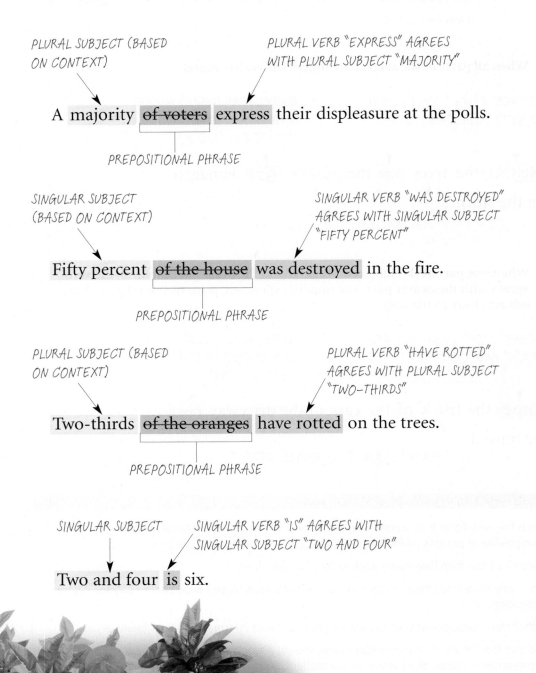

PLURAL SUBJECT (BASED ON CONTEXT)

PLURAL VERB "EXPRESS" AGREES WITH PLURAL SUBJECT "MAJORITY"

A majority of voters express their displeasure at the polls.

PREPOSITIONAL PHRASE

SINGULAR SUBJECT (BASED ON CONTEXT)

SINGULAR VERB "WAS DESTROYED" AGREES WITH SINGULAR SUBJECT "FIFTY PERCENT"

Fifty percent of the house was destroyed in the fire.

PREPOSITIONAL PHRASE

PLURAL SUBJECT (BASED ON CONTEXT)

PLURAL VERB "HAVE ROTTED" AGREES WITH PLURAL SUBJECT "TWO-THIRDS"

Two-thirds of the oranges have rotted on the trees.

PREPOSITIONAL PHRASE

SINGULAR SUBJECT

SINGULAR VERB "IS" AGREES WITH SINGULAR SUBJECT "TWO AND FOUR"

Two and four is six.

444

- **Titles** are singular subjects and require a singular verb.

SINGULAR SUBJECT PREPOSITIONAL PHRASE

War of the Worlds ~~with Tom Cruise~~ was a disappointing movie.

SINGULAR VERB "WAS" AGREES WITH
SINGULAR SUBJECT "WAR OF THE WORLDS"

PREPOSITIONAL PHRASE
SINGULAR SUBJECT

"Irreplaceable" ~~by Beyoncé~~ was recorded for the album *B-Day*.

SINGULAR VERB "WAS RECORDED" AGREES
WITH SINGULAR SUBJECT "IRREPLACEABLE"

Some **words that end in -s** (for example, *thanks, assets, glasses*) seem to refer to a single idea or item but are plural and require a plural verb. Others (for example, *mathematics, economics*) are singular and require a singular verb.

My assets have increased over the past ten years.

PLURAL SUBJECT   PLURAL VERB "HAVE" AGREES WITH
                     PLURAL SUBJECT "ASSETS"

Economics is my favorite subject.

PLURAL SUBJECT   PLURAL VERB "HAVE" AGREES WITH
                     PLURAL SUBJECT "ASSETS"

SUBJECT-VERB AGREEMENT: FRACTIONS, TITLES, AND WORDS

Choose the verb form that agrees with the subject in each of the following sentences. Cross out the prepositional phrases. Underline the subject. Circle the appropriate verb.

1. My glasses (is are) broken.
2. Thirty percent of my life earnings (is are) paid in taxes.
3. Eighty percent of students (turns turn) their work in on time.
4. "Waiting on the World to Change" (is are) the first single release from John Mayer's studio album *Continuum*.
5. Write a sentence using a fraction, title, or plural word that seems singular. Suggested topic: A favorite DVD.

Practice 12

Subjects after Verbs

In some instances, a writer may choose to place the subject after the verb. To ensure subject-verb agreement, identify the verb, identify (and cross out) prepositional phrases, and ask who or what completes the action or state of being stated by the verb.

There and *Here* are never the subject of a sentence. Both of these words signal that the subject comes after the verb.

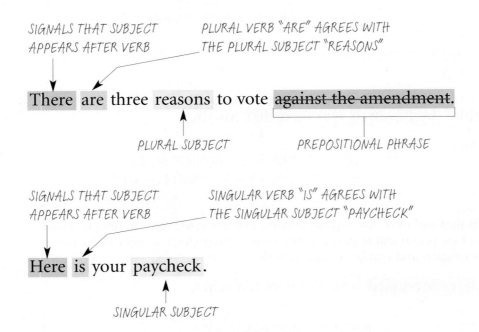

SIGNALS THAT SUBJECT APPEARS AFTER VERB

PLURAL VERB "ARE" AGREES WITH THE PLURAL SUBJECT "REASONS"

There are three reasons to vote against the amendment.

PLURAL SUBJECT

PREPOSITIONAL PHRASE

SIGNALS THAT SUBJECT APPEARS AFTER VERB

SINGULAR VERB "IS" AGREES WITH THE SINGULAR SUBJECT "PAYCHECK"

Here is your paycheck.

SINGULAR SUBJECT

Agreement in Questions relies on understanding that the subject comes after the verb or between parts of the verb.

SINGULAR VERB

SINGULAR SUBJECT

Where is the closest fast-food restaurant?

PLURAL VERB "DO" AGREES WITH THE PLURAL SUBJECT "LIGHTS"

How do the lights from the boardwalk harm the turtles' nesting season?

PLURAL SUBJECT

PREPOSITIONAL PHRASE

Writers having difficulty determining the subject in a question can identify it by reversing the word order into a statement—in the examples above, "The closest fast-food restaurant is…" and "The lights do harm…"

SUBJECT-VERB AGREEMENT: SUBJECTS AFTER VERBS

Choose the verb form that agrees with the subject of each of the following sentences. Cross out prepositional phrases. Underline the subject. Circle the appropriate verb.

1. There (is are) four reports due by the end of the month.

2. Here (is are) the pliers, hammer, and screwdriver that have been missing.

3. (Do Does) the chicken in the refrigerator need to be cooked tonight?

4. Where (is are) the first aid station?

5. Write a question. Suggested topic: How to get to a specific location.

Agreement with Relative Pronouns

Agreement with relative pronouns relies on identifying the relationships among a **relative pronoun** (a pronoun such as *that, which, who,* and *whom* that introduces a dependent clause), its **antecedent** (the word the pronoun refers to), and its verb. When a relative pronoun refers to a plural antecedent, it requires a plural verb. When a relative pronoun refers to a singular antecedent, it requires a singular verb. Note that relative pronouns signal a dependent clause. The antecedent for the relative pronoun is often found in the independent clause.

Relative Pronouns			
who	which	that	whom

SUBJECT-VERB AGREEMENT: RELATIVE PRONOUNS

Choose the verb form that agrees with the subject of each of the following sentences. Underline the antecedent of the relative pronoun once. Underline the relative pronoun twice. Circle the appropriate verb.

1. Robert, who (has have) an impressive résumé, will apply for the management position.

2. The three sandwiches, which (is are) in the brown paper bag, belong to me.

3. The buildings are on a block that (overlooks overlook) the park.

4. The computer virus that (has have) affected your computer also caused my system to crash.

5. Write a sentence using a relative pronoun. Suggested topic: A necessary item.

SUBJECT-VERB AGREEMENT REVIEW

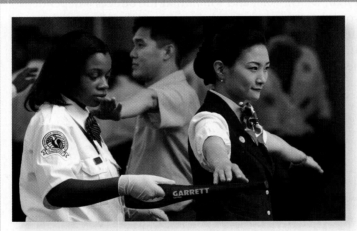

Read the following short paragraph. Edit to ensure subject-verb agreement in the present tense.

We is about to walk through the security scanner at the airport when we is asked by the airport personnel to step aside into a special area. They asks us to sit quietly and wait for the security supervisor. My mother becomes impatient and begin demanding an explanation. She wants to know why we is being stopped from boarding our plane. She worry that we will miss our flight. My sister and her husband is having their first baby, so we wants to be sure we get there in time for the birth. My mother whisper under her breath to me, "This is a situation that are meant to test one's patience!"

Writing Assignments

Writing for Everyday Life

Read the following testimonial written as an endorsement by a member of a local gym. Edit the paragraph to ensure subject-verb agreement. Use your own paper.

If you is looking to make a dramatic change in how you looks and feels, then you need to hire **Ryan Belcher** with **Gold's Gym** as your personal trainer.

My progress is the result of his training. He creates routines that is based on your specific needs. For example, my friend and I has been out of shape and overweight for years. Every training session, Ryan do his best to push us to work harder than we believes we can. We lift weights for strength; we does aerobics for endurance, and we stretch for flexibility. **"I now has more lean muscle than fat."**

One hundred percent of Ryan's clients reaches their goals.

Writing for College Life

The following paragraph was written by a student to earn five points on a math exam. The student had to explain the steps he took to correctly solve the math problem. Edit to ensure subject-verb agreement. Use your own paper.

I has repaired my answer to the question I missed on this week's quiz. To correctly solve this equation, I use the distributive law. The test question is "What is the value of x in the problem: $2(x + 3) + 4(x - 5) = 10$?" These is my steps to solve this problem.

Step 1: I multiplies each of the terms in the first expression in parentheses by two. 2 times x are 2x, and 2 times 3 are 6. The equation now is $2x + 6 + 4(x - 5) = 10$.

Step 2: I multiply each of the terms in the second expression in parentheses by four. 4 times x equal 4x, and 4 times −5 equal −20 = 10. The equation is now $2x + 6 + 4x - 20 = 10$.

Step 3: Now I add and subtracts like terms, so the equation is now $6x - 14 = 10$.

Step 4: I add 14 to both sides of the equation: $6x = 24$.

Step 5: Finally I divides each side by six. Six go into six one times, and six go into 24 four times. $x = 24 \div 6$. x is 4.

Writing Assignments CONTINUED

Writing for Working Life

Read the following flyer written by an entrepreneur who is starting up a landscaping and lawn maintenance business. Edit to ensure subject-verb agreement. Use your own paper.

Does your garden beds need weeding or replanting?

Does your grass need mowing?

Are you one of those people who needs help selecting the right plant for the right location?

Lush Lawns are the company to meet your needs. **Lush Lawns** employ experts who knows how to create and maintain beautiful landscapes. **Lush Lawns** plant, weed, mulch, edge, and mow for a low monthly price. It don't pay to wait.

Call now and begin enjoying a lush lawn of your own.

mywritinglab

WANT A BETTER GRADE?

For more practice with subject-verb agreement in the present tense, go to **www.mywritinglab.com > Recognizing and Avoiding Errors > Subject-Verb Agreement: Present Tense.**

Academic Learning Log

WHAT HAVE I LEARNED ABOUT SUBJECT-VERB AGREEMENT?

To test and track your understanding, answer the following questions.

1. What is the rule for subject-verb agreement? ....

   ....

2. How is the third-person singular verb formed?

   ....

3. What are the three forms of the present tense of the verb *to be*? ....

4. .... sometimes separate subjects from their verbs.

5. Indefinite and collective pronouns are singular or plural based on the ....

   of the sentence.

6. When either/or joins part of a subject, the verb agrees with the .... part

   of the subject.

7. Sums and products of mathematical expressions require .... verbs.

8. The words .... and .... are never the subject of a sentence; rather, they signal that the subject follows the verb.

9. In a _____ , the subject comes after the verb or between parts of

the verb.

10. Agreement with relative pronouns relies on identifying the relationship among a relative

pronoun, its _____, and its verb.

11. **How will I use what I have learned about subject-verb agreement?**
In your notebook, discuss how you will apply to your own writing what you have learned
about subject-verb agreement.

12. **What do I still need to study about subject-verb agreement?**
In your notebook, discuss your ongoing study needs by describing what, when,
and how you will continue studying subject-verb agreement.

25

The Past Tense of Verbs

The past tense of verbs describes actions or events that have already occurred.

The past tense is one of the most commonly used verb tenses in English. Thinking about a real-life situation helps us to understand the need for the past tense as we communicate. The following photograph illustrates the challenges of mountain climbing. Study the picture, complete the activity, and answer the question "What's the point of the past tense of verbs?"

What's the Point of the Past Tense of Verbs?

PHOTOGRAPHIC ORGANIZER: THE PAST TENSE OF VERBS

Assume your friend has survived a dangerous situation and has been asked to share his experience with others. He asks you to read what he has written so far. What do you notice about his use of the past tense? How does his use of verb tense affect his message?

Surviving a Fall Off the Mountain

Our 7,400-foot climb up the winter slopes of Mt. Hood challenges and exhilarated us. Thankfully, we decide to take Mountain Locator Units, small beacons that could send out radio signals to rescuers. When a storm moved in, we start our descent in blowing snow. We had no visual reference around us, so we couldn't know if we were going up or down. Then the three of us who were roped together with Champion, a black Labrador mix, disappear over an icy ledge. Champion provided warmth for us as we huddled under sleeping bags and a tarp. She takes turns lying on each one of us during the night. The activation of an emergency radio beacon bringed rescuers to us. We survived because we were prepared, we didn't panic, and Champion keeps us warm.

What's the point of the past tense of verbs?

....

....

....

Understanding the Point of the Past Tense of Verbs: One Student Writer's Response

The following paragraph offers one writer's reaction to the paragraph "Surviving a Fall Off the Mountain."

> When I first read this paragraph, I noticed that the writer kept shifting between the present and past tenses for no real reason. The shifts were so noticeable that I really couldn't focus on his story because the verb errors jumped out so much. So my advice is to edit each of the following verbs from the present tense to the past tense: "challenges" becomes "challenged"; "decide" becomes "decided"; "start" becomes "started"; "disappear" becomes "disappeared"; "takes" becomes "took"; and "keeps" becomes "kept." The misspelling of the verb "bringed" also caught my attention. The proper spelling is "brought." By the way, I had to look some of these verbs up in the dictionary to make sure of their spelling. Once the writer makes these edits, his message will be much stronger.

Applying the Point: The Past Tense of Verbs

The **simple past tense** is used to describe a completed action or event. The action or event might have taken place long ago or it might have happened recently, but either way, the past tense is used to indicate that it has already occurred. The simple past tense is also often used to tell a story. Frequently, the use of the past tense is also signaled by particular expressions of time: *yesterday, last night, last week, last year, three years ago*, and so on. The following time line illustrates the sequence of tenses.

Past
action/event

Present
action/event

Future
action/event

The past tense takes on different forms for regular and irregular verbs.

Regular Verbs in the Past Tense

The following chart shows the general rule for forming the past tense of regular verbs, the spelling rules for exceptions, and examples of each rule.

Rules for Forming Past Tense of Regular Verbs		
	Base Form	**Past Tense**
General Rule:		
Regular verbs form the past tense by adding **-ed** to the base form of the verb.	walk ⟶	walk**ed**
Spelling Exceptions:		
There are several exceptions to the way in which regular verbs form the past tense:		
1. When the base form of the verb ends in **-e**, only add **-d**.	live ⟶ save	live**d** save**d**
2. When the base form of the verb ends with a consonant and **-y**, delete the **-y** and add **-ied** in its place.	cry ⟶ try	cr**ied** tr**ied**
3. When the base form of the verb ends with **-p** or **-it,** double the last letter before adding the **-ed.**	stop ⟶ permit	stop**ped** permit**ted**

REGULAR VERBS IN PAST TENSE

Fill in each blank with the past tense form of the regular verb in parentheses.

1. Chimpanzees possibly _____ (use) "hammers" at least as 4,300 years ago.

2. Researchers _____ (discover) the hammers in the West African country, Ivory Coast.

3. The chimpanzees _____ (crack) nuts with the hammers.

4. A "chimpanzee stone age" _____ (start) in ancient times.

5. Write a sentence with a regular verb in the past tense. Suggested topic: An important invention.

_____

_____

Practice 2

Irregular Verbs in the Past Tense

Unlike regular verbs, irregular verbs do not use *-ed* to form the past tense. Nor does the past tense of irregular verbs conform to uniform spelling rules with clear exceptions. In fact, some of the most commonly used verbs are irregular, and most writers commit these words to memory so their proper use is automatic. The chart lists the base form and past tense form of some commonly used irregular verbs. When in doubt about the correct form of a verb, consult a dictionary to check the spelling of the past tense of an irregular verb.

Some Common Irregular Verbs in the Past Tense

Base Form	Past Tense	Base Form	Past Tense
be	was, were	light	lit
become	became	lose	lost
break	broke	make	made
bring	brought	mean	meant
buy	bought	meet	met
choose	chose	pay	paid
come	came	put	put
cut	cut	quit	quit
deal	dealt	read	read
dig	dug	ride	rode
drink	drank	ring	rang
drive	drove	rise	rose
eat	ate	run	ran
fall	fell	say	said
feed	fed	see	saw
feel	felt	sell	sold
fly	flew	send	sent
forget	forgot	shake	shook
forgive	forgave	shine	shone (shined)
freeze	froze	sing	sang
get	got	sit	sat
give	gave	sleep	slept
go	went	speak	spoke
grow	grew	spend	spent
hang	hung	swim	swam
have	had	take	took
hear	heard	teach	taught
hide	hid	tear	tore
hold	held	tell	told
hurt	hurt	think	thought
keep	kept	throw	threw
know	knew	understand	understood
lay (to place)	laid	wake	woke (waked)
lead	led	wear	wore
leave	left	win	won
let	let	write	wrote
lie (to recline)	lay		

Practice 3

IRREGULAR VERBS IN PAST TENSE

Fill in the blanks with the past tense form of the irregular verbs in the parentheses.

1. A slave named James Armistead .... (make) history as the most important Revolutionary War spy.

2. Armistead .... (take) on the role of an escaped slave to enter the camp of the traitor Benedict Arnold.

3. As an orderly and a guide, Armistead .... (go) North with Arnold to learn about British war plans without being detected.

4. As a double agent, he also .... (give) incorrect information to the British troops.

5. Write a sentence using the past tense of an irregular verb. Suggested topic: The Civil War.

....

....

....

Key Verbs in the Past Tense: *To Have, To Do, To Be*

Three key verbs are used both as main verbs and as helping verbs to express a wide variety of meanings: *to have, to do,* and *to be.* These three verbs are irregular verbs, so it's essential to memorize their correct forms in the past tense.

To Have	To Do	To Be
had	did	was (singular)
		were (plural)

Practice 4

IRREGULAR VERBS IN PAST TENSE

Fill in the blanks with the past tense form of the verbs *to have, to do,* or *to be.*

1. Researchers recently .... a large study that showed how midday napping reduces one's chance of coronary mortality by more than a third.

2. The most effective nappers .... those who took naps at least three times per week for an average of at least 30 minutes.

3. These men and women .... a 37 percent lower coronary mortality risk than those who took no naps.

4. The protective effect of napping .... especially strong among working men.

5. Write a sentence using the past tense of *to have, to do,* or *to be.* Suggested topic: Sleep problems.

....

....

....

Can/Could/Would

Helping verbs are auxiliary verbs that team up with main verbs for precise expression of an action or state of being. Three helping verbs are often confused in usage: *can, could,* and *would.* These auxiliary verbs help express the meaning of ability, opportunity, possibility, permission, and intention. The following provides definitions and examples for each of these three helping verbs.

Three Commonly Confused Helping Verbs: *Can, Could, Would*

- *Can* expresses physical or mental ability in the present tense.

  "CAN" EXPRESSES A PHYSICAL ABILITY

  I can run a marathon.

  "CAN" EXPRESSES A MENTAL ABILITY

  I can solve mathematical equations.

- *Could* expresses physical or mental ability, opportunity, possibility, or permission in the past tense.

  "COULD" EXPRESSES A PHYSICAL OR MENTAL ABILITY

  She could run a marathon.

  "COULD" EXPRESSES A LOST OPPORTUNITY

  You could have tried harder than you did.

  "COULD" EXPRESSES POSSIBILITY

  He could have been the culprit.

  "COULD" EXPRESSES PERMISSION

  He said that we could begin the driving test.

- *Would* expresses past routine or intention in the past tense.

  "WOULD" EXPRESSES PAST ROUTINE

  He would win every race.

  He would have won every race, but he lost the last one.

  "WOULD" EXPRESSES PAST INTENTION

  She said she would do the dishes.

Practice 5

USING *CAN, COULD,* AND *WOULD*

Complete each sentence with the helping verb that best completes the idea: *can, could,* or *would.*

1. In the early 19th century, communication technology was very limited and news _____ travel between Europe and the United States only at the speed of ships.

2. Later, thanks to the development of the telegraph and then of radio, news _____ travel almost instantaneously between Europe and the United States.

3. In the early 20th century, radio became enormously popular, and every night families _____ stop what they were doing and gather around the radio to listen to news and other programs.

4. Today, we _____ instantly access information, regardless of time or location.

5. Write a sentence about the past using *would* or *could.* Suggested topic: My childhood summers.

Practice 6

Read the following passage. Edit to ensure proper use of past tense and proper spelling of past tense forms.

In the late eighteenth and early nineteenth centuries many immigrants come to the United States from Europe, especially from eastern and southern Europe. Between 1870 and 1914 about 20 million people arrive. And many of them past through Ellis Island. Often they can barely scrape together enough money for the ship passage to the United States. Sometimes they didn't have much more than the clothes they weared on their backs. The passage was difficult—they lay on the ship decks and slept there. Like immigrants today, they endure these innumerable difficulties because they wanted to escape oppression and to pursue economic opportunity. Once they get settled, they often tryed to bring other family members in. In 1914, the outbreak of World War I stoped them from coming.

Writing Assignments

Writing for Everyday Life

Read the following letter to the editor about a local issue. Edit the paragraph to ensure proper usage of the past tense. Use the chart on page 456 of this chapter or a dictionary to confirm the spellings of irregular verbs. Use your own paper.

Just recently, two major insurance companies announced that they will no longer write insurance policies in Mississippi. The next day, the Insurance commissioner says he hopes these companies will have changed their stance. What he should have said was "good riddance." After Hurricane Katrina, fair-weather insurance companies cause added grief and expense by denying valid claims. These insurance companies was eager to write policies as long as we policy holders have no losses. Once they see the extent of our loss, they bailed on us. Even as Hurricane Katrina striked, I just know I would lose everything. So I say what the Commissioner should have said, "Good riddance, fair-weather insurance companies!"

Writing for College Life

The following paragraph was written by a student for a psychology class to define and illustrate the concept of *gunnysacking*. Edit to ensure proper usage of the past tense. Use the chart on page 456 of this chapter or a dictionary to confirm the spellings of irregular verbs. Use your own paper.

A gunnysack is a large burlap bag, and gunnysacking is a conflict strategy that stores up grievances for later use. Early in their relationship, Chris and Pat frequently resort to gunnysacking. For example, when they first begin living together, Chris could come home late every night, and every night, Pat can recount a long list of past wrongs that he had committed. "You forget my birthday," she says, "and you leave my car on empty last Thursday. You are so inconsiderate." Of course, gunnysacking leads to gunnysacking, so Chris always threw his own accusations. To save their relationship, Chris and Pat learn to focus on the here-and-now. Once they keep their focus on the issue of the moment, they were much happier.

Writing for Working Life

Read the following letter written by an employee who is requesting a performance-based raise. Edit to ensure proper usage of the past tense. Use the chart on page 456 of this chapter or a dictionary to confirm the spellings of irregular verbs. Use your own paper.

Dear Ms. Diaz:

As the Webmaster for our company, I have created a record of hard work and achievement that qualifies me for a promotion and a raise. My accomplishments include the following. I make fourteen web sites for various departments. I turned words and art selected by each department into Internet sites that people were able to use. I check to see that employees with different computers can use the web sites. As the Webmaster, I also tryd to make the sites work faster. I keep the size of files small so that they do not take much time to download. I tested web sites, too. I watch people using a site to see if there were any parts that were hard to use. I also meet with designers, helping to decide how the sites should look and work. I also update web sites, and I fixed mistakes, such as broken links. Due to my expertise and hardwork as Webmaster, our Internet presence remain interesting and effective. Thank you for considering my request for a promotion and a raise based on my performance.

Respectfully,

Donald Malik

Academic Learning Log

WHAT HAVE I LEARNED ABOUT THE PAST TENSE OF VERBS?

To test and track your understanding, answer the following questions.

1. What is the general rule for forming the past tense of regular verbs? Give an example.

....

....

2. What are three exceptions to the way in which regular verbs form the past tense? Give examples.

a. ....

....

b. ....

....

c. ....

....

3. What can be said about the past tense forms of irregular verbs?

....

....

....

4. What are the past tense forms of the irregular verbs *to be*, *to have*, and *to do*?

....

5. List three often-confused helping verbs.

....

6. How will I use what I have learned about the past tense?
In your notebook, discuss how you will apply to your own writing what you have learned about the past tense of regular and irregular verbs.

7. What do I still need to study about the past tense?
In your notebook, discuss your ongoing study needs by describing what, when, and how you will continue studying the past tense of regular and irregular verbs.

26

The Past Participle

A participle is a verb form that can be used to establish tenses or voices, or it can be used as a modifier, which describes, restricts, or limits other words in a sentence.

CHAPTER PREVIEW

LEARNING OUTCOMES

● What's the Point of the Past Participle?

● Understanding the Point of the Past Participle: One Student Writer's Response

● Applying the Point: The Past Participle

● Writing Assignments

Thinking about a real-life situation helps us to understand the purpose of the past participle in our communication. The photograph documents a bee keeper handling a colony of bees. Study the picture, complete the activity, and answer the question "What's the point of the past participle?"

What's the Point of the Past Participle?

Practice 1

PHOTOGRAPHIC ORGANIZER: THE PAST PARTICIPLE

Assume you subscribe to a news blog, and that a correspondent has filed the following report, which contains misuses of the past participle. Where are the errors? What is the impact of the errors?

Honey Bees Dropping Like Flies

Colony Collapse Disorder (CCD) has hurt bee colonies in Pennsylvania, North Carolina, Florida, Georgia, and California. So far, some beekeepers have loss up to 80 percent of their colonies to the mysterious disorder. Whatever kills the bees targets adult workers, which die outside the colony. Few adults left inside, either alive or dead. The worker bee population wiped out in a matter of weeks by the disorder. Aside from making honey, honey bees are essential for the pollination of tens of million of dollars worth of cash crops all over the United States. That's why farmers across the country are worry. A fungus, virus, or a variety of microbes and pesticides are thought to be some of the possible causes.

What's the point of the past participle?

Adapted from Larry O'Hanlon, "Honey Bee Die-off Alarms Beekeepers," *Discovery News*, February 5, 2007

Understanding the Point of the Past Participle: One Student Writer's Response

The following paragraph offers one writer's reaction to the paragraph "Honey Bees Dropping Like Flies."

> I thought this was a really interesting article, but there were some confusing errors. The verb "have loss" just doesn't sound right. I looked up the spelling for "loss," and the past participle form is "lost." The statement, "Few adults left inside, either alive or dead" is missing something. Maybe the helping verb "are" needs to be inserted so the verb is "are left." This same kind of error is in the sentence, "The worker bee population wiped out... ." The helping verb "is" needs to be inserted so the verb is "is wiped." Finally, "are worry" sounds wrong, too. "Worry" should be spelled "worried." The paragraph has too many misspelled or missing words and is hard to follow.

Applying the Point: The Past Participle

A **participle** is a verb form that can be used to establish tenses or voices, or it can be used as a modifier, which describes, restricts, or limits other words in a sentence. The **past participle** of a verb joins with helping verbs to form the present perfect and past perfect tenses and the passive voice. In addition, the past participle can act as an adjective that describes another word. Just as with the simple past tense, the past participle takes on different forms for regular and irregular verbs.

Past Participles of Regular Verbs

In general, regular verbs form the past participle by adding *-ed* to the base form of the verb. Just as with the simple past tense, there are several spelling exceptions for the past participle of regular verbs.

Base Form	Past Tense	Past Participle
live	live**d**	live**d**
cry	cr**ied**	cr**ied**
permit	permit**ted**	permit**ted**

For more about past tense forms, see pages 452–463.

Practice 2

PAST PARTICIPLE OF REGULAR VERBS

Complete the following chart with the proper forms of the past tense and the past participle of each verb.

Base		Past Tense	Past Participle
1.	accept		
2.	agree		
3.	bang		
4.	bat		
5.	cheat		
6.	clip		
7.	hurry		
8.	relax		
9.	supply		
10.	whine		

Past Participles of Irregular Verbs

As with the simple past tense, irregular verbs do not use *-ed* to form the past participle. Nor does the past participle of irregular verbs conform to uniform spelling rules with clear exceptions. In addition, the past participle forms of many irregular verbs vary from their past tense forms. Practice 3 and the chart that follows it list the base form, past tense form, and past participle of some commonly used irregular verbs. It is not a comprehensive list, however. As with the simple past forms of irregular verbs, when in doubt, careful writers consult a dictionary to find the form and spelling of the past participle of an irregular verb. Throughout the rest of this chapter, the activities dealing with irregular verbs focus on those that, based on research, occur most frequently in English.

Practice 3

PAST PARTICIPLE OF IRREGULAR VERBS

The following chart contains the top ten irregular verbs listed by frequency of use. Supply the proper forms of the past tense and the past participle of each verb. Consult pages 468–469 or a dictionary as necessary.

Base	Past Tense	Past Participle
1. say		
2. make		
3. go		
4. take		
5. come		
6. see		
7. know		
8. get		
9. give		
10. find		

Some Common Irregular Past Participles

Base Form	Past Tense	Past Participle
be	was, were	been
become	became	become
break	broke	broken
bring	brought	brought
buy	bought	bought
choose	chose	chosen
come	came	come
cut	cut	cut
deal	dealt	dealt
dig	dug	dug
drink	drank	drunk
drive	drove	driven
eat	ate	eaten
fall	fell	fallen
feed	fed	fed
feel	felt	felt
find	found	found
fly	flew	flown
forget	forgot	forgotten
forgive	forgave	forgiven
freeze	froze	frozen
get	got	gotten
give	gave	given
go	went	gone
grow	grew	grown
hang	hung	hung
have	had	had
hear	heard	heard
hide	hid	hidden
hold	held	held
hurt	hurt	hurt
keep	kept	kept
know	knew	known
lay *(to place)*	laid	laid
lead	led	led
leave	left	left
let	let	let
lie *(to recline)*	lay	lain
light	lit	lit
lose	lost	lost
make	made	made
mean	meant	meant
meet	met	met
pay	paid	paid
put	put	put
quit	quit	quit
read	read	read
ride	rode	ridden
ring	rang	rung
rise	rose	risen
run	ran	run
say	said	said

Some Common Irregular Past Participles

Base Form	Past Tense	Past Participle
see	saw	seen
sell	sold	sold
send	sent	sent
shake	shook	shaken
shine	shone *(shined)*	shone *(shined)*
sing	sang	sung
sit	sat	sat
sleep	slept	slept
speak	spoke	spoken
spend	spent	spent
swim	swam	swum
take	took	taken
teach	taught	taught
tear	tore	torn
tell	told	told
think	thought	thought
throw	threw	thrown
understand	understood	understood
wake	woke *(waked)*	woken *(waked)*
wear	wore	worn
win	won	won
write	wrote	written

PAST PARTICIPLE

You already have experience using part participles in everyday speech. Complete the following well-known phrases. Fill in the blanks with the past participle form of the **irregular** verb in parentheses. Consult a dictionary or the chart on pages 468–469 as needed.

1. A .... heart (break)

2. A .... few (choose)

3. .... a rotten hand (deal)

4. .... up (feed)

5. .... and .... (lose)/(find)

6. .... in full (pay)

7. A .... for your money

8. .... out (wear)

9. Well .... (read)

10. Hand .... (write)

Practice 4

Using the Present Perfect Tense

(*Has* or *Have* and the Past Participle)

The **present perfect tense** connects the past to the present. The present perfect tense states the relationship of a past action or situation to a current, ongoing action or situation. The present perfect tense is formed by joining the helping verbs **has** or **have** with the past participle.

The purposes of the present perfect tense are:

- **to express change from the past to the present.**

PRESENT PERFECT "HAS IMPROVED" EXPRESSES
CHANGE FROM THE PAST ACTION TO A PRESENT ONE

PAST ACTION

Jamel was sick for three weeks, but he has improved.

- **to express a situation or action that started in the past and continues to the present.**

PRESENT PERFECT "HAVE RACED" EXPRESSES AN ONGOING
ACTION, WHICH STARTED IN THE PAST AND IS CONTINUING NOW

Carmen and Michelle have raced stock cars for several years.

PRESENT PERFECT

| Past action/event | Present action/event | Future action/event |

Practice 5

PRESENT PERFECT TENSE

Fill in the blanks with the present perfect tense of the **regular** verbs in the parentheses in order to complete these sentences about events reported by Ripley's Believe It or Not! Use the helping verbs *has* or *have* to form the present perfect tense.

1. Franz Spohn .... (create) a portrait of President Barack Obama from thousands of gumballs.

2. A bright pink dolphin .... (surface) in Lake Calcasieu, in southwest Louisiana.

3. U.S. researchers .... (create) a new material that is blacker than the blackest material.

4. Artist Nathan Sawaya .... (sculpt) full-size replicas of people entirely from Legos.

5. Write a sentence using the present perfect tense of a regular verb. Suggested topic: Something amazing that I've done. ....

....

[Adapted from Ripley's Believe It or Not! online, which has photos of all of the above]

PRESENT PERFECT TENSE

Fill in the blanks with the present perfect tense of the **irregular** verbs in parentheses. Use the helping verbs *has* or *have* to form the present perfect tense.

1. As a photojournalist, I _____ (go) to many parts of the world, looking for stories to tell.

2. I _____ (take) photos of some amazing people—from children to old people, and everyone in between.

3. My editor _____ (tell) me that he doesn't know how I manage to keep going.

4. I keep going because I _____ (get) so many thrills from my work!

5. Write a sentence using the present perfect tense of an irregular verb. Suggested topic: Photos I've taken. _____

_____

_____

PRESENT PERFECT TENSE

Fill in the blanks with the present perfect tense of the verbs in parentheses. The verbs may be either **regular** or **irregular** verbs. Use the helping verbs *has* or *have* to form the present perfect tense.

1. Fashion week _____ (come) to be the fashion industry event.

2. Fashion week _____ (bring) designers and buyers together to showcase the latest fashion trends.

3. Milan, London, and Paris _____ (influence) the fashion scene throughout the years.

4. New York _____ (dominate) fashion since World War II.

5. Write a sentence using the present perfect tense of either a regular or irregular verb. Suggested topic: Your favorite piece of clothing. _____

_____

_____

Using the Past Perfect Tense

(*Had* and the Past Participle)

The **past perfect** connects two past actions or situations. The past perfect is formed by joining the helping verb ***had*** with a past participle.

The purposes of the past perfect tense are:

- **To connect a previous action or event with a later action or event.**

PAST ACTION #2

PAST ACTION #1 THE PAST PERFECT "HAD LEFT" SHOWS THAT THIS ACTION OCCURRED BEFORE THE OTHER PAST ACTION "SAMUEL WENT..."

Samuel went to Starbucks, but everyone had left.

PAST ACTION #1

- **To express an action or event that happened before a certain past time.**

A PAST TIME

THE PAST PERFECT "HAD STUDIED" SHOWS THAT THIS ACTION OCCURRED BEFORE THE PAST TIME "DINNERTIME"

By dinnertime, Suzanne had studied for hours and hours.

PAST PERFECT

| Past action/event #1 | Past action/event #2 | Present | Future |

PAST PERFECT TENSE

Fill in the blanks with the past perfect tense of the **regular** verbs in the parentheses. Use the helping verb *had* to form the past perfect tense.

1. Although Juneteenth was made a Texas state holiday in 1980, African Americans
_____ (celebrate) Juneteenth for many decades before that.

2. Juneteenth was established to commemorate June 19, 1865, the day when word of the
end of the Civil War _____ (reach) Galveston, Texas.

3. More than two years before that, on January 1, 1863, Abraham Lincoln _____
(issue) the Emancipation Proclamation, declaring an end to slavery in the slave states.

4. Nonetheless, slavery _____ (continue) in Texas, until June 19, 1865, when Union
troops brought the news to Galveston.

5. Write a sentence using the past perfect tense of a regular verb. Suggested topic:
A national holiday. _____

_____

PAST PERFECT TENSE

Fill in the blanks with the past perfect tense of the **irregular** verbs in the parentheses. Use the helping verb *had* to form the past perfect tense.

1. During my annual checkup, I discovered that my previous physician, Dr. Griffin,

_____ (hold) on to my records instead of sending them to my current

physician, Dr. Doughney.

2. Six months before, I _____ (write) Dr. Griffin to request that he forward my

records to Dr. Doughney.

3. By the time I filled out all the required forms for a new patient and another form

requesting my records, I _____ (stand) at the receptionist's window for 30

minutes.

4. I _____ (hear) from several friends that Dr. Doughney was an excellent

doctor.

5. Write a sentence using the past perfect tense of an irregular verb. Suggested topic: An

annoying event. _____

_____

Using the Passive Voice
(*To Be* and the Past Participle)

In English, verbs establish two types of voices: the active voice and the passive voice. So far, you have only worked with the active voice. Expressing what the subject of a sentence does, action verbs establish the **active voice.** When the subject of a sentence receives the action (or is acted upon), the sentence is in the **passive voice.** The passive voice is formed by joining *to be* with a past participle. In addition the passive voice can be expressed in every tense.

The purpose of the passive voice is to tell the reader what is done to a subject.

Active Voice

SUBJECT "CONSTANCE" PERFORMS THE ACTION

Constance took her daughter to the hospital.

Passive Voice

SUBJECT "CONSTANCE" RECEIVES THE ACTION

Constance was taken to the hospital by her neighbor.

Examples of the tenses of the passive voice

Present Tense

SUBJECT
PRESENT TENSE OF "TO BE"
PAST PARTICIPLE OF "PACK"

The clothes are packed.

Past Tense

SUBJECT
PAST TENSE OF "TO BE"
PAST PARTICIPLE OF "STORE"

The furniture was stored.

Present Perfect Tense

SUBJECT
PRESENT PERFECT TENSE OF "TO BE"
PAST PARTICIPLE OF "WRAP"

The china has been wrapped in bubble pack.

Past Perfect Tense

SUBJECT
PAST PERFECT TENSE OF "TO BE"
PAST PARTICIPLE OF "TAKE"

Their possessions had been taken to a storage facility.

Practice 10

PASSIVE VOICE WITH REGULAR VERBS

Fill in the blanks with the passive voice of the **regular** verbs in the parentheses. Use the proper form of *to be* as a helping verb to form the passive voice.

1. The restaurant _____ (open) in 2006.

2. Before the restaurant opened, the market for Italian food _____ (analyze).

3. After the owners had argued for months over the name for the restaurant, finally, the name Pantheon _____ (agree) upon.

4. To ensure high-quality customer service, the wait staff _____ (train) by experts in hospitality management.

5. Write a sentence using the passive voice of a regular verb. Suggested topic: A new neighborhood business. _____

_____

PASSIVE VOICE WITH IRREGULAR VERBS

Fill the blanks with the passive voice of the **irregular** verbs in parentheses. Use the proper form of *to be* with the past participle to form the passive voice.

1. We've been waiting almost an hour—maybe our order ....(lose) somewhere in the recesses of the kitchen.

2. From the looks of it, your spinach soufflé probably .... (sit) on.

3. From the taste of it, my crabmeat casserole probably .... (throw) into the microwave.

4. Customers .... not .... (make) to feel very welcome here!

5. Write a sentence using the passive voice of an irregular verb. Suggested topic: A customer complaint.

....

....

Using the Past Participle as an Adjective

The past participle is often used as an adjective that modifies a noun or pronoun. Both regular and irregular forms of the past participle are used as adjectives.

The purposes of the past participle as an adjective are:

• **to describe a noun or pronoun with a word or phrase.**

PARTICIPLE "FALLEN" DESCRIBES NOUN "HEROES"

We honor our fallen heroes.

PARTICIPLE PHRASE

Destroyed by the wind, these houses will be raised again by hope.

PARTICIPLE "DESTROYED" DESCRIBES NOUN "HOUSES"

- **to describe the subject by completing a linking verb in the sentence.**

LINKING VERB

The vegetables are washed and peeled.

SUBJECT "VEGETABLES" IS DESCRIBED BY COMPOUND PAST PARTICIPLES "WASHED AND PEELED"

LINKING VERB

She seems worried.

SUBJECT "SHE" IS DESCRIBED BY PAST PARTICIPLE "WORRIED"

Practice 12

PAST PARTICIPLE AS AN ADJECTIVE

Fill in the blanks with the past participle forms of the verbs in parentheses.

1. Some athletes become highly _____ (respect) for their contributions to their sports.

2. David Beckham, an _____ (accomplish) soccer player, enjoys worldwide recognition.

3. _____ (watch) by 300 million fans, Yao Ming towers as a star in the National Basketball Association.

4. _____ (give) to long hours of practice, Tiger Woods constantly breaks golf's longest-standing records.

5. Write a sentence using the past participle as an adjective. Suggested topic: A sports figure.

_____

_____

_____

_____

_____

Practice 13

Review what you have learned throughout this chapter by completing the following activity. Read the following short news release from the U.S. Department of Health and Human Services Website. Edit to ensure use of the appropriate form of the past participle to create proper, logical verb tenses.

FDA Approves First ADHD Patch

The first skin patch to treat attention-deficit hyperactivity disorder (ADHD) in children was gave the U.S. Food and Drug Administration's blessing late Thursday, the *Associated Press* reported.

Design to be worn for nine hours, the patch contains a methylphenidate, a stimulant that has been effective in treating ADHD for decades. Know as Daytrana and maked by Noven Pharmaceuticals Inc. in Miami, the wire service said the patch is consider an alternative treatment for children aged 6 to 12 with ADHD if taking pills is too difficult. The patch, which will be available in four doses, can also be remove immediately if side effects develop.

More than 3 million Americans under the age of 19 have use ADHD medications in the last year, according to Medco Health Solutions Inc., a prescription drug benefit program manager.

According to the *AP*, Daytrana's label will carry the same standard warnings of side effects as other methylphenidates, which have include insomnia, decreased appetite, and nausea.

Writing Assignments

Writing for Everyday Life

Read the following blog. Edit the paragraph to ensure proper usage of the past participle. Use your own paper.

Here at last is the long promised summary of what I have be up to lately. Guess what? I have good news. I have find my dream job! I had gave up hope. I had even think about signing up as a temporary worker with an agency in the city. Then I ran into Caitlyn Myers who has graduated a year ahead of me. Delight to help a classmate, she told me about an opening in an art gallery near Central Park. I was hire last week as the director of the gallery. This is the very kind of job I has hoped to get. Well, my cell phone has rang the whole time I have sit here typing, so I am going to post my good news and sign off for now. – Ciao, Danni

Writing for College Life

The following lab report was written by a student for a science class. The professor required the use of the passive voice. Edit to ensure proper usage of the past participle. Use your own paper.

LAB REPORT

Cheri Jackson   May 15/24

Lab 7: Responses to Abiotic Factors   (Name)   (Date/ Lab Section)

Overview

This lab was design to understand the responses to abiotic factors by tracking transpiration by plants. Abiotic factors are made up of air, water, or temperature. Transpiration is known as the loss of water from a plant through evaporation. The behavior and structure of an organism are affect by the loss of water through evaporation.

Procedure and Results

A long branch with healthy leaves was select. Next, a clean cut at the base was made, and the cut end was immediately transfer to a pan of water. The leaves were keep dry. A second cut was made a cm or so above the first. The cut end was not exposed to the air since an air bubble could form in plant's tissue. The cut end was kept under water, and the stem was carry through a rubber stopper. Petroleum jelly was spread at the top and bottom of the cork to seal and hold the stem in the stopper attached to a length of tubing. A bubble was introduced into the tubing. As water was took up by the plant, the bubble moved. Water uptake was measured by marking regular gradations on the tube. Next, the prepared plant leaf was placed under a lamp, and the movement of the air bubble were measured at one-minute intervals for five minutes. The light was turn off, and a small fan was move next to plant. This effect of wind was measured at one-minute intervals for five minutes. The results indicated that light and wind speed up transpiration of plants.

Writing for Working Life

Read the following report written by a manager to be submitted at a meeting. Edit to ensure to ensure proper usage of the past participle and related forms. Use your own paper.

BASIC WEB DESIGN

Prepared and Submitted by Diane Lipari

As requested, I have analyze our website for its appeal and usability. The information I have gathers indicates a need for the application of basic Web design principles. Through a survey, our users have send us two messages. They don't care about new features. They just want easy usability. Before 2006, our Website has followed the basic guidelines of Web design. However, since our company's reorganization, we have not designate a person responsible for updating the Web. Two actions have recommended. The first recommendation has already been implemented. Qualify and experience, Raul Mendez have taken responsibility for our company's Web design. He has promises to carry out the second recommendation, which is to follow these guidelines:

- Provide text they can read.

- Answer their questions with detailed information.

- Provide easy-to-use navigation and search options.

- Eliminate bugs, typos, corrupted data, dead links, and outdated content.

mywritinglab

WANT A BETTER GRADE?
For more practice with the past participle, go to **www.mywritinglab.com > Recognizing and Avoiding Errors > The Past Participle.**

Academic Learning Log

LEARNING OUTCOMES
SELF-EVALUATION

WHAT HAVE I LEARNED ABOUT THE PAST PARTICIPLE?

To test and track your understanding, answer the following questions.

1. The present perfect tense is formed by joining the helping verbs .... or .... with the past participle.

2. What are two purposes of the present perfect tense?

   a. ....

   b. ....

3. The past perfect tense is formed by joining the helping verb .... with the past participle.

4. What are two purposes of the past perfect tense?

   a. ....

   b. ....

5. The passive voice is formed by the combination of .... with a past participle.

6. The passive voice can be expressed in every ....

7. What are two purposes of the passive voice?

   a. ....

   b. ....

PORTFOLIO

8. What are two purposes of the past participle as an adjective?

   a. ....

   b. ....

9. How will I use what I have learned about the past participle?

In your notebook, discuss how you will apply to your own writing what you have learned about the past participle of regular and irregular verbs.

10. What do I still need to study about the past participle?

In your notebook, discuss your ongoing study needs by describing what, when, and how you will continue studying the past participle of regular and irregular verbs.

27

Nouns and Pronouns

A noun names a person, animal, place, or thing. A pronoun stands in the place of a noun that has been clearly identified earlier in the text.

Thinking about a real-life situation helps us to understand the purpose of nouns and pronouns in our communication. The following photograph captures the essence of a controversial tourist attraction. Study the picture, complete the activity, and answer the question "What's the point of learning about nouns and pronouns?"

What's the Point of Learning About Nouns and Pronouns?

Practice 1

PHOTOGRAPHIC ORGANIZER: NOUNS AND PRONOUNS

The following passage is adapted from a news story about the Skywalk bridge over the Grand Canyon that was built as a tourist attraction by the Hualapai tribe. All of the nouns and pronouns have been omitted from the passage. Work with a small group of your peers. Use the picture to help you fill in the blanks with nouns and pronouns that make the passage sensible. Answer the question "What's the point of learning about nouns and pronouns?"

WRITING FROM LIFE

Skywalk

A Native American _____ fastened a massive glass-bottomed _____ to the _____ of the _____. The ambitious tourist _____ has angered _____ and some tribal _____. The _____ (pronounced WALL-uh-pie) are an impoverished _____ of about 2,200 _____. _____ live at the _____ remote western _____. A private _____ constructed the $30 million _____ to lure _____ to the _____.

What's the point of learning about nouns and pronouns?

_____

_____

Understanding the Point of Learning About Nouns and Pronouns: One Student Writer's Response

The following paragraph offers one writer's reaction to the activity based on "Skywalk."

I couldn't believe how hard this activity was! It was like trying to solve a riddle or a mystery. At least we had the picture to give us some clues. I was glad to be able to work with a group, too. Together we came up with more ideas, but we still couldn't figure out what all the words should be. This activity taught me that nouns and pronouns give really important information. You can't say what you want to say without using nouns and pronouns. I also learned that the words around pronouns and nouns can act like clues. Several times we chose a word that matched the word in front of it, like "the edge" and "an impoverished tribe."

Applying the Point: Nouns

Often, nouns are the first words we learn to speak as we hear the names of people. The word "noun" comes from the Latin word *nomen*, which means "name." A **noun** names a person, animal, place, object, element, action, or concept.

What a Noun Names	
Person:	Chris Rivers; a sales clerk
Animal:	Kitty; the cat
Place:	Lake Tahoe; a state park
Object:	Kleenex; tissue paper
Element:	water; air; gas
Action:	running
Concept:	Islam; a religion

One type of noun is the proper noun. A **proper noun** names an individual person, place, or thing. A proper noun is always capitalized. The second type of noun is the common noun. A **common noun** is a general name for any member of a group or class. A common noun is not capitalized.

Two Types of Nouns	
Proper Noun	**Common Noun**
Barnes & Noble	bookstore
Olive Garden	restaurant
Levi's	blue jeans
Batman	action hero
Polk County	county

Practice 2

TYPES OF NOUNS

Identify the following words as proper nouns or common nouns. Edit to capitalize the proper nouns.

1. museum

2. smithsonian museum

3. basketball team

4. news anchor

5. katie couric

6. alcohol

7. development

8. miami heat

9. adolescents

A proper or common noun can function in a sentence as a subject, an object of a verb, an object of a preposition, or an appositive (which describes another noun).

Uses of a Noun

Function in Sentence	Example

PROPER NOUN AS SUBJECT

• Subject

Roberto finished first.

Function in Sentence	Example

VERB

COMMON NOUN AS OBJECT OF VERB "DRANK"

• Object of a verb

Maria drank coffee.

PREPOSITION

PROPER NOUN AS OBJECT OF PREPOSITION "TO"

• Object of a preposition

Justin went to AutoZone.

SUBJECT (PROPER NOUN)

COMMON NOUN AS APPOSITIVE DESCRIBING "SIMON"

• Appositive (describes another noun)

Simon, the manager, has arrived.

USES OF A NOUN

Identify the following aspects of each of the nouns in the following sentences: the noun, what the noun names, type of noun, and function of the noun.

1. The Surgeon General filed a report with the following information.

----

2. In the United States, 11 million youths drink alcohol as underage drinkers.

----

3. Of the 11 million underage drinkers, 7.2 million drink as binge drinkers.

Count and Noncount Nouns

For more information on irregular spellings, see pages 604–620, "Improving Your Spelling."

Count nouns name distinct individual units of a group or category. Count nouns usually refer to what we can see, hear, or touch. Count nouns are typically common nouns and can be singular or plural. Most singular count nouns are formed by adding *–s* or *–es*. However, many singular count nouns use irregular spellings in their plural form.

Examples of Count Nouns		
	Singular	**Plural**
Regular	age baby dress garden	ages babies dresses gardens
Irregular	calf deer man person	calves deer men people

   Noncount nouns name a nonspecific member of a group or category. Noncount nouns, which are typically common nouns, do not have plural forms. Noncount nouns name things that cannot be divided into smaller parts. Often, noncount nouns represent a group of count nouns. The following chart illustrates the differences between count and noncount nouns.

Examples of Noncount Nouns and Corresponding Count Nouns			
Noncount Noun		**Count Noun**	
air, oxygen, steam anger, happiness, grief	English, Spanish, Latin beauty, honesty, truth	gases emotions	languages concepts

---

COUNT AND NONCOUNT NOUNS

Read the following sentences. Identify the **boldfaced** nouns as a count or noncount noun.

1. A video **game** for **kids** offers the same sort of **humor** as watching a **cartoon**.

_____

2. For example, **nose-picking** is a favorite **type** of **animation** found in both.

_____

3. In addition, both offer **acts** of **violence** involving bad **guys** and **guns** as **entertainment**.

_____

4. In the **game** "Secret Rings," the **player** tries to win **rings** of **gold** floating in the **air**.

_____

5. The **game** gets off to a slow **start**, but the **pace** picks up quickly.

_____

Articles and Nouns

An **article** is a type of adjective that describes a noun as being general or specific.

> **Indefinite articles:** *A* and *an* are used before a singular noun that refers to any member of a larger group: *a cat, an umbrella*. These articles are often used to introduce a noun for the first time in the discussion. Use *a* before a noun that begins with a consonant: *a cat*. Use *an* before a noun that begins with a vowel: *an umbrella*.

> **Definite article:** *The* is used before a singular or plural noun that refers to a specific member of the larger group: *the cat, the hat*. The article *the* is often used to indicate a noun that has already been introduced into the discussion. "A cat is at the front door; the cat looks hungry." *The* is the most commonly used word in the English language.

> **Zero article:** No article is used before the noun. An example: *Time is money*. Use zero article to refer to general ideas.

- *A Chinese woman moves to a different country.*
- *The Chinese woman has a difficult time communicating.*
- *Chinese is a foreign language in her new country.*

Deciding which article to use with a noun can be a challenge. You must determine if the article refers to a count noun or a noncount noun, and you must determine if the noun is singular or plural. The following chart illustrates the proper combinations.

Nouns and Their Articles		
	Count Nouns	**Noncount Nouns**
Singular	A, An	The
Plural	The	—

ARTICLES

Read the sentences below. Insert the correct article (*a*, *an*, or *the*) in the blanks provided.

(1) Dry, irritated skin is _____ threat to _____ person's well-being. (2) To understand _____ threat, you need to understand skin. (3) Well-moisturized skin offers _____ barrier against bacteria and viruses. (4) As _____ individual ages, one's cell turnover slows down, and damage occurs.

(5) _____ damage comes from weather, from chilly temperatures and dry indoor heat. (6) Long, hot baths and showers also damage _____ skin. (7) _____ natural protective layer of oil is stripped away by too much washing.

(8) _____ lotion treatment can restore _____ protective barrier of moisture.

(9) Many of _____ lotion treatments contain petrolatum, glycerin, or shea butter, _____ oil that prevents water loss.

Applying the Point: Pronouns

Pronouns and antecedents work closely together to communicate an idea. A pronoun refers to or stands in the place of a noun that has been clearly identified earlier in the discussion. An **antecedent** is the noun to which a pronoun refers. Every pronoun should refer clearly and specifically to one particular antecedent.

ANTECEDENT OF PRONOUN "IT"   *PRONOUN "IT" REFERS TO ANTECEDENT "PACKAGE"*

When the FedEx package arrived, the receptionist put it on the front counter.

In the preceding example, the pronoun "it" clearly refers to the antecedent "package."

How to Make Clear Pronoun References

Because a pronoun takes the place of a noun, careful writers make the relationship between a pronoun and its antecedent obvious and clear. Remembering a few guidelines can help you make clear pronoun references.

> For more information on using precision in drafting sentences, see pages 360–373, "Sentence Clarity: Point of View, Number, and Tense."

Guidelines for Clear Pronoun Reference
• A pronoun refers clearly and unmistakably to one antecedent.
• The antecedent of a pronoun is clearly stated.
• A pronoun appears near its antecedent.
• A pronoun does not make a broad or sweeping reference to an entire group of words.

Faulty pronoun references usually occur when the guidelines for clear reference are ignored. Once you understand why faulty pronoun references occur and how they can be corrected, you can avoid them in your writing; then you can make clear pronoun references.

How to Correct Faulty Pronoun References

Faulty Pronoun Reference to More Than One Antecedent

PROBLEM:

The pronoun does not clearly and unmistakably refer to one specific antecedent.

PRONOUN "IT" REFERS TO ?

Jared threw the remote control at the television because it was broken.

ANTECEDENT OF "IT"?

CORRECTION:

Correct by replacing the pronoun with a noun.

Jared threw the remote control at the television because the remote control was broken.

ADDED NOUN REPLACES PRONOUN WITH NO CLEAR ANTECEDENT

Faulty Pronoun Reference to Implied or Missing Antecedent

PROBLEM:

The antecedent is not stated or is missing.

ANTECEDENT OF PRONOUN "IT"?   *PRONOUN "IT" REFERS TO ?*

The donut box is empty. Who ate it?

CORRECTION #1:

Correct by replacing the pronoun with a noun.

ADDED NOUN REPLACES PRONOUN WITH NO CLEAR ANTECEDENT

The donut box is empty. Who ate the last donut?

SUBJECT AND VERB IMPLY THAT "IT" IN THE ABOVE SENTENCE REFERS TO A DONUT

CORRECTION #2:

Correct by rewording to include a clear antecedent for the pronoun.

ANTECEDENT OF PRONOUN "IT"   *PRONOUN "IT" REFERS TO ANTECEDENT "DONUT"*

The last donut is gone. Who ate it?

Faulty Pronoun Reference due to Distant Pronoun Reference

PROBLEM:

The pronoun does not appear near its antecedent.

ACTUAL ANTECEDENT OF PRONOUN "WHICH"

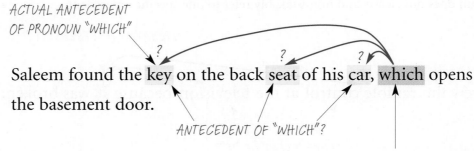

Saleem found the key on the back seat of his car, which opens the basement door.

ANTECEDENT OF "WHICH"?

DISTANCE OF RELATIVE PRONOUN "WHICH" FROM ITS ANTECEDENT "KEY" MAKES THE ANTECEDENT UNCLEAR AND THE SENTENCE AWKWARD

CORRECTION:

Correct by rewording to place the pronoun closer to its antecedent.

ANTECEDENT OF PRONOUN "WHICH"

PRONOUN "WHICH" REFERS TO ANTECEDENT "KEY"

Saleem found the key, which opens the basement door, on the back seat of his car.

Faulty Pronoun Reference due to Broad Pronoun References

PROBLEM:

The pronoun refers to a group of words, such as an entire sentence.

ANTECEDENT OF PRONOUN "WHICH" ?

PRONOUN "WHICH" REFERS TO ?

Mick told Megan about his date with Kanesha, which annoyed Megan.

CORRECTION:

Correct by rewording to eliminate the pronoun.

Megan was annoyed because Mick told her about his date with Kanesha.

CLEAR PRONOUN REFERENCE

Revise the following sentences for clear pronoun reference.

1. Maxine spewed coffee into her food because it tasted terrible.

....

2. Colleen told Samantha that her dress was torn.

....

3. Employees must check with their managers who need sick-leave forms.

....

4. Henry approached the baby's high chair and it screamed.

....

5. That guy is walking a big shaggy dog who was Carlos's roommate in college.

....

....

Practice 6

How to Make Pronouns and Antecedents Agree

A pronoun and its antecedent must agree with each other in three ways: person, number, and gender. The following chart presents pronouns based on these traits.

Pronouns: Person, Number, and Gender		
	Singular	**Plural**
First Person	I, me, my, mine	we, us, our, ours
Second Person	you, your, yours	you, your, yours
Third Person	he, him, his (**masculine**) she, her, hers (**feminine**) it, its (**neutral**)	they, them, their, theirs(**neutral**)

Pronoun agreement makes the relationship between a pronoun and its antecedent obvious and clear. **Faulty pronoun agreement** reflects vague wording and results in reader confusion. Remembering a few guidelines can help you establish pronoun agreement.

Guidelines for Clear Pronoun Agreement
• Pronoun choice establishes consistent use of the person of pronouns.
• Singular pronouns refer to or replace singular nouns.
• Plural pronouns refer to or replace plural nouns.
• Feminine pronouns refer to or replace feminine nouns.
• Masculine pronouns refer to or replace masculine nouns.
• Use gender-neutral plural pronouns and antecedents in statements that could apply to women or men.

Faulty pronoun agreement usually occurs when the guidelines for clear agreement are ignored. Once you understand why faulty pronoun agreement occurs and how it can be corrected, you can avoid vague agreements in your writing; then you can create agreement based on person, number, and gender.

How to Correct Faulty Pronoun Agreement

Faulty Pronoun Agreement Due to Shift in Person

PROBLEM:

When the person of the pronoun differs from the person of the antecedent, it is called a faulty **shift in person**. In the example below, the faulty shift is from third person to second person.

THIS ANTECEDENT OF THE SECOND-PERSON
PRONOUN "YOUR" IS A THIRD-PERSON NOUN
↓

As soon as a contestant finishes a song, the judges evaluate

your performance.

SECOND-PERSON PRONOUN "YOUR" DOES NOT AGREE
WITH ITS THIRD-PERSON ANTECEDENT "CONTESTANT"

CORRECTION #1:

Correct the shift in person by changing the antecedent to agree with the pronoun.

ADDED SECOND-PERSON ANTECEDENT AGREES WITH SECOND-PERSON PRONOUN

As soon as you finish a song, the judges evaluate your performance.

"-ES" IN VERB IS DELETED TO AGREE WITH ADDED PRONOUN "YOU" IN NUMBER

CORRECTION #2:

Correct by changing the pronoun to agree with the antecedent.

THIRD-PERSON ANTECEDENT AGREES WITH ADDED THIRD-PERSON PRONOUN

As soon as a contestant finishes a song, the judges evaluate her performance.

Faulty Pronoun Agreement Due to Shift in Number

PROBLEM:

In a sentence with a faulty **shift in number,** the pronoun is a different number than the number of the antecedent. In the two examples below, the faulty shift is from singular to plural; the revised sentences show two different ways to correct the same problem.

SINGULAR ANTECEDENT

PLURAL PRONOUN DOES NOT AGREE WITH SINGULAR ANTECEDENT "ATHLETE"

A college athlete must keep their grades at a B average to be eligible to play.

CORRECTION:

Correct by making the antecedent the same number as the pronoun.

PLURAL ANTECEDENT AGREES WITH PLURAL PRONOUN

College athletes must keep their grades at a B average to be eligible to play.

PROBLEM:

SINGULAR ANTECEDENT

PLURAL PRONOUN DOES NOT AGREE WITH SINGULAR ANTECEDENT "EVERYONE"

Everyone on the women's soccer team has their gear loaded on the bus.

CORRECTION:

Correct by making the pronoun the same number as the antecedent.

SINGULAR ANTECEDENT AGREES WITH SINGULAR PRONOUN

Everyone on the women's soccer team has her gear loaded on the bus.

Faulty Pronoun Agreement Due to Shift in Gender

PROBLEM:

In a sentence with a faulty **shift in gender**, the pronoun is a different gender than the gender of the antecedent. Most often, gender agreement problems are due to using the masculine pronoun to refer to antecedents that could apply to either men or women.

SINGULAR ANTECEDENT IS NEUTRAL ("STUDENT" COULD BE EITHER MASCULINE OR FEMININE)

A student at Carleton College can buy his parking permit at the Campus Safety Office.

MASCULINE, SINGULAR PRONOUN "HIS" DOES NOT AGREE WITH NEUTRAL ANTECEDENT "STUDENT"

CORRECTION #1:

Correct by rewording to make the pronoun the same gender as the antecedent.

NEUTRAL, SINGULAR ANTECEDENT AGREES WITH NEUTRAL, SINGULAR PRONOUN "HIS OR HER"

A student at Carleton College can buy his or her parking permit at the Campus Safety Office.

If you reword the sentence by making the pronoun and its antecedent (neutral and) plural, make sure all other parts of the sentence are plural as necessary.

NEUTRAL, PLURAL ANTECEDENT AGREES WITH NEUTRAL, PLURAL PRONOUN

Students at Carleton College can buy their parking permits at the Campus Safety Office.

"–S" ADDED TO AGREE WITH PLURAL PRONOUN "THEIR" IN NUMBER

CORRECTION #2:

Correct by rewording to make the antecedent the same gender as the pronoun. In the instance below, this requires adding a masculine proper noun ("John") to match the masculine pronoun.

ADDED MASCULINE, SINGULAR ANTECEDENT

MASCULINE, SINGULAR PRONOUN "HIS" REFERS TO MASCULINE, SINGULAR ANTECEDENT "JOHN"

John, a student at Carleton College, can buy his parking permit at the Campus Safety Office.

ADDED COMMAS SET OFF NEW APPOSITIVE PHRASE

Practice 7

Edit the following sentences to create pronoun agreement. Cross out the faulty pronoun and insert the appropriate pronoun.

1. People should check their credit reports to find out if you have been victimized by identity theft.

2. A person can have his credit report sent to him for free.

3. A victim of identity theft loses more than money; they lose peace of mind.

4. A consumer should be diligent about paying bills; your payment history counts for 35 percent of your credit score.

5. Write a sentence that requires subject-verb agreement. Suggested topic: Physical fitness.

How to Clearly Use Pronoun Case

Pronoun case identifies the function of a pronoun in a sentence. The definitions and examples of the three cases of pronouns are shown in the following chart.

Pronoun Case					
Subjective Case		**Objective Case**		**Possessive Case**	
Singular	**Plural**	**Singular**	**Plural**	**Singular**	**Plural**
1st Person	I	we	me	us	my, mine	our, ours
2nd Person	you	you	you	you	your, yours	your, yours
3rd Person	he, she, it	they	him, her, it	them	his, his her, hers its whose	their, theirs
	who whoever		whom whomever			

    Subjective case pronouns act as subjects or predicate nouns. A **predicate noun** restates the subject, usually by completing a linking verb such as *is*.

SUBJECTIVE CASE PRONOUN

We are going to audition for a gig at the Comedy Club.

SUBJECT

SUBJECTIVE CASE PRONOUN RENAMES THE SUBJECT "COMEDIAN"

The funniest **comedian** is **she**.

Objective case pronouns act as an object of a verb or preposition. The **object** of a verb is the noun or pronoun to which the action of a verb is directed or to which the verb's action is done.

VERB

OBJECTIVE CASE PRONOUN "THEM" IS THE OBJECT OF THE VERB "CAPTIVATED"

The comedian captivated them.

PREPOSITION

OBJECTIVE CASE PRONOUN "WHOM" IS THE OBJECT OF THE PREPOSITION "TO"

To whom are you speaking?

Possessive case pronouns show ownership.

POSSESSIVE CASE PRONOUN "HIS" INDICATES THAT THE GLASSES BELONG TO "TOM"

Tom put his glasses on the bookshelf.

POSSESSIVE CASE PRONOUN "THEIR" INDICATES THAT THE CAR BELONGS TO "JASON AND CINDY"

By the time Jason and Cindy parked their car, the baseball game was over.

Practice 8

PRONOUN CASE

Underline the pronouns in each sentence. Then, identify the case of each pronoun.

1. The Library of Congress has added a popular Rolling Stones song to its archives.

---

2. The song "(I Can't Get No) Satisfaction" was first recorded in 1965; it was an instant hit.

3. The Library of Congress wants to preserve significant recordings because many of them have disappeared over the years.

4. The panel who choose the recording is made up of members of the public and a panel of music, sound, and preservation experts.

5. Write a sentence that requires the use of a subjective case pronoun. Suggested topic: Favorite musical group.

▲ Mick Jagger and Charlie Watts of the Rolling Stones

Use of pronoun cases relies upon understanding the function of the pronoun in the context of its use. Remembering a few guidelines can help you choose the appropriate case of a pronoun.

Guidelines for Use of Pronoun Cases
• Choose the appropriate pronoun case in comparisons using *as* or *than* based on the meaning of the sentence.
• Use the appropriate pronoun case in compound constructions, such as compound subjects, compound objects of verbs, or compound objects of prepositions.

Misuse of pronoun case usually occurs when the function of the pronoun is ignored or misunderstood. Once you understand why misuse of pronoun case occurs and how it can be corrected, you can choose the appropriate pronoun case based on the context of its use.

How to Correct Faulty Use of Pronoun Case in Comparisons Using "as" or "than"

Pronouns in comparisons using "as" or "than" can be in the subjective, objective, or possessive case. Most writers have no difficulty using the possessive case correctly: *Sam's car is prettier than* **mine**. However, writers often confuse the subjective and objective cases (for example, incorrectly substituting "I" for "me," "he" for "him," or "she" for "her" because they think it sounds more formal).

PROBLEM:

The objective case pronoun is being used as the subject of a clause.

DEPENDENT CLAUSE WITH UNSTATED VERB "IS"

Jerome is as concerned as her .

INCORRECT USE OF OBJECTIVE CASE PRONOUN

CORRECTION:

If the pronoun is a subject, correct by replacing the pronoun with a subjective case pronoun. To identify whether a pronoun in a comparison is a subject or an object, mentally complete the comparison by filling in the implied words and then choose the pronoun that matches it logically.

SUBJECTIVE CASE PRONOUN ACTS AS SUBJECT OF IMPLIED VERB "IS"

Jerome is as concerned as she [is].

IMPLIED VERB

PROBLEM:

The subjective case pronoun is being used as the object of a verb.

INCORRECT USE OF SUBJECTIVE CASE PRONOUN

The transit strike affected Marion as much as I.

CORRECTION:

If the pronoun is an object, correct by replacing the pronoun with an objective case pronoun. To identify whether a pronoun in a comparison is a subject or an object, mentally complete the comparison by filling in the implied words and then choose the pronoun that matches it logically.

OBJECTIVE CASE PRONOUN "ME" ACTS AS OBJECT OF IMPLIED VERB "AFFECTED"

The transit strike affected Marion as much as [it affected] me.

In some cases, the pronoun in a comparison could function as either a subject or an object and still make sense either way, but it would change the sentence's meaning. Both examples below are correct, but the first sentence means that Miguel respects Carlotta more than you respect her and the second sentence means that Miguel respects Carlotta more than he respects you.

SUBJECTIVE CASE PRONOUN "I" ACTS AS THE SUBJECT OF THE IMPLIED VERB "RESPECT"

Miguel respects Carlotta more than I [respect Carlotta].

OBJECTIVE CASE PRONOUN "ME" IS THE OBJECT OF THE IMPLIED VERB "RESPECTS"

Miguel respects Carlotta more than [he respects] me.

Faulty Use of Case in Compound Constructions

In some instances, a pronoun is joined with a noun or another pronoun to form a **compound.**

- **Joseph and I** went to a concert together.

- The mailman delivered the letter to **Joseph and me**.

To decide whether the subjective or objective case should be used for a pronoun in a compound, use the same rules that apply for a pronoun that is not in a compound. Use the subjective case for pronouns that function as subjects and the objective case for pronouns that function as objects.

PROBLEM:

The objective case pronoun is being used in a compound subject.

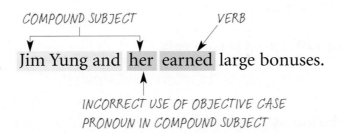

COMPOUND SUBJECT   VERB

Jim Yung and her earned large bonuses.

INCORRECT USE OF OBJECTIVE CASE PRONOUN IN COMPOUND SUBJECT

CORRECTION:

If the pronoun is a subject, correct by replacing the pronoun with the subjective case pronoun. To identify a pronoun as part of a compound subject, delete the other part of the compound so the pronoun stands alone, and see whether the sentence still makes sense. In the example here, you would delete "Jim Yung." The revised sentence, "Her earned large bonuses," does not make sense, which indicates that the pronoun used is part of a compound subject and should be subjective, not objective.

COMPOUND SUBJECT OF VERB "EARNED"   *VERB*

Jim Yung and she earned large bonuses.

SUBJECTIVE CASE PRONOUN

PROBLEM:

The subjective case pronoun is being used in a compound object.

COMPOUND OBJECTS

VERB

The supervisor told Bob and I the news.

MISUSED SUBJECTIVE CASE PRONOUN

CORRECTION:

If the pronoun is an object of either a verb or a preposition, correct by replacing the pronoun with the objective case pronoun. To identify a pronoun as part of a compound object, delete the other part of the compound so the pronoun stands alone, and see whether the sentence still makes sense. In the example, you would delete "Bob." The revised sentence, "The supervisor told I the news," does not make sense, which indicates that the pronoun used is part of a compound object and should be objective, not subjective.

VERB   *COMPOUND OBJECTS OF THE VERB "TOLD"*

The supervisor told Bob and me the news.

OBJECTIVE CASE PRONOUN

PRONOUN AGREEMENT

Edit the following sentences to ensure proper use of pronoun cases.

1. Michael, a highly skilled massage therapist, says that John is as effective as him.

2. In fact, many customers like John better than he.

3. Michael and him charge the same rates for a deep tissue massage.

4. Daniella strongly recommends both Michael and he as massage therapists.

5. Write a sentence that requires the proper use of pronoun case. Suggested topic: A good friend.

Practice 9

Reflexive and intensive pronouns include all the pronouns ending in *-self or -selves.* Often, in everyday, informal speech, the irregular forms of reflexive or intensive pronouns can be heard: *hisself, theirself,* and *theirselves.* However, these forms are to be avoided in standard, written English. The following chart lists the standard forms and uses of reflexive and intensive pronouns.

Reflexive and Intensive Pronouns		
Person	**Singular**	**Plural**
First Person	myself	ourselves
Second Person	yourself	yourselves
Third Person	himself, herself, itself	themselves

Reflexive pronouns refer back to the subject.

REFLEXIVE PRONOUN "HERSELF" REFERS
TO SUBJECT "JEANNIE"

Jeannie rewarded herself with a two-week cruise to the Bahamas.

Intensive pronouns add emphasis to another noun or pronoun.

INTENSIVE PRONOUN EMPHASIZES "DR. GILLON"

Dr. Gillon himself made a surprise appearance.

PROBLEM:
Because reflexive and intensive pronouns always refer to other nouns or pronouns, reflexive and intensive pronouns are never used on their own as the subject of a sentence.

REFLEXIVE PRONOUN MISUSED AS SUBJECT

My wife and myself went to the movies last night.

CORRECTION:
Correct by replacing the reflexive pronoun with a subjective pronoun.

ADDED SUBJECTIVE PRONOUN

My wife and I went to the movies last night.

REFLEXIVE AND INTENSIVE PRONOUNS

Complete each sentence by filling in the blank with the appropriate reflexive or intensive pronoun.

1. I do not need assistance; I can lift the weight by ....

2. Gil .... heard the diagnosis from the doctor.

3. Charlene gives .... a daily shot of her medicine for diabetes.

4. The President and the Vice President .... appeared at the rally.

5. You need to tell .... that success is possible.

NOUN AND PRONOUN REVIEW

Test your understanding of nouns and pronouns by filling the blanks with the nouns, articles, and pronouns that best complete each idea.

(1) Cheating is often .... key to success for video gamers. (2) At some point in ....

game, everyone has gotten stuck. (3) Today's gamers use cheat sites to get unstuck and to

learn how to master difficult games. (4) When .... pay $60 for .... game,

.... want to get .... money's worth. (5) While cheating can get ....

gamer blackballed in competitive video game play, solo cheating is widely practiced. (6) Still,

few gamers want to admit that .... cheat. (7) This .... for cheating

has given rise to dozens of dedicated Web ....

Writing Assignments

Writing for Everyday Life

Assume you got into a fight last night with your significant other, and you are writing a note of apology. Edit the following apology to ensure proper use of nouns, articles, and pronouns. Use your own paper.

> *Dear Jess,*
>
> *Too often disagreement come between you and I. Yesterday, our arguing seemed to upset others more than it upset ourselves. As you know, the quick tempers run in my family. And your family is just as fiery as us. Yesterday, however, a faults was all me. I can't blame anyone but me. I should not have embarrassed you by arguing with your brother Jonathan, whose also full of the remorse. You and me have been together an long time. One hopes you can find within yourself to forgive Jonathan and me.*
>
> *Regretfully, Pat*

Writing for College Life

Assume you are taking a test for a unit in Interpersonal Communication 101. On the written portion of the test, you are asked to explain some of the differences between individualistic cultures and collective cultures. You have ten minutes left to proofread your response. Edit to ensure proper use of nouns, articles, and pronouns. Use your own paper.

Exam question: What are the major contrasting traits between individualistic and collective cultures?

Individualistic and collective cultures differ in several aspect. Individualist cultures focus on the goales of an individual. You're responsible for yourself, and perhaps your immediate family. Your values are guided by your own consciences. A person's success is measured by surpassing other members of his group. Members of individualist culture are competitive, individualistic, and direct. Individualist cultures include American, Swedish, and German. In contrast, collective cultures focus on the goales of the group. Members of collective cultures are cooperative, submissive, and polite. You're responsible for a entire group and to group's values and rules. Collective cultures include Japaneses, Arabic, and Mexican.

Writing for Working Life

Assume you are a hairstylist who has recently opened a new salon. You have composed a letter to send to your customers to inform them about your move. Edit the letter to ensure proper use of nouns, articles, and pronouns. Use your own paper.

Dear Friends,

I would like to invite you to share in me new venture. I will now be at a following location: Waves & Day Spa, The Renaissance Center, 453 S. Oleander Street. We will offer your the same services at the same prices and also the addition of massage, facials, spa pedicures and manicures. There is also an selection of spa packages and escapes available. I will be working your same days Tuesday through Saturday with same flexible hours to accommodate yours schedule. I welcome you to join my new team and I at my new location and assure you that there will be same comfortable jovial atmosphere of a small salon with the offer of Day Spa services I appreciate your loyalty over the years and hope you will come see me at the new salon for a fresh new start to this new year.

Sincerely,

Denise Cossaboon

Academic Learning Log

WHAT HAVE I LEARNED ABOUT NOUNS AND PRONOUNS?

To test and track your understanding, answer the following questions.

1. A noun names a ...., animal, place, object, or concept.

2. A .... noun names an individual person, place, or thing; a .... noun is a general name for any member of a group or class.

3. A noun can function as a ...., object of a verb, object of a ...., or appositive.

4. .... nouns name distinct individual units of a group or category; .... nouns name a nonspecific member of a group or category.

5. An .... article is used before a singular noun that refers to any member of a larger group.

6. The definite article .... is used before a singular or plural noun that refers to a specific member of a larger group.

7. A pronoun refers clearly and specifically to .... antecedent.

8. An antecedent is the .... to which a pronoun refers.

9. A pronoun and its antecedent must agree with each other in three ways: ...., ..., and ....

10. The three pronoun cases are .... case, ... case, and .... case.

11. A reflexive pronoun refers back to the ....

12. An intensive pronoun adds .... to another noun or pronoun.

13. **How will I use what I have learned about nouns and pronouns?**
    In your notebook, discuss how you will apply to your own writing what you have learned about nouns and pronouns.

14. **What do I still need to study about nouns and pronouns?**
    In your notebook, discuss your ongoing study needs by describing what, when, and how you will continue studying pronouns and nouns.

28

Adjectives and Adverbs

An adjective describes a noun or a pronoun. An adverb describes a verb, an adjective, or another adverb.

Thinking about a real-life situation helps us to understand the purpose of adjectives and adverbs in our communication. The following photograph captures the action of a highly skilled basketball player, LeBron James. Study the picture, complete the activity, and answer the question "What's the point of learning about adjectives and adverbs?"

What's the Point of Learning About Adjectives and Adverbs?

PHOTOGRAPHIC ORGANIZER: ADJECTIVES AND ADVERBS

Assume you are a sports reporter for your college newspaper and you are writing a series of articles on great NBA basketball players. This week your column features LeBron James. Work with a small group of your peers. Use the picture to help you fill in the blanks with adjectives and adverbs that best describe the action in the photo.

The Amazing LeBron James

LeBron James is an _____ basketball player. His vertical leap is usually the _____ of all the players on the court. Other players' attempts to block James' shots are _____, because James' moves to the basket are _____ and _____ than his opponents could cope with. His _____ arms let him release the ball _____ to the basket while his body is _____ feet _____ from the basket. LeBron James is one of the _____ players in the NBA.

What's the point of learning about adjectives and adverbs?

....

....

Understanding the Point of Learning About Adjectives and Adverbs: One Student Writer's Response

The following paragraph offers one writer's reaction to the paragraph about LeBron James.

> This activity taught me how important adjectives and adverbs are. They paint a vivid picture so the reader can see the point of a topic or issue. I also noticed that each member of our group chose different words to describe LeBron James and the action in the photograph. For example, one person in our group described James as an "unbelievable basketball player" while another person said he is "an aggressive basketball player." So my choice of adjectives and adverbs helps me to get my own point across. I also noticed that adjectives describe people and things; while adverbs describe actions.

Applying the Point: Adjectives and Adverbs

Adjectives and adverbs are descriptive words that describe, modify, or limit the meaning of other words. Adjectives and adverbs have specific functions in a sentence and thus express precise meanings. Understanding the function and purpose of adjectives and adverbs allows a writer a thoughtful and effective expression of ideas.

An **adjective** modifies—in other words, it describes or limits—a noun or a pronoun. It answers one or more of the following questions:

- What kind?
- Which one?
- How many?

ADJECTIVE "LOUD" DESCRIBES NOUN "VOICE"

Maya has a loud voice.

PRONOUN "SHE" DESCRIBED BY ADJECTIVE "HAPPY"

She is happy.

An **adverb** modifies, or describes, a verb, an adjective, or another adverb. It answers one or more of the following questions:

- How?
- Why?
- When?
- Where?
- To what extent?

VERB "TALKS" DESCRIBED BY ADVERB "LOUDLY"

Maya talks loudly.

NOUN "MAYA" DESCRIBED BY ADJECTIVE "HAPPY"

Maya is loudly happy.

ADVERB "LOUDLY" DESCRIBES ADJECTIVE "HAPPY"

ADJECTIVES AND ADVERBS

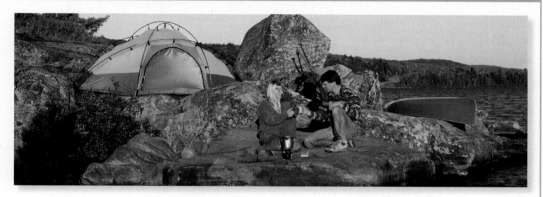

Identify the **boldfaced** words in each sentence as adjectives or as adverbs.

1. Camping has **persistently** remained one of life's **greatest** bargains.

----

2. A couple can camp **inexpensively**.

----

3. An **entire** set of **high-quality** equipment can cost **less** than $500.

----

4. Nights in **many** areas can get **very** cold.

----

5. Sleeping bags are **widely** available in **various** weights at **reasonable** prices.

Practice 2

Participles as Adjectives

Many adjectives are formed by adding *-ed* or *-ing* to verbs. These **participle adjectives** serve two purposes: The *-ed* form describes a person's reaction or feeling; the *-ing* form describes the person or thing that causes the reaction.

—ED PARTICIPLE ADJECTIVE DESCRIBES HOW THE CROWD FEELS

The amazed crowd watched the fireworks display.

—ING PARTICIPLE ADJECTIVE DESCRIBES THE FIREWORKS CAUSING THE REACTION

The amazing fireworks display lit up the entire sky.

The following chart lists some of the most common participles used as adjectives.

Common Participles Used as Adjectives			
alarmed	alarming	exhausted	exhausting
amused	amusing	fascinated	fascinating
annoyed	annoying	frightened	frightening
bored	boring	horrified	horrifying
concerned	concerning	irritated	irritating
confused	confusing	pleased	pleasing
depressed	depressing	satisfied	satisfying
discouraged	discouraging	shocked	shocking
encouraged	encouraging	stimulated	stimulating
engaged	engaging	terrified	terrifying
excited	exciting	worried	worrying

Practice 3

PARTICIPLES AS ADJECTIVES

Complete the following ideas by filling in the blanks with the proper participle adjective. Create the participle adjectives from the following words: *amaze, amuse,* and *bore.*

1. I've been impressed before, but never like last night, when we saw a truly .... spectacle, Cirque du Soleil's show "O."

2. This year, Cirque du Soliel's shows will be seen by almost 90 million people in over 200 cities around the world, and I'm willing to bet that not a person will feel ....

3. Watching "O," we were riveted from beginning to end—there wasn't a .... moment.

4. The .... crowd gasped as they watched the gymnastic and trapeze feats pulled off by incredibly brave performers.

5. Cirque du Soleil's shows have themes; some shows are serious while others are more light and ....

Nouns and Verbs Formed as Adjectives

In addition to the -ed and -ing word endings, many adjectives are formed by other types of word endings. Just as a suffix transforms a verb into a specific type of adjective or adverb, a suffix can also create adjectives out of nouns. Adjectives come in so many forms that using a few carefully chosen adjectives can add power and interest to your writing. For your reference, the following chart lists a few frequently used adjectives by some of their word endings.

Common Adjectives							
Word Endings	*-able* *-ible*	*-ful*	*-ic*	*-ish*	*-ive*	*-less*	*-ly* *-y*	*-ous*
Examples	acceptable	bashful	alcoholic	boorish	abusive	cheerless	actually	ambiguous
	accessible	cheerful	aquatic	oafish	combative	jobless	cagy	auspicious
	capable	forgetful	dramatic	devilish	decisive	mindless	daffy	courageous
	honorable	graceful	erratic	elfish	instinctive	needless	earthy	glamorous
	laughable	joyful	gigantic	lavish	receptive	noiseless	lively	industrious
	obtainable	merciful	majestic	skittish	reflective	pointless	manly	malicious
	plausible	peaceful	melodic	snobbish	secretive	senseless	seemly	nervous
	tangible	rightful	organic	squeamish	selective	useless	smelly	righteous

Placement of Adjectives

A careful writer not only chooses the precise word for impact, but also arranges words in the most effective order for the greatest impact on the reader. As you work with adjectives, be aware that the placement of adjectives varies based on its relationship to other words.

Adjectives can appear before a noun.

ADJECTIVE "NERVOUS" DESCRIBES NOUN "SUSPECT"

The nervous suspect offered an alibi.

Adjectives can appear after **linking verbs** such as *is, are, were, seems,* and *appears.*

LINKING VERB "SEEMED" JOINS ADJECTIVE "PLAUSIBLE" TO NOUN "ALIBI"

The alibi seemed plausible.

NOUN "ALIBI" DESCRIBED BY ADJECTIVE "PLAUSIBLE"

Adjectives can appear after **sensory verbs**—those that describe physical senses—such as *look, smell, feel, taste,* and *sound.*

SENSORY VERB "LOOKED" JOINS ADJECTIVE "FRIGHTENED" TO NOUN "SUSPECT"

The suspect looked frightened.

NOUN "SUSPECT" DESCRIBED BY ADJECTIVE "FRIGHTENED"

Practice 4

PLACEMENT OF ADJECTIVES

Fill in the blanks by choosing the phrase that best completes the sentence's idea by appropriate placement of adjectives.

1. _____ in every aspect of daily life.
   a. Needless conflicts arise   **b.** Conflicts needless arise   **c.** Conflicts arise needless

2. Many _____ after they are over.
   a. senseless conflicts seem   **b.** conflicts seem senseless   **c.** conflicts senseless seem

3. Frequently, conflicts arise because _____ to the needs or wants of others.
   a. people insensitive are   **b.** are people insensitive   **c.** people are insensitive

4. _____ often looks for conflict.
   a. A boorish person   **b.** A person boorish   **c.** Boorish a person

5. In contrast a person _____ strives to resolve conflicts in everyone's best interest.
   a. peaceful who is   **b.** is peaceful who   **c.** who is peaceful

Order of Adjectives

Adjectives that appear before a noun follow a particular order. Effective writers use adjectives sparingly. Rarely are more than two or three used in one sequence. The chart below outlines the preferred order of adjectives in English arranged by common types and includes three examples of expressions that follow that order. Notice that the order moves from the subjective description of *opinion* to objective descriptions such as *material* and *purpose*.

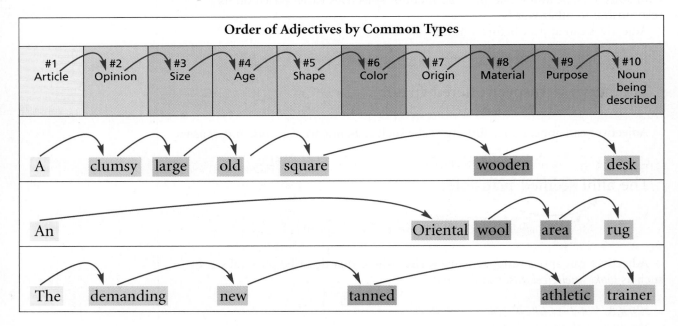

Order of Adjectives by Common Types

#1 Article	#2 Opinion	#3 Size	#4 Age	#5 Shape	#6 Color	#7 Origin	#8 Material	#9 Purpose	#10 Noun being described
A	clumsy	large	old	square			wooden		desk
An						Oriental	wool	area	rug
The	demanding		new		tanned			athletic	trainer

ORDER OF ADJECTIVES

A. Choose the option that best completes the idea by listing adjectives in appropriate order.

1. A .... bird hopped on the birdfeeder.

    a. small, brown, skittery **b.** brown, small, skittery **c.** skittery, small, brown

2. A .... cat bounded into the backyard.

    a. Siamese, young, silver **b.** young, silver Siamese **c.** young, Siamese, silver

3. The .... creature sounded the alarm.

    a. tiny, feathered **b.** feathered, tiny

4. As the bird chattered and hopped in alarm, it tipped the birdfeeder and spilled the

    .... birdseed.

    a. ample, fresh, organic **b.** fresh, ample, organic **c.** organic, ample, fresh

5. The scene remains a .... memory.

    a. fond, vivid childhood **b.** vivid, fond childhood **c.** childhood vivid, fond

B. Describe each noun with a set of two or more adjectives. List adjectives in proper order.

1. .... iPod

2. .... Website

3. .... mother

4. .... Johnny Depp

5. .... *American Idol*

Adverbs

The most common use of adverbs is to describe verbs. In addition, adverbs modify other types of words such as adjectives and other adverbs. In purpose, adverbs answer the reporter's questions *When? Where?* and *How?*

Many adverbs are derived from adjectives, many adverbs end in *-ly*, and many adverbs are gradeable based on degree or quantity. In fact, adverbs provide very specific types of information. The following chart lists some of the most frequently used adverbs based on the type of information they provide.

Common Adverbs				
Time, Frequency, or Sequence **When?**	**Place** **Where?**	**Manner** **How?**	**Certainty or Negation** **How?**	**Degree or Quantity** **How much?**
after	everywhere	automatically	certainly	absolutely
already	here	badly	clearly	almost
always	inside	beautifully	perhaps	a lot
at first	outside	cheerfully	probably	completely
consequently	somewhere	fast	maybe	enough
during	there	happily	obviously	entirely
early		hard	surely	extremely
every		quickly		fully
finally		seriously	not	hardly
often		slowly	never	least
once		well		less
never				little
next				more
now				most
rarely				much
recently				not
regularly				partly
seldom				rather
sometimes				really
soon				too
then				too little
thus				too much
tomorrow				totally
usually				very
when				
while				
yesterday				

ADVERBS

Add three adverbs to each sentence pair, so that the sentences give more information.

1. Beat the eggs. Add sugar.

2. Watch the ball. Be prepared to hit it and run.

3. When I was a child, we went to the beach. My father drove the car.

4. I've studied for the science test. I find that class difficult.

5. Write your own pair of sentences using three adverbs. Suggested topic: A childhood memory.

How to Use the Comparative and Superlative

A common error in using adjectives and adverbs occurs when a writer uses the wrong form to make degrees of comparisons between two things or among three things. Adjectives and adverbs take the form of three degrees: **absolute**, **comparative**, and **superlative**. The degrees of adverbs are formed by adding the suffixes *-er* or *-est* or by using *more* or *most*. For example, *more* or *most* establishes a degree of comparison with adverbs that end in *-ly*.

Absolute

The absolute degree makes no comparison, or makes a one-to-one comparison (in which the adjective or adverb describes both things equally).

ABSOLUTE ADJECTIVE "SWEET" DESCRIBES
COMPOUND SUBJECT "RAISINS AND PRUNES"

Raisins and prunes are sweet.

NOUNS "RAISINS" AND "PRUNES" ARE BEING COMPARED, BUT THE
ABSOLUTE ADJECTIVE "SWEET" DESCRIBES BOTH EQUALLY

Raisins are as sweet as prunes.

Comparative

The comparative degree compares and makes distinctions between two people or things, usually by using the adverb *more* or *less* or by adding the suffix *-er*. Sentences often include *than*.

COMPARATIVE ADJECTIVE "SWEETER"
COMPARES "RAISINS" WITH "PRUNES"

Raisins are sweeter than prunes.

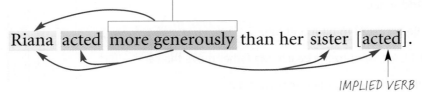

COMPARATIVE ADVERB "MORE GENEROUSLY" DESCRIBES VERB "ACTED" AND COMPARES THE ACTION OF "RIANA" (HOW RIANA ACTED) WITH THE ACTION OF "SISTER" (HOW HER SISTER ACTED)

Riana acted more generously than her sister [acted].

IMPLIED VERB

Superlative

The superlative degree makes distinctions among three or more people or things, usually by using the adverb *most* or *least* or by adding the suffix *-est*.

SUPERLATIVE ADJECTIVE "SWEETEST" COMPARES "PRUNE" TO ALL THE OTHER PRUNES "I" HAVE EATEN

This is the sweetest prune I have ever eaten.

SUPERLATIVE ADVERB "MORE GENEROUSLY" DESCRIBES VERB "ACTED" AND COMPARES THE ACTION OF "RIANA" (HOW RIANA ACTED) WITH THE ACTION OF NOUN "ALL THE STUDENTS ON THE DEBATE TEAM" (HOW ALL THE OTHER DEBATE TEAM STUDENTS ACTED)

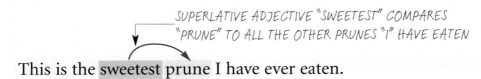

Riana acted the most generously of all the students on the debate team.

Degrees of Adjectives and Adverbs			
Degree of Comparison	**Absolute:** One as _____ as	**Comparative:** Two *-er* _____ than	**Superlative:** Three or More *-est* the _____
Adjectives	good	better	best
	bad	worse	worst
	large	larger	largest
	little	less	least
	much	more	most
	far	further/farther	furthest /farthest
Adverbs	busy	busier	busiest
	early	earlier	earliest
	carefully	more carefully	most carefully
	slowly	more slowly	most slowly
	well	better	best

Practice 7

Complete each of the following sentences with the appropriate comparative or superlative.

1. If the choice is between a diet and exercise to lose weight, exercise is the .... choice.

    a. good **b.** better **c.** best

2. Lifting weights is a .... way to burn calories.

    a. good **b.** better **c.** best

3. Working out instead of just dieting is a .... healthier way to control weight.

    a. good **b.** more **c.** much

4. Dieters lose .... muscle mass than exercisers.

    a. much **b.** more **c.** most

5. Write a sentence using a comparative or superlative. Suggested topic: A day in life.

....

....

Spelling Guidelines Comparative and Superlative Adjectives and Adverbs			
Number of Syllables	Word Ending	Comparative	Superlative
One-syllable adjectives or adverbs	any kind	add *-er*	add *-est*
Examples	fast hard young	faster harder younger	fastest hardest youngest
One-syllable adjectives	consonant-vowel-consonant	double last consonant add *-er*	double last consonant add *-est*
Examples	big sad wet	bigger sadder wetter	biggest saddest wettest
Two-syllable adjectives	ending in *-y*	change *-y* to *-i*; add *-er*	change *-y* to *-i*; add *-est*
Examples	busy pretty silly	busier prettier sillier	busiest prettiest silliest
Two- or more-syllable adjectives or adverbs	not ending in *-y*	no change in spelling; use *more*	no change in spelling; use *most*
Examples	exciting dangerous difficult	more exciting more dangerous more difficult	most exciting most dangerous most difficult

SPELLING COMPARATIVES AND SUPERLATIVES

Fill in the following chart with the correct spellings of each form of the comparatives and superlatives. Use *more* and *most* as needed.

Absolute	Comparative	Superlative
1. afraid		
2. chilly		
3. creepy		
4. fat		
5. handsome		

Mastering *Good* and *Well*

Two of the most often-confused words in the English language are *good* and *well*. One reason these two words are so often confused is that *well* can be used as either an adverb or an adjective to discuss health issues.

- **Good** is an adjective that describes a noun or pronoun.

NOUN "VOICE" IS DESCRIBED BY ADJECTIVE "GOOD"

Sally's singing voice sounds good.

ADJECTIVE "GOOD" DESCRIBES NOUN "JOB"

You did a good job.

- **Well** is an **adverb** that usually describes a **verb**.

VERB "DID" IS DESCRIBED BY ADVERB "WELL"

I did well on my test.

VERB "HEAR" IS DESCRIBED BY ADVERB "WELL"

You hear well with your hearing aid.

- Exception *Well* is an **adjective** when used to describe a person's health issues.

PRONOUN "I" IS DESCRIBED BY ADJECTIVE "WELL"

I feel well.

PRONOUN "HE" IS DESCRIBED BY ADJECTIVE "WELL"

He was sick, but he seems well now.

Practice 9

GOOD AND WELL

Fill in each blank with *good* or *well*.

1. Your new office looks really ....

2. Jeremiah is not feeling ....

3. Donald Trump lives ....

4. My mother hasn't been in .... health lately.

5. Write a sentence that appropriately uses *good* or *well*. Suggested topic: The condition of a person or thing.

....

Practice 10

ADJECTIVES AND ADVERBS REVIEW

Complete the following sentences by filling in the blanks with the appropriate form or order of the adjective or adverb in parentheses.

1. The .... audience laughed at the antics of the performers. (amused/ amusing)

2. The .... performance entertained everyone. (amused/ amusing)

3. The .... singer leapt about the stage with great energy. (athletic, youthful/ youthful, athletic)

4. The show .... sells out to a packed house. (quick/ quickly)

5. Some fans attend .... by traveling to each city where the group performs. (faithful/ faithfully)

LEARNING OUTCOMES
WRITING PROCESS

Writing Assignments

Writing for Everyday Life

Assume you own a parrot whose behavior has been highly amusing. You want to share his antics with a friend so you have composed the following email. Edit the email to ensure proper use of adjectives and adverbs. Use your own paper.

> Dear Jim,
>
> You won't believe what Charlie, my African Grey large parrot, did to our family during this past month. For weeks, our doorbell rang every night in the middle of the night. I first angry blamed the neighbors. They repeatedly reassured me that they knew nothing about the situation. After several nights, we became frightened, so we called the police. The police seemed most skeptical than our neighbors about our story, yet they diligent watched our house every night. Derrick, finally my son, noticed Charlie. The whole time, Charlie had been mimicking the sound of our doorbell. That bird had never seemed happiest.
>
> LOL, Jen

Writing for College Life

Assume you are taking a study skills course, and you have been asked by your professor to reflect upon your progress as a learner as part of your midterm assessment. You are to describe what and how you have learned. Edit to ensure appropriate use of adjectives and adverbs. Use your own paper.

> *Self-Assessment Reflection:*
>
> Even though I have learned muchly this semester, I feel as if I have more to learn. One of the best important things I learned is that I am an auditory learner. I do my better when something is explained to me. So I now read out loud important information that I want to remember, or I pair up with a study buddy and talk about what we are studying. I need to hear information, so attendance is much important for me than it is for someone who isn't an auditory learner. Time management is another vital important skill that I am trying to apply. I then always have a study schedule. I want to do good in college. I have become a well student.

Writing for Working Life

Assume you have written the following letter resigning from a job you really enjoy. Edit to ensure appropriate use of adjectives and adverbs. Use your own paper.

Dear Ms. Brown:

It is with great regret that I must submit my resignation due to my family's relocation to Texas. I have thorough enjoyed working as a team leader for the area's region. This area is the larger in the state, and our team has had the higher ratings for customer service and productivity. I remember as an exciting new employee how much I looked forward to all the wonderfully opportunities available under your leadership. I have not been disappointed in the least. My success is due to your encouraged mentorship. I thank you for your support, and I wish you and the company all the best.

Sincerely,

Sam Yoo

WANT A BETTER GRADE?
For more practice with Adjectives and Adverbs, go to www.mywritinglab.com > Recognizing and Avoiding Errors > Adjectives and Adverbs.

WHAT HAVE I LEARNED ABOUT ADJECTIVES AND ADVERBS?

To test and track your understanding, answer the following questions.

1. An adjective modifies a _____ or _____.

2. An adverb modifies a _____, an _____, or another _____.

3. Participle adjectives are formed by adding _____ or _____ to verbs.

4. Adjectives often appear in the following order: _____, opinion, size, age, shape, _____, origin, material, purpose.

5. Adverbs answer the questions _____, where, and _____.

6. Adjectives and adverbs take the form of three degrees: _____, _____, and _____.

7. The _____ degree makes distinctions between two things, usually by using the adverb *more* or *less* or by adding the suffix -er.

8. The _____ degree makes distinctions among three or more things, usually by using the adverb *most* or *least* or by adding the suffix -est.

9. *Good* is an _____.

10. Most often, *well* is an _____.

11. **How will I use what I have learned about adjectives and adverbs?**
   In your notebook, discuss how you will apply to your own writing what you have learned about adjectives and adverbs.

12. **What do I still need to study about adjectives and adverbs?**
   In your notebook, discuss your ongoing study needs by describing what, when, and how you will continue studying adjectives and adverbs.

Academic Learning Log

LEARNING OUTCOMES
SELF-EVALUATION

PORTFOLIO

29

The Comma

A comma is a valuable, useful punctuation device because it separates the structural elements of a sentence into manageable segments.

Misuse of the comma ranks as one of the most common errors in punctuation. Thinking about a real-life situation helps us to understand the purpose of commas in our communication. Complete the following activity and answer the question "What's the point of commas?"

What's the Point of Commas?

PHOTOGRAPHIC ORGANIZER: COMMAS

Assume you are working with a civic group to educate the public about the effects of pollution and the need for clean fuels. You have written the following paragraph to post on the group's Web blog. This draft does not include any commas. As you read the paragraph, think about where and why commas are needed.

One Type of Clean Fuel: Alcohol

(1) Pollution occurs when the air, water, or land become dirty through the actions of people. (2) Some types of pollution, litter along the beach, are easy to see. (3) Other types of pollution, such as chemicals in the water or air, are not as easy to see but can be even more harmful. (4) To reduce chemical pollution, we need to use clean fuels. (5) One type of clean fuel is alcohol, and two types of alcohol fuel are ethanol and methanol. (6) Historically, ethanol has been made from corn or sugarcane. (7) New processes can make ethanol from paper, yard trimmings, or sawdust. (8) Methanol is usually made from natural gas, but it could also be made from wood or sugarcane. (9) Alcohol fuels produce less carbon monoxide.

What's the point of commas?

Adapted from "Hawaii's Fun-Fueled Activity Book: Clean Fuels," *Honolulu Clean Cities* Website, <www.hawaii.gov/dbedt/ert/cc/index.html>

Understanding the Point of Commas: One Student Writer's Response

The following paragraph offers one writer's reaction to the paragraph "One Type of Clean Fuel: Alcohol."

> The paragraph "One Type of Clean Fuel: Alcohol" was confusing. I had to reread several sentences to make sense of what the writer was saying. One sentence that confused me was "Some types of pollution litter along the beach are easy to see." Another confusing sentence was "New processes can make ethanol from paper yard trimmings or sawdust." When I first read this sentence, my mind read "paper yard" as the name of something. It took a second to pick up on the word "trimmings." It would help to put a comma between "paper" and "yard trimmings." Now that I think about it, I guess, commas keep a reader from getting confused.

Applying the Point: Commas

The primary purpose of the **comma** is to make a sentence easy to read by indicating a brief pause between parts of the sentence that need to be separated.

Commas with Items in a Series

Use commas to separate a **series of items** in a list. A series of items in a list can be **three** or more words, phrases, or clauses. In addition, a series of items can be made up of subjects, verbs, adjectives, participles, and so on. Items in a series are parallel and equal in importance.

Series of Words

COMMAS SET OFF SERIES OF WORDS   COMMAS SET OFF SECOND SERIES OF WORDS

Marissa, Evan, and Kanisha skate, swim, and ski.

COMMAS SET OFF SERIES OF WORDS

Marissa enjoys skating, swimming, and skiing.

Series of Phrases

COMMAS SET OFF SERIES OF PHRASES

Marissa enjoys skating on ice, swimming in the ocean, and skiing down a snowy slope.

For more information about parallel structure, see pages 374–385, "Parallelism."

Series of Clauses

Marissa is an athlete who trains consistently, who eats sensibly, and who competes well.

COMMAS SET OFF SERIES OF CLAUSES

Note: Journalists for newspapers and magazines often omit the comma before the coordinating conjunction that joins the last item in the series; however, in academic writing, this comma, which is called the **serial comma**, is usually included.

Comma Misuses to Avoid with Items in a Series

- **Do not place a comma before the first item in a series.**

Incorrect

INCORRECT COMMA USE SEPARATES THE THREE OBJECTS IN THE SERIES BELOW FROM "DAMAGED," THE VERB THAT REFERS TO THEM

The storm damaged, the roof, the windows, and the carpet.

Correct

VERB   OBJECTS OF VERB "DAMAGED"

The storm damaged the roof, the windows, and the carpet.

COMMAS SEPARATE THREE OBJECTS OF VERB "DAMAGED"

- **Do not place a comma after the last item in a series.**

Incorrect

SUBJECT   INCORRECT COMMA USE SEPARATES THE ADJECTIVES IN THE SERIES BELOW FROM THE PREPOSITIONAL PHRASE "BECAUSE OF FLOODING"

The carpet was soggy, moldy, and smelly, because of flooding.

Correct

SUBJECT   ADJECTIVES DESCRIBING SUBJECT "CARPET"

The carpet was soggy, moldy, and smelly because of flooding.

COMMAS SEPARATE
THREE ADJECTIVES
DESCRIBING SUBJECT
"CARPET"

PREPOSITIONAL PHRASE MODIFIES
THE THREE ADJECTIVES DESCRIBING
WHY THE CARPET BECAME SOGGY,
MOLDY, AND SMELLY

- **Do not place a comma between two words or phrases of equal importance joined with a coordinating conjunction** (FANBOYS: *for, and, nor, but, or, yet, so*).

Incorrect

INCORRECT COMMA USE DIVIDES COMPOUND SUBJECT
AND SEPARATES PART OF IT FROM VERB "DESTROYED"

The twisting wind, and the unrelenting rain destroyed the house.

COMPOUND SUBJECT   VERB

Correct

COMPOUND SUBJECT [NO COMMA NEEDED]   VERB

The twisting wind and the unrelenting rain destroyed the house.

Incorrect

INCORRECT COMMA USE DIVIDES COMPOUND VERB
AND SEPARATES PART OF IT FROM SUBJECT "WIND"

The wind lifted the car, and threw it across the street.

SUBJECT   COMPOUND VERB

Correct

COMPOUND VERB [NO COMMA NEEDED]   PREPOSITIONAL PHRASE

The wind lifted the car and threw it across the street.

SUBJECT   COMPOUND OBJECT (OF COMPOUND VERB)

Incorrect

INCORRECT COMMA USE DIVIDES COMPOUND ADJECTIVE AND
SEPARATES PART OF IT FROM THE SUBJECT IT DESCRIBES, "WIND"

The strong, and wet wind blew for hours.

COMPOUND   SUBJECT   VERB
ADJECTIVE

Correct

COMPOUND ADJECTIVE [NO COMMA NEEDED]

The strong and wet wind blew for hours.

SUBJECT   VERB

COMMAS FOR ITEMS IN A SERIES

Edit the following sentences by inserting commas to separate a series of items in a list. Cross out any incorrectly placed commas.

1. A graphic novel is, a type of comic is often long and complex and is written for mature audiences.

2. Graphic novels, and comic books are excellent reading materials because they assist poor readers connect with visual learners and engage adult readers.

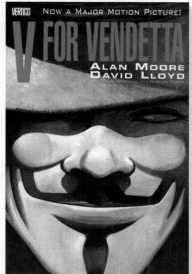

3. Graphic novels spark interest make reading fun and develop the reading habit, for many.

4. Graphic novels address important themes such as acceptance rebellion prejudice injustice and personal growth.

5. Write a sentence that lists a series of items. Suggested Topic: Your favorite possession.

Commas with Introductory Elements

Use commas to set off the introductory element of a sentence. **Introductory elements** are ideas that appear at the beginning of a sentence. Introductory elements come before a main clause. Introductory elements can be a word, phrase, or clause.

Introductory Word

COMMA SETS OFF INTRODUCTORY WORD

Overall, good health is achieved through wise choices.

Introductory Phrase

COMMA SETS OFF INTRODUCTORY PHRASE

To achieve good health, one should exercise on a regular basis.

Introductory Dependent Clause

COMMA SETS OFF INTRODUCTORY DEPENDENT PHRASE

As Maria increased her physical activity, her sense of well-being improved.

COMMA MISUSES TO AVOID WITH INTRODUCTORY ELEMENTS

- An introductory element—a word, phrase, or clause—that precedes an independent (or main) clause must be followed by a comma.

Incorrect

INTRODUCTORY PHRASE

ABSENCE OF COMMA MAKES IT DIFFICULT TO DISTINGUISH INTRODUCTORY PHRASE FROM MAIN CLAUSE

An extraordinary tennis player Roger Federer won his 15th Grand Slam title.

MAIN CLAUSE

Correct

COMMA SETS OFF INTRODUCTORY PHRASE

An extraordinary tennis player, Roger Federer won his 15th Grand Slam title.

MAIN CLAUSE

Practice 3

COMMAS WITH INTRODUCTORY ELEMENTS

Edit the following sentences by inserting commas to set off introductory elements.

1. If you decide to use one of the online dating sites be sure to write an honest description of yourself and your accomplishments.

2. For example do not say that you climbed Mount Everest when you have never put on a pair of hiking boots.

3. However do not shy away from mentioning those things that make you most proud.

4. After you have finalized your description read it to a trusted friend and ask her opinion.

5. Write a sentence that uses an introductory element. Suggested Topic: Online dating.

Commas to Join Independent Clauses

Use a comma with a coordinating conjunction to join two or more equally important and logically related independent clauses. An **independent clause** is a complete thought or sentence. To join sentences with a coordinating conjunction, place the comma before the conjunction. The acronym **FANBOYS** identifies the seven coordinating conjunctions: *for, and, nor, but, or, yet,* and *so.* The following chart lists these conjunctions and the logical relationships they establish between ideas.

Coordinating Conjunctions and the Relationships They Establish: **FANBOYS**						
For	**A**nd	**N**or	**B**ut	**O**r	**Y**et	**S**o
reason, result	addition	negation	contrast	choice, condition, possibility	contrast	addition, result

Correct Use of a Comma to Join Independent Clauses

COMMA MISUSES TO AVOID WITH INDEPENDENT CLAUSES

- **Do not place a comma *after* the coordinating conjunction that joins independent clauses.**

Incorrect

Correct

COMMAS TO JOIN INDEPENDENT CLAUSES

Edit the following sentences by inserting commas to join independent clauses with coordinating conjunctions. Cross out any incorrectly placed commas.

1. Darfur is a region in Western Sudan and, the vast majority of its population is black and Muslim.

2. Darfur is roughly the size of France yet it is home to around 8 million people.

3. The conflict in Darfur is often described as Arabs against African blacks but conflicts in the region are really between herders and farmers over the use of Sudan's land.

4. African rebel groups in Darfur believe the government favors Arabs over non-Arabs so they accuse the government of Sudan of neglecting the Darfur region.

5. Write a sentence that contains two independent clauses properly joined with a coordinating conjunction and a comma. Suggested topic: Your home town.

Commas with Parenthetical Ideas

Use commas to set off a parenthetical idea. A **parenthetical idea** is an idea that interrupts a sentence with information that is **nonessential** to the meaning of the sentence. Such an idea could be enclosed in parentheses. However, more often, a comma comes before and after such an idea. These interruptions can be words, phrases, or clauses.

Parenthetical Word

COMMAS SET OFF PARENTHETICAL WORD

The demanding customer was, however, a generous tipper.

Parenthetical Phrase

COMMAS SET OFF PARENTHETICAL PHRASE

The polite customer, surprisingly heartless, left no tip.

Parenthetical Clause

COMMAS SET OFF PARENTHETICAL CLAUSE

Jennifer, who had been working a 12-hour shift, smiled at the sight of the generous tip.

Note: Two specific types of parenthetical ideas are the **nonessential clause** and the **nonessential appositive** (word or phrase). The uses and misuses of commas with these specific types of words, phrases, and clauses are discussed in greater detail in the next two sections.

COMMAS WITH PARENTHETICAL IDEAS

Edit the following sentences by inserting commas to set off parenthetical ideas.

1. Dr. Randy Pausch a 46-year-old computer science professor at Carnegie Mellon University is a hero to many.

2. Pausch who was diagnosed with pancreatic cancer at the prime of his life wrote an inspirational speech called "The Last Lecture" in which he offered advice on how to achieve goals and reach personal happiness.

3. The lecture which has been viewed by millions on YouTube was later turned into a book that became a *New York Times* bestseller.

4. Throughout his illness in which he endured painful rounds of chemotherapy and radiation Pausch focused his attention on fulfilling childhood dreams and sharing lessons he learned on his life journey.

5. Write a sentence that contains a parenthetical idea. Suggested Topic: A Real-Life Hero.

Commas with Nonessential and Essential Clauses

A parenthetical idea, the **nonessential clause,** offers additional and unnecessary information that does not change the meaning of the sentence. Often nonessential information appears in a relative clause introduced by the relative pronouns *who* or *which*. A nonessential relative clause gives information about a nearby noun.

Use commas to set off a nonessential clause. Commas come before and after a nonessential clause that interrupts a sentence. A single comma sets off a nonessential clause at the end of a sentence.

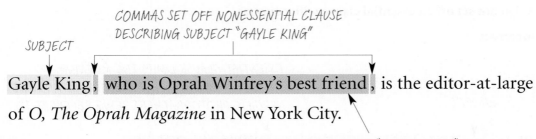

COMMAS SET OFF NONESSENTIAL CLAUSE
DESCRIBING SUBJECT "GAYLE KING"

SUBJECT

Gayle King, who is Oprah Winfrey's best friend, is the editor-at-large of *O, The Oprah Magazine* in New York City.

NONESSENTIAL CLAUSE DESCRIBES SUBJECT "GAYLE KING," BUT
COULD BE OMITTED WITHOUT CHANGING THE SENTENCE'S MEANING

COMMA SETS OFF NONESSENTIAL CLAUSE
DESCRIBING NOUN "LARRY KING LIVE"

Celebrity interviews are the main attraction of Larry King Live, which is a one-hour show seen all over the world.

NOUN

NONESSENTIAL CLAUSE DESCRIBES NOUN "LARRY KING LIVE," BUT
COULD BE OMITTED WITHOUT CHANGING THE SENTENCE'S MEANING

An **essential clause** also offers information about a nearby noun, but by contrast with a nonessential clause, it restricts or limits the meaning of a nearby noun and is necessary to the meaning of the sentence. Essential clauses should not be set off with commas. The following examples illustrate the differences between an essential and a nonessential clause.

Essential Clause

SUBJECT (COMMON NOUN) "ACTOR" IS DESCRIBED AND LIMITED IN MEANING BY ESSENTIAL CLAUSE

ESSENTIAL CLAUSE LIMITS THE MEANING OF SUBJECT "ACTOR" BY IDENTIFYING THE SPECIFIC ACTOR BEING REFERRED TO

The actor who fled the scene of the car accident was arrested.

NO COMMAS NEEDED BEFORE AND AFTER ESSENTIAL CLAUSE

Nonessential Clause

SUBJECT (PROPER NOUN) "LINDSAY LOHAN" IS UNALTERED IN MEANING BY NONESSENTIAL CLAUSE

ESSENTIAL CLAUSE GIVES EXTRA INFORMATION ABOUT SUBJECT "LINDSAY LOHAN," BUT THE SUBJECT'S MEANING WOULD NOT BE AFFECTED IF THE CLAUSE WERE OMITTED

Lindsay Lohan, who fled the scene of the car accident, was arrested.

COMMAS SET OFF NONESSENTIAL CLAUSE

COMMA MISUSES TO AVOID WITH ESSENTIAL AND NONESSENTIAL CLAUSES

- **Do not set off an essential clause with commas.**

Incorrect

ESSENTIAL CLAUSE LIMITS THE MEANING OF SUBJECT "PHOTOGRAPHERS" BY IDENTIFYING THE SPECIFIC PHOTOGRAPHERS BEING REFERRED TO

SUBJECT

Photographers, who pursue stars in high-speed chases, are irresponsible.

INCORRECT COMMA USE DIVIDES ESSENTIAL CLAUSE FROM THE SUBJECT IT DESCRIBES: "PHOTOGRAPHERS"

Correct

SUBJECT

Photographers who pursue stars in high-speed chases are irresponsible.

NO COMMAS NEEDED BEFORE OR AFTER ESSENTIAL CLAUSE

- **Do not omit the comma before or after the nonessential clause that interrupts an idea. Place a comma before and after a nonessential clause.**

Incorrect

CORRECT COMMA USAGE SETS OFF
BEGINNING OF NONESSENTIAL CLAUSE

MISSING COMMA AFTER
NONESSENTIAL CLAUSE

Scarlett Johansson **,** who tried to escape photographers had a minor car accident.

SUBJECT

NONESSENTIAL CLAUSE DESCRIBES SUBJECT
"SCARLETT JOHANSSON," BUT COULD BE OMITTED
WITHOUT CHANGING THE SENTENCE'S MEANING

Incorrect

MISSING COMMA BEFORE
NONESSENTIAL CLAUSE

CORRECT COMMA USAGE SETS OFF
END OF NONESSENTIAL CLAUSE

Scarlett Johansson who tried to escape photographers **,** had a minor car accident.

SUBJECT

Correct

COMMAS SET OFF NONESSENTIAL CLAUSE
DESCRIBING SUBJECT "SCARLETT JOHANSSON"

Scarlett Johansson **,** who tried to escape photographers **,** had a minor car accident.

SUBJECT

COMMAS WITH NONESSENTIAL CLAUSES

Edit the following sentences by inserting commas to set off nonessential clauses.

1. Tyler Perry who is one of Hollywood's most successful writers and directors came from humble beginnings.

2. Perry who was born into poverty used his background as a foundation for his many works.

3. Mabel "Madea" Simmons who is a wise-cracking main character in many of Perry's plays and films is played by Perry himself.

4. Perry who opened Tyler Perry studios in 2008 has recently expanded into television with *Tyler Perry's House of Payne* and *Meet the Browns*.

5. Write a sentence that contains a nonessential clause. Suggested Topic: Famous Hollywood directors.

Practice 6

Commas with Appositives

Use commas to set off an appositive. An **appositive** is a word or phrase that renames a nearby noun. As a parenthetical idea, a **nonessential appositive** offers information that could be left out without changing the meaning of the sentence. A comma comes before and after a nonessential appositive when it interrupts an idea. A single comma sets off a nonessential appositive at the end of a sentence.

SUBJECT

NONESSENTIAL APPOSITIVE RENAMES THE SUBJECT "MOLE," BUT COULD BE OMITTED WITHOUT CHANGING THE SENTENCE'S MEANING

The star-nosed mole, a fast-eating mammal, can consume food in 120 milliseconds.

COMMAS SET OFF NONESSENTIAL APPOSITIVE DESCRIBING SUBJECT "MOLE"

COMMA SETS OFF NONESSENTIAL APPOSITIVE DESCRIBING NOUN "KOTETSU"

The *Guinness World Records* says the highest jump by a pig is 27.5 inches by Kotetsu, a pot-bellied pig.

NOUN

NONESSENTIAL APPOSITIVE RENAMES THE NOUN "KOTETSU," BUT COULD BE OMITTED WITHOUT CHANGING THE SENTENCE'S MEANING

An **essential appositive** restricts or limits the meaning of a nearby noun and is necessary to the meaning of the sentence. Essential appositives should not be set off with commas. The following examples show the differences between an essential and a nonessential appositive.

Essential Appositive

SUBJECT

ESSENTIAL APPOSITIVE LIMITS THE MEANING OF SUBJECT "ACTOR" BY IDENTIFYING THE SPECIFIC ACTOR BEING REFERRED TO

The actor Daniel Radcliffe plays Harry Potter.

NO COMMAS NEEDED BEFORE AND AFTER ESSENTIAL APPOSITIVE

Nonessential Appositive

SUBJECT

NONESSENTIAL APPOSITIVE RENAMES THE SUBJECT "DANIEL RADCLIFFE," BUT COULD BE OMITTED WITHOUT CHANGING THE SENTENCE'S MEANING

Daniel Radcliffe, the actor, plays Harry Potter.

COMMAS SET OFF NONESSENTIAL APPOSITIVE

COMMA MISUSES TO AVOID WITH APPOSITIVES

• **Do not set off an essential appositive with commas.**

Incorrect

SUBJECT

ESSENTIAL APPOSITIVE LIMITS THE MEANING OF SUBJECT "PRESIDENT" BY IDENTIFYING THE SPECIFIC PRESIDENT BEING REFERRED TO

The controversial former president , Bill Clinton , remains popular.

INCORRECT COMMA USE DIVIDES ESSENTIAL APPOSITIVE FROM THE SUBJECT IT DESCRIBES "PRESIDENT"

Correct

SUBJECT

The controversial former president Bill Clinton remains popular.

NO COMMAS NEEDED BEFORE OR AFTER ESSENTIAL APPOSITIVE

• **Do not omit the comma before or after the nonessential appositive that interrupts an idea. Place a comma before and after a nonessential appositive.**

Incorrect

CORRECT COMMA USAGE SETS OFF BEGINNING OF NONESSENTIAL APPOSITIVE

MISSING COMMA AFTER NONESSENTIAL APPOSITIVE

Andy Warhol , a pop artist designed art for mass production.

SUBJECT

NONESSENTIAL APPOSITIVE RENAMES SUBJECT "ANDY WARHOL," BUT COULD BE OMITTED WITHOUT CHANGING THE SENTENCE'S MEANING

Incorrect

SUBJECT

CORRECT COMMA USAGE SETS OFF END OF NONESSENTIAL APPOSITIVE

Andy Warhol a pop artist , designed art for mass production.

MISSING COMMA BEFORE NONESSENTIAL APPOSITIVE

Correct

SUBJECT

Andy Warhol , a pop artist , designed art for mass production.

COMMAS SET OFF NONESSENTIAL APPOSITIVE DESCRIBING SUBJECT "ANDY WARHOL"

Practice 7

COMMAS WITH APPOSITIVES

Edit the following sentences by inserting commas to set off appositives.

1. Connie Culp the first face transplant recipient in the United States was shot in the face by her husband.

2. The injury which ripped away the entire mid-section of Culp's face left Culp unable to smell or speak very well.

3. As a result of the 22-hour surgery in which tissue from a deceased donor's face was shaped and fitted to Culp's face Culp no longer experiences constant physical and mental pain.

4. Culp who will require a few more cosmetic procedures asked the public to have empathy for people with facial disfigurements.

5. Write a sentence that contains an appositive. Suggested Topic: A person of interest.

Commas with Dates and Addresses

Use commas to set off information in dates and addresses. When a date or address is made up of two or more parts, a comma separates the parts. When the parts of a date are both words or are both numbers, a comma separates the parts. And a comma follows the last item unless it is the final detail of a list or sentence.

- **Place commas after the day and year of a date.**

Beyoncé was born September 4 , 1981 , to Tina and Matthew Knowles.

COMMAS SET OFF THE DAY AND YEAR OF A DATE

- **When writing the day and the date, place a comma after the day.**

COMMA SETS OFF THE DAY FROM DATE

COMMAS SET OFF THE DAY AND YEAR OF A DATE

Beyoncé released the album *B'Day* on Tuesday , September 4 , 2006 , to coincide with the celebration of her 25th birthday.

- **Place commas after the street name, town or city, and state of an address.**

Jay-Z is part owner of an all-American sports bar and lounge at 6 West 25th Street , New York , New York that attracts many celebrities .

COMMAS SET OFF STREET, TOWN OR CITY, AND STATE OF AN ADDRESS

- **Separate two or more geographical names with a comma.**

Jay-Z is originally from a housing project in Brooklyn , New York , where he was abandoned by his father.

COMMAS SET OFF TWO OR MORE GEOGRAPHICAL NAMES

Edit the following sentences by inserting commas to set off dates and addresses.

1. The Apollo 7 space vehicle was launched from Cape Kennedy Florida on October 11 1968.

2. The first manned mission to the moon, Apollo 8 entered lunar orbit on Christmas Eve December 24 1968.

3. Man first stepped on the surface of the Moon on Sunday July 20 1969 during the Apollo 11 mission.

4. Explorer 1 was the first satellite launched by the United States on January 31 1958.

5. Write a sentence that contains a date. Suggested Topic: A current event.

Other Uses of the Comma

Commas are also used in two additional ways.

1. Use commas to separate consecutive coordinate adjectives of equal importance. **Coordinate adjectives** are a series or two or more adjectives that could be arranged in any order or could be strung together with the word *and*. They each modify the noun directly. By contrast, **cumulative adjectives** are a series or two or more adjectives that accumulate before a noun, with each adjective modifying the adjectives that follow. Cumulative adjectives must follow a certain order to make sense. Commas should not be used with cumulative adjectives.

2. Use commas to set off direct speech.

   • **Commas between consecutive coordinate adjectives:** Use two questions to determine whether adjectives are coordinate.

      A. Can the word *and* be smoothly placed between the adjectives?

      B. Can the order of the adjectives be reversed?

   If the answer is *yes* to either of these questions, then separate these coordinate adjectives with a comma.

Commas and Coordinate Adjectives

INSERTING "AND" BETWEEN ADJECTIVES
"LONG" AND "TEDIOUS" MAKES SENSE.
SWITCHING ORDER OF ADJECTIVES TO
"TEDIOUS, LONG" WOULD STILL MAKE SENSE.

COORDINATE ADJECTIVES
"LONG" AND "TEDIOUS" BOTH
MODIFY SUBJECT "JOURNEY"

The long , tedious journey finally ended.

COMMA SEPARATES COORDINATE
ADJECTIVES "LONG" AND "TEDIOUS"

For more information about the proper sequence of cumulative adjectives, see pages 507–508, "Adjectives and Adverbs."

Commas and Cumulative Adjectives

SWITCHING ORDER OF ADJECTIVES
TO "PLANNING TEDIOUS" WOULD
NOT MAKE SENSE.

INSERTING "AND" BETWEEN ADJECTIVES
"TEDIOUS" AND "PLANNING" MAKES NO SENSE.

ADJECTIVE "TEDIOUS" MODIFIES ENTIRE PHRASE "PLANNING
SESSION" AND ADJECTIVE "PLANNING" MODIFIES SUBJECT
"SESSION," SO THE ADJECTIVES ARE CUMULATIVE.

The tedious planning session finally ended.

NO COMMA NEEDED BETWEEN CUMULATIVE
ADJECTIVES "TEDIOUS" AND "PLANNING"

- **Commas after a verb that introduces a quotation:** The comma is used to set off the "said" clause, called the **speech tag**, and the comma is placed before the quoted information.

COMMA SEPARATES SPEECH TAG FROM THE QUOTATION,
WHICH ENCLOSES THE EXACT WORDS OF THE SPEAKER

Mr. Newell said , "Let's begin the meeting promptly, please."

SPEECH TAG

QUOTATION MARKS ENCLOSE THE EXACT
WORDS OF THE SPEAKER "MR. NEWELL"

For more information about proper use of quotation marks, see pages 550–563, "Quotation Marks."

Practice 9

OTHER USES OF THE COMMA

Edit the following sentences by inserting commas as needed to separate adjectives or to introduce a quotation.

1. The Net Generation is made up of curious self-confident consumers.

2. The Net Generation will dominate their economic social, and political worlds.

3. One member of the Net Generation says "I go online for everything from shopping for running shoes to finding a job."

4. A study by the Department of Commerce said "89.5% of all school-aged children between the ages of 5 and 17 use computers."

5. Write a sentence that separates adjectives or introduces a quotation. Suggested Topic: You or someone you know as a consumer.

Practice 10

COMMA REVIEW

Write five sentences that illustrate five different comma rules. Identify the rule you used to write each sentence. Suggested topic: A pleasant memory.

1. _____

_____

2. _____

_____

3. _____

_____

4. _____

_____

5. _____

_____

Writing Assignments

LEARNING OUTCOMES
WRITING PROCESS

Writing for Everyday Life

Assume you have been struggling with sleep issues, and you have decided to write and post your feelings about your experience on a blog about sleep disorders. Proofread and edit the posting to ensure appropriate use of commas. Use your own paper.

Dreams! I have them too. They plague me nightly. They swarm in on me as soon as I fall asleep and relentlessly tear through my mind until I wake. Always they are of pain loss suffering and violence. They often feature those people who are in my life. The cast is an unpredictable rotation through the night or from one night to the next. These dreams make me loathe sleep. They have though become the only companion that I can count on every night. Their fidelity is unsurpassed. Because of them there is no rest in my sleep. I wake more exhausted than I was the previous night.

Dreams! I know them too well. The word is usually associated with optimism hope for the future. I know the ugly truth behind the façade and it's a false promise to lull me into a false sense of security only to crush me from the inside out.

Writing Assignments CONTINUED

Writing for College Life

Assume your government professor has asked you to write a one-paragraph report about a local person who takes an active role in civic life. Proofread and edit the report to ensure appropriate use of commas. Use your own paper.

Billie Jean Young

Billie Jean Young is a poet actor activist and educator. She lives in her rural Choctaw County Alabama hometown of Pennington from which she travels the world to work with young people and perform her one-woman play *Fannie Lou Hamer*: *This Little Light*. For nearly three decades Young has shared the life story of Fannie Lou Hamer a human rights activist and sharecropper from Sunflower County Mississippi. Billie Jean Young seeks to make change in the world in the spirit of Fannie Lou Hamer.

Writing for Working Life

Assume you have written a letter of recommendation for a former employee who is seeking employment closer to her home. Proofread and edit the letter to ensure appropriate use of commas. Use your own paper.

THE DENTAL CLINIC

36 Big Buck Trail
Atlanta GA 30308

Dionne Brown Office Manager
The Aim Dental Group
2 Old Kings Road Suite 303
Atlanta GA 30301

June 15, 2009

Dear Ms. Brown:

As you requested in our phone conversation on June 10 2009 I am sending you this written recommendation to hire Sophia Larson as a full-time dental hygienist. Ms. Larson who has worked in our office for five years is a highly skilled personable hygienist. In addition you will find her to be an excellent educator advocate and manager. Ms. Larson a licensed clinician has 15 years of experience. I offer my strongest recommendation on behalf of Sophia Larson.

Sincerely,

Winston Ferrell

Academic Learning Log

WHAT HAVE I LEARNED ABOUT COMMAS?

To test and track your understanding, answer the following questions.

1. Use commas to separate a series of items in a list; a series of items in a list can be .... or more words, phrases, or clauses.

2. Use commas to set off the .... elements, ideas that appear at the beginning of a sentence.

3. Use commas in union with a coordinating conjunction to create a .... sentence, which is a sentence made up of two or more independent clauses.

4. Use a pair of commas to set off a .... idea, which is an idea that interrupts a sentence.

5. Use commas to set off a nonessential clause; often nonessential information appears in a relative clause introduced by .... or ....

6. Use commas for appositives, a word or phrase that .... a noun.

7. When a date or address is made up of .... parts, use a comma to separate the parts.

8. Use commas between .... adjectives.

9. Ask two questions to determine whether adjectives are coordinate:

   A. ....

   B. ....

10. Use a comma .... a verb that introduces a quotation.

11. **How will I use what I have learned about commas?**
    In your notebook, discuss how you will apply to your own writing what you have learned about commas.

12. **What do I still need to study about commas?**
    In your notebook, discuss your ongoing study needs by describing what, when, and how you will continue studying commas.

30

CHAPTER PREVIEW

LEARNING OUTCOMES

●— What's the Point of the Apostrophe?

●— Understanding the Point of the Apostrophe: One Student Writer's Response

●— Applying the Point: The Apostrophe

●— Writing Assignments

The Apostrophe

The apostrophe is used to show ownership and to form contractions by replacing omitted letters or numbers.

Thinking about a real-life situation helps us to understand the purpose of the apostrophe in our writing. Complete the following activity and answer the question "What's the point of the apostrophe?"

What's the Point of the Apostrophe?

Practice 1

WRITING FROM LIFE

PHOTOGRAPHIC ORGANIZER: THE APOSTROPHE

Apostrophes are often used in signs for businesses and in highway billboards. For example, the signs depicted in these photographs illustrate two different uses of the apostrophe. Study the signs shown in the photographs on pages 538–539 and explain why an apostrophe was used in each one.

....

....

....

....

....

What's the point of apostrophes?

....

....

....

....

....

OKLAHOMA CITY

← Civic Ctr Music Hall

← Municipal Crt/Police

← Museum of Art   Ⓟ

↑ OKC Nat'l Memorial

Understanding the Point of the Apostrophe: One Student Writer's Response

The following paragraph offers one writer's reaction to the pictures that use apostrophes.

> The sign for the trading post uses an apostrophe to show that Tanner owns the trading post. The sign about Oklahoma City uses an apostrophe to shorten a word. Some letters are left out of the word "national."

Applying the Point: The Apostrophe

An **apostrophe** is used for two general purposes:

- To show ownership
- To form contractions

The apostrophe is often misused because words with apostrophes sound similar to other words, as in the following sentence:

INCORRECT USE OF APOSTROPHE

The cat loves it's toy mouse.

The use of the word *it's* in this sentence is incorrect because the contraction *it's* means *it is* or *it has*, as in the phrases *it's a shame* or *it's been a long time*. Instead, the correct word to use is the possessive pronoun *its* to state that the toy mouse belongs to the cat. Understanding the purposes of an apostrophe will help you reduce its misuse.

The Apostrophe for Ownership

The **possessive form** of a noun and some pronouns is created by using an apostrophe followed, at times, by an *-s*. The possessive tells the reader that someone or something owns or possesses the next stated thing.

OWNER   POSSESSION

George's Camry

OWNER   POSSESSION

the Camry's front tire

The following chart lists and illustrates the rules for using an apostrophe to show possession.

Using the Apostrophe for Ownership		
To Show Possession for	**Correct Use of Apostrophe**	**Example**
A singular noun	add 's	my husband's job Henry's car
A singular noun ending with -s	add ' or add 's	the boss' memo the boss's memo James' home James's home
A regular plural noun ending with -s	add '	the writers' colony
An irregular plural noun	add 's	women's clothing
Compound words	add 's	vice president's speech sister-in-law's business (Note: Do not confuse the possessive form with the plural form, as in *sisters-in-law*)
Joint ownership of an item	add 's to the last noun	Abbott and Costello's comedy
Individual ownership	add 's to the end of both nouns	Bush's and Obama's approaches to public speaking (Each president has his own approach.)
Indefinite pronouns ending with "*one*" or "*body*"	add 's	someone's computer

Practice 2

APOSTROPHES AND POSSESSION

Change the phrases below into possessives by using 's or adding an apostrophe.

1. the homework of the students ....

2. the credit score of the average person ....

3. the Facebook profile of Charles ....

4. the association of business women ....

5. the vacation of my sister-in-law ....

Practice 3

APOSTROPHES AND POSSESSION

◀ The First Lady, Michelle Obama

Edit the sentences for the correct use of the apostrophe to indicate possession.

1. Who would have known that Michelle LaVaughn Robinson from Chicagos South Side would grow up to make history?

2. Of course, we are talking about Michella Obama, Americas first African American first lady.

3. Whether shes breaking ground on the new organic garden at the White House, reading to school children, or accompanying her husband on diplomatic trips around the world, Mrs. Obamas ease in her position is fast making her one of the most popular first ladies America has seen in some time.

4. Mrs. Obama has said that she want's to concentrate her energy and influence as first lady on supporting military families and working families. She is also very involved in daughter's Sasha and Malias day-to-day lives.

5. Write a sentence that correctly uses an apostrophe to show possession. Suggested Topic: Famous women In history.

....

APOSTROPHES AND POSSESSION

Edit the paragraph for the correct use of the apostrophe to indicate possession.

My husbands family and I loved each other the moment we first met. My mother's-in-law Southern hospitality made me feel at home, and right away, my three future brothers-in-law began teasing me just like I was a little sister. Everyones sense of humor makes the family so much fun to be with. Some of my familys favorite memories are of Christmas at my in-laws house. Just like me, my childrens excitement always grows as we get ready to go to Pop's and Mimi's house on Christmas morning. One year, their cats mischievous nature created the days' excitement. Kitty, who liked to climb the Christmas tree, suddenly sprung out of the tree and toppled it over. Many of the gifts wrapping papers were soaked from the water in the tree stand. Everyone laughed, undisturbed by the mess.

Write a sentence that correctly uses an apostrophe to show possession. Suggested Topic: An item that has special meaning.

The Apostrophe for Contractions

An apostrophe is used to indicate the omission of letters to form a *contraction*. Most often, a **contraction** is formed to join two words to make one shorter word such as *don't* for *do not*. However, sometimes an apostrophe is used to form a one-word contraction such as *ma'am* for *madam* and *gov't* for *government*. An apostrophe (') takes the place of the letter or letters that are dropped to form the contraction.

The use of contractions gives a piece of writing an informal tone that records on paper the way we speak in general conversation. Writing for college courses usually requires a formal, academic tone. Thus, many professors discourage the use of contractions. Check with your professors about the required tone of your writing assignments. To ensure proper use of the apostrophe, the following chart illustrates how contracted verbs are formed.

Apostrophe Use in Common Contractions The apostrophe replaces omitted letters.	
'm APOSTROPHE REPLACES "A" IN "AM" I am = I'm	's APOSTROPHE REPLACES "I" IN "IS" it is = it's
're APOSTROPHE REPLACES "A" IN "ARE" you are = you're	've APOSTROPHE REPLACES "HA" IN "HAVE" I have = I've
n't APOSTROPHE REPLACES "O" IN "NOT" is not = isn't	'll APOSTROPHE REPLACES "WI" IN "WILL" I will = I'll

Practice 5

APOSTROPHES IN CONTRACTIONS

Use apostrophes to form contractions for the following words.

1. I am ....

2. he is............................

3. could not............................

4. let us............................

5. they are ....

6. should not ....

7. he has ....

8. it has ....

9. it will ....

10. they have ....

Common Misuses of the Apostrophe

Quite often, the apostrophe is misused in several specific ways. The following chart lists and illustrates these common misuses of the apostrophe. Always base your use of an apostrophe on a specific rule. Proofread your writing for these common mistakes.

- **Do not use an apostrophe to form a plural noun.**

Correct Plural	Incorrect Plural
homes	home's
books	book's

- **Do not use an apostrophe to form a possessive pronoun.**

Correct	Incorrect
ours	our's
hers	her's
theirs	their's

- **Do not omit the apostrophe to form the possessive indefinite pronoun.**

Correct	Incorrect
one's	ones
everybody's	everybodys

- **Do not confuse contractions with similar sounding words.**

Contraction	Possessive Pronoun
it's (it is)	its
who's (who is)	whose
they're (they are)	their

CORRECT USE OF THE APOSTROPHE

Edit the paragraph to ensure correct use of the apostrophe.

Los Angeles Dodgers outfielder Manny Ramirez was once the toast of Los Angeles. From the outfield, fans held up the letters, "Mannywood" as they cheered him on. All of that changed when it was discovered that Ramirezs performance may have been enhanced by a womens fertility drug that boost's testosterone levels.   Ramirez was suspended for 50 games. He join's a growing list of professional athlete's accused of using performance enhancing drugs. Los Angeles Dodgers team manager, Joe Torre, is supporting Ramirez for now saying, "Im not going to abandon the guy. Theres' a human being there that I'm concerned about."

Write a sentence that correctly uses the apostrophe. Suggested Topic: A present you would like to give to someone.

REVIEW OF THE APOSTROPHE

Edit the paragraph to ensure correct use of the apostrophe.

The Hatfield's feud with the McCoys became one of the most infamous feuds in history. They're feud may be explained by a rare disease that may cause rage and violence. Dozens of the McCoys, who's symptoms have been documented, suffer from Hippel-Lindau disease. It's symptoms include headaches, excessive sweating, racing heart, anxiety, and excess adrenaline.

Write a sentence that correctly uses the apostrophe. Suggested Topic: The causes or effects of road rage.

Writing Assignments

Writing for Everyday Life

Assume you have been having problems with a cell phone you just bought, and you are writing a letter of complaint to the manufacturer. Proofread and edit the body of the letter to ensure appropriate use of apostrophes. Use your own paper.

Recently, I purchased the Diamond Phone your currently advertising. Im writing to express my disappointment with you're product. I no longer use my phone for several reasons. First, the callers voice sounds muffled, or I cant hear someones voice message because of an echo in the phone. Im also disappointed in the quality of pictures taken with this phones camera. Bright colors looked washed out, and the prints didnt look crisp. In addition, the devices video feature isnt working. Overall, its been a disappointing purchase!

Writing for College Life

Assume you have been required to write a one-paragraph summary about stress for your psychology class. Proofread and edit the paragraph to ensure appropriate use of apostrophes. Use your own paper.

Human action takes place within a persons' life space. Forces or demands within the life space cause ones movement from activity to activity. An individuals motivation leads to many demands. However, a human beings resources often cant meet those demands, so a person feels the strain to perform. Stress is the normal reaction. Its harmful to well-being and results in negative feelings and behaviors. Examples of stressors range from tolerating a neighbors loud music to losing a loved one. A natural disasters' impact, like a major earthquake, is so vast that it's known as a cataclysmic event. Demands or stressors cause an individual to make adjustments. An individual whose stressed needs to develop coping behaviors.

Writing Assignments CONTINUED

Writing for Working Life

Assume you must resign from your job. You have asked a colleague to proofread your letter, and she suggested that you eliminate all contractions to sound professional. In addition, she noticed several apostrophe errors. Edit the letter of resignation to ensure appropriate use of apostrophes and to eliminate contractions. Use your own paper.

218 Elm Drive
New Haven, GA 33215

Ms. Anna Rivers
Rivers Advertising Agency
2 Summit Drive
New Haven, GA 33215

July 6, 2009

Dear Ms. Rivers:

I'd like to inform you that I'm resigning from my position as an office assistant for the Rivers Advertising Agency, effective August 1. I'll be starting as Alcott Companys office manager in September. Thank you for the opportunities that you have provided me during the last five years. I've enjoyed working for your're agency and appreciate the support provided me during my time with the company. Even though I will miss my colleagues, I'm looking forward to this new challenge and to starting a new phase of my career. If I can be of any help during this transition, please don't hesitate to let me know.

Sincerely,

John Olarte

WHAT HAVE I LEARNED ABOUT THE APOSTROPHE?

To test and track your understanding, answer the following questions.

1. What are two general purposes of an apostrophe?

　a. To show --

　b. To form _____

2. What are four common misuses of the apostrophe to avoid?

　a. Using apostrophes to form _____

　b. Using apostrophe to form _____

　c. -- to form possessive indefinite pronouns

　c. Confusing contractions with _____

How will I use what I have learned about the apostrophe?

In your notebook, discuss how you will apply to your own writing what you have learned about the apostrophe.

What do I still need to study about the apostrophe?

In your notebook, discuss your ongoing study needs by describing what, when, and how you will continue studying the apostrophe.

Academic Learning Log

LEARNING OUTCOMES
SELF-EVALUATION

PORTFOLIO

31

Quotation Marks

Quotation marks are used to set off exact words either written or spoken by other people or to set off titles of short works.

Quotation marks help us to record the ideas of other people. Thinking about a real-life situation helps us to understand the purpose of quotation marks in our communication. Complete the following activity and answer the question "What's the point of quotation marks?"

◀ Helen Phillips on "The Biggest Loser"

What's the Point of Quotation Marks?

Practice 1

WRITING FROM LIFE

PHOTOGRAPHIC ORGANIZER: QUOTATION MARKS

Assume you are an avid fan of *The Biggest Loser*. You love the show so much that you have joined a blog about the weight-loss competition, and you read the following posting on the blog about the latest winner, Helen Phillips. As you read the paragraph, underline the ideas that you think should be in quotation marks.

Phillips Is the Biggest Loser

(1) Forty-eight-year-old mother of two Helen Phillips just walked away with the grand prize of $250,000 for losing the most weight on The Biggest Loser: Couples. (2) Phillips exclaimed, 140 pounds! Yes! Yes! on the season finale. (3) Phillips went on to say I haven't worn a dress in at least 10 years. (4) I actually feel beautiful today. (5) Although there is much joy for Phillips' extreme weight loss, critics say that the conditions under which contestants lose weight on the show are extreme and unrealistic. (6) Critics also call the show misleading, noting that such tremendous weight loss in a controlled environment often leads to quick weight gain once the contestants enter the real world. (7) It is worth mentioning here that several Biggest Loser contestants have regained much of the weight they lost while on the show. (8) All of this criticism doesn't seem to affect Phillips, who has a message for middle-aged moms like herself, it's never too late!

What's the point of quotation marks?

....

....

....

Understanding the Point of Quotation Marks: One Student Writer's Response

The following paragraph offers one writer's reaction to the paragraph "Phillips Is the Biggest Loser."

> As I read the paragraph, I tried to figure out which ideas belonged to the writer of the paragraph and which ideas belonged to other people. This was hard! I don't think quotation marks should go around the show's title because I remember learning that TV show titles don't need quotes. I underlined parts of sentences 2, 3, and 4 because they sound like Phillips' direct words when she won the contest. I was a little confused about which words in sentences 5 and 6 should be underlined, although I'm sure that some words in these sentences should be put in quotation marks because the comments are directly from critics of the show. I'm pretty sure that sentence 7 is in the author's words, so no quotations needed for that sentence. I thought quotes should go around the words "its never to late" in sentence 8 because the sentence says that Phillips has a message to share.

Applying the Point: Quotation Marks

Use **quotation marks** (" ") to set off **direct quotes**—the exact words spoken by someone or quoted from another source—and for titles of short works. Always use quotation marks in pairs. The first quotation mark ("), also called the **opening quotation mark**, indicates the beginning of the quoted material. The second quotation mark ("), also called the **closing quotation mark**, indicates the end of the quoted material. Four general rules guide the use of quotation marks with other pieces of punctuation.

General Guidelines for Using Quotation Marks

1. Place commas (,) and periods (.) inside the quotation marks (" ").

QUOTATION MARKS ENCLOSE EXACT WORDS OF THE JUSTICE DEPARTMENT

According to a recent article, the Justice Department promised to "combat gangs and guns," lower crime rates, and help local police in crimes involving juveniles.

COMMA GOES INSIDE QUOTATION MARK

The article also said gangs and guns contributed to "a nationwide crime spike."

PERIOD GOES INSIDE
QUOTATION MARK

QUOTATION MARKS ENCLOSE EXACT
WORDS FROM THE ARTICLE

2. Place semicolons (;) and colons (:) outside the quotation marks.

QUOTATION MARKS ENCLOSE EXACT
WORDS OF THE SPEAKER "WE"

We must say "no more violence"; we must strengthen gun control laws.

SEMICOLON GOES OUTSIDE QUOTATION MARK

QUOTATION MARKS ENCLOSE EXACT
WORDS OF THE SPEAKER "WE"

There is one sure way we can say "no more violence": we can shut down violent media.

COLON GOES OUTSIDE QUOTATION MARK

3. Place a question mark (?) inside quotation marks when it is part of the quotation. Place a question mark outside quotation marks when the larger sentence is a question, but the quotation included in it is not.

QUOTATION MARKS ENCLOSE EXACT
WORDS OF THE SPEAKER "WE"

We should ask, "How does violence in movies and music affect youth?"

QUESTION MARK GOES INSIDE QUOTATION MARK BECAUSE IT IS
PART OF THE QUOTATION. (THE QUOTATION IS A QUESTION.)

QUOTATION MARKS ENCLOSE EXACT
WORDS OF THE SPEAKER "WE"

Did she really say "no more violence"?

QUESTION MARK GOES OUTSIDE QUOTATION MARK BECAUSE THE SENTENCE
ITSELF IS A QUESTION, BUT THE QUOTATION INCLUDED IN IT IS NOT.

4. Use single quotation marks for quoted information—or titles of short works—that appear within a direct quotation.

DOUBLE QUOTATION MARK INDICATES START
OF QUOTED MATERIAL FROM NEWSPAPER

The *USA Today* article reports, "The Justice Department promises '$50 million this year to combat gangs and guns.'"

SINGLE QUOTATION MARK INDICATES
START OF QUOTED MATERIAL FROM
JUSTICE DEPARTMENT

SINGLE QUOTATION MARK INDICATES END OF
QUOTED MATERIAL FROM JUSTICE DEPARTMENT.
DOUBLE QUOTATION MARK INDICATES END OF
QUOTED MATERIAL FROM NEWSPAPER.

Practice 2

QUOTATION MARKS WITH OTHER PUNCTUATION

Edit each sentence to ensure correct punctuation of quoted information and titles. Insert quotation marks and other punctuation as needed.

1. According to author Deborah Tannen, in her 2006 article in *The Los Angeles Times* Daughters and mothers agree on what the hurtful conversations are

2. I love your hair when it's combed back a mother says to her grown daughter.

3. The daughter snaps back Are you saying my hair looks unattractive this way

4. The teacher asked Do you agree with Tannen's statement Attention to hair reveals—and creates—intimacy

5. Write a quotation that records an idea stated by someone else. Suggested Topic: An opinion that differs from your own.

_____

_____

_____

_____

Adapted from Deborah Tannen, "My Mother, My Hair"

Formatting and Punctuating Direct Quotations

One part of a direct quotation is the **speech tag** or the credit given to the source, the person who spoke or wrote an idea. A speech tag is formed by a subject (the speaker) and a verb that indicates the subject is speaking. The location of the speech tag affects the punctuation of a direct quotation. A speech tag can appear at the beginning, in the middle, or at the end of a quote. The following examples highlight the correct use of commas, periods, capitalization, and quotation marks based on the placement of the speech tag.

Punctuating Direct Quotations

- **Speech tag at the beginning of quote**

COMMA SETS OFF SPEECH TAG

QUOTATION MARKS ENCLOSE EXACT WORDS OF THE SPEAKER "MOTHER"

Mother said, "Your brother is depressed."

SPEECH TAG

CAPITAL LETTER BEGINS QUOTED MATERIAL

PERIOD INSIDE QUOTATION MARK

- **Speech tag in the middle of quote**

1 Quotation is stated in one sentence:

QUOTATION MARKS ENCLOSE FIRST HALF OF THE SENTENCE OF THE SPEAKER "I"

QUOTATION MARKS ENCLOSE SECOND HALF OF THE SENTENCE OF THE SPEAKER "I"

LOWERCASE LETTER BEGINS SECOND PART OF INTERRUPTED QUOTE

"I think you're right," I replied, "because he isn't eating or sleeping."

COMMA INSIDE QUOTATION MARK

SPEECH TAG

COMMA SETS OFF SPEECH TAG

PERIOD INSIDE QUOTATION MARK

2 Quotation is stated in two sentences:

QUOTATION MARKS ENCLOSE FIRST SENTENCE OF THE SPEAKER "I"

PERIOD ENDS FIRST SENTENCE

QUOTATION MARKS ENCLOSE SECOND SENTENCE OF THE SPEAKER "I"

CAPITAL LETTER BEGINS SECOND SENTENCE OF QUOTE

"I think you're right," I replied. "He isn't eating or sleeping."

COMMA INSIDE QUOTATION MARK

SPEECH TAG ENDS FIRST SENTENCE OF QUOTE STATED IN TWO SENTENCES

OPENING QUOTATION MARK BEGINS SECOND SENTENCE OF QUOTE

PERIOD INSIDE QUOTATION MARK

- **Speech tag at the end of quote**

QUOTATION MARKS ENCLOSE EXACT WORDS OF THE SPEAKER "MOTHER"

SPEECH TAG

"Do you think he would agree to get some professional help?" Mother asked.

QUESTION MARK INSIDE QUOTATION MARK

PUNCTUATING DIRECT QUOTATIONS

Edit each sentence to ensure correct punctuation of direct quotes and titles. Insert quotation marks and other punctuation as needed. Discuss your answers with your classmates.

1. According to *ConsumerReportsHealthGuide.org* Abuse of common cough suppressants may be increasing among teens

2. Dr. Suydam said Parents should educate themselves about the dangers of cough medicine abuse

3. High doses of cough suppressants can have serious side effects Dr. Gavin warns yet young people are not aware of the dangers

4. I can tell you firsthand that teens don't realize how dangerous the abuse of cough medications can be said Toren Volkmann, a former abuser of cough suppressants.

5. Write a direct quotation to record something someone else said. Suggested Topic: Advice you have received.

Formatting and Punctuating Dialogue

Including dialogue in a piece of writing adds interest, details, and authenticity. Dialogue conveys action, time, place, and the traits and values of the speakers. Most often, dialogue is associated with creative writing, story telling, and journalism, but a well-crafted or carefully chosen piece of dialogue can also effectively support a point in an academic paper. The following chart offers a few basic tips for formatting and punctuating dialogue.

Tips for Formatting and Punctuating Dialogue
• Follow the formatting and punctuation rules for direct quotations.
• Use quotation marks to indicate a speaker's exact words.
• Use speech tags to make sure the reader knows who is speaking.
• Vary the placement of speech tags.
• Begin a new paragraph to change speakers; record each person's turn at speaking, no matter how brief, in a separate paragraph.
• When a speaker's speech is longer than one paragraph: Begin the speech with a quotation mark. Do not use a quotation mark at the end of the first paragraph or subsequent paragraphs. Instead, begin each new paragraph in the speech with a quotation mark. End the speech with a closing quotation mark at the end of the last paragraph.

Applying Appropriate Formatting

Note the ways in which the writer below applies appropriate formatting and punctuation rules for writing dialogue.

In *The Interpersonal Communication Book,* 10th edition, Joseph DeVito writes, "Many problems between people result from failure to recognize the distinction between the content and relationship dimensions of communication. Many couples argue because of the message communicated on the relationship level." He also points out that sensitivity can resolve conflicts. The following interchange, adapted from DeVito's book, illustrates DeVito's point.

He said, "I'm going bowling tomorrow night. The guys at the plant are starting a team."

"Why can't we ever do anything together?" she asked.

"We can do something together anytime," he replied. "Tomorrow's the day they're organizing the team."

"If it weren't a bowling team, there would be something else that you just had to do. You never make time to be with me."

He sat quietly for a while and then said, "Listen, I'd sure like to be on the team. And I should have asked if it would be a problem if I went to the meeting tomorrow. I know you were looking forward to having some fun and being together.

"Hey, why don't we meet at Joe's Pizza. We can have dinner after my meeting ends. Let's order the deep dish with extra cheese. You ought to think about taking up bowling, too. It would be fun to do something like that together."

She replied, "The pizza sounds great! I'm not so sure about the bowling, but I get your point. We should plan to do things together that we both enjoy."

Comment: New paragraphs signal changes in speakers.

Comment: Varied use of the speech tag.

Comment: No closing quotation mark because this one speech is two paragraphs long.

Comment: Quotation mark signals end of two-paragraph speech.

FORMATTING AND PUNCTUATING DIALOGUE

Write out the dialogue between Jeremy and his parents in this cartoon strip. Use appropriate formatting and punctuation.

Practice 4

ZITS **BY JERRY SCOTT AND JIM BORGMAN**

©Zits Partnership, King Features Syndicate.

Practice 4

Direct and Indirect Quotations

The spoken or printed words of other people are written in two ways: as a direct quotation or as an indirect quotation. So far, you have been learning about the **direct quotation**, which uses a pair of quotation marks to indicate someone else's exact words. In contrast, an **indirect quotation** rephrases or rewords what someone said or wrote. An indirect quotation is a **paraphrase** of someone else's words. Never use quotation marks with indirect quotations. To paraphrase a direct quotation into an indirect quotation, follow these steps:

How to Paraphrase a Direct Quote into an Indirect Quote
1. Remove quotation marks and internal capital letters.
2. Add the word *that* to introduce the paraphrased idea.
3. Revise verbs into past tense, except for actions continuing in the present.
4. Revise verbs that command into infinitive form; revise speech tag for logical sense.
5. Revise pronouns and signal words as needed.

Original Direct Quotation:

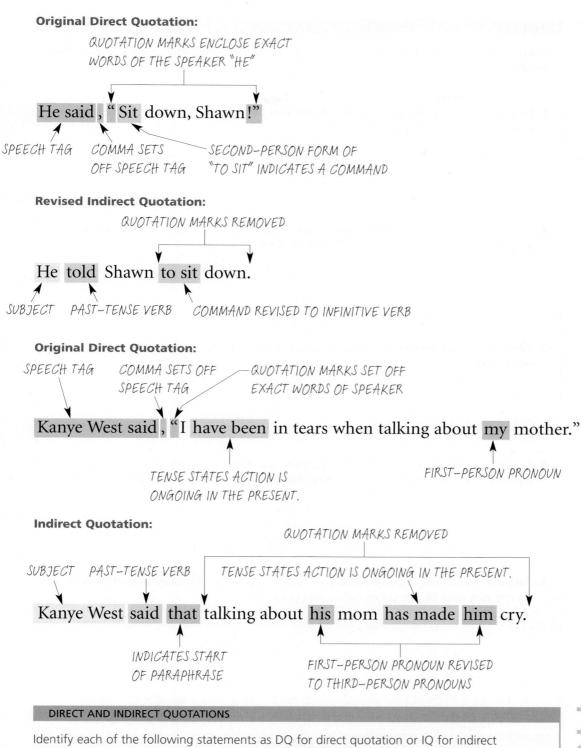

QUOTATION MARKS ENCLOSE EXACT WORDS OF THE SPEAKER "HE"

He said, "Sit down, Shawn!"

SPEECH TAG

COMMA SETS OFF SPEECH TAG

SECOND-PERSON FORM OF "TO SIT" INDICATES A COMMAND

Revised Indirect Quotation:

QUOTATION MARKS REMOVED

He told Shawn to sit down.

SUBJECT

PAST-TENSE VERB

COMMAND REVISED TO INFINITIVE VERB

Original Direct Quotation:

SPEECH TAG

COMMA SETS OFF SPEECH TAG

QUOTATION MARKS SET OFF EXACT WORDS OF SPEAKER

Kanye West said, "I have been in tears when talking about my mother."

TENSE STATES ACTION IS ONGOING IN THE PRESENT.

FIRST-PERSON PRONOUN

Indirect Quotation:

QUOTATION MARKS REMOVED

SUBJECT   PAST-TENSE VERB   TENSE STATES ACTION IS ONGOING IN THE PRESENT.

Kanye West said that talking about his mom has made him cry.

INDICATES START OF PARAPHRASE

FIRST-PERSON PRONOUN REVISED TO THIRD-PERSON PRONOUNS

DIRECT AND INDIRECT QUOTATIONS

Identify each of the following statements as DQ for direct quotation or IQ for indirect quotation. Then, insert appropriate punctuation for direct and indirect speech.

.... **1.** Ralph Waldo Emerson said   It is not length of life, but depth of life

.... **2.** According to Donald Trump   Everything in life is luck

.... **3.** Thomas Jefferson said   I find that the harder I work, the more luck I seem to have

.... **4.** An African proverb teaches that it takes more than parents to raise a child

.... **5.** A Chinese proverb states   A book is like a garden carried in the pocket

Practice 5

DIRECT AND INDIRECT QUOTATIONS

Paraphrase the following direct quotes into indirect quotes. Work with a classmate or small group of peers.

1. Dr. Martin Luther King, Jr. once said, "In the end, we will remember not the words of our enemies, but the silence of our friends."

_____

_____

2. Author and journalist Anna Quindlen wrote, "The thing that is really hard, and really amazing, is giving up on being perfect and beginning the work of becoming yourself."

_____

_____

3. World-renowned opera singer Beverly Sills once said, "There are no shortcuts to any place worth going."

_____

_____

4. Comedian Chris Rock quips, "I don't get high, but sometimes I wish I did. That way, when I messed up in life I would have an excuse. But right now there's no rehab for stupidity."

_____

_____

5. President Franklin D. Roosevelt declared, "When you see a rattlesnake poised to strike, you do not wait until he has struck before you crush him."

_____

_____

Titles

Quotation marks are also used to set off the titles of short works such as essays, short stories, short poems, songs, articles in magazines, TV episodes, and chapter titles in books.

- Follow the general rules for using quotation marks.

- Do not use quotation marks to set off titles of larger publications such as magazines, newspapers, and books. These larger publications are set off with italics or underlining.

Poems

QUOTATION MARKS SET OFF POEM TITLE

Maya Angelou read her poem "On the Pulse of Morning" at President Clinton's 1993 inauguration.

Songs

QUOTATION MARKS SET OFF SONG TITLE

Enrique Iglesias scored a big hit with the release of his single "Dimelo."

Television Shows

QUOTATION MARKS ARE NOT USED FOR THE TV SHOW TITLE

My favorite episode of the *George Lopez* show is "George's Mom Faces Hard Tambien."

QUOTATION MARKS SET OFF EPISODE TITLE OF A TV SHOW

QUOTATION MARKS AND TITLES

Edit each sentence to ensure correct punctuation of titles.

1. Did you read the *New York Times* article, Vitamins Found to Curb Exercise Benefits ?

2. I don't get it. About a week ago, I read a magazine article called, Vitamins and Good Health that said that some vitamins help boost metabolism.

3. I guess I need to do more research. First, I'll look at the chapter, Helping Others Achieve Good Health at Any Age in my nursing textbook.

4. I will also look at the website WebMD because I remember seeing a page called, Vitamins and Your Health.

5. Write a sentence that includes a title. Punctuate the title correctly.

REVIEW OF QUOTATION MARKS

Write a dialogue of five to ten sentences based on a recent conversation you have had or you have heard. Use appropriate format and punctuation. Work in pairs or with a small group of your classmates. Use your own paper.

Practice 7

Practice 8

Writing Assignments

Writing for Everyday Life

Assume you have been in an automobile accident that is not your fault. The person who caused the accident denies that she is responsible. You have decided to make a written record of the event for your insurance company. Edit the following excerpt from the report. Insert quotation marks and other punctuation as needed. Use your own paper.

I was traveling north on Clyde Morris Avenue when I stopped for a red light. Once the light turned green, I began to accelerate and pulled out to cross over Highway 1. Suddenly, a 2006 white Ford pick-up truck slammed into the rear of the passenger's side of my 2008 Maxima. At the same time, my daughter cried out from the seat behind me, She ran a red light! The force of the impact sent me spinning. Before I could get out of my car, Roxanne DeVille, the driver who caused the accident, ran up to me. Are you all right? she asked. I am so sorry, she sobbed, because it's all my fault. I was trying to answer my cell phone and didn't notice the red light. I am so sorry!

Writing for College Life

Assume you have written a summary paragraph about an article you read for a psychology course. Edit the paragraph. Insert quotation marks and other punctuation as needed. Use your own paper.

In the *Psychology Today* article How to Be Popular, Hara Estroff Marano talks about the eight traits that make people popular. Marano also argues that popularity is a trait that can be and should be learned. She writes having social contact and friends, even animal ones, improves physical health. Some of the traits of popular people include positive thinking and a good sense of humor.

Writing Assignments CONTINUED

Writing for Working Life

Assume you are working at the customer service desk of a retail store like Sears and you need to report a customer's complaint to your supervisor. Edit the paragraph. Insert quotation marks and other punctuation as needed. Use your own paper.

> Mr. Saul Richey was upset by the treatment he received from sales associate Martin Hawkins in the jewelry department. According to Richey, Hawkins refused to honor a discount coupon. Mr. Richey pointed out that the coupon was part of a promotion mentioned in the *Sunday Times* article A Jewelry Buyer's Dream: High Value at Low Cost. Mr. Richey said Your sales clerk was loud and rude; I was very embarrassed. I will never deal with that man again.

WHAT HAVE I LEARNED ABOUT QUOTATION MARKS?

To test and track your understanding, answer the following questions.

1. Quotation marks are used in pairs to indicate .... and ....

2. .... and .... go inside the quotation marks.

3. Semicolons and colons go .... the quotation marks.

4. Use a pair of quotation marks to set off a ...., which records the exact words of another person.

5. A .... is the credit given to the source of a quotation.

6. A speech tag can be placed ...., ..., or ....

7. How will I use what I have learned about quotation marks?
In your notebook, discuss how you will apply to your own writing what you have learned about quotation marks.

8. What do I still need to study about quotation marks?
In your notebook, discuss your ongoing study needs by describing what, when, and how you will continue studying quotation marks.

Academic Learning Log

32

End Punctuation: Period, Question Mark, and Exclamation Point

End punctuation marks the end of a complete thought.

Thinking about a real-life situation helps us to understand the purpose of end punctuation in our communication. Complete the following activity and answer the question "What's the point of end punctuation?"

What's the Point of End Punctuation?

Practice 1

PHOTOGRAPHIC ORGANIZER: END PUNCTUATION

Assume you have witnessed the liftoff of the Space Shuttle *Discovery*. You have been asked by your college newspaper to write your eyewitness account. You quickly freewrite a draft with no concern for punctuation. As you read this early draft, think about the need for end punctuation. Also, think about the different types of end punctuation that could be used. How do you know when one complete thought ends and another begins? Try revising the draft below, inserting end punctuation where you think it is needed and changing capitalization of words as you see fit.

An Awesome Sight

Have you ever been at a concert so loud that the music made your heart vibrate was it so loud that you couldn't hear anyone talking around you as loud as a concert can be, it is nothing compared to the sound of the Space Shuttle lifting off the ground the sound of the Space Shuttle rattles both Earth and people what an awesome sight great plumes of smoke billow from a white-hot column of flame we all hold our breath as the shuttle soars into the blue sky.

What's the point of end punctuation?

....

....

....

Understanding the Point of End Punctuation: One Student Writer's Response

The following paragraph offers one writer's reaction to the paragraph "An Awesome Sight."

Without any end punctuation, I had to keep rereading to make sense of the ideas. I had to really stop and think about where one sentence ended and another one started. I am used to seeing capital letters at the beginning of a new idea. If I put a period to end a sentence, then I capitalize the first word of the next sentence. So both end punctuation and capital letters are needed. I also would use question marks to end the first two sentences because they are asking questions. All sentences end with some kind of punctuation mark.

Applying the Point: End Punctuation

A **sentence** is a complete thought that begins with a capital letter and ends with a specific type of end punctuation. The **punctuation marks** that indicate the end of a sentence (called **end punctuation**) are **the period**, **the question mark**, and **the exclamation point**. Each of these end punctuation marks indicates the purpose or type of a sentence. The following sections present a series of charts that show the relationship among end punctuation, the type of sentence, and the purpose of the sentence. Several sections also explain common end punctuation misuses to avoid.

The Period

For more information on types and purposes of sentences, see pages 340–359, "Sentence Variety."

End Punctuation	Type of Sentence	Purpose of Sentence
The Period (.)	Ends a declarative statement	To inform
	Ends an imperative statement	To command without urgency

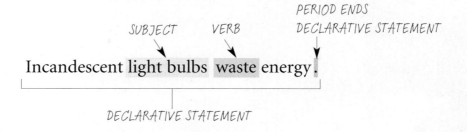

SUBJECT   VERB   PERIOD ENDS DECLARATIVE STATEMENT

Incandescent light bulbs waste energy.

DECLARATIVE STATEMENT

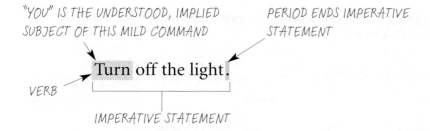

"YOU" IS THE UNDERSTOOD, IMPLIED SUBJECT OF THIS MILD COMMAND

PERIOD ENDS IMPERATIVE STATEMENT

VERB

IMPERATIVE STATEMENT

Common Misuses of Periods

A complete sentence without a period to signal its end often becomes a **fused sentence** or contains a **comma splice** error. Although there are several ways to correct these two errors, one simple correction for both is the insertion of the period. When you end a sentence with a period, capitalize the first word of the next sentence.

> For more information on comma splices and fused sentences and how to correct these errors, see pages 386–401, "Comma Splices and Fused Sentences."

- **A fused sentence occurs when two independent clauses are joined without any punctuation.**

Incorrect

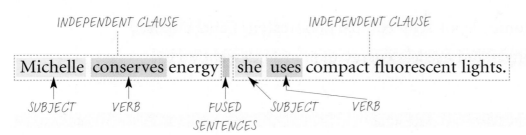

INDEPENDENT CLAUSE · INDEPENDENT CLAUSE

Michelle conserves energy she uses compact fluorescent lights.

SUBJECT · VERB · FUSED SENTENCES · SUBJECT · VERB

- **A comma splice occurs when a comma is used by itself (without a coordinating conjunction like *so*) to join two independent clauses.**

Incorrect

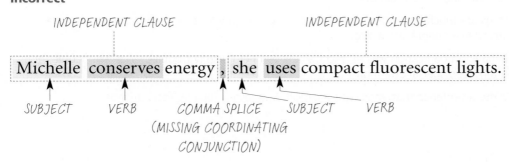

INDEPENDENT CLAUSE · INDEPENDENT CLAUSE

Michelle conserves energy, she uses compact fluorescent lights.

SUBJECT · VERB · COMMA SPLICE (MISSING COORDINATING CONJUNCTION) · SUBJECT · VERB

Correct

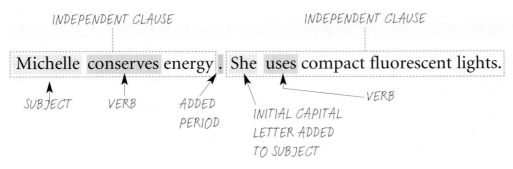

INDEPENDENT CLAUSE · INDEPENDENT CLAUSE

Michelle conserves energy. She uses compact fluorescent lights.

SUBJECT · VERB · ADDED PERIOD · INITIAL CAPITAL LETTER ADDED TO SUBJECT · VERB

For more information on fragments and how to correct them, see pages 402–421, "Fragments."

- **An improperly placed period can separate a dependent clause from the main clause and create a fragment.**

Incorrect

Correct

Home Depot sells compact fluorescent lights that last longer and use less energy than incandescent bulbs.

SUBJECT   VERB   COMPLETE THOUGHT CREATED BY REMOVING A PERIOD

Practice 2

THE PERIOD

Edit the following sentences to ensure appropriate use of capital letters and end punctuation.

1. Dogs are prone to stress mistreatment by humans is a leading cause of stress in dogs.

2. There are recognizable signs of stress in dogs the symptoms include shaking, loss of weight, and restless behavior.

3. Dogs are much less prone to stress if they lead happy lives loud noises or a disruptive lifestyle can aggravate a dog.

4. Behavior modification classes and trainers can help deeply troubled dogs like people, dogs often need special attention.

5. Write a sentence that ends with a period. Suggested Topic: Effects of stress.

The Question Mark

End Punctuation	Type of Sentence	Purpose of Sentence
The Question Mark (?)	Ends an interrogative statement	To question
	May invert order of subject and helping verb	To question
	May begin with *what, who,* or *how*	To ask a direct question
	Often uses a helping verb such as *do, can, will,* or *would*	To make a request

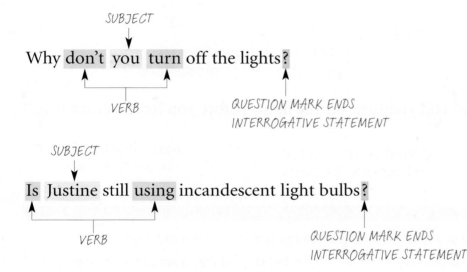

Common Misuses of Question Marks

Do not use a question mark at the end of an indirect question. An **indirect question** tells about or reports a question asked by someone by paraphrasing it rather than reporting the exact words used. An indirect question usually begins with phrases like *I wonder if* or *he asked.* Place a period at the end of an indirect question.

Incorrect

Correct

I wonder if I turned off the lights before I left the house this morning.

For more information on punctuating quotations, see pages 550–563, "Quotation Marks."

In direct quotations, writers are often confused about what punctuation to use and where it should be placed. They have particular trouble punctuating the **speech tag**, which is formed in the sentence by a subject and a verb (and an object, if any) and identifies the person speaking. To correctly punctuate a **direct question** asked by another person, follow these basic steps: (1) Set off the speech tag with a comma; (2) place a quotation mark before and after the exact words of the speaker's question; (3) capitalize the first letter of the first word in the quotation; and (4) place the question mark inside the end quotation mark.

Incorrect

MISSING QUOTATION MARKS THAT SET OFF EXACT WORDS OF THE SPEAKER "DANNY"

SPEECH TAG

Danny asked me did you turn off the lights before you left this morning.

MISSING COMMA SETTING OFF SPEECH TAG

INCORRECT USE OF INITIAL LOWERCASE "D" IN "DID," THE FIRST WORD IN THE QUOTATION

INCORRECT PERIOD USE IN DIRECT QUESTION

Correct

A PAIR OF QUOTATION MARKS SETS OFF THE EXACT WORDS OF THE QUESTION

Danny asked me, "Did you turn off the lights before you left this morning?"

SPEECH TAG SET OFF WITH COMMA

CAPITAL LETTER USED FOR FIRST WORD IN THE QUOTATION

QUESTION MARK GOES INSIDE THE QUOTATION MARK

Practice 3

THE QUESTION MARK

Insert a period or a question mark as needed to appropriately end each idea.

1. What did your boss say when you told her that she was the reason you wanted to quit

2. Will you get unemployment if you quit

3. Sometimes a difficult boss can make a good job seem bad

4. Jose's wife asked, "Are you sure you want to quit such a high paying job"

5. Write a direct quotation. Suggested Topic: Job dissatisfaction.

The Exclamation Point

End Punctuation	Type of Sentence	Purpose of Sentence
The Exclamation Point (!)	Ends an exclamatory statement	To express strong emotion
	Ends a strong imperative (command)	To express urgency, warning, or a forceful command
	Ends an interjection, a single word or phrase used as an exclamation that stands apart from the rest of a sentence	To cry out, to utter an emotion
	Used with interjections beginning with *how* or *what*	To emphasize an idea

Examples

EXCLAMATORY STATEMENT

I hate war!

EXCLAMATION POINT ENDS EXCLAMATORY STATEMENT

SUBJECT   VERB

STRONG IMPERATIVE

VERB

Stop the war!

EXCLAMATION POINT ENDS STRONG IMPERATIVE

"YOU" OR "WE" IS THE UNDERSTOOD, IMPLIED SUBJECT OF THIS FORCEFUL COMMAND

INTERJECTION: DESCRIPTIVE PHRASES WITH HOW AND WHAT

INTERJECTIONS ADD EMOTION AND EMPHASIS, BUT STAND APART FROM THE MAIN SENTENCE

Oh! How dreadful! What a calamity! I lost my passport.

INTERJECTION: SINGLE WORD

EXCLAMATION POINTS END INTERJECTIONS

Common Misuses of Exclamation Points

- Use the exclamation mark sparingly. Overuse makes the point less meaningful.

- Use only one exclamation mark for a sentence; avoid using several at a time to emphasize a point.

Incorrect

INCORRECT USAGE OF MULTIPLE
EXCLAMATION POINTS FOR EACH SENTENCE

Save your life!!!!! Stop smoking, now!!!!!!

EXCLAMATION POINTS OVERUSED

Correct

USE OF PERIODS TO END IMPERATIVES MAKES
USE OF EXCLAMATION POINT MORE EFFECTIVE

Save your life. Stop smoking. Now!

EXCLAMATION POINT ENDS
SINGLE INTERJECTION

- Do not use exclamation marks in academic writing.

Practice 4

THE EXCLAMATION POINT

Insert a period or an exclamation mark as needed to appropriately end each idea. Use periods and capital letters as needed to make your point. Discuss your responses with your classmates.

1. Be quiet we are trying to watch the movie and you keep talking

2. This is ridiculous when we paid $10.50 each to see this movie, we didn't think we would have to deal with noisy people like you

3. Oh, come on you do not need to look at your BlackBerry in a dark theater

4. It's your fault we are so angry that we are leaving. Thanks a lot

5. Write a sentence of exclamation. Suggested Topic: An urgent need.

Practice 5

END PUNCTUATION REVIEW

Insert the appropriate end punctuation for each sentence. Capitalize words as needed.

1. Get up and shout a college education should be a right not a privilege

2. Is it fair that someone is denied a good education simply because she can't afford it

3. What can we do to make education affordable for everyone

4. I wonder why education is so expensive

5. Write a sentence with a purpose of your own choosing. Use appropriate end punctuation. Suggested Topic: The cost of a college education in the United States.

Writing Assignments

Writing for Everyday Life

Assume you are writing an email to a family member about a travel experience. You write your first draft as a freewrite without concern for punctuation. You take time to proofread before you click the send button, and you see the need to insert end punctuation. Edit the email to insert appropriate end punctuation. Capitalize words as needed. Use your own paper.

Hi Aunt Jo,

You wouldn't believe what happened to me at the airport. When I tried to check in at the ticket counter, I couldn't find my wallet. I had left my new wallet with all my identification at home and had mistakenly picked up my old wallet. Now, you may be asking how that could have happened I know this was so avoidable an airline representative asked, "Do you have any government issued identification with you" Thank goodness I still had a library card in my old wallet she marked my ticket for "special screening" from security. Those folks took me aside, patted me down, and went through all my belongings. I got through security in time to board my plane I was so relieved. How stressful it all was

Writing Assignments CONTINUED

Writing for College Life

Assume you are working with a group of peers on a science project. You have been appointed the group recorder. You have started a rough draft of your group's lab report. Proofread and edit the report for correct use of end punctuation. Use your own paper.

Airfare Price to Miles Traveled Correlation Report

On Wednesday October 19, 2005 a research experiment was performed in order to detect whether or not there is a correlation between the price of a flight ticket and the actual mileage from origination to destination the three researchers conducting this research utilized the Internet Web sites Expedia.com and Mapquest.com to acquire the necessary data for the experiment. The following criteria were established in order to qualify the data for the experiment first, the flight must have at least, but not more than one layover second, the original flight must depart between six in the morning and noon. Third, the passenger must be an adult 19 to 64 years of age. Fourth, the flight must be for one adult in economy/coach class. Fifth, Delta Airlines must be the flight provider. Sixth, the data must be collected only from cities in the United States seventh, the flight must be a round trip airfare. The researchers randomly chose 25 cities in the United States to collect the required data for the experiment the researchers used Expedia.com to obtain the price of each of the 25 flights. The researchers then used Mapquest.com to collect the mileage data, from origination to destination. The researchers, by using data were able to determine that there is no correlation between the price of a flight ticket and the number of miles traveled

Writing for Working Life

Assume you are working in a local restaurant to gain experience in the industry. You want to learn about running a small business because your long-term goal is to open your own restaurant. You notice a way to improve customer satisfaction, so on your break, you quickly write down your thoughts. As you read your first draft, you see the need for end punctuation. Edit this draft to insert appropriate end punctuation. Use your own paper.

> ### My First Thoughts: Ways to Improve Customer Satisfaction
>
> In what ways can we improve customer satisfaction We need to improve our music and our napkins. Different age groups come at different times of the day the early crowd is older and quieter. The late evening crowd is younger and more active our music should be customized to meet their different tastes. I suggest classical or soft rock music to play quietly as background music for the early crowds the evening crowds are more likely to enjoy the hard-driving, party sound of hard rock or pop music. The quality of our napkins is another detail that needs improvement. I wonder how much we spend on our current small, thin paper napkins they need to be replaced with super-large, high quality paper napkins. Good napkins are well worth the money!!!!

WANT A BETTER GRADE?
For more practice with end punctuation, go to **www.mywritinglab.com > Punctuation and Mechanics > End Punctuation: Period, Question Mark, and Exclamation Point.**

Academic Learning Log

LEARNING OUTCOMES
SELF-EVALUATION

WHAT HAVE I LEARNED ABOUT END PUNCTUATION?

To test and track your understanding, answer the following questions.

1. The .... ends a declarative or a mild .... statement.

2. The purpose of a declarative sentence is to ....; the purpose of an imperative sentence is to ....

3. The question mark ends an ....; the purpose of this sentence type is to ....

4. A question mark is not used at the end of an .... question.

5. An exclamation point ends an .... statement, a strong ...., and an ....

6. The purpose of an exclamatory sentence is to express ...., urgency, ..., or a forceful ....

7. **How will I use what I have learned about end punctuation?**
   In your notebook, discuss how you will apply to your own writing what you have learned about end punctuation.

8. **What do I still need to study about end punctuation?**
   In your notebook, discuss your ongoing study needs by describing what, when, and how you will continue studying end punctuation.

PORTFOLIO

33

Capitalization

Capitalization clearly identifies the beginning of a new idea or the names of specific people, places, and things.

Thinking about a real-life situation helps us to understand the purpose of capitalization in our communication. Complete the following activity and answer the question "What's the point of capitalization?"

What's the Point of Capitalization?

PHOTOGRAPHIC ORGANIZER: CAPITALIZATION

Many experts fear that excessive text messaging harms an individual's ability to write well. Other experts believe text messaging can teach students the appropriate use of language for different situations and audiences. For example, the use of capitalization in text messages differs from standard rules. The person in the photo is text messaging her family about a delay in her travel plans. Read her text message and consult the glossary of text message lingo, common expressions used in text messages. Explain how she uses capitalization in her message. Next, identify standard uses of capitalization you have seen in written language. Do you think text messaging harms an individual's ability to write well?

Text Message Glossary

AFAIK (As Far As I Know)

BFN (Bye for Now)

CYA (See You)

FYI (For Your Information)

L8R (Later)

2NITE (Tonight)

What's the point of capitalization?

Understanding the Point of Capitalization: One Student Writer's Response

The following paragraph offers one writer's reaction to the text message.

> I do a lot of text messaging, so I know that some people capitalize everything in their messages while others don't capitalize anything. Just like the woman at the airport, I like to use capital letters in my messages because each group of caps makes up a word. Using capitals helps me see what I am writing. As I think about standard capitalization rules, I think of the names of people, places, days of the week, days of the month, and the first word of a sentence. I always follow these rules when I write for school or work, but I am not so sure about some capitalization rules, like people's titles. I can see how experts think text messaging hurts written language. Sometimes, if I'm in a hurry, I use text lingo like "4" for "four." I just make sure I proofread.

Applying the Point: Capitalization

Capitalization refers to writing letters (and sometimes words) in uppercase letters. The most frequent usage of capitalization, however, is writing a word with its first letter in uppercase (and the rest of its letters in lowercase) to indicate the beginning of a sentence.

Following seven basic rules will ensure proper use of capitalization in your writing.

RULE 1: Capitalize the first word of every sentence.

INITIAL CAPITAL LETTERS IN THE FIRST WORD OF EVERY SENTENCE INDICATE THE START OF A NEW SENTENCE AND A NEW THOUGHT

➤Extreme horror films provide thrill rides for loyal fans.

➤The core audience of horror is made up of 18- to 22-year-old males. Many criticize horror films for being too graphic.

Practice 2

Edit the following paragraph for proper use of capitalization.

an unknown actress plays a tourist visiting a foreign country in a popular horror film. the tourist and her friends are terrorized in the cheap lodgings recommended by a beautiful model. the plot contains gruesome details. although horror films are very popular, some critics condemn them for showcasing violence against women. however, other experts say that watching horror films provides a healthy outlet for aggression.

Write a sentence that requires the appropriate use of capitalization. Suggested Topic: Your opinion about horror movies.

RULE 2: Capitalize the pronoun *I*.

ALWAYS CAPITALIZE THE FIRST-PERSON SINGULAR PRONOUN "I"

►I do not enjoy watching horror movies. Because I keep my eyes closed through most of a horror movie, I think they are a waste of my money.

Practice 3

Edit the following paragraph for proper use of capitalization.

My boyfriend really enjoys horror movies, but i prefer romantic comedies. i enjoy movies that don't keep me awake all night with horrible images of dismembered bodies. i like to escape problems when i watch a movie. i don't want to think about murder, rape, and mayhem. i just want to watch a good love story. Most often, i have to watch the movies i like without my boyfriend. That's fine with me because he certainly has to watch horror movies without me.

Write a sentence that requires the appropriate use of capitalization. Suggested Topic: Your favorite kind of movie.

RULE 3: Capitalize the first letter of the first words in written greetings and salutations (for example, *Dear friends,* or *Best regards*).

ALWAYS CAPITALIZE THE FIRST LETTER OF THE FIRST WORDS IN WRITTEN GREETINGS OR CLOSINGS (IN LETTERS, MEMOS, E-MAILS, ETC.)

➤ Dear Mr. Sanchez:

I am writing to protest your support of horror films. As a sponsor of this type of film, you foster fear and violence in our culture. Until you stop sponsoring horror films, I will no longer buy items from your company.

➤ Sincerely,

Dorothea Simmons

CAPITALIZATION

Edit the following letter for proper use of capitalization.

dear Ms. Simmons:

our company appreciates your concern about horror films. we also appreciate the time you took to write to us about your concerns. our board of directors is taking this matter into consideration. we will make a public statement in the near future.

best regards,

Steve Sanchez

RULE 4: In titles of publications, such as books, magazines, newspapers, songs, poems, plays, and articles, capitalize the first letter of the first and last words, the principal words, and the first word that comes after a semicolon or a colon.

Do not capitalize the first letters of the following in titles, unless they are the first or last word or come after a semicolon or colon: articles (*a, an, the*), prepositions (such as *in, of,* and *with*), and conjunctions (such as *and, but,* and *for*). Keep in mind that capitalization styles for titles differ in certain academic disciplines, so always check with your teacher for style guidelines.

Article:

ALWAYS CAPITALIZE THE FIRST LETTER OF THE FIRST WORD IN A PUBLICATION TITLE

"Eight Top Jobs for Parents"

ALWAYS CAPITALIZE THE FIRST LETTER OF THE PRINCIPAL WORDS IN A PUBLICATION TITLE

Book:

ALWAYS CAPITALIZE THE FIRST LETTER OF THE PRINCIPAL WORDS IN A PUBLICATION TITLE

The Grapes of Wrath

Magazine/Journal:

Sociology: The Journal of the British Sociological Association

Newspaper:

The New York Times

Play or Movie:

UNLESS THEY ARE THE FIRST OR LAST WORD, DO NOT CAPITALIZE THE FIRST LETTER OF MINOR WORDS, ARTICLES, PREPOSITIONS, OR CONJUNCTIONS IN TITLES

The Taming of the Shrew

Poem:

"Death Be Not Proud"

Song:

"Dearly Beloved"

Website:

Health.gov

Note: Digital terms, such as Internet or the World Wide Web, use initial capitalization.

Practice 5

Edit the following paragraph for proper use of capitalization.

In 2009, the film star trek debuted to packed theaters around the country. The film is a chronicle of the early days of James T. Kirk and his fellow USS Enterprise crewmembers. The movie has received praise from critics worldwide. According to the boston globe, the film is "the greatest prequel of all time." The magazine entertainment weekly calls the movie "clever and infectious." Hardcore star trek fans can read more about the movie characters at the website, startrek.com. Fans new to the star trek phenomena can read books based on the popular science fiction series such as star trek: the original series and star trek: challenger.

Write a sentence that requires the appropriate use of capitalization. Suggested Topic: A popular movie, song, or website.

RULE 5: Capitalize the first letters in all essential words in proper nouns.

Proper nouns name specific people, places, things, and events. Proper nouns include people's names; certain titles of people (see Rule 6 on page 584 for details), places, and regions; organizations and associations; and publications. Each of the examples in the following chart illustrates various rules for capitalizing proper nouns.

Note the capitalization of initials and abbreviations. Do not capitalize common nouns.

ALWAYS CAPITALIZE THE FIRST LETTER IN EACH PART OF A PERSON'S NAME   *ALWAYS CAPITALIZE A PERSON'S INITIALS*

THE FIRST LETTER OF THE TITLES OF FAMILY RELATIVES (PARENTS, AUNTS AND UNCLES, ETC.) REMAIN LOWERCASE AS COMMON NOUNS, BUT BECOME CAPITALIZED WHEN A SPECIFIC RELATIVE (THE SPEAKER'S) IS REFERRED TO

	Common Nouns	**Proper Nouns**
People	a woman	Ms. Eileen Long
	a man	Mr. D. O. Nape
	a professor	Professor Walker
	an officer	Captain Rivera or Capt. Rivera
	a relative, an aunt	Aunt Jo
	a father, my mother	Father, Mother
	a believer of a religion	Christian, Catholic, Muslim
	member(s) of an organization	Republican(s), Boy Scout(s)

	Common Nouns	Proper Nouns
Places and Regions	a lake	Lake Tahoe
	a country	Mexico
	a street	Main Street
Things	a language	English
	an academic course	Psychology 101
	a history course	World History I
	a ship	Titanic
	south (a direction)	the American South (a region)
	a religion	Christianity, Judaism, Islam
	a sacred text	the Koran, the Qur'an, the Bible
	a god	God, Christ, Allah, Buddha, Zeus
	a group/organization	the Rolling Stones, the Kiwanis Club
	a department, office, or institution	the Senate, the Department of Commerce, Daytona State College
	a monument	Lincoln Memorial
	a company	Apple, Inc.
Events, Time Periods	a day	Friday
	a month	January
	an era	the Middle Ages
	a movement	the Civil Rights Movement
	a war	the Vietnam War
	a holiday	Easter, Passover, Thanksgiving, Ramadan

CAPITALIZATION

Edit the following paragraph for proper use of capitalization.

The enlightenment was a movement that started among a small group of people and slowly spread to influence society. In contrast, romanticism was more widespread in both its origins and its influence. Many experts believe that no other intellectual or Artistic Movement has had such influence since the end of the middle ages. Beginning in germany and england in the 1770s, by the 1820s

▲ *Beethoven*

romanticism had swept through europe and traveled quickly to the western hemisphere. romanticism transformed poetry, the Novel, drama, painting, sculpture, and all forms of concert music. beethoven and mozart are two well-known composers from this era. The influence of Music from this romantic era is heard in the soundtracks for Epic Films such as *star wars*.

Write a sentence that requires the appropriate use of capitalization. Suggested Topic: Person of Influence.

Practice 6

RULE 6: **Capitalize the first letter of the title of a person when the title precedes the person's name.**

Some writers capitalize the first letter of a title of very high rank even when it follows a proper name. Capitalization of the first letter of a title is also common if it appears at the end of a letter, e-mail, or other correspondence, following the person's name. Do not capitalize those titles when they appear on their own as common nouns (without modifying a particular person's name).

ALWAYS CAPITALIZE THE FIRST LETTER OF A PERSON'S TITLE WHEN IT APPEARS BEFORE THE PERSON'S NAME

WHEN A PERSON'S TITLE APPEARS AFTER THE PERSON'S NAME, THE INITIAL LETTER OF THE TITLE REMAINS LOWERCASE

Doctor Kit Doughney

Kit Doughney, a medical doctor

Professor Rivers

Van Rivers, a professor of science

IN SOME CASES, IF IT'S A HIGH-RANKING TITLE, WRITERS WILL CAPITALIZE A TITLE EVEN IF IT APPEARS AFTER THE NAME

Prime Minister Brown

Gordon Brown, Prime Minister of the United Kingdom of Great Britain and Northern Ireland

Secretary of State Clinton

Hillary Clinton, the Secretary of State

CAPITALIZATION

Edit the following paragraph for proper use of capitalization.

> One of my favorite teachers, professor Gladiz Ricci in the Political Science department at my university, told our class about one of her heroes – Political Activist Aung San Suu Kyi. A Nobel Peace Prize winner, Aung San Suu Kyi has spent most of her life fighting for democracy in Burma, a military-ruled country in Southeast Asia. On one of the walls in doctor Ricci's office, there is a quote from Aung San Suu Kyi that truly inspires me. The quote reads: "It is not power that corrupts, but fear. Fear of losing power corrupts those who wield it…" The work of this great Freedom Fighter makes me appreciate living in a democracy. In fact, I am considering being a State Senator or Legislator so that I can be a part of the political process.

Write a sentence that requires the appropriate use of capitalization. Suggested Topic: A person you admire.

RULE 7: Capitalize proper adjectives. Proper adjectives are formed from proper nouns.

Proper Noun	Proper Adjective
Africa	Africans
America	Americans
Florida	Floridian
Japan	Japanese
Spain	Spanish
Shakespeare	Shakespearean

Use and capitalize brand-name trademarks as proper adjectives:

Kleenex tissue

Scotch tape

Practice 8

CAPITALIZATION

Edit the following paragraph for proper use of capitalization.

Terrell loves to try different types of foods. He and a few of his college friends recently visited New york city, where they sampled dim sum at a chinese restaurant, a rich, creamy dessert called crème brule at a french restaurant, and crunchy, spicy empanadas at a columbian restaurant. Of all of the dishes the group sampled, Terrell's favorite was a thick chicken stew called Wat that is a staple of ethiopian cuisine. Terrell loved the dish so much that he purchased an ethiopian cookbook at a bookstore around the corner from the restaurant. Terrell knows that cooking his new favorite dish will certainly be better than eating at mcDonald's or grabbing a snickers bar.

Practice 9

CAPITALIZATION REVIEW

Edit the following paragraph for proper use of capitalization.

i love to watch the travel channel on tv. Every time I turn to that channel, there is something new to learn about the world. Sometimes the places being shown are very close to my home, but often the episodes showcase far away countries that I know little about. For example, last week I watched a program about korean food. It was on a show called no reservations, which is hosted by the famous nyc Chef anthony bourdain. In this episode he and his korean coworker, nari, made their own kimchi. kimchi is the national dish of korea. It is spicy pickled cabbage that is buried in the earth for months to ferment. Hopefully, I will have the chance to eat this some day. However, something that I do not plan on tasting is the live octopus that bourdain and his cohost sampled.   They said the tentacles stuck to their tongues as they tried to swallow! That is very different from the foods we eat here in my home town of princeton, new jersey.

Writing Assignments

Writing for Everyday Life

Assume you are writing an e-mail to a friend about a horror movie you just saw. Edit the paragraph for proper use of capitalization. Use your own paper.

i did not want to go see this movie. horror movies are not my thing, but I gave in and reluctantly went along to see *hostel ii.* i probably won't sleep soundly again for years. the motion picture association Of america gave it an r rating for "sadistic scenes of violence and torture." i have to say i didn't see a lot of the movie. i kept covering my eyes with my hands. but i heard every blood curdling sound. it was awful! i couldn't even enjoy my snacks; my coca-cola and twizzlers remained untouched. i would never recommend this movie.

Writing for College Life

Assume you are taking a health course and you have been assigned to write about the importance of sleep. Edit the paragraph for proper use of capitalization. Use your own paper.

according to the national sleep foundation, every person has Individual Sleep Needs, so there is no set number of hours that everyone needs. however, in general, an adult needs seven to eight hours of sleep each night. a constant lack of sleep can lead to several serious consequences. according to dr. dement, lack of sleep increases risk of motor vehicle accidents. lack of sleep may lead to a greater chance of obesity, diabetes, and heart problems. lack of sleep can also lessen a person's ability to pay attention or remember new information. dr. dement is a cofounder of the stanford sleep disorders clinic in stanford, california.

Writing Assignments CONTINUED

Writing for Working Life

Assume you are working as a supervisor of the maintenance department for a small printing company. You are writing a letter that claims damages and payment for those damages. Edit this draft of the letter for proper use of capitalization. Use your own paper.

dear mr. rodriguez:

as someone who has used your services for several years, i am very disappointed with the quality of the work performed by your company, best electronic company, on thursday, may 18th of this year. during the repair, your crew damaged carpets, base-boards, and walls. as stated in the work order, you guarantee that you "leave no mess behind." i expect you to pay for the cost of the damages done by your workers denise brown and kevin allgood. photographs of the damages and an estimate of the repair cost are enclosed.

yours truly,

anna b. wright, supervisor
maintenance department
quality print shop

Academic Learning Log

WHAT HAVE I LEARNED ABOUT CAPITALIZATION?

To test and track your understanding, answer the following questions.

1. Capitalize the .... of every sentence.

2. Capitalize the pronoun ....

3. Capitalize the first letter of the first words of .... and ....

4. Capitalize the first letter of .... words in ....

5. Capitalize the first letter of the .... of a person when the title

.... the person's name.

6. Capitalize the first letter of .... nouns. Do not capitalize

.... nouns.

7. Capitalize the first letter of .... adjectives.

8. How will I use what I have learned about capitalization?
Discuss how you will apply to your own writing what you have learned about capitalization.

PORTFOLIO

----

9. What do I still need to study about capitalization?
Discuss your ongoing study needs by describing what, when, and how you will continue studying capitalization.

34

Revising for Effective Expression

Effective expression makes language clear and interesting.

Thinking about a real-life situation helps us understand the purpose and need for effective expression in our communication with others. Complete the following activity and answer the question "What's the point of effective expression?"

What's the Point of Effective Expression?

PHOTOGRAPHIC ORGANIZER: EFFECTIVE EXPRESSION

Assume you received the following e-mail from a coworker. What is your impression of the person based on the language used in the e-mail?

FROM: Kendis Moore Kendis@ITsolutions.com

Date: January 15, 2009

TO: Dwayne <Dwayne@ITsolutions.com>

SUBJECT: FW: A Good Cause

FYI

--------Forwarded Message

From: "Douglas Whitten"

Date: January 15, 2009

To: All Employees of Clarke Photography & Printing

Subject: A Good Cause!

I know everyone is busy as a bee, so I am not going to beat around the bush. It's time to get the United Way Campaign under way. Last year, we let it fall through the cracks, but this year, we are going to hit the nail on the head and raise a boat load of money. You may think this is not important, but you're dead wrong. Now don't drop the ball. Be sure to give to the United Way.

What's the point of effective expression?

Understanding the Point of Effective Expression: One Student Writer's Response

The following paragraph offers one writer's reaction to the e-mail from the coworker.

> I am not impressed with the coworker based on the sound of the memo. It's too informal; it doesn't sound professional at all. And it's boring and uninspiring. I would hit delete after the first sentence. It doesn't sound like the writer takes the campaign very seriously.

Applying the Point: Effective Expression

Effective expression is a result of thoughtful word choice. Mark Twain once said, "The difference between the almost right word and the right word is really a large matter—it's the difference between the lightning bug and the lightning." During early drafts, writers often relate thoughts and ideas without concern for word choice. Words or phrases are needlessly repeated, and clichés—overused expressions or ideas—are sometimes included in the draft. This rush to record ideas as they occur makes good use of the writing process *if* we take time to revise for effective expression after we have completed a draft. Effective expression involves concise, active, positive, concrete, creative, and fresh writing. Use the revision process to achieve effective expression.

Use Concise Language

The most effective writing is concise and to the point. Concise language avoids wordiness—the use of unnecessary or redundant words and phrases that add nothing to the writer's meaning. The following example illustrates the difference between wordiness and concise writing.

Wordy

TWO ADJECTIVES THAT MEAN THE SAME THING DESCRIBE SUBJECT "COUNTY"

TWO-WORD VERB; USE OF PASSIVE VOICE

The whole, entire county was warned of flooding by the National Weather Service for the preparation of evacuations.

MULTIPLE, LONG PREPOSITIONAL PHRASES

Concise

SUBJECT   *VERB; USE OF ACTIVE VOICE*   *ONE CLEAR ADJECTIVE DESCRIBES OBJECT "COUNTY"*

The National Weather Service warned the entire county to prepare to evacuate due to flooding. *MORE CONCISE REVISION OF THE THREE ORIGINAL PREPOSITIONAL PHRASES*

592

Wordy Expressions with Revisions for Conciseness	
Wordy	**Concise**
absolutely certain	certain
advanced notice	notice
has the ability	can
he is a man who; she is a woman who	he; she
disappear from view	disappear
during the same time that	when
given the fact that	because
in an impatient manner	impatiently
in order to	to
in spite of the fact	although, though
in this day and age	today
in today's world	today, currently
personal opinion	opinion
personally, I think	I think
reason why is that	because
red in color	red
refer back	refer
repeat again	repeat
small in size	small
summarize briefly	summarize
there is no doubt but that	no doubt, doubtless
the fact that she had not succeeded	her failure
this is a topic which	this topic
very unique	unique
whole entire	whole; entire

USE CONCISE LANGUAGE

Read each sentence and revise it using concise language.

1. A lake in southern Chile mysteriously disappeared from view.

....

....

2. The disappearance of a lake five acres in size is a situation that is puzzling in nature.

....

....

Practice 2

Practice 2

3. In March, the lake was exactly the same level as it had always been; by May the whole entire lake had vanished.

4. A river that flowed out of the lake was reduced to a trickle during the same time the lake vanished.

5. Experts suggest that the lake disappeared due to the fact that an earth tremor opened a crack in the ground that acted like a drain.

Use Active and Positive Language

The most effective writing uses active, positive language to state ideas. The **active voice** states what somebody or something did. The **passive voice** states what was done to someone or something. Sentences written in the active voice are more concise because the active voice uses fewer words to state an action, and it clearly states the relationship between the subject and the action. In contrast, the passive voice uses more words to state an action, and the relationship between the subject and the action is less clear. The active voice is more direct and more powerful than the passive voice.

Passive Voice

THE SUBJECT "ANNA" RECEIVES THE ACTION PERFORMED BY SOMEONE ELSE.

Anna was surprised by her family.

Active Voice

THE SUBJECT "FAMILY" PERFORMS THE ACTION.

Anna's family surprised her.

Effective writing also involves stating ideas in the positive, which is more powerful than stating them in the negative. Too often, the use of a negative expression makes language seem unclear. The following chart offers some tips and examples for creating positive language.

Tips for Creating a Positive Voice
• Say what something **is** instead of what it **is not**.   *Negative:* The diet does not allow you to eat as much as you want of such favorites as sweets, chips, and fried foods.   *Positive:* The diet allows you to eat your favorite foods in moderate amounts.
• Say what **can** be done instead of what **cannot** or **should not** be done.   *Negative:* Bridget should not consider auditioning for the singing competition because she has never sung in front of an audience.   *Positive:* Bridget can practice singing in front of friends and family to get used to singing in front of an audience; she will then be better prepared for the audition.
• Propose an **action** in addition to offering an **apology** or **explanation**.   *Negative:* I'm sorry I didn't call last night, but what do you expect? I worked all day and had school until 9:00 p.m.   *Positive:* I'm sorry I didn't call last night, but I was feeling overwhelmed with school and work. Perhaps we can meet for coffee when my schedule is less hectic.

The following chart lists negative expressions in one column and positive revisions to those expressions in the other column.

Negative Expressions with Revisions to the Positive	
Negative Expression	**Positive Expression**
cannot lie	must tell the truth
cannot reconnect without	reconnect by
cannot waste resources	value resources
do not forget	remember
do not be late	be on time
do not be negative	be positive
never delay a response	respond quickly
never be rude	be polite
sorry, we cannot respond until	we will respond by
you misunderstood	let me clarify

USE ACTIVE AND POSITIVE LANGUAGE

Revise these sentences from passive voice to active voice or from negative statements to positive statements. Share and discuss your answers with a peer or your class.

1. Severe weather warnings must not be taken lightly by the public.

....

2. Severe weather alerts are issued by the National Weather Service (NWS), yet many do not pay attention to these official warnings.

....

Practice 3

3. No one in the warning zone of a weather alert is free from danger.

....

....

4. Minor flooding, moderate flooding, and major flooding are used by the NWS as flood severity categories.

....

....

5. Write a sentence that uses active, positive language. Suggested Topic: A weather alert.

....

....

Use Concrete Language

Another key to effective writing is using **concrete language**. When writers use concrete language, they give readers vivid descriptions that can be visualized. Concrete language is the result of the thoughtful choice of nouns, verbs, adjectives, and adverbs. Your choice of words can mean the difference between writing that is **abstract** (vague, nonspecific writing) and writing that is concrete. Let's look at the difference between abstract and concrete nouns, verbs, adjectives, and adverbs.

An **abstract noun** names an emotion, feeling, idea, or trait detached from the five senses. A **concrete noun** names an animal, person, place, or object that the reader can see, touch, taste, hear, or smell (sensory details). The following chart illustrates the difference between concrete and abstract nouns.

Abstract Noun	Concrete Noun
beauty	rainbow
love	kiss
strength	steel
work	sweaty

An **abstract verb** or verb phrase tells about a state of being or describes a general or nonspecific action. A **concrete verb** or verb phrase shows a specific action or creates a clear picture for the reader. The following chart illustrates the difference between abstract and concrete verbs and verb phrases.

Abstract Verb	Concrete Verb
He is angry.	He spews curses.
I got an "A" on the exam.	I earned an "A" on the exam.
Jerome went in the room.	Jerome walked into the room.
Jerome went, "Hey."	Jerome said, "Hi."

An **abstract adjective** is a broad and general description that is open to interpretation based on opinion. A **concrete adjective** shows a specific trait or sensory detail and is not open to interpretation. The best writing relies on the strength of concrete nouns and verbs, so use adjectives only when necessary.

Abstract Adjective	Concrete Adjective
awesome sound	echoing canyon
good taste	salty ocean
weird behavior	quiet disposition
loud music	heavy-metal concert

An **abstract adverb** is a broad and general description that is open to interpretation based on opinion. A **concrete adverb** shows a specific trait or sensory detail and is not open to interpretation. The best writing relies on the strength of concrete nouns and verbs, so use adverbs only when necessary.

Abstract Adverb	Concrete Adverb
a lot	daily
kind of	quietly
sort of	gently
pretty much	most
really	intensely
very	extremely

USE CONCRETE LANGUAGE

Revise these sentences from abstract language to concrete language. Share and discuss your answers with a peer or your class.

▲ Lake Tahoe

1. Pretty much all of us go to Lake Tahoe a lot.

----

2. Lake Tahoe is a beautiful place that we really enjoy visiting.

Practice 4

3. The children have a wonderful time and a lot of fun in the water.

....

4. It feels really good to get some rest on the beach.

....

....

5. Write a sentence that uses concrete language. Suggested Topic: A favorite vacation spot.

....

....

....

Use Creative Expressions: Similes and Metaphors

Creative expressions deepen the reader's understanding of a writer's meaning. Similes and metaphors are two ways you can include creative expression in your writing. Similes and metaphors are figures of speech that compare two unrelated ideas.

A **simile** is an indirect comparison between two ideas that uses *like, as, as if,* or *as though.*

"LIKE" CREATES AN INDIRECT COMPARISON OF TWO NOUNS/IDEAS

"I put my hands in the pockets and flapped the jacket like a bird's wings."

—Gary Soto, "The Jacket"

A **metaphor** is a direct comparison between two ideas that does **not** use *like, as, as if,* or *as though.*

"OF" CREATES A DIRECT COMPARISON OF TWO NOUNS/IDEAS

"I returned to the sea of necessity."

—E. B. White, "The Sea and the Wind that Blows"

HELPING VERB "IS" CREATES DIRECT COMPARISON OF TWO NOUNS/IDEAS

"Poverty is an acid that drips on pride until all pride is worn away."

—Jo Goodwin Parker, "What is Poverty?"

Note: In the last two examples, the writers clarified or deepened the meaning of an abstract noun by connecting it to a concrete noun. To create similes and metaphors, make a logical connection between an abstract noun and a concrete noun.

USE CREATIVE EXPRESSIONS

Complete the following sentences with a simile or a metaphor. Share and discuss your answers with a peer or your class.

1. Jealously is like ....

2. Courage is ....

3. .... struck the family to its core.

4. The Supreme Court nominee's hearing created a storm of ....

....

5. Write a sentence that uses a simile or metaphor. Suggested Topic: A lifelong goal.

....

....

....

Use Fresh Language

Effective writing also relies on using fresh language as opposed to clichés. Clichés are weak statements because they have lost their originality and forcefulness. See the example below.

Cliché:

OVERUSED NOUN PHRASE TO REPRESENT NATURE   *OVERUSED PHRASE TO DESCRIBE SNOWY WEATHER*

Mother Nature covered the ground with a snowy white blanket.

Fresh language:

STRONG, ORIGINAL NOUNS AND ADJECTIVES DESCRIBE SNOWY WEATHER IN VIVID DETAIL

"On top of this ice were as many feet of snow. It was all pure white, rolling in gentle undulations where the ice-jams of the freeze-up had formed."

—Jack London, "To Build a Fire"

The following chart lists popular clichés and their meanings.

Clichés and Their Meanings	
Cliché	**Meaning**
a needle in a haystack	hard to find
all thumbs	clumsy
as easy as pie	easy
beat around the bush	to speak indirectly about something
backstabber	an untrustworthy or deceitful person
busy as a bee	always working, very busy
drop the ball	to fail at a task
fall between the cracks	overlooked, not attended to
fit to be tied	angry
hidden agenda	sneaky
hit the nail on the head	to be correct about something
like a bull in china shop	tactless, clumsy
like a chicken with its head cut off	inefficient, erratic
never a dull moment	exciting
off your rocker	crazy, poor judgment
one foot in the grave	terminally ill
one in a million	rare; well-liked
splitting hairs	focusing on unimportant details
wishy-washy	lack of conviction, unclear
water over the dam	a past event that cannot be changed

Instead of relying on clichés such as the ones presented here, use fresh language as you revise your writing. When logical, create your own similes and metaphors to express your meaning.

USE FRESH LANGUAGE

Revise the following sentences by eliminating clichés and replacing them with fresh, creative language. Share and discuss your answers with a peer or your class.

1. The money Nyeeta won at the Las Vegas casino was burning a hole in her pocket.

_____

_____

2. Although she just lost her job at the factory, Stacey believed there was light at the end of the tunnel.

_____

_____

Practice 6

3. When Tony turned 50, he felt over the hill.

_____

_____

4. Rochelle's new position at the hospital kept her busy as a bee.

_____

_____

5. People around the country were fit to be tied when filthy rich executives from AIG walked away with million-dollar bonuses.

_____

_____

EFFECTIVE EXPRESSION REVIEW

Revise the following sentences for effective expression. Remember to use the key ingredients of effective expression—concise, active, positive, concrete, creative, and fresh language.

1. Despite its continued years on the television screen, _Sesame Street_ is a breath of fresh air in children's television.

_____

_____

2. Muppets such as Elmo, Cookie Monster, and Oscar the Grouch have withstood the test of time due to the fact that children love them as much today as in the past.

_____

_____

3. A very popular character on _Sesame Street_, Maria, is played by Sonia Manzano who joined the show in 1973.

_____

_____

4. _Sesame Street_ has had the fortune of winning a truckload of Emmy awards, and different versions of the show are broadcast throughout the world.

_____

_____

5. Write a sentence using effective expression. Suggested Topic: Popular children's television shows.

_____

_____

Writing Assignments

Writing for Everyday Life

Assume you are writing a thank-you letter for a graduation gift you received from a relative. Revise this letter using effective expression. Use your own paper.

Dear Grandfather,

Thank you for the wallet and money I got from you. I personally think that you are a man who is very generous and thoughtful. I am as happy as a lark with my new wallet, and the hundred dollars you put inside it made my day. I have always been supported by you. I am filled with gratitude.

Writing for College Life

Assume you are taking a sociology class and you are studying current events. You are required to write a paragraph discussing the impact on society of a new technological invention. Revise this draft for effective expression. Use your own paper.

The "brain-machine interface" has been developed by Hitachi, Inc. This development has the ability to totally change the way we use technology. The device can be controlled by brain activity, so you don't have to lift a finger to make anything happen. Slight changes in the brain's blood flow are analyzed, and the brain motion is converted to electrical signals. To demonstrate, a reporter was given a cap to wear that was also connected with optical fibers to a toy train. When she did simple math in her head, the train moved. A TV remote controller is being developed by Hitachi's scientists. Soon we may be able to turn on any electrical device with a simple thought.

Writing for Working Life

Assume you are working at an entry-level position for a firm that offers opportunities for advancement. You need to schedule a week off for personal reasons. Revise the following memo using effective expression. Use your own paper.

> To: Mr. Gordon
>
> From: Raul Estevez
>
> RE: Request for Personal Leave
>
> I am writing you to request personal leave due to the fact that surgery must be performed on my knee that will require a week's recovery time. I wanted to give you advanced notice given the fact that we are short on staff, but I absolutely must be off on the days of July 1 through July 8.

WANT A BETTER GRADE?
For more practice with revising for effective expression, go to www.mywritinglab.com > Punctuation and Mechanics > Revising for Effective Expression.

WHAT HAVE I LEARNED ABOUT USING EFFECTIVE EXPRESSION?

To test and track your understanding, answer the following questions.

What have I learned about effective expression?

1. The most effective writing is .... and to the point.

2. .... avoids wordiness.

3. .... is the use of unnecessary or redundant words and phrases that add nothing to the writer's meaning.

4. The .... voice states what somebody or something did.

5. The .... voice states what was done to somebody or something.

6. Stating ideas in the .... is much more powerful than stating them in the ....

7. .... language is the result of the thoughtful choice of nouns, ..., adjectives, and adverbs.

8. A .... is an indirect comparison between two apparently unrelated ideas.

9. A .... is a direct comparison between two apparently unrelated ideas.

10. A .... is a trite or overused expression.

11. **How will I use what I have learned about effective expression?**
   In your notebook, discuss how you will apply to your own writing what you have learned about effective expression. When during the writing process will you apply this knowledge?

12. **What do I still need to study about effective expression?**
   In your notebook, discuss your ongoing study needs by describing what, when, and how you will continue studying effective expression.

35

Improving Your Spelling

To spell correctly is to understand the rules for properly arranging letters in a word.

Do you have trouble spelling words? If so, you are not alone. Many people have trouble spelling. Despite these difficulties, it is important to work toward accurate spelling because it is an important part of effective expression. Complete the following activity and answer the question "What's the point of improving your spelling?"

What's the Point of Improving Your Spelling?

PHOTOGRAPHIC ORGANIZER: IMPROVING YOUR SPELLING

Assume a friend of yours has applied for an internship as a nurse at your local hospital. He is going to send a follow-up letter to express his interest in the position. He has asked you to proofread the first few sentences of the letter he wants to send. Can you find the ten misspelled words in this draft? What impact would misspelled words in this follow-up letter have on your friend's chances of getting the internship?

> I submitted a letter of aplication and a résumé earler this month
>
> for a nurseing internship with Memrial Hospital. To date, I have
>
> not herd from your office. I would like to confirm reciept of my
>
> leter and agian state my intrest in the job.

What's the point of improving your spelling?

_____

_____

_____

Understanding the Point of Improving Your Spelling: One Student Writer's Response

The following paragraph offers one writer's reaction to the spelling in the follow-up letter for the nursing internship.

> *Too many misspellings makes the writer of the letter seem uneducated or careless. I would say his poor spelling could cost him the internship. I mean he is probably competing against people who will make a better first impression. It's a good thing he asked someone to read over his letter. I don't know if my spelling is as bad as that of the writer of the letter, but I do seem to misspell a lot of words. I would love to be a better speller. I want to make a good impression on paper. I mean if it's worth my time to write, it's worth my time to do it correctly, right?*

LEARNING OUTCOMES
STRUCTURE

Applying the Point: Improving Your Spelling

You can improve your spelling by identifying and correcting patterns of misspellings in your writing. Each writer develops his or her own system for learning and using correct spelling. For example, some writers keep a vocabulary journal of new words or difficult-to-spell words, and most writers use a spell checker as a last step before publishing a piece of writing. The steps, rules, and practices in this chapter are designed to help you develop a system to improve your spelling.

Five Steps to Improve Your Spelling

Five of the best ways to improve your spelling are to use a spell checker, dictionary, mnemonics, spelling error tracking, and the writing process.

1. Use a Spell Checker

Word processing programs such as Microsoft Word provide spell checkers to verify the spellings of words in a document. Beware, however, because spell checkers seldom catch all the errors in a text. In particular, spell checkers fail to spot words that sound alike but differ in meaning, such as *to*, *too*, and *two*. In addition, spell checkers sometimes flag proper nouns (nouns that name specific people, places, and things) as misspellings even though they may be spelled correctly. Thus, carefully consider the reason the spell checker highlights a word. Be cautious about clicking the "change" or "change all" button too quickly. With thoughtful use, however, a spell checker offers helpful assistance in catching commonly misspelled words.

2. Use a Dictionary

Look up misspelled words in a dictionary. Place a dot next to each word you look up in your dictionary to flag it as a word for further study.

Most print dictionaries have guide words at the top of each page to help you locate a word. For each entry, the spelling of the main word is given first in bold type. The word is also divided into syllables. The function or part of speech and the etymology, the history of the word, are also given. It is often helpful to understand the origin of a word since many words in the English language came from other languages. Additional spellings of the word appear at the end of the entry. This listing is especially helpful when letters are dropped or added to create a new word.

Online dictionaries locate words through a search box instead of using guide words. If you misspell a word during your search, online dictionaries usually offer alternate spellings to help you find the word you are looking for. As you study the example shown on the next page from the *Merriam-Webster Online Dictionary*, think about how you will use the information in a dictionary to improve your spelling.

jealous

Main Entry: **jeal·ous**

Pronunciation: \ˈje-ləs\

Function: *adjective*

Etymology: Middle English *jelous*, from Anglo-French *gelus*, from Vulgar Latin **zelosus*, from Late Latin *zelus* zeal — more at ZEAL

Date: 13th century

1 a: intolerant of rivalry or unfaithfulness **b:** disposed to suspect rivalry or unfaithfulness

2: hostile toward a rival or one believed to enjoy an advantage

3: vigilant in guarding a possession <new colonies were *jealous* of their new independence

— Scott Buchanan>

— **jeal·ous·ly** *adverb*

— **jeal·ous·ness** *noun*

Source: By permission. From *Merriam-Webster Online Dictionary* © 2009 by Merriam-Webster, Incorporated
www.merriam-webster.com

3. Use Mnemonics

Mnemonics are different types of memory tricks that can help you remember the correct spelling of words. For example:

- Create a mental or visual image: Picture a person screaming "e-e-e" as he passes a cemetery.

- Chunk a word into visual parts: unforgettable = un for get table

- Color-code trouble spots in a word: rec**ei**ve (*not* recieve).

- Create a silly saying using each letter of the word: The first letter of each word in the following sentence combines to spell *geography*:
  George's **E**lderly **O**ld **G**randfather **R**ode **A** **P**ig **H**ome **Y**esterday.

4. Track Spelling Errors

Identify your misspellings through teacher feedback, peer edits, or a spell checker. In a journal, create a list of words that you have misspelled. Contrast the way you misspell the word with the rule and the correct spelling. Identify information that helps you remember the correct spelling such as the word's function or etymology. Create a memory trick as needed. Choose from the headings in the following example to create your own journal system for improving your spelling.

Correct Spelling	Function	Etymology	My Misspelling	Spelling Rule	Memory Trick
argument	noun	Latin *argumentum* (from the verb *arguere*)	arguement	Drop the silent e when a vowel comes right before it.	I lost an "e" in my argument.

5. Use the Writing Process to Improve Your Spelling

As you write, use these tips to ensure accurate spelling:

☐ **Decide when during the writing process you will identify and correct misspellings.**
Some writers who compose as they type or write pause frequently to revise and edit what they just wrote. Others prefer to complete a draft and then check for misspellings during the revision and proofreading phases of the writing process.

☐ **Identify and study specialized or difficult words that are connected to your writing assignment.**
Verify the spelling and etymology (how the word originated) of these words before you begin writing. Find correctly spelled synonyms (words that have similar meanings) for these words. Use this group of correctly spelled words to brainstorm additional details for your writing.

☐ **Use one proofreading session to focus only on spelling accuracy.**
By devoting time to proofreading your spelling, you are more likely to catch errors.

☐ **During the proofreading phase, edit on a printed copy of your writing if you are using a word processor.**
It's easy to overlook text errors on a computer screen.

☐ **Decide how you will track your misspelling patterns as you write.**
Will you make a list as you go, or will you list troubling words after you have completed your final edit?

Commit to improving your spelling by creating an individual study process.

Practice 2

STEPS TO IMPROVING YOUR SPELLING

Write out the steps you will take to improve your spelling. When possible, tie your steps to the writing process: Prewriting, Drafting, Revising, and Editing. Include additional steps if necessary. Share and discuss your responses with your class or a classmate.

Step 1 ....

....

Step 2 ....

....

Step 3 ....

....

Step 4 ....

....

Step 5 ....

Rules for Improving Your Spelling

Improving your spelling involves understanding rules about vowel and consonant patterns, as well as rules about the use of suffixes and prefixes.

Recognize Vowel and Consonant Patterns

Many spelling rules are based on the use of vowels and consonants to form words, so to improve your spelling, take note of the patterns of vowels and consonants in words. Take a moment to look at the following examples to refresh your memory about consonant (c) and vowel (v) patterns in words.

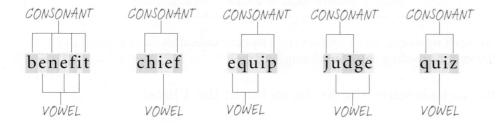

Understand How Suffixes Are Used

A **suffix** is added to the end of a **base word** (a word's original meaning) to change the use or meaning of the word. For example, the suffixes *-ing* or *-ed* can either change the tense of a verb or change the verb into a noun or an adjective. For example, *walk* is a verb, but adding *-ing* creates the present participle *walking*; adding *-ed* creates the past participle *walked*. The present and past participles can function as verbs, adjectives, or nouns depending on the context in which they are used.

Suffixes begin with either a vowel or a consonant, which affects the spelling rules for adding them to base words. You will learn about the specific ways in which vowels and consonants impact spelling throughout this chapter. The following chart lists a few common vowel and consonant suffixes, along with their meanings and examples.

Vowel Suffix	Meaning	Example
-able, -ible	able to	touch**able**, vis**ible**
-ed	past tense of a verb	talk**ed**, walk**ed**
-en	present or past participle	bitt**en**, writt**en**
-er	one who is or does	play**er**, adopt**er**
-er	comparison	bigg**er**, small**er**
-es	plural of a noun	dress**es**, box**es**
-es	singular present tense of a verb	wash**es**, finish**es**
-ous	full of	danger**ous**, luxuri**ous**

Consonant Suffix	Meaning	Example
-ful	full of	wonder**ful**, care**ful**
-ly or *-y*	like	gent**ly**, week**ly**
-ness	state of being	happi**ness**, faithful**ness**
-ment	state of	govern**ment**, state**ment**
-s	plural of a noun	doctor**s**, worker**s**
-s	singular present tense of a verb	run**s**, quit**s**

The rules for spelling words with suffixes vary. The next several sections explain and illustrate the various spelling rules for adding suffixes.

Add *-s* or *-es* to Nouns and Verbs to Form the Plural

- **Add *-s* to form the plural of most regular nouns, including those that end with *o*.**

book + s ⟶ books

video + s ⟶ videos

- **Add *-es* to nouns that end with a consonant immediately before a final *o*.**

hero + es ⟶ heroes

- **Add *-s* to most regular verbs to form the singular present tense in the third person.**

ask + s ⟶ asks

- **Add *-es* to form the plural of nouns and to third person present tense verbs that end in *ch*, *sh*, *s*, *x*, or *z*.**

Nouns

watch + es   watches

marsh + es   marshes

bus + es   buses

mix + es   mixes

Verbs

catch + es   catches

wash + es   washes

pass + es   passes

buzz + es   buzzes

ADD -S OR -ES TO NOUNS AND VERBS TO FORM THE PLURAL

Complete the chart by choosing the appropriate suffix to each of the following base words. Consult a dictionary to check your answers.

Base Words	Suffixes	
	-s	*-es*
1. store		
2. boy		
3. potato		
4. fox		
5. echo		
6. embargo		
7. wish		
8. stereo		
9. rock		

Double the Final Consonant in Words with One Syllable

Many **one syllable** words end in a **consonant** with a **vowel** immediately **before** it. (*Hint*: Remember **CVC**.) For a word with one syllable, one consonant, and one vowel, double the final consonant when adding a vowel suffix. The final consonant is *not* doubled when adding a consonant suffix.

Exception: Do not double the final consonant of words that end in *w*, *x*, or *y* as in the following examples: snowing, boxer, obeys.

Practice 4

Complete the chart by adding each of the suffixes to the base words. Consult a dictionary to check your answers.

Base Words	Suffixes			
	-s or *-es*	*-er*	*-ed*	*-ing*
1. fit				
2. hop				
3. flip				
4. fix				
5. plan				

Double the Final Consonant in Words with More Than One Syllable

Words with more than one syllable often end with a vowel immediately before a **consonant**. (*Hint*: Remember **VC**.) If the final syllable is stressed or emphasized in its pronunciation, **double the final consonant**.

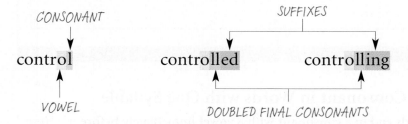

Practice 5

Complete the chart by adding the appropriate suffixes to the base words. Consult a dictionary to check your answers.

Base Words	Suffixes			
	-s	*-ed*	*-er*	*-ing*
1. acquit			— — —	
2. begin		— — —		
3. infer				
4. propel				
5. submit				
6. transmit				

Drop or Keep the Final *E*

- Drop the *e* when the base *word ends* with a *silent e* and the *suffix begins* with a *vowel.*

advance + -ing ⟶ advancing

- Drop the *e* when a *vowel comes immediately before* the silent *e.*

true + -ly ⟶ truly

- Keep the *e* when the base *word ends* with a silent *e* and the *suffix begins* with a *consonant.*

advance + -ment ⟶ advancement

DROP OR KEEP THE FINAL *E*

Complete the chart by adding the appropriate suffixes to the base words. Consult a dictionary to check your answers.

Base Words	Suffixes				
	-s	*-ful*	*-ing*	*-ly*	*-ment*
1. hope				_ _ _	_ _ _
2. live		_ _ _			_ _ _
3. manage		_ _ _		_ _ _	
4. state		_ _ _			
5. use				_ _ _	_ _ _

Change or Keep the Final *Y*

- When a *consonant* appears before the final *y*, change the *y* to *i*.

supply + -ies ⟶ supplies

- When a *vowel* appears before the final *y*, keep the *y*.

obey + -ed ⟶ obeyed

- Keep the *y* when adding the suffix *-ing*.

cry + -ing ⟶ crying

Practice 7

CHANGE OR KEEP THE FINAL Y

Complete the chart by adding each of the suffixes to the base words. Consult a dictionary to check your answers.

Base Words	Suffixes					
	-es	*-ed*	*-er*	*-ier*	*-est*	*-ing*
1. bury			_ _ _	_ _ _	_ _ _	
2. dry						
3. carry			_ _ _		_ _ _	
4. hurry			_ _ _	_ _ _	_ _ _	
5. play			_ _ _	_ _ _		

Understand How Prefixes Are Used

A prefix added to the beginning of a base word changes the word's meaning, but it does not change the word's spelling. The following chart lists a few common prefixes, their meanings, and example words.

Prefix	Meaning	Example
bi-	two	bicycle
de-	not	deregulated
dis-	not	disagree
im-	not	impossible
mis-	not	misunderstood
pre-	before	preview
re-	again	rewrite
un-	not	unknown

Adding a prefix to a word does not alter its spelling.

PREFIXES MEAN "NOT"

unusual   misspelled

BASE WORDS

USE PREFIXES TO BUILD AND CORRECTLY SPELL NEW WORDS

Use your dictionary to match words to the correct prefix. Complete the chart by writing the new words created by adding the appropriate prefixes. Consult a dictionary to check your answers.

Base Words	Prefixes				
	dis-	*pre-*	*pro-*	*re-*	*un-*
1. infect		— — —	— — —		— — —
2. qualified			— — —		
3. satisfied		— — —	— — —	— — —	
4. heat	— — —		— — —		— — —

Choose *ie* or *ei*

A helpful way to remember how to use *ie* and *ei* in spelling is to think of the following rhyme:

"***i*** before ***e*** except after ***c*** or when sounds like *ay* as in *nei**gh**bor* or *weigh*"

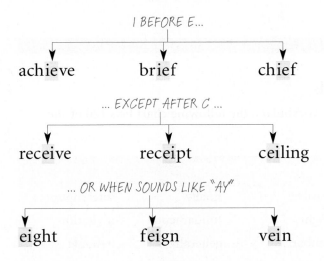

I BEFORE E...

achieve   brief   chief

... EXCEPT AFTER C ...

receive   receipt   ceiling

... OR WHEN SOUNDS LIKE "AY"

eight   feign   vein

There are, however, some exceptions to the *ie*, *ei* rule that should be memorized:

ie: species, science, conscience

ei: height, either, neither, leisure, seize, counterfeit, foreign, forfeit, sleight, weird

Practice 9

CHOOSE *IE* OR *E*

Underline the correctly spelled word in each pair of words. Consult a dictionary to check your answers.

1. *pierce*   *peirce*

2. *veil*   *viel*

3. *cashier*   *casheir*

4. *freind*   *friend*

5. *speceis*   *species*

6. *wieght*   *weight*

7. *piece*   *peice*

8. *decieve*   *deceive*

9. *preist*   *priest*

10. *thief*   *theif*

Commonly Misspelled Words

To aid in your efforts to improve your vocabulary, the following chart lists 120 of the most commonly misspelled words.

120 Commonly Misspelled Words				
absence	calendar	easily	finally	interruption
accommodate	ceiling	eight	fundamental	invitation
acquire	cemetery	embarrass	generally	irritable
across	chief	environment	grammar	island
advertise	coming	exaggerate	guarantee	judgment
advice	criticize	excellent	humorous	knowledge
apparent	definite	except	imaginary	laboratory
argument	describe	exercise	imitation	length
becoming	develop	experience	incidentally	license
beginning	difference	experiment	independent	loneliness
believe	dilemma	explanation	intelligent	losing
business	disappoint	fascinating	interesting	mathematics

120 Commonly Misspelled Words (continued)

medicine	peculiar	prejudice	repetition	succeed
minute	perceive	privilege	restaurant	surely
miscellaneous	permanent	probably	ridiculous	surprise
naturally	persevere	promise	sacrifice	temporary
necessary	persuade	proof	scissors	through
noticeable	picture	quiet	secretary	twelfth
occasion	piece	quit	separate	unusual
occurred	planning	quite	shining	using
omission	political	receive	sincerely	village
optimism	possess	recognize	soldier	weird
original	possible	recommend	stopping	whether
parallel	prefer	reference	studying	writing

CORRECT MISSPELLED WORDS

Edit the following sentences to correct misspelled words. Cross out each misspelled word and write the correct spelling above it.

1. *Staphylococcus aureus* or a Staph skin infection develops pimples or boils that are ususaly swollen, painful, and filled with pus.

2. People are more likly to aquir a Staph infection thruogh skin-to-skin contact with someone who has a Staph infection.

3. Most Staph skin infections are minor and may be easuly treated.

4. Generaly, a doctor prescribes an antibiotic and drains the infection if necesary.

5. Surly, one way of stoping the spread of Staph infections is to avoid sharing personal items like towels or razors.

Practice 10

Practice 11

SPELLING REVIEW

Edit the following sentences to correct misspelled words. Cross out each misspelled word and write the correct spelling above it.

1. The scare over the swine flu (also known as the H1N1 virus) emphasised the importanse of proper hand hygeine.

2. During the hieght of the scare, the Centers for Disease Control recomended that people be especially vijilant about washing hands.

3. In schools throughout the country, children were encourajed to sneeze into thier elbows insted of into their hands.

4. Schol workers washed down entire classrroms if an infekted child was in the classroom.

5. Virus or not, washing hands freqently is always a good idea.

LEARNING OUTCOMES
WRITING PROCESS

Writing Assignments

Writing for Everyday Life

Assume you recently visited an emergency clinic to get stitches in your foot. You believe you have contracted a Staph infection from one of the clinic's health care providers. You are writing to officially document your complaint against the clinic. Edit the misspellings in the following draft. Use your own paper.

> To Whom It May Concern:
>
> On September 24 of this year, I recieve stitchs at your clinic for a deep cut on the bottom of my left foot. While I waited in the examination room for the doctor, a nurse took my blood pressure and my temperature. Then she closly examined my foot. As I lay down to be examined, she lifted my foot onto the table. Much later, it occured to me that she had not washed her hands. I beleive she is the source of the Staph infection that I developed within days of that visit. By writing, I am hopeing to persuade all the staff members of your clinic to remember to wash thier hands.
>
> Sincerly, Jean Martinez

Writing for College Life

Assume you are taking a college health class. You have been assigned to write a report about the importance of hand washing. Edit the misspellings in the following draft. Use your own paper.

A recent survey of people in restrooms confirms that the spread of at least some infectious deseases could be curbbed if greater attention were spent on hand washing after going to the bathroom. Dirty hands can spread deseases such as colds and diarrhea and other intestinal problems. Experts say that the problem occurres across the country. According to research, only 60 percent of people useing the restrooms at Pennsylvania Station in New York City washed up. Other cityes have higher rates: 71 precent washed up at a casino in New Orleans, 69 precent at the Golden Gate Park in San Francisco, and 64 precent at a Braves game in Atlanta. Apparantly, women washed up more than men; however, men used soap more often than women did.

Writing for Working Life

Assume you are working as a health care provider for a hospital in a small community. You have been asked to research ways to improve the quality of care in your area. You are to present your recommendations in a PowerPoint presentation. Edit the misspellings in the following slide created for the presentation. Use your own paper.

Monitoring Hand Hygeine Monitoring

A hand hygeine audit determines health care worker (HCW) compliance with hand hygeine practice. Each department appointes a quality controler. The quality controler observes and records missed opportunites to carry out hand hygiene. Examples of hand hygeine opportunities include:

- Before and after touching a pateint
- After handleing body fluids
- After touching objects involved in the pateint's care
- After removeing gloves

A total of 10 observations should be performed each month. Completed forms will be submited to the Infection Control Department by the 5th of each month.

mywritinglab

WANT A BETTER GRADE? For more practice with spelling, go to www.mywritinglab.com > Punctuation and Mechanics > Improving Your Spelling.

PORTFOLIO

WHAT HAVE I LEARNED ABOUT IMPROVING SPELLING?

To test and track your understanding, answer the following questions.

1. Add .... to form the plural of regular nouns and regular verbs in the present tense for the singular third person.

2. Add .... to nouns that end with a consonant immediately before a final *o*.

3. Add .... to form the plural of nouns and to the third person present tense of verbs that end in *ch, sh, s, x,* or *z*.

4. When a word has one syllable, one consonant and one vowel, ... the final consonant before adding the suffix.

5. When words with more than one syllable end with a .... immediately before a consonant and the final syllable is stressed, double the final consonant.

6. Drop the *e* when the base word ends with a .... *e* and the suffix begins with a vowel.

7. Drop the *e* when a .... comes immediately before the silent *e*.

8. Keep the *e* when the word ends with a silent *e* and the suffix begins with a ....

9. When a .... appears before the final *y*, change the *y* to *i*.

10. When a .... appears before the final *y*, keep the *y*.

11. Keep the *y* when adding the suffix ....

12. Adding a .... to a word does not alter its spelling.

13. "*I* before *e* except after *c* or sounds like .... as in n*ei*ghbor or w*ei*gh."

14. **How will I use what I have learned about improving spelling?**
   In your notebook, discuss how you will apply to your own writing what you have learned about improving spelling.

15. **What do I still need to study about improving spelling?**
   In your notebook, discuss your ongoing study needs by describing how you will continue to improve your spelling.

Reading Selections

Reading Selections

Reading and writing are
mirror reflections of the
thinking process.

SECOND EDITION

Writing for Life

Paragraphs and Essays

D. J. Henry

- → What's the Point of Reading to Write?
- → Applying the Point: Effective Strategies for Responding to Reading Selections
- → Nineteen Reading Selections

Reading Selections

Reading and writing are mirror reflections of the thinking process.

The connection between reading and writing is a natural one. Effective writers are often avid readers. They read and study well-written pieces by other writers as a strategy to become a better writer. To begin your thinking about the connection between reading and writing, complete the following activity.

What's the Point of Reading to Write?

LEARNING OUTCOMES
READING AND WRITING

By reading, writers can learn new vocabulary, see how other writers organize ideas, add information to their bank of knowledge, and find ideas to write about.

Practice 1

USING READING STRATEGIES TO RESPOND TO WRITING SELECTIONS

Read the following excerpt from the selection, "Don't Call Me Middle Class: I'm a Professional" by Mark Penn (p. 644). Answer the questions that follow.

Not long ago, everyone in America wanted to be a member of the "middle class." In fact, as many as 53% of Americans described themselves that way to pollsters. 1

But with the information age and the rise of two-career incomes, being just middle class is a little old hat. The new aspiration for most Americans is to be a member of the new professional class. Rising numbers—as high as 64%—report that they consider themselves "professionals." The census shows a significant rise over the years, from 4% being professionals and skilled workers in 1910, to 36% today. The numbers have doubled since just 1980. 2

These new professionals, whose incomes were rising steadily until the financial crisis, have been at the heart of reshaping the country's economic and political life. Barack Obama more than any other president represents this shift and has uniquely appealed to these Americans. Everyone today wants to be a professional and most people believe they are. 3

1. What writing topics come to mind as you read these opening paragraphs?

2. What new words can you learn from reading this selection?

3. Based on these paragraphs, what kind of information do you need to define a concept?

What's the point of reading to write?

Applying the Point: Effective Strategies for Responding to Reading Selections

The fundamental connection between reading and writing is thinking: thinking about the meaning of what you read and what you say, and thinking about the connection between what you read and what you write. To fully realize the connection between reading and writing, you need to be an active and focused thinker. Two active thinking-reading-writing tasks are annotating a text and writing a summary. The following discussions take you through several steps that show you how to think, read, think again, reread, and then write—as a strategy to improve your writing.

How to Annotate a Text

Use your writing skills throughout the reading process to ensure that you are an active thinker. Annotate the text, take notes, and write journal entries, summaries, and critical responses to what you read. Annotating the text before and during reading is an active thinking-reading-writing strategy. You have been taught to ask questions as a prereading thinking task. When you read, annotate your text as you find the answers to your questions.

The word *annotate* suggests that you "take notes" on the page of the text. Writing notes in the margin of the page as you read focuses your attention and improves your concentration. Annotating also will improve your understanding of the writer's purpose and point. You can note questions or answers quickly where they occur, move on in your reading, and later return to those details for clarification. In addition to writing notes, you can underline, circle, or highlight important terms, definitions, examples, or other key ideas. After reading, a review of your annotations will make responding to the material easier and more efficient. The following techniques are often used to annotate a text. Use these as guidelines to develop your own system for annotating a text.

Annotation Techniques
• Underline the main idea once.
• Underline major supporting details twice.
• Circle or highlight key words or special terms.
• Place small question marks above unknown words.
• Signal steps in a process or list by using numbers.
• Point out important concepts with symbols such as a star or a check.
• Write recall questions in the margin where the answer is found.
• Write a statement for an implied idea.
• Write a summary.

Use your annotations to guide your written response to a piece of writing. The following selection has been annotated for you as an illustration.

The Death of President Lincoln

By Walt Whitman

April 16, '65.—I find in my notes of the time, this passage on the death of

Abraham Lincoln: He leaves for America's history and biography, so far, not only

its most dramatic reminiscence—[*memories*] he leaves, in my opinion, the <u>greatest</u>, best, most

characteristic, artistic, <u>moral personality</u>. Not but that he had faults, and show'd

them in the Presidency; but honesty, goodness, shrewdness, conscience, and (a new

virtue, unknown to other lands, and hardly yet really known here, but the founda-

tion and tie of all, as the future will grandly develop,) UNIONISM, [*keeping the United States undivided!*] in its truest and

amplest sense, form'd the hard-pan of his character. These he <u>seal'd with his life</u>.

The tragic splendor of his death, purging, illuminating all, throws round his form,

his head, an aureole [*?crown?*] that will remain and will grow brighter through time, while his-

tory lives, and love of country lasts. By many has this Union been help'd; but if one

name, one man, must be pick'd out, he, most of all, is the <u>conservator</u>, [*legal guardian or keeper*] of it, to the

future. He was assassinated—but the Union is not assassinated—*ca ira!* [*?French expression for "it will be fine"*] One falls,

and another falls. The soldier drops, sinks like a wave—but the ranks of the ocean

eternally press on. Death does its work, obliterates [*?*] literates [*?*] a hundred, a thousand—

President, general, captain, private—but <u>the Nation is immortal</u>.

—Whitman, Walt. *Prose Works*. Philadelphia: David McKay, 1892;
Bartleby.com, 2000. www.bartleby.com/229/. 12 August 2007.

> *Implied Main Idea:*
> *Lincoln preserved the*
> *UNION of the states;*
> *both he and the*
> *United States are*
> *immortal.*

Choose a selection from the nineteen reading selections. Annotate the text. After you have annotated the text, recall and record in your notebook what you remember about the selection.

Practice 2

How to Write a Summary

A summary includes only the most important points of a text. A summary is a restatement of the main idea and the major supporting details. The length of the summary should reflect the length of the passage you are trying to understand. For example, a paragraph might be summarized in a sentence or two; an article might be summarized in a paragraph, and a much longer document may be summarized in several paragraphs.

Writing a summary by relying on the annotations you make during reading is an excellent way to check your understanding of what you read. Always use the writer's name and the title of the text in your summary. The following summary is based on the annotations of the Walt Whitman piece about Abraham Lincoln's death.

> In his short note "The Death of President Lincoln," dated April 16, 1865, Walt Whitman honors the memory of the fallen president for his devotion to "Unionism," for being a faithful keeper of the future, for ensuring that it will be fine and that the "Nation is immortal."

Practice 3

Write a summary based on the annotations you made for the reading selection you used in Practice 2. Use your own paper.

A Reading Strategy for a Writer

As you read the nineteen selections included in this section, use the following reading strategy to make the connection between reading and writing. Read each selection three times. Read it once just to enjoy the writing. Then, reread the piece to annotate it for understanding. Then, read a third time to study the piece more closely to prepare for a written response. The following steps are a guide to how to get the most out of your reading.

Reading Like a Writer

Before Reading Write a journal entry about the topic, title, and vocabulary. What do you already know, believe, or feel about the topic? Skim the text to identify and look up new or difficult words.

During Reading Annotate the text. Underline or highlight key terms, definitions, and main ideas. Generate questions to guide your thinking as you read; these questions will help you recall information after you read. Look for the answers to these questions and annotate the text when you come across the answers. Many college textbooks provide comprehension questions after a section of information. Feel free to use these after reading questions to focus your attention as you read.

After Reading Think, discuss, and write about what you read. Each of the nineteen reading selections has four discussion questions about the writer's main idea, relevant details, logical order, and effective expression. These directed thinking activities are called "After Reading Discussion Questions: Meaning, Structure, and Expression." Your writing will improve as you learn how other writers handle these elements.

Discuss it Use your annotations to compare your views about a text with those of your classmates. Be open to ideas you had not considered. Add information to your notes. Discuss possible written responses.

Write about it Respond in writing to the text. Each of the nineteen reading selections has two activities called "Thinking Prompts to Move from Reading to Writing."

Nineteen Reading Selections

Description

Snow

JOHN HAINES

John Haines, born in Norfolk, Virginia, in 1924, spent more than twenty years homesteading in Alaska. He is also an award-winning author of more than ten collections of poetry and has published a book of essays entitled *Fables and Distances: New and Selected Essays* (1996). The following essay is an excerpt from *The Stars, the Snow, the Fire: Twenty-five Years in the Northern Wilderness*.

Before Reading Write a journal entry about your experience with the outdoors. Do you enjoy being outdoors? Why or why not? What is your favorite season?

To one who lives in the snow and watches it day by day, it is a book to be read. 1
The pages turn as the wind blows; the characters shift and the images formed by their combinations change in meaning, but the language remains the same. It is a shadow language, spoken by things that have gone by and will come again. The same text has been written there for thousands of years, though I was not here, and will not be here in winters to come, to read it. These seemingly random ways, these paths, these beds, these footprints, these hard, round pellets in the snow: they all have meaning. Dark things may be written there, news of other lives, their sorties and excursions, their terrors and deaths. The tiny feet of a shrew or a vole make a brief, erratic pattern across the snow, and here is a hole down which the animal goes. And now the track of an ermine comes this way, swift and searching, and he too goes down that white-shadow of a hole.

A wolverine, and the loping, toed-in track I followed uphill for two miles 2
one spring morning, until it finally dropped away into another watershed and I gave up following it. I wanted to see where he would go and what he would do. But he just went on, certain of where he was going, and nothing came of it for me to see but that sure and steady track in the snowcrust, and the sunlight strong in my eyes.

Snow blows across the highway before me as I walk—little, wavering trails 3
of it swept along like a people dispersed. The snow people—where are they

going? Some great danger must pursue them. They hurry and fall, the wind gives them a push, they get up and go on again.

I was walking home from Redmond Creek one morning late in January. On a divide between two watersheds I came upon the scene of a battle between a moose and three wolves. The story was written plainly in the snow at my feet. The wolves had come in from the west, following an old trail from the Salcha River, and had found the moose feeding in an open stretch of the overgrown road I was walking.

4

The sign was fresh, it must have happened the night before. The snow was torn up, with chunks of frozen moss and broken sticks scattered about; here and there, swatches of moose hair. A confusion of tracks in the trampled snow—the splayed, stabbing feet of the moose, the big, furred pads and spread toenails of the wolves.

5

I walked on, watching the snow. The moose was large and alone, almost certainly a bull. In one place he backed himself into a low, brush-hung bank to protect his rear. The wolves moved away from him—those moose feet are dangerous. The moose turned, ran on for fifty yards, and the fight began again. It became a running, broken flight that went on for nearly half a mile in the changing, rutted terrain, the red morning light coming across the hills from the sun low in the south. A pattern shifting and uncertain; the wolves relenting, running out into the brush in a wide circle, and closing again: another patch of moose hair in the trodden snow.

6

I felt that I knew those wolves. I had seen their tracks several times before during that winter, and once they had taken a marten from one of my traps. I believed them to be a female and two nearly grown pups. If I was right, she may have been teaching them how to hunt, and all that turmoil in the snow may have been the serious play of things that must kill to live. But I saw no blood sign that morning, and the moose seemed to have gotten the better of the fight. At the end of it he plunged away into thick alder brush. I saw his tracks, moving more slowly now, as he climbed through a low saddle, going north in the shallow, unbroken snow. The three wolves trotted east toward Banner Creek.

7

What might have been silence, an unwritten page, an absence, spoke to me as clearly as if I had been there to see it. I have imagined a man who might live as the coldest scholar on earth, who followed each clue in the snow, writing a book as he went. It would be the history of snow, the book of winter. A thousand-year text to be read by a people hunting these hills in a distant time. Who was here, and who has gone? What were their names? What did they kill and eat? Whom did they leave behind?

8

Vocabulary Before, during, and after reading the selection, annotate the text and write in your journal. Create a list of vocabulary words, along with their definitions. Give examples of their use from the selection you just read.

After Reading Discussion Questions: Meaning, Structure, and Expression

1. **Main Idea:** Work as a group to write a summary that answers the following questions: What purpose did John Haines have for writing this essay? Who is his intended audience? What is the main idea of the essay?
2. **Relevant Details:** Haines states "To one who lives in the snow and watches it day by day, it is a book to be read." How does the incident with the moose support this point?
3. **Logical Order:** Paragraphs 1 through 3 and paragraph 8 focus on the snow, and paragraphs 4 through 7 tell about the wolves and the moose. Would the essay be just as effective if it began with the incident about the wolves and the moose and then made the point about snow? Why or why not?

4. Effective Expression: According to a *Washington Post Book World* review, "Haines is a poet who crafts each sentence piece by piece . . . slowly, carefully, each word examined meticulously for rightness before being slid into place." Identify three examples of Haines's use of words that you find particularly effective. Discuss the reasons for your selections.

Thinking Prompts to Move from Reading to Writing

1. Haines uses vivid sensory details in his descriptions of the snow, the wolves, and the moose to create strong visual images in his reader's mind. No doubt, he wrote what he had closely observed through experience. Use vivid sensory details to describe a place or event in nature that you have experienced. Choose details that make a point about the scene such as *nature soothes in times of trouble* or *nature teaches harsh lessons*.

2. Haines effectively describes the nature or temperament of the wolves and the moose based on their physical traits and behaviors. Write a description of a pet or animal that reveals its personality, temperament, or nature.

Maya Lin's Design Submission to the Vietnam Memorial Competition

MAYA LIN

Born in 1959 in Athens, Ohio, Maya Lin, as a senior at Yale University, submitted the winning design in a national competition for the Vietnam Veterans Memorial that now stands in Washington, D.C. Lin, a Chinese American, designs spaces that make room for individuals within the landscape.

Before Reading Write a journal entry about the Vietnam Memorial. What do you know about it? Have you seen it? What was its impact on you? If you have not seen it, do you want to? Why or why not? Why are monuments and memorials important?

Walking through this park-like area, the memorial appears as a rift in the earth—a long, polished black stone wall, emerging from and receding into the earth. Approaching the memorial, the ground slopes gently downward, and the low walls emerging on either side, growing out of the earth, extend and converge at a point below and ahead. Walking into the grassy site contained by the walls of the memorial we can barely make out the carved names upon the memorial's walls. These names, seemingly infinite in number, convey the sense of overwhelming numbers, while unifying those individuals into a whole. For this memorial is meant not as a monument to the individual but rather, as a memorial to the men and women who died during this war, as a whole.

The memorial is composed not as an unchanging monument, but as a moving composition, to be understood as we move into and out of it; the passage itself is gradual, the descent to the origin slow, but it is at the origin that the meaning of the memorial is to be fully understood. At the intersection of these walls, on the right side, at the wall's top, is carved the date of the first death. It is followed by the names of those who have died in the war, in chronological order. These names continue on this wall, appearing to recede into the earth at the wall's end. The names resume on the left wall, as the wall emerges from the earth, continuing back to the origin, where the date of the last death is carved, at the bottom of this wall. Thus the war's beginning and end meet; the war is "complete," coming full circle, yet

1

2

broken by the earth that bounds the angle's open side, and contained within the earth itself. As we turn to leave, we see these walls stretching into the distance, directing us to the Washington Monument, to the left, and the Lincoln Memorial, to the right, thus bringing the Vietnam Memorial into an historical context. We the living are brought to a concrete realization of these deaths.

Brought to a sharp awareness of such a loss, it is up to each individual to resolve or come to terms with this loss. For death, is in the end a personal and private matter, and the area contained with this memorial is a quiet place, meant for personal reflection and private reckoning. The black granite walls, each two hundred feet long, and ten feet below ground at their lowest point (gradually ascending toward ground level) effectively act as a sound barrier, yet are of such a height and length so as not to appear threatening or enclosing. The actual area is wide and shallow, allowing for a sense of privacy, and the sunlight from the memorial's southern exposure along with the grassy park surrounding and within its walls, contribute to the serenity of the area. Thus this memorial is for those who have died, and for us to remember them.

3

The memorial's origin is located approximately at the center of the site; its legs each extending two hundred feet towards the Washington Monument and the Lincoln Memorial. The walls, contained on one side by the earth, are ten feet below ground at their point of origin, gradually lessening in height, until they finally recede totally into the earth, at their ends. The walls are to be made of hard, polished black granite, with the names to be carved in simple Trajan letter. The memorial's construction involves recontouring the area within the wall's boundaries, so as to provide for an easily accessible descent, but as much of the site as possible should be left untouched. The area should remain as a park, for all to enjoy.

4

Vocabulary Before, during, and after reading the selection, annotate the text and write in your journal. Create a list of vocabulary words, along with their definitions. Give examples of their use from the selection you just read.

After Reading Discussion Questions: Meaning, Structure, and Expression

1. **Main Idea:** Work as a group to write a summary that answers the following questions: What purpose did Maya Lin have for writing this essay? Who is her intended audience? What is the main idea of the essay?
2. **Relevant Details:** Lin writes, "For death, is in the end a personal and private matter, and the area contained with this memorial is a quiet place, meant for personal reflection and private reckoning." Based on the details in her description, how does the memorial represent this belief?
3. **Logical Order:** As Lin gives her physical description of the memorial, she explains the significance of each detail. Do her explanations help create a mental image of the memorial? Would it have been just as effective to give an uninterrupted physical description and then explain the purpose of each detail in a separate section? Why or why not?
4. **Effective Expression:** Of the 1,421 essays submitted in the design competition for the Vietnam Memorial, this essay won. In what ways did Lin use effective expression to communicate her vision? Identify three effective expressions in the essay. Discuss the reasons for your selections.

Thinking Prompts to Move from Reading to Writing

1. Just as the memorials erected in Washington, D.C. represent people and events of historical significance, many communities build memorials to honor local individuals, groups of people, or events. Describe such a memorial in your community. Use your description to convey the significance of the memorial.
2. Identify a person, place, or event that is worthy of a memorial. Design a memorial and write an essay that describes your design and the significance of the honor.

Narration

New Directions

MAYA ANGELOU

An acclaimed poet, award-winning writer, activist, performer, director, and teacher, Maya Angelou was born on April 4, 1928, in St. Louis and raised in Stamps, Arkansas. Dr. Angelou has authored twelve bestselling books including *I Know Why the Caged Bird Sings* and her current bestseller *A Song Flung Up to Heaven.* In January 1993, she became only the second poet in U.S. history to have the honor of writing and reciting her original work at a Presidential Inauguration. Angelou is hailed as one of the great voices of contemporary literature. The following essay is an excerpt from her book *Wouldn't Take Nothing for My Journey Now* (1993).

Before Reading   Write a journal entry about making a life change. Have you ever made a significant change in your life? What were the advantages or disadvantages of making the change? Was it easy? If life has not changed for you, what would you change about your life if you could?

In 1903 the late Mrs. Annie Johnson of Arkansas found herself with two toddling sons, very little money, a slight ability to read and add simple numbers. To this picture add a disastrous marriage and the burdensome fact that Mrs. Johnson was a Negro.   1

When she told her husband, Mr. William Johnson, of her dissatisfaction with their marriage, he conceded that he too found it to be less than he expected and had been secretly hoping to leave and study religion. He added that he thought God was calling him not only to preach but to do so in Enid, Oklahoma. He did not tell her that he knew a minister in Enid with whom he could study and who had a friendly, unmarried daughter. They parted amicably, Annie keeping the one-room house and William taking most of the cash to carry himself to Oklahoma.   2

Annie, over six feet tall, big-boned, decided that she would not go to work as a domestic and leave her "precious babes" to anyone else's care. There was no possibility of being hired at the town's cotton gin or lumber mill, but maybe there was a way to make the two factories work for her. In her words, "I looked up the road I was going and back the way I come, and since I wasn't satisfied, I decided to step off the road and cut me a new path." She told herself that she wasn't a fancy cook but that she could "mix groceries well enough to scare hunger away from a starving man."   3

She made her plans meticulously and in secret. One early evening to see if she was ready, she placed stones in two five gallon pails and carried them three miles to the cotton gin. She rested a little, and then, discarding some rocks, she walked in the darkness to the saw mill five miles farther along the dirt road. On her way back to her little house and her babies, she dumped the remaining rocks along the path.   4

That same night she worked into the early hours boiling chicken and frying ham. She made dough and filled the rolled-out pastry with meat. At last she went to sleep. 5

The next morning she left her house carrying the meat pies, lard, an iron brazier, and coals for a fire. Just before lunch she appeared in an empty lot behind the cotton gin. As the dinner noon bell rang, she dropped the savors into boiling fat, and the aroma rose and floated over to the workers who spilled out of the gin, covered with white lint, looking like specters. 6

Most workers had brought their lunches of pinto beans and biscuits or crackers, onions and cans of sardines, but they were tempted by the hot meat pies which Annie ladled out of the fat. She wrapped them in newspapers, which soaked up the grease, and offered them for sale at a nickel each. Although business was slow, those first days Annie was determined. She balanced her appearances between the two hours of activity. 7

So, on Monday if she offered hot fresh pies at the cotton gin and sold the remaining cooled-down pies at the lumber mill for three cents, then on Tuesday she went first to the lumber mill presenting fresh, just-cooked pies as the lumbermen covered in sawdust emerged from the mill. 8

For the next few years, on balmy spring days, blistering summer noons, and cold, wet, and wintry middays, Annie never disappointed her customers, who could count on seeing the tall, brown-skin woman bent over her brazier, carefully turning the meat pies. When she felt certain that the workers had become dependent on her, she built a stall between the two hives of industry and let the men run to her for their lunchtime provisions. 9

She had indeed stepped from the road which seemed to have been chosen for her and cut herself a brand-new path. In years that stall became a store where customers could buy cheese, meal, syrup, cookies, candy, writing tablets, pickles, canned goods, fresh fruit, soft drinks, coal, oil, and leather soles for worn-out shoes. 10

Each of us has the right and the responsibility to assess the roads which lie ahead, and those over which we have traveled, and if the future road looms ominous or unpromising, and the roads back uninviting, then we need to gather our resolve and, carrying only the necessary baggage, step off that road into another direction. If the new choice is also unpalatable, without embarrassment, we must be ready to change that as well. 11

Vocabulary Before, during, and after reading the selection, annotate the text and write in your journal. Create a list of vocabulary words, along with their definitions. Give examples of their use from the selection you just read.

After Reading Discussion Questions: Meaning, Structure, and Expression

1. **Main Idea:** Work as a group to write a summary that answers the following questions: What purpose did Maya Angelou have for writing this piece? Who is her intended audience? What is the main idea of the essay? What is the significance of the title of the book from which the selection was taken? How does this piece reflect that title?

2. **Relevant Details:** Angelou captures the reality of daily life in 1903 for Annie Johnson and her community. List the details that paint this realistic picture; consider organizing your list based on sensory details. Describe the society or type of community in which Johnson lived. Are any of the details of this story similar to or different from today's society or parts of your community? In what ways?

3. **Logical Order:** Angelou ends her essay with a paragraph that explains the lesson she wants her reader to learn from Johnson's life. What is the impact of this paragraph on you as a reader? Is the concluding paragraph necessary? Why or why

not? Why do you think Angelou waits to the end of the essay to explain her point? Would the essay be as effective if she began by stating this point? Why or why not?

4. **Effective Expression:** A key statement in the essay is made by Annie Johnson, "I looked up the road I was going and back the way I come, and since I wasn't satisfied, I decided to step off the road and cut me a new path." Explain the meaning of the metaphors "road" and "path." What "road" was Johnson on? What "path" did she cut for herself? Are these metaphors effective? Why or why not?

Thinking Prompts to Move from Reading to Writing

1. Think of an important lesson you have learned, or a truth about life that you think everyone needs to know. Write a narrative essay that illustrates this lesson or important truth about life.

2. Have you or someone you know made a decision to make a major life change? Was the change positive or negative? Was the change difficult to make? In the end, was the change worth the effort? Write a narrative that illustrates the significance of making a decision to change.

Confessions
AMY TAN

Born in 1952 to immigrant parents from China, Amy Tan is the award-winning author of several novels, including her widely popular and critically acclaimed novel *The Joy Luck Club*. Tragically, Tan's father and oldest brother both died of brain tumors within a year of each other, and Tan was in constant conflict with her mother. Tan's work has been translated into 35 languages, including Spanish, French, Chinese, Arabic, and Hebrew. The following selection is an excerpt from her autobiographical collection of essays *The Opposite of Fate*.

Before Reading Write a journal entry about the conflicts within a family. Have you ever had a terrible fight with a family member? How did it make you feel? Do mothers and daughters or fathers and sons experience a particular kind of conflict?

My mother's thoughts reach back like the winter tide, exposing the wreckage of a former shore. Often she's mired in 1967, 1968, the years my older brother and my father died. 1

1968 was also the year she took me and my little brother—Didi—across the Atlantic to Switzerland, a place so preposterously different that she knew she had to give up grieving simply to survive. That year, she remembers, she was very, very sad. I too remember. I was sixteen then, and I recall a late-night hour when my mother and I were arguing in the chalet, that tinderbox of emotion where we lived. 2

She had pushed me into the small bedroom we shared, and as she slapped me about the head, I backed into a corner, by a window that looked out on the lake, the Alps, the beautiful outside world. My mother was furious because I had a boyfriend. She was shouting that he was a drug addict, a bad man who would use me for sex and throw me away like leftover garbage. 3

"Stop seeing him!" she ordered. 4

I shook my head. The more she beat me, the more implacable I became, and this in turn fueled her outrage. 5

"You didn't love you daddy or Peter! When they die you not even sad." 6

I kept my face to the window, unmoved. What does she know about sad? 7

She sobbed and beat her chest. "I rather kill myself before see you destroy you life!" 8

Suicide. How many times had she threatened that before? 9

"I wish you the one die! Not Peter, not Daddy." 10

She had just confirmed what I had always suspected. Now she flew at me with her fists. 11

"I rather kill you! I rather see you die!" 12

And then, perhaps horrified by what she had just said, she fled the room. Thank God that was over. I wished I had a cigarette to smoke. Suddenly she was back. She slammed the door shut, latched it, then locked it with a key. I saw the flash of a meat cleaver just before she pushed me to the wall and brought the blade's edge to within an inch of my throat. Her eyes were like a wild animal's, shiny, fixated on the kill. In an excited voice she said, "First, I kill you. Then Didi and me, our whole family destroy!" She smiled, her chest heaving. "Why you don't cry?" She pressed the blade closer and I could feel her breath gusting. 13

Was she bluffing? If she did kill me, so what? Who would care? While she rambled, a voice within me was whimpering, "This is sad, this is so sad." 14

For ten minutes, fifteen, longer, I straddled these two thoughts—that it didn't matter if I died, that it would be eternally sad if I did—until all at once I felt a snap, then a rush of hope into a vacuum, and I was crying, I was babbling my confession: "I want to live. I want to live." 15

For twenty-five years I forgot that day, and when the memory of what happened surfaced unexpectedly at a writers' workshop in which we recalled our worst moments, I was shaking, wondering to myself, Did she really mean to kill me? If I had not pleaded with her, would she have pushed down on the cleaver and ended my life? 16

I wanted to go to my mother and ask. Yet I couldn't, not until much later, when she became forgetful and I learned she had Alzheimer's disease. I knew that if I didn't ask her certain questions now, I would never know the real answers. 17

So I asked. 18

"Angry? Slap you?" she said, and laughed. "No, no, *no*. You always good girl, never even need to spank, not even one time." 19

How wonderful to hear her say what was never true, yet now would be forever so. 20

Vocabulary Before, during, and after reading the selection, annotate the text and write in your journal. Create a list of vocabulary words, along with their definitions. Give examples of their use from the selection you just read.

After Reading Discussion Questions: Meaning, Structure, and Expression

1. **Main Idea:** Work as a group to write a summary that answers the following questions: What purpose did Amy Tan have for writing this essay? Who is her intended audience? What is the main idea of the essay? What is the significance of the title?

2. **Relevant Details:** Tan often implies a main idea through the use of well-chosen details that draw a vivid picture. Paragraph 13 describes a shocking scene. What point is Tan making with these details? How do these details fulfill her purpose and support her main idea? Why would Tan reveal so much personal and painful information?

3. **Logical Order:** Tan sets her narrative up as a flashback to an unpleasant memory. Later, in paragraph 16, she tells us she remembered this incident in a writing workshop 25 years after it occurred. Why do you think she waited to tell us when or how she

remembered the incident? Would the essay be as effective if she had begun the narrative from the moment she recalled the incident in the workshop? Why or why not?

4. **Effective Expression:** Tan begins the essay with a simile, an indirect comparison between two things using *like* or *as*: "My mother's thoughts reach back like the winter tide, exposing the wreckage of a former shore." How are her mother's thoughts similar to the *winter tide*? To what do *wreckage* and *former shore* refer?

Thinking Prompts to Move from Reading to Writing

1. The conflict between parent and child is age-old and universal. In her essay, Tan shows us how this timeless conflict affected her relationship with her mother. Write a narrative about a conflict between a parent and child that shows the impact of the conflict.

2. "Confessions" is a painful admission of a "worst moment" in both Amy Tan's life and her mother's life. Her confession reveals personal and potentially embarrassing information. Often, we gain wisdom and understanding through conflict and suffering. However, not every writer feels comfortable making a point through a personal confession. Find a story in the news about a "worst moment" in someone's life. Write a narrative that makes a point about the incident.

Process

How to Write a Personal Letter

GARRISON KEILLOR

Born in Anoka, Minnesota, in 1942, Garrison Keillor is the host and writer of *A Prairie Home Companion* and *The Writer's Almanac* heard on public radio stations across the country and the author of more than a dozen books, including *Lake Wobegon Days, The Book of Guys, Love Me, Homegrown Democrat,* and *Pontoon: A Novel of Lake Wobegon.*

Before Reading   Write a journal entry about letter writing. Do you or does anyone you know write letters? Why do you think letter writing is declining? How is writing a personal letter different from other kinds of writing?

We shy people need to write a letter now and then, or else we'll dry up and blow away. It's true. And I speak as one who loves to reach for the phone, dial the number, and talk. The telephone is to shyness what Hawaii is to February; it's a way out of the woods. *And yet* a letter is better.   1

Such a sweet gift—a piece of handmade writing, in an envelope that is not a bill, sitting in our friend's path when she trudges home from a long day spent among savages and wahoos, a day our words will help repair. They don't need to be immortal, just sincere. She can read them twice and again tomorrow: "You're someone I care about, Corinne, and think of often, and every time I do, you make me smile."   2

We need to write; otherwise, nobody will know who we are. They will have only a vague impression of us as "A Nice Person" because, frankly, we don't shine at conversation, we lack the confidence to thrust our faces forward and say, "Hi, I'm Heather Hooten; let me tell you about my week." Mostly we say "Uh-huh" and "Oh really." People smile and look over our shoulder, looking for someone else to meet.   3

So a shy person sits down and writes a letter. To be known by another person—to meet and talk freely on the page—to be close despite distance. To escape from anonymity and be our own sweet selves and express the music of our souls. The same thing that moves a giant rock star to sing his heart out in front of 123,000 people moves us to take ballpoint in hand and write a few lines to our dear Aunt Eleanor. *We want to be known.* We want her to know that we have fallen in love, that we have quit our job, that we're moving to New York, and we want to say a few things that might not get said in casual conversation: "Thank you for what you've meant to me. I am very happy right now."   4

The first step in writing letters is to get over the guilt of *not* writing. You don't "owe" anybody a letter. Letters are a gift. The burning shame you feel when you see unanswered mail makes it harder to pick up a pen and makes for a cheerless letter when you finally do. "I feel bad about not writing, but I've been so busy," etc. Skip this. Few letters are obligatory and they   5 are "Thanks for the wonderful gift" and "I am terribly sorry to hear about George's death" and "Yes, you're welcome to stay with us next month." Write these promptly if you want to keep your friends. Don't worry about other letters, except love letters, of course. When your true love writes, "Dear Light of My Life, Joy of My Heart, O Lovely Pulsating Core of My Sensate Life," some response is called for.

Some of the best letters are tossed off in a burst of inspiration, so keep your writing stuff in one place where you can sit down for a few minutes, and—"Dear Roy, I am in the middle of an essay but thought I'd drop you a line. Hi to your sweetie too"—dash off a note to a pal. Envelopes, stamps, address book, everything in a drawer so you can write fast when the pen is hot. A blank white 8" × 11" sheet can look as big as Montana if the pen's not so hot; try a smaller page and write boldly. Get a pen that makes a sensuous line, get a comfortable typewriter, a friendly word processor—whichever feels easy to the hand.

Sit for a few minutes with the blank sheet of paper in front of you, and meditate on the person you will write to; let your friend come to mind until you can almost see him or her in the room with you. Remember the last time you saw each other and how your friend looked and what you said and what perhaps was unsaid between you, and when your friend becomes real to you, start to write. Write the salutation, "Dear You," and take a deep breath and plunge in. A simple declarative sentence will do, followed by another and another. Talk about what you're doing and tell it like you were talking to us. Don't think about grammar, don't think about style, don't try to write dramatically, just give us your news. Where did you go, who did you see, what did they say, what do you think?

If you don't know where to begin, start with the present: "I'm sitting at the kitchen table on a rainy Saturday morning. Everyone is gone, and the house is quiet." Let your description of the present moment lead to something else; let the letter drift gently along. The toughest letter to crank out is one that is meant to impress, as we all know from writing job applications; if it's hard work to write a letter to a friend, maybe you're trying too hard to be terrific. A letter is only a report to someone who already likes you for reasons other than your brilliance. Take it easy.

Don't worry about form. It's not a term paper. When you come to the end of one episode, just start a new paragraph. You can go from a few lines about the sad state of pro football to the fight with your mother to your cat's urinary tract infection to a few thoughts on personal indebtedness and on to the kitchen sink and what's in it. The more you write, the easier it gets, and when you have a true friend to write to, a *compadre*, a soul sibling, then it's like driving a car; you just press on the gas.

Don't tear up the page and start over when you write a bad line; try to write your way out of it. Make mistakes and plunge on. Let the letter cook along and let yourself be bold. Outrage, confusion, love—whatever is in your mind, let it find a way to the page. Writing is a means of discovery, always, and when you come to the end and write "Yours ever" or "Hugs and Kisses," you'll know something that you didn't when you wrote "Dear Pal."

Probably your friend will put your letter away, and it'll be read again a few years from now, and it will improve with age. And forty years from now, your friend's grandkids will dig it out of the attic and read it, a sweet and precious relic that gives them a sudden clear glimpse of you and her and the world we old-timers knew. Your simple lines about where you went, who you saw, what they said, will speak to those children, and they will feel in their hearts the humanity of our times.

You can't pick up a phone and call the future and tell them about our times. You have to pick up a piece of paper.

Vocabulary Before, during, and after reading the selection, annotate the text and write in your journal. Create a list of vocabulary words, along with their definitions. Give examples of their use from the selection you just read.

After Reading Discussion Questions: Meaning, Structure, and Expression

1. **Main Idea:** Work as a group to write a summary that answers the following questions: What purpose did Garrison Keillor have for writing this essay? Who is his intended audience? What is the main idea of the essay?

2. **Relevant Details:** Keillor's advice about how to write a personal letter does not begin until the fifth paragraph. How are the details in the first four paragraphs related to his main point? Would the essay be as effective without these paragraphs? Why or why not?

3. **Logical Order:** Keillor describes a step-by-step process for writing a personal letter. Map out the steps in the order he suggests them. Do you agree with his advice? Would you change the order of any of the steps? Would you add or delete any steps? Why or why not?

4. **Effective Expression:** Keillor is often praised for his light-hearted, easy-to-read style. Find three expressions that are amusing in tone. Explain the reasons for your selections.

Thinking Prompts to Move from Reading to Writing

1. This essay offers clear instructions about how to write a letter based on Keillor's expertise in and understanding of the writing process. Think of a task or process that you understand or have mastered through experience. Write an essay that explains the significance of the task or process and the steps necessary to successfully accomplish it.

2. Keillor advises in paragraph 9, "Don't worry about form. It's not a term paper." His statement indicates differences among writing a personal letter for everyday life, writing a term paper for college life, and writing letters and reports for working life. How might the writing process change for each of these situations? Write an essay that describes how to write a term paper or a letter of application for a job. Use Keillor's essay as a model.

How to Twitter
JULIA ANGWIN

Julia Angwin is a mathematics major who fell in love with journalism after writing for her campus newspaper, *The Chicago Maroon*. Angwin became an award-winning journalist covering technology, media, copyright issues, and corporate corruption. She currently serves as technology editor and columnist for the *Wall Street Journal*. She has also authored the book *Stealing MySpace*, about the "swift rise and deep cultural impact" of the social networking site MySpace.

Before Reading Write a journal entry about your experiences with electronic communication. Do you e-mail, text, or blog? Do you use Facebook, MySpace, or Twitter? Which do you prefer and why?

When I first joined Twitter, I felt like I was in a noisy bar where everyone was shouting and nobody was listening. 1

Soon, I began to decode its many mysteries: how to find a flock of followers, how to talk to them in a medium that blasts to lots of people at once and how to be witty in very tiny doses. 2

Twitter is a mass text-messaging service that allows you to send short 140-character updates—or "tweets"—to a bunch of people at once. They are your "followers." It was designed to be read on a cellphone, though many people read it online, too. 3

Suddenly a lot of non-tweeters are starting to feel left out. On "The Daily Show" this week, host Jon Stewart reported on Twitter with a wink (or was it a twink?) at the narcissism of the personal broadcasting system. It has a world-wide audience of six million unique visitors a month, up from 1.2 million a year ago, according to ComScore Media Metrix. 4

But I have to admit I didn't understand the appeal of Twitter when I joined, at the prodding of friends, in November. One answer that explains its popularity: It's not about chatting with your friends—it's about promoting yourself. 5

My name was available, so I set up a profile at twitter.com/JuliaAngwin. On Twitter, however, you do not exist without followers, who subscribe to receive your messages. So I set out to follow some people in the hope that they would follow me. 6

I had to learn the crucial distinction between a "follower" and a "friend." On Facebook, if I'm your friend, you're my friend, and we can read all about each other. Relationships on Twitter are not reciprocal: People you follow do not have to follow you or give you permission to follow them. You just sign up and start following them. It's a bit like stalking. Heather Gold, a comedian and Twitter devotee, points out that for all its flaws, the term follower "is more honest than friend." 7

At first, I was the loneliest of social creatures—a leader without followers. I tried searching for my actual real-world friends using Twitter's "Find People" function, but it was down the day I joined. (Twitter is growing so fast that short outages are not unusual.) 8

So I asked a few colleagues for their Twitter addresses and began following them. I also searched their public lists of followers and who they followed. 9

Eventually, I cobbled together a mix of people I could follow: media colleagues, friends, bloggers and various people who are known as great "tweeters," such as the chief executive of online retailer Zappos.com, Tony Hsieh, who has written quite movingly on his blog about how Twitter has changed his life. He says that being forced to bear witness to his life in 140-character bursts of prose has made him more grateful for the good moments and more amused by the bad moments. 10

I discovered that a better way to get followers was to tweet. Every time I tweeted, I got a surge of followers. 11

Where were they coming from? The likely answer illuminates Twitter's greatest strength: It's easily searchable. 12

During the terrorist attacks in Mumbai in November, people scoured Twitter for postings from eye witnesses. When US Airways Flight 1549 landed in the Hudson River, one of the first pictures was posted as a link on Twitter. 13

Similar news items may have appeared on other social networks, but they were not as easy to discover. On Facebook, most people's information is viewable only by their approved friends. MySpace profile pages are searchable, but not its blogs or status updates, and it is hard to find anyone you know because most people obscure their real names. 14

Now, a gaggle of unknown followers were finding something in my tweets—and following me! 15

I quickly found that my general musings about life such as—"thank god they have wifi on jury duty"—fell like a dead weight, eliciting no response. A larger problem was that it was 16 hard to tweet when I didn't know whom I was tweeting to. Unlike Facebook, where I know each and every one of my 287 friends, I have never met or heard of the majority of the 221 people following me on Twitter.

To understand the medium, I studied others' tweets. Former *Time* magazine writer Ana Marie Cox's tweets are a poetic mix of moments like this: "Afternoon walk. Beautiful day, I now see."

17

And she included wry political commentary. Forwarding a tweet from Sen. John McCain during the presidential election, she wrote: "See, if only he had sent this a year earlier . . . RT@senjohnmccain 'YEs!! I am twittering on my blackberry but not without a little help!' "

18

I spent a surprising amount of time trying out tweets in my head before tweeting. I aimed to tweet once a day, but often came up short. I found it difficult to fit in both news and opinion. Without a point of view, though, my updates were pretty boring. So, for instance, I changed "eating strawberries during a snowstorm." Into "eating strawberries during a snowstorm. not carbon efficient but lovely."

19

Another trick: including a short link to a Web site, or my own stories (using link-shrinking services like TinyURL), let me use most of the rest of the 140 characters to compose a thought.

20

I found a good way to get followers was to get "retweeted"—meaning that someone would pick up my tweet and send it to their followers preceded by the code "RT @juliaangwin." When I tweeted about being interviewed by Wired.com recently, two colleagues retweeted my tweet. Seven of their followers then retweeted it. As a result, I gained 22 new followers.

21

People also seem eager to answer questions on Twitter. I came across 25-year-old Justin Rockwell, who was spending so much time answering people's tweets about how to build better Web pages that he says he decided to try it as a business. He now makes about $350 a week scouring Twitter for people tweeting about their problems building Web pages. Using the Twitter ID ThatCSSGuy (which refers to a Web program called CSS), he offers to help solve their problems and asks for a tip in return.

22

But I found it difficult to acknowledge answers I received on Twitter. Twitter's reply features felt clumsy. The easiest way to reply to a tweet is to hit the @reply icon which broadcasts your answer to all your followers, essentially Twitter's equivalent of the "reply all" email function. As a result, I often didn't reply because I didn't want to spam everyone with a bunch of "thanks for your feedback" messages. So I was silent—which made me feel even more antisocial.

23

Twitter wasn't designed for these kinds of social interaction or conversations. As Twitter co-founder Biz Stone told me, "Twitter is fundamentally a broadcast system." The messaging features were add-ons.

24

Twitter is useful precisely because so many people are talking about different things at once. When he was president of Sling Media, for instance, Jason Hirschhorn constantly monitored the keyword "sling" on Twitter. "It's an up-to-the minute temperature of what people are saying about your brand," he said. He left the consumer electronics company last month.

25

There are more than 2,000 Twitter applications made by other people to help you sort through all the tweets. One of my favorites is Twitturly.com, which tracks the most popular URLs (or Web links) being shared across Twitter. Others such as Tweetdeck and Twhirl, help you manage and organize your tweets.

26

Still, the beauty of Twitter is that you don't have to commit to it; no one expects you to read all the tweets rolling in. As a result, Twitter makes for very good people watching—even if you don't go home with anyone you meet there.

27

Vocabulary Before, during, and after reading the selection, annotate the text and write in your journal. Create a list of vocabulary words, along with their definitions. Give examples of their use from the selection you just read.

After Reading Discussion Questions: Meaning, Structure, and Expression

1. **Main Idea:** Work as a group to write a summary that answers the following questions: What purpose did Julia Angwin have for writing this essay? Who is the intended audience? What is the main idea of the essay?
2. **Relevant Details:** Angwin offers details that explain some of the difficulties she faced as she started to "tweet." Why does she offer these details? Would readers be more likely to use Twitter if she hadn't talked about the barriers she faced? Angwin also offers helpful hints about how to use Twitter. Are these hints distracting or are they effective pieces of information? Why?
3. **Logical Order:** Angwin describes the steps she took to join and use Twitter. Based on the details in her essay, create an outline guide that anyone could follow to join and use Twitter.
4. **Effective Expression:** Based on Angwin's choice of words, how would you describe the tone of this essay? Is the tone objective, humorous, critical, or supportive, or does it communicate some other attitude about Twitter? How does the tone of the essay help Angwin make her point? Explain your reasoning.

Thinking Prompts to Move from Reading to Writing

1. According to the passage, messages on Twitter are "140-character updates—or 'tweets'". Critics of these "tweets" complain that this type of writing hurts the development of good writing skills. Supporters disagree and argue that using Twitter will actually improve writing skills. What do you think? Explain how the process of tweeting can improve or harm a person's writing style.
2. Compare or contrast "How to Write a Personal Letter" with "How to Twitter." Choose an audience and writing situation such as the following: an academic paper for a communication class, a letter to the editor of a local newspaper, an article for a magazine or newspaper's online community forum.

Illustration

Don't Call Me a Hot Tamale

JUDITH ORTIZ COFER

Born in 1952 in Puerto Rico and raised in Paterson, New Jersey, Judith Ortiz Cofer is an acclaimed poet, novelist, and essayist. Her writings explore the experiences of being a minority as a Hispanic woman. She is currently the Regents' and Franklin Professor of English and Creative Writing at the University of Georgia.

Before Reading Write a journal entry about your experiences with stereotypes. Have you ever been stereotyped? Describe the incident. What are some common stereotypes in our culture? How are these stereotypes harmful?

On a bus to London from Oxford University, where I was earning some graduate credits one summer, a young man, obviously fresh from a pub, approached my seat. With both hands over his heart, he went down on his knees in the aisle and broke into an Irish tenor's rendition of "Maria" from *West Side Story*. I was not amused. "Maria" had followed me to London, reminding me of a prime fact of my life: You can leave the island of Puerto Rico, master the English language, and travel as far as you can, but if you're a Latina, especially one who so clearly belongs to Rita Moreno's gene pool, the island travels with you. 1

Growing up in New Jersey and wanting most of all to belong, I lived in two completely different worlds. My parents designed our life as a microcosm of their *casas* on the island—we spoke in Spanish, ate Puerto Rican food bought at the *bodega,* and practiced strict Catholicism complete with Sunday mass in Spanish. 2

I was kept under tight surveillance by my parents, since my virtue and modesty were, by their cultural equation, the same as their honor. As teenagers, my friends and I were lectured constantly on how to behave as proper *señoritas.* But it was a conflicting message we received, since our Puerto Rican mothers also encouraged us to look and act like women by dressing us in clothes our Anglo schoolmates and their mothers found too "mature" and flashy. I often felt humiliated when I appeared at an American friend's birthday party wearing a dress more suitable for a semiformal. At Puerto Rican festivities, neither the music nor the colors we wore could be too loud. 3

I remember Career Day in high school, when our teachers told us to come dressed as if for a job interview. That morning, I agonized in front of my closet, trying to figure out what a "career girl" would wear, because the only model I had was Marlo Thomas on TV. To me and my Puerto Rican girlfriends, dressing up meant wearing our mother's ornate jewelry and clothing. 4

At school that day, the teachers assailed us for wearing "everything at once"—meaning too much jewelry and too many accessories. And it was painfully obvious that the other students 5 in their tailored skirts and silk blouses thought we were hopeless and vulgar. The way they looked at us was a taste of the cultural clash that awaited us in the real world, where prospective employers and men on the street would often misinterpret our tight skirts and bright colors as a come-on.

It is custom, not chromosomes, that leads us to choose scarlet over pale pink. Our mothers had grown up on a tropical island where the natural environment was a riot of primary colors, where showing your skin was one way to keep cool as well as to look sexy. On the island, women felt freer to dress and move provocatively since they were protected by the traditions and laws of a Spanish/Catholic system of morality and machismo, the main rule of which was: *You may look at my sister, but if you touch her I will kill you.* The extended family and church structure provided them with a circle of safety on the island; if a man "wronged" a girl, everyone would close in to save her family honor.   6

Off-island, signals often get mixed. When a Puerto Rican girl who is dressed in her idea of what is attractive meets a man from the mainstream culture who has been trained to react to certain types of clothing as a sexual signal, a clash is likely to take place. She is seen as a Hot Tamale, a sexual firebrand. I learned this lesson at my first formal dance when my date leaned over and painfully planted a sloppy, overeager kiss on my mouth. When I didn't respond with sufficient passion, he said in a resentful tone: "I thought you Latin girls were supposed to mature early." It was only the first time I would feel like a fruit or vegetable—I was supposed to *ripen,* not just grow into womanhood like other girls.   7

These stereotypes, though rarer, still surface in my life. I recently stayed at a classy metropolitan hotel. After having dinner with a friend, I was returning to my room when a middle-aged man in a tuxedo stepped directly into my path. With his champagne glass extended toward me, he exclaimed, "Evita!"   8

Blocking my way, he bellowed the song "Don't Cry for Me, Argentina." Playing to the gathering crowd, he began to sing loudly a ditty to the tune of "La Bamba"—except the lyrics were about a girl named Maria whose exploits all rhymed with her name and gonorrhea.   9

I knew that this same man—probably a corporate executive, even worldly by most standards—would never have regaled a white woman with a dirty song in public. But to him, I was just a character in his universe of "others," all cartoons.   10

Still, I am one of the lucky ones. There are thousands of Latinas without the privilege of the education that my parents gave me. For them every day is a struggle against the misconceptions perpetuated by the myth of the Latina as whore, domestic worker or criminal.   11

Rather than fight these pervasive stereotypes, I try to replace them with a more interesting set of realities. I travel around the U.S. reading from my books of poetry and my novel. With the stories I tell, the dreams and fears I examine in my work, I try to get my audience past the particulars of my skin color, my accent or my clothes.   12

I once wrote a poem in which I called Latinas "God's brown daughters." It is really a prayer, of sorts, for communication and respect. In it, Latin women pray "in Spanish to an Anglo God / with a Jewish heritage," and they are "fervently hoping / that if not omnipotent, / at least He be bilingual."   13

Vocabulary

Before, during, and after reading the selection, annotate the text and write in your journal. Create a list of vocabulary words, along with their definitions. Give examples of their use from the selection you just read.

After Reading Discussion Questions: Meaning, Structure, and Expression

1. **Main Idea:** Work as a group to write a summary that answers the following questions: What purpose did Judith Ortiz Cofer have for writing this essay? Who is her intended audience? What is the main idea of the essay? What is the significance of the title?

2. **Relevant Details:** Cofer relies mostly on personal experience to make her point about stereotypes based on race or gender. Does she provide enough details to make her point convincingly? Would the use of facts or expert opinions strengthen her point? Why or why not?

3. **Logical Order:** Cofer opens her essay with an example from her personal life. Is this an effective opening for the essay? Why or why not? Compare the introduction of the essay to the conclusion. How does the conclusion relate to the introduction? Is this an effective conclusion? Why or why not? What other ways could Cofer have opened or closed her essay?

4. **Effective Expression:** Based on Judith Ortiz Cofer's choice of words, how would you describe the tone of this essay? Is it angry, embarrassed, disappointed, confrontational, or candid, or does it communicate some other attitude about stereotypes? Identify three expressions that illustrate the tone of the piece. Explain the reasons for your selections.

Thinking Prompts to Move from Reading to Writing

1. Cofer makes a connection between culture and fashion. According to her description, Hispanic fashion for women is "flashy," "mature," and "sexy" with "ornate jewelry" and "tight skirts and bright colors." Write an essay in which you illustrate how fashion represents a particular culture. For example, illustrate fashion in the Hip-Hop culture.

2. Cofer's essay illustrates the stereotypes she faces as a Hispanic woman. Identify and describe a stereotype that you or someone you know has encountered. For example, what are some stereotypes that elderly people face?

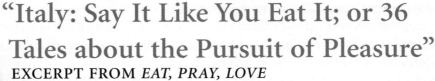

"Italy: Say It Like You Eat It; or 36 Tales about the Pursuit of Pleasure"
EXCERPT FROM *EAT, PRAY, LOVE*

Elizabeth Gilbert is a noted author of short stories, novels, and nonfiction. Her most recent book is the *New York Times* #1 best-selling memoir *Eat, Pray, Love* about the year she spent traveling the world alone after a difficult divorce. Much of her writing has been optioned by Hollywood. Her *GQ* memoir about her bartending years became the Disney movie "Coyote Ugly."

Before Reading Write a journal entry about self-discovery and growth. How can going through difficult times make you—or anyone—stronger or wiser? If you could go anywhere, where would you go to learn more about the world and yourself? Why?

In every major city in the Western World, some things are always the same. The same African men are always selling knockoffs of the same designer handbags and sunglasses, and the same Guatemalan musicians are always playing "I'd rather be a sparrow than a snail" on their bamboo windpipes. But some things are only in Rome. Like the sandwich counterman so comfortably calling me "beautiful" every time we speak. *You want this panino grilled or*   1 *cold, bella?* Or the couples making out all over the place, like there is some contest for it, twisting into each other on benches, stroking each other's hair and crotches, nuzzling and grinding ceaselessly . . .

And then there are the fountains. Pliny the Elder wrote once: "If anyone will consider the abundance of Rome's public supply of water, for baths, cisterns, ditches, houses, gardens, villas; and take into account the distance over which it travels, the arches reared, the mountains pierced, the valleys spanned—he will admit that there never was anything more marvelous in the whole world."

A few centuries later, I already have a few contenders for my favorite fountain in Rome. One is in the Villa Borghese. In the center of this fountain is a frolicking bronze family. Dad is a faun and Mom is a regular human woman. They have a baby who enjoys eating grapes. Mom and Dad are in a strange position—facing each other, grabbing each other's wrists, both of them leaning back. It's hard to tell whether they are yanking against each other in strife or swinging around merrily, but there's lots of energy there. Either way, Junior sits perched atop their wrists, right between them, unaffected by their merriment or strife, munching on his bunch of grapes. His little cloven hoofs dangle below him as he eats. (He takes after his father.)

It is early September, 2003. The weather is warm and lazy. By this, my fourth day in Rome, my shadow has still not darkened the doorway of a church or a museum, nor have I even looked at a guidebook. But I have been walking endlessly and aimlessly, and I did finally find a tiny little place that a friendly bus driver informed me sells The Best Gelato in Rome. It's called "Il Gelato di San Crispino." I'm not sure, but I think this might translate as "the ice cream of the crispy saint." I tried a combination of the honey and the hazelnut. I came back later that same day for the grapefruit and the melon. Then, after dinner that same night, I walked all the way back over there one last time, just to sample a cup of the cinnamon-ginger.

I've been trying to read through one newspaper article every day, no matter how long it takes. I look up approximately every third word in my dictionary. Today's news was fascinating. Hard to imagine a more dramatic headline than *"Obesita! I Bambini Italiani Sana i Piu Grassi d'Europa!"* Good God! Obesity! The article, I think, is declaring that Italian babies are the fattest babies in Europe! Reading on, I learn that Italian babies are significantly fatter than German babies and very significantly fatter than French babies. (Mercifully, there was no mention of how they measure up against American babies.) Older Italian children are dangerously obese these days, too, says the article. (The pasta industry defended itself.) These alarming statistics on Italian child fatness were unveiled yesterday by—no need to translate here—*"una task force internazionale"* It took me almost an hour to decipher this whole article. The entire time, I was eating a pizza and listening to one of Italy's children play the accordion across the street. The kid didn't look very fat to me, but that may have been because he was a gypsy. I'm not sure if I misread the last line of the article, but it seemed there was some talk from the government that the only way to deal with the obesity crisis in Italy was to implement a tax on the overweight . . .? Could this be true? After a few months of eating like this, will they come after me?

It's also important to read the newspaper every day to see how the pope is doing. Here in Rome, the pope's health is recorded daily in the newspaper, very much like weather, or the TV schedule. Today the pope is tired. Yesterday, the pope was less tired than he is today. Tomorrow, we expect that the pope will not be quite so tired as he was today.

It's kind of a fairyland of language for me here. For someone who has always wanted to speak Italian, what could be better than Rome? It's like somebody invented a city just to suit my specifications, where everyone (even the children, even the taxi drivers, even the actors on the commercials!) speaks this magical language. It's like the whole society is conspiring to teach me Italian. They'll even print their newspapers in Italian while I'm here; they don't mind! They have bookstores here *that only sell books written in Italian!* I found such a bookstore yesterday morning and felt I'd entered an enchanted palace. Everything was in Italian—even Dr. Seuss. I wandered through, touching all the books, hoping that anyone watching me might think I was a native speaker. Oh, how I want Italian to open itself up to me! This feeling reminded me of when I was four years old and couldn't read yet, but was dying to learn. I remember sitting in the waiting room of a doctor's office with my mother, holding a *Good Housekeeping* magazine in front of my face, turning the pages slowly, staring at the text, and hoping the grown-ups in the waiting room would think I was actually reading. I haven't felt so starved for comprehension since then. I found some works by American poets in that bookstore, with the original English version printed on one side of the page and the Italian translation on the other. I bought a volume by Robert Lowell, another by Louise Gluck.

There are spontaneous conversation classes everywhere. Today, I was sitting on a park bench when a tiny old woman in a black dress came over, roosted down beside me and started bossing me around about something. I shook my head, muted and confused. I apologized, saying in very nice Italian, "I'm sorry, but I don't speak Italian," and she looked like she would've smacked me with a wooden spoon, if she'd had one. She insisted: "You do understand!" (Interestingly, she was correct. That sentence, I *did* understand.) Now she wanted to know where I was from. I told her I was from New York, and asked where she was from. Duh—she was from Rome.

8

Hearing this, I clapped my hands like a baby. *Ah, Rome! Beautiful Rome! I love Rome! Pretty Rome!* She listened to my primitive rhapsodies with skepticism. Then she got down to it and asked me if I was married. I told her I was divorced. This was the first time I'd said it to anyone, and here I was, saying it in Italian. Of course she demanded, *"Percher?"* Well . . . "why" is a hard question to answer in any language. I stammered, then finally came up with *"Tabbiamo rotto"* (We broke it).

9

She nodded, stood up, walked up the street to her bus stop, got on her bus and did not even turn around to look at me again. Was she mad at me? Strangely, I waited for her on that park bench for twenty minutes, thinking against reason that she might come back and continue our conversation, but she never returned. Her name was Celeste, pronounced with a sharp *ch* as in *cello.*

10

Later in the day, I found a library. Dear me, how I love a library. Because we are in Rome, this library is a beautiful old thing, and within it there is a courtyard garden which you'd never have guessed existed if you'd only looked at the place from the street. The garden is a perfect square, dotted with orange trees and, in the center, a fountain. This fountain was going to be a contender for my favorite in Rome, I could tell immediately, though it was unlike any I'd seen so far. It was not carved of imperial marble, for starters. This was a small green, mossy, organic fountain. It was like a shaggy, leaking bush of ferns. (It looked, actually, exactly like the wild foliage growing out of the head of that praying figure which the old medicine man in Indonesia had drawn for me.) The water shot up out of the center of this flowering shrub, then rained back down on the leaves, making a melancholy, lovely sound throughout the whole courtyard.

11

I found a seat under an orange tree and opened one of the poetry books I'd purchased yesterday. Louise Gluck. I read the first poem in Italian, then in English, and stopped short at this line:

12

Dal centro delta mia vita venne una grande fontana . . .

13

"From the center of my life, there came a great fountain . . ." I set the book down in my lap, shaking with relief.

14

Vocabulary Before, during, and after reading the selection, annotate the text and write in your journal. Create a list of vocabulary words, along with their definitions. Give examples of their use from the selection you just read.

After Reading Discussion Questions: Meaning, Structure, and Expression

1. **Main Idea:** Work as a group to write a summary that answers the following questions: What purpose did Elizabeth Gilbert have for writing this essay? Who is the intended audience? What is the main idea of the essay?

2. **Relevant Details:** Elizabeth Gilbert uses the power of descriptive details to give life to her examples and illustrations. Find examples of her use of the following descriptive details: sight, sound, taste, smell, and touch or physical sensations. How do these details help her make her point?

3. **Logical Order:** Elizabeth Gilbert does not state the main idea of this selection in a thesis sentence. Instead, she makes her point by describing examples of her favorite fountains and illustrating her attempts to learn Italian. Then, she concludes the selection by inferring her main idea in the last two sentences. Do you think the selection would have been more effective if she had stated her main idea? Why or why not?

4. **Effective Expression:** Some have described Gilbert's tone in this selection as poetic. Do you agree or disagree? How would you describe Gilbert's tone? Give examples to support your views.

Thinking Prompts to Move from Reading to Writing

1. Throughout literature, authors use fountains to illustrate certain key principles or values in the human experience. In paragraphs 3 and 11, Elizabeth Gilbert describes two examples of fountains in Rome. What does each fountain represent to her? What life principle(s) does each one illustrate? Why do you think she was so affected by the line from Louise Gluck's poem "From the center of my life, there came a great fountain . . ."?

2. In paragraph 7, Elizabeth Gilbert describes herself as "starved for comprehension." What examples does she give from her life to illustrate her hunger to learn? Discuss the relationship between the desire to understand and learning. What causes the desire to understand?

Classification

Michelle Obama

OPRAH WINFREY

"Through the power of media, Oprah Winfrey has created an unparalleled connection with people around the world. As supervising producer and host of the top-rated, award-winning *The Oprah Winfrey Show*, she has entertained, enlightened and uplifted millions of viewers for the past two decades. Her accomplishments as a global media leader and philanthropist have established her as one of the most respected and admired public figures today" (Oprah.com). Winfrey wrote the following article for *Time* magazine's annual *Time 100* issue, which names the people who most affect our world.

Before Reading Write a journal entry about an influential person. Whom do you think has most affected our world? Why?

1   Michelle Obama doesn't just inspire us. She affirms us with her intelligence, authenticity, depth and compassion. We see the best of ourselves in her and marvel that no matter what she's doing, she brings 100% of herself to the experience.

2   I first met Michelle almost five years ago, shortly after Senator Barack Obama's riveting 2004 DNC speech. Long before there was serious talk of a campaign for the presidency, I remember going to the Obamas' house for dinner. I figured there would be takeout since I knew that, like me, Michelle had worked all day. But no, there she was in the kitchen, calm and organized, preparing linguine with shrimp and vegetables.

3   The woman I witnessed five years ago, with her graciousness, care and attention to detail, is the same woman I visited in the White House in February. Her very presence makes you feel welcome. Her political power is secondary to her heart power, and I salute her for that. I trust her. I know that whatever she gives her attention to, the truth will always be present. She doesn't make false moves.

4   The joy Michelle, 45, brings to her roles as First Mother and First Lady is what makes her so intoxicating. We want that joy in the roles we inhabit as mothers, wives, workers, daughters and friends. And while we admire those arms and applaud her fashion choices (from J. Crew to top designers), her greatest influence is that she makes us want to be our own best selves— and maybe lift a few weights too.

5   Watching her on the global stage greeting the Queen and chatting with dignitaries and representing us the way we imagine presenting ourselves on our best day, I was reminded of lines from Maya Angelou's poem "Phenomenal Woman": "It's the fire in my eyes, / And the flash of my teeth, / The swing in my waist, / And the joy in my feet. / I'm a woman / Phenomenally."

6   How sweet it is that America has a First Lady who embodies the vibrancy and confidence of a seriously prepared 21st century woman. A phenomenal woman indeed.

Vocabulary Before, during, and after reading the selection, annotate the text and write in your journal. Create a list of vocabulary words, along with their definitions. Give examples of their use from the selection you just read.

After Reading Discussion Questions: Meaning, Structure, and Expression

1. **Main Idea:** Work as a group to write a summary that answers the following questions: What purpose did Oprah Winfrey have for writing this essay? Who is the intended audience? What is the main idea of the essay?
2. **Relevant Details:** Do you think Oprah Winfrey gave enough details to convince the reader that Michelle Obama is a hero or icon of great influence? Which details are the most convincing to you? What additional details would you add to strengthen the point of the essay? What would you have liked to have learned about Michelle Obama from someone who knows her as well as Winfrey does? Where in the tribute would you place this additional information?
3. **Logical Order:** Why did Oprah Winfrey choose to use the lines from Maya Angelou's poem "Phenomenal Woman" as part of her conclusion? Would her essay have been more effective if she had used the lines from the poem in the introduction to grab our attention? Why or why not?
4. **Effective Expression:** In her article, Oprah Winfrey uses words such as "marvel," "intoxicating," "vibrancy," and "phenomenal." How would you describe the tone set by these words? Is Oprah Winfrey expressing just her personal opinion or does she speak for a majority? If she speaks for a majority, does she speak for women, men, or both? Explain your reasoning.

Thinking Prompts to Move from Reading to Writing

1. In her tribute to Michelle Obama, Oprah Winfrey uses the phrases "the best of ourselves" and "our own best selves." What do you think she means by these phrases? What are the traits of "our best selves"? Do these traits vary from person to person or are they universal traits common to everyone? Who makes you want to be your own best self? How do you encourage others to be their best selves? Assume you are writing an essay for a college psychology course. Describe the traits of a role model who inspires others to be their "best selves," such as a teacher or a parent.
2. *Time* magazine divides its list of most influential people into four categories: Builders & Titans; Artists & Entertainers; Heroes & Icons; Scientists & Thinkers. Oprah Winfrey wrote about Michelle Obama as a Hero & Icon. Whom would you nominate to the annual *Time 100*? In which group does your nominee belong? What role does this person play in society? What admirable traits does this person possess? Assume you are writing for the 2010 *Time 100* issue. Write a tribute about a person who has most affected our world.

The Truth about Lying

JUDITH VIORST

Judith Viorst was born in Newark, New Jersey, in 1931. As the author of several works of fiction and nonfiction, for children as well as adults, she has been honored with various awards for her journalism and psychological writings.

Before Reading Write a journal entry about your experiences with lying. Have you ever told a lie or been lied to? Why was the lie told? How do you feel when you lie or are lied to? Is lying necessary sometimes? If so, when?

I've been wanting to write on a subject that intrigues and challenges me: the subject of lying. I've found it very difficult to do. Everyone I've talked to has a quite intense and personal but often rather intolerant point of view about what we can—and can never *never*—tell lies about. I've finally reached the conclusion that I can't present any ultimate conclusions, for too many people would promptly disagree. Instead, I'd like to present a series of moral puzzles, all concerned with lying. I'll tell you what I think about them. Do you agree?   1

Social Lies

Most of the people I've talked with say that they find social lying acceptable and necessary. They think it's the civilized way for folks to behave. Without these little white lies, they say, our relationships would be short and brutish and nasty. It's arrogant, they say, to insist on being so incorruptible and so brave that you cause other people unnecessary embarrassment or pain by compulsively assailing them with your honesty. I basically agree. What about you?   2

Will you say to people, when it simply isn't true, "I like your new hairdo," "You're looking much better," "It's so nice to see you," "I had a wonderful time"?   3

Will you praise hideous presents and homely kids?   4

Will you decline invitations with "We're busy that night—so sorry we can't come," when the truth is you'd rather stay home than dine with the So-and-sos?   5

And even though, as I do, you may prefer the polite evasion of "You really cooked up a storm" instead of "The soup"—which tastes like warmed-over coffee—"is wonderful," will you, if you must, proclaim it wonderful?   6

There's one man I know who absolutely refuses to tell social lies. "I can't play that game," he says; "I'm simply not made that way." And his answer to the argument that saying nice things to someone doesn't cost anything is, "Yes, it does—it destroys your credibility." Now, he won't, unsolicited, offer his views on the painting you just bought, but you don't ask his frank opinion unless you want *frank,* and his silence at those moments when the rest of us liars are muttering, "Isn't it lovely?" is, for the most part, eloquent enough. My friend does not indulge in what he calls "flattery, false praise, and mellifluous comments." When others tell fibs, he will not go along. He says that social lying is lying, that little white lies are still lies. And he feels that telling lies is morally wrong. What about you?   7

Peace-Keeping Lies

Many people tell peace-keeping lies; lies designed to avoid irritation or argument; lies designed to shelter the liar from possible blame or pain; lies (or so it is rationalized) designed to keep trouble at bay without hurting anyone.   8

I tell these lies at times, and yet I always feel they're wrong. I understand why we tell them, but still they feel wrong. And whenever I lie so that someone won't disapprove of me or think less of me or holler at me, I feel I'm a bit of a coward, I feel I'm dodging responsibility, I feel . . . guilty. What about you?   9

Do you, when you're late for a date because you overslept, say that you're late because you got caught in a traffic jam?   10

Do you, when you forget to call a friend, say that you called several times but the line was busy?   11

Do you, when you didn't remember that it was your father's birthday, say that his present must be delayed in the mail?   12

And when you're planning a weekend in New York City and you're not in the mood to visit your mother, who lives there, do you conceal—with a lie, if you must—the fact that you'll be in New York? Or do you have the courage—or is it the cruelty?—to say, "I'll be in New York, but sorry—I don't plan on seeing you"?   13

(Dave and his wife Elaine have two quite different points of view on this very subject. He calls her a coward. She says she's being wise. He says she must assert her right to visit New York sometimes and not see her mother. To which she always patiently replies: "Why should we have useless fights? My mother's too old to change. We get along much better when I lie to her.") 14

Finally, do you keep the peace by telling your husband lies on the subject of money? Do you reduce what you really paid for your shoes? And in general do you find yourself ready, willing, and able to lie to him when you make absurd mistakes or lose or break things? 15

"I used to have a romantic idea that part of intimacy was confessing every dumb thing that you did to your husband. But after a couple of years of that," says Laura, "have I changed my mind!" 16

And having changed her mind, she finds herself telling peace-keeping lies. And yes, I tell them too. What about you? 17

Protective Lies

Protective lies are lies folks tell—often quite serious lies—because they're convinced that the truth would be too damaging. They lie because they feel there are certain human values that supersede the wrong of having lied. They lie, not for personal gain, but because they believe it's for the good of the person they're lying to. They lie to those they love, to those who trust them most of all, on the grounds that breaking this trust is justified. 18

They may lie to their children on money or marital matters. 19

They may lie to the dying about the state of their health. 20

They may lie about adultery, and not—or so they insist—to save their own hide, but to save the heart and the pride of the men they are married to. 21

They may lie to their closest friend because the truth about her talents or son or psyche would be—or so they insist—utterly devastating. 22

I sometimes tell such lies, but I'm aware that it's quite presumptuous to claim I know what's best for others to know. That's called playing God. That's called manipulation and control. And we never can be sure, once we start to juggle lies, just where they'll land, exactly where they'll roll. 23

And furthermore, we may find ourselves lying in order to back up the lies that are backing up the lie we initially told. 24

And furthermore—let's be honest—if conditions were reversed, we certainly wouldn't want anyone lying to us. 25

Yet, having said all that, I still believe that there are times when protective lies must nonetheless be told. What about you? 26

If your Dad had a very bad heart and you had to tell him some bad family news, which would you choose: to tell him the truth or lie? 27

If your former husband failed to send his monthly child-support check and in other ways behaved like a total rat, would you allow your children—who believed he was simply wonderful—to continue to believe that he was wonderful? 28

If your dearly beloved brother selected a wife whom you deeply disliked, would you reveal your feelings or would you fake it? 29

And if you were asked, after making love, "And how was that for you?" would you reply, if it wasn't too good, "Not too good"? 30

Now, some would call a sex lie unimportant, little more than social lying, a simple act of courtesy that makes all human intercourse run smoothly. And some would say all sex lies are bad news and unacceptably protective. Because, says Ruth, "a man with an ego that fragile 31 doesn't need your lies—he needs a psychiatrist." Still others feel that sex lies are indeed protective lies, more serious than simple social lying, and yet at times they tell them on the grounds that when it comes to matters sexual, everybody's ego is somewhat fragile.

"If most of the time things go well in sex," says Sue, "I think you're allowed to dissemble when they don't. I can't believe it's good to say, 'Last night was four stars, darling, but tonight's performance rates only a half.'" 32

I'm inclined to agree with Sue. What about you? 33

Trust-Keeping Lies

Another group of lies are trust-keeping lies, lies that involve triangulation, with *A* (that's you) telling lies to *B* on behalf of *C* (whose trust you'd promised to keep). Most people concede that once you've agreed not to betray a friend's confidence, you can't betray it, even if you must lie. But I've talked with people who don't want you telling them anything that they might be called on to lie about. 34

"I don't tell lies for myself," says Fran, "and I don't want to have to tell them for other people." Which means, she agrees, that if her best friend is having an affair, she absolutely doesn't want to know about it. 35

"Are you saying," her best friend asks, "that if I went off with a lover and I asked you to tell my husband I'd been with you, that you wouldn't lie for me, that you'd betray me?" 36

Fran is very pained but very adamant. "I wouldn't want to betray you, so . . . don't ask me." 37

Fran's best friend is shocked. What about you? 38

Do you believe you can have close friends if you're not prepared to receive their deepest secrets? 39

Do you believe you must always lie for your friends? 40

Do you believe, if your friend tells a secret that turns out to be quite immoral or illegal, that once you've promised to keep it, you must keep it? 41

And what if your friend were your boss—if you were perhaps one of the President's men—would you betray or lie for him over, say, Watergate? 42

As you can see, these issues get terribly sticky. 43

It's my belief that once we've promised to keep a trust, we must tell lies to keep it. I also believe that we can't tell Watergate lies. And if these two statements strike you as quite contradictory, you're right—they're quite contradictory. But for now they're the best I can do. What about you? 44

Some say that truth will out and thus you might as well tell the truth. Some say you can't regain the trust that lies lose. Some say that even though the truth may never be revealed, our lies pervert and damage our relationships. Some say . . . well, here's what some of them have to say. 45

"I'm a coward," says Grace, "about telling close people important, difficult truths. I find that I'm unable to carry it off. And so if something is bothering me, it keeps building up inside till I end up just not seeing them any more." 46

"I lie to my husband on sexual things, but I'm furious," says Joyce, "that he's too insensitive to know I'm lying." 47

"I suffer most from the misconception that children can't take the truth," says Emily. "But I'm starting to see that what's harder and more damaging for them is being told lies, is *not* being told the truth." 48

"I'm afraid," says Joan, "that we often wind up feeling a bit of contempt for the people we lie to." 49

And then there are those who have no talent for lying. 50

"Over the years, I tried to lie," a friend of mine explained, "but I always got found out and I 51
always got punished. I guess I gave myself away because I feel guilty about any kind of lying.
It looks as if I'm stuck with telling the truth."

For those of us, however, who are good at telling lies, for those of us who lie and don't get 52
caught, the question of whether or not to lie can be a hard and serious moral problem. I liked
the remark of a friend of mine who said, "I'm willing to lie. But just as a last resort—the
truth's always better."

"Because," he explained, "though others may completely accept the lie I'm telling, I don't." 53

I tend to feel that way too. 54

What about you? 55

Vocabulary
Before, during, and after reading the selection, annotate the text and write
in your journal. Create a list of vocabulary words, along with their definitions. Give
examples of their use from the selection you just read.

After Reading Discussion Questions: Meaning, Structure, and Expression

1. **Main Idea:** Work as a group to write a summary that answers the following questions:
   What purpose did Judith Viorst have for writing this essay? Who is her intended
   audience? What is the main idea of the essay? What is the significance of the title?
2. **Relevant Details:** Viorst describes four types of lies. Examine the examples she gives for
   each type of lie. Do you agree that she chose the best examples? Why or why not?
3. **Logical Order:** Throughout the essay, Viorst poses questions directly to the audience.
   Locate those questions. Why did she place these questions where she did? What impact
   do the questions have on the effectiveness of the essay?
4. **Effective Expression:** Based on her word choice, who is the intended audience for this
   essay? Identify several expressions that you used as clues to identify the audience. Does
   the point of the essay have meaning for other audiences? What changes in words or
   examples would you recommend to make this essay appealing to a specific audience that
   is different from the one Viorst intended?

Thinking Prompts to Move from Reading to Writing

1. Throughout the essay, Viorst asks her readers if they agree with her. Discuss your views
   about these four types of lies. Write a classification essay that answers the questions she
   poses to the reader.
2. Lying is an act that leads to a variety of emotional reactions for both the one who lies
   and the one who is lied to. How do you feel when you lie? How do you feel when you
   know you have been lied to? Write an essay that classifies and explains the types of
   reactions people have in response to lying.

Comparison–Contrast

The Talk of the Sandbox; How Johnny and Suzy's Playground Chatter Prepares Them for Life at the Office

DEBORAH TANNEN

Deborah Tannen is best known as the author of *You Just Don't Understand*, which was on the *New York Times* bestseller list for nearly four years, including eight months as #1, and has been translated into 30 languages. Professor Tannen serves on the linguistics department faculty at Georgetown University. She has published twenty-one books and over 100 articles, and is the recipient of five honorary doctorates. The following article first appeared in the "Outlook" section of the *Washington Post*.

Before Reading Write a journal entry about the differences between men and women. For example, do men and women differ in the ways they fight, apologize, compete, or learn? How so?

1   Bob Hoover of the Pittsburgh *Post-Gazette* was interviewing me when he remarked that after years of coaching boys' softball teams, he was now coaching girls and they were very different. I immediately whipped out my yellow pad and began interviewing him—and discovered that his observations about how girls and boys play softball parallel mine about how women and men talk at work.

2   Hoover told me that boys' teams always had one or two stars whom the other boys treated with deference. So when he started coaching a girls' team, he began by looking for the leader. He couldn't find one. "The girls who are better athletes don't lord it over the others," he said. "You get the feeling that everyone's the same." When a girl got the ball, she didn't try to throw it all the way home as a strong-armed boy would; instead, she'd throw it to another team member, so they all became better catchers and throwers. He went on, "If a girl makes an error, she's not in the doghouse for a long time, as a boy would be."

3   "But wait," I interrupted. "I've heard that when girls make a mistake at sports, they often say 'I'm sorry,' whereas boys don't."

4   That's true, he said, but then the girl forgets it—and so do her teammates. "For boys, sports is a performance art. They're concerned with how they look." When they make an error, they sulk because they've let their teammates down. Girls want to win, but if they lose, they're still all in it together—so the mistake isn't as dreadful for the individual or the team.

5   What Hoover described in these youngsters were the seeds of behavior I have observed among women and men at work.

6   The girls who are the best athletes don't "lord it over" the others—just the ethic I found among women in positions of authority. Women managers frequently told me they were good managers because they did not act in an authoritarian manner. They said they did not flaunt their

power, or behave as though they were better than their subordinates. Similarly, linguist Elisabeth Kuhn found that women professors in her study informed students of course requirements as if they had magically appeared on the syllabus ("There are two papers. The first paper, ah, let's see, is due. . . . It's back here [referring to the syllabus] at the beginning"), whereas the men professors made it clear that they had set the requirements ("I have two midterms and a final").

A woman manager might say to her secretary, "Could you do me a favor and type this letter right away?" knowing that her secretary is going to type the letter. But her male boss, on hearing this, might conclude she doesn't feel she deserves the authority she has, just as a boys' coach might think the star athlete doesn't realize how good he is if he doesn't expect his teammates to treat him with deference. 7

I was especially delighted by Hoover's observation that, although girls are more likely to say, "I'm sorry," they are actually far less sorry when they make a mistake than boys who don't say it, but are "in the doghouse" for a long time. This dramatizes the ritual nature of many women's apologies. How often is a woman who is "always apologizing" seen as weak and lacking in confidence? In fact, for many women, saying "I'm sorry" often doesn't mean "I apologize." It means "I'm sorry that happened." 8

Like many of the rituals common among women, it's a way of speaking that takes into account the other person's point of view. It can even be an automatic conversational smoother. For example, you left your pad in someone's office; you knock on the door and say, "Excuse me, I left my pad on your desk," and the person whose office it is might reply, "Oh, I'm sorry. Here it is." She knows it is not her fault that you left your pad on her desk; she's just letting you know it's okay. 9

Finally, I was intrigued by Hoover's remark that boys regard sports as "a performance art" and worry about "how they look." There, perhaps, is the rub, the key to why so many women feel they don't get credit for what they do. From childhood, many boys learn something that is very adaptive to the workplace: Raises and promotions are based on "performance" evaluations and these depend, in large measure, on how you appear in other people's eyes. In other words, you have to worry not only about getting your job done but also about getting credit for what you do. 10

Getting credit often depends on the way you talk. For example, a woman told me she was given a poor evaluation because her supervisor felt she knew less than her male peers. Her boss, it turned out, reached this conclusion because the woman asked more questions: She was seeking information without regard to how her queries would make her look. 11

The same principle applies to apologizing. Whereas some women seem to be taking undeserved blame by saying "I'm sorry," some men seem to evade deserved blame. I observed this when a man disconnected a conference call by accidentally elbowing the speaker-phone. When his secretary re-connected the call, I expected him to say, "I'm sorry; I knocked the phone by mistake." Instead he said, "Hey, what happened?! One minute you were there, the next minute you were gone!" Annoying as this might be, there are certainly instances in which people improve their fortunes by covering up mistakes. If Hoover's observations about girls' and boys' athletic styles are fascinating, it is even more revealing to see actual transcripts of children at play and how they mirror the adult workplace. Amy Sheldon, a linguist at the University of Minnesota who studies children talking at play in a day care center, compared the conflicts of pre-school girls and boys. She found that boys who fought with one another tended to pursue their own goal. Girls tended to balance their own interests with those of the other girls through complex verbal negotiations. 12

Look how different the negotiations were: 13

Two boys fought over a toy telephone: Tony had it; Charlie wanted it. Tony was sitting on a foam chair with the base of the phone in his lap and the receiver lying beside him. Charlie 14 picked up the receiver, and Tony protested, "No, that's my phone!" He grabbed the telephone cord and tried to pull the receiver away from Charlie, saying, "No, that—uh, it's on MY couch. It's on MY couch, Charlie. It's on MY couch. It's on MY couch." It seems he had only one point to make, so he made it repeatedly as he used physical force to get the phone back.

Charlie ignored Tony and held onto the receiver. Tony then got off the couch, set the phone base on the floor and tried to keep possession of it by overturning the chair on top of it. Charlie managed to push the chair off, get the telephone and win the fight.

15

This might seem like a typical kids' fight until you compare it with a fight Sheldon videotaped among girls. Here the contested objects were toy medical instruments: Elaine had them; Arlene wanted them. But she didn't just grab for them; she argued her case. Elaine, in turn, balanced her own desire to keep them with Arlene's desire to get them. Elaine lost ground gradually, by compromising.

16

Arlene began not by grabbing but by asking and giving a reason: "Can I have that, that thing? I'm going to take my baby's temperature." Elaine was agreeable, but cautious: "You can use it—you can use my temperature. Just make sure you can't use anything else unless you can ask." Arlene did just that; she asked for the toy syringe: "May I?" Elaine at first resisted, but gave a reason: "No, I'm gonna need to use the shot in a couple of minutes." Arlene reached for the syringe anyway, explaining in a "beseeching" tone, "But I—I need this though."

17

Elaine capitulated, but again tried to set limits: "Okay, just use it once." She even gave Arlene permission to give "just a couple of shots."

18

Arlene then pressed her advantage, and became possessive of her property: "Now don't touch the baby until I get back, because it IS MY BABY! I'll check her ears, okay?" (Even when being demanding, she asked for agreement: "okay?")

19

Elaine tried to regain some rights through compromise: "Well, let's pretend it's another day, that we have to look in her ears together." Elaine also tried another approach that would give Arlene something she wanted: "I'll have to shot her after, after, after you listen—after you look in her ears," suggested Elaine. Arlene, however, was adamant: "Now don't shot her at all!" What happened next will sound familiar to anyone who has ever been a little girl or overheard one. Elaine could no longer abide Arlene's selfish behavior and applied the ultimate sanction: "Well, then, you can't come to my birthday!" Arlene uttered the predictable retort: "I don't want to come to your birthday!"

20

The boys and girls followed different rituals for fighting. Each boy went after what he wanted; they slugged it out; one won. But the girls enacted a complex negotiation, trying to get what they wanted while taking into account what the other wanted.

21

Here is an example of how women and men at work used comparable strategies.

22

Maureen and Harold, two managers at a medium-size company, were assigned to hire a human-resources coordinator for their division. Each favored a different candidate, and both felt strongly about their preferences. They traded arguments for some time, neither convincing the other. Then Harold said that hiring the candidate Maureen wanted would make him so uncomfortable that he would have to consider resigning. Maureen respected Harold. What's more, she liked him and considered him a friend. So she said what seemed to her the only thing she could say under the circumstances: "Well, I certainly don't want you to feel uncomfortable here. You're one of the pillars of the place." Harold's choice was hired.

23

What was crucial was not Maureen's and Harold's individual styles in isolation but how they played in concert with each other's style. Harold's threat to quit ensured his triumph— when used with someone for whom it was a trump card. If he had been arguing with someone who regarded this threat as simply another move in the negotiation rather than a non-

24

negotiable expression of deep feelings, the result might have been different. For example, had she said, "That's ridiculous; of course you're not going to quit!" or matched it ("Well, I'd be tempted to quit if we hired your guy"), the decision might well have gone the other way.

Like the girls at play, Maureen was balancing her perspective with those of her colleague and expected him to do the same. Harold was simply going for what he wanted and trusted Maureen to do likewise.   25

This is not to say that all women and all men, or all boys and girls, behave any one way. Many factors influence our styles, including regional and ethnic backgrounds, family experience and individual personality. But gender is a key factor, and understanding its influence can help clarify what happens when we talk.   26

Understanding the ritual nature of communication gives you the flexibility to consider different approaches if you're not happy with the reaction you're getting. Someone who tends to avoid expressing disagreement might learn to play "devil's advocate" without taking it as a personal attack. Someone who tends to avoid admitting fault might find it is effective to say "I'm sorry"—that the loss of face is outweighed by a gain in credibility.   27

There is no one way of talking that will always work best. But understanding how conversational rituals work allows individuals to have more control over their own lives.   28

Vocabulary
Before, during, and after reading the selection, annotate the text and write in your journal. Create a list of vocabulary words, along with their definitions. Give examples of their use from the selection you just read.

After Reading Discussion Questions: Meaning, Structure, and Expression

1. **Main Idea:** Work as a group to write a summary that answers the following questions: What purpose did Deborah Tannen have for writing this essay? Who is the intended audience? What is the main idea of the essay?

2. **Relevant Details:** The details of this passage explain the similarities and differences in the conversation styles of four groups of people. What are those four groups? Which groups are compared to each other? Which groups are contrasted with each other? Tannen uses several comparable points such as playing sports, fighting, and apologizing. Why do you think she chose these three specific activities to make her comparisons?

3. **Logical Order:** How does Deborah Tannen organize her ideas? Does she talk about the similarities and differences between men and women point by point? Or does she organize her comparison and contrast by presenting one block of ideas (the communication styles of males) and then another (the communication styles of females)? Do you think she chose the more effective method for ordering her details? Why or why not?

4. **Effective Expression:** Deborah Tannen uses transitional words and phrases to clearly identify her specific points of comparison. For example, reread the first sentence in paragraph 6. Circle the phrase that connects the topic "girl athletes" to "women in positions of authority." Does this transitional phrase indicate a comparison or a contrast between the two groups of females? Find two additional transitional words or phrases that identify comparable points in the passage. What are the comparable points or topics? Based on the transitional words or phrases, are these topics being compared, contrasted, or both? Discuss the importance of transitional expressions in a piece of writing.

Thinking Prompts to Move from Reading to Writing

1. In this essay, Deborah Tannen reports her observation and study of human behavior. For example, reread paragraphs 13 through 28. This section objectively reports the differences between the communication styles of boys and girls—like a case study. First she narrates fight between the boys; then she narrates girls' fight. Simply by recording their behaviors, she illustrates their differences. Use this method of reporting to compare two topics of your choosing. For example, for a college health class report about the differences between effective and ineffective reactions to stress.

2. Deborah Tannen illustrates the differences between males and females by comparing and contrasting their communication styles as children and adults. What other differences between men and women have you observed? For example, do men and women prefer different types of movies, sports, books, cars? Do they differ in the way they act in their roles as parents, siblings, children, or friends? Write an essay using your own set of comparable points that discusses other important differences between men and women. Choose an audience and writing situation such as the following: an academic paper for a social science class or an article for the college newspaper.

A Fable for Tomorrow
RACHEL CARSON

Born in Springfield, Pennsylvania, in 1902, Rachel Carson lived the rugged life of a farmer's daughter. A biologist, environmentalist, and nature writer, Carson became a foreleader in the environmental movement. Her book *Silent Spring* raised the alarm and instigated change in national attitudes and policies about pesticides. She was awarded the Presidential Medal of Freedom.

Before Reading Write a journal entry about your views about the environment. Are you concerned about the environment? Why or why not? What do you think is the greatest threat to our environment? Why? What should be done?

There was once a town in the heart of America where all life seemed to live in harmony with its surroundings. The town lay in the midst of a checkerboard of prosperous farms, with fields of grain and hillsides of orchards where, in spring, white clouds of bloom drifted above the green fields. In autumn, oak and maple and birch set up a blaze of color that flamed and flickered across a backdrop of pines. Then foxes barked in the hills and deer silently crossed the fields, half hidden in the mists of the fall mornings.   1

Along the roads, laurel, viburnum and alder, great ferns and wildflowers delighted the traveler's eye through much of the year. Even in winter the roadsides were places of beauty, where countless birds came to feed on the berries and on the seed heads of the dried weeds rising above the snow. The countryside was, in fact, famous for the abundance and variety of its bird life, and when the flood of migrants was pouring through in spring and fall people traveled from great distances to observe them. Others came to fish the streams, which flowed clear and cold out of the hills and contained shady pools where trout lay. So it had been from the days many years ago when the first settlers raised their houses, sank their wells, and built their barns.   2

Then a strange blight crept over the area and everything began to change. Some evil spell had settled on the community: mysterious maladies swept the flocks of chickens; the cattle   3 and sheep sickened and died. Everywhere was a shadow of death. The farmers spoke of much illness among their families. In the town the doctors had become more and more puzzled by new kinds of sickness appearing among their patients. There had been several sudden and unexplained deaths, not only among adults but even among children, who would be stricken suddenly while at play and die within a few hours.

There was a strange stillness. The birds, for example—where had they gone? Many people spoke of them, puzzled and disturbed. The feeding stations in the backyards were deserted. The few birds seen anywhere were moribund; they trembled violently and could not fly. It was a spring without voices. On the mornings that had once throbbed with the dawn chorus of robins, catbirds, doves, jays, wrens, and scores of other bird voices there was now no sound; only silence lay over the fields and woods and marsh.   4

On the farms the hens brooded, but no chicks hatched. The farmers complained that they were unable to raise any pigs—the litters were small and the young survived only a few days. The apple trees were coming into bloom but no bees droned among the blossoms, so there was no pollination and there would be no fruit.   5

The roadsides, once so attractive, were now lined with browned and withered vegetation as though swept by fire. These, too, were silent, deserted by all living things. Even the streams were now lifeless. Anglers no longer visited them, for all the fish had died.   6

In the gutters under the eaves and between the shingles of the roofs, a white granular powder still showed a few patches; some weeks before it had fallen like snow upon the roofs and the lawns, the fields and streams.   7

No witchcraft, no enemy action had silenced the rebirth of new life in this stricken world. The people had done it themselves.   8

This town does not actually exist, but it might easily have a thousand counterparts in America or elsewhere in the world. I know of no community that has experienced all the misfortunes I describe. Yet every one of these disasters has actually happened somewhere, and many real communities have already suffered a substantial number of them. A grim specter has crept upon us almost unnoticed, and this imagined tragedy may easily become a stark reality we all shall know.   9

Vocabulary Before, during, and after reading the selection, annotate the text and write in your journal. Create a list of vocabulary words, along with their definitions. Give examples of their use from the selection you just read.

After Reading Discussion Questions: Meaning, Structure, and Expression

1. **Main Idea:** Work as a group to write a summary that answers the following questions: What purpose did Rachel Carson have for writing this essay? Who is her intended audience? What is the main idea of the essay? What is the significance of the title?

2. **Relevant Details:** When Carson begins her concluding paragraph by stating, "This town does not actually exist," she admits that she has used a fictitious example to make her point. Does she provide enough details to make her point convincingly? Would the use of facts or expert opinions strengthen her point? Why or why not? What is the effect of her sudden admission of using a fictitious example?

3. **Logical Order:** Carson contrasts two descriptions of a fictional place: what the place was like before it was damaged by pesticides and what the place looked like after the damage occurred. Does she organize these contrasting views point by point or by presenting one block of ideas (description of the place before it was damaged) and then another (description of the place after it was damaged)? Do you think she chose the more effective method for ordering her details? Why or why not?

4. **Effective Expression:** To make her point, Carson describes sensory details of sights and sounds to create vivid mental images in the reader's mind. Identify four sensory details: two that depict the town before it changed and two that depict the town after it changed. What impact do these details have on the reader?

Thinking Prompts to Move from Reading to Writing

1. Carson uses sensory details to describe the change of seasons in this fictitious town, such as "in spring, white clouds of bloom drifted above the green fields." Write an essay that contrasts the seasons as they occur in a particular place. Use sensory details to depict the contrast of sights, sounds, aromas, or textures among the seasons.
2. "A Fable for Tomorrow" is a story that warns the reader about the negative effects of pesticide by contrasting before and after images. Identify a specific problem such as gangs, graffiti, drug abuse, alcoholism, an eating disorder, or obesity. Write a fable that warns against this problem by contrasting before and after situations.

Definition

What is Poverty?

JO GOODWIN-PARKER

The following selection was published in *America's Other Children: Public Schools Outside Suburbs*, by George Henderson in 1971 by the University of Oklahoma Press. The author specifically requests the right to her privacy and offers no additional information about herself for public use. In her essay, a personal testimony about living in poverty, she speaks directly to the reader.

Before Reading Write a journal entry about your response to poverty. How would you define poverty? Why are people poor? How does society react to the poor? Do you think our government does enough to help poor people? What can be done to fight poverty?

You ask me what is poverty? Listen to me. Here I am, dirty, smelly, and with no "proper" underwear on and with the stench of my rotting teeth near you. I will tell you. Listen to me. Listen without pity. I cannot use your pity. Listen with understanding. Put yourself in my dirty, worn out, ill-fitting shoes, and hear me. 1

Poverty is getting up every morning from a dirt- and illness-stained mattress. The sheets have long since been used for diapers. Poverty is living in a smell that never leaves. This is a smell of urine, sour milk, and spoiling food sometimes joined with the strong smell of long-cooked onions. Onions are cheap. If you have smelled this smell, you did not know how it came. It is the smell of the outdoor privy. It is the smell of young children who cannot walk the long dark way in the night. It is the smell of the mattresses where years of "accidents" have happened. It is the smell of the milk which has gone sour because the refrigerator long has not worked, and it costs money to get it fixed. It is the smell of rotting garbage. I could bury it, but where is the shovel? Shovels cost money. 2

Poverty is being tired. I have always been tired. They told me at the hospital when the last baby came that I had chronic anemia caused from poor diet, a bad case of worms, and that I needed a corrective operation. I listened politely—the poor are always polite. The poor always listen. They don't say that there is no money for iron pills, or better food, or worm medicine. The idea of an operation is frightening and costs so much that, if I had dared, I would have laughed. Who takes care of my children? Recovery from an operation takes a long time. I have three children. When I left them with "Granny" the last time I had a job, I came home to find the baby covered with fly specks, and a diaper that had not been changed since I left. When the dried diaper came off, bits of my baby's flesh came with it. My other child was playing with a sharp bit of broken glass, and my oldest was playing alone at the edge of a lake. I made twenty-two dollars a week, and a good nursery school costs twenty dollars a week for three children. I quit my job. 3

Poverty is dirt. You can say in your clean clothes coming from your clean house, "Anybody can be clean." Let me explain about housekeeping with no money. For breakfast I give my 4 children grits with no oleo or cornbread without eggs and oleo. This does not use up many dishes. What dishes there are, I wash in cold water and with no soap. Even the cheapest soap has to be saved for the baby's diapers. Look at my hands, so cracked and red. Once I saved for two months to buy a jar of Vaseline for my hands and the baby's diaper rash. When I had saved enough, I went to buy it and the price had gone up two cents. The baby and I suffered on. I have to decide every day if I can bear to put my cracked sore hands into the cold water and strong soap. But you ask, why not hot water? Fuel costs money. If you have a wood fire it costs money. If you burn electricity, it costs money. Hot water is a luxury. I do not have luxuries. I know you will be surprised when I tell you how young I am. I look so much older. My back has been bent over the wash tubs every day for so long, I cannot remember when I ever did anything else. Every night I wash every stitch my school age child has on and just hope her clothes will be dry by morning.

Poverty is staying up all night on' cold nights to watch the fire knowing one spark on the newspaper covering the walls means your sleeping child dies in flames. In summer poverty is watching gnats and flies devour your baby's tears when he cries. The screens are torn and you pay so little rent you know they will never be fixed. Poverty means insects in your food, in your nose, in your eyes, and crawling over you when you sleep. Poverty is hoping it never rains because diapers won't dry when it rains and soon you are using newspapers. Poverty is seeing your children forever with runny noses. Paper handkerchiefs cost money and all your rags you need for other things. Even more costly are antihistamines. Poverty is cooking without food and cleaning without soap.   5

Poverty is asking for help. Have you ever had to ask for help, knowing your children will suffer unless you get it? Think about asking for a loan from a relative, if this is the only way you can imagine asking for help. I will tell you how it feels. You find out where the office is that you are supposed to visit. You circle that block four or five times. Thinking of your children, you go in. Everyone is very busy. Finally, someone comes out and you tell her that you need help. That never is the person you need to see. You go see another person, and after spilling the whole shame of your poverty all over the desk between you, you find that this isn't the right office after all—you must repeat the whole process, and it never is any easier at the next place.   6

You have asked for help, and after all it has a cost. You are again told to wait. You are told why, but you don't really hear because of the red cloud of shame and the rising cloud of despair.   7

Poverty is remembering. It is remembering quitting school in junior high because "nice" children had been so cruel about my clothes and my smell. The attendance officer came. My mother told him I was pregnant. I wasn't, but she thought that I could get a job and help out. I had jobs off and on, but never long enough to learn anything. Mostly I remember being married. I was so young then. I am still young. For a time, we had all the things you have. There was a little house in another town, with hot water and everything. Then my husband lost his job. There was unemployment insurance for a while and what few jobs I could get. Soon, all our nice things were repossessed and we moved back here. I was pregnant then. This house didn't look so bad when we first moved in. Every week it gets worse. Nothing is ever fixed. We now had no money. There were a few odd jobs for my husband, but everything went for food then, as it does now. I don't know how we lived through three years and three babies, but we did. I'll tell you something, after the last baby I destroyed my marriage. It had been a good one, but could you keep on bringing children in this dirt? Did you ever think how much it costs for any kind of birth control? I knew my husband was leaving the day he left, but there were no goodbye between us. I hope he has been able to climb out of this mess somewhere. He never could hope with us to drag him down.   8

That's when I asked for help. When I got it, you know how much it was? It was, and is, seventy-eight dollars a month for the four of us; that is all I ever can get. Now you know why there is no soap, no needles and thread, no hot water, no aspirin, no worm medicine, no hand cream, no shampoo. None of these things forever and ever and ever. So that you can see clearly, I pay twenty dollars a month rent, and most of the rest goes for food. For grits and cornmeal, and rice and milk and beans. I try my best to use only the minimum electricity. If I use more, there is that much less for food.

Poverty is looking into a black future. Your children won't play with my boys. They will turn to other boys who steal to get what they want. I can already see them behind the bars of their prison instead of behind the bars of my poverty. Or they will turn to the freedom of alcohol or drugs, and find themselves enslaved. And my daughter? At best, there is for her a life like mine.

But you say to me, there are schools. Yes, there are schools. My children have no extra books, no magazines, no extra pencils, or crayons, or paper and most important of all, they do not have health. They have worms, they have infections, they have pink-eye all summer. They do not sleep well on the floor, or with me in my one bed. They do not suffer from hunger, my seventy-eight dollars keeps us alive, but they do suffer from malnutrition. Oh yes, I do remember what I was taught about health in school. It doesn't do much good.

In some places there is a surplus commodities program. Not here. The country said it cost too much. There is a school lunch program. But I have two children who will already be damaged by the time they get to school.

But, you say to me, there are health clinics. Yes, there are health clinics and they are in the towns. I live out here eight miles from town. I can walk that far (even if it is sixteen miles both ways), but can my little children? My neighbor will take me when he goes; but he expects to get paid, one way or another. I bet you know my neighbor. He is that large man who spends his time at the gas station, the barbershop, and the corner store complaining about the government spending money on the immoral mothers of illegitimate children.

Poverty is an acid that drips on pride until all pride is worn away. Poverty is a chisel that chips on honor until honor is worn away. Some of you say that you would do something in my situation, and maybe you would, for the first week or the first month, but for year after year after year?

Even the poor can dream. A dream of a time when there is money. Money for the right kinds of food, for worm medicine, for iron pills, for toothbrushes, for hand cream, for a hammer and nails and a bit of screening, for a shovel, for a bit of paint, for some sheeting, for needles and thread. Money to pay in money for a trip to town. And, oh, money for hot water and money for soap. A dream of when asking for help does not eat away the last bit of pride. When the office you visit is as nice as the offices of other governmental agencies, when there are enough workers to help you quickly, when workers do not quit in defeat and despair. When you have to tell your story to only one person, and that person can send you for other help and you don't have to prove your poverty over and over and over again.

I have come out of my despair to tell you this. Remember I did not come from another place or another time. Others like me are all around you. Look at us with an angry heart, anger that will help.

Vocabulary Before, during, and after reading the selection, annotate the text and write in your journal. Create a list of vocabulary words, along with their definitions. Give examples of their use from the selection you just read.

After Reading Discussion Questions: Meaning, Structure, and Expression

1. **Main Idea:** Work as a group to write a summary that answers the following questions: What purpose did Jo Goodwin-Parker have for writing this essay? Who is her intended audience? What is the main idea of the essay?

2. **Relevant Details:** Parker offers her own life experiences to define poverty. Does she provide enough details to make her point convincingly? Would the use of facts or expert opinions strengthen her point? Why or why not?

3. **Logical Order:** Parker defines poverty with a series of seven statements that begin with "Poverty is." Summarize her definition of poverty using these seven statements. Do you agree with the order in which she presents these statements? Why or why not?

4. **Effective Expression:** Based on Parker's choice of words, how would you describe the tone of this essay? Is it angry, embarrassed, disappointed, reflective, sad, or optimistic, or does it communicate some other attitude about poverty? Identify three expressions that illustrate the tone of the piece. Explain the reasons for your selections.

Thinking Prompts to Move from Reading to Writing

1. Often, people do not understand what they have not experienced. Parker defines poverty for people who have never experienced it. In the last sentence in the first paragraph, she commands her readers to step into her shoes so they can learn from her experiences. Assume the view of one who understands an issue such as depression, addiction, or prejudice based on experience. Write an essay that defines the issue so that someone who has not experienced it can better understand the problem.

2. In her essay, Parker defines the problem of poverty, but she does not offer a solution, other than to say "look at us with an angry heart, anger that will help." What kind of anger will help this situation? Respond to Parker by writing an essay that defines this kind of anger. Consider using a phrase like "Anger that will help is" to reply to specific points she raises in her essay.

Don't Call Me Middle Class: I'm a Professional

MARK PENN

Mark Penn is the worldwide CEO of the public relations firm Burson-Marsteller, president of the polling firm Penn, Schoen and Berland Associates, and author of *Microtrends: The Small Forces Behind Tomorrow's Big Changes.* Penn has helped to elect over twenty-five leaders in the United States, Asia, Latin America, and Europe in addition to serving as chief adviser to President Bill Clinton in the 1996 presidential election and to Hillary Rodham Clinton through her Senate and presidential races. The following article appeared in the *Wall Street Journal.*

Before Reading Write a journal entry about your understanding of "class" in America. For example, what does it mean to be "middle class"? What does it mean to be "blue collar"? What does it mean to be a "professional"?

Not long ago, everyone in America wanted to be a member of the "middle class." In fact, as many as 53% of Americans described themselves that way to pollsters.

But with the information age and the rise of two-career incomes, being just middle class is a little old hat. The new aspiration for most Americans is to be a member of the new professional class. Rising numbers—as high as 64%—report that they consider themselves "professionals." The census shows a significant rise over the years, from 4% being professionals and skilled workers in 1910, to 36% today. The numbers have doubled since just 1980.

These new professionals, whose incomes were rising steadily until the financial crisis, have been at the heart of reshaping the country's economic and political life. Barack Obama more than any other president represents this shift and has uniquely appealed to these Americans. Everyone today wants to be a professional and most people believe they are.

The seeds of this surging class were in the new economy. As President Clinton used to point out all the time, 24 million new jobs were created during his eight-year tenure. None, however, were in the manufacturing sector, which now covers less than one in 10 jobs overall.

The traditional definition of a professional still applies: people with an advanced degree in areas like law, medicine or divinity. They have reached record numbers, approaching 100,000 a year. There are about 43,000 law degrees awarded annually, a 20% increase in the past decade. Even larger professions today are those of teachers and nurses, who number just over 6.5 million.

But the definition of professional has expanded. Most people in the fields of advertising, communications, health care and computer science consider themselves professionals. Often they even have new titles to convey this—for example what used to be called "headhunters" are now Career Management Professionals.

A look at the fastest-growing jobs shows how new-information professionals are emerging in high numbers. Network engineers are projected to be the fastest growing group in America, with computer software engineers also high on the list. Other groups with record numbers: home health aides for aging baby boomers, and veterinarians, for all the animals affected by the growing humanization of pets.

An analysis of the last election showed the emergence of this new class. Exit polls showed that in 1996, just 9% of households earned over $100,000. In last year's election, one in four (26%) earned over $100,000. And the fabled 1% earning over $200,000 in income were actually 6% of the voters. The lowest economic class over the same period saw its numbers fall nearly in half. (Of course inflation accounts for some of the change, but not all of it.)

In the past, the $100,000+ earners voted solidly Republican. In the last election, they were evenly split, with the $200,000+ voters picking Obama over McCain by 52/46. This was a sea change in political behavior for this group, now dominated by the emergence of the new professional class.

But while these political numbers are surprising, they depict a change that is much wider than the last presidential election or just politics. In the past the $100,000+ earners were dominated by small business owners and corporate executives—people who ran organizations and were strongly antigovernment—viewing government action as an intrusion into their freedom.

Today's new professional is better educated, better read, more plugged-in, more socially tolerant, more environmentally conscious—and while they like individuality in how they dress and act, they are much more open to having government solve our problems. Jobs like "network" engineer are all about improving collaboration.

But if "new professionals" were the "soccer moms" of the last election, how will this spill over into commercial life? Soccer moms needed minivans. What do new professionals need?

Clearly they are the heart of the marketplace for high-end technology. Apple marketing and pricing goes right to the core of this group. More than anything else, smart phones are the SUVs of the new professional class. Currently one in 10 phones in the U.S. is a smart phone, but that is growing at 35% a year. The Amazon Kindle would be attractive to technology-savvy professionals who like to read. 13

The titles of young professionals may be loftier and more formal—everyone these days is "chief" of something, from "chief talent officer" to "chief of creativity." But their clothing, of course, is more casual—neat, modern and green. And while hybrids are just 2.5% of all car purchases, 42% of hybrid drivers are in this class. Toyota and Lexus hit the sweet spot of these buyers over the last few years while Audi is making a comeback. Mercedes lost ground with them. 14

Younger professionals are pouring into the cities, creating unexpected revivals there while older professionals are retiring to the Sunbelt, creating new stresses in those communities. 15

In many ways, we are catching up to Europe. Those societies made the transition away from manufacturing earlier, producing professionals who wanted more stable lives with state-provided healthcare, longer maternity leaves and social help for raising children. And so the convergence of these attitudes and the collapse of the Republican Party are tied to the growth of the new professional voter and their changed outlook. 16

In the 1950s it was Levittown and the middle class that changed our society by creating the suburbs and a renewed focus on individual opportunity as the key to success. Today it's the professional class that is reshaping where and how we live, and its emphasis on the network, teamwork and collaboration is spearheading a new outlook on everything from technology to government intervention. 17

Vocabulary
Before, during, and after reading the selection, annotate the text and write in your journal. Create a list of vocabulary words, along with their definitions. Give examples of their use from the selection you just read.

After Reading Discussion Questions: Meaning, Structure, and Expression

1. **Main Idea:** Work as a group to write a summary that answers the following questions: What purpose did Mark Penn have for writing this essay? Who is the intended audience? What is the main idea of the essay?
2. **Relevant Details:** Mark Penn describes the traits and gives examples of the "new professional." Identify three traits of the new professional. Then, identify at least one example of each trait.
3. **Logical Order:** Mark Penn waits until paragraphs 5 and 6 to clearly define the term "professional." Should he have defined this term earlier in the article? Why or why not?
4. **Effective Expression:** At times, Mark Penn uses slang such as "old hat," "plugged-in," and "sweet spot." Other times, he uses the jargon of a market researcher such as "the humanization of pets" and "political numbers . . . predict a change." Is this mixture of informal and formal tones effective? Why or why not?

Thinking Prompts to Move from Reading to Writing

1. In paragraph 13, Mark Penn states that high-end technology is as important to the new professional as the minivan was to a soccer mom. What is high-end technology? Why is high-end technology so important to the new professional? Assume you are a new professional such as a personal trainer, lawyer, or Web page designer. You are writing a business plan to submit to the Small Business Association for a start-up loan. Define

your profession, and describe the kind of technology you need to purchase to succeed in your profession.

2. In his essay, Mark Penn claims that the professional class has changed our society. Based on his article, in what ways has the professional class reshaped society? What other cultures have had an impact on American life? Define a culture of your choice, such as the Hip-hop culture. In your definition, discuss the influence this culture has had—or is having—on American society. Assume you are writing an academic paper for a humanities class or a posting for a blog about diversity and tolerance.

Cause–Effect

Through Young Eyes

MICHAEL S. MALONE

Michael S. Malone is the author of a dozen best-selling business books including *The Virtual Corporation, Going Public, Infinite Loop* (the Apple story), and *Virtual Selling*. In addition, Malone writes *The Silicon Insider*, a popular weekly technology column for ABCNews.com. He also contributes regularly to the *Wall Street Journal, Wired,* and *Fast Company*. Currently, Malone serves as Editor-in-Chief of Edgelings.com, a news and features website founded by a team of prominent Silicon Valley media and technology executives. The following article appeared in Edgelings.com in the Consumer Electronics and Lifestyle/Culture section.

Before Reading Write a journal entry about your experiences with technology. Does technology—such as social networks, smart phones, the Web, instant messaging, online gaming—improve a person's life? In what ways? Can these forms of technology be harmful? In what ways? Does the good of technology outweigh the bad? Why or why not?

1 Technology in all of its forms—social networks, smart phones, the Web, instant messaging, on-line gaming—is a net loss for today's young people. At least according to one group of Silicon Valley 8th graders.

2 "It's bad for us, but it sure is fun," says Eric Bautista, 13, one of the students in Sister Jolene Schmitz's junior high school class at Resurrection School in Sunnyvale, California.

3 Admittedly, this informal survey offers, at best, only anecdotal evidence. Still, it is pretty shocking that a group of young teenagers, all of them technologically very astute, and living in the very heart of Silicon Valley, would come to such a conclusion.

4 These kids, born about the time the Internet became widely adopted, live within blocks of where the Intel microprocessor, the Apple computer and the Atari video game were all invented. They spend their days (and nights) surfing the web, playing on-line games and instant messaging. Most have cell phones in their backpacks. And many have at least one parent who works in the electronics industry.

5 Yet, when asked to weigh the benefits of having high technology in their lives versus the costs—intellectually, emotionally, socially—of that technology, the class voted 31–3 negative . . . a ratio so extreme that it argues against an aberration and towards a larger question about the overall impact of technology on the lives of our young people.

6 "We try to find the happy medium," says Stephanie Abreu, 13, "But we don't know where it is."

7 This isn't to say that the 8th graders, all of them heading off to top-tier Silicon Valley high schools, don't love their tech toys and tools. On the contrary, when asked to list all of the positives about tech, they weren't short of answers: access to information with unprecedented scope, the ability to socialize with large groups over vast distances, 24/7 multi-media communication, and perhaps best of all, whole new worlds of entertainment.

Moreover, this brave new digital world has always been part of their lives and, perhaps a bit jaded by it all, they find the idea of world without computers and cell phones surprisingly appealing: in a class vote, one-third of the students said they would prefer to have lived in the long-ago, pre-tech world of the late 1950s.

When asked what they find wrong with living in our modern Wired Web World, the students had no shortage of answers, most of which fell into a half-dozen categories. I'll let the students largely speak for themselves—voices describing the dark side of the tech revolution with a sincerity few of us adults have ever heard before:

- *Time-waster*: "Technology is the key to procrastination," says Kenny Kobetsky, 14. Eighty percent of the class said they had missed sleep due to playing on the Internet, fifty percent said they had forgotten to do homework for the same reason. "The Internet is just so tantalizing," says Nick Gregov, 14. "I actually think McDonalds is healthier than my computer," adds Blake Billiet, 13. Though the students did admit that the Web and cellphone can save time that used to be burned up driving to the store or library, few felt that these gains exceeded the many hours wasted on text or web surfing.

- *Loss of motivation*: "With all of these toys, it's hard to get out of the house," says Sybile Moser, 14. Many of the students said that while technology makes it easier to access information and learn new things, the lack of interaction with others often makes that learning biased and distorted—you only learn what you want to learn. "The students miss the give and take, the debate of learning together when they are on the Web," says Sister Jolene. Because of this, the students say, it's hard for them to keep their attention fixed on any one topic, but prefer instead to drift along in the information flow, letting it take them wherever it leads.

- *Addictive*: "The Internet is like a gateway drug," says Christine Doan, 13. Alex Nguyen, 13, compared the experience to eating ice cream—you love it even though it's bad for you. Even at their young age, many of the students already have Facebook pages and spend as much time there as watching television. Not surprisingly then, when asked if, despite all of their worries about the cost of technology in their lives, if any of them would give up their laptop or their cellphone, almost no one raised a hand.

- *Second Hand Knowledge*: This answer was probably the biggest surprise. The eighth graders seemed to intuitively appreciate that the experiences and information they received from the Web and other digital sources was essentially a simulacrum of reality—a re-creation on a glowing flat screen of the three dimensional natural world . . . and that something was being lost in the translation. "We don't get as much out of things if we don't experience them ourselves," says Lauren Fahey, 13. "We seem to spend a lot of our lives as bystanders," adds Katherine Wu, 13.

- *Exposure*: The news is regularly filled with stories of Internet predators preying on naïve young people, or about the easy availability to adolescents of on-line pornography and other vices. But these eighth graders were anything but innocents about the dark side of the Web—and indeed, showed surprising maturity in their strategies for coping with threats all-but unknown to previous generations. "Look, when you're talking to a 'friend', you don't really know if it's really them—especially if they are introduced by someone else," says Peyton Yniguez, 14. "The nature of friendship changes," says Jonathon Robbins, 14. But the most astute, and disturbing, comment belonged to Jenna Kunz, 14: "You have to develop your own special conscience for the Internet."

- *Disturbed Values*: All of these forces can't help but affect a young person's sense of values. The eighth graders, in some ways sophisticated beyond their years, instinctively understand that. "We can't respect anything anymore," says Eric Bautista. Adds Jenna Kunz, "You don't care about things as much; you aren't as passionate as you should be." And yet, that said, these are still kids who are excited about graduation and the prospects of the impending four years of high school. And world-weary as they might sound, each one of the above comments provoked conversation so loud and lively that Sister Jolene spent most of the time just trying to keep the noise down to a dull roar.   15

In the end, if the news is surprising to us adults that teenagers believe technology is a net loss in their lives, there is consolation in knowing that these young people —themselves creations of the digital age—are not starry-eyed acolytes of the latest computer game or web site. Rather, technology is the world they casually operate within and they have a deep understanding of its rewards and its costs, what it gives and takes away. And for all of our fears for them, they themselves show an extraordinary sense of perspective.   16

Stephanie Abreu said it best: "Technology is like family. Sometimes it's good, sometimes bad. But you love it all the same."   17

Special thanks to Sr. Jolene's 8th grade class at Resurrection School, Sunnyvale, California for its assistance in the preparation of this article.   18

Vocabulary   Before, during, and after reading the selection, annotate the text and write in your journal. Create a list of vocabulary words, along with their definitions. Give examples of their use from the selection you just read.

After Reading Discussion Questions: Meaning, Structure, and Expression

1. **Main Idea:** Work as a group to write a summary that answers the following questions: What purpose did Michael S. Malone have for writing this essay? Who is the intended audience? What is the main idea of the essay?
2. **Relevant Details:** In paragraph 9, Malone states "I'll let the students largely speak for themselves—" to signal his use of direct quotes as supporting details. Why does he use so many direct quotes? Does he use too many? Would the essay be more effective if he had paraphrased the students' ideas? Why or why not? Are these students a good source of information? Why or why not?
3. **Logical Order:** In paragraphs 10 through 15, Malone lists the things these young people think is wrong with technology—a list of six harmful effects arising from the "dark side of the tech revolution." Do you think Michael Malone presented the list in a particular order of importance? For example, is "time waster" less harmful than "disturbed values"? Are all these effects equally harmful? Assume Malone did list the effects from least to most significant. Do you agree with the given order? Would you reorder these effects based on their significance? How and why?
4. **Effective Expression:** Reread paragraph 14. In the last sentence of the paragraph, Jenna Kunz, 14, states "You have to develop your own special conscience for the Internet." Malone describes her statement as "the most astute, and disturbing." What does she imply in her use of the word "conscience" in her statement? What kind of "special conscience" is needed for the Internet? Do you agree with Malone's assessment about her comment? Why or why not?

Thinking Prompts to Move from Reading to Writing

1. "Through Young Eyes" generated some online comments from readers. One reader criticized the article by writing, "Interview 'normal' teens at a non-Catholic school and

you will get a different answer." Do the students' views as expressed in this article represent the views of "normal" youth? Would most youth agree that technology is harmful? Work with a group of your peers and conduct your own research into this topic. Create a survey based on the information in this article. Ask students in your classes to fill out the survey. Then, write a report on your findings based on the anecdotal evidence you gather from the survey. Assume you are writing an academic paper for a sociology class.

2. Michael Malone introduces his topic in the first sentence as "technology in all of its forms." His article explores the effects of technology on a general level. Narrow this line of thought by focusing on a specific type of technology. For example, think about the views expressed in the reading selections "How to Write a Personal Letter" by Garrison Keillor and "How to Twitter" by Julia Angwin. Write an essay that explains how technology has impacted written communication for better or worse. Assume you will post your writing as a comment to Malone's article "Through Young Eyes" on Edgelings.com. Or write an academic paper for a humanities course that explains how technology in transportation has affected society for better or worse.

Why We Crave Horror Movies
STEPHEN KING

Stephen King, born in Portland, Maine in 1947, has been writing full-time since the 1973 publication of his novel *Carrie*. He has since published over 40 books and has become one of the world's most successful writers.

Before Reading Write a journal entry about your reaction to horror movies. Do you enjoy horror movies? Why or why not? Why do you think horror movies are so popular? Do graphically violent horror movies have a harmful effect on society? Explain your reasons.

I think that we're all mentally ill: those of us outside the asylums only hide it a little better—and maybe not all that much better, after all. We've all known people who talk to themselves, people who sometimes squinch their faces into horrible grimaces when they believe no one is watching, people who have some hysterical fear—of snakes, the dark, the tight place, the long drop . . . and, of course, those final worms and grubs that are waiting so patiently underground.   1

When we pay our four or five bucks and seat ourselves at tenth-row center in a theater showing a horror movie, we are daring the nightmare.   2

Why? Some of the reasons are simple and obvious. To show that we can, that we are not afraid, that we can ride this roller coaster. Which is not to say that a really good horror movie may not surprise a scream out of us at some point, the way we may scream when the roller coaster twists through a complete 360 or plows through a lake at the bottom of the drop. And horror movies, like roller coasters, have always been the special province of the young; by the time one turns 40 or 50, one's appetite for double twists or 360-degree loops may be considerably depleted.   3

We also go to re-establish our feelings of essential normality; the horror movie is innately conservative, even reactionary. Freda Jackson as the horrible melting woman in *Die, Monster, Die!* confirms for us that no matter how far we may be removed from the beauty of a Robert Redford or a Diana Ross, we are still light-years from true ugliness.   4

And we go to have fun.   5

Ah, but this is where the ground starts to slope away, isn't it? Because this is a very peculiar sort of fun indeed. The fun comes from seeing others menaced—sometimes killed. One critic has suggested that if pro football has become the voyeur's version of combat, then the horror film has become the modern version of the public lynching.

6

It is true that the mythic, "fairytale" horror film intends to take away the shades of gray. . . . It urges us to put away our more civilized and adult penchant for analysis and to become children again, seeing things in pure blacks and whites. It may be that horror movies provide psychic relief on this level because this invitation to lapse into simplicity, irrationality and even outright madness is extended so rarely. We are told we may allow our emotions a free rein . . . or no rein at all.

7

If we are all insane, then sanity becomes a matter of degree. If your insanity leads you to carve up women like Jack the Ripper or the Cleveland Torso Murderer, we clap you away in the funny farm (but neither of those two amateur-night surgeons was ever caught, heh-heh-heh); if, on the other hand your insanity leads you only to talk to yourself when you're under stress or to pick your nose on the morning bus, then you are left alone to go about your business . . . though it is doubtful that you will ever be invited to the best parties.

8

The potential lyncher is in almost all of us (excluding saints, past and present; but then, most saints have been crazy in their own ways), and every now and then, he has to be let loose to scream and roll around in the grass. Our emotions and our fears form their own body, and we recognize that it demands its own exercise to maintain proper muscle tone. Certain of these emotional muscles are accepted—even exalted—in civilized society; they are, of course, the emotions that tend to maintain the status quo of civilization itself. Love, friendship, loyalty, kindness—these are all the emotions that we applaud, emotions that have been immortalized in the couplets of Hallmark cards. . . .

9

When we exhibit these emotions, society showers us with positive reinforcement; we learn this even before we get out of diapers. When, as children, we hug our rotten little puke of a sister and give her a kiss, all the aunts and uncles smile and twit and cry, "Isn't he the sweetest little thing?" Such coveted treats as chocolate-covered graham crackers often follow. But if we deliberately slam the rotten little puke of a sister's fingers in the door, sanctions follow—angry remonstrance from parents, aunts and uncles; instead of a chocolate-covered graham cracker, a spanking.

10

But anticivilization emotions don't go away, and they demand periodic exercise. We have such "sick" jokes as, "What's the difference between a truckload of bowling balls and a truckload of dead babies?" (You can't unload a truckload of bowling balls with a pitchfork . . . a joke, by the way, that I heard originally from a ten-year-old.) Such a joke may surprise a laugh or a grin out of us even as we recoil, a possibility that confirms the thesis: If we share a brotherhood of man, then we also share an insanity of man. None of which is intended as a defense of either the sick joke or insanity but merely as an explanation of why the best horror films, like the best fairy tales, manage to be reactionary, anarchistic, and revolutionary all at the same time.

11

The mythic horror movie, like the sick joke, has a dirty job to do. It deliberately appeals to all that is worst in us. It is morbidity unchained, our most base instincts let free, our nastiest fantasies realized . . . and it all happens, fittingly enough, in the dark. For those reasons, good liberals often shy away from horror films. For myself, I like to see the most aggressive of them—*Dawn of the Dead*, for instance—as lifting a trap door in the civilized forebrain and throwing a basket of raw meat to the hungry alligators swimming around in that subterranean river beneath.

12

Why bother? Because it keeps them from getting out, man. It keeps them down there and me up here. It was Lennon and McCartney who said that all you need is love, and I would agree with that.

13

As long as you keep the gators fed.

14

Vocabulary   Before, during, and after reading the selection, annotate the text and write in your journal. Create a list of vocabulary words, along with their definitions. Give examples of their use from the selection you just read.

After Reading Discussion Questions: Meaning, Structure, and Expression

1. **Main Idea:** Work as a group to write a summary that answers the following questions: What purpose did Stephen King have for writing this essay? Who is his intended audience? What is the essay's main idea?
2. **Relevant Details:** In paragraphs 10 and 11, King uses children as examples to support his point. Why do you think he uses these examples? Do you think these examples are typical of most children? Do you agree that these examples effectively support his point? Why or why not?
3. **Logical Order:** King declares his thesis in paragraph 11. Locate his thesis statement. Why do you think King waited until this late in the essay to state his thesis? Reread his introduction. What is his opening point? Why do you think he opened his essay with this idea? How would the impact of the essay change if King had stated his thesis in the opening paragraph?
4. **Effective Expression:** To make his point, King appeals to our senses and prior experiences with references to roller coasters, Jack the Ripper, lynching, and alligators. Discuss how each of these images supports his point.

Thinking Prompts to Move from Reading to Writing

1. King offers reasons that explain the positive effects of horror movies. However, many disagree with this view and see the violence in horror movies as a negative factor in our society. Write an essay that explains the negative impact of horror movies.
2. King claims that we are "all mentally ill" and that horror movies appeal to the "worst in us." However, many believe that humans are basically good. The famous American essayist Emerson once encouraged us "to look into yourselves and do good because you are good." Write an essay that illustrates the goodness and positive impact of human nature. Consider, for example, the reasons and effects of Habitat for Humanity or other charities or volunteer organizations.

Persuasion

Let's Tell the Story of All America's Cultures

YUH JI-YEON

Yuh Ji-Yeon, born in 1965, immigrated with her parents to Chicago from Seoul, Korea. She is best known for her book *Beyond the Shadow of Camptown* that examines the experiences of Korean women who immigrated to this country as brides of U.S. soldiers. She currently teaches history at Northwestern University.

Before Reading Write a journal entry about the positive contributions of minorities to the culture of the United States. For example, how have African Americans, Asians, or Latinos affected music, movies, fashion, or politics? Identify a particular person who has made a specific contribution. Do you think history books adequately record the contributions made by minorities? Explain your reasons.

I grew up hearing, seeing and almost believing that America was white—albeit with a little black tinge here and there—and that white was best. 1

The white people were everywhere in my 1970s Chicago childhood: Founding Fathers, Lewis and Clark, Lincoln, Daniel Boone, Carnegie, presidents, explorers and industrialists galore. The only black people were slaves. The only Indians were scalpers. 2

I never heard one word about how Benjamin Franklin was so impressed by the Iroquois federation of nations that he adapted that model into our system of state and federal government. Or that the Indian tribes were systematically betrayed and massacred by a greedy young nation that stole their land and called it the United States. 3

I never heard one word about how Asian immigrants were among the first to turn California's desert into fields of plenty. Or about Chinese immigrant Ah Bing, who bred the cherry now on sale in groceries across the nation. Or that plantation owners in Hawaii imported labor from China, Japan, Korea and the Philippines to work the sugar cane fields. I never learned that Asian immigrants were the only immigrants denied U.S. citizenship, even though they served honorably in World War I. All the immigrants in my textbook were white. 4

I never learned about Frederick Douglass, the runaway slave who became a leading abolitionist and statesman, or about black scholar W.E.B. Du Bois. I never learned that black people rose up in arms against slavery. Nat Turner wasn't one of the heroes in my childhood history class. 5

I never learned that the American Southwest and California were already settled by Mexicans when they were annexed after the Mexican-American War. I never learned that Mexico once had a problem keeping land-hungry white men on the U.S. side of the border. 6

So when other children called me a slant-eyed chink and told me to go back where I came from, I was ready to believe that I wasn't really an American because I wasn't white. 7

America's bittersweet legacy of struggling and failing and getting another step closer to democratic ideals of liberty and equality and justice for all wasn't for the likes of me, an immigrant child from Korea. The history books said so. 8

Well, the history books were wrong. 9

Educators around the country are finally realizing what I realized as a teenager in the library, looking up the history I wasn't getting in school. America is a multicultural nation, composed of many people with varying histories and varying traditions who have little in common except their humanity, a belief in democracy and a desire for freedom. 10

America changed them, but they changed America too. 11

A committee of scholars and teachers gathered by the New York State Department of Education recognizes this in their recent report, "One Nation, Many Peoples: A Declaration of Cultural Interdependence." 12

They recommend that public schools provide a "multicultural education, anchored to the shared principles of a liberal democracy." 13

What that means, according to the report, is recognizing that America was shaped and continues to be shaped by people of diverse backgrounds. It calls for students to be taught that history is an ongoing process of discovery and interpretation of the past, and that there is more than one way of viewing the world. 14

Thus, the westward migration of white Americans is not just a heroic settling of an untamed wild, but also the conquest of indigenous peoples. Immigrants were not just white, but Asian as well. Blacks were not merely passive slaves freed by northern whites, but active fighters for their own liberation. 15

In particular, according to the report, the curriculum should help children "to assess critically the reasons for the inconsistencies between the ideals of the U.S. and social realities. It should provide information and intellectual tools that can permit them to contribute to bringing reality closer to the ideals." 16

In other words, show children the good with the bad, and give them the skills to help improve their country. What could be more patriotic? 17

Several dissenting members of the New York committee publicly worry that America will splinter into ethnic fragments if this multicultural curriculum is adopted. They argue that the committee's report puts the focus on ethnicity at the expense of national unity. 18

But downplaying ethnicity will not bolster national unity. The history of America is the story of how and why people from all over the world came to the United States, and how in struggling to make a better life for themselves, they changed each other, they changed the country, and they all came to call themselves Americans. 19

E pluribus unum. Out of many, one. 20

This is why I, with my Korean background, and my childhood tormentors, with their lost-in-the-mist-of-time European backgrounds, are all Americans. 21

It is the unique beauty of this country. It is high time we let all our children gaze upon it. 22

Vocabulary
Before, during, and after reading the selection, annotate the text and write in your journal. Create a list of vocabulary words, along with their definitions. Give examples of their use from the selection you just read.

After Reading Discussion Questions: Meaning, Structure, and Expression

1. **Main Idea:** Work as a group to write a summary that answers the following questions: What purpose did Yuh Ji-Yeon have for writing this essay? Who is her intended audience? What is the essay's main idea?
2. **Relevant Details:** Yuh blends details from her personal experiences with expert opinions. Identify the details based on her experiences. Are the personal details she

provides convincing enough to persuade her reader to agree with her? Identify the details based on expert opinions. Does Yuh provide enough expert opinions and factual details to make her point? Why did she choose to include both personal experiences and expert opinions? Is the mixture persuasive? Why or why not?

3. **Logical Order:** An effective persuasive technique is to answer the concerns of the opposing view. Yuh waits to address the opposing view until paragraph 18. Why did she choose to do so at this point in her essay? Would her point be better made if she addressed the opposing view earlier in the essay? Why or why not?

4. **Effective Expression:** In paragraphs 1 through 6, Yuh repeats the parallel phrases "I never heard" or "I never learned." What is the impact of repeating these phrases and other parallel expressions on the essay's effectiveness? Explain your answer.

Thinking Prompts to Move from Reading to Writing

1. Yuh identifies and argues against one problem in education that she sees as particularly troubling. What problems have you noticed in our country's educational system or at your institution? For example, some suggest school uniforms as a solution to behavior problems and underachievement in public education. Another example is the acute problem of binge drinking on college campuses. Identify a problem or a solution to a problem in education. Take a stand on the issue. Write an essay that convinces others to agree with your stand; be sure to answer the opposing view.

2. Yuh calls for educators to "tell the story of all America's cultures," and she offers several examples of important historical figures that she never learned about in school. Identify a person, place, or event that students should study. Write an essay to convince your teacher, school board, or community to include this person, place, or event in the curriculum. Anticipate and answer the opposing view.

I Have a Dream
MARTIN LUTHER KING, JR.

Dr. Martin Luther King, Jr., born in Atlanta, Georgia, became a Baptist minister and one of the greatest civil rights leaders of the twentieth century. Influenced by Henry David Thoreau and Mahatma Gandhi, King transformed the civil rights movement of the 1950s and 1960s with his message of nonviolent civil disobedience as a means to achieve racial equality. He received the Nobel Peace Prize in 1964. King was assassinated on April 4, 1968, at the age of 39. The following passage is considered one of his most memorable speeches, delivered on the occasion of the March on Washington, a demonstration in the nation's capital in support of equal rights, on August 28, 1963. Dr. King spoke to more than 200,000 marchers from the steps of the Lincoln Memorial that day.

Before Reading Write a journal entry about Dr. Martin Luther King, Jr. and the civil rights movement. What do you know about what happened? What impact has Dr. King had on our society?

I am happy to join with you today in what will go down in history as the greatest demonstration for freedom in the history of our nation.

Five score years ago, a great American, in whose symbolic shadow we stand today, signed the Emancipation Proclamation. This momentous decree came as a great beacon light of hope to millions of Negro slaves who had been seared in the flames of withering injustice. It came as a joyous daybreak to end the long night of their captivity. But one hundred years later, the Negro still is not free. One hundred years later, the life of the Negro is still sadly crippled by the manacles of segregation and the chains of discrimination. One hundred years later, the Negro lives on a lonely island of poverty in the midst of a vast ocean of material prosperity. One hundred years later, the Negro is still languished in the corners of American society and finds himself an exile in his own land. And so we've come here today to dramatize a shameful condition.

In a sense we've come to our nation's capital to cash a check. When the architects of our republic wrote the magnificent words of the Constitution and the Declaration of Independence, they were signing a promissory note to which every American was to fall heir. This note was a promise that all men, yes, black men as well as white men, would be guaranteed the "unalienable Rights" of "Life, Liberty and the pursuit of Happiness." It is obvious today that America has defaulted on this promissory note, insofar as her citizens of color are concerned. Instead of honoring this sacred obligation, America has given the Negro people a bad check, a check which has come back marked "insufficient funds."

But we refuse to believe that the bank of justice is bankrupt. We refuse to believe that there are insufficient funds in the great vaults of opportunity of this nation. And so, we've come to cash this check, a check that will give us upon demand the riches of freedom and the security of justice.

We have also come to this hallowed spot to remind America of the fierce urgency of Now. This is no time to engage in the luxury of cooling off or to take the tranquilizing drug of gradualism. Now is the time to make real the promises of democracy. Now is the time to rise from the dark and desolate valley of segregation to the sunlit path of racial justice. Now is the time to lift our nation from the quicksands of racial injustice to the solid rock of brotherhood. Now is the time to make justice a reality for all of God's children.

It would be fatal for the nation to overlook the urgency of the moment. This sweltering summer of the Negro's legitimate discontent will not pass until there is an invigorating autumn of freedom and equality. Nineteen sixty-three is not an end, but a beginning. And those who hope that the Negro needed to blow off steam and will now be content will have a rude awakening if the nation returns to business as usual. And there will be neither rest nor tranquility in America until the Negro is granted his citizenship rights. The whirlwinds of revolt will continue to shake the foundations of our nation until the bright day of justice emerges.

But there is something that I must say to my people, who stand on the warm threshold which leads into the palace of justice: In the process of gaining our rightful place, we must not be guilty of wrongful deeds. Let us not seek to satisfy our thirst for freedom by drinking from the cup of bitterness and hatred. We must forever conduct our struggle on the high plane of dignity and discipline. We must not allow our creative protest to degenerate into physical violence. Again and again, we must rise to the majestic heights of meeting physical force with soul force.

The marvelous new militancy which has engulfed the Negro community must not lead us to a distrust of all white people, for many of our white brothers, as evidenced by their presence here today, have come to realize that their destiny is tied up with our destiny. And they have come to realize that their freedom is inextricably bound to our freedom.

We cannot walk alone. 9

And as we walk, we must make the pledge that we shall always march ahead. 10

We cannot turn back. 11

There are those who are asking the devotees of civil rights, "When will you be satisfied?" We 12
can never be satisfied as long as the Negro is the victim of the unspeakable horrors of police
brutality. We can never be satisfied as long as our bodies, heavy with the fatigue of travel,
cannot gain lodging in the motels of the highways and the hotels of the cities. We cannot be
satisfied as long as the Negro's basic mobility is from a smaller ghetto to a larger one. We can
never be satisfied as long as our children are stripped of their self-hood and robbed of their
dignity by signs stating: "For Whites Only." We cannot be satisfied as long as a Negro in
Mississippi cannot vote and a Negro in New York believes he has nothing for which to vote.
No, no, we are not satisfied, and we will not be satisfied until "justice rolls down like waters,
and righteousness like a mighty stream."

I am not unmindful that some of you have come here out of great trials and tribulations. 13
Some of you have come fresh from narrow jail cells. And some of you have come from areas
of persecution and staggered by the winds of police brutality. You have been the veterans of
creative suffering. Continue to work with the faith that unearned suffering is redemptive. Go
back to Mississippi, go back to Alabama, go back to South Carolina, go back to Georgia, go
back to Louisiana, go back to the slums and ghettos of our northern cities, knowing that
somehow this situation can and will be changed.

Let us not wallow in the valley of despair, I say to you today, my friends. 14

And so even though we face the difficulties of today and tomorrow, I still have a dream. It is 15
a dream deeply rooted in the American dream.

I have a dream that one day this nation will rise up and live out the true meaning of its 16
creed: "We hold these truths to be self-evident, that all men are created equal."

I have a dream that one day on the red hills of Georgia, the sons of former slaves and the 17
sons of former slave owners will be able to sit down together at the table of brotherhood.

I have a dream that one day even the state of Mississippi, a state sweltering with the heat of 18
injustice, sweltering with the heat of oppression, will be transformed into an oasis of freedom
and justice.

I have a dream that my four little children will one day live in a nation where they will not 19
be judged by the color of their skin but by the content of their character.

I have a *dream* today! 20

I have a dream that one day, down in Alabama, with its vicious racists, with its governor 21
having his lips dripping with the words of "interposition" and "nullification"—one day right
there in Alabama little black boys and black girls will be able to join hands with little white
boys and white girls as sisters and brothers.

I have a *dream* today! 22

I have a dream that one day every valley shall be exalted, and every hill and mountain 23
shall be made low, the rough places will be made plain, and the crooked places will be made
straight; "and the glory of the Lord shall be revealed and all flesh shall see it together."

This is our hope, and this is the faith that I go back to the South with. 24

With this faith, we will be able to hew out of the mountain of despair a stone of hope. With this 25
faith, we will be able to transform the jangling discords of our nation into a beautiful symphony of
brotherhood. With this faith, we will be able to work together, to pray together, to struggle together,
to go to jail together, to stand up for freedom together, knowing that we will be free one day.

And this will be the day—this will be the day when all of God's children will be able to sing 26
with new meaning:

My country 'tis of thee, sweet land of liberty, of thee I sing.   27

Land where my fathers died, land of the Pilgrim's pride,   28

From every mountainside, let freedom ring!   29

And if America is to be a great nation, this must become true.   30

And so let freedom ring from the prodigious hilltops of New Hampshire.   31

Let freedom ring from the mighty mountains of New York.   32

Let freedom ring from the heightening Alleghenies of Pennsylvania.   33

Let freedom ring from the snow-capped Rockies of Colorado.   34

Let freedom ring from the curvaceous slopes of California.   35

But not only that: 36

Let freedom ring from Stone Mountain of Georgia.   37

Let freedom ring from Lookout Mountain of Tennessee.   38

Let freedom ring from every hill and molehill of Mississippi.   39

From every mountainside, let freedom ring.   40

And when this happens, when we allow freedom ring, when we let it ring from every village and every hamlet, from every state and every city, we will be able to speed up that day when *all* of God's children, black men and white men, Jews and Gentiles, Protestants and Catholics, will be able to join hands and sing in the words of the old Negro spiritual: 41

Free at last! Free at last!   42

Thank God Almighty, we are free at last!   43

Vocabulary

Before, during, and after reading the selection, annotate the text and write in your journal. Create a list of vocabulary words, along with their definitions. Give examples of their use from the selection you just read.

After Reading Discussion Questions: Meaning, Structure, and Expression

1. **Main Idea:** Work as a group to write a summary that answers the following questions: What purpose did Martin Luther King, Jr. have for giving this speech? Who is the intended audience? What is the main idea of the speech?

2. **Relevant Details:** Martin Luther King, Jr. is known for his powerful style. At times, he draws on sensory details such as "an invigorating autumn of freedom and equality" (paragraph 6). He also creates word pictures as in "the manacles of segregation" (paragraph 2). These figures of speech create vivid mental images that support his point and set the tone. Find at least three additional powerful figures of speech in this reading. What is Dr. King describing in these figures of speech—historical facts, emotions, ideals?

3. **Logical Order:** Martin Luther King, Jr. presents his argument for change in three phases or sections. The first section, paragraphs 1 through 6, describes the social conditions surrounding the speech. The second section, paragraphs 7 through 14, calls for action. The third section, paragraphs 15 through 43, describes his "dream." Why did he choose this order for his ideas?

4. **Effective Expression:** Martin Luther King, Jr. skillfully phrases his ideas. His use of parallelism and certain repeated phrases adds drama and emphasis to his words. For example, in paragraph 25 every sentence is parallel; each is a simple sentence that begins with a prepositional phrase that is followed by a subject and verb. In fact, King creates this parallelism by repeating the wording in certain phrases such as "with this faith" and "we will be able to." Search the entire speech for other examples of parallelism and repeated phrases. Discuss the impact of each example. How do parallelism and repeated phrasing affect the pace of the speech?

Thinking Prompts to Move from Reading to Writing

1. In this speech, Dr. King confronted prejudice and shared his dream of a world where all people enjoy justice and peace. What is a current problem that we must confront to improve our society? How would Dr. King respond to a major issue we face today, such as drug abuse, global warming, or human trafficking? Write about a dream you have for making the world a better place. Assume you are competing in a "Freedom of Expression" writing contest sponsored by local merchants in honor of Black History month. Winners will receive $200 in cash, and the winning essay will be read on the local radio station throughout the month of February.
2. Identify one problem in your local community. Explain why the problem is significant and discuss the steps necessary to correct it. Assume you are writing a letter to the editor of your newspaper.

Remarks by the President at the Holocaust Days of Remembrance Ceremony
BARACK OBAMA

The Holocaust was the systematic, state-sponsored persecution and murder of approximately six million Jews by the Nazi regime and its partners. *Holocaust* is a word of Greek origin meaning "sacrifice by fire." The United States Congress established the Days of Remembrance as our nation's annual commemoration of the Holocaust. Congress also created the United States Holocaust Memorial Museum. The museum is a lasting living memorial to the victims. On Tuesday, April 21, 2009, President Barack Obama gave the following speech at the Holocaust Remembrance Day in Washington, D.C. The Museum chose ***Never Again: What You Do Matters*** as the theme for the 2009 observance. President Obama spoke to that theme.

Before Reading   Write a journal entry about what you know about the Holocaust. Also, respond to the theme the museum chose for the 2009 Days of Remembrance. What do you think is meant by Never Again: What You Do Matters? How could this theme apply to current events around the world or in our country?

We gather today to mourn the loss of so many lives, and celebrate those who saved them; honor those who survived, and contemplate the obligations of the living. 1

It is the grimmest of ironies that one of the most savage, barbaric acts of evil in history began in one of the most modernized societies of its time, where so many markers of human progress became tools of human depravity: science that can heal used to kill; education that can enlighten used to rationalize away basic moral impulses; the bureaucracy that sustains modern life used as the machinery of mass death—a ruthless, chillingly efficient system where many were responsible for the killing, but few got actual blood on their hands. 2

While the uniqueness of the Holocaust in scope and in method is truly astounding, the Holocaust was driven by many of the same forces that have fueled atrocities throughout history: the scapegoating that leads to hatred and blinds us to our common humanity; the justifications that replace conscience and allow cruelty to spread; the willingness of those who are neither perpetrators nor victims to accept the assigned role of bystander, believing the lie that good people are ever powerless or alone, the fiction that we do not have a choice. 3

But while we are here today to bear witness to the human capacity to destroy, we are also here to pay tribute to the human impulse to save. In the moral accounting of the Holocaust, as we reckon with numbers like 6 million, as we recall the horror of numbers etched into arms, we also factor in numbers like these: 7,200—the number of Danish Jews ferried to safety, many of whom later returned home to find the neighbors who rescued them had also faithfully tended their homes and businesses and belongings while they were gone.

4

We remember the number five—the five righteous men and women who join us today from Poland. We are awed by your acts of courage and conscience. And your presence today compels each of us to ask ourselves whether we would have done what you did. We can only hope that the answer is yes.

5

We also remember the number 5,000—the number of Jews rescued by the villagers of Le Chambon, France—one life saved for each of its 5,000 residents. Not a single Jew who came there was turned away, or turned in. But it was not until decades later that the villagers spoke of what they had done—and even then, only reluctantly. The author of a book on the rescue found that those he interviewed were baffled by his interest. "How could you call us 'good'?" they said. "We were doing what had to be done."

6

That is the question of the righteous—those who would do extraordinary good at extraordinary risk not for affirmation or acclaim or to advance their own interests, but because it is what must be done. They remind us that no one is born a savior or a murderer—these are choices we each have the power to make. They teach us that no one can make us into bystanders without our consent, and that we are never truly alone—that if we have the courage to heed that "still, small voice" within us, we can form a minyan for righteousness that can span a village, even a nation.

7

Their legacy is our inheritance. And the question is, how do we honor and preserve it? How do we ensure that "never again" isn't an empty slogan, or merely an aspiration, but also a call to action?

8

I believe we start by doing what we are doing today—by bearing witness, by fighting the silence that is evil's greatest co-conspirator.

9

In the face of horrors that defy comprehension, the impulse to silence is understandable. My own great uncle returned from his service in World War II in a state of shock, saying little, alone with painful memories that would not leave his head. He went up into the attic, according to the stories that I've heard, and wouldn't come down for six months. He was one of the liberators—someone who at a very tender age had seen the unimaginable. And so some of the liberators who are here today honor us with their presence—all of whom we honor for their extraordinary service. My great uncle was part of the 89th Infantry Division—the first Americans to reach a Nazi concentration camp. And they liberated Ohrdruf, part of Buchenwald, where tens of thousands had perished.

10

The story goes that when the Americans marched in, they discovered the starving survivors and the piles of dead bodies. And General Eisenhower made a decision. He ordered Germans from the nearby town to tour the camp, so they could see what had been done in their name. And he ordered American troops to tour the camp, so they could see the evil they were fighting against. Then he invited congressmen and journalists to bear witness. And he ordered that photographs and films be made. Some of us have seen those same images, whether in the Holocaust Museum or when I visited Yad Vashem, and they never leave you. Eisenhower said that he wanted "to be in a position to give firsthand evidence of these things, if ever, in the future, there develops a tendency to charge these allegations merely to propaganda."

11

Eisenhower understood the danger of silence. He understood that if no one knew what had happened, that would be yet another atrocity—and it would be the perpetrators' ultimate triumph.

12

What Eisenhower did to record these crimes for history is what we are doing here today. 13
That's what Elie Wiesel and the survivors we honor here do by fighting to make their
memories part of our collective memory. That's what the Holocaust Museum does every day on
our National Mall, the place where we display for the world our triumphs and failures and the
lessons we've learned from our history. It's the very opposite of silence.

But we must also remember that bearing witness is not the end of our obligation—it's just 14
the beginning. We know that evil has yet to run its course on Earth. We've seen it in this
century in the mass graves and the ashes of villages burned to the ground, and children used
as soldiers and rape used as a weapon of war. To this day, there are those who insist the
Holocaust never happened; who perpetrate every form of intolerance—racism and anti-
Semitism, homophobia, xenophobia, sexism, and more—hatred that degrades its victim and
diminishes us all.

Today, and every day, we have an opportunity, as well as an obligation, to confront these 15
scourges—to fight the impulse to turn the channel when we see images that disturb us, or
wrap ourselves in the false comfort that others' sufferings are not our own. Instead we have
the opportunity to make a habit of empathy; to recognize ourselves in each other; to commit
ourselves to resisting injustice and intolerance and indifference in whatever forms they may
take—whether confronting those who tell lies about history, or doing everything we can to
prevent and end atrocities like those that took place in Rwanda, those taking place in Darfur.
That is my commitment as President. I hope that is yours, as well.

It will not be easy. At times, fulfilling these obligations require self-reflection. But in the 16
final analysis, I believe history gives us cause for hope rather than despair—the hope of a
chosen people who have overcome oppression since the days of Exodus; of the nation of Israel
rising from the destruction of the Holocaust; of the strong and enduring bonds between our
nations. It is the hope, too, of those who not only survived, but chose to live, teaching us the
meaning of courage and resilience and dignity. I'm thinking today of a study conducted after
the war that found that Holocaust survivors living in America actually had a higher birthrate
than American Jews. What a stunning act of faith—to bring a child in a world that has shown
you so much cruelty; to believe that no matter what you have endured, or how much you have
lost, in the end, you have a duty to life.

We find cause for hope as well in Protestant and Catholic children attending school 17
together in Northern Ireland; in Hutus and Tutsis living side by side, forgiving neighbors who
have done the unforgivable; in a movement to save Darfur that has thousands of high school
and college chapters in 25 countries, and brought 70,000 people to the Washington Mall—
people of every age and faith and background and race united in common cause with
suffering brothers and sisters halfway around the world.

Those numbers can be our future—our fellow citizens of the world showing us how to 18
make the journey from oppression to survival, from witness to resistance, and ultimately to
reconciliation. That is what we mean when we say "never again."

So today, during this season when we celebrate liberation, resurrection, and the possibility 19
of redemption, may each of us renew our resolve to do what must be done. And may we strive
each day, both individually and as a nation, to be among the righteous.

Thank you, God bless you, and God bless the United States of America. 20

Vocabulary Before, during, and after reading the selection, annotate the text and
write in your journal. Create a list of vocabulary words, along with their definitions. Give
examples of their use from the selection you just read.

After Reading Discussion Questions: Meaning, Structure, and Expression

1. **Main Idea:** Work as a group to write a summary that answers the following questions: What purpose did President Obama want to fulfill by giving this speech? Who is the intended audience? What is the main idea of the speech?

2. **Relevant Details:** In paragraph 5, President Obama refers to "the five righteous men and women who join us today from Poland." Does President Obama give us enough information about these people? Who are they and what did they do? What clues does President Obama give us about the actions of these people? Why did he include paragraph 5? Should he have given us more information? Why or why not?

3. **Logical Order:** In paragraph 10 President Obama shares with the audience the personal experience of his great uncle as a soldier and returning veteran of World War II. Why did he include this personal example? And why did he choose to place it where he did in the speech? Would this information have been more effective as part of the introduction or conclusion instead of its current location? Why or why not?

4. **Effective Expression:** How would you describe the overall tone or mood of the speech? What tone does President Obama take in paragraphs 1 through 3? What tone does he use in paragraphs 4 through 6? What is his attitude in paragraphs 11 through 16? What is the relationship between his tone and the event at which he is speaking? What impact does he want to have on his audience? Give examples of specific words to support your interpretation of his tone.

Thinking Prompts to Move from Reading to Writing

1. In paragraph 14, President Obama condemns those "who perpetrate every form of intolerance—racism and anti-Semitism, homophobia, xenophobia, sexism, and more—hatred that degrades its victim and diminishes us all." Assume you are writing an essay for a college sociology class. Choose one of the forms of intolerance listed by President Obama. Define the term you chose and explain how this form of intolerance "degrades its victim and diminishes us all." Then, suggest ways to confront or resist this form of intolerance.

2. In his speech, President Obama calls us to "bear witness" against injustice by "fighting the silence that is evil's greatest co-conspirator." Assume you are an officer of your college's Student Government Association (SGA). SGA is organizing a Holocaust Remembrance Day at your college. As the SGA representative, you are asked to give a speech of remembrance. Also assume a copy of your speech will be printed in the college newspaper. Go to the homepage of the Holocaust Museum at <http://www.ushmm.org/>. Browse the site for information for your speech. Use the following MLA format to document your information.

   United States Holocaust Memorial Museum. "Title of Article." *Title of Page or Resource within Museum's Webpage.* [Date of access in the following form: day month year.] <URL>.

   Example of a Citation:

   United States Holocaust Memorial Museum. "The Holocaust." *Holocaust Encyclopedia.* 18 Oct. 2009 <http://www.ushmm.org/wlc/en/index.php?ModuleId=10005143>.

Text Credits

Photo Credits

All photos not credited below are courtesy of the author

Image Source Pink/Alamy: 2. Page 3 (top to bottom): Helene Rogers/Alamy, ©fotofresh/Alamy, ©Abode/Beateworks/Corbis, ©Gary Conner/PhotoEdit, Inc. Ilene MacDonald/Alamy RF: 5; Comstock/Corbis: 18; Chuck Savage/Corbis: 19 (top left); Image Source/Getty Images RF: 19 (top right); AP photo: 19 (bottom left); Royalty-Free/Corbis: 19 (bottom right); Michigan Board of Education 1994: 20; Myrleen Ferguson/PhotoEdit, Inc.: 22 (top left); Jessica Rinaldi/Reuters/Corbis: 22 (top right); Merry Alpern/Corbis: 22 (bottom left); Royalty-free/Corbis: 22 (bottom right); Jon Feingersh/Getty Images RF: 24 (top left); Royalty-Free/Corbis: 24 (top right); Royalty-Free/Corbis: 24 (bottom left); Bettmann/Corbis: 24 (bottom right); Royalty-Free/Corbis: 26 (left); Aristide Economopoulos/Star Ledger/Corbis: 26 (top right); Royalty-Free/Corbis: 26 (center right) Bettmann/Corbis: 26 (bottom right); Fancy/Veer/Corbis: 30; National Archives/©1943 SEPS: The Curtis Publishing Company: 32; Buddy Mays/Corbis: 34; mediablitzimages(UK), Ltd/Alamy: 35; Bernd Mellmann/Alamy: 52-53; Page 54 (top to bottom): ©Jerome Sessini/Corbis ©Bob Krist/Corbis, ©Steve Chenn/Corbis, RF ©Image Source/Corbis. ©David Muench/Corbis: 56 (top); ©Gene Blevins/LA Daily News/Corbis: 56 (bottom); ©Jeff Greenberg/PhotoEdit, Inc.: 59 (left); ©Michael Newman/PhotoEdit, Inc.: 59 (center); ©Bill Varie/Corbis: 59 (right);©David Wells/Corbis: 65 (top); ©John Miller/Robert Harding World Imagery/Corbis: 65 (bottom); ©David Pollack/Corbis: 72; Corbis/Bettmann: 73; Corbis/Bettmann: 74 (all); Corbis/Bettmann: 75 (all); Corbis/Bettmann: 77; Joseph Sohm/Corbis: 83; Douglas Kirkland/Corbis: 90 (all); Frank Micelotta/Getty Images: 91 (top); Mike Blake/Corbis: 91 (center); Frank Polich/Reuters/Corbis: 91 (bottom); © Rebecca Emery/Corbis: 106; Dorling Kindersley Media Library: 107 (all); Dorling Kindersley Media Library: 109 (all); Richard Hutchings/PhotoEdit, Inc.: 111. Page 113 (top to bottom): David Young-Wolff/PhotoEdit, Inc., Image100/Corbis RF, Michael Newman/PhotoEdit, Inc., Jeff Greenberg/Alamy, Elizabeth Lippman, Image100/Corbis RF. Gregor Schuster/zefa/Corbis: 114 (top); Ray Coleman/Photo Researchers, Inc: 114 (bottom);. Richard Drury/The Image Bank/Getty Images: 122; Sean Justice/Corbis RF: 123 (top) Fancy/Veer/Corbis RF: 123 (center); Image Source/Corbis: 123 (bottom); Sean Justice/Corbis RF: 125 (top); Fancy/Veer/Corbis RF: 125 (center); Image Source/Corbis: 125 (bottom) DInspirestock/Corbis: 128; Blend Images/Alamy: 129 (left); George Shelley/Corbis: 129 (center); David Young-Wolff/PhotoEdit,

Inc.: 129 (right): Radius Images/Alamy: 132; ©Envision/Corbis: 133; Hans Neleman/Corbis: 140; John Atashian/Corbis: 141 (left); Jessica Rinaldi/Reuters/Corbis: 141 (center); Chad Batka/Corbis: 141 (right); John Atashian/Corbis: 143 (top); Jessica Rinaldi/Reuters/Corbis: 143 (center); Chad Batka/Corbis: 143 (bottom); Jon Ragel/Corbis: 147; mypyramid.com: 149; Dorling Kindersley Media Library: 158 (left); Klaus Hackenberg/Corbis: 158 (right); Alan Look/Corbis: 159 (top left); Alan Look/Corbis: 159 (top right); Transtock/Corbis: 159 (center left); Car Culture/Corbis: 159 (center right); Robert Llewellyn/zefa/Corbis: 159 (bottom left); Ashley Cooper/Corbis: 159 (bottom right). Page 161 (top to bottom): Alan Look/Corbis, Alan Look/Corbis, Transtock/Corbis, Car Culture/Corbis, Robert Llewellyn/zefa/Corbis, Ashley Cooper/Corbis. ©Robert W. Ginn/PhotoEdit, Inc.: 166 (top); ©Richard M. Abarno/Corbis: 166 (bottom); Chloe Johnson/Alamy: 174; David James/Warner Bros/ZUMA/Corbis: 175 (left); SW Productions/BrandX/Corbis: 175 (top right); Simon Jarratt/Corbis: 175 (center right); Gabe Palmer/Corbis: 175 (bottom right); ©Thunderdog Studios, Inc./Thunderdog Collective/Corbis: 181 (left); Art Kowalsky/Alamy: 181 (center); Chloe Johnson/Alamy: 181 (right); Gene Blevins/La Daly News/Corbis: 182; George Diebold/Corbis: 190; Courtesy Habitat for Humanity: 191 (all except top left); Joseph Sohm, ChromoSohm Inc./Corbis: 191 (top left); Courtesy Habitat for Humanity 193 (all except 193 top); Joseph Sohm, ChromoSohm Inc./Corbis: 193 (top); Tim Shaffer/Reuters/Corbis: 196; Michael Newman/PhotoEdit, Inc.: 197 (both); John Lund/Nevada Wier/Blend Images/Corbis RF: 203; Hill Street Studios/Blend Images/Corbis: 206; Alan Shein Photography/Corbis: 207 (top); Benelux/zefa/Corbis: 207 (second row left); James Leynse/Corbis: 207 (second row right); Lisa B./Corbis: 207 (third row left); Fancy/Veer/Corbis: 207 (third row right); Ariel Skelley/Corbis: 207 (bottom). Page 209 (top to bottom): Alan Shein Photography/Corbis, Benelux/zefa/Corbis, Lisa B./Corbis, Ariel Skelley/Corbis, James Leynse/Corbis, Fancy/Veer/Corbis. Michael Newman/PhotoEdit, Inc.: 213; Phil Klein/Corbis: 222; Wesley Hitt/Alamy: 225; Julie Eggers/Terra Corbis: 228; Buzz Pictures/Alamy: 230; David Young-Wolff/PhotoEdit, Inc.: 231 (top); © Image100/Corbis RF: 231 (bottom left); Andrew Fox/Alamy: 231 (bottom center); Jose Luis Pelaez, Inc./Alamy: 231 (bottom right); Peter Endig/epa/Corbis: 234; Page 235 (top to bottom): Pinellas County Department of Environmental Management, Inspirestock/Corbis,

Mediscan/Corbis, Radius/Corbis RF. Thomas & Pat Leeson/Photo Researchers, Inc.: 248; Dorling Kindersley Media Library: 249 (left); Explorer/Photo Researchers, Inc.: 249 (center); Calvin Larsen/Photo Researchers, Inc.: 249 (right); Dorling Kindersley Media Library: 258; Steve Lewis/Getty ImagesRF: 259 (left); Richard Levine/Alamy: 259 (center); © Bojan Brecelj/Corbis: 259 (right); © Dennis Hallinan/ Alamy: 262; Reinhard Dirschert/Peter Arnold, Inc.: 266; ©Jeff Greenberg/PhotoEdit, Inc.: 269; ©Richard Melloul/Sygma/Corbis: 275; Hulton Archive/Getty Images: 279 (top); © Rune Hellestad/Corbis: 279 (center); © Goss Images/Alamy: 279 (bottom); Aly Song/Reuters: 289; Brand X Pictures/Alamy: 294; John Greim/Science Library/Photo Researchers, Inc.: 295; © Thinkstock/Corbis RF: 300; Joshua Lott/Getty Images: 306; Jordan Siemens/Aurora Photos/Corbis: 310; Corbis: 311; Courtesy UNHCR/Corbis: 318; Ray Stubblebine/Reuters/Corbis: 324; Envision/Corbis: 325;Yellow Dog Productions/The Image Bank/ Corbis: 336; Bill Varie/Somos Images/Corbis: 340; Jose Luis Pelaez/Blend Images/Corbis RF: 341; © Corbis RF: 345; Antiques and Collectables/Alamy: 354; Stephen Frink/Science Faction/Corbis: 360; ©Myrleen Ferguson Cate/PhotoEdit, Inc.: 361; Lon Diehl/PhotoEdit, Inc.: 364; Image Source/Corbis RF: 366; Dorling Kindersley Media Library: 372; Bettmann/Corbis: 374; Library of Congress: 375 (all); Museo Nacional de Antropologia, Mexico City, Mexico/Index/The Bridgeman Art Library: 377; Doug Armand/Getty Images: 386-387; Steven Puetzer/Iconica/Getty Images: 389; Bettmann/ Corbis: 392; juice Images/Corbis RF: 402; ©Rolf Bruderer/Corbis: 403; Bernard Annebicque/ Sygma/Corbis: 407; Beau Lark/Corbis: 408; The Advertising Archive: 413; Cassy Cohen/PhotoEdit, Inc.: 415; Alfred Pasieka/Photo Researchers, Inc.: 417; Dorling Kindersley Media Library: 419; Reuters/ Corbis: 422; AFP/Getty Images: 423; Inspirestock/ Corbis RF: 432; RF Masterfile: 433; Apple Handout/ Corbis: 438; Jeremy Walker/Getty Images: 444; Tim Boyle/Getty Images: 448; Age fotostock/Superstock: 452; George Harris/Retrofile/Getty Images: 459; Age Fotosearch: 464; Frank Greenway/Dorling Kindersley Media Library: 465; Stephen Dunn/Getty Images: 476: David Kadlubeowski/Corbis: 480-481; MedioImages (RF)/Jupiter Images: 483; Bettmann/ Corbis: 494; NBAE/Getty Images: 502; Comstock/ Jupiter Images: 505; Foodpix/Jupiter Images: 518; Radius Images RF/Jupiter Images: 519; *V is for Vendetta* by Alan Moore and David Lloyd, Cover and Compilation © 1989 DCComics. All Rights Reserved. Used with Permission: 523; Terry Eggers/Corbis: 538; Richard Cummins/Corbis: 539; Martin H. Simon/ Corbis: 542; Ariel Shelley/Blend Images/Getty Images RF: 543; AP Images: 550; ©Zits Partnership, King Features Syndicate: 557; Roger Ressmeyer/Corbis: 564-565; Lisa F. Young/Alamy: 570; Jack Hollingsworth/Corbis RF: 576; Dorling Kindersley Media Library: 577; Lebrecht Music and Arts Photo Library: 583; Fotosearch: 590; Visions of America/ Alamy: 597; ©Kristy-Anne Glubish/Design Pics/ Corbis RF: 604; Dorling Kindersley Media Library: 606; Center for Disease Control Public Health Foundation: 617; RF Comstock/Corbis: 622; Jon Feingersh/Blend Images/Corbis: 623; Thos Robinson/ Getty Images: 627, 629; Dylan Martinez/Reuters/ Corbis: 627, 648; Jemal Countess/WireImage/Getty Images: 627, 631; Hulton Archie/Getty Images: 627, 633; Colin McPherson/Corbis: 627, 636; David Brabyn/Corbis: 627, 638; Dorothy Alexander: 627 (left), 642; Scott McDermott/Corbis: 627, 644; Isabel Cutler Photography: 627, 649; Miriam Berkley: 627, 654; Bettmann/Corbis: 627, 658; PhotoEdit, Inc.: 627, 661; Martin H. Simon/Corbis.: 627, 664; Kim Kulish/Corbis: 627, 668; AFP/Getty Images: 627, 671; Rob Crandall: 627, 674; Bettmann/Corbis: 627, 676; Pete Souza/CNP/Corbis: 627, 680.

Index